RESEARCH DESIGN IN COUNSELING

Fourth Edition

P. Paul Heppner
University of Missouri

Bruce E. Wampold
University of Wisconsin-Madison &
Modum Bad Psychiatric Center, Vikersund, Norway

Jesse Owen
University of Denver

Mindi N. Thompson
University of Wisconsin-Madison

Kenneth T. Wang
Fuller Theological Seminary

CENGAGE
Learning®

Australia • Brazil • Mexico • Singapore • United Kingdom • United States

CENGAGE
Learning·

Research Design in Counseling,
Fourth Edition

P. Paul Heppner, Bruce E. Wampold,
Jesse Owen, Mindi N. Thompson, and
Kenneth T. Wang

Product Director: Jon–David Hague

Product Manager and Content
   Developer: Julie Martinez

Product Assistant: Stephen Lagos

Media Developer: Kyra Kane

Marketing Manager: Margaux Cameron

Art and Cover Direction, Production
   Management, and Composition:
   Carolyn Deacy and Jitendra Kumar,
   MPS Limited

Manufacturing Planner: Judy Inouye

Text Researcher: Kavitha Balasundaram

Text and Cover Designer: Ellen Pettengell

Cover Image: Paul Tomlins/
   Ubiquitous/Corbis

For product information and technology assistance, contact us at
Cengage Learning Customer & Sales Support, 1-800-354-9706.

For permission to use material from this text or product,
submit all requests online at **www.cengage.com/permissions**.
Further permissions questions can be e-mailed to
permissionrequest@cengage.com.

Library of Congress Control Number: 2014959102

ISBN: 978-1-305-08731-6

Cengage Learning
20 Channel Center Street
Boston, MA 02210
USA

Cengage Learning is a leading provider of customized learning
solutions with employees residing in nearly 40 different countries
and sales in more than 125 countries around the world. Find your
local representative at **www.cengage.com**.

Cengage Learning products are represented in Canada by
Nelson Education, Ltd.

To learn more about Cengage Learning Solutions, visit
www.cengage.com.

Purchase any of our products at your local college store or at our
preferred online store **www.cengagebrain.com**.

Printed in the United States of America
Print Number: 03   Print Year: 2016

To my bright, inquisitive, and passionate students from whom I have learned so much; and to Mary, my loving partner and best friend for 46 years whose love and support have been so central to my life journey.
P.P.H

To my students, whose passion for investigation provides renewal and inspiration; and to Anna and all of our children, whose love and support provide the foundation on which all else is built.
B.E.W

To my students who have enriched my life, and to my family and friends who provided endless support to me over the years. Lastly, to Drs. S. A. Fras and M. F. Hank who are my inspiration.
J.O

To the many mentors, students, collaborators, family, participants, clients, and friends who have contributed to my journey—and to you, Ben, for making every day brighter. Thank you!
M.N.T

To my students who have made teaching research a joy, and to my wife Joanne, and kids Justin and Katelyn, who have been such wonderful support on a daily basis.
K.T.W

Contents

Chapter 3   **Ethics in Counseling Research: Being and Doing Right**   48

Chapter 4   **Professional Writing: A Critical Skill for Scientists and Practitioners**   84

Preface

The seeds of great discoveries are constantly floating around, but they only take root in minds well prepared to receive them.

—Joseph Henry

So much of the field of counseling is discovery—discovering new techniques for helping people lead better, healthier, happier, and more meaningful lives. As Galileo said, "All truths are easy to understand once they are discovered; the point is discovering them." The counseling field is in many ways a new profession, and there are many truths left to be discovered. We are writing this book for the next generation of discoverers—those students and researchers who will enhance our professional skills to help more people at home and abroad. This discovery process is so critically important for the growth, health, and productivity of the specialty, as well as the next generation of practitioners and scholars who are the stewards of the profession. Moreover, critical scientific thinking is needed to extend our knowledge bases in counseling and counseling psychology; we need new scholars who can use the scientific method to further our understanding of the many complexities within human behavior across different cultural contexts. In this book we hope to provide a foundation to enhance students' scientific thinking and to help them make those discoveries.

There are several challenges in teaching the next generation of counselors and counseling psychologists to be inquisitive, passionate, and competent researchers. Perhaps first and foremost, many students learn about research methods in general research methods courses in education or psychology, which utilize what seem like very distant and even sometimes irrelevant examples from other disciplines. Subsequently, students in the counseling profession often do not see the utility, or full applicability, of research methods taught abstractly or apart from the typical domains of counseling research. We must teach research methods with meaningful examples for the next generation of counselors and counseling psychologists. In addition, when counseling students learn research methods when applied to, let us say clinical psychology or higher education, our students do not learn about the recent counseling literature and the creative approaches being utilized by contemporary scholars in our profession. Such a lack of knowledge and role models makes it difficult for counseling and counseling psychology students to even become aware, much less get excited about, the research topics within our profession. Although the book is not comprehensive of all research in counseling, it not only provides a strong foundation in research methods, but also provides students with a broad and impressive overview of many of the current research topics in the profession, along with many of our foremost researchers.

The fourth edition of *Research Design in Counseling* represents a substantial revision from the earlier editions. Because the first three editions were well received by students and faculty, we retained the basic content and style of coverage. However, this new edition reflects the work of five very well established authors in counseling and counseling psychology; Heppner and Wampold continue to provide the primary vision for this successful textbook, but now in collaboration with three very productive rising stars in our counseling profession. The combination of our areas of expertise provides a deep and rich conceptual understanding of research design from very productive researchers and scholars, with an emphasis on acknowledging the strengths and weaknesses of all the designs including quantitative and qualitative. Each chapter contains the most up-to-date information students need for utilizing the different research designs, as well as informative and concrete illustrations to enhance students' knowledge of research design and their application to the many exciting topics in our profession today. The book does not favor one design over another per se, but rather emphasizes the need to consider the type of questions being addressed, as well as the inherent strengths and weaknesses in the previous research literature. Moreover, each chapter has been revised and updated to reflect new information since the third edition.

The writing style of the book is aimed squarely at educating graduate students about the intricacies of both qualitative and quantitative research methods. Moreover, questions as well as applications of the material are highlighted in three different types of boxes (Research Journey, Research Application, and Research in Action)throughout each chapter to actively involve students in their education. Each chapter ends with a broad array of stimulus questions to enhance student learning and increase retention. We encourage the reader to use these questions to deepen awareness and understanding of each chapter. Through such reflection as well as talking with other students, both critical thinking skills as well as skills associated with designing rigorous research can become integrated more thoroughly into the way students think about important issues in the field.

We have dramatically reorganized the chapters into four major categories to help students organize the basic content areas needed to become an educated and skillful researcher. Part 1 consists of four chapters aimed at the philosophy of science, ethical issues within research, research training, and scholarly writing. It is critically important that students quickly comprehend basic philosophical and ethical issues pertaining to the role of science in creating strong foundational knowledge bases in our profession. For example, Chapter 3 on ethics provides a great deal of information about what students must know about ethical issues throughout all stages of their research. Science and ethics must go hand in hand, and this chapter offers many examples to illustrate this relationship. Moreover, Chapter 2 is totally devoted to graduate research training, and addresses the concerns and misconceptions about both science and research in counseling and counseling psychology.

We not only highlight the current research on this topic, but also most importantly discuss the implications for students' development in acquiring research competencies. In addition, we are very pleased that the chapter includes stories from a diverse group of seasoned researchers who share critical aspects of their research journey. With openness and candor they share some of their own fears as well as joys along their path of becoming experts within their research areas. Chapter 4 focuses on professional writing, a critical skill for both scientists and practitioners. A great deal of research is being conducted, but good research questions and even well-designed studies often do not get published in our journals. Certainly good research questions and well-designed studies are necessary components, but strong writing skills are needed to accurately depict the study and explain the results. This chapter is aimed at helping students and researchers with the unique skills of scientific writing. We believe that more attention needs to be given to the process of writing, and how one acquires the skills to write scientifically, clearly, succinctly, and yet address important topics with heart.

Part 2 consists of six chapters all aimed at establishing the foundation for any particular study. Thus we focus on identifying and operationalizing topics of most interest to students, balancing ideals and realities when choosing a research design, and the central role of validity in conducting research. In addition, we focus on population issues and underscore that *who we study matters* in terms of the knowledge bases that we create, or do not create. For example, in Chapter 9 on diverse perspectives we discuss a number of conceptual and methodological considerations related to studying diverse populations throughout all phases of a research project in both U.S.-based as well cross-cultural or cross-national samples. This chapter has been greatly expanded and emphasizes a broad perspective that includes multiple identities and the intersection of identities. We have also greatly revised the other chapters to have a stronger emphasis on diversity issues to portray the increasing breadth of knowledge bases across populations, as well the increasing complexities in the counseling profession. Finally, in Chapter 10 on scale construction we underscore the critical role of scale construction, and how we operationalize the constructs that are most central to our study. Our research can only be as strong as the measurement of our constructs. We encourage students to carefully consider the adequacy of the existing inventories to measure the constructs that are most important to them; most importantly, if we do not have an adequate assessment tool, we suggest that a good alternative is to take a step back, and develop a new scale to measure the construct of interest. This chapter also provides easy-to-follow guidelines and practical examples that guide the researcher toward the demystification of scale development, as well as those who want to understand more about the psychometric properties of existing inventories. In short, all of these chapters are aimed at helping students to provide a strong foundation for their study.

Part 3 provides an in-depth discussion of seven major designs. Our comprehensive coverage of research designs includes both quantitative and qualitative research, and single-subject as well as survey research. For example, Chapter 11 on true experimental designs discusses the power of these designs, most notably the power of between-groups and within-subjects designs. Moreover, Chapter 12 on quasi-experimental designs discusses relationships examined in applied settings, including longitudinal designs. Chapter 13 on quantitative descriptive designs discusses the utility describing, explaining, and predicting phenomena; this chapter also includes some of the latest thinking and writing about the importance of examining mediating and moderating variables, and provides information on the latest in all of the regression family designs. Statistical methods are also integrated throughout Part 3.

Although the strength of the book rests on the presentation of numerous intricacies of quantitative designs, the fourth edition also includes an updated and greatly expanded Chapter 16 on qualitative research. The chapter defines qualitative research and places it within constructivism and critical theory paradigms. The chapter describes three strategies of qualitative inquiry that have a great deal of applicability for counseling research: grounded theory, phenomenology, and consensual qualitative research. In addition, the chapter discusses common strategies to gather and analyze data, and also provides a wide range of references for further study with qualitative methods. In sum, this chapter not only provides a compelling need for qualitative research, but also provides detailed illustrations of most commonly used qualitative methods in counseling and counseling psychology, all of which provides students with an excellent introduction to qualitative methods. In addition, Chapter 17 on mixed methods designs provides not only a strong conceptual explanation of mixed methods (combining quantitative and qualitative approaches), but also includes several studies to illustrate the power of mixed methods.

Part 4 discusses a wide array of methodological issues, most notably a number of complexities surrounding the independent variable, as well as skillfully measuring intended outcomes with the dependent variable. In addition, we discuss methodological issues pertaining specifically to counseling outcome research, and provide the most up to date information regarding the effectiveness of counseling and psychotherapy. For example, Chapter 21 on process research focuses on the most recent research that examines the how's and why's of what makes counseling work. Chapter 22 on program evaluation applies science and practice to real-life programs that are designed to help a wide array of people. The field of counseling has increasingly become one that emphasizes intervention and social change at the program and systems level. Many counselors have jobs where conducting program evaluation and assessing the efficacy of interventions are a critical part of their position. This chapter offers many insights about the field of program evaluation and provides a great deal of information and support for researchers involved in assessing the effectiveness of programs and services. Chapter 23, the last chapter, focuses on a very important methodological topic, biases that create error variance from multiple sources, such as investigators, experimenters, and participants; most importantly, this chapter not only highlights biases, but also suggests ways to minimize their impact on our research.

We have so many individuals to thank for their contributions to this book. We especially want to thank the staff of Cengage for all of the technical support, patience, and help through this revision process; we very much appreciate the guidance of Julie Martinez who helped us through all phases of this book. Although a number of staff have changed over the years, the early vision of Claire Verduin lives on in this fourth edition, and she deserves special attention for her good judgment in developing the first edition of this book. In addition, we give a special thanks to the coauthors of several of the chapters, who added greatly to the depth and breadth of critical topics within research design: Drs. Germaine Awad, Matrese Benkofske, Kevin Cokley, Dong-gwi Lee, Hyun-Woo Lim, and Yu-Wei Wang. And another thanks to the researchers who have been willing to share some of their journey of becoming researchers; their voices added greatly to the discussion of the developmental process of becoming a researcher. In addition, we want to thank so many of you for sending in your comments about the book—how it was helpful to you and also where you would like more examples or suggestions.

Finally, we would like to thank all of the authors of the articles and books that we cite in this text; their dedication to conducting high quality research provides the profession not only with important new knowledge, but also with very helpful models on the "how to's" of conducting meaningful research.

As American folklorist Zora Neale Hurston commented, "Research is formalized curiosity. It is poking and prying with a purpose." We hope this text gives you many tools to "poke and pry with a purpose" and discover important truths for the betterment of humankind.

Part 1

PHILOSOPHICAL, ETHICAL, TRAINING, AND PROFESSIONAL ISSUES

Philosophies of Science and Counseling: Why Science Matters to Counseling

Chapter 1

Counseling and counseling psychology are founded on the integration of science as applied to clinical practice—or the integration of science into practice and of practice into science (e.g., Benjamin & Baker, 2003; Packard, 2009). We live in an evidence-based world, and practitioners are expected to be knowledgeable of both evidence-based findings as well as our scientific methods in order to ensure that our practice is grounded in evidence. In today's world, counselors or psychologists whose practice is not evidence based puts both themselves and their clients at risk. In fact, many have claimed that practicing without scientific knowledge is inherently unethical (e.g., APA Presidential Taskforce on Evidence-Based Practice in Psychology, 2006; Baker, McFall, & Shoham, 2008).

Counselors and counseling psychologists assume responsibility for promoting the welfare of the people who seek our services and for protecting clients from harm (e.g., Lambert, Bergin, & Collins, 1977). As professionals, therefore, we must continually update and extend our knowledge about human nature, and consistently evaluate the efficacy of our interventions so as to ensure that our clients receive competent treatment. Consider the real-life example of a husband and wife who sought career planning assistance described in the following box.

RESEARCH IN ACTION 1.1

After a thorough intake, the individuals were assigned to a computerized career planning program. Both of them completed the program and were amazed to learn that they received exactly the same results. As Johnston, Buescher, and Heppner (1988) described:

> Careful checking of the program revealed that the program was reporting scores accurately for the first individual who used the program each day. The second, and all subsequent users that day, however, were getting an identical printout of the first user's

results. The first user's results continued to appear until the machine was turned off. In essence, every user, except the initial user each day, was receiving invalid results. For us, this resulted in many hours of calling clients to inform them that they had received invalid results. After expressing our shock to the manufacturer, we were told simply: "Oh, yes, we found that out a month ago and it has been fixed on new discs. We'll send you a new set." One wonders how many other career centers never found this error and continued to use a program that gave users blatantly invalid results. (p. 40)

This example involves a computer programming error that was not found through careful evaluation. Many other examples could be listed in which clients receive less than desirable treatments because of outdated information, ineffective or inappropriate counselor interventions, or erroneous knowledge about human behavior and the change process.

Scholars and practitioners (e.g., Heppner et al., 2000; Neimeyer & Diamond, 2001; Stoltenberg et al., 2000; Watkins, 1994) have both advocated for the continued integration of science and practice. Such an integration is needed not only so that practitioners maintain updated knowledge that they can integrate into their clinical work, but also so that researchers stay at the forefront of the pursuits of knowledge that are likely to be the most applicable to clients and to the general public. Wedding science and practice allows trainees and professionals to advance knowledge of the profession and conduct research that has the potential to directly affect social and policy agendas (Heppner et al., 2000; Krumboltz, 2002).

In this book, we will examine in depth the foundations of the scientific method and research design. The purpose of the book is to guide the reader through the fundamental aspects of research design with a core emphasis on the integration of science and practice. Moreover, throughout the book we discuss both the advantages and disadvantages of a wide array of research designs that are commonly used in counseling and counseling psychology. We guide the reader through the process of research, beginning with identifying topics, operationalizing variables, selecting a research design that best fits a particular research question, evaluating the results, and finally the intricacies of publishing one's research. Throughout, we discuss common errors, biases, and the complexities inherent in creating scientific knowledge across different cultural contexts. Finally, we utilize a wide array of published research in counseling and counseling psychology to illustrate not only different research designs, but also to concretely describe the complexities inherent in research.

In this chapter, we look at different sources of knowledge and introduce scientific inquiry as a mechanism by which to develop a dependable knowledge base for the counseling profession. We believe that it is absolutely essential to develop evidence-based knowledge on which to build the counseling and counseling psychology profession. We begin by reviewing four philosophical foundations of science and highlight the central role of theory in guiding our science and our practice. In addition, we emphasize the integration of science and practice as a foundation of graduate training programs in counseling and counseling psychology; moreover, we highlight the critical role of scientific or critical thinking as a central outcome of graduate training, and in essence, as a major goal of this book.

SOURCES OF KNOWLEDGE

Charles Peirce, a 19th-century American mathematician, philosopher, and logician, stated that there are at least four ways of knowing, or of "fixing belief" (Buchler, 1955). The first method is the method of tenacity, or the notion that whatever belief one firmly adheres to is truth. These "truths," therefore, are known to be true because we have always known them to be true and the frequent repetition of these "truths" seems to enhance their validity (Kerlinger & Lee, 2000). A second method of knowing is the method of authority, which can be human (e.g., the president of the United States, a well-known psychologist) or superhuman (e.g., God, a higher power). In other words, if your clinical supervisor (an authority figure) says that it is so, then it is "truth." A third method of knowing is the a priori method, or method of intuition (e.g., Cohen & Nagel, 1934). Accordingly, if something makes sense and has previously been believed to be true, then it is indeed true. The fourth method of knowing is the scientific method, which involves empirical tests to establish verifiable facts. A fifth way of knowing not included in Buchler's conceptualization is knowledge learned through one's direct experiences in the world. Through countless experiences, each individual construes a "reality" of the world; some of the individual's perceptions may match those of others with similar experiences, whereas some may be different.

Given the overwhelming complexity of life and the vast amounts of knowledge needed even in daily living, people most often acquire "truths" through all five of these ways of knowing. In his annual philosophical lecture read before the British Academy, On the Sources of Knowledge and of Ignorance, Popper (1962) argued that there are a variety of sources of knowledge, but all are prone to error. He reasoned that our mission should be to detect and eliminate error by "criticizing the theories or guesses of others and—if we can train ourselves to do so—by criticizing our own theories or guesses." (p. 26). Reliance upon any one type of knowledge without critique and analysis can be dangerous. Individual biases can develop based upon a limited information and experiences can be distorted, which in turn can lead to inaccurate conclusions. We must, therefore, keep in mind that error can be involved in any of the five ways of knowing.

SCIENCE AS A WAY OF KNOWING

Science, as derived from Latin, means knowledge. The true meaning or definition of science, however, has long been disputed and numerous perspectives exist. Ziman (1968) captured this well in his statement: "To attempt to answer the question 'What is Science?' is almost as presumptuous as to try to state the meaning of Life itself." (p. 1). Science represents one of a variety of perspectives (e.g., philosophy, religion, art, literature, mythology) and sources of knowledge (Buchler, 1955) in its attempt to describe and explain human nature.

According to Pedhazur and Schmelkin (1991), science is perhaps best distinguished from other descriptions of human nature by the methods used to arrive at answers. Popper's opening statement in *The Logic of Scientific Discovery* (1959) described the scientist as follows:

> A scientist, whether theorist, or experimenter, puts forward statements or systems of statements, and tests them step by step. In the field of experimental sciences, more particularly, he [sic] constructs hypotheses, or systems of theories, and tests them against experience by observation and experiment. I suggest that it is the task of the logic of scientific discovery, or the logic of knowledge, to give logical analysis to this procedure; that is to analyze the method of empirical sciences.

In this way, Popper described the tasks and methods of the scientist. He argued against Hume's deductive perspective (or perspective that general rules hold and it is our job to uncover these rules) by suggesting that science is also inductive (i.e., conclusions drawn from science are probable rather than absolute). Popper also questioned Kant's positivist perspective by suggesting that knowledge is never determined as finality, but rather that it can and should be continuously subject to additional testing and possible refutation.

More recent descriptions of science, and the scientific method, extend the perspective held in the early-to-mid 1900s, which described scientists as objective observers who were both methodical and detached in their use of the scientific method to uncover "truth." For example, Lakatos (1976) subsequently extended Popper's theory of knowledge in its application to mathematical theorems. Specifically, Lakatos claimed that no theorem is final or perfect, but rather that no counterexample has yet been discovered. As such, he argued that knowledge must accumulate with time, evidence, and instances of contradictions. In other words, he argued for a programmatic view of research and of the development of knowledge over time.

We believe that maintaining a critical attitude or reasoning (i.e., critical inquiry) is an essential component of being a scientist. Scientific inquiry is understood to be a critical attitude toward findings and interpretations based upon the findings. Indeed, scientific inquiry is perhaps best described as a never-ending process of successive approximations in which the scientist has a tolerance for ambiguity, a willingness and ability to question, and an ability to entertain competing answers, and conduct empirical tests among them.

In essence, the scientist uses the scientific method, or a set of assumptions and standardized rules about collecting and evaluating data, in an effort to reduce bias and develop credible "ways of knowing." Collecting data allows investigators to put their ideas to an empirical test. The basic functions of the scientific approach are twofold (e.g., Kerlinger, 1986; Kerlinger & Lee, 2000). The first is to advance knowledge, make discoveries, and learn facts. The second is to establish relations among events and develop theories, thereby helping professionals to make predictions of future events.

PHILOSOPHICAL FOUNDATIONS OF HUMAN BEHAVIOR

Philosophical foundations guide our understanding of the world and affect the methods by which scientists conduct research. We will briefly discuss four philosophical underpinnings of research: positivism, postpositivism, constructivism, and critical theory. Although these four philosophical underpinnings are often discussed as distinct philosophies, it is important to understand that two or more paradigms often "interbreed" (Lincoln & Guba, 2000, p. 146) and the boundaries among these perspectives are in constant flux. With this caveat, we will present a brief discussion of four paradigms according to assumptions across three dimensions (ontology, epistemology, and methodologies—see Table 1.1).

Positivism

Positivism is the paradigm that most closely depicts the scientific method as traditionally taught in the physical sciences. According to this paradigm, the nature of the universe can be known and the scientist's goal is to discover the natural laws that govern objects in the universe. For example, physical laws that describe gravitation, magnetism, and electricity may be considered as statements about the universe that are universal in terms of both time and context. A key principle is that "truth" exists, and given time, brilliance, and sophisticated methods, discoveries will be made that illuminate the truth. In the positivistic realm, the scientist is "objective." In this way, the scientist neither affects the world that is studied nor is affected by world under investigation. A given experiment is expected to lead to the same outcome and conclusion, regardless of who conducts the experiment. In the end, the data yield results that are self-evident to the scientific community and confidence in results derives from the scientific method rather than from the scientist.

The scientific method involves well-defined steps. First, the scientist makes a conjecture about the nature of the universe. Next, the scientist designs an experiment such that its results will either confirm or disconfirm the conjecture. Knowledge is contained only in statements based on or linked to direct observation. If the data conform to the prediction, the conjecture is verified. If the data do not conform to the prediction, then the scientist concludes that the phenomenon being studied does not follow the conjecture. Positivism is often characterized as a hypothetico-deductive process. In other words, deductions are derived from testing hypotheses.

There are other important characteristics of positivistic research. First, relations typically are expressed in terms of causality—X causes Y. Second, theories are reductionistic such that complex processes are understood by being broken down into simpler subprocesses, which can be studied more easily. Third, laws are usually expressed mathematically, measurements are quantitative, and conclusions are dichotomous (either the data conform to the prediction, or they do not). According to positivism, human nature is lawful, the accumulation of facts or knowledge will result in conclusions regarding whether a law is true or not true, and the goal is to identify causal relationships among variables. This contributes to the overall goal of science: to develop theories of human behavior, which consist of a network of knowledge statements that are grounded in observation and tied together by deductive logic.

TABLE 1.1 Major Tenets of Philosophical Underpinnings

	Ontology	Epistemology	Methodology
	The nature of reality	The relationship between the inquirer and the known	Processes for gaining knowledge of the world
Positivism	There is a "real" reality Truth exists and can be known Dichotomous conclusions are possible	The scientist is objective The scientist does not affect the research and is not affected by it	Scientific method Hypothetico-deductive process Absolute truth can be uncovered Linear
Postpositivism	There is a "real" reality Truth can never be fully known Dichotomous conclusions are not possible because systems are complex	All research is flawed The scientist has biases that may affect the research	Scientific method Hypothetico-deductive process Linear Reliance upon inferences based on probability
Constructivism	There is no "real" reality or absolute truth There are no conjectures or tests of conjectures Ideas about the world are constructed in the minds of individuals Perceptions are reality	Constructions can only be understood via interactions between (a) the investigator and the participant or (b) between the investigator and the world of the participant	Reliance upon hermeneutics as data Dialectics (interactions between the participant and the investigator) are critical to the interpretation of data Recursive
Critical theory	Social constructions are shaped by social, political, cultural, historical, and economic forces Social constructions results from power structures that have become embedded within a societal context over time	Social constructions are deeply embedded in the investigator and the participant The values of the investigator are vital to the inquiry The investigator and the participant form a relationship	Constructions are refined or altered via the process of interpretation Interpretations facilitate social action designed to emancipate from oppression Dialectism is used to alter constructions Recursive

Postpositivism

Postpositivism shares with positivism the belief in a "real" reality and the goal of discovering "truth." Postpositivists, however, recognize that truth cannot be fully known and that (at best) we make probabilistic statements rather than absolute statements about truth. For example, the statistical models that underlie research in the social sciences are saturated with this probabilistic interpretation. The values of p associated with statistical tests represent probabilities, given the assumption that the null hypothesis is true. Statistical tests assert that we can never conclude with certainty that our results can differentiate among competing hypotheses. When we reject the null hypothesis (i.e., obtain a statistically significant result), we decide to accept the alternate hypothesis knowing that there is a small probability that we made the wrong conclusion. In addition, because postpositivism is characterized by a belief that absolute "truth" cannot be known, the logic of the positivistic scientific method is altered. In the postpositivistic paradigm, theories lead to conjectures, and the statements about truth are altered to recognize that the inferences are probabilistic. If the data are consistent with the conjecture, then confidence in the theory as an accurate description of "truth" is increased.

The term *corroborated* is often used to indicate that a study produced results consistent with prediction and that the conjecture has survived another test. If, however, the data are inconsistent with theoretically derived conjectures and the study is valid, then the theory has failed to be corroborated. A succession of studies that fail to conform to prediction would constitute evidence that the theory should be revised or abandoned. The goal in postpositivistic research is to produce, through a succession of experiments, descriptions that are closer approximations to the truth. For example, to prove that smoking leads to various detrimental health outcomes, multiple experiments of various types (e.g., passive designs, experimental designs using lab animals) were needed.

Postpositivism also recognizes that there is error and bias in the scientific process. For example, classical test theory rests on the proposition that any observed score represents "true score" (or the true amount of a characteristic that a person possesses) plus error. We acknowledge that random error renders our assessment of any construct imperfect. In addition, postpositivists recognize that all research is flawed and that bias has the potential to affect all research. Finally, there is recognition that the researcher may affect the research process. Truths, therefore, are not considered to be self-evident but rather must be arbitrated by the scientific community. The process of peer review is an admission that the validity of a conclusion is open to interpretation and that it is scientists' opinions about the veracity of a claim that dictate whether or not a result adds to the cumulative knowledge of a field.

Constructivism

In the constructivism paradigm, notions of "truth" and "reality" are abandoned in favor of the belief that ideas about the world, particularly the social world, are constructed in the minds of individuals. Constructivists recognize that these constructions are based on the experiences of individuals as they interact with the physical and social environment, are shaped by cultural context, and may be idiosyncratic. Constructions can be simple or complex, naive or sophisticated, uninformed or informed, but they cannot be proven true or false.

Constructivists believe that the meaning attributed to the event by the participants of the system, rather than the event itself, defines reality. Suppose that we consider the example of an individual who has been bullied. Constructivists recognize the reality of the event, but then argue that it is the meaning that is attributed to that event by the individual that is important in determining social relations and behavior. Because social constructions are developed through interactions with the environment and involve mental representations and interpretations of those interactions, the investigator and the participant(s) are linked. A participant's internal constructions, therefore, can only be understood via interactions between the investigator and the participant or the interaction between the investigator and the world of the participant.

Constructivists use hermeneutics and dialectics to facilitate understanding of the participant's constructions. Hermeneutics refers to the activity of interpretation of data (e.g., language, behavior, text, artifacts, other aspects of human behavior or thought). Constructivists use these data to develop an interpretation that is a description of the constructions of the participants. Constructivists also attend to dialectics, or the interactions between the participant and the investigator, in their interpretation of data. At the most basic level, the interaction is a conversation in which words are exchanged and interpretations of language contributes to an understanding of constructions. At the next level (which is more commonly associated with critical theory), the exchange involves discussing these constructions (e.g., an investigator shares her or his interpretations with the participant). At the last level, dialectics involve refining or altering constructions based upon the process of interpretation.

In the constructivist paradigm, there can be no conjectures (i.e., predictions based upon hypothesized truths) or tests of conjectures. Data are not collected with the aim of determining whether or not observations are consistent with conjecture. Rather, data lead to interpretations that then lead the investigator in directions that may not have been anticipated. The investigator subsequently may reinterpret data or collect additional data that may have been unimaginable when the investigation began. Constructivist and critical theorists (discussed next), therefore, recognize that methods are recursive (i.e., the results and method influence each other).

Critical Theory

Critical theory posits that people's social constructions are shaped by the social, political, cultural, historical, and economic forces in the environment that often have been created by individuals who were in positions of power. Over time, the constructions take on the appearance of reality such that the social reality grown out of the social context is assumed to be truth. Because the constructions are so deeply embedded in society (including in researchers themselves), it can be extremely difficult to comprehend that these constructions were spawned in the societal context and are not truths. For example (and any examples chosen are necessarily controversial), the belief that the monogamous union of one male and one female for the purpose of reproduction (i.e., heterosexual marriage) is "natural" is a socially derived position. Critical theorists would concede that marriage is necessary and important for the social order (as we know it), but they would contend that marriage, as an institution, was generated by the social system. They would argue that there are alternatives (e.g., same-sex unions, polygamous marriages) and that the "truth" of any "natural" propensity to marry is unfounded.

In critical theory, the investigator and the participant form a relationship, and the values of the investigator are vital to the activity. Inquiry involves the level of dialectism that changes constructions (i.e., the third level mentioned previously). That is, the investigation involves a dialogue between investigator and participants in such a way that the participants come to realize that their understanding of the world is derived from the precepts of the social order, and that these precepts can (and should) be altered. In other words, a goal of critical theory is to facilitate individuals' realization that constructions are socially constructed beliefs rather than unchangeable truths. Through this process, the dialectic leads individuals to understand that social action is needed to change the social order so as to facilitate emancipation from oppression (e.g., racism, classism, heterosexism, sexism).

Scholars have argued that "no single critical theory" exists, but that there are some "commonalities among the variants of critical theory" (e.g., Ponterotto, 2005b, p. 130). For example, feminist theory can be considered within the critical theoretical realm in that it contends that traditional roles for women have been socially determined, that the power in society has been allocated to men, and that these social realities can be altered. One goal of feminist theory is to raise the consciousness of individuals so that individuals come to recognize the historical context that led to the current social situation and subsequently move toward rejecting traditional roles and norms. Some critical theorists would contend that this worldview involves more than social action, which tends to change society at the margins, and instead necessitates radical change that dramatically replaces current social structures with others.

Summary of the Philosophical Foundations

Philosophers, since the beginning of humankind, have wrestled with ideas about knowledge and knowing. It is impossible (or irrelevant) to "prove" that one of the four paradigms is correct, more appropriate, better, or more useful than another. Each paradigm has different systems for understanding the world but no method, either logical or empirical, can establish the superiority of any given foundation. The debate over the philosophy of science is exceedingly complex and intertwined with our view of human nature, the adequacy of our research methods, the content of our research investigations, and the perceived utility of our research findings. Nevertheless, it is vital to understand the philosophical foundations of various paradigms to ensure that the research approach is appropriate for the question. Some (e.g., Morrow, Rakhasha, & Castañeda, 2001) have recommended that researchers select paradigms in accordance with an understanding of belief systems, values, personality, and knowledge of research design.

SCIENTIFIC METHOD AS APPLIED TO COUNSELING AND COUNSELING PSYCHOLOGY

The scientific method provides a mechanism to contribute to knowledge that is credible, reliable, and effective. This knowledge, in turn, is applied to work with individuals to facilitate growth and positive change. Within the field of counseling, the goal of the scientific method is multifaceted and is to advance knowledge, make discoveries, increase our understanding of human behavior, and use knowledge to solve practical problems. Because phenomena of interest in the realm of counseling include both observable events as well as subjective and self-reported experiences, researchers examine a range of phenomenological or self-report variables.

Not surprisingly, many counseling scholars argue that the adequacy of our research can be evaluated by how relevant the findings are for practitioners and for the public (Krumboltz & Mitchell, 1979; Zimbardo, 2004). Scientific research can advance our knowledge base or understanding of human behavior by providing data that describe and help us understand a wide range of human behaviors. This understanding contributes to an ability to alter such behaviors via counseling, advocacy, and consultation interventions.

The expansion of knowledge in the counseling profession is guided by pressing societal needs as well as by questions or problems that arise in our professional work. For example, a pressing question is whether the effectiveness of psychotherapy is related to common factors or specific ingredients (e.g., see Wampold & Imel, 2015). Our research is also guided by current societal needs that merit immediate attention, such as social advocacy and social justice for marginalized groups (for more details see Speight & Vera, 2003; Toporek, Gerstein, Fouad, Roysircar, & Israel, 2005; Toporek, Kwan, & Williams, 2012). For example, the increased national and international attention to immigration and the effects of recent legislation have spurred the development of an emerging body of research relevant to the counseling profession (see Yakushko & Morgan, 2012).

A common defining element of the counseling profession is that we conceptualize a person's behavior as a function of the environment (Fretz, 1982). People do not think, feel, or behave in isolation, but rather in the context of a rich personal and social history. Research that increases understanding of how individuals interact within a broader social and personal environmental context is crucial to the development of knowledge about counseling. A goal of science, therefore, is to expand our knowledge about interactions between individuals and a larger personal, social, cultural, and historical context. Ignoring these contexts ignores critical elements in understanding current behavior and can lead to ineffective or inappropriate interventions and unethical behavior (American Psychological Association [APA], 2003; Toporek, Kwan, & Williams, 2012).

There are costs to acquiring knowledge by using the scientific method. Empirical investigations are costly in terms of time, energy, and resources. Putting complex and internal cognitive and affective processes to empirical test is a difficult and elusive task. Sometimes when we try to identify specific processes or variables we become mechanistic and lose the gestalt, or whole picture. The lack of sophistication of our research methods may result in conclusions that tell us little about real-life processes. Further, relying upon culturally homogeneous samples or on theories based on majority culture to draw conclusions can lead to inappropriate interpretations and harmful consequences to individuals who are members of underrepresented groups.

Despite these challenges and limitations, we argue that the risks of building a profession on nonscientific evidence are far greater. As such, the knowledge on which the profession is built must be based on objective or verifiable information that can be put to empirical or quantifiable tests. In this way, the methods used to establish our "truths" have a built-in self-correction process; each empirical test is independent of previous findings and can either verify or disconfirm the previous knowledge.

In summary, the knowledge of a profession must be empirically based and verifiable rather than subjective and untestable. Even though the scientific method has costs and is not problem-free, building a helping profession without it is too risky. The credibility of the counseling profession would be significantly challenged without a strong scientific foundation and reliance upon theory to guide our research and interventions.

THE ROLE OF THEORY IN THE COUNSELING PROFESSION

Theories seek to establish general relations and conditional statements among events that help professionals to understand phenomena. Theories are relevant to science in that they provide a mechanism by which to organize and understand explanations for the dynamics that underlie a given psychological phenomenon (Karr & Larson, 2005; Strong, 1991). Theories also guide our practice by providing us with the tools to conceptualize human behavior and develop testable hypotheses to apply to our work with clients.

Another critical role of theory in science is that theories provide a foundation for hypothesis development and testing (Tracey & Glidden-Tracey, 1999). De Groot (1969) defined a theory as "a system of logically interrelated, specifically non-contradictory, statements, ideas, and concepts relating to an area of reality, formulated in such a way that testable hypotheses can be derived from them" (p. 4). In this way, theories function as a foundation from which scientists understand logical inferences and develop testable hypotheses (Forster, 2000; Karr & Larson, 2005).

Although it is exceedingly difficult to develop broadscale theories aimed at predicting human behavior, it is useful for counseling professionals to organize facts and knowledge into theoretical frameworks that can be used as ingredients within more complex and conditional models of behavior. Theoretical frameworks that consist of sets of conditional statements that can be qualified by specific information about an individual allow both the needed specificity and complexity in explaining and predicting individuals' behavior. In this way, theory drives our science and practice, and our science and practice explicate theory. We discuss both of these functions next.

Theory-Driven Research

Many scholars highlight the importance of conducting research that is theory driven. For example, Meehl (1978) advocated for the usefulness of theory to guide researchers to ask meaningful questions and Strong (1991) suggested that theory provides a way to avoid falling into the trap of a "generation of a multitude of unconnected facts" (Strong, 1991). Theory-driven research involves a process whereby theory is used to guide the development of hypothesis generation, which leads to testing and observations. Findings obtained from data are subsequently interpreted through the context of discovery (Strong, 1991). In this way, research explicates and refines theory. Attending to theory and viewing science as a continuous accumulation of knowledge (Kline, 2009) is consistent with Lakatos's (1976) value of science as programmatic. Indeed, we argue that theory development, specification, and refinement are central goals of the scientific endeavor: little is more useful than a solid theory!

Concerns regarding the status of theory-driven research in counseling have been raised. In their review of the literature from three major counseling journals from 1990 to 1999, Karr and Larson (2005) demonstrated that less than half of the sampled empirical quantitative studies published in *Journal of Counseling Psychology*, *Journal of Career Development*, and *Journal of Vocational Behavior* met their criteria for consideration as theory-derived research. These authors concluded that 57% of quantitative empirical research published at this time lacked a theoretical or conceptual framework.

One area of counseling research that has been noted for its theory-driven approach is vocational psychology. For example, Holland's hexagon of career interest areas (i.e., RIASEC) has generated a large body of empirical research since its inception (Swanson & Gore, 2000). Consistent with the cyclical process of theory-driven research, Holland's RIASEC has been tested over time and has been extended and refined according to tests of its structure of interests across cultures (e.g., Wilkins, Ramkissoon, & Tracey, 2013; Zhang, Kube, Wang, & Tracey, 2013).

Theory-Driven Practice

Theory-driven research also allows counseling professionals to ensure that they are engaging in interventions with individuals that are theory driven. This allows us to ensure that our counseling interventions are informed by, and grounded in, scientific evidence. Theories of psychotherapy offer a framework from which to explain the characteristics and progression of psychological phenomena for clients that informs counseling professionals' approach to treatment.

Pepinsky and Pepinsky (1954) articulated a prescriptive model of counselor thinking based on the scientific method. Strohmer and Newman (1983) summarized their model in this way:

> The counselor observes the client, makes inferences about his or her current status and the causal inferences, and then, based on these inferences, makes a tentative judgment about the client. The counselor then proceeds in an experimental fashion to state the judgment as a hypothesis and to test it against independent observations of the client. Through a series of such tentative judgments and tests based on these judgments, the counselor constructs a hypothetical model of the client. This model then serves as the basis for making predictions (e.g., which treatment approach is most appropriate) about the client. (p. 557)

In essence, Pepinsky and Pepinsky (1954) suggested that the counselor incorporate a scientific or critical thinking model by (a) generating hypotheses based on (b) the data that the client presents, followed by (c) empirical testing of the hypotheses, to develop (d) a model that can be used (e) to make predictions about the client. The essence of this approach is that it is *data based* or *empirical,* which lessens the chance of personal biases or subjectivity.

Since Pepinsky and Pepinsky's early writing, many others have offered approaches to clinical work based on the scientific method (e.g., Stricker, 2007). Evidence-based practice policies, by their very nature, require that psychotherapists' practice be grounded in theory and research (APA Presidential Task Force on Evidence-Based Practice, 2006). One of the hallmarks of our profession that highlights the integration of science and practice is that of psychotherapy outcome research. Specifically, this research seeks to answer the question: How do we know that our interventions are effective? This question has led to a large body of research that has sought to identify the interventions, therapeutic effects, common factors, and mediating contextual factors that contribute to positive client outcomes (e.g., Wampold & Imel, 2015). The accumulation of evidence from these data has demonstrated that merely relying upon a person's (such as your clinical supervisor or instructor) opinion about which interventions, under which conditions, lead to effective outcomes is insufficient. Instead, we must rely upon sound research methods to build the *knowledge* upon which the counseling profession is based.

In summary, theories have an integral role in the science and practice of the counseling profession. We all have theories, and these theories inform our perspectives as researchers and practitioners. In this book, you will learn how to examine theories, test theories, and develop theories (e.g., grounded theory). But most importantly, it is this combination, or the integration of science and practice, that is a foundation of our profession.

Science and Practice Integration

The integration of science and practice is a foundation of graduate training programs. The basic assumption is that students trained in both science and practice will be better prepared as professionals, regardless of where a particular job falls on the science versus practice continuum. Students entering a graduate training program in counseling typically have a wide range of interests along the scientist-practitioner continuum. These interests often change over time throughout their graduate training and career.

Training Models   The scientist-practitioner model is espoused in the majority of graduate training programs. The first national conferences for the training of clinical and counseling psychologists were held in Boulder, Colorado, and Ann Arbor, Michigan, in 1949 and 1950, respectively (see Baker & Benjamin, 2000, for a more detailed historical overview). One major purpose of the Boulder conference was to develop a broad scientist-practitioner model of training that came to be known as the Boulder model (Raimy, 1950). The creators of that model stressed the philosophy that students need to be trained to do research and to learn the skills of the practitioner. The integration of these two skill sets was believed to create a strong foundation for future research and practice. The field of counseling psychology reiterated its commitment to the scientist-practitioner model, most notably in 1951 at the Northwestern conference (Whiteley, 1984), in 1964 at the Greystone conference (Thompson & Super, 1964), again in 1987 at the Atlanta conference (Meara et al., 1988), and into the 1990s (Watkins, 1994). Meara and colleagues described the model in this way:

> The scientist-practitioner model is an integrated approach to knowledge that recognizes the interdependence of theory, research, and practice. The model emphasizes systematic and thoughtful analyses of human experiences and judicious application of the knowledge and attitudes gained from such analyses. In this way, an attitude of scholarly inquiry and critical thinking is deemed as essential to all of the activities in which a counseling professional engages. (p. 368)

Other models of graduate training have emerged. For example, the local clinical scientist model was presented as an alternative model to bridge science and practice and has been adopted by several programs that emphasize practitioner training (Stricker & Trierweiler, 1995). In this model, clinicians are encouraged to apply what they have learned from the research literature into their counseling work and embody a scientific attitude through "disciplined inquiry, critical thinking, imagination, rigor skepticism, and openness to change" (Stricker, 2007, p. 86) when facing evidence from their work with clients. The local clinical scientist model focuses on how clinicians develop and test hypotheses in the session while working with their clients. Local clinical scientists treat each client as a test of a model and the counseling room as a research laboratory. A group of clinicians can then collaborate to collect data from their clinical work, share the data with one another, and aggregate results across individuals.

The Association for Psychological Science also has moved to adopt an accreditation process for clinical science training programs. The clinical science model emphasizes training that is "grounded in science, practiced by scientists, and held accountable to the rigorous standards of scientific evidence" (McFall, 1990). Its advocates argue that other training models have shifted in their focus toward practice training that occurs outside of solid and intentional training in the use of science to inform effective practice and the ability for practitioners to adequately consume and integrate findings from the scientific literature.

Although the particular training emphasis differs among each of these models, and their merits have been the subject of some debate (e.g., Sanchez & Turner, 2003), all share the commitment to training counseling professionals who are committed to the reciprocal nature of science and practice. Further, they share a core foundation in scientific or critical thinking that forms the foundation for all professional activities.

The Role of Scientific and Critical Thinking

Scientific or critical thinking is a central outcome of graduate training. The most important outcome is whether the graduate can utilize scientific or critical thinking in all professional activities rather than the actual level of engagement in science or practice activities. Scientific thinking refers to a controlled method of inquiry and reasoning, typically to collect data of some kind for the purpose of testing a hypothesis. Indeed, graduate students are trained to solve problems and to possess the methodological skill to think critically about a problem in order to conceptualize the problem.

A crucial characteristic of a professional counselor is the integration of scientific thinking into the daily activities of professional practice (e.g., Gambrill, 2005; Pepinsky & Pepinsky, 1954). Scientific thinking is instrumental in how counselors process information about a specific client during counseling as well as evaluate the counseling process. One of the hallmarks of graduate work in counseling is to acquire critical thinking skills, the ability to identify and process information with fewer biases, stereotypes, and assumptions; formulate hypotheses; gather data; and make informed decisions.

Research clearly indicates that people are selective or biased in the type of information to which they attend and do not think as "objective computers" (e.g., Gambrill, 1990, 2005; Nisbett & Ross, 1980). In particular, people often attend to information that confirms their existing beliefs or discount information that is contrary to their existing beliefs (e.g., Kahneman & Tversky, 1973; Kahneman & Tversky, 1979). We develop worldviews that are culture bound and prone to stereotypes and assumptions about a variety of characteristics and identities, including but not limited to race/ethnicity, age, gender, social class, sexual orientation, and ability status (e.g., see APA, 2003). These biases, along with others that will be discussed throughout this book, can lead to problems for psychotherapists as they process information about clients. Tracey, Wampold, Lichtenberg, and Goodyear (2014) argued that psychotherapists are prone to a number of errors, particularly in their assessment of their level of expertise in their work with clients. In particular, they explained the need for psychotherapists to adopt a disconfirming scientific approach, avoid the overuse of hindsight bias, and utilize hypothesis testing in work with clients. It is, therefore, essential that we think critically and utilize the scientific literature to inform our practice so as to prevent harm in our professional work with clients.

Becoming an active consumer of the professional research literature is a basic expectation of graduate training (e.g., Goodyear & Benton, 1986). Reading the literature affects our thinking, refines our conceptualizations of the counseling process, and informs our treatment interventions. In this book, you will learn how to consume the research literature, assess findings from research, and utilize the knowledge in your own professional practice and scholarship.

SUMMARY AND CONCLUSIONS

The counseling profession helps people with a wide variety of personal, educational, and career-related problems. We must remain cognizant that we are working with real people, many of whom need critically important information and/or are experiencing psychological pain and are in need of professional assistance. In this chapter, we discuss different ways to acquire knowledge. To be credible, reliable, and effective, the profession must be built on a dependable knowledge base rather than on tenacity, decrees from authority figures, or subjective opinions.

Science represents a way of knowing and a way of establishing relevant knowledge bases for the profession. We can debate about the best way to establish suitable knowledge bases for our profession. Regardless of the perspective, however, it is critical to understand that science plays an essential role in developing the knowledge upon which the counseling profession is based. Without a strong science to promote the continual development of our field, our profession will be significantly weakened. It is, therefore, incumbent upon the counseling profession to protect and promote the development of science to continually refine a wide range of knowledge relevant for the diverse forms of counseling practice.

Although science promotes the development of relevant knowledge bases, it is essential that the members of our profession are careful in applying our knowledge bases and do not automatically assume that any particular knowledge base represents a "truth" that can be applied across different personal and historical contexts. In fact, we are at greatest risk when we consciously or unconsciously assume universal truths within counseling research and practice. Researchers, therefore, must be vigilant when applying even well documented findings across social and cultural contexts.

In summary, we highlight two important conclusions. First, the role of science is essential for the well-being, growth, and survival of the counseling profession. Second, the ability of counseling professionals to appropriately apply scientific knowledge to facilitate the development of a diverse clientele is essential. It is critical that we think scientifically and question assumptions, biases, and stereotypes. In the next chapter, we outline steps to ensure these goals.

2 Chapter Research Training: Joys and Challenges

It takes many years to become truly skilled at a complex set of tasks, such as becoming a skilled potter. For example, in Japan, it is common for an apprentice potter to make the same vase form for many months just to acquire the specific skills to consistently make 15–20 identical vases in a row. Expertise develops over time within an environment that fosters development.

In this chapter we discuss the process of becoming a skilled researcher and the type of training environments that seem to be most helpful for students to acquire the necessary skills and attitudes. For many students in counseling, graduate school is their first introduction to research and research design, and it evokes many emotional reactions that come with any novel experience, from joy and excitement to anxiety and disenchantment. We seek to prepare students to approach research with enthusiasm for the creativity involved and with a willingness to learn the intricacies of the craft and the joy of creating new knowledge for the profession. In addition, we want to promote an awareness of the anxiety that may be created by learning a technical skill that may not be central to one's interests but is required to accomplish a goal (that is, obtaining a graduate degree and becoming a professional in counseling).

We address four topics in this chapter. First, we provide a brief overview of how science intersects with counseling and psychology training through the scientist-practitioner model and the topic of evidence-based practice. Second, we identify and discuss some issues related to the developmental process of acquiring research competencies, specifically the joy as well as the challenges and fears. Third, we discuss ways in which counselors and counseling psychologists can train others to become competent, eager, and productive researchers. In this part of the chapter, we discuss what is known about research training, and how training environments can be structured to create the opportunity for students both to learn about research, and to consume and produce quality research products. Fourth, we discuss ways to broaden the concept of scientific training to include scientific thinking skills as well as research application skills. Most important, throughout this chapter we emphasize the developmental process of acquiring skills step by step to become a skilled researcher and scientist.

SCIENCE AND PRACTICE

The Scientist-Practitioner Model

Bridging the gap between research and practice in counseling is an important issue (Murray, 2009). As we mention in Chapter 1, many graduate training programs in counseling espouse the *scientist-practitioner model* of training. Basically, this model consists of training in both scientific and practitioner activities; the basic assumption is that students trained in both science and practice will be better prepared for the multitude of employment demands in the counseling profession. The scientific activities include courses that focus on the philosophy of science, qualitative and quantitative designs and methods, statistics, evaluation, counseling research literature, and often involvement in research projects (Larson & Besett-Alesch, 2000). The practice-oriented side includes courses such as counseling methods, counseling theories, personality, assessment, and involvement in a variety of practicum experiences. When students enter a graduate training program in counseling, they typically have a wide range of interests along with the scientist-practitioner continuum. These interests often change over time, not only during graduate training but also throughout their career; thus, students need to prepare themselves broadly to allow for career changes over time.

The scientist-practitioner model goes back to over 60 years. The clinical psychologists developed what they dubbed the scientist-practitioner model of training, which is also referred to as the Boulder model (Raimy, 1950).

Meara et al. (1988) succinctly captured the scientist-practitioner model:

> Psychologists, whatever their work, are professionals and their attitude toward their work is scientific. The scientist-professional model is an integrated approach to knowledge that recognizes the interdependence of theory, research, and practice. The model emphasizes systematic and thoughtful analyses of human experiences and judicious application of the knowledge and attitudes gained from such analyses. An attitude of scholarly inquiry is critical to all the activities of those educated in the scientist-professional model. The model encompasses a variety of research methods, assessment techniques, and intervention strategies. The counseling psychologist is engaged in the pursuit and application of psychological knowledge to promote optimal development for individuals, groups, and systems (including families), and to provide remedies for the psychological difficulties that encumber them. To implement these goals, the scientist-professional psychologist adopts a scientific approach based on observation of psychological phenomena. This approach generates theoretical constructs and propositions, which are in turn tested as hypotheses (Claiborn, 1987; Pepinsky & Pepinsky, 1954). (p. 368)

The scientist-practitioner model has been the predominant model of most counseling psychology programs with 73% of the programs specifically referring to the scientist-practitioner model in their program description (Horn et al., 2007). However, over the years there have been some critiques, especially in the earlier years about the utility of the scientist-practitioner model, which students may also have concerns about today. These included questions such as whether most practitioners use research findings in their practice. Moreover, it could also be that graduate training in practitioner activities does not adequately incorporate scientific activities, and vice versa (e.g., Stoltenberg et al., 2000). Some people might think that perhaps the type of research being conducted is too distant from the reality of the practitioner (see, e.g., Howard, 1984), or perhaps our research methods reduce counseling phenomena to meaningless numbers (see, e.g., Goldman, 1976). Yet another factor could be that students admitted to graduate programs have predominantly social or interpersonal interests (see, e.g., Magoon & Holland, 1984).

Therefore, other training models have emerged. These models share the core goals of integrating science and practice, but with different emphasis. For example, the *practitioner-scholar model* places more emphasis on the training of practitioners and was closely associated with the emergence of professional schools of psychology and Psy.D. degrees. This model also parallels the idea of local clinical scientists (Stricker & Trierweiler, 1995) and practice-based evidence (Barkham & Mellor-Clark, 2000) that emphasize using clinical work and observations of clients to collect data and test clinical hypotheses. On the other end of the science-practice training spectrum, the *clinical science model* (Academy of Psychological Clinical Science, 2014) is similar to the scientist-practitioner model in theory, but places even more emphasis on science and uses empirical approaches to advance clinical science.

The importance of science in the psychology field has not diminished, but rather has grown over the past few decades. There has been increased emphasis on utilizing scientific findings in mental health practices. Thus, it is important for students to have the scientific skills to critically evaluate research findings rather than simply accepting knowledge from research as authoritative prescriptions (Stoltenberg et al., 2000). Integrating the scientist-practitioner model with current trends in the mental health field is important, and there are recommendations on how the scientist-practitioner model can be better implemented (see Stoltenberg et al., 2000). Chwalisz (2003) suggested that evidence-based practice is the framework for training scientist-practitioners in the 21st century. The evidence-based practice movement in psychology has become a main focus over the past decade.

Evidence-Based Practice

The increased demands from health care systems and policies to integrate science and psychology practice have made evidence-based practice an important movement in the psychology and mental health field (Baker, McFall, & Shoham, 2008). Evidence-based practice in psychology (EBPP) is "the integration of the best available research with clinical expertise in the context of patient characteristics, culture, and preferences." (APA Presidential Task Force on Evidence-Based Practice, 2006, p. 273). The field of medicine is an example of how EBPP has shaped the improvement of patient outcomes in utilizing research in clinical practice (Woolf & Atkins, 2001). EBPP is a more comprehensive concept than a closely related movement of establishing empirically supported treatments

(ESTs), which refers to the specific treatment that works for certain disorders or problems. Whereas ESTs focus on the treatment approach, EBPP starts with the client and with the attempt to utilize research evidence to inform treatment to achieve the best possible outcome for the client. Moreover, EBPP includes a broader scope of clinical/counseling aspects, such as assessment, case formulation, counseling relationships, etc.

In APA's 2006 Presidential Task Force on Evidence-Based Practice, research evidence, clinical expertise, and patient characteristics were all emphasized as critical components leading to best practices. In terms of this research evidence, a broad array of scientific results related to intervention strategies, assessment, clinical problems, and client populations are all included. Multiple types of research evidence such as efficacy, effectiveness, cost effectiveness, cost benefit, epidemiological, and treatment utilization are all recognized as contributors to informing best psychological practices. EBPP also requires mental health practitioners to recognize that treatment method (Nathan & Gorman, 2007), counselors/therapists (Wampold, 2001), therapy relationship (Norcross, 2002), and the client (Bohart & Tallman, 1999) are all critical components to achieve best outcomes in psychological practices, and therefore research evidence on any of these aspects should not be overlooked.

Clinical expertise is also a critical component of EBPP (APA Presidential Task Force on Evidence-Based Practice, 2006). Counselors and psychologists are recognized as essential contributors in identifying the best research evidence based on the client's characteristics, background, presenting issue, and preferences. Thus, it is important that counselors and psychologists are trained not only as practitioners but also as scientists so that their practice is informed by scientific literature. Client characteristics, culture, and preferences are also important parts of EBPP. Counselors and psychologists should take into account what works for whom when providing guidelines for effective practice. EBPP requires attention to client characteristics such as gender, sexual orientation, culture, ethnicity, race, age, religion, nationality, disability status, etc. In addition to client characteristics, it is also important to consider the client's values, religious beliefs, worldviews, goals, and preferences for treatment when determining and utilizing the best available treatment for the client.

Although APA and many training programs have supported EBPP, there has also been resistance toward EBPP. Similar to the critiques of the scientist-practitioner model, there have been several reasons that EBPP raises concerns. Lilienfeld and colleagues (2013) examined the roots of resistance to EBPP by clinical psychologists and summarized six sources:

> (a) naïve realism, which can lead clinicians to conclude erroneously that client change is due to an intervention itself rather than to a host of competing explanations; (b) deep-seated misconceptions regarding human nature (e.g., mistaken beliefs regarding the causal primacy of early experiences) that can hinder the adoption of evidence-based treatments; (c) statistical misunderstandings regarding the application of group probabilities to individuals; (d) erroneous apportioning of the burden of proof on skeptics rather than proponents of untested therapies; (e) widespread mischaracterizations of what EBP entails; and (f) pragmatic, educational, and attitudinal obstacles, such as the discomfort of many practitioners with evaluating the increasingly technical psychotherapy outcome literature. (Lilienfeld, Ritschel, Lynn, Cautin, & Latzman, 2013, p. 883)

In addition to highlighting the roots of resistance, Lilienfeld et al. (2013) also offered suggestions on how to address these resistances among students in training. They suggested exposing students to a better awareness that they are not immune from cognitive biases, such as confirmation bias, hindsight bias, and illusory correlation. They also suggested graduate instructors to not only convey accurate information, but also disabuse students of inaccurate information, especially around misunderstandings of the human nature. They also argue that students should not just be taught the "hows" of implementing therapy techniques, but more so the "whys" of how these approaches have been established as effective. In sum, Lilienfeld et al. stressed the importance of critical thinking and scientific training of students in the mental health field. For more detailed information on EBPP, as well as the resistance toward EBPP, please see APA Presidential Task Force on Evidence-Based Practice (2006) and Lilienfeld et al. (2013).

Science and Practice Training

The focus between research and practice has been an issue for training programs that emphasize both. Sometimes the model has been interpreted as a 50–50 split of performing science and practice activities. The type of model in its ideal form (i.e., implicitly 50% practitioner and 50% scientist/researcher) may be just that—an ideal that is rarely found in reality. Gelso (1979) proposed that it may be more realistic to train students in both domains (in varying degrees depending on their interests) with the expectation that students will find a suitable place for themselves in performing relevant activities on the scientist-practitioner continuum. Thus, one student might prefer a 20–80 split while another might choose a 75–25 split. Sometimes there have been implicit values attached to either science or practice; that is, some educators might value science more than practice, and thus feel more satisfaction when a new graduate obtains the "best" job, which to them is an academic position complete with a myriad of scientific pursuits. We strongly believe that science and practice are both highly valued activities in the counseling profession, and that as a profession we are stronger (and only can survive) when we train students to be competent in both science and practice. In short, it is important for the profession to equally value various points along this performance continuum.

We prefer to conceptualize the *core* of the scientist-practitioner model in terms of scientific or critical thinking. In short, we are suggesting that the role of scientific or critical thinking is a central outcome of a wide range of science and practice activities. The choice of whether a graduate engages in science or practice activities is not the most important outcome, but rather whether the graduate can utilize scientific or critical thinking in whatever professional activities she or he chooses. For example, a counseling center staff member might be engaged primarily in direct client service and, say, one program evaluation project (see Chapter 22); this might be a 5%–95% science-practice split of *professional activities*. A faculty member (three-quarters time) with a quarter-time direct service appointment in the counseling center might have a 75%–25% split of professional activities. In addition to the quantitative difference in how research and practice is split, the role of research can also be qualitatively different. Gelso and Fretz (2001) proposed a three-level model of how research functions for counselors. First, the minimum level involves counselors being able to consume and apply research in their work with clients. The second level involves counselors being able to use critical thinking to develop and test hypotheses during their work with clients. The third level involves being able to conduct empirical studies and to present the research findings. Regardless of the type of professional activities a person selects along the scientist-practitioner continuum, we maintain that counselors utilize scientific thinking within their practice and science activities.

Baker, McFall, and Shoham (2008) suggested that the lack of adequate scientific training and utilization of scientific knowledge has been a major problem in the development of the clinical psychology field, which is also a reflection of the mental health profession:

> Clinical psychologists' failure to achieve a more significant impact on clinical and public health may be traced to their deep ambivalence about the role of science and their lack of adequate science training, which leads them to value personal clinical experience over research evidence, use assessment practices that have dubious psychometric support, and not use the interventions for which there is the strongest evidence of efficacy. Clinical psychology resembles medicine at a point in its history when practitioners were operating in a largely prescientific manner. Prior to the scientific reform of medicine in the early 1900s, physicians typically shared the attitudes of many of today's clinical psychologists, such as valuing personal experience over scientific research. (p. 67)

In the end, there is no doubt that research has enhanced the practice of counseling. Even though a practitioner may not be able to cite a specific reference, his or her graduate school training was likely based on a tremendous amount of research data, all the way from personality theory to intervention strategies. The accumulation may be slow, but the data eventually advance our working knowledge of the field. The scientific method and research have advanced the field, but they could be even more helpful. In addition, training in both science and practice has become more sophisticated with not only more integration but also more emphasis on critical thinking, which is the core of all science and practice activities of the counseling profession. For more information on a broad array of recommendations for enhancing training in the scientist-practitioner model and how EBPP is a framework for training scientist-practitioners in the 21st century, see Chwalisz (2003).

JOYS AND CHALLENGES IN ACQUIRING RESEARCH COMPETENCIES

Students will often experience a number of different reactions to research training, and these emotional reactions can change throughout the course of their graduate training and actually many years beyond (see Table 2.1). Sometimes students will be elated with the joy of discovering new and useful information from their research. Other times students will become restless and disgruntled with the minutiae

TABLE 2.1 Common Student Reactions toward Research and Our Suggestions

Student Feelings	Our Suggestions
I don't know enough to conduct any meaningful research.	Volunteer to help on a research project; slowly work your way up to learn the more advanced skills.
I am a fraud and really don't know how to do research.	Feelings of anxiety and doubt associated with research are normal; they are often due to having limited experiences.
What if I make a mistake and report inaccurate findings?	It is a learning process; allow yourself time to learn and develop more advanced skills.
I'm scared of running into debilitating writing blocks in my research.	Acquiring research and thinking skills occurs over a long period of time; sometimes it is a sign that you may need to acquire more knowledge of the literature.
I am afraid that my results will be statistically nonsignificant.	Programmatic research often results in the accrual of knowledge over time; nonsignificant results are also helpful information.
The whole thesis process seems overwhelming, tedious, long, anxiety producing, confusing, and complicated.	The more you get involved in research, the more self-efficacious you will feel.
I just want to practice; I am not interested in science/research.	Be open to learning more about the research process as well as the research literature.
science = statistics	Science and research are broader than quantitative studies that utilize statistics. Critical thinking is the core of science.
I don't believe that research in counseling can make a difference in the profession.	Read literature review and meta-analysis articles to get a better understanding of cumulative knowledge base.
Science is too intellectual, too cognitive, and unrelated to the experiences of real people.	As you obtain more experience with research activities, your research interests may increase and you might see a higher value on the role of research.

associated with research. In addition, some students will experience obstacles such as negative self-talk, procrastination, perfectionist tendencies, and a range of "shoulds" (e.g., I should be better at math; see Heppner & Heppner, 2004).

The developmental process of acquiring research competencies takes considerable time, years in fact, and often differs across students. Throughout this chapter are reflections from experienced and skillful researchers who provide some useful glimpses into this developmental process of acquiring an array of research competencies. A great deal of wisdom is communicated by these prolific and creative scholars, and we appreciate their candid perspectives on their own developmental journey.

These reflections on their journeys throughout the chapter depict various aspects of the developmental process of acquiring research competencies. From our collective experiences as authors of this text, we have observed that many students question whether they can adequately learn the skills associated with research and science: How can I, a mere graduate student, come up with a good research idea? What if I get bogged down in my research and never finish my degree? Statistics scare me—what if I make a mistake in analyzing my data? We contend that these and other fears are common and developmentally normal. We believe it is essential to discuss the negative affective and cognitive components associated with research, and thus the first section focuses on such common student reactions, namely (a) performance anxiety and efficacy; (b) the false dichotomous conceptualization as research versus practice; and (c) belief in oneself as a researcher, and science in general.

Performance Anxiety and Efficacy   From our experience working with students, we have found that performance anxiety is a central and crucial affective issue. For example, common student disclosures include: "I don't know enough to conduct any meaningful research on my own. How can I do a thesis?" "Any study that I could do would be so basic and bland as to make it worthless." "I feel completely inadequate in even conceiving a study that examines counseling from a unique perspective." "Although I made it through the statistics and research design courses, once I start to do some research, I'll be 'found out'; I am a fraud, and really don't know how to do research." "What if I make a mistake and report inaccurate findings?" "I've had trouble writing before, and I'm scared to death that I will run into debilitating writing blocks again in my research." "I am afraid that my results will be statistically nonsignificant, and all of my research efforts and time will just be one big waste." "I've seen other students in the throes of a dissertation. The whole process seems overwhelming, tedious, long, anxiety producing, confusing, and complicated."

It is important to put these and similar feelings into the context of the typical entering graduate student. Most incoming graduate students have had some experience (or even a lot) with helping other people, and consequently the benefits of counseling and other practitioner activities are abundantly clear. Moreover, for most of us, helping people is a personally rewarding experience, and students have an understanding of those rewards. Conversely, it has been our experience that most incoming students have had considerably less experience with science. Typically, students do not imagine themselves making contributions to the profession by publishing in our professional journals. Since students have had little, if any, research experience, they often have legitimate reasons to question and doubt their skills and abilities—these feelings, concerns, and fears are thus developmentally normal. In fact, it is not uncommon even for faculty to experience performance anxiety and question their efficacy (e.g., see Research Journey 2.1).

This suggests to us that acquiring the necessary research and thinking skills occurs over a long period of time; it does not happen all at once. In fact, expert performance is found associated with active engagement in deliberate practice, which involves training on particular tasks, receiving immediate feedback, having time for evaluation, problem solving, and the opportunity to refine behaviors (Ericsson, 2008).

RESEARCH JOURNEY 2.1

Developing competencies in research is not an event. Instead, it is a slow journey; as some markers are achieved, new competency goals quickly surface, even as a senior faculty member. I am committed to life-long learning! This applies to life in general and also to my life as a researcher. I did not always hear encouraging words from others about my ability to carry out a project or the importance of my work. Early in my career, I focused on the negative messages that I received. It took a while for me to tune out the naysayers and find ways to identify growth areas to strengthen my research so that it could contribute to the literature in the ways that I found important. I have had to learn how to believe in what I do and in my ideas. I was able to do this by seeking feedback from those who conducted similar research—from people who "got" my work and thus were able to identify strengths and limitations of the work in a constructive way. I now recognize that to be a good researcher requires feedback and input from a number of sources. To help develop a research project, it is absolutely essential to share your work with others and get feedback at all stages. Over the years, I have learned that it is okay to have a project be underdeveloped in its initial conceptualization— others do not judge me on where I start, but rather on where I end up. That is, how I have incorporated the ideas and suggestions from others and how much the project has developed over time. Knowing this has provided me the space to make mistakes, learn, and grow.

—Helen Neville, Ph.D.

As students acquire and begin to apply their knowledge about research design, we have been struck by *many* students' surprise and actual delight about research as they get past their initial fears. We often have heard comments like, "I'm actually *enjoying* this research course"; "I never thought I would be a researcher; now I'm beginning to reconsider my career goals"; "This research stuff is contagious; I'm starting to think about research studies a lot and I want to collect data now!" (e.g., see Research Journey 2.2). In sum, the major point is that beginning graduate students often have considerably less information about research and science than about practitioner activities. Moreover, there is evidence that as students obtain more experience with research activities (especially if it is early in their training), their research interests increase and they place a higher value on the role of research (e.g., Gelso, Baumann, Chui, & Savela, 2013).

RESEARCH JOURNEY 2.2

When I started graduate school, my dream was to become a director of a counseling center. Research was not part of my career dreams, and I had no sense that I could ever publish in a professional journal. However, subsequent research experiences in my coursework, especially with my doctoral advisor, David N. Dixon, shifted my career aspirations toward academia. Several years later after having a modicum of success in publishing, I realized that the most important goal was the accumulation of knowledge from the systematic study of a particular topic, and subsequent theory development. Several more years later, I more fully realized the importance of the context surrounding my research topic, and in particular, the many variables (age, SES, race) within participants' cultural context that greatly affected our research findings. I also realized our research efforts alone were insufficient to create the knowledge bases needed for tomorrow, and that the worldviews and power of journal editors, editorial boards, and others in leadership positions in our profession played a critical role in the creation of our future knowledge bases. This realization led me to engage in a number of professional roles (e.g., editorial boards, assuming editorships, involvement and leadership positions in professional organizations), all aimed at improving knowledge bases and promoting social justice in counseling psychology. In the end, one of the things I greatly value in our profession is the many ways that we can join hands with diverse partners to create knowledge bases and theories to promote the development of a broad array of people.

—Puncky Heppner, Ph.D.

Thus, our advice to students regarding performance anxiety is first of all to recognize that feelings of anxiety and doubt associated with research are normal, and often reflect where one is in the developmental process of acquiring new competencies, in this case research competencies. Second, we strongly recommend that students get involved with research projects to slowly develop various research competencies. We believe the best way to create a sense of research efficacy is to learn and perform those skills. For example, students might offer to volunteer to help on a research project to learn the basic research skills, and slowly work their way up to learn the more advanced skills (e.g., see Research Journey 2.3). In essence, both our experience and our research have suggested that the more students get involved in research, the more self-efficacy they tend to feel; the more efficacious students feel about conducting research, the more positive they are about the training environment and interest in research (Gelso et al., 2013; Kahn, 2001).

RESEARCH JOURNEY 2.3

I had the good fortune of becoming Professor Donald Atkinson's doctoral advisee in counseling psychology at the University of California, Santa Barbara, back in 1996. I learned firsthand via Don's work the power of research—that is, good research work can lead to significant changes in our profession and society (e.g., increased attention to multiculturalism). It was also during that time that my research training became more solidified through several courses on research methods and statistics (by the way, I used the first edition of this book in my main research methods course and it couldn't have offered me a better start!). Most importantly, however, it was the day-to-day work on several research studies with Don and other students that taught me the intricacies of research, starting from problem conceptualization and moving into research design, data collection, data analyses, and manuscript publication. So in hindsight, I mostly "learned by doing." And I've come to understand that there is no magic formula to becoming a good researcher but to have good people around you who also are enthusiastic about research. At this point in my career, as a full professor with tenure and the editor of Asian American Journal of Psychology, I continue to believe that research success is a function of inquisitive and informed researchers working together for a common goal. So my recommendation continues to be: "Get involved, join a research team, study the topic of your passion, and don't forget to enjoy the process! The outcome will then take care of itself."

—Bryan S. K. Kim, Ph.D.

Threats, Unrewarding Training, and Disenchantment   For any of a number of reasons, students' research training is often less than rewarding, and actually often rather threatening, all of which can result in student disenchantment. It is not uncommon for students to enter graduate school with ambivalence and anxiety about the academic and research requirements that they have to meet over the next several years. Many students are intimidated by their instructors and professors; in particular those that teach courses in which the students feel less competent in (such as statistics and research methodology, which are less directly associated with counseling practice). Moreover, the idea of coming up with an innovative research topic for their thesis is quite daunting. It is hard enough to generate adequate research questions for a study, let alone finding measures, collecting data, statistical analysis, and writing all these up into a lengthy thesis! With the anxiety experienced around research, the program and training can feel quite threatening. Unfortunately, when students have little experience with research and science, one bad experience can create tremendous attitudinal and motivational damage and move a student a long way from future scientific activities. Some training programs may actually decrease students' interest in research.

The profession has come a long way in enhancing research training over the last two decades. Consideration of students' affective reactions, values, and individual differences, and of the training environment will most likely continue to enhance the development of students' research efficacy. In addition, consideration of cultural values and social connections are especially important issues for some racial/ethnic minority and international students whose cultural values make it more difficult to seek and participate in the research groups without others' invitation or help.

The False Dichotomous Conceptualization of Science versus Practice   Another developmental issue is how students conceptualize science and research, and their relationship to practice. A common statement is, "I just want to practice; I am not interested in science/research." Sometimes the scientific enterprise is erroneously conceptualized as totally separated from applied work in counseling. Thus, a false dichotomy is established, science versus practice. Actually there is interplay between science and practice. Our belief is that those students who develop skills in both arenas will be better equipped to do the work of the counseling profession (for example, see Research Journey 2.4).

RESEARCH JOURNEY 2.4

When I started my undergraduate studies, I was sure that I wanted to be a police detective. Although I realized that path was not in the cards for me, the drive to find solutions to mysteries has never left. I quickly realized when it comes to research that the world is far more complex than I originally thought. Additionally, with complex questions come complex answers that frequently result in multiple equally valid solutions. This process is what draws me into doing research and at the same time the multitude of possibilities and enormous amounts of information can be paralyzing—a common theme I hear from my students. Yet I have found two sources of inspiration: (a) working with others (counselors, researchers, and clients) to be sure I am expanding the way I am thinking about any given topic and to stay connected to the lived experience of those who matter the most, and (b) tackling specific questions so that each study is manageable. In this way, each study is akin to adding to an ongoing conversation, and developing a research agenda or doing multiple studies in the same area allow for the conversation to continue. I find this process very gratifying and rewarding!

—Jesse Owen, Ph.D..

Moreover, one of the hallmarks of graduate work in counseling is to acquire critical thinking skills, the ability to identify and process information with fewer biases, stereotypes, and assumptions; formulate hypotheses; gather data; and make informed decisions. These critical thinking skills are essential in both the practice and science arenas. Higher critical thinking ability has been found as a key characteristic of master therapists (identified as having exceptional mastery of therapy by their peers; Jennings & Skovholt, 2015; Ronnestad & Skovholt, 2013; Skovholt, 2012). A qualitative meta-analysis of six studies that examined characteristics of master therapists in different countries found that master therapists have developed more sophisticated and complex conceptualization of clients' presenting issues (Jennings & Skovholt, 2015). One of the key themes identified across master therapists in all the studies was the capacity for cognitive complexity and intricate conceptualization. This capacity was developed through ongoing learning through reflection, feedback, and teaching others.

Our advice to students is to avoid a narrow conceptualization of research and science and to not prematurely conclude that research and science have little or nothing to offer the practitioner (Skovholt, 2012). Rather, we encourage practice-oriented students to be open to learning more about the research process as well as the research literature, and how these experiences can inform practice and improve their counseling competence. The scientific method is simply a set of tools to establish a controlled mode of inquiry about all of our professional activities, research and practice.

Disbelief in Oneself as a Researcher and Science in General   A critically important belief in the process of becoming a competent researcher is believing in one's ability to conduct meaningful research as well as belief in the utility of research, that research does contribute to the profession's knowledge bases, and that our research can and does make a difference in clients' lives (e.g., see Research Journey 2.5).

RESEARCH JOURNEY 2.5

Being involved in research that has the potential to make a difference is a meaningful aspect of my work and motivates me to persist when encountering inherent obstacles in the research process. After graduating from college with degrees in Biology and Sociology (and a minor in Women's Studies), I worked in an inner city battered women's shelter. At the shelter, I became interested in what differentiated women who returned to the abuser from women who struggled to create nonviolent lives for themselves and their children. In part, this desire to understand critical social problems motivated me to purse a master's degree, where I focused my thesis on shelter workers' perceptions of battered women. I loved how my work in the shelter informed and was informed by my research. I also began to see that while helping people individually was rewarding to me, I might be able to make a difference through sharing my research findings with others. My doctoral program solidified my passion for research as I was given the opportunity to study topics of interest that had real-world applications, including helping women to achieve economic self-sufficiency. I sometimes struggle with a component of research (e.g., collecting data from difficult to obtain samples), but as soon as this task becomes very painful, the next step in research brings new and exciting challenges (e.g., analyzing the data!). Also, working with students and colleagues on research teams makes the research process a wonderful, fun, and memorable adventure.

—Karen O'Brien, Ph.D.

It is common for students to not initially feel efficacious as a researcher nor to believe that our research in counseling can make a difference in the profession. Most beginning students do not have much of an understanding of the role of science in our profession, and since they do not have a long history in the profession they are unable to identify how previous research has contributed to the profession. Similarly, students do not have a clear understanding of the utility of the scientific method as a way of thinking about either research or clients. Finally, the student typically has had relatively little experience of expanding his or her understanding about clients and applied problems by engaging in research, reading the professional literature, and contemplating the implication of empirical findings. One unfortunate outcome is that students sometimes fill this void with misinformation, like "science = statistics." Or students believe that "science is too intellectual, too cognitive, and unrelated to the experiences of real people." Or "the scientific method is so mechanical and reductionistic that it cannot be used adequately to study the complexities of real human behavior." Conversely, seasoned researchers understand both the challenges of conducting meaningful research and the gradual but steady accumulation of knowledge from our research. Even though it is rare that any one study has a major impact on the profession, programmatic research often does result in the accrual of knowledge over time, and often achieves significant conclusions. For example, many of the chapters in the *APA Handbook of Counseling Psychology* (Fouad, Carter, & Subich, 2012) are based on extensive literature reviews and nicely reflect the utility of our research in creating knowledge as well as enhancing the sophistication of our conceptualization of relevant constructs in counseling.

Clara Hill, a creative and prolific counseling researcher, was invited to write a personal account of her evolution as a researcher. Her account illustrates how she made decisions, how complex the process of research can be, and how she coped with the ups and downs along the way and, most important, her "crisis of faith in research":

> After this series of studies I underwent a crisis in terms of research. I had achieved tenure, had my first baby, and turned 30. I started questioning everything. Because I could see so many imperfections in my research, I was not very proud of my work. It had taken an incredible amount of time for little "hard information." I could not even remember the results of many of my studies. Further, I seemed woefully far from even describing what happens in the counseling process let alone understanding what counselor behaviors were useful in effecting change. I despaired that counseling was far too complex to be studied. I had previously had lots of doubts about my research, but it was mostly related to self-confidence in my research abilities. This crisis seemed to have more to do with whether I felt that research was a viable means to answer questions about the counseling process. (Hill, 1984, p. 105)

Hill's behind-the-scenes disclosures are illuminating as well as often relieving for many students and faculty. We strongly encourage students to read this article, perhaps during their first course on research methods. We have found that Hill's frustrations, jubilations, feelings of inadequacy, and doubts about the role of research resonate strongly with students. The evolution of Hill's confidence in the utility of conducting research in her own way not only sends a useful message, but also illuminates the developmental processes of students and faculty in becoming skilled and competent researchers.

From our experience, it is critical not only that researchers feel efficacious in conducting relevant and important research, but also that they begin to perceive that their research is important, that it contributes useful information to our professional knowledge bases, and that it can make a difference in the profession as well as the lives of our clients. Such beliefs often are the result of identifying implications of your research findings to practice, being cited in the professional literature in meaningful ways, or seeing either that others are using your research findings in applied settings or that your research is helping other researchers subsequently ask other important questions.

Belief in the utility of research can also result from reading the professional literature to learn the impact of others' research. Our advice is for students to not only read and reflect on the literature, but also to read literature reviews in particular (see Major Contributions in *The Counseling Psychologist* or review papers in *Psychological Bulletin*). In addition, we advise students to get involved in conducting research on topics that are really important to them, either topics that they are very interested in or ones that reflect their personal values in some way (e.g., see Research Journey 2.6).

RESEARCH JOURNEY 2.6

I firmly believe that the best researchers usually have a connection and passion about their research. I developed my research program, in part, to help me understand and make sense of my own experiences as an African American man in a predominantly White college environment struggling to do well academically, while at the same time trying to learn more about my history and culture. This desire to better understand myself and the experiences of other people like me led to a dissertation, my first publication, several other articles, and a book. Everyone has experienced challenges in writing and conducting research at some point, and everybody has experienced rejection when trying to publish something. I have learned that it is not always the "smartest" people who can successfully carry out a research project and publish it, but often it is those individuals who are the most resilient.

—Kevin Cokley, Ph.D.

A MODEL FOR RESEARCH TRAINING

The purpose of this section is to discuss a number of factors that are important in enhancing research training. Our goal is not only to enhance students' awareness of what appears to be some of the major constructs in research training, but also to promote additional attention and research on this important developmental process. Based on the culminated research on effective research training, Kahn (2001) proposed a model that incorporated various factors, which is presented

FIGURE 2.1 Parameter Estimates for the Modified Structural Model of Kahn (2001)

Source: From Kahn, J. H. (2001). Predicting the scholarly activity of counseling psychology students: A refinement and extension. *Journal of Counseling Psychology, 48,* 344-354. doi:10.1037/0022-0167.48.3.344.

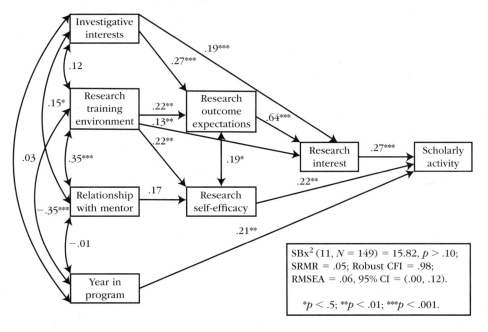

in Figure 2.1. We will discuss this model and the empirical evidence that supports parts of it, as well as add a few other important aspects of research training not included in the model. We begin by discussing each of the major constructs in the model: (a) investigative interests, (b) research training environment, (c) relationship with mentor, (d) research outcome expectations, (e) research self-efficacy, (f) research interest, (g) scholarly activity, and (h) year in program.

Constructs of the Model

Investigative Interests Most students in counseling and counseling psychology can be categorized into one of Holland's (1992) three personality types: social, artistic, or investigative. Research has shown that the personality type of counseling students is related to their level of interest in research and in research courses, choice of graduate program types with varying levels of research focus, and to research productivity (Mallinckrodt et al. 1990; Tinsley, Tinsley, Boone, & Shim-Li, 1993). Specifically, it appears that students who are investigative types have more interest in research activities and ultimately produce more research (e.g., see Research Journey 2.7). Accordingly, Kahn (2001) found that a student's investigative interest would be directly related to expectations of research outcome and research interest, which in turn would be related to research productivity. In particular, investigative types are hypothesized to be more interested in research, and social types less interested.

RESEARCH JOURNEY 2.7

My passion for science originated at a very early age, when I found myself setting up mini "experiments" to test various questions. I was curious about the world and about human interactions in the world. At this young age I also was acutely aware of individuals whose experiences in the world were different from my own. I viewed humans as equal with unequal opportunities. After multiple undergraduate transfers, I was fortunate to have ended up in a college that provided me access to mentoring and advising that enabled my interests, skills, and efficacy in science to flourish. Were it not for these individuals and my experiences, I would have never realized that a doctoral degree or a career as a scientist-practitioner was a viable option. Throughout my graduate training and career, my passion to share my excitement for the scientific process in a way that is meaningful for others (e.g., via knowledge in research design and analysis, consultation with organizations, developing and testing hypotheses with clients in psychotherapy) has continued to blossom. As I reflect upon my research journey, I appreciate the combination of factors that have contributed. These personal characteristics (I am deeply curious about the world), beliefs (I believe that science has the potential to impact practices and prompt positive change in the world), and values (opportunities, and access to them, matter) continue to shape the work in which I choose to engage and the questions that I choose to ask.

Mindi Thompson, Ph.D.

Research Training Environment   Gelso, Baumann, Chui, and Savela (2013) discussed 10 ingredients of graduate training programs that foster positive attitudes toward research. These components have been identified as important features of the research training environment: (a) faculty modeling of scientific behavior; (b) the positive reinforcement of scientific activity, both formally and informally; (c) early and minimally threatening involvement in research; (d) emphasizing science as a partly social-interpersonal experience; (e) emphasizing that all studies are limited and flawed; (f) teaching and valuing varied approaches to research; (g) teaching students to look inward for research ideas when they are developmentally ready to do so; (h) the wedding of science and practice; (i) relevant statistics and the logic of design; and (j) teaching how research can be done in practice settings.

An illustration of a positive training environment that included the 10 components would be having an environment that involved students in research as early as possible and in ways that are interesting, involving, and consistent with their skill level. Many counseling students are socially oriented, increasing the social aspects of research through the forms of advising, and research teams will increase the attractiveness of the endeavor for them. In research groups, students of various levels can participate to the extent that they feel comfortable and have something to contribute. Research advising and modeling is beyond transferring skills and involves having research mentors exhibit healthy attitudes toward research including both the excitement and disappointment in response to its trials and tribulations. Honest expressions of reinforcement to students all along the way in the research process are an important part of building interest. Providing a nonintimidating atmosphere for learning is important. Students should not feel pressured to design the perfect study; rather, they should feel motivated to create a study that can address their research questions. Also, many counseling students have little fondness for statistics and are turned off to *research* because they equate doing research with studying for statistics examinations. Some students will be attracted to quantitative methods and others to qualitative methods, and these preferences should be respected and honored. Not only do students benefit by using a method that they enjoy, but the field benefits from this methodological pluralism (Gelso et al., 1988). A true integration of science and practice will make research more attractive, especially to the majority of students whose primary interest is in practice. Looking inward to rely on clinical experience is an example of wedding science and practice. Students who have a deep interest in their topic finish their dissertations faster than those who are motivated to finish their programs but who pick a convenient topic of study. Not all research environments are ideal, but it is important to make the most out of them (e.g., see Research Journey 2.8).

RESEARCH JOURNEY 2.8

I applied to graduate school with the goal of conducting community-engaged research on Asian immigrant families and disseminating this research through community organizations and churches. However, I ended up at a graduate program that did not have such research opportunities at the time. Rather than get disheartened, I had to make the most of what was available to me, so I pursued more mainstream research on individual differences. But I kept my interests alive by independently reading ethnic minority psychology research, writing papers on ethnic minority issues, and finding support and inspiration through my membership with the Asian American Psychological Association. It was just a dream deferred, but not like a raisin in the sun (h/t Langston Hughes). Ideas percolated; studies were imagined and reimagined over and over again. And then when I finally had the chance to pursue my original research interests, I felt so relieved, happy, and completely scared. Was I really ready? Could I do it? Like most things in life, you have to just do it and don't stop. Keep pushing yourself to do it better. Learn from mistakes. Collaborate with others. Dare to be different, but be sure you are ready to defend your decisions. My program of research today is consistent with my original research interests, but also ever changing—almost always for the better. You need to have passion and commitment to pursue a research career, but don't get stubborn or set in your ways. Be adaptive and open to new ideas and opportunities.

—Richard Lee, Ph.D.

Gelso and colleagues (Gelso et al., 1996; Kahn & Gelso, 1997; Royalty et al., 1986) developed an instrument (the Research Training Environment Scale, RTES, and its revision, RTES-R) that operationalized these nine components of the training environment. Because it was unlikely that these aspects are independent, Kahn and Miller (2000) later developed a short version of the RTES-R (RTES-R-S), which included two higher order factors that underlie the nine aspects operationalized by the RTES-R. The first factor, labeled *instructional dimension,* contains aspects of the environment that are present because of curricular components of graduate training, which included teaching statistics and the logic of design, teaching students to look inward, teaching that experiments are flawed, teaching varied approaches, and wedding science and practice. The second factor was labeled *interpersonal dimension* because the components involved the interaction of trainer and trainee, which includes modeling, reinforcing, involving students early, and conducting science as a social experience. Although the nine components of the research environment can be reduced to two factors statistically, the examination of the individual components that follow reveals how research trainers can construct curricula and experiences to foster the development of skilled and motivated consumers and producers of research. Thus, we recommend that professionals involved in research training read Gelso's (1979) seminal article on research in counseling and Gelso et al's (2013) review of empirical evidence over the past three decades supporting the importance of the research training environment.

Relationship with Mentor   Similar to the research training environment, a graduate student's relationship with his or her mentor is an important aspect associated with research outcomes (e.g., see Research Journey 2.9). The quality of research mentoring that a student receives is a critical aspect of the environment, which has been found to be related to students' attitude toward research and their research self-efficacy (Hollingsworth & Fassinger, 2002; Morrison & Lent, 2014). A qualitative study identified four main factors related to students' satisfaction of the mentoring relationship: (a) the ability to choose their own advisors, (b) the frequency of individual and group meetings with their advisors, (c) how conflict was handled in the advisory relationship, and (d) the benefits and costs associated with the advisory relationship (Schlosser, Knox, Moskovitz, & Hill, 2003). Schlosser et al. categorized each of the 16 participants in their study based on whether they were satisfied ($n = 10$) or unsatisfied ($n = 6$) with her or his relationship with her or his advisor.

Most of the satisfied students were found to have had the option to choose their advisors, whereas all the unsatisfied students were assigned to their advisors. As for meetings with advisors, satisfied students were found typically to have frequent individual or group meetings, whereas unsatisfied students generally had infrequent individual meetings (e.g., once or twice a semester). Conflict in advising relationships was dealt more openly and difficult issues were addressed among the satisfied students, whereas conflict was avoided for those that were unsatisfied. All unsatisfied students reported that their needs were being met outside of their advisory relationship, whereas only some of the satisfied students sought out external resources when their advisors were unable to meet their needs. These findings provide some important insights for developing a positive advisory relationship.

RESEARCH JOURNEY 2.9

As I was approaching the end of my doctoral training and about to start my dissertation study, I vividly remember a meeting with Puncky Heppner, one of my mentors in graduate school. This meeting stands out clearly to me because his advice on what I could do as a graduate student to start laying a foundation for a career in research was so critical at this stage of my career. He suggested that I consider doing my dissertation study in an area that could develop into a programmatic line of research—and that this area be one that sustains my interest over the years and fills a void in the current literature. This incident and many other teaching moments from valued mentors have taught me that the world of research operates on a unique time frame that requires patience, perseverance, planning, and good advice from research mentors because we often don't see immediate outcomes for the behaviors we are engaged in as early career researchers.

—Lisa Flores, Ph.D.

Research Self-Efficacy   Social cognitive models of academic and career interest and choice hypothesize that self-efficacy mediates the relationship between direct and vicarious experiences and attainment of goals (Lent, Brown, & Hackett, 1994). Research self-efficacy is defined as the confidence in one's ability to successfully complete various research-related tasks (Kahn & Schlosser, 2014). Research self-efficacy is an integral part of building interest and shaping one's career goals (e.g., see Research Journey 2.10). There have been a few measures developed to assess the research self-efficacy of counseling students. Among these scales, Self-Efficacy in Research Measure (SERM; Phillips & Russell, 1994) is one widely used to measure research self-efficacy (Gelso & Lent, 2000). The SERM includes four subscales measuring the design, practical, writing, and quantitative aspects of research skills (see Table 2.2 for a list of the scale items), and can be a tool used to assess your own research self-efficacy. Kahn (2001), based on social cognitive models and past research in this area (see, e.g., Brown et al., 1996; Phillips & Russell, 1994), found that research training environment and mentorship predict research self-efficacy, which in turn would predict scholarly activity.

TABLE 2.2 : Self-Efficacy in Research Measure (Phillips & Russell, 1994)

The following items are tasks related to research. Please indicate your degree of confidence in your ability to successfully accomplish each of the following tasks on a scale of 0–9 with 0 representing no confidence and 9 representing total confidence.

| 1 | 2 | 3 | 4 | 5 | 6 | 7 | 8 | 9 |

No Confidence   **Total Confidence**

1. Selecting a suitable topic for study

2. Knowing which statistics to use

3. Getting an adequate number of subjects

4. Writing a research presentation for a conference

5. Writing the method and results section for a research paper for publication

6. Manipulating data to get it onto a computer system

7. Writing a discussion section for a thesis or dissertation

8. Keeping records during a research project

9. Collecting data

10. Designing an experiment using nontraditional methods (e.g., ethnographic, cybernetic, phenomenological approaches)

11. Designing an experiment using traditional methods (e.g., experimental, quasi-experimental designs)

12. Making time for research

13. Writing the introduction and literature review for a dissertation

14. Reviewing the literature in an area of research interest

15. Writing the introduction and discussion sections for a research paper for publication

16. Contacting researchers currently working in an area of research interest

17. Avoiding the violation of statistical assumptions

18. Writing the method and results sections of a dissertation

19. Using simple statistics (e.g., t test, ANOVA, correlation)

20. Writing the introduction and literature review for a thesis

21. Controlling for threats to validity

22. Formulating hypotheses

23. Writing the method and results sections of a thesis

24. Utilizing resources for needed help

25. Understanding computer printouts

26. Defending a thesis or dissertation

27. Using multivariate statistics (e.g., multiple regression, factor analysis)

28. Using statistical packages (e.g., SPSS-X, SAS)

29. Selecting a sample of subjects from a given population

TABLE 2.2 Self-Efficacy in Research Measure (Phillips & Russell, 1994) *(continued)*

30. Selecting reliable and valid instruments

31. Writing statistical computer programs

32. Getting money to help pay for research

33. Operationalizing variables of interest

Scoring:

Sum items within each subscale for subscale scores, or sum all 33 items for a total score.

Research Design Skills = 1, 10, 11, 21, 22, 29, 30, 33

Practical Research Skills = 3, 8, 9, 12, 16, 24, 26, 32

Quantitative and Computer Skills = 2, 6, 17, 19, 25, 27, 28, 31

Writing Skills = 4, 5, 7, 13, 14, 15, 18, 20, 23

RESEARCH JOURNEY 2.10

Having been a Taiwanese international student and now a scholar in the United States, I encountered additional challenges in my research journey. My research interests started when working as an assistant to Professor Kuo-Shu Yang in conducting Chinese indigenous psychology research. I was intrigued by how much I learned about myself within my cultural context through this approach as opposed to simply utilizing findings from Western studies. A first challenge was how to incorporate the Chinese cultural context into my research of Chinese populations while conducting the studies in the United States. I was privileged to have an advisor, Dr. Robert B. Slaney, who supported me to study perfectionism across cultures. A second challenge was academic writing with English as my second language. Writing has not been easy, but I have learned and improved through the process of simply writing, revising, rewriting, etc. It also takes reminding myself that research design, conceptualization, and data analyses are more essential to conducting quality research than writing skills. My research efficacy grew through utilizing my statistical analyses skills, which facilitated a greater interest in research, and eventually led me to pursue an academic career. One of the important things I've learned as a developing researcher is that most scholars have relative strengths and weaknesses. It is important for me to utilize my strengths and also have patience with my weaker areas. It has been helpful when I refocus my attention to growth and development as opposed to only productivity. Being mentored and normalizing my learning curve have helped me develop. Also, collaborating with others whose skill set complement mine has made research much easier and more fun.

—Kenneth Wang, Ph.D.

Research Outcome Expectations Students' expectation of the consequences and outcome of conducting research is also a factor related to their research experience. These expectations can include how much they perceived conducting research and impact their future career or job opportunities. Negative expectations might be related to how involvement in research may take away from opportunities to enhance their counseling skills or time for leisure activities. Research outcome expectations have been found associated with one's level of interest in research and research self-efficacy (Bishop & Bieschke, 1998).

Research Interest Kahn (2001) hypothesized that research interest serves as a mediator between the relationships of various research-related predictors mentioned previously and scholarly activity. Put another way, the established relationship between personality type and research productivity is due to interest. Investigative types have more interest in research and therefore have goals related to research and produce more research products. A multilevel study has also shown that counseling programs with positive research training environments had students with stronger research interests (Kahn & Schlosser, 2010).

Scholarly Activity The outcome construct in Kahn's model (2001) is scholarly activity, which was defined broadly to include past accomplishments related to published journal articles, unpublished empirical manuscripts, manuscript submission and research in process, presentations presented or in process, and conferences attended, as well as current involvement in data collection or data analyses. Research productivity has a long history as an outcome variable due to many observations that the research productivity of graduates from counseling programs is low.

Research productivity as a goal is somewhat controversial. Increasing research productivity has often been advocated by leaders in the field. However, we feel that the quantity of research published by students, before and after they graduate, should not be the primary indicator of the quality of a training program. We think students should be skilled researchers who can conduct quality research (and who do so in their dissertations), and also intelligently consume research, cogently think about scientific issues, balance research and practice from an informed standpoint, appreciate and value the scientific method, and most important apply critical thinking skills to a broad range of research and applied contexts. Hill (1997) noted that even though few of her students had taken academic positions or produced much research, she should not as a result be judged as an inadequate research mentor.

Year in Program Kahn (2001) also found that the amount of research training that a student has received, which was approximated by the year they were in their program, was directly associated with their scholarly activity. This is an important factor to consider as we mentioned about how research skills take time to develop, and students should take into account the developmental process as they assess their research abilities and potential.

RESEARCH IN ACTION 2.1

Complete the Self-Efficacy in Research Measure (SERM) presented in Table 2.2 to assess your self-efficacy levels in the four different aspects of research skills. What did you learn about yourself? How do your results from the SERM relate to the concerns, obstacle, and fears that you have about scientific training? What steps can you take now to enhance the development of your research skills?

Testing the Model

Kahn (2001) tested the path model and the results are presented in Figure 2.1. Several aspects of the model are informative. The critical mediating construct was research interests along with research self-efficacy and research outcome expectations. All four predictive factors (investigative interests, research training environment, relationship with mentor, and year in program) were directly or indirectly associated with predicting scholarly activity. Among these factors, the research training environment appeared to be most predictive of scholarly activity through research outcome expectations and self-efficacy. The relationship with the mentor was significantly associated with scholarly activity through research self-efficacy. As for year in program, it was directly associated with scholarly output, which points to the importance of multiple research experiences. This study highlights the importance of students having research interests and self-efficacy, and then provides the kind of research environment and mentorship that helps to foster those interests and self-efficacy. See Kahn (2001) and Kahn and Scott (1997) for more details.

Research Competence: The Missing Construct

From our perspective, the missing construct in the Kahn (2001) model is research competence. As counselors and counseling psychologists we appropriately attend to how we structure environments to foster positive attitudes and self-efficacy. However, having competencies to conduct and consume research is also critical to producing quality research. Wampold (1986b) found that training programs did not teach their students various statistical procedures that were used in typical counseling research. In addition, Royalty and Reising (1986) surveyed professionals and found that respondents felt confident of their research skills, with the exception of statistical and computer skills, two skills that were highly correlated with productivity. Although the respondents indicated that graduate programs adequately contributed to their skill level, they became less confident of their skills later in their careers, and they indicated that it is unlikely that they would augment their research skills after graduation. Self-efficacy is due in part to a research environment that fosters positive attitudes toward research, but it is also built upon competencies.

Based on the empirical evidence for competence in statistics and design, Wampold (1986b, p. 44) listed the following design and statistics competencies: (a) knowledge of designs including, but not limited to, traditional experimental designs, quasi-experimental designs appropriate for field settings, single-subject designs, survey designs, and qualitative designs; (b) an understanding of design issues, such as validity, methods of sampling, and power; (c) knowledge of the statistical analyses commonly used in counseling research; (d) an understanding of statistical issues, such as the role of assumptions, hypothesis-testing strategies, and confirmatory versus exploratory analyses; and (e) the ability to perform analyses with computer assistance, when appropriate. It is hoped that this book, statistics classes, and other experiences will provide readers these competencies. In addition, professional writing skills, which are covered in the last chapter of this book and in a more detailed way in Heppner and Heppner (2004), are critically important skills for students to develop.

THE NEED TO BROADEN SCIENTIFIC TRAINING

Most counselor training programs have a number of training components aimed at promoting the development of an array of research competencies (e.g., research design, statistics). However, we want to discuss two additional competencies that merit attention: basic scientific or critical thinking skills and basic research application skills.

Training in Basic Scientific Thinking Skills

All counselors, regardless of where their professional activities fall on the scientist-practitioner continuum, need basic scientific or critical thinking skills. Scientific thinking refers to a controlled method of inquiry and reasoning, typically to collect data of some kind for the purpose of testing a hypothesis. A crucial characteristic of a professional counselor is the integration of scientific thinking into the daily activities of professional practice (e.g., Gambrill, 2005; Pepinsky & Pepinsky, 1954). Scientific thinking can be instrumental in how counselors process information about a specific client during counseling as well as evaluate the counseling process.

How a person thinks is an exceedingly complex process. It is becoming increasingly clear over time that human beings often think or process information in both rational and irrational ways, in systematic and unsystematic ways, and in linear and nonlinear ways. Moreover, there is reason to believe that one's cognitive processes (that is, how one thinks) interact with one's affective processes and behaviors, thereby creating a complex triadic process (Heppner & Krauskopf, 1987). Research clearly indicates that people do not think as "objective computers," but rather are selective or biased in the type of information to which they attend (Garb, 1998). In particular, people often attend to information that confirms their existing beliefs or discount information that is contrary to their existing beliefs. Moreover, most therapists and counselors give more weight to their personal experiences than to science when making decisions while working with clients (Stewart & Chambless, 2007). Such biases can lead to problems for professional counselors as they process information about clients and evaluate the effectiveness of their work.

Carl Rogers was very aware of this danger of counselor bias; in 1955 he observed that he could "deceive himself in regard to my creatively formed subjective hunches" about a client (p. 275). He believed that the scientific method, as a way of thinking, led him to check "the subjective feelings or hunch or hypothesis of a person with the objective fact" (p. 275). Rogers would often check his hunches very directly by asking the client, "Do you mean this?" or "Could it be this?" Rogers would sometimes go a step further and develop a written transcript of an interview to analyze the relationships between counselor and client statements. Years later his face would still light up with excitement about what he would learn about a particular client, or the counseling process, by stepping back from the immediacy of an interview to analyze those transcripts (Rogers, personal communication with P. P. Heppner and L. A. Lee, January 1984).

Training in scientific thinking may be particularly important in evaluating counseling outcomes. Lilienfeld et al. (2014) provide an illustration of how mental health providers can be biased:

> A clinically depressed client obtains psychotherapy; 2 months later, she is free of serious symptoms. Was her improvement due to the treatment?
>
>   The correct answer is "We don't know." On the one hand, ample data demonstrate that scientifically supported psychotherapies can alleviate many mental health difficulties (Barlow, 2004), so the client's improvement may well stem at least partly from the intervention. On the other hand, as most mental health professionals know, we cannot draw valid conclusions regarding a treatment's effectiveness in the absence of methodological safeguards against errors in inference, such as well validated outcome measures, randomized control groups, and blinded observations (Gambrill, 2012). Yet even seasoned clinicians and researchers can easily fall prey to the error of concluding that a treatment worked when the evidence for this inference is insufficient. They can commit this mistake when evaluating the effectiveness of treatment for a given client, the effectiveness of a specific school or modality of psychotherapy, or both. (p. 355)

Thus, training in scientific thinking and methodologies can help counselors evaluate the effectiveness of counseling interventions more objectively and with less personal or subjective bias.

More recently, there has been a strong movement for empirically validated treatments or evidence-based practice to enrich the training and practice of counselors (McHugh & Barlow, 2010; Norcross, 2011; Waehler, Kalodner, Wampold, & Lichtenberg, 2000). Scientific thinking is a crucial feature that distinguishes the counselor from a nonprofessional layperson, in large part because of its self-corrective characteristics. That is, whereas laypeople tend to fit what they see or hear into preconceived notions of their world view, well-trained counselors should view their assumptions or observations as subject to change based on scientific evidence (Lilienfeld et al., 2014).

Thus, the difference between the counselor-as-scientist and the scientist is more a matter of goals than of procedure. We believe that it would be worthwhile to pursue more thorough training in basic scientific thinking skills to reflect train-ing outcomes associated with a more integrated scientist-practitioner model. To facilitate the development of scientific thinking, particularly with practice-oriented students, Hoshmand (1994) developed a practice-oriented approach to research supervision; her experiences led her to conclude that a practice-oriented approach engages students' interest and prepares them for contributing scholarly research relevant to practice. At this point, more attention is needed on the efficacy of dif-ferent approaches of scientific thinking for different types of students. Thus, critical thinking, hypothesis testing, and other scientific methodology should be integrated into all aspects of training.

Training in Basic Research Application Skills

The counseling research literature contains a great deal of information about cli-ent populations, counseling processes and outcomes, assessment, interventions, crisis intervention, professional issues, human behavior, and a variety of special topics (see *APA Handbook of Counseling Psychology* edited by Fouad et al., 2012, for various topics related to the counseling profession). This information is obviously essential for any person engaging in counseling research and practice. This information also can be an extremely useful database or tool in helping a practitioner solve particular client problems. In a world that is constantly chang-ing, counselors' knowledge bases can quickly become out of date. Thus, counsel-ors in the field need to train themselves continually to work effectively with new client problems.

The professional research literature is a resource that can both provide a wealth of useful information about specific client problems and suggest topics for additional research. Moreover, reading the literature may affect the coun-selor's thinking and refine his or her conceptualizations of the counseling process. Thus, a basic activity for all graduate students in counseling is to become active consumers of research. Learning how to use the research literature (e.g., becom-ing familiar with the types of articles in different journals, learning how to access information most efficiently) and making the literature a part of one's problem-solving repertoire does not simply happen, but rather typically involves specific training.

SUMMARY AND CONCLUSIONS

The trainers of future researchers are the students of today. In this chapter we dis-cuss some basic issues related to research training, which we hope will help to create positive attitudes toward research as well as increase research competence not only for future researchers but also for future research trainers.

We strongly believe that there can be a much greater integration between the science and practice domains, not only within counselor training, but also within the professional activities of all counselors. Carl Rogers's hope for the future was that researchers would practice in some field and practitioners would be engaged in some research. This is one type of integration; we have also suggested that scientific research training be broadened to emphasize scientific thinking and basic research application skills. In our personal experience, our research has clearly been facilitated by observations made during many hours of counseling practice. Moreover, our experience has been that our thinking and counseling skills have been sharpened, extended, and clearly enhanced by subjecting our thinking to empirical tests as well as contemplating and applying new ideas from the research literature. Integration might also happen on another level: between those who are primarily research oriented and those who are practice oriented. In some ways, the people who have the most well developed set of observations of the counseling process are those who are heavily engaged in counseling practice; it behooves the typical researcher to develop collaborative relationships with such practitioners. In short, we suspect that both scientific and practice-oriented professional activities could be enhanced by a more complete integration of the two domains.

We have also maintained that a basic issue in scientific training is scientific thinking. Such an outcome requires not only scientific skills, but also scientific values. The latter are also important goals and need specific attention in training (perhaps by way of discussions about the philosophy of science, research methods, the slow but steady accumulation of knowledge, and students' own research experiences).

An attitude of scholarly inquiry goes beyond scientific thinking and involves curiosity, inquisitiveness, healthy skepticism, exploration, and a desire to learn (e.g., see Research Journey 2.11). In a way, all counseling professionals are pioneers in extending the boundaries of their own knowledge throughout their careers, and possibly extending the knowledge bases of the profession as well. In this way, scholarly inquiry involves discovery, excitement, and even a sense of adventure. Not surprisingly, pioneers in the field of counseling and development report that they were motivated to achieve, in part, by the joys of intellectual discovery, "the thirst to know something" (Pepinsky, cited in Claiborn, 1985, p. 7).

RESEARCH JOURNEY 2.11

Looking back at my career as a counseling researcher, I find gratification in observing that foremost my research has been driven by curiosity. Curiosity is the desire to know something—to probe, to inquire, to design studies, and to examine data until a coherent story about the phenomenon under scrutiny appears. The psychotherapy story is not exactly what I expected but that is what science is about—discovering something unexpected. For many years, I believed and taught my students that some forms of psychotherapy for some problems were more scientifically sound and more effective than others. Yet, when I examined the process and outcome evidence about psychotherapy, the purported scientific bases of psychotherapy appeared to be fragile. So I set out to conduct meta-analyses and analyses of large naturalistic psychotherapy data to examine these issues more fully. Increasingly, evidence from many different types of designs, in different areas, some from my research group but much from others, including advocates of particular treatments, was telling a different story—but what story was it? It was not enough to observe that the evidence was not consistent with existing psychotherapy theory. The evidence demanded an alternative explanation, a new theory that would parsimoniously explain the current research evidence and anticipate evidence produced by future research. This led me to read more widely—evolutionary psychology, anthropology, social psychology, neuropsychology, placebo studies, religiosity, and epidemiology. This quest, which was immensely fascinating, led to the development of the contextual model of psychotherapy. One has to be humble in such an endeavor because scientific progress dictates that theories will be abandoned and replaced by superior ones, not something I look forward to but inevitable nevertheless.

—Bruce Wampold, Ph.D.

Maintaining a pioneering attitude in professional scholarly inquiry can also be a way of life. Enos Mills was an early pioneer in the mountainous area of Colorado that is now Rocky Mountain National Park. In the following quote, Mills (1924) aptly describes the qualities of a pioneer's life. Even though he was referring to pioneering in the American West, the qualities of life he describes also apply to the pioneering attitude involved in discovering professional knowledge through scholarly inquiry:

Those who live pioneer lives are usually the most fortunate of people. They suffer from no dull existence. Each hour is full of progressive thought, and occasions which call for action accompanied by the charm of exploration—action that makes their lives strong, sincere, and sweet. Their days are full of eagerness and repose, they work with happy hands. The lives of pioneers are rich with hope and their future has all the promise of spring. (p. 9)

We hope that your life in the counseling profession will be a good place for you to be a pioneer and that scientific thinking will enrich your life with discoveries that are exciting to you and beneficial to the various clienteles we serve.

RESEARCH IN ACTION 2.2

After reading about the research joys and challenges of various researchers, are there particular journeys that stood out for you? Which aspects of their journey were more helpful and in what ways?

STIMULUS QUESTIONS

Reflections on Research Training

1. In what ways do you think scientific thinking might be useful for both practice and science activities?
2. Identify five activities you can do to incorporate scientific thinking into your counseling practice.
3. What do you see as the most important advantages of integrating science and practice in the counseling profession?
4. How do you see yourself in terms of being a researcher and/or practitioner?
5. What do you feel very passionate about in your future as a counselor? Can you see any way that research could help you enhance the work you will do within the areas that excite you the most?
6. What concerns, obstacles, and fears do you have about scientific training?
7. Examine the reactions you listed in question 6; why do you think you have these reactions?

3

Ethics in Counseling Research: Being and Doing Right

Ethical principles are at the heart of counseling professions. They are expressions of the values that guide our field, mold our way of being with others, and inform the ways in which we embark on answering essential questions in counseling research. Ethics principles give voice to the rights and dignity of others and serve as a moral compass in our work. Moreover, ethical principles help researchers achieve their goals while avoiding strategies that compromise their values, and ethics help them make decisions when their values are in conflict (Kitchener & Anderson, 2011). We believe that ethics are nothing less than central to the conduct of research. Because of the centrality of ethics in research, this chapter is placed toward the beginning of the book so that ethical reasoning can be integrated into basic design considerations as an intrinsic feature of the research endeavor. Indeed, research suggests that students in counseling training programs regard ethical training as essential for their professional roles (Wilson & Ranft, 1993). Becoming a counseling researcher involves a delicate mixture of technical research design skills and ethical awareness to ensure that research is conducted in a way that enhances the field as well as honors those who contribute to the creation of knowledge including research participants, coworkers, the profession, and society.

In this chapter we focus on the investigator's responsibility in two general categories: ethical issues related to scholarly work and ethical issues related to participants. In today's multifaceted world these topics take on a complexity not even imagined several decades ago. It is important to underscore at the outset that ethical issues in research are rarely cut and dried, and sometimes one ethical principle will conflict with another to create a tangled and murky dilemma. Yet, as researchers we need to be able to make the best decision based on empirical information, theory, expertise, and ethical/legal guidance. These decisions are made, at times, with incomplete and conflicting information. Yet, researchers cannot flee responsibility from making these difficulty decisions, nor can they rely solely on authorities (e.g., ethical principles, professors) to make the final decisions (King & Kitchener, 2002; Owen & Lindley, 2010). Accordingly, our main goals in this chapter are to (a) introduce common ethical issues involved in counseling research; (b) underscore the complexity of real-life ethical dilemmas, which sometimes do not have clear answers; and (c) discuss decision-making approaches highlighting ethical reflectivity for designing research with rigor.

The first section of this chapter discusses fundamental ethical principles as well as virtue ethics that form the core of our professional values. Specifically, we discuss the fundamental ethical principles of nonmaleficence, beneficence, autonomy, justice, and fidelity/veracity. In addition, we introduce ethical guidelines that have been provided by the American Psychological Association and the American Counseling Association. In the second section of the chapter we discuss ethical issues related to scholarly work, specifically (a) execution of the research study, (b) reporting the results, (c) duplicate and piecemeal publication, (d) publication credit, and (e) plagiarism. In the third section we discuss ethical issues pertaining to participants: (a) risks and benefits, (b) informed consent, (c) deception and debriefing, (d) confidentiality and privacy, and (e) special considerations for treatment issues. In the final section we describe an ethical decision-making model to assist researchers in responding to ethical dilemmas they may face in the process of conducting research.

FUNDAMENTAL ETHICAL PRINCIPLES

To facilitate professionals' decision making with regard to ethics, both the American Counseling Association (ACA) and the American Psychological Association (APA) have developed a set of ethical principles or guidelines: *Code of Ethics,* referred to hereafter as *CE* (ACA, 2014), and *Ethical Principles of Psychologists,* referred to hereafter as *EPP* (APA, 2010), respectively. These principles are presented in Appendixes A and B and will be referred to in the discussion of ethical issues throughout the chapter. Both *CE* and *EPP* are evolving documents, with continual changes based on new developments in society and advancements in our fields' collective ethical knowledge. Yet, at the heart of these documents are more general and fundamental ethical principles—many of which have lasted the test of time. In essence, the fundamental ethical principles are far reaching in application and can provide guidance when the specific principles are unclear, inadequate, or incomplete. Moreover, the fundamental ethical principles move the counseling profession away from the rule-bound conception of ethics to one that focuses on identifying and applying foundational ethical principles in difficult ethical dilemmas (Kitchener & Anderson, 2011).

We focus on five fundamental ethical principles: nonmaleficence, beneficence, autonomy, justice, and fidelity/veracity. In essence, these fundamental ethical principles are central but implied building blocks for the professional codes of the ACA and APA. We briefly discuss these general principles to clarify the essence of ethical issues and facilitate an understanding of professional ethical codes. Readers interested in a fuller discussion of such fundamental ethical principles are directed to Beauchamp and Childress (2001), Kitchener and Anderson (2011), and Koocher and Keith-Spiegel (2008).

Nonmaleficence

Diener and Crandall, in their classic book *Ethics in Social and Behavioral Research* (1978), succinctly concluded "the most basic guideline for social scientists is that subjects not be harmed by participating in research" (p. 17). This central principle has been referred to as the principle of nonmaleficence (above all do no harm; Beauchamp & Childress, 2001). This includes not inflicting intentional harm and avoiding the risk of harming others. Thus, it is the responsibility of the investigator to plan and act thoughtfully and carefully in designing and executing research projects, because harm can occur intentionally or unintentionally.

Although this principle appears to be commonsense, there is a long history of researchers inflicting harm in the name of science. Currently, there are safeguards to prevent harm (e.g., institutional review boards), and yet there are still more subtle ways that researchers may inflict harm. As an example, consider a study on adult romantic relationships, where the researchers would like to know if the quality of the romantic relationships is associated with experiences in childhood. The researcher includes questions regarding childhood sexual abuse. These questions may trigger negative thoughts and feelings for some participants—thus causing harm. Given the potential impact on participants, most ethicists have suggested that professionals have argued that if we must choose between harming someone and perhaps helping another person, the strongest obligation would be to avoid harm (e.g., Beauchamp & Childress, 2001; Kitchener & Anderson, 2011). Diener and Crandall (1978) have argued that nonmaleficence can be superseded only if volunteers knowingly participate and the benefits are of great import. Consequently, in our example, researchers would want to consider ways to protect the welfare of participants as well as ask whether the potential gains from the study warrant the potential discomfort.

Beneficence

Acting ethically not only involves preventing harm, but also contributes to the health and welfare of others (Beauchamp & Childress, 2001). Doing good for others is beneficence. This central ethical principle is the essence of the goal of counseling—to help people resolve problems that they have been unable to resolve on their own. Moreover, beneficence constitutes the core of the ethical principles advocated by the APA and ACA. In the Preamble to the *EPP* (APA, 2010b, p. 3), the *Ethics Code* noted an imperative "to improve the condition of individuals, organizations, and society." Likewise, in the Preamble to Ethical Standards (ACA, 2014, p. 3) proclaims at the core of the profession is "enhancing human development throughout the lifespan."

Inherent in beneficence is competence. If our value is to help others, particularly those in need who come to rely on our services, then we have an obligation to help others as competently as possible. Such reasoning has a number of implications for service delivery, professional training, and research. With regard to research, the beneficence principle calls the profession to conduct research that will be advance counselors' competencies and maximize benefit for our clients. To do so, there is a call for researchers to have an active, altruistic, group/community-oriented approach that "gives back" to the research participants and the community. For example, consider a researcher team who conducts a study that demonstrates a significant advancement in the way that we can treat depression for racial/ethnic minority clients, but they never publish the results. This failure to contribute to the field is inherently not living up to the principle of beneficence. In short, an important aspect of beneficence is for researchers to take an active, altruistic approach in order that the results of their research provide benefits to the community under investigation (Ponterotto & Casas, 1991).

Autonomy

The principle of autonomy centers around the liberty to choose one's own course of action, including freedom of action and freedom of choice (Kitchener & Anderson, 2011). The principle of autonomy is woven into American political institutions, law, and culture. In many ways, autonomy is the cornerstone of subjects' rights to voluntarily participate in psychological research, or conversely to decline to participate. Since the Nuremberg trials after World War II, the principle of autonomy has received increased attention in research. At the center of this attention is the notion of informed consent, or educating potential subjects about a particular research project so that they can make informed decisions about participation. Making decisions about autonomy in research can be difficult. Are researchers living up to the principle if they mandate that *all* survey items must be completed in order to get full credit for participating, for instance? Alternatively, a professor of an undergraduate course would like to do a study on students' attitudes about college life and asks his or her students to complete the survey. Do the students have the autonomy to *really* say no? Is the power that the professor may have over their grades enough to influence students' sense of autonomy? Ultimately, researchers need to be aware about their relationship with participants and how that may influence their sense of autonomy.

Justice

The principle of justice implies fairness, rightness, and equity (Kitchener & Anderson, 2011). Because the quantity of services and goods in any society is limited, there are conflicts between people. Thus, a vast array of laws has developed as part of our judicial system for deciding what is fair. In essence, the principle of justice is based on the assumption that people are equals. Thus, as initially suggested by Aristotle, equals should be treated as equals, and unequals should be treated unequally only in proportion to their relevant differences (Beauchamp & Childress, 2001). For example, would it be fair to offer therapeutic services at a rate of $500.00 per session for everyone? Clearly, some clients could easily afford this rate, but others could not. It could be a better policy to offer a rate for services based on the client's income (i.e., sliding scale). The principle of justice also applies to the type of research that is conducted. For example, is there justice if primarily White middle to upper socioeconomic status clients are included in counseling treatment studies? The concept of justice also implies just rewards for one's labor, and ownership of the fruits of one's labor. For instance, are the authors receiving appropriate credit for their work in publications or other dissemination efforts (e.g., talks, media).

Fidelity/Veracity

The principle of fidelity/veracity implies faithfulness, truthfulness, keeping promises or agreements, and loyalty (Ramsey, 1970). This principle applies directly to inter-personal relationships, including counselor-client, student-teacher, and researcher-participant. Not fulfilling a contract (by, e.g., engaging in deception or breaching confidentiality) is a violation that infringes upon the other individual's choice to enter into a mutually agreed-upon relationship. Issues of fidelity and trustworthiness are central to the helping professions such as counseling. The principle of fidelity is important for the reputation of the profession as well as for individual profession-als in their work as counselors, supervisors, consultants, educators, and researchers. Consider an example of a researcher who is conducting a study on long-term coun-seling (e.g., 50 sessions of counseling). However, after 30 weeks the researcher shuts down the study and refers all of the clients to other counselors. Although transfer-ring the participants to other counselors may be a good step, the researcher is not upholding the initially agreed-upon obligations. What options could the researcher have to avoid violating the principle of fidelity/veracity?

Weighing the fundamental ethical principles at the same time can also be complex. For practice, apply the fundamental ethical principles to the following case example:

RESEARCH IN ACTION 3.1

You are a therapist in a psychotherapy research study testing the efficacy of a new manualized treatment for test anxiety among college students. All participants are screened before entering the 10-week (one session per week) program to assess whether their participation is appropriate. One of your study clients, a 19-year-old, Latina American woman, disclosed on the third session that along with test anxiety, she experiences bouts of depression and anxiety-related childhood trauma. She informs you that she did not disclose this information during the screening, because she was hoping that you could accommodate discussing both of those challenges during the 10 sessions, and that she cannot afford alternative services. Not diverg-ing from the treatment manual was stressed during your training.

Questions

What would you do based on fundamental ethical principles? What principles are most salient?

What steps would you take to make a decision in this case? What other informa-tion would you want to have?

ETHICAL ISSUES RELATED TO SCHOLARLY WORK

The study of human behavior is constantly changing and progressing. This evolu-tion reflects that counselors "are committed to increasing scientific and professional knowledge of behavior and people's understanding of themselves and others…" (*EPP,*

Preamble, p. 3). One of the basic purposes of scientific endeavors in counseling is to increase our knowledge about topics of value to the counseling profession and to do so in a way that is "honoring diversity and embracing a multicultural approach in support of worth, dignity, potential, and uniqueness of people within social and cultural contexts" (*CE*, Preamble, p. 3). It can be argued that accurate information promotes the profession's knowledge bases, and that inaccurate and misleading information may distort or even falsify the profession's knowledge bases. In short, given the role of science within the profession, scientists have the responsibility "to undertake their efforts in a totally honest fashion" (Drew, 1980, pp. 58–59). Although any of a number of factors may tax the typical researcher (e.g., publication pressure or fatigue), it is imperative that the researcher keep in focus the ultimate aim of the scientist—to extend our knowledge bases with accurate, reliable, and thus usable information. If researchers lose sight of this essential goal, then in our opinion they have no business conducting research and may only hinder the profession and the people we try to help.

It is important to note that the goal of providing accurate information and extending the profession's knowledge bases can sometimes be at odds with promoting the welfare of others and society. Even though it can be argued that research that led to the atomic bomb extended existing knowledge bases and was instrumental for the Allied victory in World War II, it can also be argued that this research did not promote the welfare of many innocent people, because it resulted in the deaths of thousands of people. Seeman (1969) aptly concluded:

> The existence of Hiroshima in man's history demonstrates that knowledge alone is not enough, and that the question "knowledge for what?" must still be asked. If knowledge in psychology is won at the cost of some essential humanness in one person's relationship to another, perhaps the cost is too high. (p. 1028)

Likewise, Jensen (1969, 1985) published research (and there was considerable controversy about whether the data were biased) that has been interpreted as showing that African Americans are intellectually inferior. Although Jensen's conclusion has not been supported over time (e.g., Sternberg, 1982), clearly Jensen's writing did not promote the welfare of African Americans. In short, the essential point is that more information does not necessarily promote human welfare. At a minimum, expanding our knowledge bases raises deeper moral issues about right and wrong (Kitchener & Anderson, 2011). Thus, it is imperative to note the complexity, and sometimes the contradictions, in the seemingly straightforward goals of extending knowledge bases and promoting human welfare.

Next we will discuss the implications of the researcher's responsibility to provide accurate information concerning five matters: execution of the research study, reporting the results, duplicate and piecemeal publication, publication credit, and plagiarism.

EXECUTION OF THE RESEARCH STUDY

A study must be properly executed if it is to establish valid knowledge bases. The researcher has a responsibility for accurately and reliably planning and conducting the research investigation (*CE*, G.1). The researcher also has the responsibility for evaluating its ethical acceptability, weighing scientific values and rights of participants, and then conducting all aspects of the study in a careful, deliberate manner that minimizes the possibility that results will be misleading in any way. Thus, to reduce methodological biases and errors, it is essential that researchers have an accurate and sensitive understanding of the target population. How would a researcher know if they have the competency to successfully execute a study?

Consider the following example:

RESEARCH IN ACTION 3.2

Bill is conducting a counseling study on the effects of cognitive-behavioral treatment (CBT) for clients who are struggling with social phobia. Although Bill has received extensive training in CBT, he has only had a couple clients with social phobia in his career. Moreover, he feels that his version of CBT is a better approach than most others, which is why he wants to do the study. Accordingly, he compares his version of CBT to a group treatment where clients will watch movies in a group setting.

Questions

What issues are most salient here?

Is Bill in a position to execute this study in a competent manner, why/why not?

Conducting research typically involves multiple tasks and requires a lot of attention to many details. Typical procedural tasks include contacting participants, arranging experimental conditions, randomly assigning participants to conditions, locating and assembling assessment instruments, administering instruments, coding data, entering the data into a computer, and analyzing the data. Within these major tasks are a myriad of steps and processes, such as collating questionnaires, checking the accuracy of the coded data against the original data set, and checking for data entry errors. In short, many tasks confront the researcher in a typical research project, and the researcher is responsible for the accuracy and reliability of carrying out all of them. Even if the researcher employs other individuals, such as research assistants, the primary researcher is ultimately responsible for the process. Research assistants can be invaluable resources, but they typically need close supervision. Indeed, investigators are responsible for the competence of assistants working with them, as well as for the ethical treatment of the research assistants themselves.

REPORTING THE RESULTS

Reporting the results of a study, although seemingly a straightforward task, entails responsibilities and often complexities. This area includes several of the fundamental ethical principles, including beneficence, nonmaleficence, justice, and fidelity/veracity. For example, the investigator has a responsibility to report accurately and prevent misuse of research results (*EPP,* 8.10; *CE,* G.4). This implies that the researcher must honestly report findings and present them in a way that is clear and understandable to readers.

The investigator has several tasks in presenting the results. Initially, the investigator should present the facts of how the study was executed. There are no perfect studies and the investigator should describe the approach they took in conducting the study (this is typically reported in the Methods section of an article) as well as describe the limitations to the study (this is typically reported in the Discussion section of an article). Discussion of limitations is especially important when the findings may be less favorable for particular groups (e.g., gender, race/ethnicity, national origin, sexual orientation, social class). Sometimes researchers believe that if limitations are discussed, their results will be weakened, perhaps so much as to prevent their publication in a professional journal. It is important to remember that the goal of the researcher is to provide the most accurate information possible about the phenomenon of interest. Specifying the limitations is helpful to the profession, and often to future researchers as well. In our view, if a study's limitations are such that they in fact substantially reduce the probability of publishing the results, then the long-term interests of the profession are probably best served if the results are not published. It is antithetical to the long-term goals of a scientist to publish information that is misleading or to suppress disconfirming data.

Next, investigators need to present the results from the study in a straightforward and transparent manner (this is typically reported in the Results section of an article). For example, the researchers should be presenting basic descriptive information regarding the findings as well as a description of how they conducted the analyses. Finally, investigators also have a responsibility to accurately interpret their findings (this is typically presented in the Discussion section of an article). Sometimes researchers believe that their data will have greater value if they confirm their hypotheses or support a well-known researcher's theory. It is probably true that most published research report statistically significant findings. However, it is imperative to note that the researcher is not responsible for whether the data do or do not support a particular theory; perhaps the theory is incorrect. As Carl Rogers once said, "The facts are always friendly," implying that one should not feel bad about data that do not support a given hypothesis (personal communication to P. P. Heppner and L. A. Lee, January 1983). Thus, the job of the investigator is to report the results honestly, regardless of any preconceived notions, predictions, or personal desires. This also includes being clear to whom the results are likely generalizable. For instance, it is good ethical practice to note that the results coming from a sample of predominately men may not be generalizable to women, transgender individuals, or those who identify as gender nonconformning.

The investigator also has a responsibility, after research results are in the public domain, to make original data available to other qualified researchers who may want to inspect them and verify claims (*EPP,* 8.14; *CE,* G.4.e). This necessitates storage of raw data for some time after a study is published, typically for five to seven years.

Perhaps one of the most serious problems is the intentional fabrication of data. It is clearly unethical to produce fraudulent data (*EPP,* 8.10). There are at least three basic methods of concocting fraudulent data: (a) inventing findings without any actual data collection, (b) tampering with or doctoring actual findings to more closely resemble the desired outcome, and (c) trimming actual findings to delete unwanted or discrepant information (Koocher & Keith-Spiegel, 2008). Tampering with the findings can also include presenting post hoc findings as if they were planned; such fabrication obviously provides misinformation to the profession and serves only to increase confusion and misunderstanding. Unfortunately, numerous instances of fraudulent research have been reported in the scientific community (see Koocher & Keith-Spiegel, 2008), attracting attention in the general media and even provoking congressional investigations (Broad & Wade, 1982).

Perhaps the most publicized report of fabricating data involves Sir Cyril Burt, a noted British psychologist whose research on identical twins was read and cited internationally. Burt was a well-known scientist who was knighted in 1946 in recognition of his work (Drew, 1980). Burt has been exposed posthumously for publishing implausible and fictitious data that supported his own theory of inherited intelligence. Not only did such fabrications mislead the psychological profession for many years, they also became a major source of embarrassment to the profession.

Clearly, the fabrication of data represents a loss of "scientific responsibility" (Keith-Spiegel & Koocher, 1985, p. 364) and does little to promote human welfare. The goals of science are then trampled in the pursuit of personal rewards and short-term gain. Although a quest for personal recognition and the pressure to publish (the academic publish-or-perish dilemma) may distort a researcher's motivations, probably the most significant inducement pertains to securing grant funds. Researchers who make startling discoveries often are awarded grant funds; grant renewals are contingent upon continued research performance and the breaking of new ground. But sometimes in this pursuit the basic aim of science—extending the knowledge bases of a profession—is lost. Fabrication of data results in especially negative consequences for the counseling profession because most of our research is also aimed at improving psychological services to people in need. Thus, fabrication of data does more than create confusion; it can also reduce the effectiveness of the counseling profession, which affects the lives of real people.

DUPLICATE AND PIECEMEAL PUBLICATION

Another issue relates to the duplicate publication of data (*CE*, G.5.g). Obviously, publishing the same data in different journal articles creates some problems. Duplicate publication may give the impression that there is more information in our knowledge base on a particular topic than is warranted. Suppose that a journal article reports a relationship between a new relaxation training technique and stress management, and that shortly thereafter another article appears in a different journal reporting the same finding—the same relaxation training technique is helpful in reducing stress. The second article appears to replicate the first study, and thus creates the impression that the effect of this new relaxation training technique on stress management is a robust finding. In reality, however, these two articles only represent one data set, and the perception of replication is inaccurate. Moreover, duplicate publications waste valuable resources, including journal space and reviewers' and editors' time. In short, "psychologists do not publish, as original data, data that have been previously published" (*EPP*, 8.13). This issue becomes a bit more complicated when multiple researchers work with shared data. For instance, there are several large-scaled databases that are available for researchers. If multiple researchers are addressing similar (or the same question) with the same data it may result in the same situation as just described—albeit with a bit less intentionality for duplication.

A related issue pertains to what is referred to as piecemeal publication. Piecemeal, or fragmented, publication involves publication of several and perhaps slightly different studies from the same data set. Piecemeal publication is not necessarily synonymous with duplicate publication, although it can be. For example, it is possible in piecemeal publication to have one study reporting findings on relationships among depression, hopelessness, and suicidal ideation, while a second study from the same data set reports on relationships among depression, hopelessness, suicidal ideation, and irrational beliefs.

The prohibition of piecemeal publication does not include reanalysis of published data to test a new theory or methodology, although the new article needs to be clearly labeled as such (American Psychological Association, 1994). Likewise, there are times when multiple reports from large longitudinal studies are warranted, especially when the time lag across data collection is significant. Similarly, sometimes multiple reports from a large data set are warranted if the studies are theoretically or conceptually distinct, and thus the data cannot be meaningfully combined into one article. Parsimoniously presenting research is desirable, however, and should be done whenever possible.

It is strongly recommended that authors clearly identify instances of multiple publications from the same data set. Moreover, authors should inform editors of the possibility of multiple publications and preferably provide the relevant articles so that editors can make informed decisions regarding fragmented publication. When in doubt, consult with journal editors and colleagues.

PUBLICATION CREDIT

Researchers have a responsibility to adequately and accurately assign credit for contributions to a project (*EPP*, 8.12; *CE*, G.5). The issues involved with publication credit primarily relate to the fundamental ethical principles of justice and fidelity/veracity. On the one hand, assigning publication credit seems like a straightforward and simple process. People who made minor contributions are acknowledged in a footnote, while those making major contributions are given authorship and listed in order of how much they contributed. In reality, these decisions can be complicated and emotional, primarily because of ambiguity surrounding the term *contribution*. What constitutes minor and major contributions? Some contend that the person who contributed the most time to a project deserves to be first author, while others argue that expertise, or even seniority, should determine author order. At other times it is reasoned that the one who conceived the idea for the study should be the principal or first author. Determining the author order often becomes difficult when the authors were primarily engaged in separate activities, such as writing the manuscript, analyzing the results, collecting the data, designing the study, and supervising the conduct of the study. Assigning publication credit becomes complicated as researchers debate whether all of these contributions are equally important, or whether some contributions should be assigned greater weight than others.

Accurately assigning publication credit is important for several reasons. First and foremost, it is important to publicly acknowledge the contributions of all the people involved in the study—to give credit where credit is due (*EPP*, 8.12; *CE*, G.5). In addition, publication credit is often important in one's professional career, helping one gain entrance into graduate school, obtain professional employment, and earn professional promotion. Moreover, public acknowledgment of one's professional contributions can serve as a "psychic reward" to compensate for the low monetary rewards associated with writing for scholarly outlets (Koocher & Keith-Spiegel, 2008). Sometimes the order of authorship on a publication is important, because the first author is accorded more credit (and responsibility) for the scholarly work than are the other authors. For example, only the first author will receive recognition in citation indices such as the Social Science Citation Index. Clearly, then, determining the order of authorship is relevant to career-related issues.

Ethical Principles of Psychologists and *Ethical Standards* are ambiguous in addressing most of these issues. The *Publication Manual of the American Psychological Association* (2010a) provides more direction; major contributions typically include writing the manuscript, formulating the research question or hypotheses, designing the study, organizing and conducting the statistical analysis, and interpreting or writing the results. It is often suggested that "minor contributions" to publications be credited in footnotes. Typically, "minor" professional contributions include such activities as giving editorial feedback, consulting on design or statistical questions, serving as raters or judges, administering an intervention, collecting or entering data, providing extensive clerical services, and generating conceptual ideas relevant to the study (e.g., directions for future research). Paid research assistants are remunerated for their contribution. Thus, a common introductory footnote (usually found at the bottom of the first page of a journal article) reads something like: "The authors would like to thank Josephine Computer for statistical assistance and Helen Grammar and Chris Critical for helpful editorial comments." Usually, these contributors went out of their way to help the authors in minor but significant ways. Thus, it is important to publicly recognize these minor contributions. However, the author should receive permission from contributors before thanking them in a footnote. Another type of footnote is a public acknowledgment of a funding source that sponsored the research. A footnote might acknowledge, "This research was supported by a grant received by the first author from the National Institute of Mental Health" (complete with reference to the grant number).

How to distinguish between a minor contributor and a major contributor (an author) and how to determine the order of multiple authors are not clearly specified in *EPP* and *CE*. *EPP* does state that "principal authorship and other publication credits accurately reflect the relative scientific or professional contributions of the individuals involved, regardless of their relative status" (8.12). Spiegel and Keith-Spiegel (1970) surveyed over 700 professionals to examine their opinions about determining authorship. They found modal trends, but not a firm consensus, for the following criteria, in their respective order: (a) generation of hypotheses and design, (b) writing the manuscript, (c) establishing the procedure and collecting the data, and (d) analyzing the data. Contributions tend to be valued according to their scholarly importance, as opposed to the amount of time they required. Moreover, respondents in two studies did not rate professional status as a determining variable (Bridgewater, Bornstein, & Walkenbach, 1981; Spiegel & Keith-Spiegel, 1970), which suggests that merit rather than degrees or status is typically a stronger determinant of professional contribution. In short, the list of authors should include those individuals who made a major scholarly contribution to the study in the ways just listed.

Consider the following example:

RESEARCH IN ACTION 3.3

You meet with your supervisor in the beginning of the school year to discuss a research opportunity. She invites you to help with the data collection and data entry for a project examining the effects of fatigue on fine motor skills. Throughout the semester, you conduct numerous study trials with participants staying awake for 24 hours, while you administer fine motor tasks every 3 hours. You then enter the data from 150 participants and help with analyzing the data. During the following semester, your supervisor asks you to check the References section on her manuscript, and you are surprised and angry to see that your name is not included as a coauthor.

Questions

Should the student in this case be given authorship?

How could the supervisor and supervisee dealt with the situation differently?

The order of authorship (in the case of multiple authorship) typically reflects differential amounts of scholarly contributions; that is, the person who made the greatest scholarly contribution to a project should be the principal or first author, with the others listed in order of their relative contributions. The process of determining authors and order of authorship is very important, perhaps as important as the outcome. Because a great deal of ambiguity enters into deciding authorship, authors may have different opinions about author order. The potential for authors to feel slighted or cheated is greater when authorship is decided by one person, such as the first author. Thus, from our experience, a mutual decision-making process is most desirable, and preferably a consensus model in which those involved discuss these issues. Yet, there can be challenges to this process when there are different levels of power among the authors (e.g., professor-student).

Sometimes the order of authorship is decided at the conclusion of a study (a post hoc strategy) and just prior to the submission of a manuscript for editorial review to a journal or to a professional convention. The advantage of assigning authorship at this time is that it is possible to assess how much each person actually contributed. The disadvantage is after-the-fact disappointments: A person might have wanted or expected to be first author but was unaware of either how the order was to be decided or other members' contributions. Or a worse scenario: A person might have thought that his scholarly contribution was sufficient to qualify him/her/them as an author, but then learned after the study that his/her/their contribution was deemed minor and would be acknowledged only in a footnote.

Another strategy (the a priori strategy) is to assign authorship before implementing a study. The advantage here is that as a result of the opportunity to discuss and clarify the relevant issues beforehand, informed decisions and agreements can be made by all participants. The disadvantages to this strategy are that a person might contribute considerably more or less than initially agreed to, or an inexperienced researcher might want to be first or second author without clearly understanding the implications of such an assignment in terms of the tasks and skills needed.

A third strategy is to combine both the post hoc and a priori strategies, discussing author-related issues before the study is conducted, perhaps developing a tentative author order, and then evaluating the accuracy of that initial order after all the tasks have been completed. This strategy offers the benefits of both of the other strategies and minimizes the disadvantages and disappointments.

A final strategy is to assign the order of authorship by chance (e.g., by drawing straws). This strategy is sometimes used when it truly seems that each author contributed equally, and it is literally impossible to differentiate among their contributions. It may also seem that any author order would misrepresent the contributions of both the first and last authors. In these situations, authors may use some arbitrary method of assigning the order of authorship. If this strategy is used, an introductory footnote should acknowledge that the author order was determined by chance. Parenthetically, assigning author order by alphabetizing names is not a random process (ask people with names like Zimmer or Zytowski).

One final note: A very complicated issue pertaining to publication credit involves graduate students' theses and dissertations. Often graduate students feel that because they have contributed a great deal of time, effort, and sometimes money, they have contributed the most to their project. Faculty advisor input might include providing encouragement and technical assistance in designing the study, developing major interpretative contributions, providing funding and other support, and writing major parts of the manuscript. However, it is unclear how much of the faculty advisor's contribution is a part of her or his teaching and training role within the university. There is a real potential for exploiting graduate students if a faculty member has them perform most (if not all) of the research tasks and then claims publication credit, particularly first authorship. *EPP* indicates that "except under exceptional circumstances, a student is listed as principal author on any multiple-authored article that is substantially based on the student's doctoral dissertation" (8.12). Similarly *CE* (G.5) indicates that "For articles that are substantially based on students' course papers, projects, dissertations or theses, and on which students have been the primary contributors, they are listed as principle authors." Indeed, the APA Ethics Committee (1983) wrote specifically about dissertations; their guidelines pertain equally well to theses. The guidelines are as follows:

1. Only second authorship is acceptable for the dissertation supervisor.
2. Second authorship may be considered *obligatory* if the supervisor designates the primary variables, makes major interpretative contributions, or provides the database.
3. Second authorship is a courtesy if the supervisor designates the general area of concern or is substantially involved in the development of the design and measurement procedures or substantially contributes to the write-up of the published report.
4. Second authorship is *not* acceptable if the supervisor provides only encouragement, physical facilities, financial support, critiques, or editorial contributions.
5. In all instances, agreements should be reviewed before the writing for publication is undertaken and at the time of submission. If disagreements arise, they should be resolved by a third party using these guidelines.

PLAGIARISM

Researchers have a responsibility to acknowledge the original contributions of other writers and to clearly distinguish their own original scholarly insights from the work of others (*EPP*, 8.11; *CE*, G.5.b). Again, these issues revolve primarily around the fundamental ethical principle of justice, fidelity/veracity, and nonmalifence. Plagiarism can occur in the direct, verbatim copying of another's work, or less explicitly, as in duplicating ideas from others' work without proper citation. Quotation marks and proper citation form should be used when quoting a passage verbatim from another article; paraphrasing sentences from other articles should include a citation to the original work. In both cases of plagiarism, the original author does not receive proper acknowledgment or credit for his or her work. Keith-Spiegel and Koocher (1985) nicely depicted this issue:

> Copying the original work of others without proper permission or citation attribution is often experienced as "psychic robbery" by the victims, producing the same kind of rage expressed by those who arrive home to find the TV set and stereo missing. When plagiarizers reap financial rewards or recognition from passing someone else's words off as their own, the insult is still greater. Readers are also misled and, in a sense, defrauded. Plagiarism and unfair use of previously published material are among the more serious ethical infractions a psychologist can commit. (p. 356)

Plagiarism can occur on several levels. A researcher might omit necessary citations through inattention, perhaps by not being sufficiently careful or conscientious. The plagiarism in such cases is unintentional and due more to oversight. Another level involves the difficulty sometimes encountered in determining what is original in a researcher's ideas. For example, after a researcher has read and written in an area for 20 years, ideas from a variety of sources often blend together in a complex knowledge base. The researcher may one day conceive of what seems like a new insight, and publish it. However, in reality the "insight" had already been published years ago; the researcher simply did not remember the original source. Or, as researchers work together and not only share ideas but also build upon each other's ideas, the ownership of ideas becomes unclear. Sometimes researchers working in slightly different areas may duplicate each other's ideas without being aware of their common work. These types of plagiarism are difficult to control; one needs to be as conscientious as possible while acknowledging that memory lapses can create less than ideal conditions.

A final level of plagiarism involves the verbatim copying of another's writing or the duplicating of ideas with the motive of presenting oneself as the original contributor, all the while knowing full well that this is not the case. In these situations the plagiarist has control and has made some deliberate choices.

The point is that acknowledging the contributions of others is basically a matter of fairness and integrity—in essence, of giving credit where credit is due. Not citing the original author may seem like a rather small issue, but it is really quite important. Imagine that you have worked very hard for two or three years, creating and building a new conceptual model. Naturally, you are very proud of this accomplishment. Then someone publishes a similar model and this person receives the credit for developing this innovative model. In addition to fairness and integrity, there is also the matter of saluting (in a small way) previous researchers for their accomplishments. From a historical perspective, it is important not only to recognize the authors whose work preceded one's own, but also to recognize where one's work fits into the bigger picture. Keep in mind as well that the federal government considers plagiarism to be misconduct in science, and that employing institutions are required to investigate all cases of suspected plagiarism and provide sanctions where appropriate.

ETHICAL ISSUES RELATED TO PARTICIPANTS

A central issue in all psychological and counseling research is the dignity and welfare of the people who participate in the study. The goal of the ethical researcher is to develop a fair, clear, and explicit agreement with participants so that his or her decision to participate in an experiment is made voluntarily, knowingly, and intelligently (Kitchener & Anderson, 2011; Koocher & Keith-Spiegel, 2008). In this manner, participants are not coerced and make informed decisions about the benefits and risks associated with taking part in a particular experiment. The most fundamental ethical principles implied in the treatment of participants involve nonmaleficence, autonomy, and fidelity.

Historically, the dignity and welfare of those participating in research have not always been of foremost concern. Probably the most notorious example of abuse of participants occurred in the experiments conducted during World War II in Nazi prison camps, where many prisoners died from lethal doses of chemicals and various levels of physical abuse. Physicians conducted research on such topics as effective ways of treating severe frostbite (which involved subjecting individuals to freezing temperatures), infected wounds, and deadly diseases such as malaria and typhus (which involved subjecting individuals to infectious germs) (Stricker, 1982). Fortunately, the Nuremberg trials at the end of World War II, which tried 23 physicians for these research atrocities, served as an initial impetus for guidelines of ethical treatment of research participants. In fact, the Nuremberg Code has been the basis for subsequent ethical principles regarding human subjects in research (Koocher & Keith-Spiegel, 2008). Unfortunately, yet other research tragedies stimulated additional concern and the need for additional regulation.

In 1962, the thalidomide scandal came to public attention because of innumerable gross neonatal deformities. Consequently, the U.S. Food and Drug Administration introduced much stricter regulations for tightly controlled experimentation on drugs and other products (Stricker, 1982). Not long afterward, public attention became focused on a program conducted by a hospital in Brooklyn, where 22 chronically ill patients were injected with cancer cells as part of a study to examine the body's capacity to reject foreign cells. The patients were not informed of their participation. This, and other studies involving excessive shock treatment conditions and subjecting participants to diseases such as syphilis, served to raise public awareness of ethical issues related to informed consent of research participants. Subsequently the issue of informed consent crystallized, and obligations to research participants were made clearer (Stricker, 1982).

Another horrific example is the Tuskegee syphilis experiment, where the U.S. Public Health Service recruited approximately 600 lower-income African American men. The study was conducted from the 1930s to the 1970s. Approximately 400 of the participants were diagnosed with syphilis prior to the study. Although the researchers provided some medical care for all of the participants, they never informed the men that they had syphilis and most troubling they did not treat their syphilis. In the late 1940s, penicillin was the gold standard of treatment for syphilis. The 40-year study resulted in the tragic loss of life and spreading of the disease to other individuals (e.g., partners and children). Clearly, this study violates many ethical principles, and raises questions about the moral character of the researchers (see Brandon, Iaasc, & LaVeist, 2005).

As awareness of and sensitivity to the rights of both human and animal participants in psychological and educational research have increased, there have been major changes in the regulation of research. One of the major changes has been development of institutional review boards (IRBs) and an ethics guidance program to protect human participants in biomedical and behavioral research. Initially, IRBs were established as five-person panels to preview research proposals and weigh potential risks and benefits for all research that sought funding from the Department of Health, Education, and Welfare (now the Department of Health and Human Services, hereafter referred to as DHHS). Although IRBs still serve this function, most institutions now routinely have all research proposals reviewed by a college or university IRB (C-IRB) committee of peers at their institution. In essence, the typical C-IRB certifies that projects comply with the regulations and policies set forth by the DHHS regarding the health, welfare, safety, rights, and privileges of human participants. The general procedure is for the investigator to complete and submit to the C-IRB a form that summarizes basic information about the research, including purpose of the study, types of participants needed, informed consent procedures, method of collecting data, and funding sources. Please contact your particular campus IRB for specific requirements and procedures.

Key issues in evaluating the ethicality of any research project are the risks and benefits involved to the participants, which can be difficult to fully ascertain. Additionally, it is important to assess whether participants have been fully informed about the study so they can make an informed decision to voluntarily participate (informed consent). In this section of the chapter we discuss a number of complexities and complications related to using human participants. Specifically, we discuss issues pertaining to risks and benefits, consent, deception and debriefing, confidentiality and privacy, and treatment.

RISKS AND BENEFITS

Assessing potential harm or risk is a difficult and sometimes imprecise process. Because there is some level of risk (even if it is minuscule) in every experiment, how much risk or harm is too much? In some research, deception is needed to adequately investigate a particular construct, and if the full truth were known to a participant, the validity of the experiment might be significantly reduced. Thus, without deception, knowledge of some aspects of human behavior may be inaccessible. But deception conflicts with informed consent and the fundamental principles of autonomy and fidelity. This section focuses on these issues in greater detail as we discuss the issues involved in protecting the dignity and welfare of the people who participate in research investigations.

The ethical researcher's goal is to conduct an investigation that creates new knowledge (the beneficence principle) while preserving the dignity and welfare of the participants (the nonmaleficence and autonomy principles). Yet, all researchers need to consider the balance of these two, as there is some level of risk (even if it is minuscule) in every experiment. Thus, the question remains for most studies is: How much risk or harm is too much?

It almost goes without saying that one would not want to harm participants in any way. Particularly for the counseling researcher, the goal is usually to alleviate human suffering; thus harm is antithetical to the immediate and long-term goals of the professional counselor. But harm can be manifested in many ways. The most obvious way involves physical harm, or even death, as in the Nazi "research" during World War II. However, harm can also consist of embarrassment, irritation, anger, physical and emotional distress, loss of self-esteem, exacerbation of stress, delay of treatment, sleep deprivation, loss of respect from others, negative labeling, invasion of privacy, damage to personal dignity, loss of employment, and civil or criminal liabilities. Part of the difficulty in predicting harm is that different people may react to the same experimental condition in very different ways. For example, most clients may feel very comfortable rating their expectations for the counseling they are about to receive; some clients might even enjoy this reflection. However, a few clients might experience distress or embarrassment, or even guilt, by participating in this exercise. Sometimes cross-cultural differences contribute to unintended reactions, which underscore the complexity of this issue. Researchers need to assess harm not only in a general sense, but also with regard to the intended participants' worldview and cultural background. Because there is some level of risk (even if it is minuscule) in every experiment, how much risk or harm is too much?

It is the researcher's responsibility to identify potential sources of risk and eliminate or minimize them to protect potential participants (*EPP*, 8.02; *CE*, G.1). The professional codes of ethics suggest that the researcher should carefully assess the potential risks of involvement for participants and take precautions to protect participants from physical and mental discomfort, harm, and danger that might occur in a study (*EPP*, 3.04; *CE*, G.1). Implied in these statements is that it is the responsibility of the investigator to reduce risk and prevent harm by detecting and removing any negative consequences associated with a study, to the extent possible.

One of the problems inherent in assessing risk potential is that the task is often subjective, ambiguous, and involves an estimation of probabilities. Typically one does not have prior, empirical, objective data about whether the experimental condition is stressful (and to collect such data would require administering the experiment to participants). Moreover, the type and level of stress that would be harmful is ambiguous and likely varies across cultures and individuals; that is, what is perceived as harmful in one culture may not be perceived as such in another culture. Thus, assessing harm may also involve cross-cultural sensitivity. In short, assessing risk is difficult, if not impossible, to quantify.

Acknowledging the difficulty, ambiguity, and imperfectness of the task, there are at least two main strategies for obtaining approval to conduct a study, typically from an institutional review board. The first strategy involves making a best estimate of the risk/benefit ratio of the study; that is, a comparison should be made of the potential benefits that might accrue from the study relative to the potential risks to participants. This involves a three-step process: (a) assessing risks, (b) assessing benefits, and (c) comparing risks and benefits. For example, a study might be considered ethically acceptable if the potential benefits greatly outweighed the potential risks, or if failure to use the experimental procedures might expose participants to greater harm. Assessing the benefits derived from a particular study, however, is also a difficult and ambiguous task. This assessment is complicated by the question of "benefit for whom?" That is, should participants be the ones to receive the benefit directly, or could it be a larger group, as when a profession's knowledge base is increased. Some may argue that benefits from any single study may be minimal, but that over time programmatic research does increase the profession's knowledge base. Still, balancing individual costs against societal benefits is a difficult task. Moreover, it can be argued that the investigator is at a disadvantage to judge the cost/benefit ratio accurately because he or she may be overly biased regarding the benefit of the study (Diener & Crandall, 1978). In short, in principle the risk/ benefit ratio is appealing, but in practice it is difficult to apply. Nonetheless, the risk/ benefit ratio is one useful strategy for assessing the ethical issues associated with a particular study.

The second strategy involves several procedures to minimize risk or reduce the probability of harm. Whenever the potential for substantial risk is present, the investigator should search for other possible designs or procedures. The researcher needs to exhaust other possibilities for obtaining the same or similar knowledge by using a slightly different design. A common practice is to consult with colleagues not only to obtain ideas regarding alternative designs or procedures, but also to obtain alternative perspectives in assessing risks and benefits.

Consultation with colleagues is particularly important in planning socially sensitive research or research in which cross-cultural or multicultural issues and investigator bias may be a factor. Researchers have a duty to consult with those knowledgeable about the individuals or groups most likely to be affected (*EPP*, 2.01; *CE*, G.1). Often the researcher's problem solving with regard to ethical issues can be greatly stimulated and facilitated by successively conferring with a wide variety of colleagues. The process of consulting with colleagues has now been formalized at many institutions and agencies, as we indicated earlier, into campus institutional review boards (C-IRBs) or human subject review committees. The C-IRBs serve the extremely valuable function of providing additional perspectives in assessing risk and suggesting possible alternative designs that are not always immediately apparent to the researcher. Even if not technically required to do so, researchers are encouraged to solicit feedback from such committees.

The researcher can also engage in other strategies to minimize risk. We indicated earlier that one of the problems in assessing risks and benefits is the lack of empirical data on which to make informed decisions. Thus, another strategy is to collect some data through safer channels, such as using pilot participants and role playing, to facilitate a more accurate assessment of risks and benefits. For example, the researcher and his or her assistants might role-play the experimental procedures in question (which is often a good idea in general), and perhaps explore alternative procedures. Perhaps colleagues could also be asked to serve as participants to review the procedures and provide feedback on potential risks. Colleagues often can provide very useful feedback because they can discuss their experience as a participant in light of their knowledge of ethical and design issues. Depending on the outcome of such role plays (that is, if the risks do not appear to be substantial), the researcher might take another step by conducting a very small-scale pilot study with two to five participants. In such a pilot, the researcher should not only monitor the experimental procedures very carefully, but also interview participants at length about their experiences and solicit suggestions for alternative procedures. Pilot feedback can be extremely valuable, and its utility should not be downplayed. Likewise, any frequency data from previous studies employing the same procedures may be very useful in assessing the degree of risk; for example, researchers might use a postexperimental evaluation to ask subjects whether they experienced any harm. In short, role plays and pilot projects provide the researcher at least minimal data from which to assess risks and benefits. Additional data can also be obtained by carefully monitoring the actual experiment and even interviewing randomly selected participants both immediately after the experiment and several days later. The researcher should not stop evaluating the potential risks of a study once the study is approved by a C-IRB committee, but rather should remain vigilant by constantly evaluating the risks and benefits as more data about the participants' experiences become available.

Another strategy to minimize risk is to screen participants for a particular study and then select only those participants who have certain characteristics that make them more resistant to the risks involved (or dismiss participants who might be particularly at risk in the study) (Diener & Crandall, 1978; Kitchener & Anderson, 2011). For example, depressed participants with very low self-esteem might be at increased risk if they participated in a protracted study that involved a great deal of interpersonal feedback from other students. In this regard, special populations (such as children, patients from a psychiatric hospital, or prisoners in solitary confinement) merit careful consideration as a group.

In summary, the ethical researcher's goal is to conduct an investigation that creates new knowledge while preserving the dignity and welfare of the participants. Thus, a major task for the researcher is to carefully assess potential risks and make every attempt to eliminate or minimize such risks. Two strategies were discussed for obtaining approval to conduct a study: (a) attempting to assess and weigh the risk/benefit ratio of the study and (b) using a variety of procedures to evaluate, minimize, or eliminate potential risks. It is important to note, however, that a great deal of ambiguity often enters assessments of costs and risks, particularly in cross-cultural and multicultural situations; the researcher may often experience conflict and struggle with the imperfection of this important task. Consultation is strongly encouraged.

Consider the following example:

RESEARCH IN ACTION 3.4

You are conducting pre- and postassessments for a reading intervention among second graders. You have received consent from all parents for their children participating in the study. After completing the intervention, you begin your postassessments, which take about 30 minutes per student. After meeting with Lilly, a 9-year-old African American girl, for the first half of the assessments, she begins to cry and says that reading aloud embarrasses her. She continues to become increasingly distressed, even with you telling her just to try her best. You are unsure if you should continue to testing, because her mother consented that it was okay.

Questions

What could the researchers have done differently to avoid this situation?

INFORMED CONSENT

After a researcher has carefully evaluated potential harm and developed the best design to answer his or her questions while preserving the participant's dignity and welfare, the researcher is then ready to approach participants with a fair, clear, and explicit agreement about the experiment in question (informed consent). The issue of informed consent revolves around the fundamental ethical principles of autonomy and fidelity/veracity. Consent refers to the process of giving participants the opportunity to decide whether or not to participate in a particular research study.

This might appear to be a rather simple matter: Simply ask the participant if he or she would like to participate. But a number of factors make obtaining consent a rather complicated process.

The professional codes of ethics clearly indicate that the investigator has a responsibility to obtain informed consent from participants (*EPP*, 6.11; *CE*, G.2). The investigator seeks to develop a specific type of relationship with potential participants and thus is ethically bound to establish a clear and fair agreement that clarifies obligations, risks, and responsibilities prior to the study.

Turnbull (1977) discussed consent in this special relationship in terms of three key elements: capacity, information, and voluntariness. *Capacity* refers to a participant's ability to process information and involves two issues: a legal age qualification and ability standards. Minors, people under the age of 18, are not considered to be legally able to make some decisions and thus do not have the needed capacity in these instances. The principle of autonomy creates difficult issues when applied to using children in research (*EPP*, 3.10, 8.02). Because children have a reduced or limited capacity, it is impossible to obtain a fully rational consent from them (Kitchener & Anderson, 2011; Ramsey, 1970). Moreover, the child's parent or legal guardian cannot know whether the child, if fully rational, would choose to participate or not. Federal regulations indicate that a child's assent (defined as an affirmative agreement to participate) is required whenever in the judgment of a C-IRB the child is capable of providing assent, taking into account age, maturity, and psychological state. We encourage counseling researchers to explain to children (and to their parents or guardians), in language they can understand, what they will be asked to do in the course of the research and to secure whenever possible their agreement to participate.

Ability typically refers to mental competence, and thereby protects individuals who may be at risk because of diminished mental capacities. Autonomy is again an issue. If a researcher uses institutionalized adults, then consent must be obtained from parents or legal guardians. We also suggest obtaining assent from adults with diminished capacity if at all possible. In short, a critical element of consent involves the capacity to process information about the merits and drawbacks of participating in a particular study.

The second key element of informed consent pertains to the type of *information* that potential participants are given about a study (*EPP*, 8.04; *CE*, G.2). Participants must be given all of the relevant information about a study so that they can make an informed decision about the merits and liabilities of participating. In doing so, it is important to provide detailed information as well as take time to process it with participants (Kitchener & Anderson, 2011; Turnbull, 1977). Thus, the information given must be complete and presented in understandable, jargon-free language. Drew (1980) referred to these issues as fullness and effectiveness. To satisfy the requirement of fullness, the information presented should contain a description of what the investigation is about and what the participant will be asked to do (such as complete two questionnaires about study habits). This should include a discussion of any type of voice or image recording (*EPP*, 8.03). Moreover, the explanation should include a discussion of possible risks or potential harm involved in the study, as well as a discussion of potential benefits that might accrue from participation. Failure to make full disclosures, as in the case of deception, requires additional safeguards that we will discuss later. Moreover, the information must be understandable to participants given their particular worldview.

The third element of consent is *voluntariness:* assent must be given without any element of explicit or implicit coercion, pressure, or undue enticement (*EPP,* 8.06). Examples of coercion include requiring students to participate in a study because they are enrolled in a class, living in an institution, part of a therapy group, or seeking individual therapy; publicly humiliating participants if they choose not to participate; paying excessive amounts of money or giving other financial rewards as an inducement to participate; repeatedly contacting clients and soliciting participation; and creating undue social pressure by indicating that all of the other clients have agreed to participate. University courses (such as large introductory psychology classes) sometimes offer bonus credits for or require participation in research studies; in such situations it is essential to offer students viable alternatives to participating in research studies in order to protect their autonomy. Voluntariness can also be a complex issue in a counseling context. For example, situations in which therapists ask their clients to participate may contain elements of undue influence (e.g., the therapist is very likable, or the client is vulnerable and wants to be a "good client"). In short, a key aspect of consent is that participants can voluntarily decide on participating free from blatant or subtle extraneous factors that may compel them to participate.

The notion of voluntariness does not end when a potential participant decides to participate in a study; it continues throughout the duration of a study. Thus, participants are typically informed prior to the commencement of a study that they have the right to withdraw from the experiment at any time, and that their initial agreement to participate is not binding. Koocher and Keith-Spiegel (2008) astutely observed that the wise investigator will be alert to signs of discomfort or anxiousness that might influence participants to withdraw, and rather than coerce continued involvement be concerned about the usefulness and validity of data collected under stressful conditions.

Consider the following example, various ethical issues that may be relevant within the scenario, and consider whether this would be acceptable:

RESEARCH IN ACTION 3.5

You are conducting a study investigating family systems coping styles in an urban, low-SES community. Participants are asked to complete three interview sessions lasting about 90 minutes each. This community understandably has a general mistrust towards research, due to devious studies conducted in the past. Your advisor suggests providing financial incentives for participation. Families are provided $100 per session to compensate for their time and to cover transportation and child care if needed.

Questions

What ethical considerations are there in this example?

Do you believe this is acceptable practice? Why or Why not?

In short, an important ethical consideration in recruiting participants in counseling research involves their informed consent. It is important that potential participants have the capacity to process information about the study, have received complete and effective information about the content and procedures of the study, and can decide on the merits of participating voluntarily, without extraneous compelling factors.

As we indicated earlier, documentation of the participant's consent is now common practice. There are a few exceptions; several categories of research are typically considered exempt from these requirements, such as observation of public behavior, the study of anonymous archival data, and certain types of survey and interview procedures. Participants are asked to sign a formal consent form indicating their informed agreement to participate if there is more than what is referred to as a minimal risk (i.e., more risk to the participant than he or she would encounter in daily life). Even in studies involving minimal risk to participants, obtaining a signed consent form is advisable to avoid misunderstandings and for the researcher's own protection. It is important to note that cross-cultural issues can also create confusion or misunderstandings that may be relevant during the process of obtaining informed consent, which again reinforces the need for sensitivity to these matters while obtaining consent.

Specifically, the following elements are to be incorporated into a written consent form:

- Name, phone number, and address of the person(s) conducting the study, and whom to contact for additional information or questions; name, phone number, and address of faculty member if the investigator is a student; whom to contact in the event of a research-related injury to the participant
- A statement that the study involves research, along with the title, purpose, and general description of the study
- A description of the procedures, including amount of time involved and any plans for contacting participants at a later time
- A description of any reasonably foreseeable risks or discomforts to the participant
- A description of the benefits to the participant, or to others that can reasonably be expected
- In cases involving treatment or therapy, a statement of appropriate alternative procedures or courses of treatment, if any, that might be advantageous to the participant
- A statement describing the extent to which confidentiality will be maintained
- A statement that the results of the study may be published or reported to government or funding agencies
- A statement indicating that participation is voluntary, and that the participant may discontinue participation at any time without any penalty
- For research involving more than minimal risk, an explanation of whether compensation or medical treatments are available if injury occurs

A sample of a typical consent form for adults is provided as Exhibit A at the end of the chapter, and a sample of a typical consent form for children (note the appropriate language level) is provided as Exhibit B.

DECEPTION AND DEBRIEFING

Deception is a topic that has received considerable attention and been the subject of much debate (*EPP*, 8.07; *CE*, G.2). Deception in psychological research refers to misinforming or withholding information from potential participants about the nature of the experiment or the procedures involved in the study. Thus, deception refers to misrepresenting the facts pertaining to a study, through acts of either omission or commission. For instance, an investigator might omit or withhold some information about a study and thus disguise the true nature of the study in some way; or the researcher might purposefully provide false or misleading information, an act of commission, to deceive the participant in some way. Either way, the thorny issues of deception revolve around the fundamental ethical principles of autonomy, fidelity, and, to some extent, nonmaleficence.

It is important to note that there are many types or levels of deception. Perhaps at the simplest and most benign level, the experimenter may accurately describe the study but not disclose all the facts about it, largely because of the tremendous amount of detail involved. Or the experimenter might accurately disclose the nature of the experiment but not reveal the hypotheses so as to not bias the participants. These acts of omission usually do not bother participants. It is typically recognized that an experimenter cannot be completely forthcoming about all aspects of a study (including the researcher's hypothesis or complete descriptions of all experimental conditions); in fact, revealing such information can bias or confound the results of a study (see Chapter 23). Other types of deception, however, mislead the participants in major ways and often lead them to feel "duped" or "bamboozled." For example, participants might be told that they failed a problem-solving test (that their score was in the fifth percentile) in order to examine their behavior following failure. In reality, participants probably did not perform so poorly on the test but were merely given bogus feedback. For the most part, the major controversy surrounding deception pertains to those situations in which participants are entirely misled. It is on these instances of deception that we will focus here.

Obviously, the use of deception is antithetical to fully informing potential subjects about the essence of a particular study. However, sometimes deception is necessary in psychological research to adequately examine certain phenomena, like the process of persuasion. Specifically, in a study of the social influence process in counseling, some participants might very well be predisposed not to change a particular belief or attitude if they were told beforehand that the study was investigating variables related to changing their beliefs. In this case, not using deception would result in a study that did not have much generalizability or resemblance to the attitude change process in counseling.

Deception may have especially troublesome consequences for counseling researchers (Schmidt & Meara, 1984). A core ingredient of the counseling relationship is perceived counselor trustworthiness; deception would most likely destroy client perceptions of trustworthiness and the working alliance. Thus, because of therapeutic considerations, researchers examining real-life counseling processes must address additional considerations and consequences involving deception.

Our view is that researchers should avoid deception whenever possible. In particular, "psychologists do not deceive prospective participants about research that is reasonably expected to cause physical pain or severe emotional distress" (*EPP*, 8.07, p. 11). Moreover, the use of certain types of deception with oppressed groups is very questionable. Still, we believe there are exceptions in which deception may be allowed. Specifically, when there is little or minimal risk and the benefits from the research are socially significant or directly benefit the participant, deception may be allowed. In addition, before conducting a study using deception, it is the responsibility of the investigator to have (a) "determined that the use of deceptive techniques is justified by the study's significant prospective scientific, educational, or applied value," and (b) determined that "effective non-deceptive alternative procedures are not feasible" (*EPP*, 8.07, p. 11). Thus, the extent or magnitude of the harm is an important consideration. In short, if an investigator decides to use deception, additional responsibilities and safeguards are required to protect the welfare and dignity of research participants, and the researcher must carefully assess the potential consequences and risks to participants. Finally, given the nature of the counseling relationship, deception in real-life counseling with actual clients would rarely seem justifiable.

If deception is justified, the investigator is responsible for informing participants about the nature of the study and removing any misconceptions as soon as is possible within the experiment (*EPP*, 8.07; *CE*, G.2). Providing a sufficient explanation is commonly referred to as debriefing. Moreover, in educational settings, if students are serving as participants to earn research credits and learn about psychological research, debriefing also should emphasize educational issues. Exhibits C and D provide examples of both oral and written debriefings for an analogue study that examined variables affecting laypersons' perceptions of grief reactions. Because this study was conducted with undergraduates who earned extra credit, the debriefing nicely emphasizes educational components. Moreover, the example explains the need for the minimal level of deception used in the analogue study.

It is important to note that the effectiveness of debriefing is unclear and probably varies with each study or experimenter. Moreover, in some cases debriefing can itself create stress or harm. For example, if the researcher preselected two groups of participants who had very high or very low self-concepts, communicating this information may not be well received by some participants. In this regard, Baumrind (1976) identified debriefing as "inflicted insight." In other situations participants may feel angry because they were misled or "duped." Thus, sometimes debriefing adds additional complications and results in delicate situations with which the investigator must contend.

CONFIDENTIALITY AND PRIVACY

Investigators ask participants for a wide array of information, often of such a very personal nature that it could be harmful if publicly released. Often experimenters promise confidentiality to increase the likelihood of honest responses from participants. If a participant agrees to participate confidentially in an experiment, the principles of fidelity, autonomy, and to some extent nonmaleficence suggest that any information that the participant discloses should be protected to safeguard the welfare of the client. The professional codes of ethics clearly indicate that care should be taken to protect the privacy of participants (*EPP*, 6.02; *CE*, G.2).

Maintaining the anonymity or confidentiality of participants is now standard in counseling research. Anonymity exists when there are no identifiers whatsoever on project materials that can link data with individual participants; often researchers assign participants coded designations that appear on their respective questionnaires in lieu of their names. Thus, the participants' responses are anonymous, and even the investigator cannot identify the participants. At other times, investigators collect data and ask for participants' names. Researchers have an obligation to maintain the confidentiality of information obtained in such research. If names are used, typically code numbers will be assigned to participants when the data are transferred to coding sheets, and the original questionnaires containing participants' names will be destroyed. If someone other than the experimenter will have access to data (e.g., a research assistant), this should be explained to the participants (and usually is stated in the consent form) along with plans for maintaining confidentiality. In field settings, researchers also should be alert to minimizing the invasiveness of data collection so as to protect the participants' privacy within a social milieu.

Schmidt and Meara (1984) indicated that because confidentiality is central to the counseling relationship, counseling researchers often need to be especially sensitive to maintaining confidentiality, particularly with regard to research conducted in an agency such as a university counseling center. For example, researchers must be sensitive to releasing demographic information that might identify participants in a small therapy group (e.g., an eating disorder group or a consciousness-raising group for men over 30); on small college campuses, demographic information about the group composition can easily identify clients. Likewise, research using an intensive single-subject design or an intrasubject design with only a few participants also demands sensitivity to identifying characteristics; typically it is advisable to provide fictitious descriptive information that is similar to the truth if it is necessary to describe a particular client in detail, and to explicitly indicate this in whatever written or oral report is made. Sometimes investigators also communicate to participants how the data will be used. They may also obtain feedback and written approval from clients on written descriptions of the study's results to further reduce any breaches of confidentiality.

Another confidentiality issue arises if researchers want to investigate some aspect of a particular treatment procedure *after* clients have already begun treatment at an agency. Suppose there is an active relaxation training program at a university counseling center, in which students, staff, and faculty are encouraged to participate. Clients enter this program with the usual assurance of confidentiality. Let's say a researcher from the counseling department (outside the agency) is interested in evaluating some aspect of the treatment program and examining the effects of certain individual difference variables (such as coping style) on the relaxation training. Given that the clients have been assured of confidentiality at the outset, it would be a breach of confidentiality at this point to reveal client names to a researcher outside the agency. Some clients might also feel their privacy has been invaded if they were identified to a researcher *in the agency*, because they did not consent to having that person know of their seeking such services. Likewise, if an investigator should conduct a study with a sample of counseling center clients that gave their consent to participate in a study with certain specified procedures, the investigator is limited to accessing only the information or data that the clients consented to disclosing or providing, as opposed to any information in the clients' agency files (see Keith-Spiegel & Koocher, 2008). In short, counseling researchers sometimes have dual responsibilities; they need to be sensitive to confidentiality issues pertaining to research endeavors as well as to confidentiality issues inherent in therapeutic relationships in general.

Consider the following example and think about what could have been done differently to avoid this outcome:

RESEARCH IN ACTION 3.6

You are conducting a qualitative study on teacher efficacy. You meet with 20 teachers in small, rural elementary school to conduct your interviews. Numerous themes were found, including teachers feeling unsupported by the administration, frustration with low reading/math scores, and anxieties common among beginner teachers. A few weeks after your manuscript is published in a popular education journal, you receive a call from one of the teachers you interviewed. He said that a few community members recognized the school in the manuscript, even though the name was kept private, due to descriptors such as midwest, rural town, with a new principal, along with curious community members remembering seeing research assistants at the school. The community members were shocked at the reports of failing reading/math scores and instantly complained to the principal, threatening to withdraw their children from the school. The principal in turn fired three teachers, with the lowest test scores, and promised to hire new staff.

Questions

What are the most salient ethical principles present in this example?

Did the researcher violate ethical priniciples? Why or Why not?

What could have been done differently to avoid this outcome?

Confidentiality and privacy issues in research settings can also intersect with a psychologist's duty to protect the welfare of participants and other individuals, thereby creating an ethical dilemma for the researcher. The most notable examples involve participants with homicidal and suicidal intentions that become evident during the course of a research investigation. For example, counseling researchers routinely assess the psychological adjustment of participants in various ways, such as by using the Beck Depression Inventory (BDI) (Beck et al., 1961). In this case, the difficult question concerns what to do when the investigator finds that a participant scored very high on the BDI. Or suppose the researcher is investigating suicidal intentions and in administering the Scale for Suicide Ideation (SSI; Schotte & Clum, 1982) learns that one or more participants scored very high on the SSI. Another ethical dilemma can arise when a participant reveals some information such that the participant or others will be liable for a violation of the law. In short, sometimes the counseling researcher obtains information about participants that either creates considerable concern for the general well-being of particular participants or other individuals, or brings up criminal or civil liabilities.

Concern for the well-being of a particular participant must also be considered in light of the individual's right to privacy. In approaching one participant who had a very high BDI score after a particular investigation, the investigator was curtly informed that the participant "consented to participate in a psychological experiment, not psychotherapy." Some participants may feel embarrassed if attention is called to them within a group setting; obviously, care must be taken to avoid breaching confidentiality to other participants and to being sensitive to the effects of isolating particular individuals.

Concern for the well-being of a particular participant must also be considered relative to the amount of information an investigator has about the participant. Whereas one researcher might have only one data point (a BDI score) that is causing some concern, another researcher might have a much broader array of information (e.g., questionnaire data, interview data, information about environmental stressors, knowledge about past suicide attempts) that more strongly suggests considerable reason for concern.

Clearly, the counseling researcher has ethical obligations beyond the research. Moreover, each situation presents a slightly different context and calls for slightly different interventions. The researcher faces a complex decision as he or she weighs the strength of the evidence, the individual's right to privacy, the consequences of approaching a participant with the topic, and the obligation to promote human welfare. Some C-IRBs now require investigators to include in the consent form a statement that indicates that if the participant reveals information that signals danger to the participant or another person, confidentiality may need to be broken. Another strategy is for researchers who collect data of a psychologically sensitive nature to routinely attach to the research questionnaire a statement communicating that it asks questions of a personal nature, and that participants are strongly encouraged to discuss the feelings reflected in the questionnaire, if they so choose. Applicable resources should then be listed, such as the address and phone number of the university counseling center or local mental health center. In addition, verbal announcements can also be made before administering the questionnaire. The following paragraph, developed as part of an introduction to the Scale of Suicide Ideation, is an example of a statement designed to facilitate such an exchange:

> The following questionnaire inquires about a variety of thoughts, feelings, attitudes, and behaviors that are sometimes related to suicide. We are interested in how frequently college students think about suicide. We realize that this is not a rare occurrence. In fact, by some estimates, up to 70% of the population at one time or another contemplate suicide. However, we want you to be aware that counseling services are available to you should your thoughts about suicide cause you some distress. To inquire about counseling, you can contact the Counseling Center [address and phone], or the Psychological Clinic [address and phone]. In the event that your score on this inventory indicates that you are seriously contemplating suicide we will contact you to express our concern and urge you to seek counseling. (Dixon, 1989, p. 42)

TREATMENT ISSUES

In the past, a common strategy among researchers was to use a between-groups design to compare two or more groups of participants; one group received a particular treatment, and instead of the treatment one of the other groups received a placebo or had treatment delayed. Although such designs offer methodological rigor, they can present ethical problems related to withholding treatment from people in need. Clients in a waiting-list or placebo group could be at risk as they continue to struggle under duress. Thus, researchers who are interested in examining questions about comparative treatments often must examine additional ethical issues.

One of the essential issues pertains to the necessity of withholding treatment. In general, if there are treatments that are known to be effective, then withholding them from participants raises serious ethical concerns. However, there is less concern about withholding an intervention of unknown effectiveness. The researcher might examine the need to compare a particular treatment against a no treatment group. The researcher might also consider alternatives, such as comparing the treatment of interest against a well-known treatment. Or the researcher might examine treatment comparisons in an alternative design, such as a within-subjects design. In short, as with the standards for using deception, researchers must assess potential risk and consider alternative designs to answer treatment questions.

Another consideration is the type of participants involved in the experiment. Kazdin (2002) suggested that volunteer clients solicited from a community setting may be more appropriate for a waiting-list group than are clients from a crisis intervention center. Assessing the risk potential not only involves an assessment of the setting from which participants are drawn, but also consideration of the type and severity of a participant's presenting problem (e.g., depression versus assertiveness).

Kazdin (2002) also suggested that assigning participants to delayed-treatment groups might be more ethically appropriate if the participants initially came from a waiting list, which is in essence delayed treatment. For example, many agencies have waiting lists because service demands are heavier than can be met by the staff. Thus, a treatment study might be conducted by randomly assigning clients from the waiting list to the experimental conditions (treatment and delayed treatment). In such a case, some clients would actually receive treatment earlier than if they had stayed on the agency's waiting list.

Other ethical considerations that merit attention in delayed-treatment conditions include informed consent and ultimately providing treatment. Ethically, participants should be informed before an investigation if there is a possibility that they may be placed in a delayed-treatment group; they then may or may not decide to participate in the study. Moreover, participants in a delayed-treatment group are entitled to treatment after the experiment has concluded, and these participants deserve the same quality of treatment as the experimental group.

In short, counseling researchers who contemplate using placebo or delayed-treatment conditions must carefully examine additional ethical issues. As with the standards for the use of deception, we suggest that researchers assess the potential risks and consider alternative designs as ways of minimizing risks.

RESPONDING TO ETHICAL DILEMMAS

It is important to note that researchers are not likely to be entirely ethical all of the time. In fact, almost all researchers will unknowingly engage in some aspect of research that might infringe upon one of the ethical principles at some time or another. Sometimes an ethical problem may not be foreseen or may be inadequately anticipated, or the researcher may be inexperienced and have an incomplete understanding of the ethical codes. Or because there can be ambiguity in the ethical codes, inexperienced researchers may make questionable decisions. Most often, infringements occur due to a lack of sensitivity, knowledge, or experience. This is not to condone infringements, but rather to acknowledge that oversights and mistakes happen. We can all help each other by consistently educating each other in our endeavors to conduct our research ethically and to uphold our professional responsibilities. Thus, it is important to talk with each other about ethical issues and dilemmas, particularly when we witness events that make us uncomfortable. Moreover, it can be useful for counselors to have a framework in order to confront ethical dilemmas.

Kitchener and Anderson (2011) suggested nine principles for responding to an ethical dilemma, and here we provide a slightly adapted version of these principles. Prior to facing an ethical dilemma, counselors should examine their cultural values, beliefs, and moral reasoning. Exercises to assist with this process could include reading articles that have been done over the years (e.g., Milgram's study) and reflect on personal reactions to the ethical and moral treatment of the participants (e.g., where do my negative or favorable reactions come from?). Given that most current published research is (hopefully) done in an ethical manner, it may be useful to gauge where the "bottom line" is for each counselor. These beliefs and values will ultimately influence how any new ethical dilemma is interpreted (Kitchener & Anderson, 2011).

When faced with an ethical dilemma, it is important to slow down and reflect on the situation. In most cases an immediate response is not needed; rather a calculated well-thought-out response may be more fruitful. Next, it is important to review all the available information. In this process it is important to consider the credibility of the evidence as well as personal biases in weighing the evidence (e.g., is more credence given to some evidence more than others, perhaps because the evidence confirms one's own beliefs?). Additionally, counselors should wonder about the information that would be needed to make a better decision. In many cases, more information can be discovered.

After available information has been collected , the next step is to consider the range of possible options and outcomes (Kitchener & Anderson, 2011). For instance, are there alternative research designs that would avoid the ethical complications? Compiling a list of options could serve to be a useful exercise in order to not prematurely foreclose on one decision. For each of the options, counselors should consult the ethics code and assess how each option fits within the foundational ethical principles. Consistently, there may be legal issues related to the potential decisions that could influence the process.

Once the potential options are developed, and the various legal/ethical concerns have been considered, the next step is to reflect upon the potential consequences of the options and develop a plan (Kitchener & Anderson, 2011). A dialectical process may be useful in the reassessment of the options. For example, counselors could undergo a process of arguing for a particular decision (or approach to deal with the ethical dilemma) and then arguing against the decision (M. Leach, personal communication, March 14, 2014). This will encourage counselors to challenge their decisions in a way that may thwart confirmatory thought processes. In addition, consulting with elders and trusted colleagues with experience in dealing with ethical dilemmas is almost always recommended at this stage. Following the selection of the decision, a specific plan should be developed and implemented (Kitchener & Anderson, 2011). Throughout the process, counselors should document their process. Afterwards, counselors should reflect on the process and gauge how well the outcome fits the situation. The use of feedback is important to help develop expertise in clinical decision making (Tracey et al., 2014). There are other decision-making models and the interested reader should consult Koocher & Keith-Spiegel (2008), who provide excellent guidelines for a range of options (and sanctions) in responding to ethical situations. We encourage readers to examine not only the *EPP* and *ES* codes in the appendixes, but also the *Publication Manual of the American Psychological Association* (2010a). Most important, whenever in doubt, consult with trusted, knowledgeable colleagues and faculty.

EXHIBIT A
Consent to Serve as a Participant in Research[1]

1. I hereby consent to take part in research directed by Dr. Mary Heppner and Meghan Davidson, and sponsored by the University of Missouri. Dr. Heppner is an Associate Professor and Meghan Davidson is a doctoral student in the Department of Educational and Counseling Psychology. I understand that other persons will assist Dr. Heppner and Meghan Davidson in conducting this research.

2. Further, I understand that:
   a. *Purpose*. The purpose is to study the validity and reliability of a new measure of empathy.
   b. *Requirements*. My part of this research will be to complete a paper and pencil survey designed to measure the way I empathize with others. Surveys will be completed by groups of students in university classrooms.
   c. *Time needed*. The total time required will be approximately 25 minutes.
   d. *Voluntary participation*. My participation is completely voluntary. Even after I begin participating, I will be free to stop at any time. I have the right to stop after I have started participating, or I have the right to decide not to participate at all in this study. Although the researchers ask that I try to answer every item, I understand that I can skip any item that I simply do not wish to answer. (I do not need to give a reason for skipping any item.) In no case will there be a negative effect for my nonparticipation or noncompletion.
   e. *New developments*. I will be told of any new information that develops during the course of this research that might affect my willingness to participate in this study.
   f. *Benefits*. I will receive a debriefing sheet that explains more about empathy. General benefits will come for myself and others in the form of an increased scientific understanding of how people relate to and understand other people.
   g. *Protections*. I understand that the following precautions have been taken for my protection: (1) no part of the surveys will ask for my name or other identifying information, my

responses will remain completely anonymous; (2) no questionnaire asks me to describe specific incidents; (3) I am free to discontinue my participation at any time for any reason; (4) although the researchers would like me to answer every item, I am free to skip any question or item that I find too sensitive or stressful; (5) when the results of this study are published, only aggregate data (for example, group averages) will be reported.

3. My questions about this research have been answered. If I have further questions, I should contact:

Dr. Mary Heppner   office phone: (573) 882-8574
16 Hill Hall   email: HeppnerM@missouri.edu
Department of Educational and Counseling
    Psychology
University of Missouri
Columbia, MO 65211

Meghan Davidson   email: mmd75b@mizzou.edu
16 Hill Hall
Department of Educational and Counseling
    Psychology
University of Missouri

Institutional Review Board   phone: 882-9585
Jesse Hall
University of Missouri
Columbia, MO 65211

Signature _____

Date _____

EXHIBIT B
Sample Youth Assent Form (Children)[2]

You are invited to participate in a research study conducted by a graduate student at the University of Missouri-Columbia. As a participant, you should read and understand the following statements. Ask any questions before you agree to participate.

1. **Goal of the Project:** The goal of this research project is to develop a new survey that measures high school students' attitudes about healthy relationships and sexual coercion in dating relationships. It is hoped that this survey will be used in evaluating educational programs about sexual coercion in dating relationships. Please note that you will be asked about information pertaining to your attitudes, beliefs, and own personal experiences.

2. **Participation Procedure and Guidelines:**
    a. You will receive an assent form (this page), get any questions that you might have answered, and then complete the surveys.
    b. The information you provide will be kept **completely anonymous.** That is, your name will not be on any of the forms.
    c. It will take about 30 minutes to complete the surveys.

3. **Participation Benefits and Risks:**
    a. Your participation in this study does not involve risks that are greater than those you experience in your daily life. You might feel some mild discomfort from reading and

responding to some items on the questionnaires. But again, the risk of discomfort is not greater than you might have in class or in other normal activities.

   b. You also might experience some benefits from participating in this project. These benefits might be positive feelings from helping with an important research study.

   c. By filling out the survey, you will be entered into a raffle to win 1 of 15 gift certificates to any store in the Columbia Mall.

4. Rights to Refuse or Withdraw: Your participation is VOLUNTARY, and there is no penalty for you not wanting to participate. This means that you are free to stop at any point or to choose not to answer any particular question.

5. Rights as a Participant: You have a right to have any questions about this research project answered. Please direct any questions to the following individuals:

M. Meghan Davidson, M.A.   Mary J. Heppner, Ph.D.
Department of Educational & Counseling   Department of Educational
   Psychology   & Counseling Psychology
16 Hill Hall   16 Hill Hall
University of Missouri-Columbia   University of Missouri-Columbia
Columbia, MO 65211   Columbia, MO 65211
(573) 884-4328   (573) 882-8574

For additional information regarding participation in research, please feel free to contact the University of Missouri-Columbia Campus Institutional Review Board office at 882-9585.

6. Agreement to Participate:

Signature _____

Date _____

EXHIBIT C
Oral Debriefing[3]

That concludes your participation in the study. Thanks so much for your help. Now that you have finished giving your opinion, I can explain more to you about the whole purpose of the study. I could not do so before now without biasing your responses. First, the study is concerned with more than "interviewing styles." We are more interested in impressions of college students about bereaved and depressed persons. Specifically, we wanted to find out both about your personal reactions to someone who is bereaved and also your attitudes about what is normal or pathological grief. We didn't want people to know exactly what we were looking for in advance, because it could have influenced who signed up for the experiment or the answers they gave. We regret that we could not more fully inform you before you participated. We strongly hope you will respect our need to withhold this information and will not discuss this experiment with your fellow classmates.

Some of you received instructions that you were listening to a tape of a middle-aged widow; some were told that she had become widowed three weeks ago and some were told she became widowed two years ago. If you received these instructions, you were in one of the experimental groups. Others received instructions that you were listening to a tape of someone who had lost a job. You were in a control group. In addition, some subjects hear a depressed woman on tape and others hear a nondepressed woman. We will be looking for differences in the answers of these various conditions depending on whether the subjects are male or female.

I want to tell you now that none of you will come back to participate in a further part of the experiment. When you leave today, your participation will end. It was important that you think you might come back, so we could get your reaction about whether you were willing to meet the woman you heard on the tape.

Next, let me explain that this is an analogue experiment. That means that the people you heard on tape were playing parts that were written for them in advance. The purpose of this is so each time a new group hears a particular conversation, it is done exactly the same as the last time a group heard that conversation. This allows for better control of the experiment and helps to eliminate unknown influences on the answers you gave.

I want to thank you for your participation today. Again, it is very important that you do not talk about this experiment with anyone once you leave this room. If people who participate later in the study are aware of its purpose or procedures, their answers may be biased. This would cause us to report misleading results. As we hope our research may some day assist actual bereaved persons, this is a serious problem. Please give others the chance to fairly contribute as you have today.

Does anyone have any questions? [Pause for questions.] I will sign your research cards and you are free to leave. I will stay for a moment in case you have other questions.

If you're having any difficulty dealing with either bereavement or depression, I have the telephone numbers of our University Psychology Clinic and of the Counseling Service, and I will be glad to give them to you when you have finished.

EXHIBIT D
Written Debriefing[4]

This sheet will further explain the purpose of this research project beyond the oral explanation you have already heard. It will outline the independent and dependent variables and research hypotheses. It is crucial that you do not discuss the information on this sheet with any of your friends (who might inadvertently communicate with future participants) or with the experimenter who is present today. She must remain blind (uninformed) concerning the hypotheses in order to avoid influencing the experiment. You may direct any questions to Carol Atwood at 484-1676 (leave a message if no answer). Please sign this sheet as soon as you finish reading it, place it back in the envelope provided, and seal the gummed flap. Thank you very much for your help.

1. *Nature of the project:* This project would best relate to the major research area of social psychology—attitudes and social perception.

2. *Findings of related studies:* There is little previous research concerning the layperson's views of what is a healthy versus an unhealthy grief reaction, and whether or not laypersons reject or avoid the bereaved. Vernon (1970) asked participants how they would respond to a recently bereaved person that they knew. Only one-fourth of participants indicated they would spontaneously mention the death; another one-fourth preferred that neither side mention the death at all. Other researchers, such as Lopata (1973) and Glick, Weiss, and Parkes (1974), have indirectly addressed the question by interviewing widows themselves, who frequently reported experiencing strained relationships or the breakup of friendships after the deaths of their husbands.

3. *Independent variables:* These are the variables in the experiment that the investigator manipulates or controls. There are three independent variables in this project. The first is gender of the participants. We will look for differences in the responses of male and female subjects. Second is the depression condition (whether the woman heard on the tape is depressed or nondepressed). Third is the "bereavement (or widowhood) status"; that is, the

woman on the tape is either recently widowed, long-term widowed, or not widowed (loss of a job is mentioned), depending on which written instructions you received.

4. *Dependent variables:* Used to measure the effects of manipulation of the independent variables. In this project, the dependent variables consisted of the written questionnaire you completed. We want to find out how much you would reject the woman heard on the tape, what your social perceptions of her were, and how pathological you found her to be.

5. *Hypotheses:* The research questions to be examined in the project. Please do not share this information with today's experimenter.
   A. How do college students' judgments of emotional disturbance compare, based on whether the woman on the tape is recently bereaved, long-term bereaved, or nonbereaved? How do ratings of disturbance differ, depending on whether the woman on the tape sounded depressed or not depressed?
   B. Do college students reject a bereaved person or a nonbereaved person more, and is this rejection affected by whether the woman sounds depressed or not depressed?
   C. How does the gender of the participant (male or female) affect participants' responses?

6. *Control procedures:* Procedures to reduce error or unwanted variance. In this study, random assignment of participants to experimental conditions was used, except that it was not possible to randomly assign participants based on participant gender. Other control procedures used include keeping the experimenter blind to the study hypotheses, not informing participants before the experiment about the true purpose, use of an analogue procedure in which actors were used on the tapes, and use of a control group of participants who listen to the tape of a woman who is neither a widow nor depressed.

I have read the above information concerning the nature of the study, Reactions to Stressful Life Experiences. I agree not to disclose this information either to potential future participants or to the experimenter present today.

Name (Print) _____

Signature _____

Date _____

SUMMARY AND CONCLUSIONS

We have suggested that ethics are central to the conduct of research and, in fact, permeate the entire research enterprise. Broadly speaking, ethics are a "set of guidelines that provide directions for conduct" (Keith-Spiegel & Koocher, 1985, p. xiii). For counselors, research on ethics provides direction for interacting with the larger profession, other professionals, and those people who participate in our research. Moreover, how we design and conduct our research reflects our basic values, such as autonomy, fairness, promoting the welfare of others, fidelity, and above all, avoiding harm to others. Sometimes it seems that the business of life overshadows our basic values, as we cut corners to save time. It is essential to keep in mind, however, that the health and longevity of our counseling profession rest on such basic values as honesty and fairness. These values need to be emphasized throughout graduate training in a wide range of situations, and particularly with regard to research. Our values may communicate more about who we are and what we do in our research than any other aspect of our behavior.

Notes

1. An earlier version of this consent form was written by Meghan Davidson. At the time this chapter was written for the third edition of the book, Meghan was a doctoral candidate in counseling psychology at the University of Missouri-Columbia.

2. An earlier version of this consent form was written by Meghan Davidson. At the time this chapter was written for the third edition of the book, Meghan was a doctoral candidate in counseling psychology at the University of Missouri-Columbia.

3. An earlier version of this oral debriefing was written by Carol Atwood. At the time this chapter was written for the first edition of the book, Carol was a doctoral student in clinical psychology at the University of Missouri-Columbia.

4. An earlier version of this written debriefing was written by Carol Atwood. At the time this chapter was written for the first edition of the book, Carol was a doctoral student in clinical psychology at the University of Missouri-Columbia.

STIMULUS QUESTIONS

Ethical Issues in the Research Process

In this chapter, we have maintained that it is essential for researchers to be aware of their ethical responsibilities to research participants, coworkers, the counseling profession, and society as a whole. The purpose of this exercise is to promote additional thinking about ethical issues related to participants and scholarly work. We suggest you reflect on the following questions, write your responses, and then discuss your responses with a peer in the class to further your understanding of ethical issues and responsibilities related to the research process.

1. Why might it be functional to focus on learning the foundational ethical principles rather than just relying on a rule-bound conception of ethics?

2. Explain why it is essential to interpret the findings of any study within the cultural context in which the data were collected. Can you list at least three problems that occur when researchers misinterpret their findings without the appropriate reference to the cultural context?

3. What, in your view, is the most serious consequence of publishing fraudulent data?

4. What do you think Carl Rogers meant when he said "the data are always friendly"?

5. What do you think is the best strategy for determining the author order of a manuscript? Why?

6. In what instances, if any, do you think deception is acceptable in counseling research? In what instances would you definitely not allow deception?

7. Identify two situations where investigators' bias could result in insensitive cross-cultural research.

8. What is the difference between confidentiality and anonymity?

9. Why do you think it is often recommended to talk directly to the relevant people when ethical issues arise?

Professional Writing: A Critical Skill for Scientists and Practitioners

Chapter 4

Scientific writing is a critical skill that is needed by practitioners and scientists. The ability to write scientifically is an essential outcome of graduate training programs. It is important to acknowledge at the beginning that everyone has difficulty in writing at one time or another. It may be due to writer's block, fatigue, a particularly complex writing task, or a myriad of fears and apprehensions about the product (e.g., "I will make a mistake, which will be there for everyone to see"; "What I have to say is really not important"; "If I can't write it perfectly, I won't write anything"). These fears and apprehensions related to writing may be particularly acute for inexperienced authors, but even veteran authors experience fears and apprehensions related to writing. Writing is a skill that can be learned with practice, feedback, analysis of successful models of writing, and editing.

Writing is personal and style varies according to the constraints of the publication in which the writing will appear. For example, the American Psychological Association (APA) carefully details the required elements of manuscripts submitted to APA journals in its *Publication Manual of the American Psychological Association* (APA, 2010a). This reference book is indispensable for authors who publish in counseling and related professional journals. Graduate schools, on the other hand, typically have their own formatting and style requirements for theses and dissertations (see Heppner & Heppner, 2004, for further information regarding dissertation and thesis writing). Guidelines have also been published for psychological assessment report writing; see the Standards for Educational and Psychological Testing (2014) developed jointly by the American Educational Research Association (AERA), the American Psychological Association (APA), and the National Council on Measurement in Education (NCME). Clinical sites often have their own specifications for style regarding case notes, termination summaries, and other patient communications depending upon the nature of the site and the software utilized.

One chapter cannot possibly cover the myriad details involved in all forms of professional writing. Our goal in this chapter is to introduce writers to the basic components and issues related to scientific writing. We describe the reasons that counselors and psychologists write. We also identify several challenges to writing and introduce some writing strategies. We then offer a description of the technical aspects involved in writing a research report to ensure that readers are prepared to write their own research reports and have the capability to appropriately evaluate the literature to be an informed consumer of the research literature. We present the major sections of a report and discuss their relation to the principles of research design discussed throughout this book.

WHY WE WRITE

Writing is a method of inquiry (Richardson, 2000). The process of writing facilitates further learning as we seek to develop a new understanding of a topic and to ensure that we are aware of knowledge in an area. Writing also forces us to delve more deeply into a subject, which facilitates a renewed perception of the subject and inspires creativity and thinking (Runco & Pritzker, 1999). When we write a psychological assessment report, we are required to consider up-to-date information about the assessment instruments and their applications to our clients. We then must consider that knowledge, in conjunction with the client-specific data obtained via the assessment. As we summarize this information into a written report, our understanding of the client inevitably increases in breadth and depth. In the same way, when we write research reports, we must revisit the current literature on the topic, organize thoughts into a coherent whole, and synthesize existing information with new knowledge gained from the study (Newell, 2000).

Writing also improves our ability to teach and to practice as we are compelled to synthesize information and generate new perspectives. In this way, writing contributes knowledge to the profession. Involvement in writing projects also offers counselors and psychologists opportunities to develop a professional community, which become sources of collaborations across institutions, geographic regions, and disciplines. Among those who wish to pursue academic positions, scientific writing is critical to tenure and promotion.

WRITING CHALLENGES AND STRATEGIES

Contrary to popular lore, many authors find writing to be challenging. Indeed, the concept of writer's block has become popular lore within many writing communities. Varying perceptions exist regarding what constitutes writers block. The term is often used but may perhaps best be considered a social construction that is indicative of some obstacle to writing (Greyser, 2014). Cvetokovich (2013) described writer's block among academics as intellectual, personal, and political. She suggested that we respect the intellectual conditions that lead to blocks, depersonalize blocks as being less about us as writers and more as a product of the institutional and sociopolitical system, be kind to ourselves, and develop communities of support.

Rockquemore and Laszloffy (2008) detailed common challenges to writing according to three primary categories: technical errors, external realities, and psychological obstacles. Technical errors encompass struggles that exist as a result of lacking a specific skill or technique, including, but not limited to: failing to set aside a specific time for writing, disorganization in space and task that prevents a person from knowing what to work on next, relying upon a list of tasks that are too complex and not specific or measurable, and underestimating how long tasks will require for completion. These authors argue that making behavioral adjustments or acquiring specific skills can easily address these skills deficits. For example, they recommended using a calendar to schedule your tasks for the week, scheduling a time for daily writing in your calendar, and tracking your writing time. External realities are best described as situational or environmental factors that are outside of your control, such as a health problem that limits the ability to work or a life transition such as a new child or an aging family member. Such challenges generally require patience and creativity in redistributing one's workload or delegating tasks while adjusting to the life circumstance.

Psychological obstacles are more complex and therefore require more time and attention to address. They include a variety of experiences, such as academic perfectionism, feelings of disempowerment related to research and writing, fear of being "exposed" by one's writing, crisis of legitimacy, lack of clarity regarding one's longer term vision or goals, and unrealistically high expectations. A variety of authors have written extensively about strategies to manage these psychological and other affective challenges to writing (for more information, see Cvetokovich, 2013; Heppner & Heppner, 2004; Greyser, 2014; Lamott, 1995; Rockquemore & Laszloffy, 2008).

Leading experts on the behavior patterns of prolific writers have highlighted the importance of developing a practice of daily writing (e.g., 30–60 minutes of writing Monday–Friday). As Furman and Kinn (2012) put it, "consistency beats brilliance" when it comes to writing (p. 26). Robert Boice (1989) provided support for this practice through following three groups of junior faculty members for one year after those faculty members attended one of his writing workshops. Participants were divided into three groups: Group 1 continued their preworkshop writing practices; Group 2 engaged in daily writing and tracked their writing time; and Group 3 engaged in daily writing, tracked their writing time, and were accountable for their writing to someone on a weekly basis. After one year, participants in Group 1 had produced an average of 17 pages, those in Group 2 had produced an average of 64 pages, and those in Group 3 had produced an average of 157 pages.

Except for the extraordinary few, authors need to rewrite and edit in order to complete a writing task. Different writers use different methods. For example, some write as fast as possible and rely heavily on the revision process to create a polished product, whereas others write the first draft carefully and minimize time with revisions. Some writers like to let the draft "age" before revising, while others progress as quickly as possible to the final product. Regardless of one's specific approach, learning how to edit one's own work and seek feedback are critical skills needed in order to write effectively.

Authors often become so absorbed with their project that they lose objectivity. After having researched, discussed, and thought about their work in great detail, writers may become convinced that their explanation of their work is clear and concise and their rationale sound. Another person, however, may have a very different view. We strongly recommend that all authors have colleagues or advisors read and critique their research reports as part of the writing and revision process. It may be best to choose individuals who can be counted on for constructive and critical feedback (rather than glowing compliments) in order to ensure that the writing improves. Because different types of readers will provide different types of feedback (e.g., those who are familiar with the content area can provide content-specific feedback, those who are unfamiliar with the content area can provide an objective perspective regarding the overall logic or writing style), it is important to solicit readers who are best suited to provide the feedback needed in order to strengthen the writing. In her guide to academic writing, Rockquemore (2012) advises academic writers to elicit feedback early and often. She recommends that academic writers develop a community of readers who can review work at varying stages of the writing process (e.g., 0%–25% complete, 26%–50% complete, 51%–75% complete, 76%–100% complete) in order to provide feedback throughout the process rather than once an author has invested countless hours until the author has deemed a manuscript "ready" for submission.

Problems related to procrastination are pervasive among academic writers. Many of us who enjoy conducting research or engaging in clinical practice avoid settling down to write. We venture to say that at one time or another, all researchers have agonized about writing the research report. Rather than stating "misery loves company," we give this suggestion: Write! Even if you think that what you are writing is terrible, write anyway! Drafts can be changed or discarded. In fact, it is usually much easier to revise a draft than to create a first draft. Write a few pages and then decide later whether it is any good. Once started, writing becomes increasingly easy.

WRITING A RESEARCH REPORT

Although results of studies can be disseminated in ways other than written reports (such as conference presentations), within the fields of counseling and counseling psychology, the research report is a very important mechanism for the dissemination of new knowledge. Journal articles, books, dissertations, and (to a lesser extent) written summaries of conference presentations are the permanent records of counseling research. Unless a study is discussed in one of these sources, it is unlikely that a researcher interested in the topic will be able to learn about the study. The preparation of a clear and informative research report, therefore, is a critical step in the research process.

The exact organization of a research report varies depending on the publication for which it is intended and the nature of the study. Nevertheless, a perusal of counseling journals reveals that articles are typically organized according to the format outlined in Table 4.1. There are a variety of resources to guide the reader through a more detailed description of each section (e.g., APA Publication Manual, 2010). The purpose of this chapter is to provide a brief overview of the research report sections, with particular emphasis on those aspects that relate to research design.

Although we discuss these components sequentially, it is important to note that all sections are held together by a common focus: the research questions and/or hypotheses. This common focus is threaded throughout each section and allows the reader to comprehend the study as a whole. In other words, each section of the research report should be consistent with all other sections.

TABLE 4.1 : Key Components of the Major Sections of a Research Report

Title	The research topic, variables, design, and outcomes are summarized in 10 to 12 words.
Abstract	Summary of the research report. Describes hypotheses, method (participants, measures, materials, design, and procedure), results, and conclusions in 100–150 words.
Introduction	Description of theoretical or conceptual rationale to clarify the purpose of the research report. Detailed review of past empirical findings and theoretical rationale provides the framework for the proposed hypotheses (quantitative designs) or research questions (qualitative designs).
Method	Summary of the participants, materials, procedures, and design (or design and analysis) used to conduct the study.
Results	Summarize the data and results of the analyses.
Discussion (or conclusions)	Summary of the findings in the context of prior research and theory. Overview of study limitations, future directions, and implications.
References	Complete list of all sources cited in the text.

Title

At its best, the title of a research report makes the report accessible to readers and offers a stand-alone explanation of the manuscript. Bem (2003) suggested that title selection should be guided by the data and contain the most important descriptive information about the study. A title should accurately summarize the research, describing the topic, the variables, the design, and the outcome(s) succinctly (in 10 to 12 words, according to most sources). For this reason, many authors suggest writing the title after much of the writing is complete. Because many users decide whether to read a manuscript based on the title that appears in services that index publications (e.g., *PsychLit, PsychInfo*), it is important to carefully select the title.

Abstract

The abstract is a brief summary of the research report that generally does not exceed 120–150 words. The abstract is also used for indexing and retrieving articles and, after the title, is the most-often read portion of a research report. As such, the abstract must be succinct, accurate, and comprehensive. It should summarize in one or two sentences the content of each of the major sections of the manuscript, including the problem under investigation, relevant characteristics of the participants and design, the results (as linked to the hypotheses or research questions), and conclusions.

The abstract should be self-contained; the reader should not need to depend on any other section of the report to make sense of the abstract. It is therefore important to avoid abbreviations and acronyms and to explain unique and technical terms. Given the need to be accurate, informative, and succinct, many authors (e.g., Bem, 2003; Kazdin, 1995) argue that this is one of the most difficult sections to write and therefore suggest that authors write this section last.

Introduction

The introduction to a research report sets the stage for the study (see Table 4.2). It orients the reader to the problem, develops the rationale for the study, and indicates as specifically as possible the research questions being explored or hypotheses being tested in the study. The list of questions presented in Table 4.2 is intended to guide readers in writing the writing of the introduction.

To answer these questions, the introduction of a research report typically contains three components: (a) an introduction to the problem, (b) a development of the framework for the study, and (c) a statement of the research questions and/ or hypotheses. The first component of an introduction includes a broad statement of the topic area used to orient the reader to the topic and to highlight why it is important to investigate. The writer then narrows to a review of the theory and empirical data that is most relevant to the topic of interest. This leads to the explication of the framework or rationale for the study, or the second component of the introduction.

The framework for the rationale is built through the logical interconnectedness of empirical results and theory that leads to a critical and (as yet) unanswered research question. We quite deliberately avoid the use of the more traditional term *literature review* because it implies (at least to some) a synopsis of one study after another, along with considerable integration and synthesis of the findings. In contrast, a *framework* consists of elements connected in some logical way.

TABLE 4.2 Research Application: Questions That Should Be Answered in Your Introduction

Question	(✓)
Why is this an important topic to study?	
What previous work (empirical and theoretical) bears on the topic?	
What is the background and context of the study?	
How does this previous work logically lead to the author's research questions and/or hypotheses?	
How will this question be researched?	
What current theory, research, or applied work makes this study useful, important, or interesting?	
What is different or unique about the study in terms of design, focus, or methods that allows this study to address a need in this area?	
Is the rationale clear regarding the constructs to be manipulated and assessed?	
What were the purposes, predictions, and hypotheses?	

The literature cited in the development of the framework should be pertinent to the particular research study. In any discussion of a previous study, describe only the pertinent aspects of that study that build the rationale for your study. These are often aspects that relate to findings from prior research and may also include a discussion of methodological issues (such as type of participants), design, and statistical tests. For example, reference to a study would not mention the number of participants unless those data were pertinent to the rationale of your study. This would be the case if you were arguing that there was inadequate power to detect an effect in the prior research. Discussion of previous findings and theories needs to be intertwined logically. When you discuss a particular study or theory, the purpose of the discussion vis-à-vis the framework should be clear to the reader. Furthermore, you should integrate the material reviewed. Often studies result in contradictory findings. In the introduction, you should speculate about the reasons for the discrepancy and indicate how these discrepancies (and the reasons behind them) relate to your research.

If the framework has been developed properly, the purpose of the present research (or the third component of the introduction) should be readily apparent. One purpose might be to reconcile discrepancies in previous research; in that case the study will explain why contradictory findings have been obtained. Another purpose might be to apply results from some noncounseling area to problems in counseling. Still another purpose of the study might be to extend previous results to a different population. In some ways, the development of a framework is similar to that of a legal brief. When the case is solid, there is one inescapable conclusion. Similarly, by the time a reader reaches the end of a well-written introduction, the reader should be able to identify the exact research question and/or research hypothesis to be examined. The research questions and/or hypotheses should follow logically from the framework built throughout the introduction. Research questions are typically used in descriptive and qualitative studies when the purpose of the research is exploratory rather than predictive. In quantitative studies, research hypotheses should be used as a critical test of an important theoretical question. Research hypotheses should be stated unambiguously and clarify how the discovered relation relates to theoretical predictions. Of course, the degree to which a hypothesis can be specific depends on the specificity of the theory. See Heppner and Heppner (2004) for a more in depth discussion of writing research questions and hypotheses.

One commonly suggested format to guide writing the entire research report, beginning with the introduction, is the hourglass format. As depicted in the Figure 4.1, the introduction covers the top portion of the hourglass, or the funnel. The method and results sections are often depicted as the center of the hourglass, which is the most narrow and specific to the particular study. The discussion section provides the bottom half of the hourglass, or the reverse funnel.

Method

The method section describes how the research questions and/or hypotheses were examined, including all aspects of how the study was conducted. Enough detail is

FIGURE 4.1 : Hourglass Image of Manuscript Sections

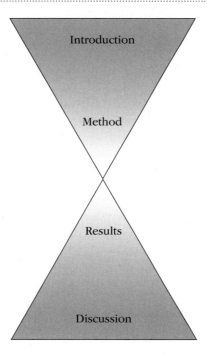

needed so that a reader can evaluate the validity of the study and replicate the study. Methodological considerations are important criteria by which reviewers and editors make decisions to reject manuscripts (Hoyt & Mallinckrodt, 2012). For this reason, it is imperative that the research design, measurement, and analyses are solid (as outlined throughout this book) and that the method section is well written.

The method section is typically divided into subsections, including participants, measures (or variables or instruments), materials, and procedures. Optional subsections depend upon the nature of the study and may include research design, analyses, coding, and data reduction. Organization of the method section depends, to a great extent, on the nature of the study. The order of the subsections may be altered (for instance, design may appear as the first or the last subsection), but they should fit together. At the end of reading a well-written method section, the reader should have a very clear picture of exactly what and how the study was completed.

Participants   The subsection on participants should indicate, at a minimum, (1) the total number of participants, (2) participant recruitment and selection pr ocedures, and (3) characteristics of the participants. Participant information should be detailed along a number of dimensions (including, but not limited to age, educational level, gender, ethnicity, geographical area of residence, and pretest level of functioning, depending on the study; see Chapter 8 for a discussion of this issue). Providing this level of detail allows the reader to assess the external validity or generalizability of the study.

For qualitative manuscripts, a description of the researchers and their biases are also summarized. The level of detail included may vary depending upon the publication outlet and method of qualitative inquiry (see Chapter 16 for a review). In general however, a summary of assumptions and biases that the members of the research team held prior to, and throughout, the research process is presented. In addition, a brief description of each researcher and relevant demographic characteristics is detailed. These descriptions are offered in an effort to situate the researchers within the work.

Measures (or Variables or Instruments)   The purpose of the measures subsection is to operationalize the constructs to which the research questions and/or hypotheses referred. For a quantitative study that utilizes participant responses to survey instruments, this subsection includes a discussion of each instrument, an overview of the scoring properties of each instrument, and a description of the psychometric support for the instrument (see Heppner & Heppner, 2004, for a more in depth review). Statements about reliability and validity estimates should refer to the context in which the estimates were calculated (e.g., the population of the cited study). Citing a variety of sources in this subsection is common as it allows the author to justify decisions regarding construct operationalization. If, however, the operationalization of a crucial construct is controversial, then discussion of these issues probably fits best in the introduction (as a part of the development of the framework). This would be the case if the researcher claims that previous attempts to corroborate a theory were unsuccessful because of improper operationalization of the dependent variable and the present study used different instruments to operationalize the dependent variable. Using the checklist in Table 4.3 may help to ensure that you have included enough detail regarding the use of each instrument.

In a treatment or other experimental study, operationalization of the independent variable is vital. Each condition or treatment needs to be described in sufficient detail so that an interested reader could replicate the treatment or conditions utilized in the study. If the amount of detail needed to describe a particular treatment intervention adequately becomes prohibitive, a detailed treatment manual to which interested readers can be directed via a footnote may be developed.

For qualitative and descriptive studies, the label for this subsection and its contents will vary depending upon the method of qualitative inquiry utilized. For example, *Interview Protocol* or *Interview Materials* may be used as labels for this subsection. This subsection generally includes information regarding the information-gathering procedures used for the study. Information regarding questions and probes used with participants, including the rationale for the questions and probes that were selected are presented. In addition, the process by which the researcher(s) made decisions regarding the extent to which questions and probes were permitted to evolve over time (or not) may be included in this subsection. Details about how interview data were transcribed (e.g., the stage of the research process at which transcription occurred, parties who were responsible for interview transcription, whether interviews were transcribed verbatim versus in summary format) may also be summarized. Finally, other sources of data that were utilized throughout the project (e.g., field notes) may be described in this subsection.

TABLE 4.3 | Research Application: Checklist for Each Instrument or Measure in Your Quantitative Study

Element	Measure 1 (✓)	Measure 2 (✓)	Measure 3 (✓)	Measure 4 ... (✓)
Instrument name				
Acronym				
Author(s)				
Key citation (manual, article, or other primary source)				
Brief description of the construct the instrument assesses				
Number of items				
Type of items (e.g., Likert-type format)				
Sample items				
Factors or subscales and their definitions (as applicable)				
Indication of the direction of the scoring, (i.e., a high score indicates __ whereas a low score indicates __)				
Evidence to support validity				
Evidence to support reliability				

Materials   The materials subsection describes any materials (other than the measures or instruments themselves) used in the study. For example, if the research involves use of functional magnetic resonance imaging (fMRI) to assess brain activity or saliva samples to assess cortisol levels, a depiction of these materials must be included. Sufficient information should be given to enable an independent researcher to reproduce the materials and to replicate the study. The level of detail required varies based upon publication outlet; some outlets encourage authors to indicate in a footnote that additional information or the materials themselves are available from the author to provide a more detailed description in supplemental materials published online.

Procedure   The procedure subsection describes the steps by which participants completed the research. It is typically organized chronologically and includes information related to interactions with participants from the beginning to the end of the study. This involves details including, but not limited to how participants were recruited or learned of the study; inclusion criteria for participation in the study and screening processes (if applicable); information shared with participants about the study; institutional review board approval and documented adherence to ethical principles, such as informed consent procedures; response rates; attrition rates, if applicable; and circumstances under which the participants participated (e.g., financial remuneration, course credit, other incentives). Additional details may also depend upon the study design utilized. For example, if the study utilized an experimental or quasi-experimental design, information regarding assignment of participants to conditions of the independent variable (including number of participants in each condition) and procedures for experimental manipulations should be presented. For qualitative investigations, information related to the length of the interviews, the location in which the interviews were conducted, and details about the interviewer may also be included.

Design (or Design and Analysis)   This subsection provides readers with a clear understanding of the overall study design. The connection between the design and the research questions and/or hypotheses should be clear. After reading this subsection, the reader should understand how the research questions were explored and/or how the hypotheses were tested. The design and analysis section(s) should include sufficient information so as to provide a very clear picture of what was done, how it was done, and how the data were analyzed so as to prime the reader for the presentation of the results.

The specific information included in the procedure or analysis section(s) depends upon the nature of the research study. For quantitative designs, additional information related to analysis may be detailed. For example, results from a power analysis used to determine the number of participants needed for sufficient power may be presented, procedures utilized for data reduction may be detailed, decisions related to the treatment of missing data may be explained, coding procedures may be specified, and complicated data analysis procedures may be overviewed. Research hypotheses may also be connected to specific analytic tests. For example, for a factorial design the factors should be labeled, the number of conditions within a factor should be indicated, and the nature of the factors (such as between versus within, or random versus fixed) should be stated. If the analyses are mentioned (e.g., a two-way analysis of variance applied to a factorial design), then the name of the subsection should include "analysis." Often (especially in a dissertation), the research hypotheses are restated in operationalized form, such as "To test the research hypothesis that [statement of hypothesis], a two-way analysis of variance was conducted. [Explain factors and indicate dependent variable.] It was predicted that a statistically significant F test for the interaction would be obtained."

The design and analysis subsections of a qualitative study generally overview the rationale for employing one's approach to data coding, analysis, and interpretation. Data analysis procedures are described, including the procedures by which the researcher or the research team examined data. Processes related to training the research team, coding procedures, the use of an auditor (if applicable) to provide evidence of triangulation, member checking procedures, participant feedback, and treatment of data from field notes may also be included in this section.

Results

The purpose of the results section is to summarize the results of the analysis utilized in the study. Although the writing style for the results section may be quite different depending upon the study methodology, results sections are designed to provide the reader an overview of the findings from the study. The results section should report the findings, but discussion of the results and interpretations based upon the findings are saved for the discussion section. Organization of the results section may be facilitated by appropriately titled subsections (e.g., "Summary Statistics" and "Tests of Hypotheses" for quantitative manuscripts and the use of themes from the findings such as "Therapist Personal Experiences and Countertransference" for qualitative manuscripts).

Results are often presented in tables or figures, which are useful when details related to the results can be understood while taking up a minimal amount of space. Locating important results in the text is much more difficult than finding them in a well organized table. Figures are particularly useful for illustrating patterns of results, such as an interaction in a test of moderation or a proposed theoretical framework that emerges from a grounded theory investigation. The writer should refer the reader to the table or figure and inform the reader of the information contained therein (e.g., "The main effects of the 3 (treatment) by 2 (gender) analysis of variance were statistically significant, as shown in Table 1.").

The results section of a quantitative study generally contains two broad sections. The first includes the presentation of evidence to support the procedures of the study design and support for the use of the statistical tests used to analyze the data (e.g., conformity to assumptions of statistical tests, manipulation checks, procedures for dealing with missing data; Bem, 2003). The second broad section generally includes a report of two types of results: (a) data screening, summary statistics, and results of preliminary analyses; and (b) results that test the research hypotheses. Means, standard deviations of the primary variables, and the correlation matrix for all variables are often presented as part of the summary data. Results specific to research hypotheses should be organized so that the reader can directly tie the results of the statistical tests to the research hypotheses stated earlier in the manuscript. There should be a one-to-one correspondence between the hypotheses and the statistical tests.

Given the technical nature of the results section, authors such as Bem (2003) caution writers to "write the results section in English prose" (p. 197). In particular, he suggests the format shown in Table 4.4 when presenting results from hypothesis testing.

TABLE 4.4 Research Application: Hypothesis Testing Format

Steps	(✓)
1. Recall the stated hypothesis.	
2. Operationalize the hypothesis.	
3. Indicate whether the stated hypothesis was supported by the data.	
4. Provide numbers based upon results of the statistical test and refer reader to table (as relevant).	
5. Provide additional details to elaborate or qualify the results and refer reader to table or figure (as relevant).	
6. Summarize results.	

APA's Task Force on Statistical Inference (TFSI; Wilkinson & Task Force on Statistical Inference, 1999) maintained that effect sizes provide a very good summary of the study findings and therefore should be included for any statistical test. The *APA Publication Manual* (2010) incorporated this recommendation in the sixth edition and provided specifics about reporting statistical tests in the text and in tables. Failure to report information other than significance levels makes it difficult or impossible for readers to verify results, calculate other indexes (such as effect size or power), and conduct meta-analyses.

For qualitative studies, the results section will vary based on the chosen strategy of inquiry (e.g., grounded theory, consensual qualitative research, phenomenology/ hermeneutics). Contents of subsections as well as the use of tables or figures will also differ depending upon the nature of the inquiry (see Chapter 16 for more details). Most qualitative results sections, however, will include detailed descriptions of participant data and excerpts from the interviews or field notes in order to exemplify the themes or dimensions using a narrative style. In general, the length of the results section for qualitative manuscripts will be greater than that for quantitative manuscripts. For this reason, many journals provide different page limits for qualitative and quantitative manuscripts.

Discussion

The discussion section allows the author to expand upon the findings and to place the results in the context of previous research and theory on this topic. This section typically includes (a) an explanation of the results of the data analyses; (b) whether or not the data support the research hypotheses (for quantitative manuscripts); (c) a statement of the conclusions and interpretations of the findings in lieu of current theory and research; (d) an honest overview of the study's limitations; (e) a discussion of directions for future research; and (f) a discussion of the implications that can be drawn from the research. Topics that were central to the introduction section will likely be integrated into the discussion section in order to contextualize the results of the current study. Using the hourglass analogy discussed at the beginning of this section, the discussion reverses the flow of the introduction in that it begins with a narrow overview of the results of the study, expands to situating the results within previous research and theory, offers alternative explanations or qualifiers to the results based upon study limitations, and concludes with a discussion of directions for the future and implications.

Every discussion of results should include a statement of the limitations, which typically are related to issues with the sample (e.g., heterogeneity of the sample, low power, geographic restrictions), procedures (e.g., attrition, recruitment procedures impacted by inclusion/exclusion criteria), measures (e.g., unreliability of measures, violated assumptions of statistical tests), and/or study design (e.g., the analogue nature of the study, confounds, ability to imply causation). Remember that no study is perfect; it is best to be forthright about the limitations and discuss how the results are interpretable in spite of the limitations. The discussion often ends with a discussion of implications of the study for theory and for practice. Taken together, the components of the discussion section commonly include those shown in Table 4.5.

TABLE 4.5   Research Application: Checklist for Subsections of the Discussion

Question	(✓)
What are the major findings from this research?	
How do these findings fit within theory and prior empirical research?	
How do these findings extend, support, or refute theory?	
What alternative explanations exist that may explain the findings?	
What are the limitations to the current study (e.g., sample, methodology, data-analytic strategy, measures)?	
What new research directions are indicated based upon results from this study?	
What implications can be drawn from the results of this study (e.g., for practice, for training, for teaching)?	
What is a broad summary or concluding statement?	

GENERAL PRINCIPLES FOR WRITING RESEARCH REPORTS

Although it is difficult to identify general principles of research report writing, we can emphasize four general rules of thumb: (a) be informative, (b) be forthright, (c) do not overstate or exaggerate, and (d) be logical and organized.

Principle 1: Be Informative

The goal of the research report is to inform the reader about the study. Provide enough detail for the reader to understand what you are explaining, but not so much that the reader becomes bogged down in the details. Of course, the publication outlet may also determine the level of detail. Dissertations require the most detail. Some journals are more technical than others and thus require more detail (and allow longer manuscripts). It is important to be knowledgeable about the publication outlet and intended audience when determining the level of detail and overall style of the report. The majority of publication outlets provide comprehensive information regarding instructions for authors as well as an overview of the aims of the journal on their websites.

In any report, discuss the central points and minimize digressions. Obviously, you should not report everything that you did, but you must provide information that readers need to understand the study. For example, preparation of stimulus materials often involves many successive stages of development. It is not necessary to explain all iterations. Instead, authors may describe the final product and summarize the development process. Similarly, when stating a decision that you made (e.g., "three outliers were omitted from the analysis,") be sure to also explain the basis upon which the decision was made (e.g., "based upon analysis of the Mahalanobis distance statistic").

Principle 2: Be Forthright

As discussed repeatedly throughout this book, every study has flaws (Gelso, 1979). It is rare that a researcher would not alter a study if given the chance to do so. Authors should be forthright and discuss the ramifications of a study's limitations, rather than trying to hide flaws. Signs of hidden flaws include obtuse language, esoteric statistical tests (with improper justification), omitted information, and overstated justifications. Red flags are often raised by reviewers of manuscripts submitted for publication who uncover hidden flaws or who have a vague (intuitive) sense that the author has not been forthright with regard to some limitation.

Flaws necessitate a fundamental decision: if a flaw is fatal to the study (e.g., a confound that cannot be minimized), then it is best to consider the study a time-consuming learning experience. If the flaw is problematic but the results of the study are informative nevertheless, then the author should indicate how the flaw affects the interpretation, highlight future directions in order to extend the current findings, and detail the contribution of the study in spite of the flaw. Of course, the ultimate decision as to whether the flaw is fatal is made by others (e.g., dissertation committee members, editors, reviewers).

Principle 3: Do Not Overstate or Exaggerate

There is a widely shared tendency to believe that every study will somehow change the course of the field. When expressed in written reports, it appears as unjustified claims about the importance of the results. It is highly unusual that any one research study is sufficient to stand alone or to change the course of research or clinical practice. As will be discussed in Chapter 6, research is best viewed as a progressive and cyclical endeavor in which evidence (including alternative or contradictory evidence) accumulates over time and adds to our knowledge.

Unsupported statements most often appear in the discussion section of a manuscript. Refrain from stating that, based on the results of your study, practitioners should change their practice or that researchers should abandon some theoretical position. If you feel strongly about a position, you might suggest something like: "the results of this study as well as previous studies [cite those studies] suggest that Theory X should be reconsidered in Y manner."

An issue related to overstatement also concerns the appraisal of other authors' work. Generally, it is not advisable to be overly critical of others. Again, let the scientific community make judgments about the worth of various schools of thought or of a researcher's contributions. It is acceptable to point out differences of opinion, but do so tactfully.

Principle 4: Be Logical and Organized

The written report is not a recitation of facts; it is the presentation of a position. Authors must persuade the reader that there is a solid rationale for the study and that the claims made therein are justified. As we indicated previously, the research question should be justified given the literature reviewed, and the logic and organization of the introduction should make the case for the research question.

Although this list is certainly not exhaustive, there are a few general strategies that can aid in organization. First, begin writing with an outline that not only lists various sections of the report, but also neatly summarizes the logical organization. One strategy that we often find useful is to review published manuscripts that utilize a similar method (e.g., if you are writing a report to summarize a scale development study, it might be useful to examine the overall structure of some published scale development studies to guide your own organization). Second, provide organizers and summaries of complex materials. Specifically, tell the reader what is to follow and how it is organized, and, if necessary, summarize at the end of long or detailed explanations. Third, use headings to organize the manuscript and assist the reader by highlighting the core components. Finally, include transition statements between topics to highlight how two different topics or logical arguments are connected (for more details and examples, see Heppner and Heppner, 2004).

MANUSCRIPT SUBMISSION PROCESS

Following completion of the research report, manuscripts are submitted for review. The manuscript submission process involves a series of steps. Although many steps may be considered "universal" in nature, each publication outlet has particular specifications that must be adhered to (e.g., manuscript length, manuscript formatting). Descriptions of the steps for submitting manuscripts to journals are listed on the webpage of that journal. There are instructions for submission, including links to the electronic manuscript submission portals. While a detailed overview of all of these steps is beyond the scope of this book, we do want to highlight some of the common characteristics of manuscript submission as well as the possible outcomes of a submission.

The four most common outcomes from a submitted manuscript to peer reviewed journals include rejection, revise and resubmit, provisional acceptance, and acceptance. A provisionally accepted manuscript is one that the editor has deemed suitable for publication, but may be requesting a few additional minor tweaks (generally in style rather than substance) before officially accepting the manuscript. An accepted manuscript, on the other hand, has been determined to be of sufficient quality to warrant publication. It is important to note, however, that once a manuscript is accepted, there are a still a number of steps that the author(s) must complete prior to the article's publication (e.g., transfer of copyright, responding to queries from the publication outlet's editorial staff). Hoyt and Mallinkrodt (2012) suggested that, in their experience working as editors for *Journal of Counseling Psychology*, manuscripts are reviewed and critiqued using the criteria of fatal versus fixable flaws. Those flaws that are determined to be fixable through revision generally translate into manuscripts that receive a disposition of "revise and resubmit." On the other hand, those that are determined as fatal flaws receive a disposition of "rejection" as it is believed that because of study design, the flaws cannot be addressed even through considerable revision.

SUMMARY AND CONCLUSIONS

The research report is critical to the research endeavor because it is the vehicle by which the results of studies are typically disseminated. The entire research process is summarized in the research report, from the statement of the problem to the discussion of the results. A coherently organized and well-written report increases the likelihood that the research study will influence the scientific community.

Although organization of the research report varies, most reports contain a title, an abstract, an introduction, a description of the method, a presentation of the results, and a discussion or conclusion. The content of these sections is determined, to a great extent, by the design of the research. The style of the written report varies, for each of us has our own style, which we in turn alter depending on the publication outlet for which our writing is intended. Professional writing is a complex skill that takes years of practice and feedback. Moreover, it is a skill that involves one's personal style of communicating. Procrastination and other avoidance patterns are common reactions of inexperienced and experienced authors alike. One of the most effective strategies to improve one's professional writing is to work closely with a successful author, writing drafts, receiving feedback, rewriting, and polishing. It is not atypical for graduate students to spend two to three years cowriting with a faculty member to enhance both their professional writing skills and their research skills in general. We strongly urge students to actively solicit feedback on their writing and seek cowriting experiences with established authors.

STIMULUS EXERCISE

Writing an Introduction to an Article

Learning to write a compelling introduction is difficult. We have found that the following exercise is helpful in learning this complex skill. This exercise is best done as a class, or with a small group of four to six students. It is best if you can have a faculty advisor or advanced student with expertise in scientific writing leading the exercise or helping the group work through it together. We will describe the exercise using a class format, but it can be adapted for a small group of students as long as one of the students is more advanced in their writing skills and can give appropriate feedback to group members. In addition, the exercise can be done with all seven steps or just a few of the steps.

1. First, the class critiques an introduction to an article the instructor selected from a recent journal.

2. Then, as an individual assignment, each student critiques the introduction to an article in their area of interest and receives feedback on their critique from the instructor.

3. The next assignment involves a published article that contains an introduction citing seven other articles (but no books or book chapters). The students are given the published article without the introduction and the seven articles cited.

4. The next assignment is to read the seven cited articles and the published article (without the introduction). At the next class meeting, the class discusses various structures that could be used to construct the introduction to the published article (i.e., the logic of the introduction, how the paragraphs would follow each other, how the case would be built for the hypotheses, and so on). In this discussion, it is

emphasized that there is no one correct way to write this introduction, but the class agrees on a common structure.

5. The next assignment is for each student to write, in APA style (i.e., in accordance with the *Publication Manual of the American Psychological Association*, 2010a), an introduction that leads logically to the hypothesis, using only the seven articles as supporting evidence (this assignment is completed in one week). The instructor grades the papers, providing feedback at every level (i.e., grammar, sentence construction, paragraph construction, logic, proper citation, and so forth) within one week.

6. Finally, students should revise the introduction according to the instructor's feedback. This revision is again evaluated by the instructor.

7. At the end, the original introduction is critiqued in a class discussion.

Part 2

GETTING STARTED: ESTABLISHING THE FOUNDATION FOR A STUDY

Identifying Interests and Operationalizing Topics: Forget That Perfect Study

5 Chapter

The purpose of this chapter is to provide an overview of the process of selecting a research topic and developing the research idea into a testable hypothesis. The chapter describes the five main components of this process: identifying research topics, specifying research questions and hypotheses, formulating operational definitions, identifying research variables, and collecting and analyzing data (see Figure 5.1). We present these activities in separate sections in order to adequately discuss each of the five components. However, in reality these activities are often intertwined, and researchers often intersperse thinking and planning across all of these activities as they progress from identifying the topic to collecting data.

FIGURE 5.1 Five Main Components

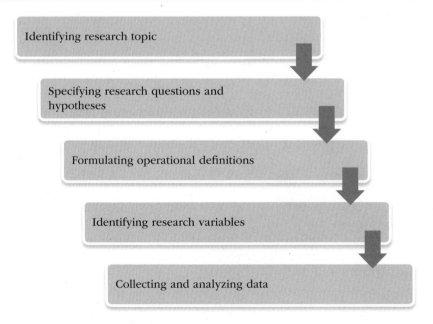

Identifying research topic

Specifying research questions and hypotheses

Formulating operational definitions

Identifying research variables

Collecting and analyzing data

IDENTIFYING RESEARCH TOPICS

A wide range of experiences can play a role in helping the researcher develop research ideas. At times, developing a research idea can involve a great deal of creativity as the researcher integrates information from diverse sources and in novel ways. Sometimes successful theses and dissertations extend previous well-established studies one step further by examining one new variable, collecting data from different groups, or using a new methodology (Heppner & Heppner, 2004). It is often exciting to identify topics and innovative ideas that may lead to important contributions of new knowledge, and it is exhilarating to think that no one has thought of this idea before (at least for a short period of time!).

Sometimes developing research ideas may seem difficult for inexperienced researchers; they cringe at the thought of developing an original research idea that *no one* has *ever* had before. Typically, the experienced researcher has little difficulty in developing research ideas. In fact, often the veteran researcher has too many research ideas, and a more difficult problem is deciding which ideas to pursue.

Several characteristics differentiate the experienced researcher from the inexperienced. The experienced researcher usually has a large knowledge base, not only about a given topic, but also about several other topics. Such a researcher can most likely process information about these topics in sophisticated ways, identifying the most important findings, combining research findings, dovetailing an idea from one topic with another, and elaborating on or extending ideas in novel ways. In addition, the experienced counseling researcher often has a considerable wealth of information from his or her applied counseling experiences that can be the source of many ideas and hypotheses. The veteran researcher also typically knows a great deal about the skills needed to conduct research, such as knowledge of research design, methodology, assessment, statistics, data collection, data analysis, and technical writing. All of these knowledge bases are important tools in facilitating the processing of large amounts of information about specific research projects in sophisticated and often innovative ways. Perhaps equally important, the experienced researcher typically has confidence that he or she can effectively conduct research, and thus has the needed level of self-efficacy.

In contrast, the inexperienced researcher has far less knowledge about specific research topics and often has trouble identifying the most important or relevant information. The novice often has less applied experience in counseling, and most likely has less-developed conceptualizations of the counseling process. The inexperienced researcher has perhaps only a vague sense of the various research activities (such as recruitment of participants and data collection) and harbors doubts about his or her ability to do research well. In fact, in many counseling programs, well-articulated guidelines for conducting research are not available to students, leaving the impression that the research process is rather mystical. Drew (1980) noted that a logical place to turn for information is a college or departmental catalog that describes a thesis or dissertation project. Typically such documents say something to the effect that the thesis "must be an original contribution to the field." When viewed literally, the word *original* can engender considerable anxiety as the trainee tries to develop a completely novel research idea. In addition, the idea must represent "a contribution to the field," which makes the task seem even more formidable. It is the rare trainee who believes at the outset that he or she can make a "real contribution" to the field; after all, we are talking about *science*! Sometimes the inexperienced researcher interprets "original contribution" much too broadly and tries to develop a new topic area by creating a new assessment instrument to measure new constructs, a new research methodology to collect data previously not collected, and new statistical procedures to handle old problems. In reality, most experienced researchers would feel quite a sense of accomplishment if they did all of these things during an entire *career*. An original contribution could simply be extending the literature to different populations, empirically testing a conceptual model, further examining the underlying variables that might affect the associations between two variables, evaluating the psychometric properties of a certain scale, replicating studies that have yielded inconsistent results, accounting for certain limitations of past studies, etc. In short, the inexperienced researcher often takes on too much in trying to develop an original contribution. Not surprisingly, our experience has been that graduate students in beginning research design courses ask questions about how to identify "good" research topics and "good" research ideas. Also not surprisingly, they often ask whether a particular idea is "enough" for a thesis.

We make some suggestions in this chapter to help beginning researchers to identify a research topic. Essentially, the task is to identify some general topic that may (a) contribute to the profession's knowledge bases in meaningful ways, and (b) simultaneously stimulate and motivate students to explore and learn more about the topic. Most inexperienced researchers in counseling need to learn more about the body of knowledge and the directions of current research efforts. Thus, for such students we do not simply recommend sitting and thinking hard about research topics and hoping that the ideal research question will present itself, but rather taking a more active, information-collecting approach.

RESEARCH IN ACTION 5.1

Brainstorm a list of topics that excite and motivate you. Are there any themes in this list? Rate the degree to which each topic interests you (1 = low, 10 = high).

A necessary first step in identifying possible research topics is to start collecting information about previous research, both within and outside of counseling (see Table 5.1). Thus, read widely in the professional journals and books. Reading widely not only will provide you with information about what is being published, but also may help you to clarify what topics are of most interest to you. Sometimes it is useful to start with a general review of the counseling literature (see *APA Handbook of Counseling Psychology* edited by Fouad, Carter, & Subich [2012] for various topics related to the counseling profession). Another strategy is to begin by looking for more focused literature reviews on specific topics. (The *Psychological Bulletin* is a journal devoted to evaluative and integrative reviews; see Cheng, Lau, and Chan [2014] for an excellent example of a meta-analytic review of the literature on coping and psychological

TABLE 5.1 : Strategies for Identifying Research Topics
....

- General review of counseling topics.

- Read literature review articles and handbooks.

- Explore topics through funding agency websites.

- Talk with faculty and peers about topics.

- Attend conference presentations.

- Consult with advisor.

- Take notes of observations, reflections, and ideas.

- Critique existing lines of research.

- Consider own interest, values, and motivation.

---

adjustment to stressful life changes, as well as another excellent example by Oyserman, Coon, and Kemmelmeier [2002] evaluating theoretical assumptions of individualism and collectivism.) Books on specific topics are often useful resources. For example, a student interested in conducting research with racial/ethnic minorities would be wise to examine Leong, Comas-Díaz, Nagayama Hall, McLoyd, and Trimble's (2014) *APA Handbook of Multicultural Psychology*. In short, there is no substitute for this time-consuming process of reading the relevant literature; at first you might peruse and read abstracts to develop a broad overview. A good beginning is to spend at least five hours a week reading and exploring the journals for six weeks or more.

In addition to examining what kind of research that has already been done, it would also be important to get a sense of what kind of research grant funding agencies have identified as new and important topics that merit investigation. Exploring grant funding agency websites is an important avenue to gain a better understanding of what kinds of topics are currently valued by funding agencies, which usually reflect the current societal issues of most significance. The National Science Foundation (NSF) (http://www.nsf.gov/funding/), National Institutes of Health (NIH) (http://grants.nih.gov/grants/oer.htm), and Institute of Educational Sciences (IES) (http://ies.ed.gov/funding/) are some major federal grant funding agencies. There are also foundation grant funding sources, such as American Psychological Foundation (APF) (http://www.apa.org/apf/funding/grants/index.aspx), Robert Wood Johnson Foundation (http://www.rwjf.org/en/grants/what-we-fund.html), and John Templeton Foundation (http://www.templeton.org/what-we-fund/core-funding-areas). Exploring the kind of studies that these agencies are funding will provide a broad sense of the topics that are perceived as pressing societal needs.

Capitalizing on the faculty and student resources on your campus is another approach. Although this sounds simplistic, it often provides useful information. Talk with these people about their past and present research projects. What are they most excited about now? What was the most stimulating idea at a recent national, regional, or state convention they attended? What do they consider as hot or promising topics? Heppner and Heppner (2004) also encouraged consultation with professionals and experts in the field in a prepared and respectful manner. Follow up your discussions with these people with readings they might suggest to you.

In addition to faculty in general, your advisor or research supervisor is often an invaluable resource. Typically, the advisor's role is to facilitate students' work on their thesis/dissertation. Thus, another strategy is to begin research training by working closely within the advisor's research interests; this approach resembles an apprenticeship model. An advantage of this strategy is that your advisor can more easily facilitate the identification of relevant readings, workable research ideas, methods, obstacles, and procedures (Heppner & Heppner, 2004).

Although we said earlier that we do not recommend simply sitting and thinking hard, we do recommend thinking and reflecting *after* you have collected a wide variety of information. What do you like and dislike about a particular line of research? Pay attention to what bothers you about a study. Was something omitted? How could you improve the study? Also try to bring your own observations and beliefs into your research topics. Many experienced counselors use their own observations about a topic (e.g., the counselor supervision process or counselor self-disclosure) as a source of ideas for research topics. This is riskier for the inexperienced counselor and researcher, however, because a lack of experience may provide less reliable observations. To facilitate reflecting and brainstorming, sometimes it is helpful to record ideas, observations, and questions in a journal or log.

While reading and thinking about previous research in counseling, it is important to keep in mind at least four issues: the utility of research in answering real-life applied questions that address important societal needs, your particular interests, a way to build on previous research, and the role of theory. Perhaps one of the most basic reasons for conducting research is to develop knowledge bases that in one way or another can help people by addressing pressing societal needs. In essence, in order for the counseling profession to be of value to the larger society, our research must address important issues and problems in society. Thus, we encourage students to reflect on some of the most significant current societal issues to identify research topics. For example, a researcher might have questions about effective interventions for treating individuals with alcohol abuse. Alcohol abuse has been the topic of a great deal of attention and has stimulated research on the efficacy of a number of psychosocial interventions (see Donoghue, Patton, Phillips, Deluca, & Drummond, 2014). Or a researcher might consider whether improvements could be made to increase the effectiveness of various treatment programs (e.g., anger management, substance abuse, or parenting training) or outreach programs (e.g., rape prevention or alcohol awareness programs). Or are there some important questions that an agency director or some other helping professional needs more information about in order to improve their services? Perhaps a career center director would like to know whether webinars online would be a cost-effective way to provide training services (see Yates, 2014). For example, using a qualitative method, Yates evaluated a series of online webinars conducted with 15 career advisors. Results indicated that although lacking peer interactions was a limitation, overall participants found the training to be helpful. In short, unresolved societal problems or questions about applied aspects of counseling are a rich source of research topics.

It is also essential to continually assess which topics are most important to you. Are there certain topics that you are motivated to pursue, or perhaps feel a special commitment to investigate because of your beliefs or values? What important topics have previous researchers overlooked? In short, pursuing research topics that you are motivated and dedicated to pursue will likely provide both the drive and intellectual stimulation needed to sustain you through the various research tasks.

It is also important to realize that a great deal of research in counseling involves extending the results of previous research. Typically, our research progresses by adding one or two new pieces of information per study. Thus, a researcher might extend a previous study by adding one or two new constructs or by developing a new assessment instrument to operationalize a construct. Often a researcher uses a data collection method similar to that used in previous research, or instruments used in three or four previous studies. In short, it is essential to focus on investigating a few constructs only, and not to try to do too much in developing an "original contribution." Most often our knowledge bases in counseling increase in small steps by building only slightly on previous research. A puzzle can be used as an analogy to depict the research literature on a certain topic, whereas each piece of the puzzle represents a study. It is by putting the pieces together for the whole puzzle that provides a comprehensive understanding of a topic area. Thus, remind yourself that your study is a piece of the puzzle that contributes to the whole picture, rather than feel the need to design a comprehensive study that will address everything on that topic matter.

A considerable amount of research within counseling applies or tests theories about personality, human behavior, and the change process as they apply to topics in counseling. Testing theory can be an important contribution to the counseling field because it helps refine our theories, especially because many theories have not been tested on diverse populations (Heppner & Heppner, 2004). For example, Stanley Strong (1968) initially conceptualized counseling as a social influence process and used research and theory on persuasion from social psychology to develop a two-phase model of influence within counseling. Subsequently, a great deal of research has examined the persuasion or social influence process within counseling (see reviews by Corrigan, Dell, Lewis, & Schmidt, 1980; Heppner & Claiborn, 1989; Heppner & Dixon, 1981; Heppner & Frazier, 1992; Hoyt, 1996; Strong, Welsh, Corcoran, & Hoyt, 1992). Likewise, another theoretical perspective that is influencing counseling research is the contextual model of psychotherapy (see Wampold & Imel, 2015).

Sometimes a new model or theory is developed by integrating different bodies of research. For example, McCarn and Fassinger (1996) developed a model of lesbian identity formation by integrating literature on lesbian/gay identity, racial/ethnic identity, and gender issues related to identity development; subsequently, a number of research directions were proposed. Or sometimes research will test and extend either competing theories or different conceptualizations of the same phenomena. For example, in 1971 Cross published a model on Black racial identity that has been modified by refinements and elaborations, as well as empirically tested (see, e.g., Cross, 1978; Cross & Vandiver, 2001; Elion, Wang, Slaney, & French, 2012; Helms, 1990; Helms & Parham, 1996; Nghe & Mahalik, 2001; Parham, 1989; Parham & Helms, 1981, 1985b). Subsequently, over the years a number of White racial identity models have been proposed, debated, and empirically tested (see, e.g., Carr & Caskie, 2010; Gushue & Carter, 2000; Helms, 1990; Johnson & Jackson Williams, 2014; Rowe & Atkinson, 1995; Rowe, Bennett, & Atkinson, 1994; Thompson, 1994).

Similarly, sometimes theory and research from one topic can be extended to another related topic. For example, women's career development has been the focus of both

FIGURE 5.2 : Brainstorming Topics

theoretical models (e.g., social cognitive career theory; Lent, Brown, & Hackett, 1994) and empirical research for some time (see, e.g., August, 2011; Betz & Fitzgerald, 1987; Farmer, Wardrop, Anderson, & Risinger, 1995; Fassinger, 1990; Harmon, 1977; Lindstrom, Harwick, Poppen, & Doren, 2012; Walsh & Heppner, 2006). Models of women's career development were then integrated with empirical research on lesbians' career development to develop a minority group model of career development (Morgan & Brown, 1991). This model of career development was extended to the career development of highly achieving women with physical and sensory disabilities (Noonan et al., 2004). Thus, another strategy in identifying research topics is to examine any theories, whether they are found within the counseling literature or outside the counseling literature, that might be helpful to the work of counselors.

RESEARCH IN ACTION 5.2

Can you narrow the list of topics that you brainstormed (see Figure 5.2) and identify two to three topics on which you might like to conduct a study (based your interest and its significance/importance)? Evaluate each of the topics (1 = low, 10 = high) in terms of how significant this topic is as well as how proud you would feel about contributing your scholarly efforts. Indicate why you rated each topic as you did.

In summary, ideas for research projects can come from a wide range of sources. It is often useful for students to use a combination of strategies as they enter the world of research.

SPECIFYING RESEARCH QUESTIONS AND HYPOTHESES

Typically, the purpose of research is to answer questions, address pressing societal problems, refine theories of interest to counseling, and ultimately add to the existing knowledge in the field. It is one thing to identify a *topic* you want to research. It is another thing to move beyond the research topic to develop a specific research question or hypothesis that can guide your research. In fact, developing testable research questions is often quite troublesome for inexperienced researchers.

After identifying a possible research topic (e.g., counselor supervision), it is important that you become knowledgeable about the previous research on that topic, perhaps even by writing a formal review paper. There is no substitute for becoming thoroughly knowledgeable about a topic by identifying current research findings, previous research obstacles, and previous researchers' suggestions for future research. As we indicated earlier, many times developing a specific research idea means extending a line of research one logical step further (e.g., exploring factors associated with effective supervision among cross-cultural supervisor-supervisee dyads). Thus, examining key studies or incisive reviews is essential. Pay particular attention to the discussion section in those studies. Often there is explicit discussion of future research needs or of the next logical step. The authors often identify these needs by phrases such as "future research should" or "additional research might examine." These suggestions could be the basis of your research idea.

After reading a number of articles on your general topic, begin to attend more closely to the constructs that have been used in the previous research. What variables or processes are interesting and important to researchers in the field? What questions have researchers been addressing in the research literature? *Research questions* are key elements in developing a topic area, and in essence are questions that explore the relations among or between constructs. For example, "Does the client's level of dysfunction affect the working alliance formed in counseling?" is a research question. In contrast, a *research hypothesis* is more specific in that it states the expected relationship between the constructs, as in "More-dysfunctional clients will form poorer alliances in counseling than will less-dysfunctional clients." Often, distinctions are not made between questions and hypotheses. However, it should be kept in mind that hypotheses specifically state the expected relationship.

From our experience, students have difficulty developing research questions and hypotheses for several reasons. Perhaps most frequently, students may lack a theoretical structure for their investigation and thus cannot conceptualize relevant research hypotheses that will empirically test or extend previous research. Research questions and hypotheses are often deduced from theory (Tracey & Glidden-Tracey, 1999; Wampold, Davis, & Good, 1990). At other times, students select constructs they have no way of measuring or testing. For example, one doctoral student was stymied because he could not clearly assess what he meant by counselor personal power and autonomy. Sometimes students have not thought in depth beyond the research topic and have not asked themselves what specific constructs they are most interested in examining. Thus, they may be unable to be more specific than being interested in "something about social media and mental health." Students also may be reluctant to decide on specific constructs, choosing instead to delay or procrastinate for an array of conscious and unconscious reasons. All these difficulties in developing research questions and hypotheses are not atypical for inexperienced researchers. Most important, such difficulties suggest that additional reading and thinking are necessary. Researchers can make serious errors by proceeding to select participants and assessment instruments without ever clarifying their research questions or hypotheses and exactly what they are looking for in their research.

TABLE 5.2 ⋮ Types of Research Questions

Descriptive questions: Describe the variables of interest with questions such as how much, how often, what percentage, what is, etc.

Difference questions: Compare between groups of people or within individual participants.

Relationship questions: Examine how two or more constructs or associated with each other.

Drew (1980) has identified three useful general categories of research questions (or hypotheses): descriptive, difference, and relationship (see Table 5.2). *Descriptive questions* essentially ask what some phenomena or events are like. Sometimes we have questions about counseling events or phenomena that are best answered by collecting information through inventories, surveys, or interviews to describe events. Experimental manipulations typically are not used in these studies.

Because there are many types of studies that examine descriptive research questions, we will provide a number of illustrative examples. For example, a researcher might want to use a survey to describe the types of events that trigger counselor anger (Fremont & Anderson, 1986) or a qualitative method to learn about gay men's experiences in mixed sexual orientations groups (Provence, Rochlen, Chester, & Smith, 2014). Other times qualitative studies might use interviews to understand therapists' experiences addressing racial issues in counseling (see Knox, Burkard, Johnson, Suzuki, & Ponterotto, 2003). Similarly Swagler and Ellis (2003) used interviews to study the cross-cultural adjustment of Taiwanese graduate students in the United States; the results revealed themes of language barriers, confidence about speaking English, social contract, and cultural differences. Later, focus groups were conducted to provide a more complete conceptualization of the relations among the constructs. If a researcher wanted to identify the professional needs and experiences of ethnic and racial minority psychologists, a survey might be a useful strategy to collect information, which was precisely the approach chosen by Constantine, Quintana, Leung, and Phelps (1995). Another survey study was conducted by Johnson and Hayes (2003) to examine the prevalence of religious and spiritual concerns among counseling center clients. At other times we use statistical procedures such as factor analysis (see Tinsley & Tinsley, 1987) or cluster analysis (see Borgen & Barnett, 1987) to describe how people or events might be categorized. For example, researchers have used cluster analysis to describe different profile types of racial identity among African Americans (Worrell, Andretta, & Woodland, 2014) and Latinos (Chavez-Korell & Torres, 2014). Similarly, Kim, Li, and Ng (2005) developed the Asian American Values Scale-Multidimensional (AAVS-M) to measure the adherence to cultural values that play an important role incounseling through factor analysis. Wei, Alvarez, Ku, Russell, and Bonett (2010) also used factor analysis to develop the Coping with Discrimination Scale (CDS); in this study they also supported their initial factor structure with confirmatory factor analysis. Descriptive research is discussed more fully in Chapters 13 and 16, and scale construction in Chapter 10.

Difference questions ask if there are differences between groups of people, or even within individual participants. The key feature in this type of question is a comparison of some sort. Such research questions tend to focus on groups of individuals; the groups may differ on some dimension or may receive different treatments. For example, a study by Mallinckrodt and Helms (1986) examined a difference question in determining whether counselors who are physically challenged have certain therapeutic advantages relative to able-bodied counselors. Likewise, Wang (2010) compared perfectionism and perceived family perfectionism between Asian and White Americans. In addition to comparing groups based on certain demographic statuses, other studies have focused on comparing differences on manipulated variables (e.g., interventions, treatment conditions). For example, Martens, Smith, and Murphy (2013) studied brief motivational interviews with at-risk college drinkers. They compared groups that received personalized normative feedback (PNF), protective behavioral strategies feedback (PBSF), and general alcohol education (AE) on drinking outcomes. Results indicated that PNF was efficacious in reducing alcohol use compared to the other two groups. Difference questions are often examined in between-group and within-group designs (see Chapter 11).

Relationship questions explore the degree to which two or more constructs are related or vary together. Such questions tend to use correlational statistics or more complex regression analyses. For example, a study by Rochlen, Land, & Wong (2004) examined men's restrictive emotionality and their perception of online and face-to-face counseling. They found that men with lower restrictive emotionality were more favorable to face-to-face counseling compared to those with higher restrictive emotionality. Similarly, Smith and Ingram (2004) studied the relationships among workplace heterosexism, unsupportive social interaction, and adjustment of lesbian/gay/bisexual individuals. Likewise, Good et al. (1995) examined the correlations between gender role conflict and several other inventories (e.g., attitudes about masculinity, fear of intimacy, social desirability) to provide estimates of construct validity for the Gender Role Conflict Scale (O'Neil, Helms, Gable, David, & Wrightsman, 1986). Cournoyer and Mahalik (1995) extended this line of research by using canonical analysis, a multivariate approach to examining relations among multiple variables. Relationship research questions are discussed more fully in Chapters 13.

What constitutes a testable research question? A research question (a) asks a question about (b) the relationships between two or more constructs that can be (c) measured in some way. First, the question should be worded clearly and unambiguously in question form. Second, the research question should inquire into a relationship between two or more constructs, asking whether Construct A is related to Construct B. (If a particular relationship is stated, the research question becomes a hypothesis.) This second criterion pertains mostly to difference and relationship questions, whereas descriptive questions often seek to collect or categorize information. Finally, not only is a relationship between constructs examined, but somehow this relationship also must be measurable.

For example, consider a research question like "Is supervision effective?" One might immediately ask, "Effective at what?" Is the researcher interested in the effectiveness of supervision to lower a trainee's stress level to conceptualize clients, or to intervene with clients? In short, such a question lacks specificity. Now consider the research questions developed by Wiley and Ray (1986), who were interested in the topic of the changing nature of supervision over the course of training. In particular, they were interested in testing Stoltenberg's (1981) counselor complexity model concerning developmental levels of counselor trainees. (Stoltenberg proposed that counselor trainees develop in a predictable way over the course of graduate training, and that counseling supervision environments should be adapted in ways that match the needs of the trainee.) Wiley and Ray developed three specific research questions, each of which inquired about relationships between two or more constructs and was amenable to being measured or tested in some way. For example, one of their questions was: To what extent do supervision dyads with a more congruent person-environment match on developmental level report higher satisfaction and learning than those with a less congruent match? The construct of the congruent person-environment match was concretely operationalized via the use of an assessment instrument called the Supervision Level Scale. Likewise, satisfaction and learning were operationalized in terms of a brief outcome instrument. Parenthetically, although Wiley and Ray obtained results that provided some support for conceptualizing supervisees and supervision environments developmentally, mean satisfaction and learning ratings did not differ by person-environment congruency.

In short, the function of a testable research question or hypothesis is to provide direction for experimental inquiry. The testable research question or hypothesis not only identifies the topic, but also identifies specific constructs of interest within that topic. For more examples about writing research questions, see Heppner and Heppner (2004). After a researcher has developed a specific research question or hypothesis, he or she can then proceed to determine what instruments to use, how data can be collected, what participants to use, and so on. Many of these methodological decisions are directly dependent on the investigator's specific question or hypothesis.

Although the research question provides direction for designing a study, it is important to note that in the formative stages—as an investigator continues to develop the design and methodology of a particular study—it is not uncommon to revise or change the original research question. The investigator may encounter measurement or participant availability problems, which may dictate a slightly different research question. Or the researcher may find new data that suggest additional complexity in the topic and thus require revision of the research question. In short, any of a number of events may lead the researcher to process more information and subsequently to revise or sharpen the research questions in the formative stages of study design.

FORMULATING OPERATIONAL DEFINITIONS

After the initial development of the research question or hypothesis, it is crucial that all terms or constructs in the question be defined concretely so that the research idea can be empirically tested. More specifically, each construct must be operationally defined, which means specifying the activities or operations necessary to measure it in this particular experiment. Kerlinger (1986) referred to operational definitions as a sort of manual of instructions that spells out what the investigator must do to measure or manipulate the variables during the procedures of the study.

For example, considerable interest has been shown concerning developmental models of supervision, which in essence postulate that trainees' skills and supervisory needs change over time as trainees attain different developmental levels (see Ellis, Ladany, Krengel, & Schult, 1996; Holloway, 1987, 1992, 1995). A critical issue is how one operationally defines developmental level. Some of the initial investigations operationally defined developmental level as the training level of the student, such as beginning practicum student, advanced practicum student, and doctoral-level intern (see, e.g., Heppner & Roehlke, 1984; Reising & Daniels, 1983; Worthington, 1984). Thus, developmental level was concretely or operationally defined in terms of training level.

The primary function of an operational definition is to define the constructs involved in a particular study. In a way, the operational definition provides a working definition of the phenomenon (Kazdin, 1980). Thus, the operational definition allows the researcher to move from general ideas and constructs to more specific and measurable events. A problem arises when researchers investigate a given construct but develop different operational definitions for it. Consider again the example of developmental levels of counseling trainees. Whereas developmental level was initially defined as trainee level (see, e.g., Reising & Daniels, 1983), Wiley and Ray (1986) defined developmental level in terms of supervisors' ratings on an instrument (the Supervision Level Scale) that assesses the trainee developmental level along five dimensions. Wiley and Ray's definition is more specific and is based on Stoltenberg's (1981) theoretical model. Interestingly, Wiley and Ray found that these two definitions of developmental level result in quite different categorizations of trainees.

This example aptly depicts the problem of different operational definitions for the same construct. As research information accrues over several investigations, it becomes difficult to summarize information on supervisees' developmental level because of the different operational definitions. More important, different operational definitions sometimes lead to very different results. This is a crucial point for the inexperienced researcher to comprehend, because it implies that the results from a particular study must be qualified or restricted according to the operational definitions used in the study. It is also important to note that as research within a topic progresses and becomes more complex, operational definitions often undergo revision as knowledge accumulates and researchers become more sophisticated, as in the supervision literature.

IDENTIFYING RESEARCH VARIABLES

Up to this point we have referred to variables rather generally. Often there is confusion and debate about the terms used to describe or designate the variables in a research study. We hope to alleviate some of this confusion by using specific terms throughout this book to describe the various types or classes of variables found in research designs. Specifically, the terms *independent variable* (see Chapter 18) and *dependent variable* (see Chapter 19) have been used in both experimental and descriptive research to define different types of variables. In true experimental designs (see Chapter 11), the researcher attempts to examine causality by systematically varying or altering one variable or set of variables and examining the resultant changes in or consequences for another variable or set of variables. In such experiments, the variable that is varied or altered is called the independent variable. More specifically, the independent variable is the variable that is manipulated or controlled in a study. Usually an experiment involves two or more levels of the independent variable (e.g., treatment and no treatment), sometimes referred to as conditions. For example, in a study that compares cognitive versus interpersonal treatments for depression, the type of treatment (cognitive vs. interpersonal) would be the independent variable.

To examine the effects of the manipulation of the independent variable, concomitant changes in another variable, the dependent variable, are observed. In an experimental study, changes in the dependent variable are supposed to depend on or be influenced by changes or variations in the independent variable. In the previous example, the comparison between cognitive versus interpersonal treatments is made by measuring some dependent variable.

One example of a dependent variable is the depression scores on a standardized test (e.g., the MMPI-Depression scale). In a true experimental design we infer that a change (if one exists) in the dependent variable was caused by the manipulation of the independent variable. Thus, the terms *independent variable* and *dependent variable* have causal implications. These terms are sometimes used to describe the variables in nonexperimental studies as well. For instance, the predictor variables in a regression equation are sometimes referred to as independent variables, and the criterion variable is sometimes referred to as a dependent variable. This can be confusing because of the notions of causality implied in the terms. To alleviate this type of confusion, we will primarily utilize the terms *independent variable* and *dependent variable* to describe variables in experimental studies, although some exceptions will have to be made. Independent and dependent variables are discussed further in Chapters 18 and 19.

COLLECTING AND ANALYZING DATA

Once the constructs referenced in the research question or hypothesis have been operationally defined and the design of the study determined, the researcher collects data. The actual process of data collection involves various steps: defining the target population, creating a participant pool, selecting participants, and determining the number of participants, which we will further discuss in detail in Chapter 8 and 16. In addition, data collection decisions also depends on the design of the experiment. Thus, the design of the study must be first determined—and that is the primary focus of the remaining chapters of this book. The final step of analyzing data is most appropriately discussed in various statistical books as well as qualitative research method books. In this book, we will only briefly address some of the analytical issues.

Once the data are collected, sense must be made of them. Data usually consist of numbers that index characteristics of the participants. The data are summarized and analyzed with the express purpose of testing the research question or hypothesis. Specifically, the data are examined to determine whether the hypothesized relationship indeed exists. Inevitably, decisions need to be made during the course of a study. At these times, always think about how various alternative methods will affect your ability to shed light on the original question. Will a course of action obscure or clarify the original research question?

SUMMARY AND CONCLUSIONS

The purpose of this chapter is to provide an overview of the process of selecting a research topic and developing the research idea into a testable hypothesis. A number of activities are involved in narrowing a general topic to a series of specific, testable research hypotheses, such as developing research questions or hypotheses, identifying specific variables, and operationalizing variables. Typically, researchers intersperse thinking and planning into all of these activities as they proceed in reading relevant research literature and developing a particular topic. The outcome should be a specific, well-defined, clearly articulated research hypothesis.

We want to emphasize that it is normal, and even expected, for inexperienced researchers to make false starts and to modify aspects of their research project as they hone the final research question and hypothesis. Sometimes students get the impression that once they have had courses in research methods, statistics, and counseling theory, they ought to be able to produce research questions that have all the bugs worked out. They fear that if they do not perform flawlessly, not only will their competence as a researcher be questioned, but also it will be clear that they do not have "the right stuff" to complete the program or have a research career.

Regardless of how many courses a student has taken, there is no reason to expect a graduate student to be an expert researcher. Rather, it may be useful for students to regard their initial research attempts as training opportunities.

It is also important to note, especially for beginning researchers, that all research studies have limitations of one kind or another (such as lack of experimental control or concerns regarding generalizability). Gelso (1979) referred to this phenomenon as the bubble hypothesis and suggested that all research studies have some type of flaw or weakness. Sometimes inexperienced researchers create problems for themselves by trying to develop the perfect study or dissertation. In truth, these entities do not exist. Thus, it is essential for the inexperienced researcher to keep in mind the goal of developing a study that provides the profession with another piece of information, not *the* definitive study. Most often our knowledge bases in counseling are increased by adding one or two more pieces of information per study, with each study building on the previous research in some relatively small way. Over time, these small pieces accumulate and our knowledge about a particular topic is substantially increased, just like the puzzle analogy.

STIMULUS QUESTIONS

Initial Reflections on Possible Research Topics

The purpose of this exercise is to promote reflection on possible research topics. You might want to respond to these questions now, or spend several hours examining recent articles in some counseling journals and then consider these questions.

1. You have identified a few research topics of interest. Now list as many resources as possible in your environment to help you find relevant literature on each of these topics to expand your knowledge.

2. Who in particular could help you to learn more about these topics?

3. Consider your responses to the previous questions, and rank order the two to three topics that might be most appropriate to further examine.

4. Finally, spend a few days beginning to explore the top ranked topic, finding a few recent articles on this topic, talking to relevant peers and faculty to collect additional information about the topic, and seeing how you now evaluate this topic. Has your interest increased or decreased? Why?

6
Chapter

Choosing Research Designs: Balancing Ideals and Realities

The purpose of this chapter is to provide an overview of some of the issues for consideration related to what is commonly referred to as research design. We begin by defining research design as a tool or framework to guide us in our pursuit of scientific inquiry. Here we briefly introduce a key concept in research: drawing inferences or conclusions from our data. The data may be of both a quantitative and qualitative nature. Next we discuss problems with the commonly held "research design myth," or the conclusion that one design is, a priori, "better" than others.

The next section of this chapter introduces ways of classifying research designs. We discuss quantitative, qualitative, and mixed methods designs. We then present one classification system for quantitative research that emphasizes the balance between experimental control and generalizability of the research findings when choosing a design. Finally, we return to the question of choosing a design based upon a number of considerations. We believe that it is inappropriate to focus only on the merits of any specific design without considering other factors, especially the match between the prior research knowledge, one's resources, and the type of research questions being examined. We conclude with an overview of the flaws inherent in all research and advocate for methodological diversity in our research design.

SCIENTIFIC INQUIRY AND RESEARCH DESIGN

In Chapter 1 we identify the role of science as extending the profession's knowledge bases and theoretical underpinnings. We describe the scientific method as a source of knowledge used to establish credible knowledge bases through systematic and controlled inquiry. We extend this discussion in this chapter by introducing research design as a critical tool used to guide our science.

Traditionally, scholars have identified three components (the research trinity) that form the backbone of all research. Specifically, the research trinity consists of (a) design, (b) measurement, and (c) analysis. Design provides the conceptual framework from which a study is structured and executed. Trochim and Donnelly (2007) highlighted five critical components of research design: sample, conditions, method of assignment to groups or conditions, data collection, and timing of study procedures. Measurement includes identifying the variables of interest, operationally defining the variables so as to allow them to be measured within a sample, and collecting data that are used for analysis. Analysis involves the use of statistical tools to test hypotheses (in quantitative designs) or coding strategies to examine research questions (in qualitative designs) using the sample data. Measurement and analysis procedures are outlined more in depth in subsequent chapters, but we introduce them here in the context of their connection to research design.

Many authors (e.g., Tracey & Glidden-Tracey, 1999; Trochim & Land, 1982; Wampold, Davis, & Good, 1990) have suggested the need to extend the concept of the research trinity by including theory. Tracey and Glidden-Tracey proposed an iterative model of reasoned research that calls for researchers to consider the components of theory, design, measurement, and analysis as an integrated whole. Like others, these authors maintained that the elements mutually impact one another and are best considered as recursive and iterative. In other words, design, measurement, analysis, and theory each continuously connect with, and inform, one another. In this way, each component of the research process (i.e., design, measurement, analysis, and theory) mutually relate to, and have implications for, one another. Indeed, Tracey and Glidden-Tracey (1999) proposed that viewing and treating these four components of research as discrete represents a major problem within the counseling literature. As a whole, our science is improved when we consider the research process in this way as we make more informed and intentional decisions at each stage of the process.

THE RESEARCH DESIGN MYTH

The basic task of the scientist is to design research in such a way as to describe a phenomenon or identify relationships between constructs while ruling out as many plausible rival hypotheses or explanations as possible. The goal, put simply, is to more fully understand a phenomenon or construct, even though many sources of bias and confounding variables might distort that understanding. Research design is the tool that researchers use to frame a study and involves developing a plan or procedure to conduct the investigation. Different research designs have different strengths and weaknesses, and each will reduce different types of bias, distortion, or error. Sometimes bias is also referred to as error, error variance, or "noise." One of the most critical decisions in research, therefore, is selecting a design whose strengths and weaknesses help the researcher to examine specific research questions, and rule out as many plausible rival hypotheses or explanations as possible.

RESEARCH IN ACTION 6.1

Perhaps an analogy might help. Ever since human beings began harvesting grains, there has been a need to separate the grain itself (the wheat) from its protective shield (the chaff), a dry, coarse, inedible material. In a way, the chaff gets in the way of digesting the wheat. In a similar way, the researcher wants to isolate the constructs of interest to his or her research question (the wheat) and remove as much as possible of any other constructs (the chaff) that might contaminate, confound, bias, or distort the constructs of interest. Although the analogy of separating the wheat from the chaff is an oversimplification, it does highlight the essential task of the scientific method: isolating the constructs of interest and trying to draw useful conclusions about those constructs while at the same time ruling out rival hypotheses. How does the researcher separate the "wheat" from the "chaff"? The basic tool of the researcher is what we call research design.

It is, unfortunately, not uncommon for researchers to assume that a given design is "better" than others. For example, researchers in the past have examined questions like: Does counseling/therapy work? What is the best type of counseling? Which clients benefit the most from therapy? The common thread among these three questions, and many like them, is their assumption of what Kiesler (1966) labeled a uniformity myth. The uniformity myth states that we have oversimplified counseling to assume that psychotherapeutic treatments are a standard (uniform) set of techniques, applied in a consistent (uniform) manner, by a standard (uniform) therapist, to a homogeneous (uniform) group of clients. Kiesler believed that this myth greatly hampered progress in unraveling and understanding psychotherapy. Instead, he advocated for researchers to address a different question: What are the best types of treatments for particular types of clients across different settings?

The uniformity myth has undoubtedly hampered, and continues to hamper, research within counseling. We believe that counseling researchers often operate under an equally pervasive, often subtle, and hindering uniformity myth about research design. We have labeled this the "research design myth." The research design myth is the belief that one design is a priori "better" than others.

The research design myth leads students, and even more experienced researchers, to assume that there is one right or best type of research design, regardless of the type of research question they are examining. Instead, we encourage researchers to consider research design as a tool to help researchers examine specific research questions. Just as a carpenter has many different kinds of tools with unique functions (e.g.,hammers, pliers, and screwdrivers), different research designs have different functions. For example, if a carpenter wanted a large nail in an oak plank, a hammer would likely be a good tool to choose; but this does not mean that using a hammer every time the carpenter needed a tool would be a wise strategy—it would take a much longer time for the carpenter to remove a screw from the oak plank with a hammer. Similarly, it is an oversimplification to assume that there is one best type of research design. For example, it was not until relatively recently that psychotherapy researchers began to attend to the influence of therapists in their research on psychotherapy processes and outcomes. Instead, the growing body of research focused on treatment efficacy and ignored the influence of the psychotherapists on the outcomes. Scholars (e.g., Serlin, Wampold, & Levin, 2003; Wampold & Serlin, 2000) have highlighted the challenges associated with the failure to consider therapists as a relevant variable in research designs used to examine psychotherapy outcomes.

As we noted, research design is one of four major elements of the research process (i.e., design, measurement, analysis, and theory). Decisions about design must be made in conjunction with the consideration of the existing theoretical and empirical knowledge about the topic area, the proposed research method, and analysis. The intended aims of the study must also be at the forefront when selecting a design. We advise that researchers avoid asking, "What is the best research design?" and instead ask, "What is the best research design for this particular problem at this time?"

CLASSIFYING RESEARCH DESIGNS

Research designs and methods are constantly evolving, as will be discussed throughout this book. As we consider various categories of research designs, it is essential that we understand the strengths and weaknesses associated with each so as to select the design that is most appropriate to our research question. In this section, we provide a brief overview of some of the research design classifications used in the past and present.

Historically, several broad categorizations of research designs have been outlined. For example, in 1963, Campbell and Stanley discussed design according to the categories of preexperimental designs, experimental designs, and quasi-experimental designs. In 1980, Kazdin classified research designs as experimental, quasi-experimental, and correlational designs. Others commonly discuss research design according to whether the research utilizes qualitative, quantitative, or mixed methods designs.

Qualitative research (described in more detail in Chapter 16) relies upon a naturalistic and interpretive approach in order to understand the research question of interest. Research is exploratory in nature and relies upon the relationship between the researcher and the subject of exploration to illuminate meaning. According to Denzin and Lincoln (2011), qualitative researchers in the social sciences seek to understand "how social experience is created and given meaning" (Denzin & Lincoln, 2011, p. 8). Unlike quantitative designs, qualitative approaches aim to understand via interviews, observation, and artifacts (e.g., review of historical records, media, or client records) and typically produce rich descriptions of the data to make interpretations of meaning. Qualitative methodologies stress the process in which individuals create and give meanings to their social experience and lived realities.

In contrast, quantitative methodologies paint a broad picture of the relationship among the constructs assessed through generating and averaging nomothetic data over a relatively large number of participants. Quantitative research is most closely aligned with a postpositivist paradigm and seeks to test research hypotheses using the scientific method as discussed in Chapter 1. Quantitative designs typically rely upon "numbers data" rather than the "language data" used in qualitative designs. These numbers data are typically analyzed via a variety of statistical tests (as will be reviewed throughout this book), and then inferences are drawn from the sample to the population.

Mixed methods designs (described in further detail in Chapter 17) utilize elements from both qualitative and quantitative designs. Using qualitative and quantitative methods together in a single study provides multiple perspectives on the data that are collected and subsequently analyzed (Creswell, 1994). Some authors (e.g., Creswell, 1994; Greene, Caracelli, & Graham, 1989) have maintained that mixed methods designs offer advantages to increasing knowledge because they allow the researcher to assess convergence of results across the qualitative and quantitative methods and allow for a complementary and more in depth understanding of the phenomenon of interest.

The traditional view of science (particularly as borrowed from the physical sciences) assumes superiority for quantitative designs, and particularly for experimental laboratory designs. In particular, it suggests that the most rigorous, and therefore, the "best," knowledge is obtained from tightly controlled quantitative experimental research that uses randomization and control groups. According to this view, there is an implicit hierarchy of research designs: experimental designs are at the top, quasi-experimental and correlational designs are in the middle, and descriptive and qualitative designs are at the bottom of the hierarchy. We disagree with such assumptions, and maintain instead that the selection of the research design must fit both the phenomenon under investigation and the research question (e.g., Ford, 1984; Howard, 1982, 1984; Patton, 1984; Polkinghorne, 1984).

Researchers are encouraged to embark upon their study after considering the strengths and limitations of each research design, some of which are discussed in the next section. These considerations, along with careful reflection on the question, "What do I wish to be able to say?" (Tracey & Glidden-Tracey, 1999), should guide design selection.

EXPERIMENTAL CONTROL AND GENERALIZABILITY

Two major issues that have implications for selection of research design are experimental control and generalizability. We recognize that it is an oversimplification to conceptualize research design in terms of these two issues alone (see Chapter 6 for a more in-depth discussion), and that these two issues adhere most closely to a positivist and postpositivist paradigm as described in detail in Chapter 1. Yet, a basic understanding of these two issues offers a very basic framework from which to consider the basic strengths and limitations of various study designs.

Experimental Control

On one side of this trade-off the experimenter might use a particular research design to exercise as much experimental control as possible to ensure an accurate investigation of his or her research question. Experimental control allows researchers to make inferences about causal relationships between variables, which is referred to as the internal validity of the study (internal validity is discussed in greater depth in Chapter 7). Research studies that are high in experimental control typically use random selection of participants from the target population, random assignment of participants to groups, and manipulation of an independent variable or variables. An intended goal is to allow the researcher sufficient control so as to be able to make inferences about causality. Studies that are low in experimental control lack random assignment to treatments (as in the case of quasi-experimental studies) or manipulation of an independent variable (as in the case of correlational designs). In studies with low experimental control, researchers can make inferences about relationships but not about causality.

A scientist might choose to design a study to allow her or him to exercise as much experimental control as possible in an effort to make accurate causal inferences from the sample data to the population. Kerlinger (1986) described this process as the MAXMINCON principle. He observed that the researcher first tries to *maximize* the variance of the variable or variables pertaining to the research questions. Second, the researcher tries to *minimize* the error variance of random variables due to errors of measurement or individual differences of participants. Third, the experimenter tries to *control* the variance of extraneous or unwanted variables that might affect or bias the variables in question. Although the MAXMINCON principle applies most directly to traditional experimental research (between-group or within-group designs), the essence of Kerlinger's principle also applies to other research designs. Specifically, this principle stresses the importance of obtaining the most accurate or complete investigation of the research question by controlling the extraneous variance, minimizing error variance, and maximizing variance related to the primary variable(s).

Generalizability

At the same time, it is important to emphasize that counseling is first and foremost an applied specialty. It is therefore important to ascertain that the phenomenon one wishes to examine has some relevance to counseling. Whereas experimental control is a central ingredient of research design, a second key issue is generalizability of the results to applied settings, which is referred to as external validity. As such, a scientist may be most interested in research findings that have the greatest applicability to an applied or real-world setting. Research that is designed to emphasize generalizability, or external validity (discussed in more detail in Chapter 7), is grounded in a real-world setting. For example, a study may use participants from the population of interest in a naturally occurring form. For psychotherapy research, this could entail using actual clients seeing experienced therapists in an agency setting. For career counseling research, this could entail using actual students who are truly undecided about a major or career choice. Inferences from such studies would likely be more generalizable to actual psychotherapy or career counseling applications.

In an applied field such as counseling, full experimental control is often difficult, sometimes impossible, and often even unethical. For example, it may be impossible to minimize error, or "noise," that is due to individual differences across clients (e.g., clients who identify as African American may have different perceptions of working alliance with their White psychotherapist than clients who identify as White). There also may be ethical dilemmas associated with particular treatment interventions or experimental manipulations (as discussed in more detail in Chapter 21). One example of an ethical dilemma related to research design relates to the use of a wait-list control or psychological placebo group (e.g., a low empathy condition) in randomized clinical trials (RCTs). Specifically, there is potential for participants to be harmed when researchers convince them that their placebo treatment is actually a legitimate form of treatment. Similarly, there is potential for harm to participants who are assigned to wait-list control conditions, and who therefore have to wait (in some cases, for several months) before receiving treatment. In addition, the research context has the potential to become increasingly simplified and artificial with further steps toward maximizing control. Experimental control, therefore, presents obstacles for the applied researcher who is interested in research that involves the lives of real people who are struggling and need psychological assistance.

A CLASSIFICATION OF RESEARCH DESIGNS

Gelso (1979) used the concepts of external and internal validity to create a typology of research designs. He essentially proposed that we could organize counseling research along these two dimensions. First, research can be either high or low in control (internal validity). Second, research can be conducted in either a field or a laboratory setting (external validity). According to his matrix, there are four types of research designs: descriptive laboratory studies, descriptive field studies, experimental laboratory studies, and experimental field studies. Although we acknowledge that these categories are oversimplifications, we summarize each of the four that follow as a basic method by which to begin to consider the strengths and limitations of various research designs. Figure 6.1 depicts a slightly modified version of Gelso's (1979) two (high and low internal validity) by two (high and low external validity) matrix of research designs.

Descriptive Laboratory Studies

Descriptive laboratory studies are characterized by investigations that do not exercise experimental controls (such as randomization or manipulation of

FIGURE 6.1 Types of Research Designs Classified by Levels of External and Internal Validity

	Internal validity	
	High	Low
External validity — High	Experimental field	Descriptive field
External validity — Low	Experimental laboratory	Descriptive laboratory

independent variables) and that are conducted in a laboratory setting. A descriptive laboratory study is low in external validity because it uses a setting that in some ways can only simulate a real-life setting. For instance, a study of some aspect of the counseling process could use undergraduate students as clients and trainees as counselors. Such "counseling" may or may not be like that which takes place between real clients and experienced psychotherapists (see Chapter 12 for more details). In other words, there would certainly be questions about the extent of generalizability of findings from this type of study to actual psychotherapy.

A descriptive laboratory study is also low in internal validity because it lacks experimental control in the sense of manipulation of an independent variable and randomization of participants to conditions. Instead, it involves observation and description of events. For example, a researcher may want to determine the frequency and depth with which clients respond to therapist interventions. Rather than manipulating therapist responses, the researcher studies them in their natural occurrence.

Although both external and internal validity are low in this instance, this design offers two advantages. First, even though a researcher may not choose to manipulate some extraneous variables, a laboratory setting allows the researcher some control over these variables. This design may also allow data to be more easily collected, and when applied to psychotherapy research, may allow the researcher more freedom to explore research questions without worry of adversely affecting the therapeutic assistance that a client receives. Second, descriptive laboratory settings allow researchers to study some phenomenon that may otherwise be difficult to study in a field or real-life setting. The data collection procedures may be so extensive and/or intensive that the very presence of these procedures alters the process under examination to the extent that it is no longer natural or real.

Descriptive laboratory studies are utilized less frequently in today's literature. We review a historical example that utilized this design to highlight its strengths and limitations. Elliott's (1985) study of helpful and nonhelpful events in counseling interviews is a good example of a descriptive laboratory study. He had counselor trainees conduct an interview with a recruited client. After the interview, the client reviewed a videotape of the interview and rated each counselor statement on a nine-point helpfulness scale. Most and least helpful counselor statements from each counseling dyad were then given to judges who sorted the statements into categories. Cluster analysis was then used to put the statements into categories. In this manner, Elliott was able to develop a taxonomy of helpful and nonhelpful events in early counseling interviews.

This study is low in internal validity because no manipulation of counselor statements occurred. Rather, statements were classified as helpful or nonhelpful on the basis of an a posteriori (after the fact) rating of helpfulness. The study is low in external validity because counselor trainees and recruited clients served as the participants, and because the video-recall procedure probably altered aspects of the counseling. This study does, however, provide important information about the counseling process that certainly advances our understanding of an important concept—perceived helpfulness to clients of counselor statements.

Descriptive Field Studies

Descriptive field studies are investigations that do not exercise experimental control (randomization, manipulation of variables) and are conducted in a real-life setting. A descriptive field study is often high in external validity because a sample of participants can be taken directly from a population of interest. In psychotherapy research, for example, this could mean the study of real clients seeing actual therapists. A descriptive field study is low in internal validity because variables are studied as they occur naturally rather than being manipulated.

For a study to be truly high in external validity, the data-gathering procedures should not greatly alter routine procedures. The two most common examples of this type of study are retrospective studies that use data routinely collected (e.g., as part of an agency policy) and single-subject studies of individual counseling. A classic study representing descriptive field research is the Menninger project (Wallenstein, 1989), a very large study conducted over a 35-year period that examined the effectiveness of counseling (thus, an outcome study) with patients who received more than 1,000 hours of analysis. Client-therapist pairs were selected for this study only after counseling had formally ended. As Wallenstein stated, clients and therapists were totally unaware during treatment of which cases would be analyzed. In addition, the study used only data that were routinely collected during treatment. Because of the lack of experimental control in this study, a number of problems regarding internal validity are raised, such as threats from history and selection (terms that are explained more fully in Chapter 7). The real-life nature of this study makes it intriguing because it has high external validity and applicability, even though the findings are only suggestive at best.

A recent example of this type of design demonstrates some of the advantages and disadvantages of descriptive field studies. Minami and his colleagues (2009) used archival data collected at a university counseling center to examine treatment effectiveness. These authors analyzed archival data that included 6,099 client responses to the Outcome Questionnaire-45.2 (OQ-45, a self-report general psychological functioning inventory) over an 8-year period and compared treatment improvement of these patients to efficacy benchmarks derived from clinical trials with adults that used similar measures. Results demonstrated that the effects attained in the counseling center were similar to the treatment effects of the trials. Further, their findings indicated that certain characteristics of clients in their sample contributed to poorer outcomes. For example, clients who indicated problems with substance use and those who were separated or divorced had poorer outcomes than those who did not report substance use problems and those who were married or partnered. This study is high on external validity because of its large number of participants and reliance upon data that were collected in a real-life setting. At the same time, the data available for analysis in this study lacked some relevant information (e.g., diagnosis, use of psychotropic medication) that may have impacted the findings. Further, the study is low on internal validity, because no variables were manipulated. It is, therefore, not possible to make causal statements concerning the effects of therapist practices or client characteristics on therapeutic outcomes.

Experimental Laboratory Studies

Experimental laboratory studies are characterized by manipulation of independent variables and are conducted in a laboratory setting. An experimental laboratory study is low in external validity because it relies upon the researcher setting up a situation to resemble one that is naturally occurring rather than observing participants in real-life settings. This research is often high in internal validity because the experimenter can randomly assign participants to treatments and manipulate one or more independent variables. Because these studies are high in internal validity, the researcher can and does make inferences about causality based upon the results from the study. The extent to which these inferences about causality can be generalized to the populations and settings of interest is the critical question about experimental laboratory studies.

A study by Kim, Wollburg, and Roth (2012) typifies some of the advantages and limitations of experimental laboratory studies. The researchers were interested in examining the effectiveness of two opposing breathing therapies among a sample of individuals who met criteria for panic disorder. The authors designed their study to address a discrepancy that had emerged from theory and prior empirical research. On the one hand, some research had demonstrated support for teaching people to stop hyperventilating when they are anxious via raising levels of carbon dioxide. On the other hand, the false-suffocation alarm theory purports that the best treatment for individuals who are hyperventilating as a result of anxiety may be to lower levels of carbon dioxide. The study was conducted at an academic research clinic and researchers randomly assigned 74 patients who met DSM criteria for panic disorder to one of three groups (Breathing Therapy A, Breathing Therapy B, and a wait-list control group who received one of the two therapies after a delay) and measured outcome with ratings on the Panic Disorder Severity Scale. Results indicated that both breathing therapies effectively reduced panic disorder severity at one month and six months posttreatment. Because of the experimental controls used (e.g., the use of a control group, random assignment to groups), the authors could conclude with a high degree of certainty that the two breathing therapies affected severity of panic symptoms. The study, therefore, has a high degree of internal validity. The study is low in external validity given its restrictions in participant selection. Specifically, out of 369 people who expressed interest in the study, only 74 met study inclusion criteria (i.e., participants had to be willing to accept the possibility of an 8-week treatment delay if assigned to the wait-list condition, participants with a history of a variety of other mental health diagnoses or symptoms were excluded from participation, and participants who reported suicidality were excluded). These experimental controls limited the ability to conclude, based upon this study, whether their results would generalize to individuals outside of these restrictions.

Experimental Field Studies

Experimental field studies are investigations that manipulate independent variables and are conducted in a real-life setting. An experimental field study attempts to examine causality through random assignment of treatments and control of independent variables. Such experimental control moves the study away from the examination of naturally occurring real-life settings, yielding moderate external validity, at best. The researcher can never exercise the same control in the field as in the laboratory, yielding moderate internal validity, at best. An experimental field study, therefore, provides an opportunity to include the best combination of inferences about cause and generalizability that is attainable within a single study. At the same time, an experimental field study can obtain neither the same level of certainty about causality as is possible in an experimental laboratory study nor the same level of certainty about generalizability as in a descriptive field study.

Addis and his colleagues (2004) provide an example of an experimental field study. These authors randomly assigned clients who presented for treatment via a managed care company to one of two treatment conditions. Specifically, 80 clients who identified panic disorder as the primary reason for seeking treatment were assigned to either a therapist who had recently been trained in a manual-based empirically supported treatment or to a therapist conducting treatment as usual. Clients in both conditions changed significantly from pretreatment to posttreatment as measured by scores on a variety of mental health inventories and ratings on a structured interview conducted by a trained therapist. Results also demonstrated that clients in the panic control therapy condition (i.e., the manualized treatment) improved slightly more than clients in the treatment as usual condition on the outcomes of interest. External validity was emphasized by using actual clients who were seeking treatment via their managed care company and experienced therapists. Threats to external validity existed because of the use of pretreatment assessments and possible reactions to experimental procedures (tape recordings).Internal validity was emphasized by random assignment of clients to treatment conditions. This study is a good example of the sacrifices that researchers must often make in external and internal validity considerations in order to conduct an experimental field study. Researchers wanting to do experimental field studies should read Chapter 11 describing between-groups and within-subjects designs, and Chapter 12 on quasi-experimental designs.

ON CHOOSING A RESEARCH DESIGN

We now return to the question of choosing the best research design. There is no a priori best design for research within the counseling profession as a whole. *At any particular time in the history of a topic area there may be more or less useful ways to approach a specific research question.*

We propose that the usefulness of a particular research design for examining a specific research question is a function of five factors. First, the researcher should review the existing knowledge bases pertaining to the specific research question. Second, the researcher should consider the types of research designs used in prior research and the inferences made to develop the existing knowledge bases. Third, the researcher should consider the available resources. Fourth, specific threats to the validity of particular designs should be evaluated. Finally, the first four factors should be considered in combination to assess the match or fit between previous research knowledge (Factors 1 and 2), the design being considered (Factor 4), and one's resources (Factor 3).

Factor 1: Existing Knowledge Pertaining to the Specific Research Question

Research on a particular question is conducted within an existing body of empirical and theoretical knowledge. It is, therefore, imperative for the researcher to ascertain what the existing literature suggests about a particular topic area and to identify the questions that remain unanswered. As a researcher formulates a particular research question, it is important to ask what kind of knowledge will add to the existing literature. At the same time, the researcher must determine the type of research design that will provide the knowledge that is needed in order to answer the research question.

For example, a qualitative study might add the most useful knowledge or basic understanding about a topic that has received minimal attention in the literature. Qualitative research can be particularly useful when we are investigating new topics about which we know very little (e.g., people's reactions to Ebola or the experience of quarantine in response to Ebola outbreak). They can also be useful when we want to examine a particular facet related to a larger topic about which we have more extensive knowledge. For example, within the vast body of psychotherapy literature (literally thousands of studies), we may know little about specific identity factors (e.g., understanding client or therapist experience of social class in the psychotherapy context; Thompson, Cole, & Nitzarim, 2012; Thompson et al., 2015). Research that addresses these questions adds to the already vast psychotherapy literature by understanding specific experiences (e.g., social class) as related to the therapy process. Another example of a way in which qualitative designs could contribute to this vast psychotherapy knowledge is through research designed to understand the specific factors that contribute to successful client outcomes. In other words, although there is a large body of scientific literature that has established evidence for specific treatments, we know little about the particular facets of a treatment that are responsible for contributing to positive outcomes. Wampold and Imel (2015), therefore, suggested that qualitative inquiries designed to dismantle a particular treatment that is known to work may be an important next step in adding to our knowledge of what actually contributes to positive therapeutic outcome for specific clients in particular psychotherapy contexts.

In short, the utility of a research design, therefore, needs to be evaluated by the researcher in the context of existing research knowledge in a given area as relevant to the question about which we want more information. Specifically, we suggest considering the following questions to guide your selection of research question and design:

Research Application: Potential Contributions of Your Research

"Big Questions" to Consider When Choosing a Research Design	Potential Contributions of Your Research
What is the most important thing yet to be known about this area?	
What is intriguing?	
What would be clinically useful to psychotherapists and clients?	
What knowledge would have the potential to positively impact the lives of individuals?	
What do I wish to be able to say?	

Factor 2: Inferences Made to Develop Existing Knowledge Base via Research Design

Researchers must consider the inferences drawn to develop the existing knowledge base when choosing a research design. Because the type of design used affects the types of inferences that can be made in developing and extending a knowledge base, researchers should carefully consider their intentions when designing a study. For example, if a particular topic has been predominantly researched in laboratory settings, then research focused on field settings may add useful knowledge to address questions about external validity (see, e.g., Heppner & Claiborn, 1989). Or, if a topic has been investigated extensively through tightly controlled experimental studies, then descriptive studies that investigate the experience of the phenomenon among individuals representing specific identities might now add useful information.

The overreliance upon a specific design in a given topic area can produce an unbalanced and weak knowledge base. For example, the reliance upon randomized clinical trials in the psychotherapy literature has told us very little about how psychotherapy actually works. As such, researchers are encouraged to choose a design that will allow the research to contribute to knowledge generation and extension.

To assist novice researchers in this process, we recommend that researchers carefully read the method sections of the existing articles on their topic and make a note of the research design used in each study. It will quickly become apparent which designs have been used, and perhaps overused, within a particular topic area.

Factor 3: Resources and Costs Associated with Research Designs

Practical considerations also impact selection of a particular design. Specifically, different designs require different resources and have distinctive associated costs. Every study requires particular costs (e.g., financial, time, physical lab or clinic space in which to conduct the study, technology) and expertise (e.g., familiarity with software and/ or computer programming needed to collect data, data analysis, intervention skills).

For example, a researcher who has decided that a descriptive field study is needed to examine the relationship between counselor techniques and clients' perception of the working alliance must decide whether to utilize a correlational design, an intensive single-subject design, or a grounded theory investigation of clients' perceptions of the working alliance. This researcher may choose among these design options after examining available resources. We offer a few examples and general time estimates: please note that all estimates are simply offered as a general guide and actual time required for each step will vary greatly by factors such as geographic region, access to recruitment sites, particular recruitment criteria, and the size of the research team. For example, a correlational study would require the researcher to sample 30 to 50 client-counselor dyads. It may take a great deal of work to find these dyads (e.g., 3–5 months), but the data analyses may be fairly quick and painless (e.g., less than 3 weeks). An intensive single-subject study design might require finding a single dyad (which may be relatively easy, perhaps one month), but would require a rather involved, intensive process of analyzing the data (e.g., perhaps several months). A grounded theory investigation would require the recruitment of 10–15 dyads to participate in one or more interviews with the researcher (perhaps 1–3 months), and would require an intensive data analysis process (e.g., perhaps several months of weekly meetings with a research team). As such, researchers must consider practical resources and costs associated with choosing a design that is feasible and allows the researcher to address the question of interest.

Factor 4: Threats to the Validity of a Specific Design

Choosing a research design also requires the researcher to acknowledge the limitations, or threats, inherent in each design, and the impact of those limitations on the conclusions that can be drawn from the study. Specific threats to validity are discussed in considerable depth in Chapter 7. We introduce the concept here as relevant to selection of research design.

As is likely obvious by now, every research design has its strengths and weaknesses and there is no perfect design. Gelso (1979) described this using the image of the bubble hypothesis, or the notion that all research will be flawed in some way. In describing the bubble hypothesis, he suggested that doing research is akin to trying to apply a sticker to a car windshield. When an air bubble forms between the sticker and the windshield, the owner presses it in an attempt to eliminate the bubble. Yet, no matter how hard the owner tries, the bubble reappears elsewhere. The only way to get rid of the bubble is to throw the sticker away, but then the owner is left without a sticker. In a similar manner, all research and every research design is flawed or has a weakness someplace (has a bubble). The different research designs will have different limitations and strengths (the different designs may change the location of the bubble), but no single design can entirely eliminate the bubble. The researcher can either stop doing research (throw the sticker away) or be cognizant of the size and location of the bubble. Reason (1998) advocated for researchers to persist in the face of the varieties of threats to our research. He stated,

> In human inquiry it is better to be approximately right than precisely wrong. It is also better to initiate and conduct inquiry into important questions of human conduct with a degree of acknowledged bias and imprecision, than to bog the whole thing down in attempts to be prematurely 'correct' or 'accurate'. (p. 229)

The bubble hypothesis clearly points out that if only one type of research design is advocated by a discipline, then the body of research will contain similar flaws or threats in each study. On the other hand, if multiple research designs are advocated, each with different threats, then the cumulative effect will be a clearer, more accurate picture of the topic under examination. Viewed in this manner, the usefulness of a particular design at a particular time is determined by the locations of the threats in the studies that have previously addressed the question of interest. As such, all types of research designs are determined to be valuable. Knowledge can be advanced when the same problem is examined using multiple design strategies, or via paradigmatic diversity (discussed in more detail as follows).

We suggest that beginning researchers use the following table when reviewing the existing literature and selecting a research design. As you are finding and reading research related to your intended topic, we recommend that you record the following pieces of information for each study that you review.

Research Application: Reviewing Literature Relevant to Your Study

Published Literature Related to Topic (Citation)	Type of Design Used	Strengths and Limitations of Inferences of This Research Based upon Design	Potential Ways to Extend the Existing Research in My Study
Citation 1			
Citation 2			
Citation 3			
...			

Factor 5: Match or Fit among Factors 1–4

It is important that researchers weigh Factors 1–4 when selecting a design for a particular study. Because each of the four factors mutually influence one another, it is essential to consider them in combination. For example, a researcher should become familiar with the literature related to the topic in order to understand the existing knowledge, as well as to understand potential ways in which to extend the knowledge (Factor 1). The researcher will simultaneously determine the types of inferences that may be drawn from the research (Factor 2). The researcher will then consider the potential designs based upon Factors 1 and 2 in terms of their associated costs and the threats that will be associated with each design. Ultimately, weighing each of these factors and their interactions should inform the final selection of the design.

At this point, we suggest that novice researchers use the information gathered in their review of the literature using the previous table to guide their assessment of the advantages and disadvantages to using a particular design in a given area. Specifically, at this stage, it would be important to identify the purpose of your intended study and to identify the specific research questions (for qualitative study designs) or research hypotheses (for quantitative study designs) that will add exciting new knowledge to the topic. As you consider potential designs that will allow you to address the topic of interest to you, you must also keep in mind practical considerations due to budget, time, and other resources, as well as the potential limitations to your identified study. It may be useful to track your selection process using the following matrix.

Research Application: Practical Considerations and Limitations Related to Your Study

Intended Study Purpose	Potential Research Question (for Qualitative Designs) or Research Hypotheses (for Quantitative Designs)	Potential Study Design	Potential Limitations to Internal Validity and External Validity	Practical Limitations of Design (e.g., Financial, Time, Energy, Other Resources)
Study Idea 1				
Study Idea 2				
Study Idea 3				
Study Idea ...				

THE IMPORTANCE OF METHODOLOGICAL DIVERSITY

For several decades, there has been a growing consensus within (and outside) the field of counseling that the discipline is strengthened when a wide array of designs are utilized. Not surprisingly, several authors (e.g., Creswell, 1994; Goldman, 1982; Hanson et al., 2005; Harmon, 1982; Haverkamp, Morrow, & Ponterotto, 2005; Hoshmand, 1989; Howard, 1982, 1983, 1984; Polkinghorne, 1984; Ponterotto, 2005; Tashakkori & Teddlie, 2003) have advocated for methodological diversity. We strongly agree that greater creativity and flexibility in using research designs is needed in order to examine research questions.

The use of multiple methods is essential for important advances in the counseling literature. This may allow the discipline to grow in its ability to address research questions and topics that have relevance to actual work with clients and to social issues. Indeed, the American Psychological Association's (2003) Guidelines on Multicultural Education, Training, Research, Practice, and Organizational Change for Psychologists highlighted the need for researchers to rely upon multiple methods when conducting multicultural research. They stated,

> Culturally centered psychological researchers are encouraged to seek appropriate grounding in various modes of inquiry and to understand both the strengths and limitations of the research paradigms applied to culturally diverse populations. . . . They should strive to recognize and incorporate research methods that most effectively complement

the worldview and lifestyles of persons who come from a specific cultural and linguistic population, for example quantitative and qualitative research strategies. (p. 389)

In any discussion that involves advocating the use of multiple research designs in order to address the flaws inherent in each study, it is essential to be cautious about the potential for conducting poor research. There is poorly designed and conducted research of all kinds in the literature and so any movement toward methodological diversity should also include an emphasis on research that is sound. Although there is no such thing as a perfect study, we hope that through learning the core concepts covered throughout this book, you will be well-prepared to contribute to the advancement of research in our field.

Programmatic research on particular topics is useful to extend our knowledge base. Put another way, a series of investigations, conducted by the same or different researchers, that successively extends our knowledge bases on a particular topic is highly desirable for the profession. As we have discussed, there is no perfect design and each research study will have its flaws. Through programmatic research on a topic, hopefully the flaws in one study will be addressed by another study even though that study will also have its flaws. In this way, a series of related investigations that build on each other tends to accumulate more useful knowledge bases than does a series of isolated investigations.

A good example of programmatic research is evident within the psychotherapy literature. Over time, researchers have utilized a variety of designs to address questions about what works in psychotherapy. Specifically, the use of randomized clinical trials grew in popularity, primarily in an effort to establish the efficacy of treatment. Over time, this body of research has permitted researchers to utilize meta-analytic methods in order to compare treatment effects across studies (e.g., Bell, Marcus, & Goodlad, 2013; Cuijpers et al., 2012; Del Re, Flückiger, Horvath, Symonds, & Wampold, 2012; Shimokawa, Lambert, & Smart, 2010). Correlational designs also continue to be utilized in order to understand the relationships among constructs relevant to psychotherapy processes and outcomes (e.g., the association of the therapeutic alliance with outcomes, Friedlander, Escudero, Heatherington, & Diamond, 2011; Horvath, Del Re, Flückiger, & Symonds, 2011; Shirk, Karver, & Brown, 2011). In addition, researchers (e.g., Ladany, Hill, Thompson, & O'Brien, 2004) have utilized qualitative designs in order to understand, for example, therapists' use of silence as related to the therapeutic alliance. More recently, researchers (e.g., Flückiger, Del Re, Wampold, Symonds, & Horvath, 2012) have added to the knowledge by using multilevel modeling designs in order to examine potential moderators of the relationships between alliance and outcomes. In some instances, the reliance upon programmatic research utilizing multiple methods has contributed to the *convergence of knowledge* regarding a specific finding. At the same time, new knowledge has corrected issues raised about old studies (for a more complete discussion, see Wampold & Imel, 2015).

SUMMARY AND CONCLUSIONS

In this chapter we have extended our discussion of science and the scientific method to basic research design considerations. We have maintained that the basic task of the experimenter is to design research in such a way as to simultaneously identify relationships between constructs as well as eliminate as many threats as possible. Kerlinger (1986) has labeled this the MAXMINCON principle. Research design involves developing both a plan and a structure for an investigation and provides a framework from which the researcher can execute the study that simultaneously reduces certain kinds of error and helps the researcher obtain empirical evidence (data) about variables of interest.

We discussed two issues related to research design, experimental control and generalizability, and highlighted four factors that researchers are encouraged to consider when choosing different types of research designs. We argue that internal and external validity are not independent and that they are not incompatible, especially across multiple investigations. We need programmatic research that is designed to maximize the benefits of both internal and external validity across investigations. Moreover, within such an investigative blend there is a useful place for laboratory research in extending theoretical issues. As Stone (1984) has argued, "a preoccupation with immediate application can lead us to dismiss important research" (p. 108) that extends our theoretical understanding. In essence, we are underscoring the need for balance in our research; we suggest that investigative styles that disregard certain types of research (e.g., naturalistic research) are dangerous because they reduce the possibility of gaining certain types of knowledge.

We have also suggested that the goodness of a particular design hinges not only on the threats to validity it allows, but also on the context provided by previous research and existing knowledge bases. In addition to evaluating the threats to validity for a particular study, the researcher needs to consider the existing research content, the type of research designs used in creating the existing knowledge bases on the topic, and the resources currently available for study. The researcher must choose a research design with strengths and weaknesses that match the needs of the research question, and a design that will provide the type of knowledge needed at this particular time in history. In this way, a series of research studies, each with different strengths and weaknesses, may add the greatest breadth to our knowledge bases. We strongly encourage using programmatic research that emphasizes paradigmatic diversity to build broad knowledge bases for the counseling profession.

STIMULUS QUESTIONS

Following is an exercise that is designed to help students to apply some of the material from this chapter to further explore the advantages and disadvantages of different types of research designs.

Utilizing Different Types of Research Designs to Investigate Your Topic of Interest

Sometimes researchers study a topic by utilizing the same type of research designs over and over. (See Chapter 14 for the consequences of overutilizing analogue methodologies.) It is often useful to initially consider a wide range of research designs when developing a study to determine what type of study you want to do. The purpose of this exercise is to practice conceptualizing studies with different types of research designs on a topic of interest to you.

1. In your topical area of interest, conceptualize a study that utilizes a descriptive laboratory design.
   a. What would be the intended purpose of this study?
   b. Describe the methods you would utilize to conduct the study.
   c. Would this study be high or low on experimental control and external validity?

d. What outcomes would you predict would be found from the study?

e. What are the advantages or limitations of the design on the conclusions you could draw from the study?

2. In your topical area of interest, conceptualize a study that utilizes a descriptive field design.

   a. What would be the intended purpose of this study?

   b. Describe the methods you would utilize to conduct the study.

   c. Would this study be high or low on experimental control and external validity?

   d. What outcomes would you predict would be found from the study?

   e. What are the advantages or limitations of the design on the conclusions you could draw from the study?

3. In your topical area of interest, conceptualize a study that utilizes an experimental laboratory design.

   a. What would be the intended purpose of this study?

b. Describe the methods you would utilize to conduct the study.

c. Would this study be high or low on experimental control and external validity?

d. What outcomes would you predict would be found from the study?

e. What are the advantages or limitations of the design on the conclusions you could draw from the study?

4. In your topical area of interest, conceptualize a study that utilizes an experimental field design.

   a. What would be the intended purpose of this study?

   b. Describe the methods you would utilize to conduct the study.

   c. Would this study be high or low on experimental control and external validity?

   d. What outcomes would you predict would be found from the study?

   e. What are the advantages or limitations of the design on the conclusions you could draw from the study?

Validity Issues in Research: The Heart of It All

To draw valid conclusions about research questions, the researcher must design a study that minimizes the potential to generate alternative explanations for the study's results. Whereas we discuss the trade-off between internal and external validity in Chapter 6, this chapter provides a more detailed analysis of four major inferences made by researchers in evaluating the validity of a particular research design. Specifically, the purpose of this chapter is to define and discuss threats to (a) statistical conclusion validity (i.e., degree to which the researcher has come to the correct conclusions through statistical analyses), (b) internal validity (i.e., degree of certainty with which one can conclude causal relationships), (c) construct validity (i.e., degree a chosen variable captures the hypothetical construct), and (d) external validity (i.e., degree the relationship can be generalized).

FOUR TYPES OF VALIDITY AND THE THREATS TO EACH

Chapter 5 presents an overview of the research process. Based on theory, clinical practice, or observation, the researcher first states one or a set of research hypotheses. Recall that a research hypothesis is a conjecture about the relationship between or among constructs. The next step is to operationalize the constructs so that they can be measured. In a true experimental design, the independent variable is manipulated by the researcher to assess the effect of the manipulation on a dependent variable. Statistical methods are often (although certainly not always) used to help the researcher decide whether the manipulation had the hypothesized effect.

RESEARCH APPLICATION 7.1

As an illustration, consider the following example. Suppose that a researcher suspects that cognitive treatments of social anxiety have had only limited success because the interventions do not generalize to behavioral situations. The researcher hypothesizes that in vivo behavioral exercises added to cognitive therapy will improve the efficacy of the therapy. In vivo behavioral exercises are operationalized carefully by designing homework that involves a progressive set of situations in which clients first smile at a stranger, later engage strangers in a short conversation, and finally arrange a social encounter. Social anxiety is operationalized by having the participants report on the (fictitious) ABC Anxiety Test the level of anxiety that they experienced after talking with a stranger that the researcher arranged for them to meet (called a confederate). The independent variable is manipulated by randomly assigning the participants to one of two conditions: cognitive therapy alone or cognitive therapy plus behavioral exercises. Further, suppose that 40 participants are randomly chosen from people who (a) answered an advertisement for a program to treat social anxiety; and (b) were assessed by the researcher in a clinical interview to be socially anxious. After the 10-week program, anxiety was assessed using the confederate and the ABC Anxiety Test; a statistical test indicates that there was a reliable difference between the groups in the hypothesized direction. That is, the mean level of anxiety, as indicated on the ABC Anxiety Test, is lower for the group that received the exercises, and this difference has a low probability of occurring by chance.

Pleased with these results, the researcher concludes that (a) a true relation exists between the independent variable and the dependent variable (i.e., participants who receive in vivo exercises in addition to cognitive therapy have reliably lower scores on the ABC Anxiety Test than participants who receive cognitive therapy only), (b) the manipulation of the independent variable was indeed the cause of the difference in scores (i.e., the exercises were the cause of the lower anxiety scores), (c) in vivo behavioral exercises increase the effectiveness of the cognitive treatment of social anxiety, and (d) the results are applicable to socially anxious participants generally (and not just to the participants in this particular study). These conclusions, or more specifically the inferences, seem reasonable in this case; however, there are always flaws in any research, and it is appropriate to keep in mind that one or more of these inferences may be incorrect. Take a few minutes and think of alternative explanations for the lower anxiety scores of the group that received in vivo behavioral exercises in addition to cognitive therapy.

The degree to which inferences reflect how things actually are is referred to as validity. If in vivo exercises in fact reduce anxiety, then the inferences made by the researcher in our example are valid. The purpose of this section is to discuss the principles of validity so that researchers and consumers of counseling research can evaluate the probable validity of the inferences made in a particular study. There are several considerations to keep in mind when reviewing threats to validity.

The first issue is that the conceptual specifics of validity and threats to validity are not concretely fixed as innate properties of research. These concepts are deeply embedded in the philosophy of science and have evolved over time as philosophers ponder what it means to conduct research and make inferences about their findings. Thus, it is not the categories of validities per say, or their descriptions that are important. Rather, what is important is that an understanding of threats to validity will lead to research that yields conclusions that have a reasonable probability of being correct, and that decisions made using those conclusions will result in clinical activities and policies that ultimately benefit people. Although there are many ways to look at the validity of research, the framework presented by Shadish, Cook, and Campbell (2002) represents the current state of this evolution. Shadish et al. have created a taxonomy that classifies validity into four types: statistical conclusion validity, internal validity, construct validity, and external validity. This typology was derived from Campbell and Stanley's (1963) original conception of internal and external validity, and further refined by Cook and Campbell (1979). Other discussions of validity are presented by Bracht and Glass (1968), Reichardt (2011), and Wampold, Davis, and Good (1990).

A second issue is that no study will be able to rule out every threat to the validity of the conclusions reached. A study for which the threats to validity are not severe enough to discredit the conclusions completely will remain useful scientifically because the conclusions reached can be tentatively accepted. Additional studies should be designed to rule out the threats that plagued the original study. Through the accumulation of studies, threats to a conclusion can be ruled out and a strong statement can be made. For example, no single study of smoking and health has unequivocally established a causal relationship between smoking and disease; however, the accumulation of many studies (and there have been thousands) rules out, with near absolute certainty, any threats to this conclusion. (At one time, the Tobacco Institute claimed that no *one* study had ever scientifically established an unequivocal causal relationship between smoking and disease—in isolation, this is a true statement, but it ignores the accumulation of evidence.)

A third issue is that, more or less, most threats discussed here are *possibly* present in any study. However, more important is the determination of the *plausibility* of a threat in a particular study and its *implication* for the conclusion. Thus, the validity of a conclusion is suspect if a threat is plausible and the threat created conditions that could have produced the evidence supporting the conclusion. However, some threats, although logically possible, are not plausible. Suppose that a treatment is found to be effective in reducing depression related to career-ending knee injuries to athletes, and the conclusion is made that the treatment is useful for the treatment of career-ending orthopedic injuries. Technically, the experiment did not include participants with nonknee orthopedic injuries, but there is little reason to believe that depression or its treatment would differ for patients with knee injuries versus those with shoulder injuries. So although a threat exists, the plausibility that it renders the conclusion invalid is low.

A fourth issue is that there are often trade-offs to be made in the design and implementation of research. Designs that increase the certainty of both causal inferences (internal validity) and statistical conclusion validity may decrease the certainty of generalizing inferences from samples to populations (external validity) or the meaning of the operations (construct validity). Likewise, designs that increase the certainty of inferences from samples to populations or about constructs may do so at the expense of decreasing the certainty of inferences about the extent of relationships or causality. The point is that there may be trade-offs with different types of research designs, not only with regard to these four types of inferences, but also with respect to other factors. As mentioned in Chapter 6, Gelso (1979) used the metaphor of trying to eliminate a bubble underneath a sticker to describe these trade-offs—removing the bubble in one place creates a new bubble somewhere else. Nevertheless, a bubble that casts grave doubts on the conclusions made from a study cannot be discounted simply because the presence of bubbles is inevitable.

A final issue is that considerations of validity are important for those who design and conduct research as well as those who consume research. A researcher who designs a study should consider each of the possible threats prior to conducting the study, and even to determine whether to undertake the study. The design of a study should be modified to reduce threats to validity, and sometimes various ancillary aspects can be incorporated to address various threats—such aspects are discussed throughout this book. Of course, there are no guarantees that the study will produce valid conclusions, because despite the researcher's best efforts unexpected events occur. Furthermore, publication or dissemination of results does not ensure that conclusions are valid, and consumers of research should examine threats independently. For example, generally accepted conclusions that interventions are effective sometimes are incorrect, as has been the case with D.A.R.E. (Drug Abuse Resistance Education, a program of classroom lessons delivered by police officers) to reduce drug use (e.g., Thombs, 2000).

Overview of the Types of Validity

We will approach Shadish et al.'s (2002) four categories by examining the four major inferences made by the researcher in the anxiety example (see Research Application 7.1). Recall that the first question was whether there was a relationship between the in vivo exercises used in this study and scores on the ABC Anxiety Test. In our example, there was a statistically significant relationship between the independent and dependent variables. Often, one of the major inferences made in interpreting research concerns the existence of a relationship between (or among) the variables in the study. The researcher may conclude that there is a relationship or that there is no relationship. *Statistical conclusion validity* **refers to the degree to which the researcher has come to the correct conclusion about this relationship.**

The second major inference to be made in interpreting research is an answer to the following question: Given that there is a relationship between the variables, is it a causal relationship? In our anxiety example, the researcher concluded that the statistically significant difference between the anxiety levels for the two groups was due to (i.e., caused by) the addition of the exercises. *Internal validity* **refers to the degree of certainty with which one can make statements about the existence of a causal relationship between variables.**

It is important that the variables chosen represent and capture the essence of the hypothetical construct. If the operationalizations of the constructs of a study were adequate, then the causality attributed to the independent and dependent variables justifies statements about the causality of the constructs used in the research hypotheses. If the construct were not measured adequately, a confounding problem might exist. Thus, *construct validity* **refers to the degree to which the measured variables used in the study represent the hypothesized constructs.**

To be of any value to researchers and practitioners, the causal relationship between the hypothesized constructs must be generalizable to units (typically persons, but not always), treatments, outcomes, and settings other than those in the particular study. In the context of our fictitious example, to what extent can we generalize the use of in vivo behavioral exercises to other socially anxious people? *External validity* refers to the degree to which the causal relationship is generalizable across units, treatments, outcomes, and settings.

Threats to Statistical Conclusion Validity

In this section we define statistical conclusion validity and delineate nine threats to this type of validity. First, however, we need to examine the role of statistics in counseling research. Although most students study statistics outside the context of design, it is necessary to realize that statistical analysis is just one of many parts of the research process. Typically, a statistical test is used to examine whether there is indeed a relation between the variables in a study. In the anxiety example, most likely a two-group independent *t* test would be performed.

Traditionally, statistical tests are employed to test two competing hypotheses: the null hypothesis and an alternative hypothesis. Usually, the *null hypothesis* predicts that there is no relationship between the variables in the study. The *alternative hypothesis* states that there is some true relationship between the variables (which is typically the relationship that the authors have reason to believe might exist). In the anxiety example, the null hypothesis would be that the mean scores on the ABC Anxiety Test for those who receive in vivo exercises would be equal to the mean scores for those who do not receive the exercises. The alternative hypothesis would be that the mean anxiety scores for those who receive the in vivo exercises would be lower than for those who do not receive this treatment. Rejection of the null hypothesis and acceptance of the alternative hypothesis lend credence to the hypothesis that in vivo exercises add to the efficacy of cognitive therapy.

Statistical tests, which are based in probability theory, are used to indicate whether one should reject the null hypothesis that there is no relationship or accept the alternative that there is a relationship. A statistically significant *t* test in the anxiety example (say with the *p* value set at $p < .05$) would indicate that one could comfortably believe that a true relationship exists between the independent and dependent variables. However, it is possible that this conclusion is in error; that is, the null hypothesis of no relationship may be true, even though a statistically significant result was obtained due to sampling error. The significance level of 0.05 indicates that the chances of incorrectly concluding that a true relationship exists are fewer than 5 in 100. **Incorrectly concluding that a true relationship exists is called a *Type I error*** (rejecting the null hypothesis when in reality it should be accepted). Type I errors are particularly troublesome because they result in claims that something is going on when it is not; for example, a Type I error in the anxiety study would perpetuate the belief that in vivo exercises were helpful when in reality they were not.

Another type of error can be made by incorrectly concluding that no relationship exists. Suppose the *t* test in the anxiety example was not statistically significant;

in this case, the researcher could not conclude that the independent variable was related to the dependent variable. Nevertheless, there might have been a true relationship between these two variables even though for any of a variety of reasons the researcher did not find it. **Incorrectly concluding that there is no relationship is called a *Type II error*** (failing to reject the null hypothesis when in reality it should be rejected). One of the major reasons for Type II errors is that variability in the participants' responses tends to obscure true relationships. This variability, often called *error variance,* can be thought of as static on a radio receiver that obscures the true signal. Even if the true signal is strong, an electrical storm can generate sufficient static that one cannot hear a favorite program. Conditions that create error variance lead to threats to statistical conclusion validity.

It is important to note that there is a trade-off between avoiding Type I and Type II errors. In Table 7.1, we illustrate how these two types of errors are related and their relationship with power (correctly concluding that a true relationship exists). In addition, we will use weighing scales as a metaphoric example to illustrate the trade-off and how to decide which error to emphasize. Scales, like bathroom scales, are not perfect and most likely will include some minor error. Oftentimes such scales have adjustment functions. Imagine that we want to ship boxes filled with materials to another country, and our goal is to pack as much as possible into each box without exceeding 20 pounds (which often results in extra charges). Our scale will likely have error as well as the scale at the local post office. Thus, we need to take into account that our scale and the one at the distribution center both could yield different results because of measurement errors. As a strategy to avoid such extra charges due to measurement error, we could set our scale to be a little conservative than the actual weight. Conversely, if we wanted to pack as much as possible in each box without much concern of being occasionally overweight, we could to set our scale to lean more towards the other direction. These two weighing strategies parallel how a researcher may weigh the costs and benefits of Type I and Type II errors. Type I and Type II errors have an inverse relationship: the more stringent the threshold for Type I error is set to be, the more lenient Type II error is. Thus, a researcher needs to decide whether it is more important to avoid falsely concluding an effect when in fact it does not exist (Type I error) or to avoid failing to detect the effect when it does exist (Type II error).

TABLE 7.1   Type I and Type II Errors

		In Reality	
		Null (H_0) Is True	**Null (H_0) Is False**
Conclusion	Reject H_0 [claim effect]	Type I error (α) [false positive]	Correct (power) [true positive]
	Accept H_0 [claim no effect]	Correct [true negative]	Type II error (β) [false negative]

TABLE 7.2 : Threats to Statistical Validity

Threats	Example of Threat	Ways to Minimize Threats
Low power	Insufficient sample size to detect true effect	Conduct power analysis to determine adequate sample size
Assumption violation	Ignoring the dependence among clients seeing the same therapist in a study	Examine and ensure assumptions of statistical tests are met
Fishing and error-rate issues	Conducting many statistical tests on a data set without specific hypotheses	Specify hypotheses for statistical tests or adjust significance level for multiple tests
Unreliable measures	Low internal consistency of a scale	Use scales with adequate reliability estimates established with similar populations of study sample
Range restriction	Measures with ceiling effects or floor effects	Use appropriate measures for the population of interest
Unreliable treatment implementation	Variations in how treatment is implemented	Standardization of treatment implementation
Extraneous variance in setting	Participants completing treatment assignment in different settings	Account and adjust for various factors that may influence outcome
Heterogeneity of units	Different attractiveness levels in a heterogeneous sample	Use statistical procedures or design methods to control for the factors that impact outcome
Inaccurate effect size estimates	Outliers impacting statistical results	Examine for outliers and their impact

It is important to realize that one is never totally certain that a statistically significant result indicates that a true relationship exists. Similarly, a nonsignificant result does not absolutely indicate that no relationship exists. Nevertheless, various factors or threats can decrease the confidence with which we conclude that there either is or is not a true relationship between variables.

The remainder of this section discusses the various threats to statistical conclusions validity. See Table 7.2 for a summary of ways to address each threat.

Low Statistical Power   Power refers to the probability of correctly deciding that there is a true relationship, if indeed a true relationship exists. In other words, power is simply 1 minus the Type II error rate. Clearly, if there is a true relationship, we want to design a study that is able to detect this relationship. Studies with low power often result in the conclusion that no relationship exists when in fact a true relationship exists. Insufficient power most often results from using too few participants.

For example, in a study with fewer than 10 participants, the probability of obtaining a statistically significant result when the null hypothesis is not true (that is, concluding that there is a relationship when such a relationship exists) will be very small. Power is discussed in more detail in Chapter 8; here we need only note that inadequate statistical power is a threat to statistical conclusion validity, thus using power analysis to determine adequate sample sizes is an important aspect when designing a study.

Violated Assumptions of Statistical Tests   All statistical tests rely on various assumptions (e.g., traditional parametric tests typically rely on the assumption that scores are normally distributed). When the assumptions are violated, the researcher and consumer may be misled about the probabilities of making Type I and Type II errors. For example, if the p level of a statistical test is set at 0.05 and the test is statistically significant (that is, $p < .05$), one commonly believes that the likelihood of incorrectly concluding that there is a true relationship is less than 5%. However, if the assumptions of the test are violated, the probability of making an incorrect conclusion may be much higher. Thus, the statistical conclusion validity is reduced because of the increased chance of making a Type I or II error. To illustrate, an assumption of most parametric statistical tests is the independence of observations. If this assumption is violated by ignoring the dependence among the clients seeing the same therapist, for example, the probability of falsely concluding that a particular treatment is effective can be dramatically increased (Wampold & Serlin, 2000). We advise you to be aware of the assumptions of statistical tests and the consequences of violating those assumptions.

"Fishing" and Error-Rate Issues   As previously discussed, when a researcher employs any one statistical analysis there is always a chance of incorrectly concluding that a relationship in fact exists. The probability of making this error is set by the significance level chosen for the test (e.g., $p < .05$, or 5% chance). However, the probability of this error escalates dramatically when more than one test is conducted. For example, if 10 statistical tests are conducted, the probability of making at least one Type I error (incorrectly concluding that a relationship exists) is at most 0.40 rather than 0.05 (see Romano & Lehmann, 2005; Shaffer, 1995, for a discussion and calculations of experiment wide error rates). The point is this: When a researcher conducts many statistical tests, some are likely to be statistically significant by chance and thus lead to false interpretations, sources of statistical conclusion invalidity. Sometimes researchers engage in "fishing," which is simply conducting many statistical tests on a data set without stating specific hypotheses. This procedure inappropriately capitalizes on chance events and increases the probability of a Type I error occurring. Matching the statistical test to the research hypothesis is preferable (Wampold et al., 1990) and often times adjusting the p value according to the number of tests conducted is recommended.

Unreliability of Measures   Unreliable measures introduce error variance and obscure the true state of affairs, and thus such measures cannot be expected to be related to other measures. For example, think of a bathroom scale that yields a dramatically different weight each time you get on it (i.e., the readings are random). It is unlikely that scores obtained from this scale will be related to any other scores (such as caloric intake) in any systematic way. Thus, the unreliability of measures provides another threat to statistical conclusion validity, and choosing measures with adequate reliability estimates established with similar populations of study sample is a way to minimize this validity threat. Reliability and its effects on research outcomes are discussed further in Chapter 19.

Restriction of Range The restricted range of a variable likely leads to an attenuated relationship with other variables. The restricted range usually occurs because the instrument measuring the variable is not sensitive to the construct being measured at the upper limit (ceiling effects) or at the lower limit (floor effects). For example, suppose that a researcher wants to determine the relationship between the cognitive complexity of counselor trainees and the sophistication of their case conceptualizations, but uses an instrument to measure cognitive complexity on which most trainees score at or near the maximum allowable score; even though there may be a true relationship between cognitive complexity of the trainee and the sophistication of the case conceptualization, it is unlikely that the statistical test will lead to rejection of the null hypothesis. Restriction of range often occurs when an instrument designed to measure pathology is used on a nonclinical population.

Unreliability of Treatment Implementation Although a researcher might have carefully developed a particular treatment intervention, it is still possible for treatments to be delivered or implemented in a variety of ways. For example, the in vivo homework exercises in our fictitious study may have been assigned in a variety of ways. One of the group therapists may have given the exercises to the clients in written form at the end of the session with no explanations, whereas another therapist may have explained to them the rationale in detail. These variations tend to lead to uncontrolled variability that obscures the true relationship between the independent and dependent variables. Thus, unreliability of treatment implementation is another threat to statistical conclusion validity. Standardization of treatments is desirable and is discussed in more detail in Chapter 18.

Extraneous Variance in the Experimental Setting Any aspect of the experimental setting that leads to variability in responding will increase the error variance and obscure a true relationship. In the fictitious anxiety study, the situations in which the exercises were practiced were not controlled. Some participants may have completed their exercises in a singles bar, others at work, and still others in the grocery store. The differences in these situations would likely lead to variability in responding, which again increases the error variance and threatens statistical conclusion validity. These extraneous factors should be accounted for and addressed either through research design or statistical procedures.

Heterogeneity of Units Differences in experimental units can also lead to variability in responding. For example, in our anxiety study, physically attractive participants may have had more success in the exercises than less attractive participants. Thus, differences in attractiveness would have led to variability in responding, adding to the error variance (and again obscuring any true relationship). From this point of view, homogeneous samples (e.g., all participants having equal attractiveness) are preferable to heterogeneous samples (participants having various levels of attractiveness) from an internal validity perspective. However, the results from homogeneous samples can be appropriately generalized only to populations with similar characteristics (see Chapter 8), which limits external validity. To some degree, statistical procedures (such as the analysis of covariance) or some design characteristic (such as matching) can be used to remove variance due to some nuisance factor, such as personal attractiveness in heterogeneous populations (see Rutherford, 2012; Wampold & Drew, 1990). The units need not be persons; in studies of school achievement, heterogeneity of schools or teacher effectiveness introduces increased error.

Inaccurate Effect Size Estimation   There are instances when effects detected in studies will be inaccurately estimated. For example, correlation coefficients, particularly in small samples, can be dramatically affected by outliers, so one unit with extreme scores on both measures will result in a sizable correlation when no true correlation exists. Some statistics are biased in the sense that they consistently overestimate population effects, which is the case for R^2 (the sample value of the proportion of variance accounted for in multiple regression). Reporting R^2, particularly in small samples, provides an inflated sense of the relationship between the independent variables and the outcome variable.

Threats to Internal Validity

Internal validity refers to the confidence one can have in inferring a causal relationship among variables while simultaneously eliminating rival hypotheses. Internal validity is concerned with the most basic aspect of research, the relationships among the variables of interest (typically the independent and dependent variables). Thus, internal validity in an experimental study focuses on whether the independent variable is the cause of the dependent variable. In our example, was it the in vivo behavioral exercises that caused the lower anxiety scores in the treatment group, or is there some other explanation for the results? Because one can never know the true state of affairs, internal validity is assessed by the extent to which alternative explanations for the results can be ruled out. The more alternative explanations that can be ruled out, the higher the internal validity. As will become evident, internal validity is directly related to experimental control, such as that achieved through random selection of participants, random assignment to groups or treatments, manipulation of the independent variable, and determination of measurement times. Our discussion of internal validity begins by examining three very basic research designs. We will then discuss in considerable detail nine specific threats to internal validity.

To illustrate internal validity, consider the three designs diagrammed in Figure 7.1. The numeric subscripts for the observations are used to indicate the order of different observations (e.g., Ob_1, Ob_2) and letter subscripts are used to differentiate the treatment (Ob_a) and control groups (Ob_{ctrl}). The first design, called a one-shot pretest/posttest design (Campbell & Stanley, 1963), involves observing a sample of participants (Ob_{1a}), administering some treatment (Tx), and then observing the participants afterward (Ob_{2a}).

FIGURE 7.1 Three Possible Research Designs

Design 1: One-shot pretest/posttest design

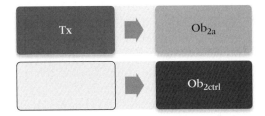

Design 2: Nonequivalent group posttest-only design

Design 3: Randomized posttest-only design

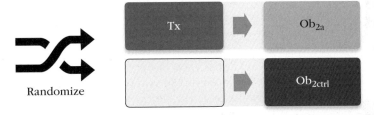

Note: Ob = Observation, Tx = Treatment, a = Intervention group, ctrl = Control group

RESEARCH APPLICATION 7.2

Consider a study designed to test the efficacy of a psychoeducational intervention to teach fifth graders about sexual abuse. Suppose that the pretest is a 30-item knowledge test related to sexual abuse (e.g., "What should you do if a stranger asks to touch you under your bathing suit?"). The psychoeducational intervention, which consists of puppet shows, plays, discussions, and workbooks, lasts throughout the school year. At the end of the school year the knowledge test is readministered. We would expect that the posttest scores would be higher than the pretest scores (i.e., $Ob_{2a} > Ob_{1a}$). Suppose that this relationship is observed; generally the participants score higher after the psychoeducational program than before it. The question is this: Was the psychoeducational program the cause of the increase in scores on the knowledge test? (Take a few minutes and think of alternative explanations for this increase.)

There are actually many alternative explanations. Perhaps over the course of the school year the participants learned about sexual abuse from their parents, friends, or television. Or perhaps they scored better at the second administration of the test because they had taken the test before and were more comfortable with the format of the questions. Or perhaps their reading ability had improved during the year and they scored better because they understood the questions better. Clearly, there are a number of problems with attributing causality in this example. Are there any other alternative explanations that you can come up with?

One of the problems with the first design is that the performance of the participants who receive the treatment is not compared to the performance of participants who do not receive the treatment. In Design 2 in Figure 7.1, there are two groups of participants; one group receives the treatment and one does not. After the treatment, observations are made. Let's say the psychoeducational program is implemented in Chris Jones's class but not in Dale Wong's class. If the psychoeducational program increased knowledge, then we would expect the scores in Chris's class (Ob_{2a}) to be higher than those in Dale's class (i.e., $Ob_{2a} > Ob_{2ctrl}$). Again, assuming that this is the case, was the psychoeducational program the cause of this difference? The answer is possibly, but again there are strong alternative explanations for the difference. The most problematic is that it is possible that Chris's class already knew more about sexual abuse before the intervention began. The students may have been placed in Chris's class because it was the accelerated track, or the students may have been placed in Dale's class because they had behavioral/emotional problems. Basically, the problem here is that there is no way of knowing or inferring that the students in the classrooms were comparable before the intervention. (There are other problems as well—e.g., Chris may have discussed sexual abuse with his students.)

The best way to make groups comparable is to randomly assign participants to the groups. Although random assignment will be discussed in more detail in subsequent chapters, the principle is that each participant has the same likelihood of being assigned to one group as to the other group. Or, said another way, participants are not assigned in any systematic way that might bias the composition of the groups. (Keep in mind that random assignment most likely will result in some small initial differences between groups. This is sampling error and is accounted for in statistical tests.) Design 3 in Figure 7.1 involves two groups containing participants who were randomly assigned. For example, students were randomly assigned either to a treatment group (they receive the psychoeducational program) or to a group that does not receive treatment (called a no-treatment control group; in this case they might have a study period during the time the other group receives the psychoeducational program). Now, if the expected pattern of scores is obtained ($Ob_{2a} > Ob_{2ctrl}$), it is more difficult to find alternative explanations to the conclusion that the psychoeducational program was responsible for the higher scores. However, there are still some alternative explanations. Perhaps a student in the treatment group had been abused, and this led to a very emotional discussion during the treatment; this event and the ensuing discussion, rather than the content of the psychoeducational program, may well have caused the higher scores for the treatment group.

The anxiety study (Research Application 7.1) described at the start of this section is an example of Design 3, which is called a randomized posttest-only design. In this context, one group receives cognitive therapy plus the in vivo behavioral exercises, whereas the other receives only the cognitive therapy. In this way, statistically significant differences can be causally attributed to the addition of the exercises (although there are still some threats to this attribution).

We now discuss the threats to internal validity. Keep in mind that each of the following is a threat to drawing the conclusion that some variable *A* causes some variable *B*. See Table 7.3 for a summary of ways to address each threat.

TABLE 7.3   Threats to Internal Validity

Threats	Example	Ways to Minimize Threats
Ambiguous temporal precedence	Preceding variables measured concurrently with other related variables through recollection	Address limitations with recollection or use longitudinal, multirater designs
Selection	Existing group differences prior to treatment due to selection method	Utilize random assignment when possible
History	An event that occurred during treatment that may have impacted the results	Use two groups, shorten treatment period, and isolate participants
Maturation	Natural development as a confounding factor for changes occurred	Use two groups to account and adjust for changes due to maturation
Regression	Research participants chosen due to their extremely high pretest scores on depression, which will likely regress towards the mean in the following test	Use a control group to account and adjust for regression toward the mean
Attrition (differential attrition)	The reasons for participants dropping out differs across two groups and effects the outcome comparison	Administer a pretest to examine and address attrition issues
Testing	Due to taking the test multiple times, the practice may affect the outcome results	Use alternate forms to measure the variable; use two groups to account and adjust for changes due to testing
Instrumentation	Changes in the measuring device or procedure	Examine for consistencies across measurement at various time points
Additive/ interactive effects	Interactive effects across various factors	Explore potential interactions that can be prevented

Ambiguous Temporal Precedence   In the previous examples, the independent variable was manipulated to determine its effect on the dependent variable. Even if the threats to the internal validity of the studies can be ruled out, it would appear that the manipulation of the independent variable caused the concomitant change in the dependent variable, and not vice versa. However, the direction is not as clear in designs in which the independent variable is not manipulated. Consider studies in counseling that examine counselor empathy and therapeutic gains in clients; several studies have found a positive relation between these two variables (e.g., Kwon & Jo, 2012). Does the empathy of the counselor cause client progress, or does client progress cause the counselor to be more empathic? In other cases, the hypothesized cause clearly precedes the effect in time, but the measurement of the cause is assessed retrospectively. In another example, it may be hypothesized that family environmental factors lead to the development of perfectionism (e.g., DiPrima, Ashby, Gnilka, & Noble, 2011). Clearly, the temporal precedence is clear; however, if family environment is measured concomitantly with perfectionistic traits, it is unclear that what is measured (i.e., recollections of family environment) precedes perfectionistic traits in time. This topic is also discussed in relations to counseling process research in Chapter 21.

Selection   Selection refers to differences between groups that exist before implementation of the treatment. Selection is often a threat when participants are initially chosen for a study based on some group membership—that is, when participants are assigned to a particular treatment or control group because they are part of an existing group. Design 2 is subject to the threat of selection. Recall that in our example (Research Application 7.2), the students in Chris's class may be very different from the students in Dale's class, and therefore observed differences (e.g., $Ob_{2a} > Ob_{1ctrl}$) could well be due to these initial differences rather than the treatment. In the absence of random assignment of participants to groups, selection is always a potentially serious threat to the internal validity of a study.

History   History refers to an event that transpires during the time when the treatment is administered and may affect the observations. Thus, history refers to any events in the participants' school, work, or home life (e.g., a television program, a newspaper article, a term paper, or the death of a family member). In our example, history is a threat in Design 1 because a television special on sexual abuse may have been aired while the intervention was being administered. There is no way to determine whether it was the television special or the psychoeducational program that resulted in the increase in knowledge.

The primary way to control history is to use two groups (as in Designs 2 and 3) so that the event affects both groups equally (or nearly equally). In our example, the participants in the treatment and control groups would have equal access to the television special, equalizing this threat. (Note that in Design 2, students in one class might stay up later, possibly due to increased homework or some other reason unique to that group, making late night specials more accessible to them than to the other class.) Still, try as the researcher might, it is possible that an event could occur that would affect only one of the groups. The threat that occurs from an event that affects only one of the groups is called local history.

Threats due to history can be reduced in a number of other ways. First, observations on the groups should be made at the same time. For example, in Design 3, Ob_{2a} and Ob_{2ctrl} should occur at the same time. Delaying observations for one group leaves open the possibility that some important event may occur after one group is tested but before the other is tested, creating a threat due to local history. Second, the shorter the treatment, the less opportunity there is that an event will occur. Third, the participants can be isolated during the treatment, thereby reducing the likelihood that an extraneous event will affect them. This is similar to sequestering a jury; however, this is extremely difficult to accomplish with human participants in naturalistic settings.

Maturation Maturation refers to normal developmental changes in participants between the pretest and the posttest that might affect the results. Obviously, studies of physical and mental abilities will be affected by maturation. Design 1 is an example of a study that is particularly vulnerable to the threat of maturation, especially if the time span between Ob_{1a} and Ob_{2a} is long. For example, if the treatment in a study is a one-year program to increase the physical strength of third graders, gains in strength (i.e., $Ob_{2a} > Ob_{1a}$) could be due to maturation instead of treatment.

Design 3 controls for maturation provided that Ob_{2a} and Ob_{2ctrl} take place at the same time. The participants in this study design were randomly assigned to groups that therefore were most likely comparable before the study began. It can be expected that participants in each group will mature at the same rate.

Regression Regression refers to changes in scores due to the fact that generally, participants who score low on the pretest will score higher on the posttest, and participants who score high on the pretest will score lower on the posttest. (For this reason, regression often is referred to as regression toward the mean.) As an example, consider a batting champion in baseball. Obviously, he obtained this title because he is a good hitter. Still, his batting average for a given year is also due in part to serendipity. Perhaps there was a warm spell in his home city in the spring, the player next in the lineup had a good year (and so the opposing team could not pitch around him), he was injury-free, he had more than his share of luck as several balls just eluded the outstretched gloves of fielders, his personal life was stable, and so on. It is unlikely that all these factors will be favorable the next year, and so it is logical to predict that although he likely will have another good year, he will not be the batting champion again. (Indeed, batting champions rarely repeat.) Likewise, someone who scores low initially is likely to score higher the next time around.

Regression is a problem, especially when an experimenter chooses research participants because of their extreme standing on some variables (such as high levels of depression). If participants are selected based on their extremely low scores, then as a group they can be expected to score higher on the posttest, *regardless of whether or not they have received any treatment*. Again, consider Design 1 in Figure 7.1. Suppose that participants were selected for a study because they fell above a certain cutoff score on a depression measure (higher scores indicate greater depression). Upon subsequent testing (i.e., at posttest), these participants generally will score lower (less depressed) than they did previously. Therefore, a statistically significant difference from pretest to posttest (i.e., $Ob_{1a} > Ob_{2a}$) may be due entirely to statistical regression. Design 3 controls for regression because the participants are randomly assigned (i.e., have comparable scores), and thus the regression toward the mean for both groups will be about the same.

Attrition   Attrition refers to the effect of participants dropping out of a study. Attrition can be a particularly pernicious threat because it can affect all designs and because its severity is difficult to assess. When participants drop out of a study, the scores that remain at posttest may not be representative. For example, consider Design 1 with participants who are depressed. If the most severely depressed participants drop out, then the observations at posttest will tend to indicate less depression because the most extreme scores are no longer considered. Therefore, the fact that $Ob_{1a} > Ob_{2a}$ could very well be due to the fact that the scores that remain at posttest are unrepresentative. (In this instance, the pretest scores for those who drop out would not be analyzed either, but the discussion illustrates the problems of attrition that ensue.)

When more than one group is involved and the attrition across the groups is not comparable, *differential attrition* is said to exist. Design 3, which has been immune to most of the threats to internal validity so far discussed, is subject to differential attrition. We will consider a few applications of Design 3 to indicate how differential attrition may work. First, consider the psychoeducational example (Research Application 7.2) in which the participants were randomly assigned to either a treatment group or a control group. Suppose that five of the participants in the treatment group moved out of the school district, whereas none of the control participants dropped out of the study. If the five participants were representative of the other participants, then their removal would have no effect on the outcome (other than to reduce power, and possibly to make the tests more sensitive to violations of assumptions).

Now consider Design 3 in our fictitious anxiety study (Research Application 7.1). Recall that one group received cognitive therapy plus in vivo exercises, whereas the second group received only cognitive therapy. Because the exercises are anxiety provoking in their own right, it may well be that the most anxious participants will drop out of the cognitive therapy plus exercises group (treatment group) rather than complete the exercises (a not uncommon avoidance reaction). Because the participants who drop out of the first group are the most anxious, their attrition will tend to decrease the anxiety scores in this group (i.e., decrease O_{2a}) and could be responsible for a significant difference between the groups (i.e., $O_{2a} < O_{2ctrl}$) in favor of the treatment group. Thus, it would be important to also have pretest scores of both groups available to address the change in the pretest and posttest scores along with group comparisons. The effects of differential attrition often can be assessed by administering a pretest. For more detailed discussion on attrition issues in outcome research, please refer to Chapter 20.

Testing   Testing refers to changes in scores on a test due to taking the test more than once. Participants' scores often improve due to familiarization with the test, recall of items and previous responses, and so forth. For example, participants might be asked to perform anagram tasks both before and after a problem-solving intervention. However, the practice performed on the first anagram task might account for improved performance on the posttest, apart from the effect due to treatment. Testing is a threat in Design 1 because improvement in scores from the pretest to the posttest could be due to taking the test a second time. Effects of testing should always be considered when pretests are given. Testing is not a threat in Designs 2 and 3 because the participants are tested only once in these designs.

Instrumentation   Instrumentation refers to changes in the measuring device or procedure over the course of a study. One might think that a "test is a test," that its properties cannot change from pretest to posttest. Realize that scores are often obtained from assessments that do not involve tests—for example, observations, interviews, electronic and/or mechanical devices, and so forth. Observations by "objective" coders are known to change or "drift" systematically during the course of a study (Kazdin, 2003). Often raters may change or refine definitions as a result of increased experience with the rating process, thereby changing their rating behavior over time. Electronic devices are subject to changes in weather. Even paper-and-pencil tests are subject to the threat of instrumentation; scoring of the tests may differ systematically from pretest to posttest, especially if the tests are subjectively scored.

Additive and Interactive Effects of Threats to Internal Validity   Many of the threats to internal validity discussed so far can work in concert with each other to affect the results of a study. Consider Design 2 in the psychoeducational example. Suppose that even though the participants were not randomly assigned to Chris's and Dale's classes, they were roughly equivalent on all relevant characteristics (intelligence, previous knowledge, motivation, socioeconomic status, and so forth). Suppose as well that a local television station ran a series about sexual abuse on the late-night news. It would appear that selection is not a threat because of the comparability of the groups, and that history is not a threat because the television series aired when both groups of participants could watch it (assuming that Ob_{2a} and Ob_{2c} occurred at the same time). However, selection and history could interact; perhaps Dale assigned a great deal of homework and children stayed up late to complete it, and therefore they were awake at the time when this series aired. In this example, the scores in the control group could be improved by the interaction of selection and history, obscuring treatment effects. This interaction would make it difficult to know whether an observed effect for the treatment group was due to the psychoeducational treatment or due to the television series.

Threats to Construct Validity

Construct validity refers to how well the independent and dependent variables represent the constructs they were intended to measure. Construct validity is an important issue in scale construction (see Chapter 10). When there is ambiguity about a construct, a confound is said to exist. More technically, a confound is an alternate construct that cannot be logically or statistically differentiated from a hypothesized construct.

RESEARCH APPLICATION 7.3

Suppose that a researcher hypothesizes that male clients with personal problems prefer female counselors, and male clients are randomly assigned to one of two groups. One group reads a description of a counselor who has a female name and views a photograph of a female counselor; the other group reads the same description, but with a male name and a male photograph. After receiving the materials, each participant indicates his willingness to see the counselor for a personal problem. Suppose that the results indicate that the clients prefer, as predicted, the female counselor (and further suppose that the statistical conclusion validity and the internal validity are adequate). A logical conclusion is that male clients prefer female counselors for personal problems. However, there is an alternative explanation: It may well be that the female in the photograph is more physically attractive than the male counselor. As a result, the willingness to see the female counselor may be due to personal attractiveness rather than to gender. Take a few minutes and think about possible ways to design the study so that it addresses this alternative explanation.

In this example (Research Application 7.3), the two constructs (physical attractiveness and gender) have been confounded. Construct validity is relevant to both the independent variable and the dependent variable. With regard to the independent variable, the groups should vary along the dimension of interest but should not systematically vary on any other dimension. If the independent variable is meant to operationalize gender (as in our previous example), then the groups should differ on this dimension (which was the case) but should not differ on any other dimensions (such as physical attractiveness). Likewise, the dependent variable or variables should only measure what they are intended to measure and should not measure irrelevant factors.

Here, we briefly review the threats to construct validity as described by Shadish et al. (2002). These threats cluster into two main groups: construct underrepresentation and surplus construct irrelevancies. Construct underrepresentation occurs when we fail to incorporate all of the important aspects of the construct. On the other hand, surplus construct irrelevancies occur when we include irrelevant aspects as part of the construct. Consider an analogy: If we use a fishing net with holes that are too big, some of the fish that we want to catch will get away (construct underrepresentation). If we use a net with holes that are too small, we will catch a lot of smaller fish that we do not want (surplus construct irrelevancies). In many ways the search for construct validity is like trying to find a net with holes that are just right for catching our target fish. See Table 7.4 for a summary of ways to address each threat.

TABLE 7.4 Threats to Construct Validity

Threats	Example	Ways to Minimize Threats
Inadequate explications	Lack of clarity with operationalizing a construct	Conduct a careful, rational analysis of the construct's important or essential components
Construct confounding	When the operationalization of a construct (gender) also inadvertently operationalizes another construct (attractiveness)	Examine how the two constructs are associated and find ways to neutralize them (use comparable attractiveness level across the two genders)
Mono-operation bias	Using a single exemplar to assess a construct	Utilize multiple exemplars and measures to assess a construct
Mono-method bias	Using a single method (self-report) to measure a construct	Use multiple ways to measure a construct (self-report and other rated)
Confounding constructs with level	Only having a restricted level of expertise of participants (e.g., novice counselors)	Expand the levels of expertise among participants, such as including a range of novice and seasoned counselors
Treatment sensitive factorial structure	Receiving treatment affects participants' responses to the treatment separate from the intended effects of the treatment (being in treatment makes participants more sensitive to what the measures are assessing)	It is often hard to detect these interactions, but limitations of the findings should be addressed if this threat is identified
Reactive self-report changes	Illusory self-reports of change due to being assigned in the treatment condition	Use instruments administered by objective raters or other nonreactive measures
Reactivity to experimental situation	Participants attempting to figure out what the researcher wants and then either comply with or rebel against the presumed outcome	Make the purpose of the study ambiguous or blind participants to treatment condition
Experimenter expectations	Experimenters consciously or unconsciously affecting results through how they communicate and interact with participants	Make the purpose of the study ambiguous to experimenters or blind experimenters to treatment conditions
Novelty and disruption	Excitement and expectation due to novelty may affect how participants respond	It is often hard to detect the effects of novelty and disruptions on outcomes, but limitations of the findings should be addressed if this threat is a concern

(continued)

TABLE 7.4 : Threats to Construct Validity (continued)

Threats	Example	Ways to Minimize Threats
Compensatory equalization of treatments	Participants in the control group seeking alternative treatment or services elsewhere	Design ways to prevent or identify it when it occurs, and account for this factor when analyzing results
Compensatory rivalry	Efforts by participants in the control group to outperform participants in the treatment group	Design ways to prevent or identify it when it occurs, and account for this factor when analyzing results
Resentful demoralization	Participants in the less desirable treatment group (or in a control group) become demoralized and tend to decrease performance	Design ways to prevent or identify it when it occurs, and account for this factor when analyzing results
Treatment diffusion	Treatment delivered to one group is unwittingly allowed to spread to other groups	Design ways to prevent the spread of treatment to participants in the control group

Inadequate Explication of Constructs To make a construct operational, one must first have a careful, rational analysis of the construct's important or essential components. A threat to construct validity from inadequate explication of constructs occurs when such an analysis has not taken place. This is an example of construct underrepresentation. To adequately operationalize a construct, it should be defined clearly. When a construct is referenced by a name but not discussed in detail, it is often difficult to ascertain exactly what is intended. *Spouse abuse* may refer to physical acts with the intent to harm, to any physical acts, to physical and verbal attacks, and so forth. Decisions about the nature of a construct should not be arbitrary; proper definitions are needed so that the research hypotheses follow from theories. Moreover, it is important to define constructs to be consistent with prior research so that conclusions about the construct can accumulate.

Construct Confounding As described earlier, confounding occurs when the operationalization of a construct also inadvertently operationalizes another construct, which is an example of surplus construct irrelevancies. In the earlier example, gender was confounded with personal attractiveness. Confounding is problematic because it is difficult to design pure operations, and extraneous constructs have a way of surreptitiously weaseling their way into studies.

Mono-Operation Bias Mono-operation bias refers to problems with single exemplars of a level of independent variable or a single measure of the dependent variable. Mono-operations are problematic because frequently the essence of a construct cannot be captured by a single exemplar or a single measure. Most likely, mono-operations underrepresent the construct and contain irrelevancies.

Mono-operations of the independent variable can result when only one exemplar of each treatment is used. For example, in the gender study mentioned earlier, all of the participants in the female-counselor group read the same name and description of the counselor and viewed the same photograph. It would have been preferable to have several descriptions, male and female names, and photographs. With regard to the dependent variable, a single measure often will not reflect the construct adequately. The ABC Anxiety Test may reflect social anxiety to some extent, but it will fail to do so perfectly. By adding other measures of social anxiety, the construct is operationalized more completely. The technical bases for the use of multiple dependent measures to operationalize a construct are found in statistics and measurement; these bases are discussed conceptually in Chapter 19.

Mono-Method Bias   As mentioned previously, multiple measures are important in capturing the essence of a construct. However, if all the dependent measures use the same method, there may well be a bias introduced by the method. For example, self-report measures often share a common respondent bias. If a participant responds in a socially desirable way to all self-report instruments, then consistent bias is introduced by this method. If two constructs are measured in the same way (e.g., self-report), the correlation between variables may result from method variance rather than any true correlation between constructs. For example, instead of using only self-report measures to assess depression, a more valid method would be to use a client self-report measure coupled with a therapist and observer measure of depression.

Mono-method bias can also apply to independent variables. Presenting written descriptions, names, and photographs (even multiple exemplars of each) operationalizes gender using one method. The question remains: Would the results be similar if gender were operationalized using a different method (such as videotapes of the counselor)?

Confounding Constructs with Levels of Constructs   Frequently, constructs that are continuous are operationalized with discrete exemplars. For example, the experience level of the counselor is often an independent variable in treatment studies. Experience is a continuous variable with a wide range. If the experience levels chosen are either at the low end of the continuum (e.g., novice counselors, those with one practicum course, and those with a master's degree) or at the high end of the continuum (doctoral-level counselors with 10, 15, or 20 years of experience), then it might be concluded that experience does not affect counseling outcomes. A very different result might be obtained with experience levels that span the continuum. When restricted levels of the construct are chosen, another example of construct underrepresentation, the construct is confounded with levels of the construct.

Treatment-Sensitive Factorial Structure   Instrumentation, as discussed earlier, can be problematic with regard to internal validity. There are times, however, when delivery of a treatment affects participants' responses to the treatment separate from the intended effects of the treatment. Occasionally, the treatment will sensitize the participants to aspects of the instrument, which changes the factor structure of the instrument. For example, an instrument measuring depression may be one-dimensional when administered to untreated depressed persons; after treatment, particularly with a psychoeducational component, the clients may now be able to differentiate aspects of their depression related to melancholy, loss of pleasure in activities, eating and sleeping, irrational thoughts, activity level, and so forth, creating a multidimensional instrument. Thus, after treatment they have become sensitized and now with their greater awareness of melancholy, they score higher on the subscale. A total score on the depression instrument for the treated subjects may misrepresent the fact that the treatment affects melancholy but not activity level, for instance.

Reactive Self-Report Changes   Self-report of functioning prior to and after assignment to condition can lead to illusory reports of change. For example, participants wishing to qualify for a treatment in a clinical trial may report increased symptomatology, which quickly dissipates if they are assigned to the treatment condition. On the other hand, participants assigned to a wait-list control may actually report an increase in symptomatology based on the belief that the researchers will not allow them to deteriorate untreated. According to this scenario, the treatment would appear to be efficacious when in fact the superiority of the treatment vis-à-vis the control group was due entirely to reactive self-reports. Posttests can also be reactive to treatments retroactively. Clients completing a course of cognitive behavioral treatment who take a depression inventory loaded with items about maladaptive cognitions may respond favorably as they recognize, due to the treatment, that these thoughts are inappropriate, whereas the same retroactive effect may not occur for participants who had received a dynamic or experiential treatment. One solution to this threat is to use instruments administered by objective raters or other nonreactive measures (see Webb, Campbell, Schwartz, & Sechrest, 1966; Webb, Campbell, Schwartz, Sechrest, & Grove, 1981).

Reactivity to the Experimental Situation   Reactivity to the experimental situation occurs when participants respond based on the reaction to aspects of the experimental situation that are incidental to the treatment condition (Hawthorne effect; Landsberger, 1957). Sometimes participants attempt to figure out what the researcher wants (sometimes called *hypothesis guessing*) and then attempt to either comply with or rebel against the presumed outcome. One of the most problematic things about hypothesis guessing is that it is very difficult to determine when it occurs, how often it occurs, and the direction and magnitude of its effect. For example, if the participants in the gender study guess that the hypothesis is actually related to their willingness to see a counselor of a specific gender, then they may respond in a certain way to please the researcher, to show that they are open minded and nonsexist, and so forth. Reactivity to the experimental situation is also related to the idea of placebo effects in medicine, which occur to a large extent because of the expectation that the treatment will work. Assignment to the desired or experimental treatment may increase the participant's expectation that the treatment will be effective, which in turn will positively affect the client, creating a treatment effect independent from the actual ingredients of the treatment.

There are some ways to reduce reactivity to the experimental situation, although these solutions are not without their own flaws and problems (Rosnow & Rosenthal, 1997). First, the experimenter can make the purpose of the study ambiguous and obscure any indication that one treatment is expected to produce better outcomes than another. However, this reduces the completeness of informed consent because ethical principles dictate that the purpose of research be explained to participants before they consent to participate (see Chapter 3 for a discussion of these ethical issues). Another action that can be taken is to blind the participants to the treatment so that they are unaware of whether they are receiving an active medication or a placebo pill.

Experimenter Expectancies Although experimenters are portrayed as objective scientists, there is evidence that this is not the case. They are often eager to find particular results, and this bias is often communicated to participants in subtle (and sometimes not-so-subtle) ways. For example, if the experimenter is also the counselor in a treatment study, he or she may be overly eager to help the clients to show the effectiveness of his or her valued treatment. When this happens, it is unclear whether the causal element is the treatment or expectation; such uncertainty threatens the construct validity of the study. Experimenter expectancies are discussed in detail in Chapter 23.

Novelty and Disruption Effects Humans respond to novelty, and it has been noted that this phenomenon might affect how participants in research would behave in novel experimental situations. Innovations create an aura of excitement and expectation that could well influence research participants. For example, when the first selective serotonin reuptake inhibitor (SSRI) fluoxetine (Prozac) was introduced in the 1980s, it was hailed as a miracle treatment and subjects enrolling in clinical trials at that time had a much different sense than those enrolling in clinical trials of later generations of SSRIs. Sometimes, however, novelty can disrupt routines and create deleterious effects. As with many threats to validity, it is difficult to know whether novelty and disruption effects would augment or attenuate the treatment.

Compensatory Equalization of Treatments Most counselors are naturally reluctant to withhold programs from participants in control groups. When personnel directly or indirectly involved in a study provide some type of service to participants in a control group to compensate for their assignment to a group that does not receive treatment, compensatory equalization of treatments is said to exist and might pose a threat to internal validity. In counseling, participants in the control group will often seek services elsewhere (clergy, other counseling services, and so forth). In school settings, administrators, feeling bad for the control group, may provide extraordinary experiences, such as field trips, movies, and so forth. These experiences may well affect the scores for these participants, especially if the dependent variable is nonspecific (e.g., self-concept).

Compensatory Rivalry   Compensatory rivalry refers to efforts by participants in the control group to outperform participants in the treatment group to prove that they are "just as good, if not better." This threat to validity occurs most often when the participants' performance will be publicized and there are consequences of not performing well. To illustrate this threat, suppose that counselors in a mental health center are randomly assigned to a treatment group or a control group. The treatment consists of refresher courses on assessment, diagnosis, and service delivery. Because the counselors find such courses remedial and demeaning, they are determined to demonstrate that they do not need the courses. Therefore, the participants in the control group work extra hard to demonstrate that they are competent in these areas.

Resentful Demoralization   Resentful demoralization is, in some ways, the opposite of compensatory rivalry. Rather than working extra hard to perform, participants in the less desirable treatment group (or in a control group) will often become demoralized, which tends to decrease performance. For example, participants in a study of depression, even if informed that they might be assigned to a control group, may feel more depressed than usual when actually assigned to the control group. Their sense of having little control over the reinforcers in their world is reiterated. The demoralization of the participants in the control group adds to the level of depression of these participants, and therefore differences between scores on the posttest (i.e., $Ob_{2a} < Ob_{2ctrl}$) may be due to the demoralization of the control participants rather than to the effectiveness of the treatment.

Treatment Diffusion   Occasionally, the treatment delivered to one group is unwittingly allowed to spread to other groups. This is particularly likely when the treatment is primarily informational and of much interest. Suppose a study is being conducted on sexual abuse. Because of the relevance of this topic, students in the treatment group may discuss it with students in the control group, thereby effectively delivering the treatment to both groups. Diffusion of treatments makes it difficult to find differences among or between groups, even when the treatment is effective.

Threats to External Validity

External validity refers to the generalizability of a study's results. To what group of units (typically persons), settings, treatments, and outcomes do the results of the study apply? Often, external validity is limited to how well the conclusions hold for persons or types of persons who did not participate in the research. However, it is important to understand that we want conclusions to be robust relative to various settings, treatments, and outcomes as well (Shadish et al., 2002).

Traditionally, the external validity of persons has been approached by examining samples from populations. First, a population of persons is defined; second, a random sample is drawn from that population. Based on the results of the research conducted with the obtained sample, conclusions are made about the population. Unfortunately, truly or even approximately random sampling is possible only infrequently. Consider the study with socially anxious participants. It is impossible to randomly sample from the population of all socially anxious individuals in the United States. The concepts of sampling and the inferences that can be drawn in the absence of random sampling are discussed in Chapter 8.

Cook and Campbell (1979) broadened the concept of external validity to include generalization *to* the population and generalization *across* populations. Random sampling from a well-defined population refers to the generalizability *to* the population; however, because true random sampling is infrequently conducted, generalization to the population is difficult. Of greater practical importance is the generalizability of results *across* different populations. Consider the social anxiety example, and suppose that the study finds that cognitive therapy plus exercises is significantly more effective than cognitive therapy alone in reducing social anxiety. (Assume that the statistical conclusion validity, internal validity, and construct validity are adequate to draw valid inferences.) Across which populations are these results generalizable? Do they apply equally to all socially anxious participants? To males and females? To adolescents and adults? To various minority groups? And do the results also apply to participants in various settings (social gatherings, public places), to people of different ages than the participants, to well-being as well as depression, to treatments other than cognitive behavioral therapy (i.e., do exercises augment the effects of process experiential therapy), and so forth?

Generalizability across populations is of particular interest to counseling researchers. It is important to determine which treatments work with which types of clients in which settings. We will briefly discuss four threats to external validity that serve to limit the generalizability of research results. See Table 7.5 for examples of issues related to external validity.

TABLE 7.5 External Validity Issues

External Validity Type	Example
Units	Characteristics of persons (e.g., gender, racial or ethnic background, experience level, degree of dysfunction, intelligence) or schools/classrooms (e.g., public/private, grade level)
Treatments	Conditions and level of adherence in the clinical trial vs. those in the community setting; selected counselors with specific training of the treatment vs. general counselors in the community
Outcomes	Outcomes measured by specific instruments (a specific self-report depression scale) vs. outcomes assessed by other measures and methods (diagnosis by psychologist)
Settings	Different settings (e.g., university counseling center, community mental health setting, hospital setting, private practice, schools)

Units   When the unit is persons, the variables relevant to counseling research include such variables as gender, racial or ethnic background, experience level, degree of dysfunction, intelligence, cognitive style, personality, level of acculturation, and sexual orientation, among others. Clearly, there are many choices for populations to be studied; some considerations in choosing populations are discussed in Chapter 8. In short, the external validity of a study is strengthened when the research examines the causal relationship between the independent and dependent variables across different categories of persons.

Units need not be persons. For example, interventions at the school level may involve classrooms as units; the question then is whether the conclusion holds for classrooms in other schools, which may or may not be similar to the school or schools at which the research was conducted.

Treatment Variations   Does the treatment have to be given exactly as it was in the clinical trial in order for it to be effective? Treatments in clinical trials are administered by selected therapists, who received supervision and training in the treatment and are required to adhere to the treatment protocol; the question is whether the treatment administered by therapists in the community, who might deviate from the protocol and use techniques from other treatments, is equally effective.

Outcomes   This is an issue that has been a source of contention between proponents of behavior therapies, who utilize behavioral and symptom outcomes, and proponents of dynamic therapies, who utilize more personality and well-being measures. Do the results obtained with one set of measures generalize to outcomes that would be assessed by a different set of measures? A similar debate occurs in schools between those who advocate for narrow achievement outcomes and those who desire a broader net that would include variables related to citizenship, altruism, creativity, general problem-solving skills, and so forth. Often, studies are designed to ignore important constructs, and the research can be criticized because these other constructs might be the most interesting piece of the psychological puzzle. There have been numerous investigations of minority group preference for types of counselors (e.g., Chang & Yoon, 2011; Coleman, Wampold, & Casali, 1995); however, missing from most of this research are constructs related to counseling outcomes. (Does the fact that an Asian American client *prefers* an Asian American counselor imply that an Asian American would produce the most desirable outcome in this context?). A meta-analysis study on this topic supported a preference toward having a counselor of one's race, and perceiving counselors of one's own race as more positive compared to others; however, results also indicated that there were no benefits of matching race on the counseling outcomes (Cabral & Smith, 2011). Thus, restriction of the constructs used in a study is a threat to the construct validity of the study.

Settings   How generalizable are results obtained in a university counseling center to a community mental health setting, a hospital setting, or private practice? There are obvious differences among these settings, and there is little reason to believe that results necessarily generalize across these settings. Much research is conducted at counseling centers, perhaps because staff members are motivated, interested, and proactive; however, there are factors that may differentiate this setting from others. Thus, the external validity of a study is strengthened when the relationship between the independent and dependent variables is examined across different settings.

SUMMARY AND CONCLUSIONS

In this chapter we discuss four types of validity in considerable detail. Statistical conclusion validity refers to the degree to which a researcher has arrived at the correct conclusion about the relationships among the variables in a research question. Internal validity refers to the degree to which statements can be made about the existence of a causal relationship among the variables. Construct validity refers to the degree to which the variables measured in the study represent the intended constructs. Finally, external validity refers to the degree to which the relationship among the variables is generalizable beyond the study to other units (usually people), settings, treatments, and outcomes. Although one can never establish each of the four types of validity with total certainty, researchers establish estimates of validity by ruling out as many threats to the validity as possible. Most important, different types of designs typically represent trade-offs with regard to the four types of validity.

A wide range of different threats to each of the four types of validity exist. How does one assess the severity of a threat? In some instances, statistical tests can be used to determine whether a threat is problematic. For example, if pretests are administered, differences among participants who drop out of a study can be compared statistically to those among remaining participants. Or external validity can be assessed by examining the statistical interaction between the independent variable and some person, setting, or time variable.

A second way to assess validity is to logically examine the likelihood of a threat's occurrence. In some instances, it is very unlikely that a particular threat is problematic, even in the absence of direct evidence. For example, although maturation may be a threat in some designs, if the treatment lasts only 1 hour, participants are very unlikely to mature much during that time. Or if the pretest is a commonly used test and the treatment is lengthy, interaction of testing and treatment probably will have little effect on the results. Diffusion of treatments will be impossible if participants are strangers and do not have the opportunity to meet.

It is also possible to reduce threats to validity by building into the study some aspects that control for the threat. Consider the example of the study in which photographs of counselors of both genders were presented to the participants. Recall that personal attractiveness was a potential confound in that study. To control for the confound, the researchers could have judges rate the personal attractiveness of various photographs and then match them so that the personal attractiveness of the photographs was constant across the groups.

In sum, our discussion of validity provides a framework for assessing the types of inferences made in research and the subsequent validity of a study. The fact that many threats were presented indicates that many things can weaken or strengthen any particular study. Keep in mind that no research can be designed that is not subject to threats to validity to some degree, which is in essence the thesis of Gelso's (1979) bubble hypothesis. The objective is to design and conduct research in a way to minimize the threats and maintain the possibility of obtaining interpretable findings. In this respect, programmatic research is needed because studies can build on each other, and a threat to one study can be ruled out in a future study. In fact, programmatic research on a given topic that examines similar variables over time is essential to creating useful knowledge bases within scientific inquiry in the counseling profession.

STIMULUS QUESTIONS

Validity Issues

1. Select two studies in your area of interest.
   a. Identify the major conclusions made by the authors.
   b. Identify three possible threats to the validity of these conclusions.
   c. Discuss how these studies could have been designed to better rule out these threats.
2. A researcher is interested in studying racial and ethnic identity. The researcher uses ethnic minorities attending the researcher's university as a sample. What would be some important validity considerations of using this sample?
3. Experimental studies are often criticized on the grounds that, due to the desire to control extraneous variables and exert experimental control, the results are not applicable to real-world situations. Discuss both sides of this argument (i.e., why experimental studies are important and why the results may not be useful).
4. Search the literature to find several studies bearing on the same question. Identify one study with high internal validity and low external validity and another with low internal validity and high external validity. Discuss how each has handled the trade-off between internal and external validity. Which study is more informative? Finally, how do the studies compliment each other in terms of building knowledge?

8
Chapter

Population Issues: Who We Study Matters!

The numerous complexities involved in selecting participants and generalizing the results based on the data collected from those participants constitute what we call *population issues*. Perhaps the one question we are most frequently asked by student researchers is "How many participants do I need?" Less frequently asked but perhaps more crucial are questions related to how applicable the results of a study are to other contexts. For example, do the results of a treatment study apply to the types of clients seen in mental health agencies? Does a study of marital satisfaction provide information that is valid for various ethnic/racial groups? Is the use of convenience samples (e.g., undergraduates) appropriate for a particular study? These and many related questions can be answered only when we understand population issues.

This chapter focuses on the ways in which population issues impinge on the design and interpretation of research in counseling. Key population issues for successful research in counseling include (a) what types of participants to use, (b) how many participants to study, (c) how to treat different types of participants in the design and analysis, and (d) to what extent the results are generalizable.

Selecting participants for a study typically involves selecting samples from a population of interest. Because the rationale for using samples from a population is based on sampling theory, we discuss this subject first. Then we address practical issues in selecting participants including (a) defining the target population, (b) creating a participant pool, (c) selecting participants, (d) establishing the validity of research in the absence of random selection, and (e) determining the number of participants. Finally, we examine the relationship of external validity and population issues by considering factorial designs involving factors related to person or status variables.

SAMPLING THEORY

Selecting participants for a study typically involves selecting samples from a population of interest. For example, it would be too cumbersome for an investigator interested in homophobia to survey all Americans about homophobia, so instead the investigator selects a sample of participants that presumably reflects the American population as a whole. For example, Poteat, Mereish, DiGiovanni, and Koenig (2011) conducted a study on how general and homophobic victimization affects adolescents' psychosocial and educational concerns. The researchers used a data set collected from the Dane County Youth Assessment (DCYA) project, in which 7th–12th grade students in 43 out of 45 public schools in this Wisconsin county were surveyed. The goal was to use this sample to make conclusions about U.S. adolescents in general. However, as will be described, a number of practical concerns lead one to question whether this was accomplished in this and other related studies.

Sampling theory provides the foundation for understanding the process and the implications of selecting participants for a particular study. We briefly discuss sampling theory and elucidate some of the real-life restrictions and subsequent problems that investigators encounter. The essence of sampling theory involves selecting samples that reflect larger or total populations (see Figure 8.1). We typically think of a population as a well-defined set of people, such as adolescents, college students seeking help at a counseling center, or counselors-in-training, but technically a population is a set of observations. Put another way, the focus is the observations (or scores) of the people, rather than the people themselves, that constitute the population. The important aspect of populations, whether viewed as people or observations, is that conclusions reached from the research sample should apply to the population. By necessity, counseling research is conducted with a limited number of participants; the results for these particular participants alone are rarely of primary interest. The object of most research is to generalize from the observations of these study participants to some larger population;

FIGURE 8.1 : Selecting a Sample from a Population

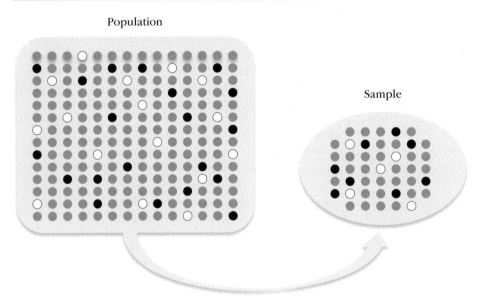

1. Define target population
2. Create participant pool
3. Select participants

that is, some inference is made about the population based on a small number of observations.

Inferences about populations are made on the basis of samples selected from populations. Technically, a sample is a subset of the population; that is, the observations in the sample are taken from the set of observations that constitute the population. This process is called sampling. Again, inferences about the population of observations are made from the observations of the sample; the validity of the inferences about the population depend on how well the sample in fact represents the population. Representativeness is a complex concept that requires further explanation.

Certainly, selecting 20 males at an Ivy League college and recording their scores on the BDI would poorly represent the population of BDI scores for all college students nationally. Samples that systematically differ from the population in some way are said to be *biased*. More technically, a biased sample is a sample selected in such a way that all observations in the population do not have an equal chance of being selected. In the example of male Ivy Leaguers, the sample is biased because female students do not have the same chance of being selected as males (i.e., the probability of selecting a female is zero), and students in non–Ivy League colleges do not have the same chance of being selected as students in the Ivy League. However, as we shall describe, sample bias often operates in much more subtle ways than just noted.

Samples that are not biased are random samples—that is, samples in which each observation in the population has an equal chance of being selected. Logistically, random samples can be selected by assigning each observation a consecutive number (1, 2, 3 . . .) and then choosing the observations by selecting numbers from a random numbers table or by using a computer-assisted random numbers generator. To randomly select a sample of size 20 from all college students, each student could be assigned an eight-digit number, a computer could be used to generate 20 eight-digit random numbers, and the BDI scores for the students whose numbers were generated would compose the sample. Clearly, this would be a laborious process (and could never realistically be accomplished), but it illustrates the ideal that researchers seek to approach when utilizing random selection.

Although random selection eliminates systematic bias, there is no guarantee that a random sample will be representative of the population. To understand representativeness, and to comprehend how inferences from samples to populations are made, we now discuss some basic principles of sampling theory. Consider a population that has a mean of 100 (i.e., the mean of the observations in the population is 100). Typically, this is denoted by writing $\mu = 100$; the Greek symbol μ (mu) indicates a population parameter. A researcher selects a random sample of 25; if the obtained mean M of the 25 observations is close to 100 (say $M = 103.04$), then in one sense the sample is representative. If the mean of the 25 observations is far from 100 (say $M = 91.64$), then it could be said that the sample is not representative.

This all seems logical; however, the situation in the real world is that the population parameter is unknown to the researcher, and the researcher selects only one sample. Therefore, it is unclear how representative any given sample in fact is. Fortunately, statistical theory helps us here by allowing calculation of the probability that an obtained mean has some arbitrary (but acceptable) distance from a specified population value (more about this later in the chapter). It should be noted that larger samples (2,000 college students) are likely to be more representative of the population than smaller samples (20 college students).

We now integrate our previous discussion of random assignment from Chapters 7 and 11 with random selection in the context of a particular design. Consider the case of a posttest-only control-group design (as discussed in Chapter 11); let's say the researcher is testing the efficacy of an innovative treatment. Two populations are of interest here: the population of individuals who have received the innovative treatment and the population of individuals who have received no treatment. Suppose that 30 participants are randomly selected from a well-defined population; the researcher does not know how well the sample represents the population, only that there are no systematic biases in the sample because the participants were selected randomly. The next step is to randomly assign the 30 participants to the two groups (15 in each). Participants in the treatment group are administered the treatment, and at some subsequent time both the treatment and the control participants are tested. At this point something crucial should be noticed: The 15 observations for the treated group are considered to be randomly selected from a hypothetical population of observations of individuals in the population *who have received the treatment*. Think of it this way: All people in the well-defined population are eligible to be treated; hypothetically, all of these people could receive the treatment and subsequently be tested. The 15 observations (i.e., the posttest scores) in the treatment group are considered to be randomly selected from the hypothetical population of posttest scores for all persons as if they had been treated. The 15 observations in the control group are considered to be randomly selected from the hypothetical population of posttest scores for persons who have not been treated. These concepts are illustrated in Figure 8.2. These are fundamental assumptions under which the majority of clinical research (both medical and psychological) rest. However, there is sufficient evidence to believe that the samples often utilized in both clinical trials and psychological research in general are not entirely representative of populations to which the results are often generalized.

Next, we discuss a crucial point about experimental design and the tests of statistical hypotheses. The null hypothesis in the previous case is that the population mean for all individuals who hypothetically could be treated is equal to the population mean for all individuals who are untreated, symbolically expressed as $\mu_T - \mu_C = 0$. An appropriate alternative hypothesis (assuming higher scores indicate a higher level of functioning) is that the population mean for all individuals who hypothetically could be treated is greater than the population mean for all individuals who are untreated: $\mu_T > \mu_C$. If the statistical test (here a two-group independent t test) is statistically significant, then the null hypothesis is rejected in favor of the alternative. Because statistical hypotheses are written in terms of population parameters, the researcher—by deciding to reject the null hypothesis and accept the alternative—is making an inference about the *population of observations* based on the sample scores. In this example, if the null hypothesis is rejected in favor of the alternative hypothesis (based on, say, a statistically significant t test), then the

FIGURE 8.2 How Sampling Is Conceptualized for a Hypothetical Posttest-Only
Control-Group Design

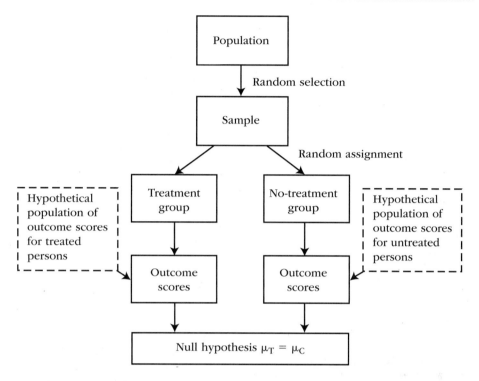

researcher concludes that the mean of scores of treated persons is in general higher
than the mean of scores of untreated persons. However, this conclusion could be
incorrect because the samples might not have been representative.

Perhaps the 15 participants assigned to the treatment condition were initially
superior in some way(s) to the other persons in the population. (Of course, this cannot be determined with this design.) Perhaps certain subsets of the population were
not adequately represented in the sample (as it is often the case that racial and ethnic
minorities are underrepresented in psychological research). When researchers generalize the results of studies to such groups, they must assume there are no systematic
differences in the variables of interest between the two groups, an assumption that
is often tenuous at best. Nevertheless, protection against this possibility is expressed
as the alpha level, the probability of falsely rejecting the null hypothesis. When alpha
(Type I error) is set at, say, .05, the probability that the null hypothesis is rejected
when it actually is true is less than .05. Because alpha conventionally is set at low
levels (for example, .05 or .01), the probability that significant results are due to
unrepresentative samples is small. Remember this central point: Rejection of a null
hypothesis does not mean that the null hypothesis is false; it means that the obtained
results would be very unusual if the null had been true, and thus the decision is made
to reject the null. However, there is still the small possibility that the null is true,
and that sampling error (i.e., Type I error) was responsible for the obtained results.

Even though we have just emphasized the importance of random selection from a population, we must point out that random selection is almost always an impossibility in applied research. A perusal of journals in counseling convincingly demonstrates that random selection is seldom used. For example, the Dane County Youth Assessment data set used in Poteat et al.'s (2011) study were from a certain county in Wisconsin which had characteristics that were limited to that region. For all practical purposes, it is not possible to select participants for a treatment study from across the country; researchers are fortunate to be able to afford to select clients locally. Even when random selection is pragmatically feasible (e.g., a survey of members of Division 17 of the American Psychological Association [APA]), not all persons selected will choose to participate, creating a bias. For example, 2 out of the 45 public schools in the DCYA project did not participate. Researchers might generate numerous hypotheses concerning how those that participated differed in important ways from those who did not. In the next section we discuss procedures for conducting research without random selection, and the attendant problems involved.

PRACTICAL CONSIDERATIONS IN SELECTING PARTICIPANTS

If true random sampling were possible, the researcher would define the target population, identify all people in the population, and randomly select from that group of people. But as we have noted, this process is not practical except in the most contrived contexts. In this section we explore the practical issues in participant selection by discussing the following topics: (a) defining the target population, (b) creating a participant pool, (c) selecting participants, (d) establishing validity in the absence of random selection, and (e) determining the number of participants.

RESEARCH IN ACTION 8.1

Think about a research topic that you would like to study. What would be the first target population that comes to mind in terms of collecting data from? Briefly describe this target population in terms of demographics (e.g., gender, age, race) and setting (e.g., college, schools, clinics). Which factors led you to choose this target population? How feasible would you be able to collect data from this target population for your study?

Defining the Target Population

The first step in the selection of participants is to define the target population, or the population to which the investigator wants to generalize. Although technically *population* refers to a set of observations, the population is typically defined in terms of the characteristics of people. Researchers must carefully consider many different characteristics in this definition, because ultimately these characteristics define the group to which the study's results will be generalized.

Defining characteristics may include diagnostic category, gender, ethnicity, age, sexual orientation, country of origin, religion, presenting problem, marital status, and socioeconomic status, among others. For example, in a study using a religious-based behavioral activation intervention for depression, Armento, McNulty, and Hopko (2012) limited participants to undergraduates who were mildly depressed (had a score of 14 or greater on the Beck Depression Inventory-II) and did not have active suicidal intent or psychosis. Participants who were undergoing pharmacological treatment for depression or had coexisting anxiety were included. In addition, there were no restrictions on one's religious orientation; although the majority identified as Christians ($n = 47$), two identified as atheists and one Jewish.

One important issue in defining the target population is deciding how heterogeneous the population should be. Heterogeneous populations are desirable because they contain a wide variety of characteristics to which the results of the study may be generalizable; conversely, homogeneous populations limit the degree to which the results are generalizable. By limiting the population to undergraduates, Armento et al. (2012) restricted the degree to which the results are generalizable; the study does not shed light on the efficacy of a religious-based behavioral activation intervention for depression with other groups, such as unemployed laborers. Nevertheless, there are problems with heterogeneous populations as well. For one thing, it is unclear how the results of a study apply to various subgroups of a heterogeneous population (a topic that we revisit in a later section); furthermore, by their very nature, heterogeneous populations show much variability in responding, such that the error variance is greater than it would be for homogeneous populations, creating less powerful statistical tests. Again, as is the case with most decisions in research design, determining a study's optimal degree of population heterogeneity depends on the nature of the problem being investigated. In terms of Kerlinger's MAXMINCON principle, this is a trade-off between maximizing variance for broader generalization and minimizing within-group variance to control for random errors due to individual differences.

As a practical example of this phenomenon, consider two examples. The findings of the Treatment of Depression Collaborative Research Protocol (TDCRP), a large treatment trial funded by the National Institute of Mental Health (NIMH), have heavily influenced treatment decision making in the United States (Elkin, Shea, & Watkins, 1989). In addition, the Task Force for the Promotion and Dissemination of Psychological Procedures (TFPDPP) has generated a list of empirically supported treatments (ESTs) that it argues should be used by all practicing psychologists (TFPDPP, 1995). However, both of these examples base their findings on predominately White American, middle-class samples. The generalizability of these findings to non-White American, non-middle-class samples is highly suspect. Therefore, it is important to conduct research with a diverse group across different dimensions, such as gender, ethnicity, age, sexual orientation, country of origin, religion, presenting problem, marital status, and socioeconomic status. There has been increasing attention and a call for counseling psychologists to address the issue of health disparity in the United States, which is a form of oppression of marginalized populations in our society (Buki & Selem, 2012).

Creating a Participant Pool

After defining the target population, the researcher needs to identify a group of people who both fit this definition and are accessible; this group is called the participant pool. Suppose that the target population is defined as university counseling center clients. Clearly it is impossible to identify all such clients, so the participant pool is often limited to possible participants in the researcher's vicinity.

The participant pool might consist of counseling center clients at the researcher's university, a not uncommon practice (see, e.g., Choi, Buskey, & Johnson, 2010). However, restricting the participant pool to a subset of all possible participants introduces various kinds of bias—in this case, those related to geography, including socioeconomic factors, ethnicity, and values. In the Choi et al. study, the participants were clients at a "midsize mid-Atlantic university counseling center." Are the results of this study applicable to clients at counseling centers at a large midwestern college, an Ivy League university, or a university in southern California? Restricting the participant pool restricts the population, and so technically the results of the Choi et al. study are generalizable only to clients at that particular mid-Atlantic university counseling center.

There is no empirical way to determine whether restricting a particular participant pool limits the generalizability of a study, other than by investigating the potential participants excluded from the participant pool. Clearly, this is not a feasible solution, because if those participants were accessible to the researcher, they would have been included in the study in the first place. Therefore, the researcher needs evidence to support the contention that restricting the participant pool does not affect the results. Background knowledge and prior research are crucial in making the decision to restrict the participant pool. For example, the physiological responses to physical stress would not be expected to vary from one area of the country to another, whereas attitudes toward abortion very well might. Of course, restriction of participant pools is not based on geographical criteria alone; often participants are recruited from local mental health agencies, undergraduate participant pools, school districts, and so forth.

Indeed biases will exist in virtually all samples. But if we repeatedly marginalize some populations in our research, then we are introducing/promoting systematic biases in counseling and counseling psychology knowledge bases. That is, the literature may have much information about the mental health of White college undergraduate students in the United States that may not apply to marginalized groups such as Latino/immigrants, European international students, or women of Muslim faith. Thus, it is important that research is extended beyond convenience samples that are mostly majority groups. To achieve a knowledge base that will apply and benefit various population groups, research needs to not restrict the participation pool, but to extend its focus towards marginalized groups that may not be as easily accessed.

In one sense, all participant pools are restricted. Because it is required that research participants take part voluntarily, all participant pools are restricted to participants who satisfy the definition of the target population and volunteer to participate. A bias is introduced here because volunteer participants have been found to be quite different from nonvolunteers. As an illustration, researchers have found that volunteers are better educated, have a higher need for social approval, are more intelligent, are less authoritarian, appear to be better adjusted, and seek more stimulation than nonvolunteers (Rosenthal & Rosnow, 1969).

Another complicating factor in composing participant pools is that because the presence or magnitude of characteristics contained in the definition of the target population may not be readily apparent, testing may be required. For example, in Armento et al.'s (2012) study of depressed undergraduates, it was necessary to assess the level of depression of many potential participants. Over 250 students were given the Beck Depression Inventory-II to identify those who were at least mildly depressed.

Selecting Participants

The next step is to determine those participants in the participant pool who will participate in the study. Ideally, participants are randomly selected from the participant pool. For example, if the participant pool comprised students seeking help at a counseling center at a particular university, then the researcher could assign each such student a number and, with the aid of a random numbers table or a computer-assisted random numbers generator, randomly select the participants for the experiment. However, even this process can be pragmatically troublesome. Often the researcher needs all participants to be at the same stage of counseling, but if there are not enough qualified clients, the researcher may solicit participants as they become available. For example, Choi et al. (2010) had university counseling center clients complete surveys prior to their intake and their termination session. To obtain a sufficient sample, the researchers invited all clients who presented themselves at the center to participate in the study; in all, 424 of 520 clients agreed to participate and completed the preintake survey; however, only 83 clients completed the pretermination survey. Thus, in this study, random selection from a participant pool did not occur because all available participants were used, and attrition was also an issue.

Establishing Validity in the Absence of Random Selection

Even though random selection has historically been considered an element critical to generalizing the results of a study sample to a larger population (Serlin, 1987), random selection does not typify research in counseling. Nevertheless, available samples may be good enough to address our research purpose. The "good enough" principle stipulates that nonrandom samples can have characteristics such that generalization to a certain population is reasonable. Accordingly, when samples are obtained by some means other than random sampling, "valid inference can be made to a hypothetical population resembling the sample" (p. 300). In this way, generalization is made rationally rather than statistically.

However, rationally based generalizations should be theory driven (Serlin, 1987); we will use two different career development theories to illustrate. First, Holland's (1997) theory of vocational types proposes that individuals' career choices and satisfaction levels are linked with their personality types. To examine this theory, a sample with a wide spectrum of career focuses and personality types would be ideal.

A sample utilizing college students across different majors would seem appropriate as this population is currently immersed in exploring their career interests and making early career-related decisions. Thus, undergraduates may constitute a sufficient sample from which to make valid inferences. Second, Super's (1980) theory of vocational development links various career developmental tasks with various stages of life. The focus of the theory spans across life stages from birth to retirement. Thus, utilizing a college student sample to address life span issues would not be sufficient. In sum, undergraduates are "good enough" to examine Holland's theory of vocational types, but they are not "good enough" for studies examining Super's vocational development theory. In reference to Poteat et al.'s (2011) study of homophobic victimization cited earlier, although the sample may not sufficiently represent the general population of all adolescents in the United States or across the world, it may be "good enough" in that results demonstrate that general and homophobic victimization affects adolescents' psychosocial and educational development among adolescents in midwest public schools that are predominately White.

Thus, in the absence of random sampling, researchers must take great care in identifying the characteristics of study participants. The burden of proof is on the researcher to establish that the characteristics of participants are such that generalizations to a relevant hypothetical population are valid. The current vogue in counseling research is to eschew studies with limited generalizability in lieu of field studies with actual clients. Accordingly, for studies investigating anxiety (including treatment studies), clients seeking treatment for anxiety are favored over mildly anxious undergraduates who had not presented themselves for counseling.

Of course, recruiting clients seeking treatment is more difficult than recruiting undergraduates. Researchers must take special care when making generalizations about differences between groups defined by categorical status variables. To understand these difficulties, consider first a true experimental design in which a treatment is compared to a control group. In such a design, questions about the cause of any differences found between the treatment and control groups are internal validity questions; if the study is well designed (specifically, if the subjects are randomly assigned), then the effects are relatively unambiguously attributed to the treatment.

The generalizability of the results is an external validity issue. Consider, for example, the study in which Armento et al. (2012) examined the efficacy of a religious-based behavioral activation intervention for depression. Using 50 college students in which 47 were Christians, findings are narrowly restricted to a sample that is predominantly Christians. To address this issue, it would be helpful to see if their sample of predominantly Christians reflected the composition of their defined population. To illustrate, using Figure 8.1 as an example, it would be important to examine whether the percentages of the black, gray, and white dots representing different types of people on a certain characteristic (e.g., religion, race) are the same between the population and sample. Let's say that the black dots represent Christians, gray dots Muslims, and white dots Buddhists. To determine whether the religious distribution of the sample is representative of the religious distribution of the population, we would use a chi-square test to examine whether the proportions of individuals from these three religious groups are statistically different between the sample and population. If the proportions of the three religious groups are similar between the sample and population, we would have more confidence that the sample is representative of the population of interest. If not, it would be harder to make the case that results found from the sample could be generalized to the population. Nevertheless, Armento's study makes an important contribution because it demonstrates, at least for this sample that is mainly Christian, the treatment works; future researchers should examine whether this intervention is effective for other groups (e.g., Buddhists, Muslims) as well.

Now consider a hypothetical status study whose purpose is to compare the anxiety, stress, and academic performance in two samples—White American and African American adolescents. Suppose that samples of White American and African American students were obtained from a school in which the White American students were transported from suburban areas, and that significant differences were found between the groups in levels of anxiety, stress, and achievement. Because there was no random assignment, the two populations might well have differed on many characteristics other than ethnicity, such as socioeconomic status (SES), family status, parental involvement and supervision, community crime rates, and so forth. Consequently, it would be difficult to attribute the differences in dependent variables to ethnicity, and therefore the sampling method causes a problem for both internal and external validity. It might well be that the differences between the two groups of students were due to the characteristics mentioned, and had the researchers selected samples that held these factors constant (which would be extremely difficult), the differences would not have been present. The point here is that when status variables are used, internal as well as external validity problems arise, whereas if a study involves a true independent variable, only external validity could potentially be problematic because the generalizability of results relies on the characteristics of the participants, researchers must carefully document the important characteristics of the sample. Given that race and ethnicity are always important considerations in generalizability for studies in the United States, Ponterotto and Casas (1991) made the following recommendation:

> Knowing simply the ethnic make-up and mean ages of one's sample is insufficient in assessing result generalizability. Describe the sample fully: mean and median age; educational level (and in immigrant groups, where the education was received); socioeconomic status; gender; preferred language and level of acculturation in immigrant samples; the level of racial identity development; geographic region of the study, and any other sample characteristics you believe your reader would consider when interpreting the results. As a rule of thumb, the more accurately you can describe your sample, the more accurate you can be in determining the generalizability of your results. (p. 107)

The National Institutes of Health's (NIH) guidelines on the inclusion of subpopulations recognize the importance of gender and race/ethnicity as critical status variables in research. The guidelines state:

> The overarching goal of this policy is to ensure the appropriate inclusion of women and minorities in all clinical research supported by the National Institutes of Health (NIH). NIH supported clinical research should address/include the population(s) at risk for the disease or condition under study and ensure that the distribution of study participants by sex/gender, race and ethnicity reflects the population needed to accomplish the scientific goals of the study. (National Institutes of Health, 2013, General NIH Inclusion Policy Questions, question 1)

Admittedly, recruiting appropriate samples of racial and ethnic groups can often be difficult. Suggestions and guidelines have been provided for conducting research with ethnic minorities as well as economically disadvantaged populations. For those interested in more detailed information, handbooks by Knight, Roosa, and Umaña-Taylor (2009) and Trimble and Fisher (2005) would be good resources.

In addition to the discussion on diverse populations in the United States, the counseling psychology field has become increasingly aware of the need for globalization and a focus on international populations (Marsella & Pedersen, 2004). In other words, most of the studies in psychology have been conducted using samples from the United States. In response to this issue, Arnett (2008) conducted an analysis of the national affiliations of study samples and authors of articles published by the American Psychological Association (APA) journals. He concluded that the APA journals have been too narrowly focused on U.S. populations, which only comprise 5% of the world population. Arnett argued that "the majority of the world's population lives in conditions vastly different from the conditions of Americans, underlining doubts of how well American psychological research represent humanity." (p. 602). Thus, he calls for more attention to study the "neglected 95%" of the people around the world. As for guidelines on studying various populations around the globe, Yang (2000) proposes a model to examine single cultures as well as make cross-cultural comparisons using indigenous approaches to achieve a more balanced global psychology. Also, Ægisdóttir, Gerstein, and Çinarbaş (2008) provide guidelines on methodological issues regarding bias, equivalence, and translation for cross-cultural research in counseling. And the *International Handbook of Cross-cultural Counseling: Cultural Assumptions and Practices Worldwide* (Gerstein, Heppner, Ægisdóttir, Leung, & Norsworthy, 2009) would also be a good resource that addresses various issues related to counseling from a global perspective.

Determining the Number of Participants

The number of participants used in a study is important because as the number of participants increases, so does the probability that the sample is representative of the population. The question "How many participants?" is intimately involved with the concept of statistical power. Recall that power is the probability of rejecting the null hypothesis when the alternative is true, or the likelihood of detecting an effect when the effect is truly present. Even given a treatment that is effective, a study comparing the treatment group to a control group will not necessarily result in a statistically significant finding—it is entirely possible that even though an effect exists (the alternative hypothesis is true), the obtained test statistic is not sufficiently large to reach significance (i.e., the null hypothesis is not rejected). Generally, the greater the power, the better the study (although after we discuss factors that lead to increased power, we will present a caveat to this general rule).

Power is dependent on (a) the particular statistical test used, (b) the alpha level, (c) the directionality of the statistical test, (d) the size of the effect, and (e) the number of participants. Even though an in-depth discussion of these factors involves statistics more than design, an elementary understanding of statistics is required before the important question "How many participants?" can be answered (see Cohen, 1988; Kraemer & Thiemann, 1987; and Wampold & Drew, 1990, for more complete discussions).

Before power can be determined, the researcher must select a statistical test. For a given situation, often a variety of statistical tests will do the job. For example, for a design with two treatment groups and a control group, the most frequently used test is an analysis of variance. However, nonparametric alternatives exist; in this case, the Kruskall-Wallis test would be appropriate. The relative power of different alternative tests varies, and this topic is beyond the scope of this book (see, e.g., Bradley, 1968). The point is that power must be calculated for each specific statistical test.

Another factor that affects power is the alpha level. If a researcher sets alpha conservatively, say at .01, then it is more difficult to reject the null hypothesis, and power is decreased. So in being careful not to falsely reject the null hypothesis (in setting alpha small), the researcher sacrifices power.

The directionality of the test also affects power. If a two-tailed (i.e., nondirectional) test is used, the researcher reserves the option of rejecting the null hypothesis in either direction. This is helpful when a researcher is interested in results in both directions and/or is unclear about the direction. For instance, when comparing two treatments, knowing whether Treatment A or Treatment B is superior is important; however, keeping options open in both directions costs the researcher power because it is more difficult to detect effects in this case than when one direction or the other is specified. One-tailed (directional) tests are more powerful when the effect is in the expected direction. For example, when testing the efficacy of a treatment vis-à-vis a control group, it makes sense to test only whether the treatment is more effective than no treatment (one is rarely interested in knowing whether the treatment is less effective than no treatment). By specifying the direction (that the treatment is superior to no treatment), the researcher increases the power of the statistical test.

The most difficult factor to specify in any determination of power is the size of the true effect. When a treatment is extraordinarily effective, the effect of the treatment is relatively easy to detect, and thus power is high. For example, if a treatment of depression reduces self-deprecating statements from an average of 20 per hour to zero, achieving a statistically significant finding will be easy. However, if the reduction is from an average of 20 self-deprecating statements to 18, then detecting this small change will be difficult. Specifying the size of the effect before the study is conducted is problematic—if one knew the effect size for any experiment beforehand, there would be no need to conduct the study. Nevertheless, the effect size must be stipulated before the number of participants can be determined. The effect size can be stipulated in a number of ways. First, prior research in relevant areas often provides clues about the size of effects. For instance, if the effect of cognitive-behavioral treatments of test anxiety is known to be a certain size, it is reasonable to expect that the effect of a cognitive-behavioral treatment of performance anxiety would be approximately the same size. A second way to stipulate effect size is to specify the effect size considered to have practical or clinical significance. For example, in a treatment study involving a treatment group and a control group, the researcher might want to stipulate the percentage of those treated that exceeds the mean of those untreated. Using normal distributions, it can be shown that an effect size of

1.0 indicates that at the end of treatment, 84% of the treatment group functioned better than the mean of the control group (assuming normality); an effect size of 1.5 indicates that 93% functioned better than the mean of the control group; an effect size of 2.0 indicates that 98% functioned better than the mean of the control group. Translation of effect size into indexes of clinical improvement allows the researcher to gauge how large the effect must be to have clinical significance. Finally, based on a number of considerations, Cohen (1988) classified effects into three categories: small, medium, and large. This scheme makes it possible for a researcher to determine the number of participants needed to detect each of these three effect sizes. Of course, the researcher must still stipulate which of the three sizes of effects the study should detect. Furthermore, Cohen's determination of effect size is arbitrary and cannot apply equally well to all areas of social and behavioral research. Nevertheless, in the absence of other guiding lights, stipulation of a medium-sized effect has guided many a researcher.

The last determination needed before deciding how many participants to use in an experiment is the level of power desired. Power of .80 has become the accepted standard (although, again, this level is arbitrary). A level of power of .80 refers to a probability level; that is, 80% of the time the stipulated effect size will be detected (i.e., the test will be statistically significant). It also means that there is a 20% chance that no statistically significant results will be found when the effect in fact exists!

Once the researcher has selected the statistical test to be used, chosen whether to use a one-tailed or two-tailed test, set alpha, stipulated a desirable level of power, and determined the effect size to be detected, he or she can ascertain the number of participants needed to obtain the stipulated level of power.

There are computer programs available to calculate the number of participants needed for a study. G*Power (Faul, Erdfelder, Lang, & Buchner, 2007) is a common free software that can be used for this purpose, which can be downloaded from http://www.gpower.hhu.de/en.html. PowerUp! is another program that calculates minimum detectable effect sizes and minimum required sample sizes for experimental and quasi-experimental design studies (Dong & Maynard, 2013). These software programs are relatively easy to use. For example, in G*Power, users will be asked to (a) select the type of statistical analysis that will be used, and (b) enter the estimated effect size, alpha level, and desired power. Then G*Power will calculate the sample size needed. Through these programs, one can also easily determine the relationships between effect size, desired power, and the sample size required.

Some caveats are needed about determining sample size. First, all of the procedures presume that the assumptions of the chosen statistical test are met. When assumptions are violated, power is typically decreased, so beware. Second, even though one often hears rules of thumb about sample sizes—10 participants for each variable in a multiple regression, 15 participants to a cell in a factorial design, 5 to 10 participants for each free parameter in structural equation modeling (Bentler & Chou, 1987), and so forth—be warned that such rules can be oversimplistic and misleading (e.g., refer to Wolf, Harrington, Clark, & Miller, 2013, for a discussion on SEM sample size issues). In some instances fewer than 10 participants per variable are needed, and in other instances many more than 10 are needed. Third, the general rule that the more participants for an experiment, the better, is also misleading. Certainly, the researcher wants to have a sufficient number of participants to have a reasonable opportunity (say 80%) to detect an effect of a specified size. However, using too many participants raises the possibility that a very small effect size can be detected (see Meehl, 1978, for an excellent discussion of this issue). Although small effects can be interesting, they often mislead the researcher into believing that something important has occurred when in fact only a trivial finding has been obtained. Given a large enough sample, a researcher might find a significant (although meaningless) correlation between, say, hours of television watched and shoe size. An interesting exercise might be to obtain the World Values Survey ($n > 200,000$) available from http://www.worldvaluessurvey.org and attempt to find two variables that are not significantly related. For example, in a regression problem, a statistically significant finding with a large number of participants that accounts for only 2% of the variance in the dependent variable will likely add little to our understanding of psychological processes. Because statistical significance can be obtained for trivial effects, it is often recommended that researchers report effect size and power in addition to significance levels (Shadish, Cook, & Campbell, 2002).

EXTERNAL VALIDITY AND POPULATION ISSUES

Recall that external validity refers to the generalizability of findings across persons (e.g., adolescents, college students, African Americans, gay men), settings (e.g., university counseling center, in-patient hospital setting, mental health center), or times (e.g., 1960s, 1990s, 2000s). The most direct way to increase the external validity of findings is to build into the design variables that represent persons, settings, or times. Because issues related to the generalizability of findings across persons are the most relevant to counseling researchers, we next illustrate these issues and indicate how they might also extend to settings or times. We first describe how population issues can be incorporated into factorial designs, and then we discuss several general considerations of studying external validity in factorial designs. It is important to note that even though factorial designs are discussed here, they are not the only designs that can examine population issues.

Use of Factorial Designs to Study External Validity

To determine how results apply to various groups of persons, a status variable related to persons can be added to the design to create a factorial design (discussed in Chapter 11). Consider a factorial design with one independent variable (with three levels) and a status variable related to persons (with two levels); for example, consider the three levels of the independent variable to be three treatments, and the two levels of the status variable related to persons to be gender. Interpretation of the main effects and the interaction effects of this factorial design will illustrate how it establishes the generality of the results across persons.

Suppose that it was found that there was no treatment effect; that is, there was insufficient evidence to establish that one treatment was more effective than any other. External validity involves answering the question of whether this result applies equally to males and females. It may well be that there was no main effect for gender as well (e.g., no effect of gender across treatments). However, the presence of an interaction (e.g., does the effect of a particular treatment vary depending on the gender of a client?) effect most clearly addresses issues related to external validity. For example, Treatment A may have been most effective with males, whereas Treatment C may have been most effective with females, indicating that the results are not generalizable across gender. Clearly, considerations of person variables can be vital to the proper understanding of research results.

Parenthetically, both gender and racial/ethnic variables are receiving increased attention in the counseling literature. Moreover, as mentioned earlier in the chapter, there are a broad array of person variables beyond gender, race, and ethnicity (e.g., sexual orientation, nationality, religion, social class, disability status). And these diverse cultural and demographic factors can have significant influence on the psychological processes of individuals. Although it is impossible to account for all these factors in one single study, cumulative research over time with different populations examining the varying effects of these factors could eventually result in more nuanced knowledge bases.

The general principle to be gleaned from this discussion is that when external validity is examined within a design (by including person as a status variable), it is the interaction effect that is most interesting. An interaction effect indicates that the levels of the independent variable interact with the person variable to produce different outcomes. Researchers with a background in educational research will recognize this phenomenon as essentially that of aptitude-treatment interactions.

Some theoretical models in counseling highlight the importance of taking into account contextual and individual factors. For example, the cross-national cultural competence (CNCC) model theorized that (a) personality, attitudes, and coping; (b) immersion experiences; and (c) mental processing of cross-national experiences are all factors that may have influences on one's level of cultural competence, specifically cross-cultural awareness, knowledge, and skills. In other words, the CNCC stresses that not all individuals have the same level of cultural competencies, and the different levels of competencies would be associated with various individual and environmental factors. Moreover, interventions to increase cultural competencies may not be equally effective for everyone. Thus, when studying the effects of interventions, it is important to take into account individual and environmental factors. Following is an example in which multicultural training on diversity awareness was found to have different levels of effects across varying types of individuals (i.e., White versus racial/ethnic minority).

Chao, Wei, Good, and Flores (2011) found a significant interaction effect between race/ethnicity (i.e., White vs. ethnic minority) and multicultural training on multicultural awareness. For students that received lower levels of training, racial/ethnic minority trainees had significantly higher multicultural awareness than their White counterparts; however, for those that received higher levels of training, there was no significant difference between White and racial/ethnic minority students. In other words, receiving more training significantly enhanced the multicultural awareness of White students but not for racial/ethnic minority students, because racial/ethnic minority students already had high levels of multicultural awareness regardless of the level of training received. This study illustrates that a particular type of training can have different types of impact for different groups of people.

Thus far we have discussed external validity in terms of a factorial design, with emphasis on the interaction effect. However, examination of interaction effects is not limited to factorial designs (and concomitant analyses of variance). For example, regression analysis also accommodates interaction effects nicely, and thus, external validity is related to the interaction of independent and person variables, regardless of the analysis.

Considerations in Examining Generalizability across Populations

Although the factorial design approach to external validity seems straightforward, there are some issues concerning group differences that need consideration. One important and difficult to resolve issue is the choice of variables related to persons, settings, or times. Furthermore, the researcher cannot know whether an interaction effect crucial to external validity would occur with other unexamined person, setting, or time variables. In this section, we address the following issues: (a) selecting which variable to examine; (b) the importance of understanding the process underlying group differences; (c) the proportion of different groups in the sample; (d) philosophical issues related to comparing groups; and (e) establishing external validity through multiple studies.

Deciding on which population variable to examine can be challenging. There are literally hundreds of such variables that might be included in the design, including gender, ethnicity, sexual orientation, SES, race, age, level of disability, intelligence, personality types, and type of clinic. Most of these variables are status variables, for which, as we have seen, sampling becomes intimately involved in both internal and external validity. Moreover, some of the most important status variables are not clearly defined. For example, although race is an important aspect of American society, there are still controversies around the lack of scientific bases for race and how it is defined (Leong & Eccles, 2010). Finally, even if the variables can be well defined and measured, related constructs may be more important. For example, gender and ethnicity appear often in counseling research, but it is possible that sex-role orientation is more critical than biological gender, or that level of acculturation and/or racial identity is more critical than ethnicity. Many psychologists have offered these alternatives to simplistic notions of race and ethnicity, and researchers are engaged in a significant and productive debate regarding the use of various cultural instruments in counseling research (see, e.g., Knight, Roosa, & Umaña-Taylor, 2009; Ponterotto & Grieger, 2008; Spanierman & Poteat, 2005). At this juncture, we invoke the usual refrain: Knowledge of the substantive area should inform the choice of variables related to external validity. If prior research or theory—or for that matter, common sense—indicates that gender is an important variable, add it to the design. Alternatively, it is unwise to include variables when there is no compelling reason for their inclusion.

The field of counseling has placed much emphasis on understanding the role of race/ethnicity/culture on counseling and psychological functioning; researchers are encouraged to investigate this area, for race/ethnicity/culture factors are everywhere. Whether or not a given study is directly focused on race/ethnicity/culture, the influence of these factors on behavior and on the research endeavor should be understood. For example, parenting styles and family relationships may look different across cultural groups and have different effects on psychological well-being. And conducting research aimed at comparing differences across ethnic groups (e.g., African Americans and White Americans) is different from understanding certain constructs within a specific ethnic group (e.g., African Americans). How the research study is designed will affect the type of findings and knowledge gained from the study.

Understanding the complexities within group differences is important. We have alluded to the problems inherent in comparing two groups formed from differences on a categorical status variable (e.g., African American and White American groups). Because the issues involved in examining group differences are so important, we explore them again, in a slightly different way. A previous example involved differences between African American and White adolescents in terms of stress, anxiety, and achievement. The goal of such a study was to identify mean differences between the two populations (e.g., are the mean levels of anxiety for the two groups different?). One of the most persistent but controversial findings in psychology involves just such a comparison—namely, the group differences found on traditional tests of intelligence.

The point that we want to make is that simply identifying group differences on some variable is often limited in usefulness; ultimately, an important goal of our research is to promote greater understanding of underlying psychological processes across and within group differences.

When differences between groups are found, a vital question arises: Are the psychosocial processes that lead to these differences the same for both groups? Suppose there are two groups, A and B, that reliably show differences in some construct, say antisocial behavior (Group A > Group B). A critical piece of the puzzle is to determine whether the factors that lead to antisocial behavior in the two groups are the same. Given that we know inadequate parental supervision to be a key causal construct in antisocial behavior, the question could be expressed as follows: "Is academic achievement in Group A higher because there is more adequate supervision, or because there is some other variable that uniquely influences behavior in Group A but not Group B?" In a comprehensive reanalysis of several large data sets, Rowe, Vazsonyi, and Flannery (1994) found racial similarity in developmental processes related to achievement and behavior; that is, they found that the variables that predicted achievement and behavior were common across groups, and that no variables were uniquely important to specific racial groups.

Clearly, if a researcher is going to examine group differences, an understanding of the processes that lead to those differences is paramount to making sense of the results. Basically, if an examination across populations reveals that the causal factors are similar, then the efficacy of interventions would be similar; if causal factors are not similar, then group-specific interventions would be needed. More research is needed to establish the efficacy of culture-specific educational and psychological interventions.

As an example of systematic examination of group differences, Fouad (2002) has investigated the cross-cultural validity of the Strong Interest Inventory and the RIASEC model of career interests, demonstrating basic support for similarity of interests and structure of interests. These findings have made important contributions to our understanding of career interests across cultures. Moreover, additional research was followed up to examine underlying factors that explain certain cultural difference. For example, factors that influence whether women persisted or left the field of engineering were explored through qualitative (Fouad, Fitzpatrick, & Liu, 2011) and quantitative (Singh et al., 2013) studies. Fouad et al. found family responsibilities such as care for children as one of the main themes for women that left the field of engineering. Singh et al.'s study found developmental opportunities at work (a form of organizational support) associated with self-efficacy and outcome expectations of female engineers.

As an example of unique processes in different groups, Eugster and Wampold (1996) found that the factors that predicted global evaluation of a counseling session were different for the counselor and the client. Although clients and therapists had some factors in common, the researchers found that clients' global evaluation of a session was positively related to their perceptions of therapist interpersonal style and of the real relationship, whereas therapists' evaluations were positively related to their perceived expertness and negatively related to perceptions of the real relationship. These differences were verified by statistically testing the differences in regression equations. The goal of this research was not to determine whether there were mean differences between client and therapist evaluation of sessions, but to determine whether the factors that form the bases of these evaluations were different.

RESEARCH IN ACTION 8.2

Revisit the research topic that you came up with earlier in this chapter. Would you expect there to be any possible differences in your findings if you had chosen a different target population? Why or why not? Identify two alternative target populations that would be interesting and meaningful to investigate with your research topic. How feasible would it be to collect data from these two alternative populations? List the kind of challenges you might face during the data collection process.

Another issue related to group differences involves the proportions of participants assigned when status variables are included in a factorial design. It is desirable in a factorial design to have equal numbers of participants in each cell; in this way, main and interaction effects are independent (provided the assumptions of the analysis of variance are met; see Wampold & Drew, 1990). Accordingly, equal numbers of participants of each type should be selected (recruited). For instance, equal numbers of males and females should be selected and then randomly assigned to the three treatments. For research on gender, this presents no problems; however, when the base rates of various person variables are different, conceptual (as well as statistical) problems occur. For example, having equal numbers of American Indians and White Americans in a sample may not be representative of the general population in the United States (i.e., the proportion of American Indians are much lower than White Americans). If one were conducting a study to examine how various types of political television commercials affected voting preferences of White Americans and Americans Indians, equal numbers of these persons would be selected. The results of this study might be theoretically interesting and applicable to real political campaign strategies. However, if one were polling to determine the expected outcome of an election, one would not want to bias the sample by having equal numbers of Americans Indians and White Americans in the sample. Generally, experimental studies that examine theoretical phenomena or treatment efficacy should have equal numbers of participants. However, for studies that examine relations between variables in society, participants should be selected so that the proportions of the various person variables reflect the proportions in the population. In sum, whether to have equal number of participants between groups depends on the nature of the research question.

The factorial design approach to external validity also has philosophical implications for various classes of persons. Typically, studies are either conducted on predominantly majority samples (e.g., White Americans) or include person variables that contrast a majority sample with a minority sample (e.g., White Americans vs. African Americans). The latter design includes the assumption that White Americans are somehow the norm, and that all other groups are to be contrasted with them (see Delgado-Romero, Galván, & Maschino, 2005; Heppner, Casas, Carter, & Stone, 2000). It is also assumed that each of these groups is homogeneous. African Americans comprise a diverse population, and typically such diversity (in, e.g., level of acculturation, racial identity, and generational status; again, see Delgado-Romero, Galván, & Maschino, 2005; Heppner et al., 2000) must be considered in research designs. Furthermore, there are phenomena that may be culture specific and for which it is not optimal or even sensible to use a design that contrasts various groups. For instance, the reasons for the underutilization of mental health clinics by ethnic minorities, which is a major concern to providers of service, may best be understood by examining intraethnic processes rather than ethnic differences. To illustrate, a comparison study on ethnic differences only provides information on the utilization rate across various ethnic groups. However, to gain an understanding of why certain groups underutilize mental health services, the study could be designed to examine the potential reasons (e.g., attitudes, perceived discrimination, stigma, accessibility) that may lead to underutilization within the particular group of interest.

External validity is often established using multiple studies. For example, single-participant designs do not include person variables because only one or a few participants are used. Therefore, researchers use a strategy called systematic replication (Barlow & Hersen, 1984), which involves replicating an experiment while varying a single element. The idea of systematic replication can apply to group studies as well. For example, interaction effects might be identified by two studies that differed only insofar as one had female participants and the other had male participants. However, there are disadvantages of such a strategy. True replication is difficult to accomplish, and thus the differences between two studies may be due to factors other than different types of participants. Furthermore, examination of external validity in one study allows direct estimation of the size of the interaction effect, a procedure that is precluded in the systematic replication strategy.

SUMMARY AND CONCLUSIONS

Population issues affect the design and interpretation of research in counseling and counseling psychology. A critical issue in the development of a study is the selection of a sample of participants from a broader target population. Considerable care is needed to (a) define the target population (the population to which the investigator wishes to generalize), and (b) select participants that fit the definition of the target population.

Theoretically, the generalizability of the results is established by randomly selecting a sample from a population. Because of the practical constraints on most counseling research, sampling is rarely achieved through true random selection. Instead, researchers often use nonrandom samples that have similar relevant characteristics to a target population, and then rationally suggest that the results apply to a population with the same characteristics.

Finally, a critical issue in selecting participants is determining how many participants are needed to adequately test the relationships among the study's constructs of interest. The number of participants needed for any study pertains to statistical power, or the probability of rejecting the null hypothesis when the alternative hypothesis is actually true. With regard to estimating statistical power (and thus the number of participants needed), we discussed

(a) the particular statistical test used, (b) alpha level, (c) directionality of the statistical test, and (d) effect size.

Thus, investigators must make a number of decisions in selecting participants for a study. Typically, researchers are interested in generalizing the results of a particular study to a larger population of individuals, which is the essence of external validity. External validity also relates to the generalizability of findings across persons, settings, or times. We suggested that the most direct means to increase the external validity of findings is to build into the design factors that represent relevant persons, settings, or times. In this way, external validity can be investigated by examining the interaction of the independent variable and a variable related to persons, settings, or times.

Because counseling is an applied profession designed to help a broad array of individuals in various settings across different times, external validity is very important. Far too often, convenience samples consisting of predominantly White American undergraduate participants are used in counseling research. We strongly encourage efforts to broaden the external validity of research in counseling in order to develop the more extensive databases that are needed in the counseling profession.

STIMULUS QUESTIONS

Exercises on Population Issues

1. A researcher is considering the relative efficacy of two treatments for depression. What population issues are important when considering the interpretation of the results?

2. Discuss the differences between random selection and random assignment. How are these concepts related to the validity of a study?

3. Select a recent issue of a counseling journal. Describe the samples used in the research in the issue and rate the adequacy of the samples vis-à-vis the purpose of the research.

4. Suppose that you are designing a study to test theoretical propositions related to career development. Discuss issues related to the definition of the population and recruitment of participants.

5. Select a population status variable that you would like to examine (e.g., gender, sexual orientation, race) to better understand group differences on a specific topic. Discuss issues to consider when comparing and interpreting group differences.

Diverse Perspectives: Conceptual and Methodological Considerations

Chapter 9

With Kevin O. Cokley and Germine H. Awad

One of the distinguishing characteristics of counseling and counseling psychology research is its emphasis on multiculturalism. "Multiculturalism, in an absolute sense, recognizes the broad scope of dimensions of race, ethnicity, language, sexual orientation, gender, age, disability, class status, education, religious/spiritual orientation, and other cultural dimensions. All of these are critical aspects of an individual's ethnic /racial and personal identity, and psychologists are encouraged to be cognizant of issues related to all of these dimensions of culture. In addition, each cultural dimension has unique issues and concerns" (American Psychological Association, 2002, pp. 9–10). As discussed throughout this book, counselors and psychologists must be culturally competent in providing mental health services to an increasingly diverse clientele. Counselors and psychologists must also be equipped to conduct and critically evaluate research in terms of its responsiveness to, and treatment of, cultural issues.

It is important for students to understand that the consideration of diverse cultural perspectives is relatively new in the counseling profession, as well as the larger psychological profession. For example, Bernal, Cumba-Aviles, and Rodriguez-Qunitana (2014) observed that until around 1999, culture, race, ethnicity, and language had not received much attention in the overall body of psychological research. Many scholars have noted that the predominant psychological literature has not usually considered factors such as race, ethnicity, and culture (Bernal & Scharró-del-Río, 2001; Burlew, 2003; Hall, 2001; Lau, Chang, & Okazaki, 2010; Miranda, Nakamura, & Bernal, 2003; Ponterotto & Mallinckrodt, 2007; Sue & Sue, 2003; Wyatt et al, 2003), and when culture and race are considered, they are often treated as nuisance variables (S. Sue, 1999).

Especially in the last 15 years, however, there has been more focus on diverse populations within counseling and psychology in general, and sparked by social movements (Hall, 2014). Pedersen (1991) initially described multicultural psychology as the "fourth force" in psychology, and is widely regarded as such today. For example, the widespread focus on multicultural issues is evident in all of the professional organizations in counseling and psychology in the United States such as the American Psychological Society (APS), American Psychological Association (APA), and American Counseling Association (ACA). Moreover, within these organizations, such as the APA, many of the Divisions focus on an array of diversity issues (e.g. Divisions 9, 17, 35, 36,

44, 45, 51, and 52). The major journals within counseling, counseling psychology, and psychology more broadly (e.g., *Journal of Counseling Psychology, Journal of Counseling and Development, The Counseling Psychologist*) regularly publish a broad array of articles that examine multicultural and cross-cultural issues. In addition, there are numerous journals that focus specifically on multicultural and cross-cultural issues, including *Cultural Diversity and Ethnic Minority Psychology, Psychology of Sexual Orientation and Gender Diversity, Psychology of Women Quarterly, Men and Masculinity,* and *International Perspectives in Psychology.* Many comprehensive books have also been written on multicultural psychology; for example, Leong (2014) has developed an impressive three-volume set, the *APA Handbook of Multicultural Psychology.* Further, there are a number of psychological organizations that focus exclusively on diverse groups such as the Association of Black Psychologists, Asian American Psychological Association, Association for Women in Psychology, National Latina/o Psychological Association, and Society of Indian Psychologists. Each of these organizations publishes journals that emphasize these perspectives.

Likewise, professional organizations also have contributed greatly to the growth of multicultural perspectives in our work (see Hall, 2014). For example, in 2003 the APA published the Guidelines in Multicultural Education, Training, Research, Practice, and Organizational Change for Psychologists; in 2006 the APA published Report of the APA Task Force on the Implementation of the Multicultural Guidelines; in 2004, the APA published the Resolution on Culture and Gender Awareness in International Psychology. Thus, program accreditation guidelines within the APA require diverse multicultural perspectives throughout the training program.

David, Okazaki, and Giroux (2014) nicely depicted the changing focus on diversity issues by comparing two time frames in the PsycINFO database for key terms such as minority, racism, oppression, and ethnic identity. For the decade 1950 to 1959, there were 546 hits, in contrast to 35,006 hits between 2000 and 2009 (as of July 14, 2011). Reflective of such growth in the multicultural literature, Leong (as Editor-in-chief in 2014) published a three-volume *Handbook of Multicultural Psychology.* In short, although the assessment of the multicultural literature before 2000 by Bernal et al. (2014) was discouraging to some, the progress in the last 15 years has been considerably more positive, and "important advances have been made since 1999" (Bernal, et al., 2014, p. 106).

Nonetheless, how to conceptualize multiculturalism has been an ongoing debate in the literature. Some scholars and practitioners (e.g., Fukuyama, 1990; Robinson & Howard-Hamilton, 2000; Sue & Sue, 2003) argue for a broad definition of multiculturalism that would include, but would not be limited to, race, ethnicity, gender, sexual orientation, religion, socioeconomic status, disability, and other social identities that are marginalized or otherwise sources of differences among people. On the other hand, some (e.g., Carter, 1995; Helms, 1994; Helms & Cook, 1999) advocate for a narrower approach that focuses on race, in part because these authors maintain that a broad definition of multiculturalism serves to obscure or avoid focusing on difficult issues of race. Others have opted to use both a narrow approach (Atkinson, 2004) and a broad approach (Atkinson & Hackett, 2004).

For an introductory research design text such as this one, our primary goal is to address several methodological issues that are relevant to conducting research on a wide array of diverse groups, although some methodological issues may be more relevant for some particular groups. Thus, our goal is *not* to promote specific research agenda for any specific population or group; rather our goal is to assist beginning multicultural researchers in the consideration of a number of methodological issues from conceptualizing a particular study to interpreting the results. This chapter will discuss a number of conceptual and methodological issues related to research on diverse samples.

The first section of this chapter discusses definitions and ways of operationalizing various groups of identities that are commonly linked together (and confused) in the literature. We acknowledge that a full review of all identities relevant to multicultural research is beyond the scope of this chapter; indeed it is the focus of entire textbooks (e.g., Ponterotto, Casas, Suzuki, & Alexander, 2010; Sue & Sue, 2012). Instead, we define and describe a few groups of identities that are commonly used and conflated in counseling and psychology literature: (a) race, ethnicity, and culture; (b) sex, gender, sexuality, sexual orientation identity; and (c) social class, socioeconomic status (SES), and social status. The important issue to understand is that these terms are hard to define and are often used loosely and interchangeably, which makes efforts to scientifically study them very challenging.

The second section of this chapter focuses on several major research design considerations relevant to conducting multicultural research. We first discuss the use of descriptive and theory-driven research. We then introduce problems related to relying on distal variables (e.g., demographic characteristics that do not, in and of themselves, directly explain observed phenomenon) rather than proximal variables (e.g., psychological characteristics that more directly and parsimoniously explain observed phenomena) when designing and conducting research including multicultural constructs. Next, we discuss the potential usefulness of using proximal variables as mediator and moderator variables in multicultural research designs in order to increase our level of understanding about a particular multicultural topic. Finally, we discuss five threats to the internal validity of a study that may be particularly salient in the design of multicultural research.

The third and final section focuses on methodological challenges. We discuss several methodological challenges in conducting multicultural research and offer suggestions for dealing with these unique challenges. Within this discussion, we highlight important considerations related to internal and external validity within multicultural research. It is important to understand and use creative approaches to address these challenges, and ultimately inform our practice with research from diverse and underrepresented backgrounds.

We conclude this chapter by underscoring the need for considerably more research on diverse cultural groups to promote more and deeper psychological insights within culturally diverse samples within counseling and counseling psychology.

OPERATIONALIZING MULTICULTURAL VARIABLES

Operationalizing and defining central concepts to multicultural research is critically important because variations of psychological phenomena often exist between groups of people. Before any meaningful interpretations regarding these concepts can take place, the researcher must have a clear definition of what the concepts actually mean. As has been noted by several scholars (e.g., Betancourt & Lopez, 1993; Diemer et al., 2013; Moradi, Mohr, Worthington, & Fassinger, 2009), particularly problematic is that these concepts are unclearly defined and understood from a psychological perspective. Lack of clear operational definitions leads to terms being used interchangeably, confusion regarding who actually participated in a study, and misinterpretation of research results. In this section, our goal is to introduce the reader to several broad categories and to offer operational definitions of distinct, yet related categories. In this discussion, we highlight some of the challenges inherent in defining and measuring multicultural variables, given historical, sociopolitical, and psychological connotations related to each of these variables.

Race, Ethnicity, and Culture

Race   Race has been defined as a "… presumed classification of all human groups on the basis of visible physical traits or phenotype and behavioral differences" (Carter, 1995, p. 15), "… a sociopolitical designation in which individuals are assigned to a particular racial group based on presumed biological or visible characteristics such as skin color, physical features, and in some cases, language" (Carter, 1995, p. 15), and "… an inbreeding, geographically isolated population that differs in distinguishable physical traits from other members of the species" (Zuckerman, 1990, p. 1297). Most definitions of race include a biological component, where the assumption is that people can be divided into groups defined by similar physical features and behavioral tendencies. These groups have been generally classified as Mongoloid, Caucasoid, and Negroid, where Mongoloid is defined as anyone whose ancestors were born in East Asia, Caucasoid is defined as anyone whose ancestors were born in Europe, and Negroid is defined as anyone whose ancestors were born in sub-Saharan Africa (Rushton, 2000). The creation of racial taxonomies, however, has been documented to have occurred in a distinctly unscientific manner (Gould, 1994). In fact, there does not exist any agreed-upon racial classification system.

There are no physical traits that are inherently and exclusively found in combination with other physical traits (e.g., "black" skin is not always linked with full lips; "white skin" is not always linked with straight hair, etc.). Most social scientists agree that race is not a biological reality, but rather a social construct used to divide people and perpetuate power relations and social inequities. Several researchers have discussed at length the problematic nature of race as a biological reality (Atkinson, 2004; Betancourt & Lopez, 1993; Helms & Cook, 1999; Zuckerman, 1990). Instead, scholars have suggested that race is best described as a social construct because there are real social consequences of being perceived to be a part of an identifiable racial group. These consequences include being the targets of prejudice and discrimination, which have long-term quality of life and mental health implications.

Ethnicity   Similar to race, there has not always been agreement or consistency on the definition of ethnicity or ethnic group. Carter (1995) defined ethnic group as "one's national origin, religious affiliation, or other type of socially or geographically defined group" (p. 13). Betancourt and Lopez (1993) defined ethnicity as "… groups that are characterized in terms of a common nationality, culture, or language" (p. 7), while Helms and Cook (1999) characterized ethnicity as a euphemism for race, and defined ethnicity as "... the national, regional, or tribal origins of one's oldest remembered ancestors and the customs, traditions, and rituals (i.e., subjective culture) handed down by these ancestors..." (p. 19). Phinney (1996) used the term *ethnicity* to encompass race and indicates that ethnicity refers to broad groups of people on the basis of culture of origin and race.

There are also broad and narrow interpretations of ethnicity (e.g., Atkinson, 2004). When ethnicity is characterized as sharing cultural characteristics and physical features, the broad interpretation of ethnicity is being used. This interpretation of ethnicity is similar to the way in which race is discussed (Atkinson). When ethnicity is restricted to cultural characteristics and differences, the narrow interpretation of ethnicity is being used (Atkinson). From our perspective, a broad interpretation of ethnicity is problematic because it primarily relies on physically distinguishable features as markers of ethnic group membership and minimizes the psychological and cultural processes believed to play a critical role in ethnic group membership.

Culture   Culture is perhaps the most difficult of these three terms to define because there are well over 100 different definitions of culture found in various psychological, anthropological, and sociological literatures. Although the definitions overlap in many instances, it is important to note that there are some central differences. These differences often depend on whether the scholar is defining culture psychologically, anthropologically, or sociologically. For example, a focus on objective culture includes studying such things as the human-made part of the environment (e.g., buildings, roads, homes, tools; Herskovits, 1955). Subjective culture, on the other hand, includes an emphasis on values, beliefs, attitudes, and role definitions (Triandis, 1972). Counselors and counseling psychologists, therefore, tend to be interested in subjective culture. Helms and Cook (1999) offered a psychological definition of culture: "... the values, beliefs, language, rituals, traditions, and other behaviors that are passed from one generation to another within any social group" (p. 24). Matsumoto (2000), also using a psychological definition, defined culture as:

> A dynamic system of rules, explicit and implicit, established by groups in order to ensure their survival, involving attitudes, values, beliefs, norms, and behaviors, shared by a group but harbored differently by each specific unit within the group, communicated across generations, relatively stable but with the potential to change across time. (p. 24)

Similar to ethnicity, culture has both broad and narrow interpretations. Broadly interpreted, culture encompasses any socially definable group with its own set of values, norms, and behaviors. Thus, culture would include but not be limited to ethnic groups; men and women; gays, lesbians, bisexuals, and transgender individuals; religions; disabled individuals; and socioeconomic statuses. Narrowly interpreted, culture encompasses countries (e.g., United States, Egypt, Philippines). More narrowly interpreted, culture refers to specific ethnic groups (e.g., African Americans, Mexican Americans). And even more narrowly interpreted, culture refers to specific ethnic groups residing in particular geographic regions who share similar customs or identities (e.g., first generation Hmong women living in the midwest region of the United States).

FIGURE 9.1 ⋮ Race, Ethnicity, and Culture

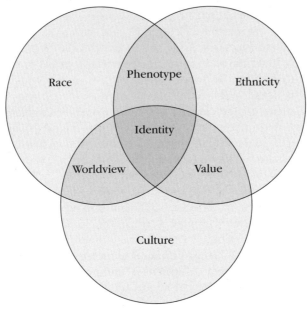

Source: Adapted from Create-Avenn system at www.venndiagram.com, 2004 Kevin Cokley, Ph.D., kcokley@siu.edu.

The interchangeable use and overlap of these concepts can be very confusing. Figure 9.1 illustrates the shared and unshared variance of these concepts. When phenotype, or physical characteristics, becomes the primary marker of ethnic group status, race and ethnicity share variance. In other words, they are being used interchangeably. When race and culture overlap, a racial worldview is created that involves classifying human groups as exclusive, ranking these human groups as superior or inferior, linking physical features with psychological qualities, and believing that the psychological qualities are inheritable, unalterable, and ordained by God (Smedley, 1999). When subjective culture (e.g., values, beliefs, attitudes, norms, behaviors) is the focus, ethnicity and culture overlap. The combination of race, ethnicity, and culture intersects to contribute to group identity.

Sex, Gender, Sexuality, and Sexual Orientation

Similarly, there are challenges in conceptualizing and defining constructs typically associated with sex and gender. Moradi and colleagues (2009) noted that there is a "lack of consensus about distinctions among separate but overlapping constructs such as sex, gender, gender expression, gender identity, transgender, gender variant, sexuality, sexual orientation, sexual identity, and sexual orientation identity (e.g., Chung & Katayama, 1996; Currah & Minter, 2000; Green, 2000; Worthington, Savoy, Dillon, & Vernaglia, 2002), as well as imprecise labels and language used in articulating these constructs in the extant literature" (p. 6). A full review of each construct is beyond the scope of this chapter. Our goal here (as with race, ethnicity, and culture) is to highlight important considerations relevant to multicultural researchers and to encourage those interested in such topics to carefully review and consider the myriad issues at hand in this work.

Sex, Intersexed, Gender, and Transgender   Historically, researchers have used sex and gender interchangeably in research. Recently, however, these variables have begun to be disentangled. In such definitions, sex denotes anatomical or biological characteristics as male or female and gender "refers to culturally ascribed characteristics associated with maleness or femaleness that are distinct from nata, assigned, or biological sex (Green, 2000)" (Moradi et al., 2009, p. 6). Intersexed refers to an individual who is born with male and female sexual anatomy. Transgender has been defined as "any person whose anatomy, appearance, identity, beliefs, personality characteristics, demeanor or behavior diverges from or is perceived to diverge from prevailing social norms about gender" (Currah & Minter, 2000, p. 17). Gender variant is a term that has emerged recently, and some (e.g., Moradi et al.) have noted its value as a broader and more inclusive term.

Counseling and psychology researchers have been particularly interested in the social and psychological aspects of these constructs, namely gender expression and gender identity. Moradi and colleagues (2009) described gender expression as the behaviors and characteristics that one chooses to outwardly display to others. In this way, gender expression captures an individual's decisions about how to present oneself in the world and may include behaviors such as attire, haircut and style, and use of makeup. Gender identity refers to individuals' decisions to intentionally claim a particular gender expression. In this way, gender identity captures individuals' decisions regarding behavioral characteristics and sense of self.

Sexuality, Sexual Identity, and Sexual Orientation Identity   Sexuality is considered to be the broadest categorization of sexual behavior in humans. Sexuality includes reference to sexual behavior, sexual values, preferences for sexual activities, and sexual needs (Moradi et al., 2009). Sexual identity is a narrower construct that includes claiming sexuality as relevant to the self, such as by self-labeling and accepting one's identity. Sexual orientation and sexual orientation identity are even more specific constructs. Moradi and colleagues (2009) defined them in this way:

> *Sexual orientation* is a specific manifestation of sexuality as expressed through sexual, affectional, and relational predispositions toward other persons on the basis of their gender, whereas *sexual orientation identity* is the inward or outward conscious claiming of those predispositions (see Worthington & Mohr, 2002, and Worthington et al., 2002, for a thorough discussion of the distinctions between sexual orientation, sexual identity, and sexual orientation identity). (p. 6)

As with race, ethnicity, and culture, there are numerous perspectives on how to best define and measure these distinct, yet related constructs. Further, there is acknowledgement that an attempt to define and measure these constructs has political and personal implications. Indeed, such tensions and disagreements are apparent in reviewing literature that has emerged from this burgeoning area of research and theory. For example, the tensions between nature and nurture as well as between essentialism and social constructionism are apparent. In practical terms, this manifests as challenges related to the reliance upon measures that have been demonstrated to have high psychometric support historically, but that are now outdated (e.g., the Kinsey Scale, which relies upon an understanding of heterosexuality and homosexuality as binary opposites on a continuum with bisexuality in the middle).

Social Class, Socioeconomic Status (SES), and Social Status

Social class, SES, and social status are terms that have been used interchangeably in the counseling and counseling psychology literature (e.g., APA Task Force on SES, 2007). Indeed, based on findings from their content analysis of three of the major counseling journals (i.e., *Journal of Multicultural Counseling and Development, Journal of Counseling and Development,* and *Journal of Counseling Psychology*) from 1981 to 2000, Liu and his colleagues (2004) noted that 484 different words have been used to describe social class. Growing attention to the challenges inherent in defining and measuring social class-related variables has become a growing concern among counseling and psychology researchers (e.g., Diemer et al., 2013; Liu et al., 2004; Thompson & Subich, 2011). As with race, ethnicity, and culture and sex, gender, and sexual orientation identity, scholars have advocated for further refinement in our operationalization and measurement of these related but unique constructs. Our intent in this section is to introduce readers to the complexities to be considered when integrating social class–related variables into research.

Social Class   Diemer and colleagues (2013) suggested that social class might best be defined as the "higher order construct representing an individual or group's relative position in an economic-social-cultural hierarchy" (p. 79). Accordingly, social class may be considered the umbrella term that encompasses the more narrow constructs of SES or perceived social status.

Socioeconomic Status (SES)   Socioeconomic status has been described as an index to denote an individual's position within a hierarchy relative to power, prestige, and control of resources (Diemer & Ali, 2009). In this way, SES is considered to be a relatively objective indicator that can be assessed via a variety of categorical measures. In particular, most measures of SES rely upon assessments of levels of prestige or access to resources (Duncan & Magnuson, 2003). Specifically, measures of prestige can include items that tap occupational prestige via categorization of job titles along a prestige ranking, educational attainment levels, income levels, and wealth. Measures that tap resources assess absolute and relative poverty. For example, researchers may categorize individuals based upon their qualification for public assistance (e.g., food stamps, housing subsidies, Temporary Assistance for Needy Families [TANF], free or reduced-price school lunches), based upon material hardship (e.g., financial hardship, food insecurity), or based upon neighborhood characteristics (e.g., percentage of households living below the poverty line). Taken together, measuring SES relies upon demographic, categorical, and objective indicators.

Subjective or Perceived Social Status (SSS or PSS)   SSS and PSS, on the other hand, tap individuals' perception of their social standing compared to others in society using more qualitative approaches (Liu et al., 2004). These measures, therefore, rely upon a multidimensional and psychological understanding of social class and assume that there are both social and psychological consequences associated with occupying a particular position on the stratification hierarchy (Fouad & Brown, 2000; Diemer et al., 2013; Thompson & Subich, 2011). In other words, this conceptualization recognizes that an individual who, for example, has a high income may not perceive oneself to have high status or have an emotional or psychological identification with others in that income level (e.g., a person whose well paid occupation is a sanitation worker).

Several new measures of PSS and SSS have emerged in the past decade. For example, Adler and colleagues (2000) developed a social class ladder that asks individuals to identify the rung to which they perceive themselves compared to others in their communities. Other researchers rely upon participant's self-identification into social class-related categories such as poor, working class, middle class that are tied to a theoretical explanation such as the social class worldview model (SCWM, Liu et al., 2004). Finally, some new measures of PSS attempt to capture individuals' perceptions of their access to social prestige, social power, and economic resources as compared to others (e.g., Thompson & Subich, 2007; 2011). This area of research is still in its infancy and continued efforts to develop theoretically consistent measures are needed.

In summary, our intent in this section was to offer operational definitions of some of the common variables used in multicultural research in counseling and counseling psychology. Moreover, the operational definitions of variables, and their measurement, have important implications for research and the interpretation of our research findings.

RESEARCH DESIGN CONSIDERATIONS

This section addresses three major considerations in utilizing different designs with diverse populations. First, we will discuss theory-driven versus descriptive research; this is a very important issue with considerable complexities within diverse groups that merits discussion. Second, we will discuss the use of distal and proximal factors to explain human behavior within diverse groups; in the past some of our research with diverse groups has been less than informative because of overreliance on distal variables. Third, we will discuss the utility of using moderator and mediator variables to extend our knowledge basis within diverse populations. Finally, we will discuss several threats to internal validity that are particularly troublesome in multicultural research.

Research involving cultural variables goes by many names (e.g., diversity research, cross-cultural research, ethnic minority research, multicultural research). Cross-cultural research is interested in determining which aspects of behavior are culture specific (i.e., emic) and which aspects of behavior are universal across cultures (i.e., etic) (Matsumoto, 1994). Typically, cross-cultural researchers are interested in examining behaviors between two or more countries. The *Journal of Cross-Cultural Psychology* is devoted to publishing cross-cultural research studies. Conversely, *International Perspectives in Psychology: Research, Practice,*

Consultation publishes research that examines human behavior around the globe from a psychological perspective, not to compare cultures but only to understand the psychological processes in different cultures; in essence, this journal publishes articles that promote the use of psychological science that is contextually informed and culturally inclusive.

Multicultural research examines groups living within the United States (e.g., African Americans and Latinas/os). As noted at the beginning of this chapter, entire journals in counseling and psychology are devoted to multicultural research (e.g., *Journal of Multicultural Counseling and Development, Cultural Diversity and Ethnic Minority Psychology*) as well as to particular multicultural topics, such as gender (e.g., *Psychology of Women Quarterly, Gender and Queer Studies*). Multicultural and cultural research within different countries/cultural contexts also are published in counseling journals (e.g., *Journal of Counseling Psychology, Journal of Counseling and Development*).

Theory-Driven versus Descriptive Research

There is nothing so practical as a good theory.

—Kurt Lewin

Kurt Lewin, father of modern social psychology, is best known for his field theory, which proposes that human behavior is the result of both the person's characteristics and the person's environment or social situation. Field theory is represented by the symbolic terms $B = f(P, E)$, where B = behavior, P = personality, and E = environment. Lewin's often-quoted statement about theory is a commonly cited driving force behind theory-driven research. In the past, concern was raised that much of the multicultural research was atheoretical and primarily descriptive (Betancourt & Lopez, 1993).

Although these criticisms were in part valid, it is important to consider two issues. The first issue is the sociohistorical context within which ethnic minority research developed. Early research pathologized ethnic minorities, operating out of a genetically deficient model whereby racial and ethnic minorities were considered to be inferior (Sue & Sue, 2003). This was later replaced with the "culturally deficient model," which assumed that the problems of racial/ethnic minorities could be attributed to being culturally deprived of White middle-class culture, which perpetuated the "myth of minority inferiority" (Sue & Sue, p. 56). The current zeitgeist emphasizes a culturally diverse model, in which it is not necessary for minority groups to be compared to majority groups as the standard (e.g., Asian Americans to White Americans), but rather cultural groups are understood on their own cultural terms in and of themselves.

In short, multicultural research was born out of the necessity to conduct research on ethnic minority populations that was not pathologically oriented or deficit driven. In many ways, its initial purpose was solely to refute the negative nature of much of the early research conducted on racial and ethnic minority populations. To that end, much of the research has focused on providing descriptive information about racial and ethnic minority populations, and describing in nonpathological terms how they differ from White Americans.

The second issue to consider is the level of existing knowledge on a particular research topic. Some topics have *not* been researched extensively with diverse groups, and thus there is presently a considerably smaller knowledge base (e.g., the efficacy of interventions with transgender youth; Hmong women's career development). As suggested in Chapter 6, qualitative research and atheoretical, descriptive research can be very informative for topics where there is a small knowledge base. Findings from these studies provide foundational knowledge from which future theory-driven research ensues.

For example, consider a topic of interest to multicultural researchers: rates of depression in racial/ethnic minority populations.

Research Application: Potential Research Questions and Associated Designs

Research Question of Interest	Type of Research Design
How is depression experienced among individuals living in the United States who identify as African American?	Qualitative research
What are prevalence rates of depression among individuals who are living in the United States and identify as Asian Americans?	Descriptive research
Are there significant differences in levels of depression as experienced among individuals living in the United States who identify as African American and Latina/o?	Atheoretical research using inferential statistics
Why do levels of depression differ among individuals living in the United States who identify as members of particular racial/ethnic groups? Are cognitive appraisals of environmental experiences responsible for these differences?	Theory-driven research
How does the intersection of identities (specifically gender, generation status, and ethnicity) impact experiences of depression among Latinas/os living in the United States?	Qualitative or descriptive research
How do American Indian's identification with their tribal group (Taos Pueblo, NM) and their personal and familial values impact rates of depression among individuals?	Theory-driven research using proximal (rather than distal) variables

The previous table depicts the process by which multicultural research can progress over time. In the example, researchers may have started by simply trying to understand how individuals who identify as belonging to the racial ethnic minority group experience depression or the prevalence rates of depression or whether some groups experience more than other groups. Qualitative (see Chapter 16 for more details), quasi-experimental (see Chapter 12), or quantitative descriptive designs (see Chapter 13) may offer the researcher a starting place from which to explore these questions. Most beginning stages of a research line rely on qualitative and atheoretical descriptive research. After numerous studies have been conducted, and trends are found across those studies, researchers might then design studies that more than simply document and describe findings, but rather examine *why* those trends/differences exist. In order for the researcher to meaningfully examine this question, it would be most useful for the researcher to (a) possess basic knowledge/theory about the nature of depression; (b) possess knowledge/theory about the stress and adjustment issues relevant to individuals from diverse ethnic groups; (c) possess considerable knowledge about the history and cultural values/dynamics of the ethnic groups of interest; and (d) have an empirical/theoretical understanding of how stress, adjustment, minority issues, history, and cultural values/dynamics may interact to influence the rates of depression among the relevant ethnic groups. In short, the researcher must be informed by the previous empirical literature/existing theory and must now hypothesize as to why the differences exist.

Using the previous examples, assume that the researcher is using a cognitive theory to understand the cause of depression. The researcher might hypothesize that the ethnic differences in depression are a result of differential social experiences with peers, neighbors, work colleagues, and other individuals (e.g., police), which result in different cognitive appraisals of the environment. The researcher would then develop a cognitive theory-driven research study that tests particular hypotheses purported by that theory. Data that allow the researcher to examine these hypotheses would be collected and analyzed.

Obviously a programmatic line of research does not stop at this point, but rather will continue to be extended and refined. Depending upon the nature of the research questions, a variety of research designs might be utilized. Some designs, including qualitative and descriptive, may be revisited in order to further explore particular nuances or intersecting identities (e.g., researchers may begin to notice that levels of depression seem to vary within racial/ethnic groups in relation to other factors such as gender and generation status). Indeed, scholars and practitioners have called for further attention to the intersection of identities as multicultural research continues to advance. The research might also progress by shifting from a focus on distal explanations (e.g., ethnic group membership) to one that is more proximal (e.g., identification with one's ethnic group, personal and familial values). We discuss the difference between these two terms in more depth in the next section.

Distal versus Proximal Explanations

An important function of research is to identify causes of human behavior (see Chapter 1). Here we want to highlight an important distinction between distal and proximal explanations in multicultural research. As previously mentioned, ethnic minority research has been criticized for being primarily descriptive in nature. Research that is descriptive in nature usually relies on distal factors to explain differences in behavior. The word *distal* means farthest from the point of origin. Distal factors are factors that, in and of themselves, do not directly explain observed phenomena. They are often not psychological in nature, but rather, they tend to be demographic. For example, when researchers collect data, they usually incorporate demographic information. The demographic information will usually include information about demographic characteristics, including race and/or ethnicity, sex, socioeconomic status, age, and so on. When researchers analyze their data, descriptive statistics are usually the first set of analyses conducted. It is common to compute the mean scores on the variables or constructs of interest, and then, using inferential statistics, compare demographic groups to see whether there are statistically significant differences. When differences are found, researchers often attribute the differences to the demographic variables themselves.

Going back to our earlier examples, suppose Latinas/os had significantly higher depression scores than other racial/ethnic groups. The researcher may attribute the difference in depression scores to *cultural differences*. In other words, the researchers would have relied on the self-reported ethnic categorization of the participants as a necessary and sufficient explanation for the observed differences. However, as Phinney (1996) indicated that ethnic categorization is problematic because of its imprecise and arbitrary nature, attributing the differences to ethnic status is insufficient. Phinney stated that ethnic categories, or ethnicity, have psychological dimensions. She maintained that ethnicity can be thought of as culture, identity, or minority status, with each dimension having a specific psychological impact.

As ethnic minority research has matured, it has moved away from purely descriptive research and from its reliance on distal explanations to more theoretically driven research with proximal explanations. The word *proximal* means situated nearest to the point of origin. Proximal factors are ones that more directly and parsimoniously explain observed phenomena. Unlike distal factors, proximal factors are usually more psychological in nature. Cokley (2004) offered a matrix of variables that serve as proximal or distal explanations for group differences in observed phenomena.

Table Proximal and Distal Explanations

Proximal Explanations	Distal Explanations
Racial identity	Race
Ethnic identity	Ethnicity
Worldview	Culture
Acculturation	Sex
Values	Age
Communication patterns	Socioeconomic status*
Spirituality/religiosity	Education
Individualism/collectivism	Generation status
Independence/interdependence	Year in school
Familial roles	Major

*If used simply as a demographic, categorical variable (e.g., low, middle, high), socioeconomic status is a distal explanation. However, socioeconomic status may also be used as a proximal explanation if race and ethnicity differences are observed, and these differences can best be explained because of differences in socioeconomic status.

Using the previous example, ethnic identity, as a psychological dimension of ethnicity, is a proximal factor that could be hypothesized to account for the differences in depression among individuals living in the United States who indicate being members of particular ethnic groups. However, we may find that ethnic identity does not account for the differences in depression, and instead, the answer may lie with the importance of familial roles and values in the lives of both groups. For example, we may discover that a disproportionate number of Latina/o individuals are financially supporting a number of family members and are feeling guilt related to their desire to provide for their family and community while also furthering their own education and career development. Thus, although the distal factor of ethnicity is not sufficient to explain why differences in depression exist between ethnic groups, a proximal factor (e.g., familial roles) may provide the specific reason for the difference. In short, researchers have found that it is important to go beyond distal factors and instead utilize proximal factors to explain observed phenomena.

Moderator and Mediator Variables

In Chapter 13, moderator and mediator variables will be discussed in more detail. Briefly, moderators are variables that affect the direction and/or strength of the relationship between a predictor (independent variable) and a criterion (dependent variable). Moderators are usually involved in questions addressing "when" or "for whom" a variable most strongly causes or predicts an outcome variable (Frazier, Tix, & Barron, 2004). Moderators are either categorical (e.g., race, ethnicity, sex) or continuous (e.g., income, amount of depression; MacKinnon, 2008). When the researcher moves beyond using distal variables like race and ethnicity in descriptive fashion, to specifying how the variable changes the direction or strength of the relation between a predictor and an outcome, the distal variable is being used as a moderator. For example, Carter, Mollen, and Smith (2014) drew upon prior research and minority stress theory (Meyer, 1995) to hypothesize that locus of control would moderate the relationship between workplace prejudice events and psychological distress among lesbian, gay, and bisexual (LGB) individuals. Results indicated that locus of control did moderate this relationship, such that the relationship between workplace prejudice and psychological distress was significant for participants with higher levels of locus of control (i.e., more external locus of control) than for those with lower levels of locus of control (i.e., more internal locus of control). The authors interpreted their findings as indicating that "it appears that an internal locus of control may serve as an important resiliency factor for both the general population, and for LGB individuals specifically" (p. 173).

Mediators are variables that account for or explain the relationship between a predictor (independent variable) and criterion (dependent variable). Mediators are usually involved in establishing "how" or "why" a predictor variable causes or predicts a criterion variable (Frazier et al., 2004; MacKinnon, 2008). Research testing mediators of established relationships can further our understanding of specific variables and inform interventions. As an example, Cramer, Miller, Amacker, and Burks (2013) used the dual-process cognitive-motivational model of ideology and prejudice (DPM; Duckitt, 2001; Duckitt & Sibley, 2009) to inform their examination of right-wing authoritarianism (RWA) as a mediator of the relationship between openness (a personality characteristic) and antigay prejudice with college students. Cramer et al. found that RWA mediated the negative relationship between openness and antigay prejudice. In short, they concluded, "the present findings suggest that RWA belief structures may explain a linkage between inflexible, unimaginative thinking and anti-gay prejudice in college students. Conversely, facilitating imaginative thinking (e.g., about alternative social conditions to the status quo) may be a particularly promising strategy for interrupting the development of authoritarian ideologies and, in turn, anti-gay prejudice" (p. 68).

Threats to Internal Validity

As we discussed in Chapter 7, internal validity is extremely important to draw accurate conclusions in our research, and specifically refers to the extent that a researcher may infer a causal relationship among variables in a given study. A study is said to have adequate internal validity when the presence of possible rival hypotheses is ruled out. When plausible rival hypotheses are not ruled out, threats to internal validity arise. Several of these threats are made more salient when conducting research with diverse samples. We will briefly discuss five threats: selection, local history, attrition, testing effects, and maturation.

Selection   Selection is one of the most pernicious threats to internal validity. Selection of the samples utilized in a study can be particularly problematic in multicultural research that utilizes a comparative framework to analyze data based on group membership (i.e., sampling). Sometimes individuals are chosen on the basis of their membership in a cultural or minority group (e.g., a research study designed to examine the hypothesis that individuals who identify as transgender will report increased mental health symptomatology as compared to individuals who identify as lesbian or gay). Other times, unfortunately, analysis is conducted post hoc (e.g., after the fact with no theoretically based hypotheses once the researcher realizes that she or he has enough participants from each group to conduct some sort of statistical analyses). One reason that selection threats are particularly dangerous to internal validity is that one cannot randomly assign culture (e.g., race, ethnicity, sex); therefore, selection biases are inherent in these types of studies. Another reason is that race or group membership is used as a proxy for numerous cultural variables. As discussed earlier, differences found among cultural groups are erroneously attributed to group membership as opposed to more proximal variables that may actually be responsible for differences (e.g., familial values, neighborhood characteristics). As described in Chapter 7, selection biases may also interact with other threats to internal validity to impact results of a study.

Local History   Another particularly relevant threat in multicultural research is local history. Consider the following example.

RESEARCH IN ACTION 9.1

Suppose that a researcher was conducting a large-scale, two-week diversity training designed to increase awareness and understanding of cultural groups on campus. A pretest measure was given before the implementation of the intervention and a posttest was planned after the workshop series was completed. Imagine that the majority of the participants in the workshop were students who identified as White,

Black, and Latino. Suppose that while this intervention was in progress, an incident occurred where on a Friday night, Black college students were seemingly targeted by university police and told that their house parties must end. Imagine that one member of a Black fraternity argued with the officer and refused to send individuals home, citing that there was a White fraternity on their street that was also having a party but was not told to send its guests home. As a response to the apparent anger displayed by the Black male student, the officer became alarmed and decided to use mace to subdue the student. Although the incident was not publicized in the school newspaper, the news spread like wildfire to all the Black students and faculty at the university. It appeared that many of the White and Latino students were seemingly unaware that this incident occurred. When the diversity training intervention was completed and the posttest was given, scores significantly decreased for the Black students, indicating a decrease in awareness, knowledge, and acceptance of other groups, whereas scores for Whites and Latinos increased, indicating the opposite finding.

In this case, if the researcher was unaware of any of the events that occurred, the researcher may conclude that the intervention did not work for students who identify as Black, but was successful for students who identify as Latino and White. This conclusion, however, would be invalid and highlights the threat of local history (e.g., the event at the Black student house) and the threat of selection-history interaction (e.g., the interaction among study participants and the event at the Black student house).

Attrition   Another threat that may have occurred in the previous example is attrition. More specifically, suppose that instead of staying in the study, the Black students were so upset with what had happened that they subsequently refused to participate in the research (i.e., dropped out of the study). These events would also lead to invalid conclusions about the intervention due to the altered composition of participants at the posttest.

Testing   Testing effects that threaten internal validity may also be particularly prevalent in multicultural research. Consider the following example.

RESEARCH IN ACTION 9.2

A researcher decides to use an intervention designed to increase levels of job search self-efficacy among a sample of individuals at a local community center for whom English is not their first language. Using a pretest-posttest research design, the researcher tests levels of job search self-efficacy before and after delivering an intervention over the course of 4 weeks designed to increase job search self-efficacy. The researcher then studies the differences between pretest and posttest scores to determine whether the intervention was effective.

If individuals are tested more than once during the implementation of an intervention (or a research study), there is a possibility of testing threats. In this example, the first time that the participants completed the pretest measures, they may not have understood all of the items. Upon repeated exposure to the same measures at posttest, however, they may begin to understand the language used on the measures. As a result, their scores might significantly differ between the pretest and posttest. Concluding that these changes were due to the intervention itself, however, would be invalid. The change in scores might actually be due to increased level of English proficiency or to the repeated exposure to the items themselves rather than to the effectiveness of the intervention.

Maturation Similarly, level of acculturation may also introduce maturation threats to internal validity in multicultural research. Consider this example.

RESEARCH IN ACTION 9.3

Let us suppose that an intervention was designed to prevent domestic violence with immigrant women. The intervention included assertiveness training and education about domestic violence laws in the United States. Moreover, the intervention was part of a three-year longitudinal study assessing several factors related to personal relationships; every six months participants were contacted and asked to complete a series of measures. At almost every data collection time, scores on assertiveness and knowledge of domestic violence laws increased.

If the researchers had concluded that the intervention was successful in increasing knowledge of domestic violence laws and level of assertiveness among participants, their conclusions would be invalid. Specifically, the researchers would not have considered the fact that as the length of the participant's residence in the United States increased, their level of acculturation also increased (i.e., maturation). Some women may have come from more patriarchal societies where domestic violence is more common, and laws to protect women from abuse were either nonexistent or not enforced. As time passed and the women learned more about the culture in the United States, these women also may have learned that what may have been more acceptable in their former countries of residence was not customary in the United States.

In sum, it is essential that counseling and counseling psychology researchers establish strong knowledge bases about all populations with whom they work. Although it is often tempting to apply what may seem like "relevant knowledge" or theories based on one population to a different population, it is important to question whether such generalizability assumptions are indeed true. A wide array of research is needed across diverse populations that utilize different research designs to establish firm knowledge bases and subsequent theories.

We want to emphasize two issues. First, when researchers are able to consistently identify when and under what conditions a variable predicts or causes another variable within a particular population, the level of understanding about that particular topic within a particular population greatly increases. Second, when researchers are able to use proximal variables to explain relationships between predictors and criterions, not only does the specificity of the research increase, but also the proximal variables are ones that often can be used in intervention studies within that particular population.

METHODOLOGICAL CHALLENGES: CULTURAL CONSIDERATIONS THROUGHOUT THE INVESTIGATION

In this section we will address methodological challenges that often confront researchers focusing on diverse populations. We will discuss challenges across five topics, beginning with the initial conceptualization of the research idea or research question, and ending with the interpretation or discussion of the research findings. Our aim is to provide specific information to help guide research across all populations of interest to counseling and counseling psychology students. Perhaps the central theme in our discussion in this section is the importance of *respectfully focusing on the cultural context (e.g., cultural values, contextual dynamics) that permeate all phases of the particular population under study.*

This inclusion of the cultural context is critical to conducting rigorous and meaningful research with diverse multicultural and cross-cultural populations (e.g., Bernal et al., 2014; Heppner, 2008; Sue, 1999). Although counseling psychology has been a leader in the broader field of psychology in promoting the highly salient role of culture in understanding human behavior (Ivey, 1977), the centrality of culture has been less apparent in our earlier research, and across psychology as a whole. In general, psychology as it has developed in the United States (and several Western countries as well) has been more focused on individual level explanations, as opposed to understanding individuals' behavior in a broader social/cultural context.

What is needed is a basic paradigm shift from behavior that occurs within the individual to behavior that occurs within a cultural context. The acknowledgement and inclusion of the cultural context is a critical part of addressing both internal and external validity within our research. Moreover, it will also negate the view that all psychological theories and constructs are universal across many different cultural contexts. In essence, such a shift in focus from individual behavior to interdependent behaviors within a cultural context will promote a more complex understanding of human psychology, and ultimately a greater overall understanding of human behavior across different cultural contexts. In short, we believe it critically important to not only have a basic understanding of research design and methods, but also to understand at a deep level the cultural contexts surrounding all human behavior in diverse populations.

Conceptualizing the Research Question

As we have discussed previously in this text, identifying the particular research question one wants to study takes considerable time and involves not only reading the professional literature on the topic, but also talking with other professionals, reflecting on life experiences, talking with elders and other members of our target population, etc. Ideally, the research question should be based not only on the existing literature within the target population and relevant existing theory but also on personal knowledge and establishing firm collaborative relationships with community leaders (see Trimble, Scharrón-del-Río,& Casillas, 2014). However, sometimes the existing literature on new topics can be relatively sparse, and often the existing theories have been primarily based on research conducted with White American participants. Thus, the existing professional literature may be relatively limited when investigating new lines of research with previously marginalized groups. Consequently, a wide array of information and theories might be used to conceptualize particular research questions during the formulation of the research question; the research question may likely change several times during this incubation phase. It is important that research conducted on any target population also be closely tied to the cultural context surrounding the target population. Researchers might draw from a wide array of existing literatures (e.g., sociology, gender studies, Black studies, historical documents), personal experiences, discussion with community leaders, colleagues and friends, and not necessarily restrict themselves to the psychological literature to initially conceptualize cutting-edge research questions in new arenas.

Early Reliance on the Comparative Research Strategies An early research strategy was to compare members of diverse groups with the majority White population on various psychological variables. This type of research was called the comparative research framework. However, before conducting group comparisons, a clear theoretically driven rationale should guide the decision to compare groups; moreover, it is critical to reflect on why and which groups are to be compared? In the past, perhaps one of the most common research strategies was to compare White American groups to racial/ethnic minority groups, particularly African Americans. Although these research studies were often theory driven, it is important to understand that most of our psychological theories were developed using White samples with little inclusion of non-White individuals. Thus, these studies compared how individuals in diverse communities compared to White majority Americans on various psychological constructs based on White American samples. Consequently, this deeply flawed research contributed little to our scholarly bases, and at times served to support stereotypic views of diverse populations.

Daudi Ajani Ya Azibo (1988) shared a vivid example of the pervasiveness of the comparative research framework from his own experiences interviewing for a faculty position in the late 1980s. After presenting two colloquia where he discussed empirical studies using culturally specific instruments normed on African Americans, he was asked the question, "Why didn't you use a White control group?" In the ensuing dialogue, Azibo simply asked "what he would be controlling for," to which there was no reply. This attitude that White Americans are the gold standard, the norm, or the standard to which others are compared was unfortunately a deeply held bias for many years. Moreover, science is neither apolitical nor neutral (Guthrie, 1998). This is perhaps most evident when research involves underrepresented ethnic groups, in which case the generalizability of the findings tends to be questioned more than research involving predominantly White populations (Sue, 1999). Azibo (1988) emphasized his point by quoting Khatib and Nobles (1997, pp. 97–98), "Whites or Europeans are no longer the standard by which the psychology of people is judged."

Earlier in this chapter, we provided a more in-depth discussion of the problems inherent in comparing two groups formed from differences on a categorical/distal status variable (e.g., race). Similarly, Azibo (1988) suggested that comparing two different ethnic groups, especially when the comparison involves an ethnic minority group with Whites, is only appropriate when "racial" groups are equated on all relevant variables, especially culture.

Azibo took a strong and in our view, methodologically sound stance on the comparison of ethnic groups. Taken to its logical conclusion, it would almost never be appropriate to do any comparisons of ethnic groups when they are not equivalent. Finding ethnic groups that are equivalent on all relevant variables is virtually impossible, because researchers obviously cannot control for differences in history and differential experiences with prejudice and discrimination, which will influence the thoughts, beliefs, attitudes, and behaviors of ethnic groups. Moreover, he stated that whenever psychological constructs are used in research, culture will always be relevant.

In essence, the comparative research framework has been criticized because of the history of ethnic minority groups being compared to White Americans as a "norm group." Comparing groups should have a clear theoretical rationale and research question (e.g., to better understand how a phenomenon manifests differently across groups) rather than to compare how minority groups differ from the dominant groups, which can unwittingly perpetuate a hegemonic approach in research (Awad & Cokley, 2009; Cokley & Awad, 2013). Today such comparisons are not typically viewed as necessary because it is more informative to study psychological constructs of various groups in and of themselves.

Understanding Psychological Constructs within a Particular Group   Since the development of our research questions or hypotheses will guide subsequent research steps, it is critical that careful and informed consideration is given to developing questions that are appropriate and relevant within the cultural contexts of the individuals being studied. Often students and seasoned professionals may feel they lack sufficient knowledge of the cultural context of their intended population and thus feel ill equipped to develop their research questions. Even researchers who are part of the diverse group they wish to study may feel they are not totally knowledgeable of the myriad of cultural values within their target population. For example, a gay male scholar may be interested in studying issues related to the LGBTQ community, and specifically the degree to which they are open about their orientation within their work setting. The scholar may feel well equipped to generate research questions for gay men in an eastern urban setting, but less equipped to generate such questions within southwestern rural communities.

We first want to emphasize how important it is to not only carefully select one's research questions, but also assess one's knowledge to sensitively and competently conduct the investigation. Sometimes researchers can unknowingly cause more harm to particular groups or communities. We also want to emphasize how important it is to carefully and sensitively involve members of the diverse population one wishes to study in the formulation of research questions, thus providing knowledge that will lead to more appropriate, culturally sensitive research questions, and most useful outcomes. Cultural consultation of this type is critical to promote the utility of our science. Community stakeholders often not only have greater sensitivity to research questions but also ultimately promote the development of research questions that focus on important and relevant topics to understand about any particular group. Investigators should carefully examine Trimble et al. (2014).

A recent dissertation by Kanagui-Muñoz (2015) nicely illustrates this process. She was aware that although coping has been one of the most widely studied constructs in psychology, research has largely reflected the behavior of White Americans. Thus, she chose to examine coping within Latinas/os to not only further understanding of distinctive coping activities within this group, but also expand current conceptualization and measurement of coping within Latinas/os. Over a period of several months, she had numerous discussions with her parents, elders, and other members of the Latina/o community, and then her dissertation advisor; based on these discussions as well as her review of the existing relevant literature, it was clear that there was a need for a broad assessment of Latina/o ways of coping. Consequently, she decided to develop a new coping inventory specifically for Latinas/os that built on the strengths of that cultural group, specifically what she referred to as a Cultural Wealth Coping Scale for Latina/os.In short, Kanagui-Muñoz collected a great deal of information by examining the existing coping literature, as well as specifically the coping literature as it pertained to her target population. In addition, she consulted a wide array of people to further elaborate her thinking. After several months of collecting information, and based on a theoretical model about cultural wealth/resources, her goal was to conduct a psychometrically strong coping inventory for Latinas/os, which she predicted would be associated with other well-established coping inventories (to provide an estimate of concurrent validity) as well as with several indices of psychological adjustment (to provide estimates of construct validity). Thus, the purpose of this research was to understand salient psychological constructs within the Latino/a population, without a need for comparison to any other ethnic groups.

Choosing Appropriate Research Designs to Fit the Target Population

Sometimes students find it difficult to decide what type of research design they should select when constructing their investigation. We have maintained in this book that the type of design chosen should be the one that best answers the research questions or hypotheses one wishes to investigate given the existing knowledge bases. It is also important that the design reduce as many alternative hypotheses or extraneous variables as possible in order to be able to draw conclusions with some degree of certainty.

Sometimes research on diverse topics poses challenges for researchers. In essence, because some research topics and some populations have historically received little attention in the literature, it may be difficult to design rigorous quantitative studies with intricate hypotheses. For example, studying the cross-cultural adjustment of Filipina immigrants who work in small midwestern communities may be challenging given the relative lack of research on this topic, and also the lack of appropriate psychological measures validated on this population. Similarly, there may be few or no theories that have been developed with the cultural context of this population, and it may be difficult to develop hypotheses. In such situations, qualitative methods may be the most appropriate research strategy to gain information about the psychological phenomena of interest.

Hsieh (2012) conducted a qualitative dissertation on this very topic, examining Filipina immigrants coping and psychological adjustment living in small rural communities in mid-Missouri who married White Americans. Her results provided a contextualized understanding of the cyclical and dynamic process of coping of the Filipina immigrants. The central and recurring theme of the experiences of Filipina immigrants was their continuous coping with, and adjustment to, a wide array of hardships. From an ecological perspective, Filipina immigrants faced adjustment challenges within the context of their own expectations and attitudes, their marriage with white American men, work and community relationships, as well as the climate in landscape of rural America. Subsequently, she found that the Filipina immigrants relied on a wide range of coping activities to respond to the innumerable acculturative demands surrounding them. Over time, the accumulation of effective and positive coping experiences further facilitated Filipina immigrants' ongoing coping efforts with a wide range of stressors associated with living in rural communities (e.g., financial hardship, racial prejudice, bicultural negotiations). In essence, this qualitative investigation contextualized the perspectives on immigrants' adjustment, coping, and outcomes within a sociocultural context, which is often lost with cross-sectional research based on U.S. college student samples. Moreover, the conceptual model developed in her dissertation was consistent with recent coping models that emphasized the transactional and bidirectional dynamics in individual's coping experiences (Heppner, Wei, Neville, & Kanagui-Muñoz, 2014; Wang & Heppner, 2011). In short, qualitative methodologies such as Hsieh's allows for the collection of extremely rich information on unique target populations, which subsequently may help build a foundation for subsequent quantitative research questions.

At times, researchers select topics and subsequent research designs not because they are the best design to answer their research questions, but rather because they are more comfortable with a particular methodological or statistical procedure. So instead of formulating the strongest and most appropriate research questions and letting that drive the research design choice, they let their comfort with the procedures be the deciding factor. This practice is similar to choosing the same tool for every maintenance job in one's home. But obviously sometimes you need a hammer and sometimes you need a screwdriver. We urge researchers to allow the existing knowledge bases and relevant instrumentation for particular cultural groups, as well as their questions and hypotheses, guide their studies.

As we have discussed previously in Chapter 1, there are three general research design typologies: experimental, quasi-experimental, and correlational designs. We have also highlighted in other chapters how each design comes with its own set of strengths and weaknesses. It is particularly important when choosing a design that the researcher carefully considers the existing knowledge bases, the cultural context of the population they are studying, and how that relates to the strengths and weaknesses of any particular design.

Since the study of diverse populations is a relatively new area in psychology, it may often be helpful to focus on the more descriptive goal of science. In essence, when we know less about an area, an important first step is gathering descriptive information that we can then later build theories, develop necessary assessment tools, and conduct quantitative studies. An example of this in psychology currently is the amount of descriptive work being done on brain mapping and psychological traits. Because of this area being in its initial stages, much of what is needed is a documentation of what specific areas of the brain are activated when they are exposed to specific stimuli. In short, descriptive studies are often a necessary early step in the topics and populations before researchers can examine more complex and even causal relationships.

Historically research in psychology has placed a great deal of emphasis on internal validity (e.g., the psychometric properties of the instruments) and some have placed less emphasis on the external validity (how generalizable are the finding to other samples, or even populations: Sue, 1999). Similarly, much of the previous psychological research was conducted using participants from introductory psychology classes that consisted of primarily White American undergraduate students who were privileged to attend college. Thus, the type of research designs utilized within the existing research on a particular topic/population may also suggest the need for particular research designs over others.

Sometimes when one is struggling with whether to use a quantitative or qualitative research design to answer a research question, an alternative is to use both. This type of strategy is referred to as mixed methods (see Chapter 17), and employs both quantitative and qualitative approaches in the same study with the goal of more thoroughly answering a particular research question. In short, a strength of mixed methods is that they combine qualitative research that is often useful when exploring a new area, along with quantitative methods that leads to the possibility of greater generalizability. Another strength of mixed methods is the opportunity to provide clarification of previously confusing findings (see Chapter 17 for examples of such studies). Given the relatively sparse literature on a number of topics across diverse groups, mixed methods can sometimes be particularly useful designs.

Sampling, Recruitment, and Data Collection Issues

Who we study matters. Arnett (2008) raised this issue when he provided data indicating the dominance of U.S. psychology primarily on U.S. samples who comprise only 5% of the world population; he persuasively argued that our psychological knowledge base does not reflect humanity, but rather a population vastly different from most of the rest of the world. He maintained that ignoring the 95% of the world's population and ignoring the cultural context have led to erroneous assumptions about the universality of our constructs. Similar observations have been raised about the oversampling of White college student populations to describe and understand human adaptation and psychological functioning. Research that addresses the full spectrum of human functioning across different cultural contexts is clearly needed in counseling and counseling psychology, and more broadly, psychology in general.

In the previous chapter (Chapter 8), we discussed a broad array of issues related to obtaining research participants or samples. Basically researchers define a target group with specific criteria (e.g., age, gender, ethnicity), and develop strategies for getting those people to participate in their study. In the past, the target population might have been vaguely defined as "undergraduate students," which created ambiguity about the sample, and how it might generalize to subgroups, such as older students, racial/ethnic minorities, etc.

More often as of this writing, researchers will specify particular inclusion and exclusion criteria in order to ensure the sample being studied meets the criteria of interest to the researcher; these criteria create the researcher's target population. In addition, representative samples from the target population are needed in order to draw sound conclusions from the results. Sometimes researchers establish a broad target population, which then makes it more feasible to collect data from sufficiently large samples. However, sometimes very broad samples may obscure cultural differences within the sample. For example, the term Latina/o is commonly used to denote a particular sample; however, this designation covers people with vastly different sociocultural histories, beliefs, and customs. Thus, although studying all subgroups of Latinas/os would lead to a more representative sample of Latinas/os in the United States, this sampling procedure (perhaps depending on the topic) could greatly obscure important cultural differences within such a broad group. Sometimes there is a tension between identifying a sufficiently narrow target population, while still allowing access for a sufficient number of participants.

Likewise, considerable research has examined the adjustment of international students as they cross cultural borders to study in the United States (e.g., Wang, Heppner, Wang, & Zhu, 2015). Most studies in the literature (probably to increase sample sizes to have sufficient power) identified their target population to include all international students. For example, some studies may have included international students who appear White, who are native English language speakers (e.g., students from Canada or an English-speaking European country) combined with other international students from China, Norway, and Botswana. It is easy to see how these highly heterogeneous samples, which cross many different cultures, could lead to inconsistent and likely erroneous conclusions about the constructs of interest in such a broad target population (see, e.g., Zhang & Goodson, 2011, for a discussion of such sampling issues with international students). In short, it is important to carefully identify a target population that allows the researcher to examine the proposed hypotheses without introducing a great deal of variability due to significant cultural differences within the sample that might result in considerable variability in the measurements of the study.

As previously discussed in Chapter 8, researchers who are designing quantitative studies will often focus on "how many participants will I need," or said a little more specifically: "How many participants will I need to find an effect if indeed a true effect exists?" (These questions revolve around what is often called statistical power.) In essence, will the researcher have sufficient power to adequately test her or his research hypotheses? Insufficient statistical power can be a serious threat to a study when there are relatively fewer individuals of a certain underrepresented and "hard to reach" communities; small samples thus make it difficult to draw valid conclusions from the data. Although identifying the target population is critically important in diversity-related research, a major challenge after identifying the target population is getting sufficient sample sizes to actually participate in the research study. There are a host of reasons why potential participants may not want to participate in a particular study. For example, there are a number of recruitment barriers when a researcher has chosen to conduct a study with undocumented immigrants living in the United States (e.g., language, legal issues, informed consent concerns associated with potential data breaches, distrust of researchers); these challenges may make it difficult for researchers to obtain the needed sample sizes. Moreover, these difficulties can be further exacerbated when researchers are attempting to account for intersections among identities (e.g., undocumented immigrants who are members of the LGB community). For some minority groups, there is also a history of using our research for further oppression, and this has made some potential participants hesitant and skeptical (at best!) of participating in psychological research. For others who may be struggling financially and taking care of their families, time is a highly valued and precious commodity; spending time to participate in a research study may not be something they would prioritize over working and family. For some, simply getting to a research site may be difficult for some who have limited mobility or transportation; for others, coming to a university setting may be uncomfortable and inhibitive.

Although it can be difficult to collect data with diverse samples, it is not impossible.In this section we discuss eight suggestions related to the recruitment and data collection of underrepresented groups that may be helpful to you as researchers plan to successfully recruit and collect data from one's target population.

Perseverance and Passion   Although our first suggestion applies to most any research endeavor, it is perhaps most important when there are significant challenges to successfully recruiting participants. After a researcher has explored/tried various data collection strategies, and repeatedly fails, perseverance is critically important. One's values, beliefs, and passions are essential for persevering through hardships to conduct important research with target populations. We have witnessed students who successfully collected data from battered women's shelters, with homeless individuals, with undocumented workers; all of these target populations were difficult to obtain access, and many attempts were made before sufficient data were collected. The reason these students persevered was because of their passion, commitments (e.g., to a particular target population, wanting their participants' stories to be known, social justice), and dedication to expanding the psychological literature in ways that were important to them. In short, starting with a topic and target population that one is passionate about is extremely important and functional to obtain the necessary sample, and to the successful completion of the study.

Making Social Connections within the Target Population   We strongly encourage researchers to build relationships with members from the community they wish to study; this is an important ethical consideration (see Trimble et al., 2014). This is often especially functional for both researchers who may be perceived as cultural "insiders" or "outsiders" to build some level of trust within the target population. It almost goes without saying, but it is very important that researchers are transparent about their intentions with members of the target population, as well as follow guidelines set forth by institutional review boards pertaining to informed consent, confidentiality, and benefit/risk assessments. It is also important to note that building trust with members from the target population takes considerable time and energy; good relationships are built over time. Leaders within the target population can often be very helpful in facilitating many activities within data collection. For example, sometimes local leaders can provide feedback on culturally appropriate collection processes, as well as raise relevant language issues in the data collection protocol. Sometimes, directors of local social organizations who work with members of the target population can be very helpful in reaching members of the target population. In addition, researchers can utilize social media or listservs of relevant groups or organizations that would include members of the target population. Sometimes it is helpful as well to be publicly endorsed by local leaders within the target population.

Using One Social Network   It is not uncommon that students and early career researchers believe they have few, if any, contacts to help establish a potential recruitment site. Perhaps they just moved to a new community and have not developed the necessary social network yet. We encourage researchers to first of all think about who they know in their own circle of friends and acquaintances, either in their current community or other communities they have lived, professional organizations, potential associations or churches, gym, etc. Moreover, we encourage researchers to try to draw their social circle wider; for example, which of their friends/contacts may know someone who could help with data collection. For example, one student wanted to study the role of religiosity in coping within an African American community. Although she did not have the connections within this community, she had friends and acquaintances that could introduce her to pastors who were able to help her in collecting community data.It is also important to remember that data collection does not have to occur in the community in which one is currently residing. For example, one of our students returned to her home community, talked to some of her former social connections, and was able to successfully collect data within that community.

Make Explicit How Your Research Can Benefit the Target Group   Rather than thinking of your research as taking from or "using" a particular sample, think about how it can and will benefit the participants and their community. For example, Heppner and Heppner (2004) identified several potential benefits: (a) provide a connection with an academic institution that might enhance the credibility of their agency's goals; (b) provide data that can be used for future grant writing by the agency to obtaining monies to support their cause; (c) provide opportunities and visibility for agency personnel to copresent at a conference; (d) help to lessen or resolve a problem or answer a question that the organization has about their constituent group; and (e) help agencies better serve their mission or role by providing them with much needed empirical data, and helping them better serve their constituent groups. Sometimes by carefully considering how a particular research project can benefit others, the researcher is not only much more prepared to make a compelling argument for recruitment of participants, but also able to develop mutually beneficial relationships that may in the end help the target population in various ways.

Giving Back   Researchers have been criticized for "using" diverse samples largely for their own benefit, and without giving anything in return. This is an important issue for any kind of research with any sample, but particularly important when studying vulnerable populations. Consider how one's results may be helpful to members of the target population. At the very least, giving back means informing the participants of the outcome of one's research. Giving back can mean volunteering one's time, giving presentations that are helpful on some topic of interest to the participants, etc. In essence, giving back means striving for mutually beneficial relationships in kind and magnitude, some of which may continue for many years.

Collecting Data through the Internet   Although there are still segments of society that do not have ready internet access, and many others that do not have the time to participate in online interviews, for some projects the internet provides access to a nationwide, and in some cases worldwide, sample. Thus, it is important for researchers to carefully examine a wider range of opportunities to collect data from their target population via the internet. At the same time, it is also important to consider the type of person who may, and may not, choose to participate in an internet data collection procedure; will such volunteers be representative of one's target population? Will internet respondents bias the findings in a significant way (e.g., only those who have access to the internet are likely to respond)?

Conservation of Sparse Target Populations   Participants from underrepresented groups are often barraged with requests for participation in research studies. For example, many master's and doctoral counseling training programs receive dozens of requests each year, seeking students of color, LGBTQ, or international students to complete questionnaires for someone's thesis or dissertation. Each year there are a limited number of counseling trainees who may fit certain characteristics; thus it is important that researchers are mindful of the demand on various target populations, and are judicious in their use.

Cultural Sensitivity Issues around Data Collection   It is critically important that researchers are sensitive to the cultural contexts within their target population, and collect data accordingly. For example, cultural sensitivity may suggest that data be collected in ways other than the traditional university classroom location. Some participants from the target population may feel uncomfortable participating in a research study in a university setting, or perhaps the distance from their home creates significant difficulties for data collection. Sometimes it may be more appropriate for data collection procedures to take place within the participants' home, and other times it may be totally inappropriate to do so. Sensitivity is also necessary to develop culturally sensitive language within the data collection materials. In some situations, the investigator may need to engage in socially appropriate behavior that matches social etiquette within the target population to avoid being what may be perceived in the target population as a detached/selfless/uppity investigator. Consulting with cultural insiders of the target population is highly recommended.

In sum, there are a wide array of culturally sensitive issues to consider when identifying the target population and obtaining representative samples, recruitment, and data collection of diverse samples in counseling and counseling psychology. Sometimes the overutilization of university undergraduate populations that have tended to dominate data collection in psychology for many years can lead to insensitive ways of thinking, and to ignore the cultural context of our participants. As the research with diverse populations continues to expand in counseling and counseling psychology, we urge researchers to carefully attend to the cultural context of our participants in all activities associated with recruitment and data collection.

Measurement Issues

In Chapter 5, we discussed the process of formulating definitions of constructs as a step toward identifying more specific and measurable variables. Later in the book (Chapters 18 and 19) we will discuss a number of measurement issues pertaining to the variables involved in a study (e.g., the independent and dependent variables). In many ways the strength of a particular research study is heavily dependent upon the instruments we used to measure the constructs in the study, or in qualitative studies, how we define and operationalize the constructs under investigation. In short, adequate validity and reliability of measures are imperative in all research, but the use of measures that have been created and normed on middle-class White participants presents additional issues in conducting culturally sensitive research in more diverse populations. Thus, identifying culturally appropriate and sensitive instruments that have acceptable estimates of validity and reliability with the particular target population of interest can sometimes be a difficult task with diverse samples. In short, the use of culturally inappropriate measures increases error variance and may mask significant relationships among variables in research related to diverse populations.

Construct validity is of critical importance in examining potential research instruments, that is, the extent to which study variables (i.e., independent and dependent variables) accurately measure the constructs that they claim to measure (see Chapters 18 and 19). It is important to examine whether or not the psychological construct is generalizable across different cultural groups, and in particular to the diverse target population of interest. Since most existing scales developed within the United States utilized White American norming samples, there is a need to determine whether an inventory of interest measures the same construct with the new target population as with the initial norming group (i.e., would the inventory have the same factor structure, validity and reliability estimates as with the original population?).

For example, consider the construct of the self. In Western, individualistic cultures the self is generally perceived as a bounded, independent entity consisting of personal needs, abilities, motives, and rights; however, in collectivistic cultures, the self is generally perceived as an unbounded, interdependent entity socialized to fit in and be a part of a group (Matsumoto, 2000). Traditional self-esteem measures in Western cultures are typically operationalized with an individualistic notion of the self. Using these measures with samples from collectivist populations, who possess a more collectivist notion of self (e.g., the self extends beyond the individual), would most likely be inappropriate and lead the researcher to erroneous construct interpretations.

In short, it is abundantly clear that constructs are not the same across cultural groups, and thus the meaning associated with any particular inventory (e.g., self-esteem) may or may not be equivalent. To determine if an instrument has acceptable reliability and validity estimates for the target population of interest, researchers specifically examine psychometric information (i.e., various validity and reliability estimates). For example, if the inventory was initially based on primarily White university students, that initial and subsequent psychometric information is examined; in addition, any relevant psychometric information based on one's target population is examined (or another target population culturally similar to one's target population). In short, the researcher attempts to determine if a particular inventory has construct validity (as well as other suitable psychometric properties) for the intended target population.

As will be discussed in Chapter 10, there are a variety of statistical tests that can be used to establish psychometric support for a measure with particular groups [e.g., factor analysis to assess the factor structure of a particular measure, differential item functioning to assess the extent to which particular items are endorsed by specific groups of participants, and Brown's (2006) four-step process for examining measurement invariance]. Research has found that sometimes a construct developed in one cultural context is equally valid in another cultural context, but other times it is not (see, e.g.,Tian, Heppner, & Hou, 2014).

Low internal consistency estimates are usually one of the first signs that a measure is not functioning properly with a particular sample. Low reliability estimates may be present for a number of reasons, but in research with a new target population, the most common reason for low levels of reliability may be a reflection of a deeper validity issue where the construct under investigation may have a different meaning for the target population under consideration.

Some researchers use extensive pilot testing before conducting their primary investigation. A methodical pilot test can help alleviate problems in the main study. For example, participants can be asked for their understanding of the construct being assessed in order to determine whether there are cultural differences between groups. Sometimes if research has not been conducted with a similar target population, it may be necessary to initially collect data on the instrument using the target population of interest, and conduct factor analytic procedures to determine if the factor structure is the same as in the original sample. In addition, additional information would ideally be collected to also establish other reliability and validity estimates of this inventory with the new target population. Given the limited state of our instrumentation at this point in time, some researchers have decided to conduct a scale construction and validation study first to provide a more psychometrically sound inventory to measure the specific constructs of interest.

Although the various statistical analyses provide useful tools for assessing construct validity, they should not be used as the only method for determining construct validity (Byrne, 2014; Byrne & Watkins, 2003; also see Chapters 7 and 10). Indeed, there are sources of error that sometimes can be identified, and many sources of error that cannot be identified for any given measure. For example, a measure may not cover all of the important aspects of a construct across different cultural groups, and thus result in construct underrepresentativeness for some groups (Shadish et al., 2002). For example, it may be easy for a researcher to assume that a measure of discrimination developed for, and normed with, a sample of Mexican American adults living in Miami, Florida, could be used with all Mexican American adults living in the United States. Such an assumption, however, would be problematic given the regional differences in the United States that likely impact the experience of discrimination for Mexican Americans (e.g., rural vs. urban; neighborhood levels of poverty and violence; bilingual public education). Thus, construct validity is not a property of the inventory per se, but rather applies to the interpretation of scores (and actions based on those interpretations) in a particular population; it is very possible that valid interpretations in one population may not be valid in a different context or in studying a different population (Hoyt, Warbasse, & Chu, 2006).

For example, suppose that a researcher is interested in understanding experiences of discrimination, and its relation to mental health symptoms, among individuals who are members of the Sikh community and living in the United States. Although a researcher may be tempted to use previously developed measures of discrimination that have been validated with other ethnic groups, the researcher must take care to ensure that the measure is appropriate to be used with a sample comprised of individuals who identify as Sikh given distinct cultural and contextual experiences that may relate to experiences of discrimination (e.g., religious practices, media portrayals of Sikh communities, diet, dress). Furthermore, the issue of the reliability of measures becomes salient when a measure that has been previously normed on a group different than the one being investigated is used to ascertain relationships among variables of interest. As will be discussed in more detail in Chapter 13, such measures are more susceptible to error variance, and may mask true relationships among study variables.

In sum, considerations of construct validity, as well as other estimates of validity and reliability, across different cultural contexts merit close attention from researchers and from consumers of such research. Given the number of threats to validity and reliability of inventories across different diverse groups, the statement is particularly important. Thus, it is essential that instrumentation be selected that has acceptable validity and reliability estimates in measuring the construct of interest with any particular target population of interest in a particular study.

Interpretation/Discussion of the Findings

The discussion section of any research article is a critically important place for the researcher to be highly cognizant of the participant's cultural context and to place the findings from the investigation into that context. This is *the* place to help the reader understand the results of this study, what these results might mean within that target population, and what might be the implications for working with the target population. Although this may sound relatively straightforward, sometimes this is actually difficult to accomplish for a number of reasons. First, there is a relatively sparse literature on a number of diverse groups and psychological topics, and sometimes with limited theory development. Such a task is very different than writing a discussion section based on a line of research with 100 previous investigations where similarities and differences are more easily identified. Second, sometimes investigators may interpret the findings from marginalized groups within the dominant White American literature on this particular topic; sometimes this can be useful, but sometimes such analyses overlook the need to understand the findings within the particular target population and the associated cultural values. Third, occasionally journal editors and reviewers may ask researchers to discuss their findings within the existing literature, even though it is most often based on different populations than the one examined by the investigator. Although sometimes this can be a useful suggestion, from our view it is important that researchers do not "stretch" or "bend" their findings to fit the existing theoretical models. In our view, it may well be the case that different empirical findings for similar psychological constructs indeed do exist across different cultural groups, and such differences are not only important to identify and accept; such findings ultimately provide greater understanding of human behavior across different cultural contexts, and that helps us to be better psychologists.

In essence, the discussion is a place for the authors to examine and discuss the findings, interpret their findings based on the cultural context of their participants, and also draw inferences from their findings as well as conclusions. Moreover, according to the *Publication Manual* (American Psychological Association, 2010), the authors might also emphasize both theoretical and applied implications of their results, and contextualize and clarify one's conclusions. Although not mentioned explicitly, the latter seems particularly important within the cultural context of the target population. After all, the authors typically bring a great deal of expertise to bear on their target population, and it is their responsibility to explain the meaning of their results within that particular cultural context. In addition, the authors may be in a particularly advantageous position to share their knowledge and understanding of future research directions to extend this particular line of research.

It is often very useful to ask members of the target group for their understanding of the findings. Such procedures are often routinely conducted within qualitative research, but less so with quantitative studies. However, especially within new lines of research and underrepresented groups, consulting with several cultural advisors about one's results can be useful to provide not only more accurate interpretations of one's findings, but often more complex understanding of specific cultural dynamics. For example, one of the authors of this text was developing an East-Asian based Coping Scale with a team of Asian doctoral students; the factor analytic structure suggested a factor that was very difficult for that White American researcher to understand at that time. But in consulting with the team, it made perfect sense to them!("Yes, that is exactly what we do!") In short, "we don't know what we don't know" is important to remember. Moreover, the story highlights not only one of the strengths of a culturally diverse team, but also consulting with members of the target group, particularly when interpreting and discussing the results of a study.

In sum, a number of methodological issues and challenges need to be considered when conducting research with diverse populations. Although other authors have raised this issue (see Bernal et al., 2014, pp. 105–123), much more work needs to be done to identify the methodological challenges when investigating diverse populations. As Bernal et al. powerfully noted: "From our perspective, the central issue at hand is the decolonization of research methods that requires a comprehensive effort at examining all aspects of the research." (p. 107). With the increased cultural awareness, knowledge and skills being developed in our training programs, and with additional application of such knowledge, we believe that a much stronger and more inclusive knowledge base will develop in psychology that will not only result in new knowledge bases that are relevant for counseling and counseling psychology, but also the development of much more complex and contextualized conceptualizations of human behavior.

SUMMARY AND CONCLUSIONS

In an ideal world, there would not be a need for a chapter on multicultural research. All methodologically sound and scientifically rigorous research would be attendant to the issues raised in this chapter. However, we live in a less than perfect world, and researchers are subject to the same biases (intentional and unintentional) and myopic mindsets as exist in the society in which they live. Scholars, scientists, and researchers have never been consistent in their definitions of multicultural constructs. A basic premise of all psychological research is that the constructs used are operationally defined. Constructs such as ethnicity, social status, and gender are psychological in nature. They constitute an important part of the subjective, phenomenological world of the observer and the observed.

Out of convenience, researchers who have access to samples who happen to be diverse along some identity (e.g., gender, ethnicity, religion) may be tempted to simply conduct post hoc analyses based on the comparative research paradigm. The problem with this approach is that it is primarily descriptive and atheoretical, reflecting little thought about the underlying causal relationships. Researchers who employ this approach unwittingly perpetuate the marginalization of multicultural research. The early stages of ethnic minority research, as in other areas of research, necessarily are predominated by descriptive

research that was not often guided by established psychological theories and principles. Multicultural researchers have rightfully been critical of traditional psychological theories and principles that were primarily created using White and often middle-class men, thereby raising serious questions about the external validity of the findings to other groups. Both etic and emic approaches are important, because by virtue of our shared humanity we all experience the full range of human emotions (e.g., happiness, love, sadness, depression, anxiety, anger, jealousy, confidence). However, the expression and manifestation of these emotions are often filtered through cultural lenses that are not always well understood.

In studies with an explicitly multicultural focus, it is critically important that proximal rather than distal variables be used to explain observed differences in behavior. The use of moderators and mediators reflects one mechanism by which researchers can move toward theoretical and methodological sophistication, thereby advancing the state of affairs of multicultural research on particular topics.

Finally, we provided examples of validity issues and threats that may occur in multicultural research. The main purpose of addressing validity in psychological research is to ensure that a study's conclusions are valid. Multicultural researchers are often driven by concerns about validity, and at their best will reflexively critique their work to ensure that state of the art science is being conducted that generates valid psychological insights relevant to culturally diverse groups of people.

STIMULUS QUESTIONS

An Integration Exercise

The purpose of this exercise is to promote integration and utilization of the material presented in this chapter. Students should respond to each question and then discuss their responses with a peer.

1. Why is it problematic to use the terms race, ethnicity, and culture interchangeably?
2. What is the difference between distal and proximal explanations for behavior in multicultural research?
3. A researcher hypothesizes that there are racial differences in intelligence test scores. What issues would the researcher need to address, and what evidence would need to be presented, in order to provide support for the hypothesis?
4. What are the advantages and disadvantages of conducting multicultural research that is primarily descriptive versus theoretically driven?
5. What are the advantages and disadvantages of adding cultural validity as an additional category of validity in research?
6. What are some ways individuals can conduct more culturally competent research studies?
7. Think of a situation where the validity issues discussed in this chapter would be at odds for a person trying to conduct culturally competent research (i.e., increasing one type of validity at the expense of another type of validity).

10
Chapter

Scale Construction: A Most Fundamental Tool

With Dong-gwi Lee and Hyun-Woo Lim

Scale construction is a widely used research methodology in the field of counseling psychology research (Worthington & Whittaker, 2006). The term *scale* in counseling research is typically defined as "a collection of items combined into a composite score and intended to reveal levels of theoretical variables not readily observable by direct means" (DeVillis, 2012, p. 11). For example, to measure the construct of acculturation, responses to multiple items that are related to acculturation are combined into a score to reflect the overall level of acculturation. Using a scale that consists of several items to measure a variable has advantages over rating a single item (e.g., asking respondents to simply rate their level of acculturation from 1 to 10). Assessing a construct using multiple items can incorporate various aspects of the construct and also account for the consistency of responses across the different items. However, all scales are not created equally. Some sets of items used in a scale may more accurately reflect the construct than a different set of items. In other words, there are accurate and reliable measures as well as poor ones. In counseling research, scales are the tools to measure psychological constructs, and strong science is built on strong measures of psychological constructs. In contrast, using poor measures could cause problems and yield inaccurate results that lead to distorted scientific knowledge. Let's use building construction as an analogy. If an inaccurate tape measure was used while constructing a house, it could lead to serious structural concerns, which could result in the house collapsing. Similarly, scale development is a crucial foundation for strong counseling research.

Scales can be categorized into one of two types (Pett, Lackey, & Sullivan, 2003): (a) a criterion-referenced scale, which measures an individual's ability (e.g., achievement tests), or (b) a norm-referenced scale, which aims to differentiate individuals standing along dimensions of a given construct, typically "portrayed along a continuum of values" (e.g., personality or attitude tests) (pp. 14–15). The majority of scale construction in the field of counseling concerns the latter (i.e., individual differences scales). In this chapter, therefore, we focus our discussion on norm-referenced scales.

The purpose of this chapter is to demystify the process of scale construction. First, commonly observed misconceptions or myths pertaining to the scale construction process will be highlighted. Subsequently, a discussion of typical steps of scale construction along with examples from journal articles will be provided. Given that an in-depth discussion of statistical analyses (e.g., various scaling methods, factor analyses) is beyond the scope of this chapter, those more interested in statistical analyses are directed to additional resources (e.g., Dawis, 2000; DeVellis, 2012; Heppner & Heppner, 2004; Pett et al., 2003).

SEVEN COMMON MYTHS ON SCALE CONSTRUCTION

This section provides a discussion of seven common myths that researchers unwittingly assume in scale construction. The first four myths concern the scale construction process in general, and the latter three myths pertain to cross-cultural or multicultural considerations germane to scale construction.

Myth 1: Item Construction Can Be Done in a Few Weeks

Researchers are tempted to believe that they can develop items in a short period of time, or if they exert high levels of concentration due to an impending deadline. However, this common myth comes from a lack of understanding of the arduous and time-consuming processes of scale construction. For instance, the item generation process itself is not linear; researchers often add, delete, and revise the items multiple times to hone their meaning or focus. This recursive process is inevitable even after pilot testing and such revisions take considerable time and effort; for example, it is not uncommon for item construction to take six months to a few years. It is critical to remember that a scale is only as good as its items, and that hurried item construction often leads to disappointing results. As for the arduous processes in item construction, some examples are provided for illustrative purpose later in this chapter. It is very important that the reader understands the complex processes of scale construction, particularly item generation, pilot testing, and, if necessary, translation and back-translation.

Myth 2: Items Can Be Easily Constructed without an Extensive Literature Review

Sometimes researchers believe that items can be created through a couple of meetings where the research team members brainstorm the content and focus of items. This certainly is not true. A sound scale requires a clear definition and operationalization of the construct (DeVellis, 2012; Pett et al., 2003; Worthington & Whittaker, 2006), and this can be achieved only from careful deliberation, a clear definition of the construct, and an extensive literature review. There is no substitute for this time- and energy-consuming process. In essence, the literature review is crucial because it can provide a solid theoretical/conceptual grounding of the construct and/or a wealth of information from previous research findings that investigated similar constructs. An example of adequate literature review in scale construction is presented later in this chapter.

Myth 3: Use a Convenience Sample Whenever Possible

Researchers typically face a situation in which scale construction is a component of a larger project (e.g., dissertations, grant proposals); thus, many want to collect data quickly. It is not surprising that a number of researchers utilize convenience samples (e.g., psychology undergraduates) for testing the psychometric properties of their scales. Although college student samples could be relevant for some cases (e.g., the development of a scale designed to measure college students' career decision-making style), this is not always the case. For example, if researchers want to develop a new scale to measure individuals' general trait of procrastination, not only should the researchers devise items relevant to trait procrastination (not procrastination specific to academia), but they also should administer the scale to a broader population rather than just college students. It is also important to note that psychology students may not be representative of all college students. In the same vein, even within psychology undergraduates, the external validity (i.e., generalizability) of the scale can be compromised by other factors such as race and ethnicity. Alexander and Suzuki (2001) cautioned against biases in assessment and measurement procedures that lack sensitivity to multicultural issues, and highlighted the importance of obtaining representative samples of various racial and ethnic populations.

Myth 4: Factor Analysis Alone Provides Sufficient Evidence of the Scale's Validity

Although statistical advancements in factor analytic techniques provide a useful tool for the researcher in testing the latent structure of the scale, which provides an estimate of construct validity, it should be noted that factor analysis alone cannot provide sufficient estimates of validity. Sometimes researchers skip the necessary steps to test validity, such as convergent and discriminant validity estimates. For example, sometimes researchers attempt to make the research packet as short as possible, and do not include extra measures for convergent and discriminant validity estimates. However, this approach may yield serious problems in terms of internal and construct validity. (See discussions on various validity issues in Chapter 7.) For example, if a scale was designed to measure individuals' attitudes toward seeking professional help but a measure for social desirability to test discriminant validity was not included, then it is difficult to determine whether the items developed actually measure the intended construct, or whether participants were simply responding in socially desirable ways. The discriminant validity of a scale can be established by providing a low correlation coefficient between the inventory and the social desirability measure. Likewise, when a scale designed to measure an individual's level of depression is developed, it is an imperative step to examine convergent validity (e.g., concurrent or predictive validity) estimates of the scale by including a more widely used measure of depression (e.g., the Beck Depression Inventory). It is desirable to have a high correlation between the two measures to support convergent validity that the new scale measures depression. Examples of testing convergent and discriminant validity estimates are presented later in this chapter. In summary, it is crucial to include measures of convergent and discriminant estimates in addition to a plan to conduct a factor analysis in establishing the validity of a new inventory.

Myth 5: A Scale with Strong Psychometric Properties Developed in a Western Culture Is Universally Valid

Sometimes researchers may mistakenly assume that a scale that has been validated in a Western culture will also be suitable for people in other cultures, and thus a careful translation and back-translation will ensure cross-cultural compatibility. Translating and back-translating the items of a scale only indicate that the *items* have been adequately translated into another language, but does not provide any estimates of the validity of the items/scale in the other culture. If an adequately translated version of a scale replicates its original factor structure or reveals a similar factor structure in another culture, such results provide one estimate of construct validity, and the scale may be potentially suitable for the second culture. However, satisfactory results in factor analyses on a scale do not always guarantee the equivalence of two versions of the scale (an original version developed in the Western culture and a translated version in a non-Western culture). Any psychological construct measured by a scale is *culture bound*. A scale developed in one culture about a particular target is based on the beliefs and assumptions of the particular cultural group, which could be similar or different from the beliefs/assumptions about this construct in another culture. Thus, it is important to not only provide cross-cultural validation of a scale, but also seek to understand the culturally based meaning of that scale in different cultures.

As an example, Lee, Park, Shin, and Graham (2005) conducted an exploratory factor analysis (EFA) with a sample of Korean college students by using the U.S.-based Frost Multidimensional Perfectionism Scales (Frost, Marten, Lahart, & Rosenblate, 1990). Frost et al. reported six factors: (a) concerns over mistake, (b) doubts about action, (c) organization, (d) parental expectations, (e) parental criticism, and (f) personal standards. Although a five-factor solution was also found in some Western cultures (e.g., Harvey, Pallant, & Harvey, 2004; Stumpf & Parker, 2000), the EFA results by Lee et al. favored a five-factor solution with parental expectations and parental criticism combined into one new factor called parental pressure. In essence, the parental criticism factor almost disappeared. A similar finding was reported by Cheng, Chong, and Wong (1999) with a Chinese adolescent sample in Hong Kong. Thus, the majority of items in the parental criticism factor failed to be retained, indicating a culturally unique factor structure found in the two studies using Asian samples.

In short, even though a scale has been carefully translated and back-translated, the factor structure of the scale may change across different cultural contexts. Such results would typically suggest that the psychological construct as measured by the scale differs across different cultural contexts. In addition, research has found that sometimes the items that comprise a particular factor on a scale can be quite similar (or even almost identical) across two cultures, but reflect slightly different constructs. For example, Tian, Heppner, and Hou (2014) found that one factor (personal control) on the Problem Solving Inventory (PSI) was nearly identical in the United States and China, but that it was more accurate to rename that factor to (emotional control) within the majority Chinese culture. In sum, scales developed in one culture should not be used across different cultural contexts without acquiring additional data.

Myth 6: A Literal Translation Ensures Linguistic and Cultural Equivalence

A literal, word-for-word translation of each item or the instruction statements of a scale may not guarantee linguistic or cultural equivalence. It is crucial to conduct appropriate translations and back-translations and to seek consultations with cultural insiders regarding how the translated items would be interpreted by people from the target culture. A literal translation sometimes can bring about unintended consequences. For example, the term *self-esteem* may not be universal across cultures or even exist in certain languages. To test this point, one of the authors used Google Translate to translate the term *self-esteem* from English into various languages (e.g. Chinese, Spanish, Persian) and asked native speakers to back-translate the terms. They identified terms and concepts that were related, but different from self-esteem! Many languages do not have a specific term that precisely reflects self-esteem as how it is conceptualized in the Western context or English language. Similarly, unique concepts such as filial piety may have different meanings and importance across cultural contexts.

In addition, the sentence structure and grammar across languages can also be different, which can present challenges around translation. For example, in some languages the literal translation puts a subordinate clause (e.g., if, when clauses) in the wrong place, resulting in a different meaning. Furthermore, such situations can be more complicated when a sentence contains two elements. Consider the following item, which was included in the initial item pool for the Collectivist Coping Styles Inventory (CCS; Heppner et al., 2006) but was modified due to its statement ambiguity as well as potential problems in translation:

> Item: To avoid family shame, only told a few people about the difficult event or my feelings about the event.

This item contains two elements (i.e., avoidance of family shame and only told a few people about the stressful event), and thus the respondents may be confused in determining which content they should respond to. For example, perhaps one respondent wanted to avoid family shame at all costs, but actually did *not* confide in any friends. But the respondent could be quickly confused on how to best respond to this item in which one part is true, but the second part is false. Therefore, we strongly advise the researcher to avoid any item that contains two or more elements at any time.

Myth 7: Structural Elements of a Scale, Such as a Likert Rating Scale, Are Universal across Cultures

Likert scales (Likert, 1932) are one of the most widely used rating scales, and typically consist of "a number of positively or negatively worded declarative sentences followed by response options that indicate the extent to which the respondent agrees or disagrees with the statement" (Pett et al., 2003, p. 32). Given its popularity, researchers and students usually believe this response system may be universally accepted because it is an ordinal scale consisting of five- or six-degree points. Unfortunately, this is not the case at all. Literature suggests that some East Asians tend to frequently endorse the middle or center points of the scale (Chen, Lee, & Stevenson, 1995;

Chia, Allred, & Jerzak, 1997; Gibbons, Hamby, & Dennis, 1997). This tendency may reflect Asians' avoidance of being extreme in their responses. Thus, it is difficult to interpret results from East Asian populations where the mean response is, let's say, a 3 on a 5-point scale; and using an even number of Likert points (e.g., 4-point, 6-point scale) would be a way to eliminate the option to pick the middle point.

RESEARCH IN ACTION 10.1

Among the seven myths of scale construction described in this chapter, which one stood out for you when reading it? What was the new knowledge that you gained from thinking about that myth?

STEPS OF SCALE CONSTRUCTION

Thus far, common myths concerning scale construction have been highlighted. In the remainder of this chapter, we provide a brief description of typical steps of scale construction, particularly in a cross-cultural or multicultural context. For more information, interested readers are encouraged to read DeVellis (2012), Kline (2005), Patten (2001), Pett et al. (2003), and Worthington and Whittaker (2006).

A brief sketch of the process by which Heppner et al. (2006) developed the Collectivist Coping Styles Inventory (CCS) may be instructive. The process of developing the CCS not only reveals the complexity of the scale construction processes, but also highlights the importance of cross-cultural or multicultural considerations in scale construction.

First, the researchers formed a research team that consisted of two European American doctoral-level counseling psychologists and three Asian-born doctoral students (one Taiwanese and two South Koreans) in a U.S. counseling psychology program, as well as one Taiwanese faculty member. It took a year for the team to develop, discuss, refine, pilot, and finalize the items for the CCS. The item generation processes involved debates and refinements of items. For example, the original 70 items developed across 13 theoretically driven categories (described later in this chapter) were subject to numerous debates, brainstorming, and modifications. The 70 items were pilot tested with eight Asian graduate students in order to ensure the relevance of the items to Asian cultures. Numerous personal communications and consultations with Taiwanese colleagues regarding the cultural relevance of the scale were also necessary. The final version of the CCS was then subject to robust translations and back-translations in order to be used in Taiwan. The translation process was repeated until consensus was reached among all the parties involved in terms of linguistic equivalence and cultural relevance. In addition, the team spent a great deal of time incorporating culturally relevant categories for common stressful or traumatic life events. For example, issues such as social ostracism or academic failure were included among 17 stressful or traumatic events because these events may be perceived as traumatic, particularly in Asia where interpersonal harmony

TABLE 10.1 : Steps of Scale Construction

1. Conceptualizing and operationalizing the construct of interest
2. Conducting the literature review
3. Generating the items, indicators, and response formats
4. Conducting content analysis, pilot testing, revising, and administering the items
5. Sampling and data collection
6. Translating and back-translating the scale, if necessary
7. Finalizing items and optimizing scale length
8. Testing the psychometric properties of the scale
9. Advanced evaluation or refinement of the scale

is extremely valued and keen competition in academic environments is prevalent. Details about testing the construct validity of the CCS (i.e., factor analyses and psychometric properties) can be found in Heppner et al. (2006).

In the following sections, we describe nine steps in scale construction (see Table 10.1).

Step 1: Conceptualizing and Operationalizing the Construct of Interest

The first step in scale construction involves identifying of the construct of interest. Before deciding to develop a new scale, a researcher should consider (a) assessing the necessity for a new scale for the construct and the population of interest, (b) conceptualizing the content of the construct and writing its operational definition, and (c) consulting with other colleagues regarding the utility of the scale and the appropriateness of the definition. In order for the definition to be operationalized, the construct should be written in a statement that is measurable. For example, Wang, Wei, Zhao, Chuang, and Li (2015) developed a scale that was designed to measure losses experienced by people who cross national borders, such as international students. The construct of cross-cultural loss was conceptualized to include both tangible (e.g., food from home country, in-person access to family members) as well as intangible losses (e.g., feeling less connected, having less relevant knowledge). Conceptualizing and operationalizing a construct necessitates a researcher's extensive knowledge of the target population.

Step 2: Conducting the Literature Review

It is essential that researchers ground their scale construction in the previous literature and relevant theories related to the construct under investigation. Perhaps previous scholars have developed a scale on the same construct, or a closely related construct. Typically, the previous studies help researchers understand the construct of interest, as well as the strengths and limitations of the existing knowledge on the construct. Often a researcher uses a theory to guide the development of the items, which typically provides guidance in generating the domain of items. Thus, after conceptualizing the construct, the next step typically is to search for relevant literature to increase one's knowledge about the construct, and search for relevant theories to guide the item generation phase.

Heppner and Heppner (2004) highlighted the importance of understanding the nonlinear nature in the literature search processes, stating "Be careful! As you plan your time for the literature search, add more time for the nonlinear, looping-back process.... These kinds of nonlinear processes generally mean that [you] are (a) critically analyzing a complex topic, [and] (b) refining [your] conceptualization of [your] study" (p. 56). In addition, Pett et al. (2003) provided practical guidelines in developing questions and evaluation criteria to guide the literature review:

> How is the construct defined conceptually and operationally in a published article?, What kind of and how many concerns about testing [this construct] does the author identify?, Were there specific empirical indicators [regarding the construct] listed in the article?, Does that author cite other authors who have studied the construct? (p. 21)

For example, in Heppner et al.'s (2006) CCS project, identifying the relevant literature or theoretical background for the construct they purport to measure was a crucial task because it identified relevant theories related to the construct. For example, the CCS was guided by three theoretical/conceptual grounds or previous research findings: (a) Kim, Atkinson, and Yang's (1999) work on Asian values; (b) Weisz, Rothbaum, and Blackburn's (1984) concepts regarding primary and secondary control; and (c) Zeidner and Saklofske's (1996) adaptational model of coping. Moreover, Heppner et al. described how the construct, Collectivist Coping Styles, and items were derived from Weisz et al.'s work on both primary control (individuals achieve control by directly influencing their realities) and secondary control (individuals obtain control by reframing or accommodating their realities). This was an important component in generating items for the CCS project because the researchers' goal was to develop a broad range of coping items specifically for Asians, which would include items related to secondary control as well as primary control (which is prominent in Western coping instruments).

Step 3: Generating the Items, Indicators, and Response Formats

Item generation is a pivotal step in scale construction, because poor items jeopardize the construct validity of the scale, which in turn misleads future researchers who wish to use the scale. Generally speaking, careful item generation takes several months. The quality of items are often enhanced in several ways such as (a) basing the items on a solid literature review and conceptual models or theories, (b) using qualitative methods such as focus groups and interviews with relevant groups of people to identify prototypical dimensions or indicators of the construct, and (c) writing conceptually and linguistically clear items. Kline (2005) suggested the following nine rules to guide the development of writing items: (a) deal with only *one* central thought in each item, (b) be precise, (c) be brief, (d) avoid awkward wording or dangling constructs, (e) avoid irrelevant information, (f) present items in positive language, (g) avoid double negatives, (h) avoid terms like *all* and *none*, and (i) avoid indeterminate terms like *frequently* or *sometimes* (pp. 34–35).

DeVellis (2012) also provided some additional guidelines around developing scale items. He suggested that it is not uncommon for the item pool to be three or four times as large as the final scale length. DeVellis recommended examining the readability of items so that they are written at the appropriate level for the intended population. For example, when developing a scale for young children, the words used in the items should be at their reading level. And there are programs available (e.g., Microsoft Word) to examine the reading level. A final issue raised was the inclusion of both positive and negatively worded items. Although experts disagree on this topic, DeVellis suggested that the disadvantages of having opposite direction items (reversed items) outweighed the benefits. Issues raised included (a) item polarity that are reversed can be confusing to participants especially if they are completing a long questionnaire, and (b) items worded in opposite directions often perform poorly (see DeVellis, 2012, for more detailed discussion on suggestions for scale development).

Consider a study by Kim et al. (1999) to develop the Asian Values Scale. Specifically, the researchers were first guided by their literature review, which generated 10 Asian value dimensions and 60 statements. Subsequently, the researchers obtained feedback on the identified Asian value dimensions and statements from 103 psychologists, selected from the list of members in Division 45 (Society for the Psychological Study of Ethnic Minority Issues) of the American Psychological Association. Finally, Kim et al. performed focus discussion groups to generate Asian value dimensions and statements. These multiple processes resulted in 14 Asian values and 202 items for the Asian Value Scale. In essence, the researchers were able to identify sound items for their scale using multiple methods of item generation.

In addition, to achieve the clarity of items and response formats, researchers should avoid an item with negatives or double negatives. This is applicable to any scale construction project, but it would be more critical in a cross-cultural study necessitating translation. Consider the following example modified from Patten (2001, p. 11):

Item: "I *can't* stop ruminating about how the accident happened."

1. Very rarely   2. Rarely   3. Sometimes   4. Often   5. Very Often

The respondent may be confused because of the negative statement in the item (i.e., can't) and the anchor choices that also include negatives (i.e., rarely). Moreover, it would likely confuse respondents more from another culture in a different language. It is generally advisable to avoid using negatives or double negatives, particularly in cross-cultural contexts, unless the researchers have a strong rationale for using them.

RESEARCH IN ACTION 10.2

Please come up with a psychological construct that you might have interest in developing a scale to measure. What would be some sample items that might reflect the construct of interest? What would be some ways to generate more items for the pool of that measures?

Step 4: Conducting Content Analysis and Pilot Testing, Revising, and Administering the Items

It is important for authors to go beyond just developing a list of items. Regardless of one's level of confidence in the validity of item content, the respondents may perceive/interpret the items quite differently from what researchers intended due to many systematic or nonsystematic errors. To enhance the construct validity of the scale (i.e., whether the scale measures what it purports to measure) researchers are advised to (a) conduct content analyses and consult with domain experts, and (b) pilot items to identify potential problems with their wording. The following example from Pinterits, Poteat, and Spanierman (2009) illustrates the importance of conducting content analyses. Pinterits et al. developed a scale designed to measure White privilege attitudes. The researchers checked the content validity of the items by seeking consultation with five experts in the topic of interest. The following is an excerpt from the Pinterits et al. study.

> To improve content validity, five psychologists and education scholars with expertise in White privilege issues (one African American and four White) rated each item on content appropriateness and clarity using a 5-point Likert-type scale ranging from 1 (not at all appropriate or clear) to 5 (very appropriate or clear), respectively. Items with average ratings below 3 were dropped or revised, resulting in 111 items. Twenty-three items were reverse scored to reduce response bias. Because many items from this initial generation were double-barreled (i.e., they mentioned several facets of White privilege within a single item), two of the authors with experience in scale construction independently reviewed and edited each item to separate double-barreled items and to delete redundant items; this improved clarity and parsimony. (p. 419)

In addition to content analysis, pilot testing of the items is another important activity in the development of items. Pilot testing involves asking participants not only to respond to the items as a participant, but also to identify unclear or ambiguous elements about the items. Sometimes this is accomplished by having participants circle ambiguous terms, identify in writing what parts are confusing or ambiguous, or even write alternative wording to enhance the items. With such a strategy, participants are given not only very specific instructions to clearly identify the task, but also ample space below each item to make comments. In this way, pilot testing provides a powerful tool for the researcher to identify items that might be misunderstood or unclear to the respondents. Following is an example from Juntunen and Wettersten (2006). Note that the authors sought pilot testing before they consulted with domain-specific experts. This strategy attempts to reduce ambiguity in the items before the content experts examine them.

> We eventually selected 28 items for the initial item pool. We structured each as a declarative sentence, and we selected a Likert scale response format. We then administered the 28-item WHS [Work Hope Scale] to a pilot sample of individuals from a northern Midwestern community. Although this varies slightly from the recommendations of DeVellis (2003), who suggested moving directly to expert review, we included the pilot study to identify items that performed poorly and to gain initial psychometric information to assist in decision making for inclusion, exclusion, and revision of items. (p. 97)

In essence, content analysis and pilot testing helped the authors to fine tune and revise their items. Readers should keep in mind that the revision processes are neither linear nor clear-cut; sometimes, the researchers repeatedly engage in numerous activities to revise and alter the items to achieve more clarity in content.

Step 5: Sampling and Data Collection

Sampling pertains to identifying the samples of the population of interest that the research intends to generalize to; data collection is the actual collection of data from the participants. The researcher must first consider (a) whether the sample is representative of the population of interest or a sample of convenience, and (b) whether the sample size is appropriate (e.g., typically at least 250–300 participants are needed for factor analyses; see Tabachnick & Fidell, 2001, for more details).

The sampling issue is a critical one. For example, when Heppner et al. (2006) were developing and validating the CCS inventory, they specifically sought an East Asian sample that would assess Asian-specific ways of coping with traumatic life events. A total of 24 universities in Taiwan were involved in the data collection procedures. The college student samples were also relevant for the study because several categories among the common stressful or traumatic events assessed academic situations. It should be noted that the research team sought data from the four different geographic regions in Taiwan (north, south, central, and east) in order to obtain a geographically representative sample of Taiwanese college students. This was extremely important because the geographic region is one of the most distinct demographic characteristics in Taiwan. The data collection procedures required a great deal of work for a senior Taiwanese faculty member and one of the research team members, which was far from collecting the data from a "convenience" sample. As a result, college students from around the island participated in the study. For more information about sampling and screening, see Kline (2005).

Data collection is also a critical step in scale construction. A typical method of data collection involves distributing questionnaires to a group of participants. Internet-based surveys are increasingly being used because of their distinctive advantages, such as being less geographically constrained, quick and economical, and easy to convert into statistical software. However, the Internet's disadvantages should also be considered; these include limited accessibility to the Internet for some people, a tendency to obtain low response rates, and issues with privacy and confidentiality (see Wright, 2005, for a more detailed discussion). For more information on survey methods, see Chapter 13 as well as Dillman (2000) and Heppner and Heppner (2004).

Step 6: Translating and Back-Translating the Scale, if Necessary

The issue concerning translation and its linguistic and cultural equivalence cannot be overemphasized; lack of care in this step not only introduces measurement error in the scale, but also misleads readers about the generalizability of the construct across cultures. Three resources that discuss enhancing the quality of translation and back-translation of the construct in cross-cultural studies are Ægisdóttir,

Gerstein, and Çinarbas (2008), Van de Vijver and Leung (1997), and Mallinckrodt and Wang (2004). These references discuss challenges in cross-cultural studies such as equivalence issues. In particular, Mallinckrodt and Wang provided a thorough discussion of the procedure to enhance the equivalence (e.g., content, semantic, technical, criterion, and conceptual equivalence) of a translated scale to the original instrument.

Following is an excerpt from Mallinckrodt and Wang (2004) pertaining to the back-translation procedure they employed to ensure linguistic and cultural equivalence in the translation and back-translation. Note that the researchers started by gaining permission from the original authors of a scale that they wanted to translate into Chinese (Mandarin). This is an important step concerning the ethics in cross-cultural validation of a scale.

> The study began by obtaining permission from the developers of the ECRS (Experiences in Close Relationships Scale; Brennan, Clark, & Shaver, 1998) to adapt the instrument (P. R. Shaver, personal communication, March 5, 2002). Next, two native speakers of Chinese (one man, one woman) who were doctoral students in counseling psychology and fluent in English independently translated the ECRS into Mandarin Chinese. (Mandarin is the official language of Taiwan and mainland China.) At this stage, there were three types of discrepancies between the two initial translations: (a) selection of an appropriate Chinese phrase for "romantic partner," (b) problems created by shifts across the English ECRS items from singular "partner" to plural "partners," and (c) finding a single Chinese referent for affect descriptors such as "feel bad" or "resent." Discrepancies between the two versions were thoroughly discussed and resolved until a new draft translation was agreed upon. This first draft of the Chinese version of the ECRS was then submitted for back-translation to a bilingual Taiwanese graduate student whose major was Translation and Interpretation. She was completely unfamiliar with the original English version of the ECRS. Next, a native English speaker, with a doctoral degree in counseling psychology and considerable familiarity with the ECRS, compared the back-translated English version with the original ECRS item-by-item, together with the instruction, to evaluate the semantic equivalence of the two versions. Two pairs of items were evaluated as not equivalent. The preceding steps were then repeated for these items in a second iteration. After this process, the back-translated version and the original ECRS were judged to be equivalent. The final Mandarin Chinese version was labeled the *ECRS-C*. Quantitative procedures for establishing equivalence of the ECRS and ECRS-C are described in the Results section. (p. 372)

Step 7: Finalizing Items and Optimizing Scale Length

Conducting factor analyses (both exploratory and confirmatory factor analyses) to finalize scale items is a critical step in the scale development process. Factor analysis is a set of statistical procedures for "theory and instrument development and assessing construct validity of an established instrument when administered to a specific population" (Pett et al., 2003, p. 3) and typically consists of two types (a) exploratory factor analysis (EFA) and (b) confirmatory factor analysis (CFA). EFA is conducted "when the researcher does not know how many factors [or underlying/ latent dimensions] are necessary to explain the interrelationships among a set of characteristics, indicators, or items" (Pett et al., p. 3), whereas CFA is utilized when the researcher wants "to assess the extent to which the hypothesized organization [i.e., the researcher already knows the underlying structure or dimensions of the construct] of a set of identified factors fits the data" (Pett et al., p. 4). Typically, a researcher performs EFA first with a sample in order to identify the underlying factor structure of a construct, and then attempts to cross-validate it with another sample via CFA. For example, a researcher might carefully develop a 50-item questionnaire to measure beliefs about social justice and social advocacy. Factor analysis could be used to identify how the 50 items could be grouped together in theoretically meaningful categories, with the end product being five distinct factors consisting of 30 items. In essence, factor analysis examines the interrelationships among a large number of items (or variables) and condenses (summarizes) that information into a smaller set of common underlying dimensions or factors. These dimensions or factors presumably correspond to underlying psychological constructs. Thus, the fundamental aim of factor analysis is to search for underlying psychological constructs seen in the common dimensions that underlie the original items or variables (Hair et al., 1987). This process is actually quite complex; in order to fully understand the conceptual and statistical issues pertaining to factor analysis, readers should refer to some of the following resources to attain more complete information on those processes: (a) Pett et al. (2003) for the steps to conduct EFA using Statistical Package for Social Sciences (SPSS), (b) Thompson (2004) for conceptual understanding and application of both EFA and CFA along with SPSS syntax, and (c) the chapter by Lee and Park in Heppner and Heppner (2004) for practical guidelines and examples regarding how to report factor analysis results.

In general, when conducting EFA, particularly for new scale development, two points are noteworthy. First, researchers should use common factor analysis (CA) instead of principal components analysis (PCA) because CA provides a more realistic estimation of factor structure assuming that "the items are measured with errors" (Kline, 2005, p. 258). Second, the use of parallel analysis (Hayton, Allen, & Scarpello, 2004) is recommended in order to more objectively determine the number of factors to retain.

As a result of the EFA, typically a number of the original scale items are deleted, leaving only those items that correlate strongly with the factors identified in the EFA. The scale items are finalized and ready for the final stage of validation, testing of the psychometric properties of the scale. If another sample is available (which is usually encouraged), researchers will also conduct a CFA for cross-validation of the factor structure. It is also recommended to use the same estimation method of both the EFA and CFA, if possible (Brown, 2006).

To illustrate the process of conducting factor analyses to select scale items, we will use Wang et al.'s (2015) study in which they developed the Cross-Cultural Loss Scale as an example. Please note how they not only used EFA to select strong items for the scale, but also made an attempt to optimize the scale length. In other words, the researchers' goal was to develop a scale as short as possible with solid psychometric properties so that it would be less of a burden on respondents.

> We first conducted exploratory factor analyses (EFA) for item selection with sample 1 ($N = 262$). Following recommendations from Brown (2006) to use consistent methods across EFA and CFA, all factor analyses were conducted in Mplus 7 with robust maximum likelihood (MLR) as the estimator and Geomin as the rotation method. To

determine the number of factors, we conducted a parallel analysis by comparing initial eigenvalues of this sample with those generated through random data; the comparison suggested a three-factor solution. Due to initially using four domains to create the item pool, we thus conducted exploratory factor analyses on the 29-items with three- to five-factor solutions using an oblique rotation method (i.e., Geomin) due to the expected inter-factor correlations in this multifactorial model (Brown, 2006). The most interpretable solution was a three-factor oblique-rotation solution ... The three factors were generally consistent with the four categories used when developing the item pool, but with two categories combined into one factor: Belonging-Competency, National Privileges, and Access to Home Familiarity. Among the 29 items tested in the three-factor solution, five items had significant cross-loadings. In addition, our goal was to create a brief scale with four to six items in each factor. We thus utilized the modification indices and significant cross-loadings as criteria to determine which items to retain. Using the modification indices that suggest correlations between item-residuals allows us to identify item-pairs that have overlapping content beyond variances associated with the factor. By removing relatively redundant items accordingly would result in more diverse sets of items that measure the same factors. Through a series of EFAs, we retained 14 items for the final CCLS (six in Belonging-Competency, four in National Privileges, and four in Access to Home Familiarity). (p. 46)

Following the EFA results, Wang et al. (2015) conducted a CFA on a separate sample to validate the initial factor structure found through the EFA. Through the CFA model fit indices, conclusions can be made about whether the data fit well with the factor structure. Please note following that the researchers also examined competing CFA models.

Confirmatory factor analysis (CFA) was conducted with sample 2 ($N = 256$) using Mplus 7 to cross-validate the measurement qualities of the CCLS using MLR as the estimator and Geomin as the rotation method. The CFA model constrained the 14 CCLS items to load onto their corresponding factors based on the EFA results. The three factors were permitted to correlate with one another. The range of standardized factor loadings for the factors was: .61 to .85 for Belonging-Competency, .52 to .72 for National Privileges, and .53 to .79 for Access to Home Familiarity. The fit statistics for this three-factor oblique model [CFI = .971, SRMR = .038, RMSEA = .041] were strong. We also examined three competing models: a three-factor orthogonal model, a bifactor model (i.e., each item loads on a general Cross-Cultural Loss factor and one of the three orthogonal factor), and a one-factor model. The fit indices for all four models are presented in Table 4. Based on the general guidelines, the CFI, SRMR, and RMSEA all indicated an adequate data to model fit for both the three-factor oblique and the bifactor models, but not the three-factor orthogonal model or one-factor model. To compare between the three-factor oblique and the bifactor model, we examined the Akaike information criteria (AIC). A slightly smaller AIC indicated that the three-factor oblique model was better, however, the bifactor model was comparable with slightly higher CFA and lower SRMR. (p. 49)

Step 8: Testing the Psychometric Properties of the Scale

It is essential to establish the psychometric properties of any new scale. This can be achieved by examining estimates of reliability (e.g., coefficient alphas and test-retest reliability) and various types of validity (e.g., convergent and discriminant validity as well as incremental validity). With regard to reliability estimates, coefficient alphas (typically referred to as Cronbach's alpha) provide the researcher with information about the degree of the homogeneity or internal consistency among a set of items. Although there is not a commonly agreed upon cutoff for the acceptable magnitude of a coefficient alpha, often .70 or higher is desired in the social sciences. Another estimate of reliability is also recommended. A test-retest reliability coefficient informs researchers of the stability of the scale over time. The time interval between pre- and posttest needs to be at least 2 weeks, preferably a month. When reporting test-retest reliability (e.g., $r = .80$), it is essential to include the specific time interval (e.g., 2 weeks) because the longer the time interval (e.g., 2 weeks versus 2 years), typically the lower the correlation.

Estimates of validity, typically convergent and discriminant, are also very important in scale construction. The following is an example of an attempt to establish both convergent and discriminant validity of a scale developed by Neville, Lilly, Duran, Lee, and Browne (2000). The researchers first examined the concurrent validity of the Color-Blind Racial Attitudes Scale (CoBRAS) by calculating its correlation coefficients with the Global Belief in a Just World Scale (GBJWS; Lipkus, 1991) and the Multidimensional Belief in a Just World Scale (MBJWS; Furnham & Procter, 1988), two established measures of social justice attitudes. They expected moderate to high correlations with these two scales. In addition, they examined the discriminant validity of the CoBRAS by calculating its correlations with the Marlowe-Crowne Social Desirability Scale (MCSDS; W. M. Reynolds, 1982), expecting a small correlation. Following is an excerpt from Neville et al. Two points are noteworthy. First, in order to establish the discriminant validity of the CoBRAS, the researchers used a short version of the MCSDS (13 true-false items), which in the past was one of the most widely used measures of social desirability. More recently, another measure of social desirability, the 20-item Impression Management (i.e., deliberate self-presentation to an audience) of the Balanced Inventory of Desirable Responding (BIDR; Paulhus, 1984, 1991) is being used more frequently. (Those interested in the psychometric properties of the BIDR should refer to Paulhus, 1991.) Second, note that Neville et al. found one significant correlation between one of the CoBRAS factors and the MCSDS. This is not an ideal situation because it indicates some items of the CoBRAS may reflect that respondents' responses are associated with social desirability. However, this does not nullify the utility of the CoBRAS because the amount of variance accounted for in the correlation was very small ($.20 \times .20 = 4\%$). This is called a "coefficient of determination," which refers to "an indication of how much variance is shared by the X and the Y variable" (Cohen, Swerdlik, & Phillips, 1996, p. 133). We recommend that researchers report the amount of variance when the correlation between their new measure and social desirability is statistically significant.

Concurrent Validity

The correlations among the CoBRAS factors and the two Belief in a Just World scales were examined to investigate the concurrent validity of the CoBRAS. Results indicate significant correlation among the GBJW, MBJWS-sociopolitical subscales (SS), the three CoBRAS factors, and the CoBRAS total score. Correlations ranged from .39 (between Institutional Discrimination and GBJW) to .61 (among MBJWS and Racial Privilege as well as the CoBRAS total).

Discriminant Validity

The correlations among the CoBRAS factors and the MCSDS were examined to provide estimates of discriminant validity. Results suggest that generally there is no strong association among the MCSDS and the CoBRAS factors. There was one statistically significant relation: MCSDS was associated with Blatant Racial Issues ($r = .20$); however, the maximum amount of variance accounted for was 4%. (p. 65)

Incremental validity assesses whether a scale adds more predictive ability of a particular outcome variable over another predictor variable (usually an existing scale that measures a similar construct). Haynes and Lench (2003) further suggest that incremental validity can be "evaluated on several dimensions, such as sensitivity to change, diagnostic efficacy, content validity, treatment design and outcome, and convergent validity" (p. 456). A most common form is incremental criterion validity that is used in counseling related studies. Following is an excerpt from Wei, Alvarez, Ku, Russell, and Bonett's (2010) study in which they evaluated the incremental validity of the Coping with Discrimination Scale (CDS).

Hierarchical regression analyses were conducted to examine the incremental validity of the CDS. All four coping strategies (i.e., active coping, self-blame, substance use, and behavioral disengagement) assessed by the Brief COPE were entered in Step 1 of the regression analysis, with the five CDS subscales (i.e., Education/Advocacy, Internalization, Drug and Alcohol Use, Resistance, and Detachment) entered in Step 2. ... The five CDS subscales accounted for an additional 5% of variance, $\Delta F(5, 209) = 3.05$, $\Delta R^2 = .05$, $p = .011$, in depression over and above the Brief COPE. ... For life satisfaction, the five CDS subscales accounted for 6% of the variance over and above the general coping measure, $\Delta F(5, 209) = 3.30$, $\Delta R^2 = .06$, $p = .007$. The Internalization and Resistance subscales uniquely and significantly predicted life satisfaction. Similarly, all five CDS subscales added 5% incremental variance in predicting self-esteem. ... These results demonstrate the incremental validity of the CDS over and above the general coping strategies. (p.339)

Step 9: Advanced Item Evaluation or Refinement of the Scale

Item response theory (IRT) is an advance approach for evaluating scale items, which have received increased attention over recent years. DeVellis highlighted three key distinctive features of IRT-based measurement approaches compared to the classical test theories: (a) the focus on items as opposed to the scale as a whole, (b) the ability to identify levels of how items measure a certain attribute, and (c) utilization of visual graphics to illustrate item-scale characteristics. Based on these features that IRT offers, the approach provides the ability to assess item difficulty, item discrimination, and guessing/false positives. Because assessing item difficulty is an integral part of IRT, it is most often used with measures, such as achievement test (e.g., SAT, GRE), which utilizes multiple-choice questions that have right/wrong answers. IRT relates a person's response patterns (e.g., correct vs. incorrect) to items of varying difficultness to determine the level of one's ability. However, IRT's focus on item performances can be used to evaluate items for norm-referenced scales used in counseling research as well. For example, using IRT to assess items on a depression scale, a researcher can identify the probability of individuals with different levels of depressive mood endorsing particular items. To illustrate, an item such as "I have thoughts about ending my life" would more likely to be endorsed by individuals who are moderate to highly depressed; however, an item such as "I feel sad" would likely be endorsed by individuals even with very low depressive mood. Moreover, through IRT approaches, scale items' ability to discriminate among different severity levels of depressive mood can also be assessed. To illustrate, the item "I feel sad" would likely be good at differentiating between lower levels of depressive mood (e.g., those that are not depressed at all from those that have minor depressive mood); however, the item may not be as good at differentiating between those at higher levels of depressive mood (e.g., severely depressed and those with moderate depression). In contrast, the "I have thoughts about ending my life" item would likely perform better in the case of differentiating between the moderate and severe depressed individuals as opposed to differentiating between mild and nondepressed individuals. In addition, IRT can also be used to examine whether different groups of individuals (e.g., gender, race, nationality) respond differently to particular scale items. This function allows for better assessment of whether scales and their items are equivalent across demographic and cultural variables.

In counseling research with norm-referenced scales, IRT are most often used to further refine scales after they have been developed through EFA and CFA. For example, Locke et al.'s (2012) study in which they developed a short form of the Counseling Center Assessment of Psychological Symptoms (CCAPS) by reducing the original scale from 62 items to 34. Locke et al. used item response theory to examine the performances of each item to determine the best items to retain. Following is an excerpt of the process in which they identified the better performing items of the Depression subscale and a graph to illustrate how each item provided different information.

> Results of the IRT item information estimation for the Depression subscale are shown in [Figure 10.1]. Consistent with the CTT item analysis results, the IRT item information also showed that Items 13, 24, 27, and 45 were the best-performing items on the Depression sub scale. These items provided the most information around the middle range of the latent trait (depression). On the other hand, Item 65 was less than ideal and was removed from the short form. It did not give much information across trait levels.... [Figure 10.1] shows that the item information curves for Items 11, 61, and 70 nearly overlapped, as did the item information curves for Items 15, 32, 41, and 55. The nearly overlapping item information curves suggested that the items gave similar amount of information in the similar range of the latent trait. In addition, Items 10 and 51 were also similar in terms of the amount of information they offered; however, the item information curve of Item 10 reached the peak in the middle of the latent trait continuum while that of Item 51 was negatively skewed, suggesting that Item 10 provided the most information in the middle range whereas Item 51 offered more information in the upper range of the latent trait. (p.155)

FIGURE 10.1 : Estimated Item Information: CCAPS-Depression Subscale

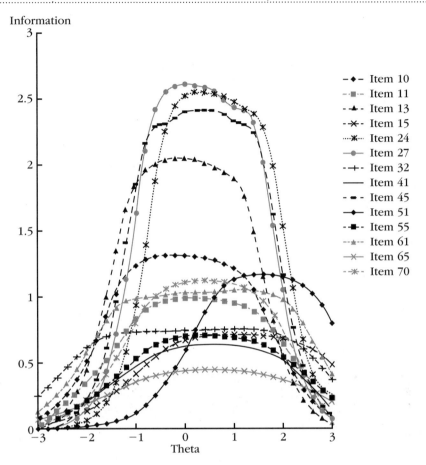

Based on the IRT results in combination with other analyses using classical test theory, Items 11, 13, 24, 27, 45, and 51 were retained for the CCAPS-34 (short form). As mentioned, Items 13, 24, 27, 45 were best performing because they were able to discriminate among individuals with midlevel depression (as seen in the graph, there is a steep bell shape curve that peaks in the middle range). In addition to these four best performing items, Items 11 and 51, each represented a group of overlapping items, were also retained. In particular, Item 51 was retained due to it providing more information on the upper range (i.e., peaking at a higher level of the depression continuum) as it assessed suicidal ideation, which was deemed important for the clinical utility of the scale. This is an illustration of the advantages of using IRT to examine the specific characteristics of each item (e.g., the ability to discriminate individuals and where the item provides most information on the continuum of the latent variable). This study provides an example of how IRT has been most commonly used in counseling research to refine scales.

There are also more sophisticated ways that IRT can be in used in the scale development process, especially in developing scales that measure ability (e.g., SAT, GRE). IRT provides information on the probability of persons at different ability levels answering the question correctly (i.e., item difficulty). And thus, computerized-adaptive testing that adapts to an examinee's ability level is developed through IRT. Computerized-adaptive testing presents questions based on the examinee's responses. If an examinee answers a question correctly, a more difficult question will be presented next; whereas if the examinee incorrectly answers the question, a simpler question will follow. The main goal of this type of testing is to determine examinees' ability level. However, these more sophistical ways of using IRT is beyond the scope of this chapter. For those interested in learning more about IRT, please refer to other examples of studies that used IRT to develop three equivalent versions of an e-measure that assesses therapist competence (Cooper et al., 2015), to examine item difficulty and item fit of a racial identity measure (Sussman, Beaujean, Worrell, & Watson, 2013), and to develop short forms of existing measures (Kim & Hong, 2004; Peters, Sunderland, Andrews, Rapee, & Mattick, 2012), as well as other readings on IRT (DeVellis, 2012; Embretson & Reise, 2000; Thomas, 2011).

SUMMARY AND CONCLUSIONS

The following seven common myths that researchers often unwittingly assume have been discussed: (a) item construction can be done in a few weeks, (b) items can be easily constructed without an extensive literature review, (c) using a convenience sample whenever possible, (d) factor analysis alone provides sufficient evidence of the scale's validity, (e) a scale with strong psychometric properties developed in a Western culture is universally valid, (f) a literal translation ensures linguistic and cultural equivalence, and (g) structural elements of a scale, such as a Likert rating scale, are universal across cultures. In addition, our discussion of the seven steps in scale construction along with examples from several inventories developed in the field of counseling (e.g., CCS and CoBRAS) guides researchers and students who may develop their own scales, particularly in a cross-cultural or multicultural context.

Creating a new scale is very important in education and psychology in general because a psychometrically sound inventory can provide an effective tool to (a) assess individual differences across various domains such as personality, attitudes, cognitions, emotions, and behaviors; and (b) examine the interface of such domains and psychological adjustment. Furthermore, scales are critical to counseling psychology research and in essence promote the development of psychometrically sound ways of assessing and promoting understanding of a new construct relevant to the counseling profession. It is also critically important to understand that a scale developed to assess *any* construct is bound to the cultural context in which the scale is developed. For example, Heppner (2006) suggested that (a) ethnocentricity, (b) difficulty in accepting others' worldview, (c) accepting cultural differences across cultures as simply differences, and (d) universal assumptions were particularly pertinent in developing a culturally sensitive scale. It is hoped that researchers and students in the field not only increase their awareness of the complex nature of scale construction, but also incorporate multicultural and cross-cultural perspectives into the construction of new inventories across different cultural contexts.

STIMULUS QUESTIONS

A 22-Item Checklist of Scale Construction

The following list of items can be used as a checklist when conducting a scale construction project.

Did you . . .

1. Identify a construct or phenomenon that you want to measure?
2. Search for other instruments that measure similar constructs or phenomena?
3. Consider the advantages and disadvantages of developing a new scale?
4. Seek consultations from your colleagues about this project?
5. Decide on the target population?
6. Define the construct with statements that can be measured?
7. Conduct an extensive literature review?
8. Consider multiple ways of item generation (e.g., focus discussion groups, interviews)?
9. Generate a clear and sufficient number of items informed by the various methods in item 8, as well as guided by theory?
10. Create response formats and directions with clarity?
11. Refine the items through content analysis from domain-specific experts as well as pilot testing?
12. Conduct translation and back-translation procedures along with permission from the original author(s), if necessary?
13. Finalize the questionnaire including items, response formats, directions, and necessary demographic information?
14. Identify a representative sample with a sufficient number of participants?
15. Identify inventories for providing estimates of convergent and discriminant validity?
16. Obtain approval from the institutional review board?
17. Consider a suitable method of data collection?
18. Enter the data into a statistical analysis package (e.g., SPSS, SAS) and clean the data?
19. Calculate descriptive statistics (e.g., means, standard deviations)?
20. Identify the factor structure of the construct and finalize the items through a series of exploratory factor analyses including parallel analysis?
21. Collect additional data and examine the stability of the factor structure through confirmatory factor analysis and administer other inventories to promote additional estimates of validity?
22. Determine reliability estimates (internal consistency, e.g., alpha coefficients) as well as various estimates of validity (e.g., convergent and discriminant), calculating correlation coefficients?

Part 3

MAJOR DESIGNS

11
Chapter

True Experimental Designs: The Power of Between-Groups and Within-Subjects Designs

Many research questions in counseling relate to the very basic question of whether what a counselor is doing is effective: Is counseling really helping people with some aspect of their lives? Whether we work in independent practice, in counseling centers, in school settings, or in academic jobs, we are a profession that helps people in a variety of ways, and we want to know if what we are doing is really having a positive impact. Whether it is a psychoeducational group for teens with eating disorders, a high school classroom intervention aimed at bringing awareness to the discrimination faced by minority group members, or a specific treatment we are using with an individual client, the most basic question we want to answer is: Is the intervention effective? Some of the most rigorous designs we have at our disposal to address such questions are what are called between-groups and within-subjects designs, both of which are often referred to as true experimental designs.

In Chapters 5 and 6 we identify the goal of research as isolating relationships among constructs of interest and operationalizing constructs into the independent and dependent variables while simultaneously eliminating sources of bias, contamination, and error. Perhaps the most essential rules of research are expressed by Kerlinger's MAXMINCON principle, in which researchers try to maximize the systematic variance of the variables under study, minimize error variance, and control extraneous variables. Extraneous variables and error variance can mask or obscure the effects of the independent variable on the dependent variable.

In this chapter we discuss two designs—between-groups and within-subjects—that are often referred to as true experimental designs because of their emphasis on experimental control, minimizing extraneous variables, and internal validity. These emphases are achieved through random assignment and manipulating the independent variable, two core elements that define true experimental designs. Even though students sometimes feel intimidated about true experimental designs because of the heavy, ominous meaning that the words sometimes convey, the designs are actually quite straightforward; the label is more ominous than the actual design. True experimental designs are commonly categorized into between-groups design and within-subjects design.

The between-groups design often adheres to the MAXMINCON principle. Differences between treatments can be maximized by making the treatment (independent variable) stronger or even exaggerated. Thus, researchers will often examine the effects of extreme treatments, such as five counselor disclosures in 50 minutes, or three counselor influence attempts in 15 minutes. Moreover, the between-groups design can be arranged to control extraneous variables and minimize error variance through random assignment of treatment condition and manipulating the independent variable, while controlling for other factors.

The essential feature of between-groups design is the comparison of variables across two or more groups under tightly controlled experimental conditions. In early counseling research, a common comparison group was some type of control group, a group that did not receive one of the active treatments in the study. Over time, differences between or among experimental treatments have been compared. To adequately make comparisons across groups necessitates that the groups do not differ in important ways before the experiment. Thus, initial differences between groups in terms of individual difference variables, demographics, and situational variables must be minimized prior to experimental manipulations to reduce threats to internal validity. Because of the emphasis on comparison and equivalent groups, assignment of participants to groups is a critical consideration in between-groups design. In fact, one of the major identifying features of between-groups design is the random assignment of participants to different treatment conditions. In short, the between-groups design is a powerful investigative tool, and often the most strongly favored design (Kazdin, 2003; Kerlinger, 1986; Shadish et al., 2002).

The hallmark of the within-subjects design is that it attempts to minimize error variance due to individual variation by having each participant serve as his or her own control because all participants are exposed to all of the treatment conditions. This design is another type of true experimental design because of the random assignment of treatment order. The random assignment that occurs in the within-subjects design is the assignment of the order in which the treatments are delivered, as opposed to the different treatment conditions in between-groups designs.

For example, perhaps a researcher has two videos that may be useful for increasing participants' empathy related to issues of poverty and social injustice. In a within-subjects design, all participants would view both videos, but not at the same time. For example, one group of participants would receive intervention Tx_1 (video 1) before Tx_2 (video 2), whereas the other group would receive the opposite sequence, Tx_2 before Tx_1. Conversely, using a between-groups design, one group of participants would receive intervention Tx_1 (video 1) only, whereas the other group of participants would only receive intervention Tx_2 (video 2). In both designs, each participant is assigned to either sequence (within-subjects) or intervention condition (between-groups) randomly, as a matter of chance. Hence, the comparison in a within-subjects design is between different time periods in which separate intervention conditions are in effect, whereas the comparison in a between-groups design is between the groups that received different intervention conditions.

PARTICIPANT ASSIGNMENT

Because a hallmark of true experiments is the random assignments of participants, we will discuss this issue prior to introducing the different types of between-groups and within-subject designs. It is critical that the people in the groups that are compared do not differ in important ways before the experiment or measurement begins. The intended outcome of assigning people to groups is to eliminate systematic differences across groups before the experiment, so that if any changes are detected in one or more of the groups after the experiment, the change can be attributed to the independent variable. Participants therefore need to be assigned to groups in an unbiased fashion and free from extraneous variables.

The most effective way of ensuring comparable groups is to assign participants to groups randomly, or in such a way that each participant has the same probability of being assigned to each group. Such assignment tends to equalize both known and unknown sources of participant variation across groups, so that extraneous variables will not bias the study.

A number of procedures exist for randomly assigning participants to groups. This can be done by generalizing random numbers through Microsoft Excel (using the RANDBETWEEN function) or online programs (e.g., www.random.org, www.psychicscience.org/randomlist.aspx) to determine the order of assigning participants to groups. Note that random assignment would most likely result in unequal numbers of participants in each of the groups. For statistical purposes it is better to have equal numbers across groups. To deal with this issue, Kazdin (2003) suggested assigning participants in blocks based on the number of groups. For example, with a study of three groups, within each block of three participants, the experimenter would simply randomly assign one participant to each of the three groups. This procedure is particularly useful when participants begin the experiment periodically, or at different times.

In counseling research, a researcher will often have a sample identified and available at the beginning of an investigation. For example, a researcher might have 20 people who are available and have expressed an interest in some kind of treatment group, such as assertiveness training or group therapy. In this situation, the investigator knows the total number of participants, their names, and their general characteristics such as age and sex. Underwood (1966) has labeled this type of participant pool as captive. In this situation, random assignment is easily accomplished at one time via a list of random numbers, or even by drawing names from a hat. Quite often in counseling research, however, we do not have the entire sample at the outset, but rather must engage in sequential assignment (Underwood, 1966). For example, imagine that a researcher is investigating the effect of two types of precounseling information on client expectations of therapy. Most counseling centers have only a few clients beginning therapy each day, which would necessitate randomly assigning clients to the two types of precounseling information each day. In this case, clients can be assigned to either treatment as they enter counseling via some sort of randomization process.

BETWEEN-GROUPS DESIGNS

In this section we first discuss the strengths and weaknesses of two specific between-groups designs. Because the central focus of between-groups designs is to compare between different treatment groups and/or with control groups (please note that having a control group is not required), the second section explicitly discusses issues pertaining to control groups. The third section discusses more complex designs that contain two or more independent variables, which are called factorial designs. In the last section we discuss related issues of matching and dependent samples designs.

Two Common Experimental Between-Groups Designs

We now discuss the two most commonly identified experimental between-groups designs. To do so, we use the following symbols to represent various processes in the research design. Ob indicates an "observation" or point where data are collected as a dependent variable; and Tx indicates the exposure of a group to an experimental variable, often a treatment intervention of some kind. The purpose of Ob, in essence, is to measure the effects of Tx. The first subscripts following Ob and Tx indicate the sequence of occurrence: Ob_1 is the first observation, Ob_2 is the second, and so on. And the second subscripts following Ob and Tx indicate the assigned condition: Ob_{1a} is the first observation of the treatment A group, Ob_{2ctrl} is the second observation of the control group.

After describing each of these two designs, we then discuss advantages and disadvantages of each, referring particularly to validity issues (see Table 11.1). It is important to note that these two designs are most easily conceptualized by using one independent variable. For example, the independent variable may represent two treatment conditions, or contain two levels—treatment and no treatment (that is, control group).

TABLE 11.1 Pros and Cons of Different Between-Groups Designs

Design	Pros	Cons
Overall between-groups designs	• Internal validity due to controlling for various threats (e.g., history, maturation, instrumentation, testing effects)	• Limited generalizability to other populations or nonexperimental settings • Withholding study treatment for control or waitlist group
Posttest only	• Cost-efficient due to no pretest • Eliminates pretest sensitization	• Limited information on group equivalence prior to treatment
Pre-post design	• Pre-scores can be controlled for • Pre-scores to select/remove cases • Pre-scores to describe participants • Pre-post scores to examine individual performances	• Sensitization due to pretest

FIGURE 11.1 : Posttest-Only Control Group Design

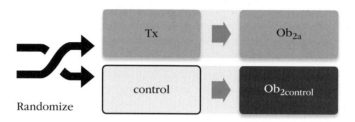

Randomly assign into two groups [A] and [ctrl]

Randomize

Posttest-Only Control Group Design   Notationally, the posttest-only control group design is conceptualized as shown in Figure 11.1. In its most basic form, this design involves the random assignment of participants to two groups; one of the groups receives exposure to a treatment while the other group serves as a control group and thus receives no treatment. Both groups receive a posttest, but neither group receives a pretest. The basic purpose of the design is to test the effect of Tx, the independent variable, on observations of the dependent variable, vis-à-vis Ob_{2a} and Ob_{2ctrl}.

Strengths   Although the posttest-only control group design is the most basic form of between-groups designs, it controls for most of the threats to internal validity. And the strengths of internal validity in which we describe as follows also apply to other between-groups designs. For example, history would have affected each group equally because Ob_{2a} and Ob_{2ctrl} occurred at the same time. Likewise, maturation, instrumentation, testing effects, and regression are controlled in that they are expected to be equally manifested in both the experimental and control groups. For example, if extreme scores were used, the control group would be expected to regress as much as the experimental group.

In many ways the posttest-only control group design is the prototypical experimental design and most closely reflects the characteristics needed to attribute a causal relationship from the independent variable to the dependent variable (Shadish et al., 2002). The difference between Ob_{2a} and Ob_{2ctrl} reflects the degree to which treated participants are different from untreated participants at the end of the treatment period. Of course, the observed difference needs to be statistically significant (have statistical conclusion validity) to justify a claim that the treatment indeed is effective (also see Chapter 7 for more discussion on validity issues).

In spite of the simplicity of the posttest-only design, there are some concerns regarding it. The primary concern is that because the dependent variable is examined only at the end of treatment, statements about actual change cannot be made; put another way, there is no evidence to show that the treatment group improved vis-à-vis their level of functioning prior to treatment. However, in our view the level of functioning of treated individuals (at Ob_{2a}) versus their level of functioning had they not been treated (Ob_{2ctrl}) is the most important comparison, not the change from before treatment to after treatment because change may be due to other factors (e.g., depressed individuals generally becoming less depressed because it is a cyclical disorder). The logic of experimentation does not require that pretreatment levels of functioning be assessed; thus, a pretest is not used.

One of the strengths of the posttest-only control group design, therefore, is that a pretest is unnecessary. Practically speaking, sometimes the repeated testing of participants is bothersome to the participants and expensive to the researcher in terms of time and effort. Furthermore, the absence of pretests removes the need to collect both the pretest and posttest scores, and hence it may be easier to have participants respond anonymously, thereby protecting the confidentiality of responses. Another advantage of the posttest-only control group design is that it eliminates pretest sensitization (which is discussed more fully as a disadvantage to the pretest-posttest control group design).

Weaknesses   The absence of a pretest in this design limits the information available to researchers, such as being able to check if group equivalence prior to the treatment was in fact established through random assignment or to know participants' level of functioning prior to treatment. More detailed arguments for using pretests are presented in the discussion of the pretest-posttest control group design.

Although the posttest-only control group design is generally considered an internally valid experimental design, like the other between-groups designs, there are issues pertaining to external validity, namely the interaction of selection and treatment (Shadish et al., 2002). From an internal validity perspective, selection of participants is not a threat because participants are randomly assigned across groups. However, from an external validity perspective, the generalizability of the results of the study to another population is unknown, like any other experimental design. For example, it is possible that a treatment (e.g., a career-planning workshop) is effective but only for the particular sample (e.g., returning adults who have a broader set of work experiences). Another threat to external validity pertains to reactivity to the experimental situation. That is, participants may react differently, perhaps in biased or socially desirable ways, because they are in an experiment, which again threatens the generalizability of the findings. Because counseling is an applied field, we are especially concerned with external validity, and these and other threats to external validity merit serious consideration (also refer to Chapter 7 and Chapter 8 for more discussion on external validity issues).

Finally, a practical issue pertaining to between-groups design is that of timing. To adequately control for history effects, the investigator must conduct the experimental and control sessions simultaneously. Sometimes this requirement places excessive time and energy constraints on the experimenter. Nonetheless, history effects may not be controlled for if the experimenter conducts the two sessions, say, one month apart. The greater the time differential between group administrations, the greater the likelihood of confounding history effects. For a more detailed discussion and an example of history effects, please refer to Chapter 7.

An Example   A study aimed at understanding the effects of music therapy on self and experienced stigma in psychiatric patients used a posttest-only design. Silverman (2013) was interested in examining whether music therapy could reduce psychiatric patients' level of stigma. Silverman used a between-groups posttest-only design to compare the effectiveness of three conditions in reducing stigma: (a) music therapy, (b) education, and (c) wait-list control group. Participants ($N = 83$) were randomly assigned through clusters to one of the three conditions. Results indicated that participants in the music therapy group reported lower posttest scores on measures of disclosure (self-stigma), discrimination (experienced stigma), and overall stigma (composite score) compared with the waitlist control group. However, the education group's stigma scores did not significantly differ from the music therapy group or the waitlist control group. In sum, music therapy was found to be an effective approach in reducing the stigma psychiatric patients had in the forms of self-disclosure and perceived discrimination from others. The study is an example of utilizing a posttest-only design to examine the effects of certain interventions.

Pretest-Posttest Control Group Design   Notationally, the pretest-posttest control group design is conceptualized as shown in Figure 11.2. This design involves the random assignment of participants to two (or more) groups, with one group receiving treatment while the other group receives no treatment and thus serves as a control group. Both groups receive a pretest and a posttest. The purpose of the design is to test the effect of the independent variable, Tx, which is reflected in the differences on the dependent variable, specifically between Ob_{2a} and Ob_{2ctrl}.

Strengths   This design controls for most of the threats to internal validity discussed by Shadish et al. (2002), and in that way it is similar to the posttest-only control group design. The unique strength of this design pertains to the use of the pretest, which allows the researcher to perform various analyses that may be helpful in making valid inferences about the effects of the independent variable.

One of the most important reasons for giving a pretest is that pretest scores can be used to reduce variability in the dependent variable, thereby creating a more powerful statistical test. In essence, such a strategy attempts to minimize error variance in line with the MAXMINCON principle. Much of the variance in any dependent variable is due to individual differences among the participants. Knowledge of the pretest level of functioning allows the researcher to use statistical methods, such as the analysis of covariance, to remove the variance found in the pretest from the variance in the posttests. Such procedures can reduce drastically the number

FIGURE 11.2 ⋮ Pretest-Posttest Control Group Design

Randomly assign into two groups [A] and [ctrl]

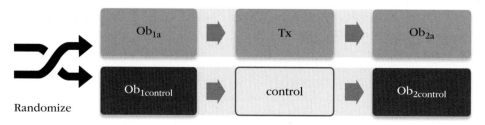

Randomize

of participants needed to achieve a desired level of statistical power (Porter & Raudenbush, 1987). Of course, the pretest in this case need not be the same measure as the posttest; however, it must be correlated with the posttest to allow a covariance analysis.

Another important reason to give a pretest is that it can be used to help eliminate post hoc threats to internal validity. In this regard, one strategic use of pretests is to compare participants who terminate or drop out to those participants who remain. If more participants terminate from the treatment group than from the control group, then differential attrition is a particularly troublesome threat; however, if pretest scores indicate that those participants who terminated did not differ significantly from those who remained, then concern about differential attrition is reduced.

Pretests can also be used to select or deselect participants. For example, in a study on depression, the researchers may wish to select only those participants who are in the moderately depressed range. For example, if participants report very few symptoms of depression, these participants may not exhibit any change on the dependent variable even though the treatment would have been effective with moderately or even severely depressed participants.

Pretest scores can also be used to describe the participants of a study. For example, it would be important to describe the level of anxiety of undergraduate participants in a study of test anxiety to determine whether the participants were representative of clients who were really affected by test anxiety.

Finally, the pretest-posttest scores allow the researcher to examine the individual performance of specific participants. Kazdin (2003) suggested that in this way, researchers might examine participants who benefited the most versus those who benefited the least from the treatment intervention. Identifying participants in such a fashion, combined with any relevant anecdotal information, may suggest hypotheses for future research. In short, the pretest provides additional information to researchers, and perhaps some clues for future research directions.

Two often-stated advantages of pretests are controversial. The first pertains to comparing posttest scores to pretest scores to determine the degree to which the treatment was beneficial. The problem with making inferences from pretest measures to posttest measures is that there are too many rival hypotheses to infer the degree to which treatment was effective by comparing pretest scores to posttest scores. For this reason, "gain scores" (differences from pretest to posttest) are typically not recommended for statistical analyses. Instead, it is better for researchers to restrict themselves to making inferences only about differences at the posttest, because fewer threats are involved. Parenthetically, statisticians typically recommend using the pretest as a covariate in analyzing the posttest scores (see Huck & McLean, 1975). These techniques adjust or reduce error variance across individuals.

There is a second controversial use of pretest scores. Recall that random assignment was a means of distributing individual differences randomly across the two groups to remove any systematic bias due to selection or assignment. But the groups will not be exactly the same in all aspects; random error, if you will, will often result in some differences between groups. Often there is a tendency to check whether random assignment succeeded—that is, to see whether the groups were indeed comparable. To do so, a researcher might examine as a preliminary analysis the pretest scores to ascertain whether there are significant differences between the groups *before* treatment. However appealing this process is, there are some complex issues that make these comparisons far from straightforward (Wampold & Drew, 1990).

First, how big a difference is necessary to decide whether random assignment failed? For small sample sizes, statistically significant differences between two groups' pretest scores are unlikely to be obtained, but in large samples, it is much more likely that relatively small differences between samples will be statistically significant. Second, pretest scores represent only possible differences on the particular characteristics measured; what about differences in age, gender, intelligence, education, and a host of other variables that were not examined? Third, if a very large number of factors are compared before treatment, by chance some differences will be found.

In short, it is important to note that however appealing it is to check the effectiveness of random assignment in eliminating differences between the groups before the independent variable was introduced, there are a number of complexities that make it difficult to conclude with absolute certainty that the two groups are "equal." Suffice it to say that there are some problems and controversy with this procedure.

Parenthetically, if one wants to ensure that a nuisance factor is evenly distributed across the groups, another alternative is to use a matching procedure. For instance, to equate groups based on intelligence, participants in the treatment and control groups could be matched on intelligence. This process, and its advantages and disadvantages, are discussed in the section on dependent samples designs.

Weaknesses It is ironic that the unique strength of the pretest-posttest control group design, namely the pretest, is also the main weakness. It is often assumed that pretesting will not sensitize participants to a particular treatment. In the two-group pretest-posttest control group design, the effect of repeatedly administering a test to the treatment group (Ob_{1a} to Ob_{2a}) is the same for the control group (Ob_{1ctrl} to Ob_{2ctrl}). Therefore, the effect of repeated testing is not a threat to internal validity.

However, the pretest may have a potential sensitizing effect pertaining to external validity, and thus generalizing the results from the study to other samples. It is unclear whether any changes found at posttest might be due to the groups being sensitized by the pretest; that is, it is unclear if the same effect of Tx on Ob_{2a} would be found again without the sensitizing effect of Ob_{1a}. For example, a pretest questionnaire on attitudes about rape might cue participants not only to reflect on this topic, but also to process information differently in the ensuing treatment, say, an awareness-enhancing workshop about date rape. Although the treatment may or may not have an effect by itself, the interactive effects of the pretest may result in substantially greater changes at posttest. A real problem could result if practitioners implemented the workshop but without the pretest, and thus the treatment had a much weaker treatment effect than they thought they would have. When researchers use the pretest-posttest control group design, they need to be cautious in generalizing the results of the study, and they must discuss this sensitization issue explicitly.

An Example Shechtman and Pastor (2005) used a between-groups pretest-posttest design to assess the effectiveness of two types of group treatment offered to 200 elementary school children in a center for children with learning disabilities in Israel. More specifically, the authors were interested in whether students would evidence better academic and psychosocial outcomes in either cognitive-behavioral treatment groups or humanistic therapy groups as compared to individual academic assistance alone. Their results suggested that either form of group therapy rather than individual academic assistance resulted in more academic (reading and math), psychological adjustment, and social adjustment gains. Moreover, they also found that the humanistic therapy group resulted in better outcomes than the cognitive behavioral therapy group. The gains were found on all measures pretest to post-test, and most of the differences were also found at a three-month follow-up. The authors interpreted their findings as suggesting that addressing children's general concerns and emotions in and of themselves without focusing on their academic failure may be constructive (Shechtman & Pastor, 2005).

To examine other examples of the pretest-posttest control group design, see Cheng, Tsui, and Lam (2015), who also employed this design to assess the effectiveness of a gratitude intervention for reducing stress of health care practitioners in Hong Kong. Participants were assigned to groups that (a) wrote work-related gratitude diaries, (b) wrote work-related hassle diaries, and (c) a control group. The results suggested that those in the gratitude intervention showed a significant larger decrease in stress and depressive symptoms over time compared to those in the other two groups. Likewise, Lemberger and Clemens (2012) examined the effects of a small group counseling intervention (versus a control group) with inner-city African American elementary school children; the results indicated that participants who received the intervention resulted in significant higher metacognitive skills and feelings of connectedness to school.

RESEARCH IN ACTION 11.1

Identify a research topic of your interest. Propose how you would examine your research question utilizing the two between-groups designs: (a) posttest-only control group design and (b) pretest-posttest control group design. Discuss the conceptual and practical advantages and disadvantages of using each design. Conclude with the most appropriate design for your study.

Use of Control Groups

To this point, the designs discussed have included a control group. The purpose of this arrangement is to compare treated participants with nontreated participants. In this way, the effect of the treatment vis-à-vis no treatment can be determined. However, there are some cases where the use of control groups is not warranted. For instance, it is unethical to withhold treatment from participants who are in need of treatment and who have a condition for which a treatment is known to work. For example, it would be unethical to have a control group of suicidal clients in a study of a new crisis-intervention technique. Furthermore, the research question may not refer to the absence of a treatment. For a study comparing the relative effectiveness of two different types of treatment approaches, a control group is not needed; inclusion of a control group, however, would answer the additional question of whether either of these two treatments is more effective than no treatment.

Although some research questions do not call for control groups, the logic of much research dictates the use of a control group. *Control group* refers generically to a class of groups that do not receive any interventions that are designed to address the outcome in the study. For example, if an intervention designed for alcohol abuse is to receive personalized feedback about one's level of alcohol use (percentile compared to a norm group), a control group can either receive no additional information or unrelated information (e.g., percentile of height, weight). It should be realized that even though this implies that the researchers do not provide any intervention, participants in such groups could seek alternative interventions or information elsewhere (e.g., internet).

Often it is practically and ethically difficult to have a group that does not receive any treatment. However, a viable control condition can be obtained by using a *waiting-list control group*. Typically, participants are randomly assigned to either the treatment condition or the waiting-list control group; at the end of the treatment phase and the posttests, the treatment is made available to the participants in the waiting-list control group. In either the pretest-posttest control group design or the posttest-only control group design, the treatment given to the waiting-list participants can be analyzed to test the reliability of the results (Kazdin, 2003) or to rule out threats to the validity of quasi-experimental designs (Shadish et al., 2002). One disadvantage of the waiting-list control group is that long-term follow-up of the control participants is lost (because they have by then received treatment). Another disadvantage is that although ultimately the participants in the waiting-list control group receive treatment, the treatment is withheld for some time. (For more details on this topic, see Chapter 20.)

Another type of control group is the *placebo control group*. Participants in a placebo control group are led to believe that they are receiving a viable treatment, even though the services rendered them are nonspecific and supposedly ineffective. For example, in a group counseling outcome study, participants in the placebo condition may be in a discussion group with no active group counseling. The rationale for including a placebo control is that it enables the researcher to separate the specific effects of a treatment from effects due to client expectations, attention, and other nonspecific aspects. Some investigators contend that the major effects of the counseling process are due to nonspecific factors (Wampold, 2001); inclusion of a placebo control group allows determination of whether the effects of a treatment are greater than those obtained under conditions that appear to clients to be viable but do not contain the major aspects of the active treatments.

A final type of control group is the *matched control group*. Participants in a matched control group are paired in some way with participants in the treatment group. The primary purpose of this type of design is to reduce variance due to a matching factor (which is discussed later in this chapter under Dependent Samples Designs).

Factorial Designs

Factorial designs are used when two or more independent variables are employed simultaneously to study their independent and interactive effects on a dependent variable. Factorial designs are extensions of these earlier designs, namely by the addition of independent variables. With factorial designs it is more useful to visualize the design by diagramming the levels of the independent variables into cells. For example, lets say a researcher were interested in testing the effectiveness of two interventions designed to enhance cross-cultural awareness in high school students. The two interventions (Tx_1 and Tx_2) and a no-treatment control are formed. In addition, the researcher is interested in examining whether male and female students might respond differently to the interventions. The study would be considered a 2 (Gender: male and female) $\times$ 3 (Tx_1, Tx_2, and control) posttest-only design containing six cells. To illustrate, please see Figure 11.3, which includes posttest cultural awareness scores in each cell.

In this hypothetical example, one intervention (Tx_1 cultural awareness score = 20) was found to be more effective than the other intervention (Tx_2 cultural awareness score = 10) for boys due to the higher posttest cultural awareness scores. In contrast, it was the other way around for girls; those that received Tx_2 intervention (Tx_2 cultural awareness score = 15) had higher posttest cultural awareness scores than those who received the Tx_1 intervention (Tx_1 cultural awareness score = 8). Alternately, if there were two independent variables that each had three levels or conditions, this would be considered a 3 $\times$ 3 design and have nine cells.

Strengths   The unique strength or advantage of the factorial design is that it tests the effects of two or more independent variables, and of their interaction with each other on the dependent variable. The factorial design provides more information than the single-independent-variable designs because it simultaneously tests two or more independent variables.

In our hypothetical study, the researcher could examine whether two interventions have an effect on the dependent variables, as well as whether a participant's gender has an effect on the dependent variables. The effect of an independent variable on a dependent variable is often referred to as a main effect. Because of the efficiency of such simultaneous tests in factorial designs, it is not uncommon for

FIGURE 11.3 Factorial Design Example

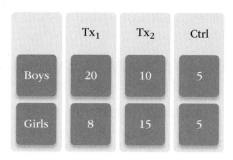

researchers to test two, three, or even four independent variables in one study. Usually these added independent variables are person (personality) variables.

More important, factorial designs allow the investigator to examine the interaction of the independent variables. An interaction means that the effect of one of the independent variables depends on the levels of one or more other independent variables. In our hypothetical example, the researcher might find that either one of the treatments does not have the same effect on all participants, but instead one intervention was more effective for boys whereas the other intervention was more effective for girls. Thus, factorial designs not only result in more information because they examine the effects of more than one independent variable, but also result in more complex information about the combined effects of the independent variables.

Another advantage of factorial designs is that if the second independent variable added to the design is related to the dependent variable as expected, then the unexplained variance in the dependent variable is reduced. Reducing unexplained variance is again related to Kerlinger's MAXMINCON, which in essence increases the power of the statistical test for analyzing factorial design (for example, in the analysis of variance, the denominator of the F ratio is reduced).

In a way, our fictitious example indicates how the factorial design can provide important qualifications about relationships between variables. The factorial design provides some answers about the conditions under which a treatment may operate, such as the gender of participants, the type of intervention, the age of clients, or the problem-solving style of clients. Whereas the single-variable study most often investigates whether a variable (most notably some treatment) has any effect, the factorial design examines more complex questions that approximate the complexity of real life.

Weaknesses   Although at first one might think the more information, the better, it is important to realize the costs involved as more variables are added to designs. With the addition of variables, the results of the study become more complex and sometimes too complex. In a 2×2 design, the researcher would typically examine the main effects of two levels of variable A, the main effects of two levels of variable B, and the interaction of A with B. In a 2 (A) $\times$ 2 (B) $\times$ 2 (C) design, the investigator would typically examine the main effects of variables for two levels of A, B, and C; the two-way interactions of A with B and B with C; and the three-way interaction among A, B, and C. Complex interactions between three, four, or more independent variables typically are difficult to interpret, and the results of the study may be unclear. Researchers should not add independent variables just to have more than one independent variable; instead, independent variables need to be carefully selected on theoretical and empirical grounds after thought is given to the research questions of interest.

Another disadvantage of the factorial design is the flip side of an advantage: If additional independent variables are added to the design and these variables turn out to be unrelated to the dependent variable, then the power of some statistical test may be reduced. There are also complications regarding the conclusions that can be drawn when the independent variable is a status variable (e.g., counselor gender) and is not manipulated. (For more details, see the discussion in Chapter 8.)

An Example   Merrill, Reid, Carey, & Carey (2014) examined the moderating effects of gender and depression level on the effectiveness of brief motivational intervention in reducing alcohol use. They found a three-way interaction effect of the intervention. For women, those with low-depression reduced their drinking more after the brief motivational intervention than the control groups, whereas women with high depression did not show any differential improvement compared to the control groups. On the contrary, high-depression men showed significant reductions in weekly drinks following the brief motivational interventions, whereas low-depression men did not show differential improvement compared to the control groups. The results of the study indicated that the effectiveness of brief motivational interventions for alcohol abuse differs across participants by gender and depression level.

Dependent Samples Designs

Dependent samples designs are a type of between-groups design that are intended to address issues related to some of the problems mentioned previously related to random assignment of participants. Dependent samples designs are based on the assumption that a particular extraneous variable, let's say intelligence or level of psychological functioning, is important to the outcome of the study. Importance in this context can be defined in two ways.

First, the variable may be theoretically important for understanding the phenomenon under investigation. In this case, the variable definitely should be examined for its own sake. For example, if intelligence is thought to be an important variable theoretically, then it should be included as an independent variable in a factorial design. In this way the effects of intelligence, as well as the effects of the interaction of intelligence with the treatments (or with other independent variables), can be determined.

Second, if the variable is not interesting for its own sake, it might best be labeled a nuisance variable. Although a nuisance factor is not examined explicitly (i.e., by inclusion as an independent variable in a factorial design), it remains an important consideration in the design of an experiment because it could affect the results in unknown ways. For example, pretest level of functioning may not be interesting to the researcher in the sense that the effectiveness of treatment for clients at different levels of psychological functioning is not a burning research question. Nevertheless, it is desirable to have the treatment and control groups comparable on psychological functioning so that psychological functioning does not confound the results. Sometimes a useful way to reduce the effects of a confounding variable is to match participants on the basis of the potentially confounding variable pretest scores and then randomly assign one of the matched participants to the treatment group and the remaining participant to the control group, as illustrated in Table 11.2. As a result, the two samples are dependent. In this way, the researcher can be relatively certain that levels of psychological functioning are comparable across the two groups. More important, if the nuisance factor is related to the dependent variable as expected, then the variance in the nuisance variable can be removed from the variance in the outcome variable, resulting in a more powerful statistical test (Wampold & Drew, 1990). The typical statistical test for this type of design is the dependent samples *t* test (sometimes called the paired *t* test or correlated *t* test).

TABLE 11.2 Assignment of Participants to Treatment and Control Groups in a
Dependent Samples Design

Pairs of Participants	Treatment		Control
1	S_{11}	is matched with	S_{12}
2	S_{21}	is matched with	S_{22}
3	S_{31}	is matched with	S_{32}
—	—		—
—	—		—
—	—		—
N	S_{n1}	is matched with	S_{n2}

Note: Paired participants have comparable scores on pretest.

Essentially, the dependent samples *t* test accomplishes the same purpose as the analysis of covariance—it reduces unexplained variance and yields a more powerful test. The analysis of covariance does not require that participants be matched, and the reduction in unexplained variance is accomplished statistically, by the design of the experiment. The dependent samples design reduces uncertainty by matching comparable participants. Two participants who have high pretest scores are also likely to have high posttest scores; differences in posttest scores for these two matched participants are due presumably to the treatment (and other uncontrolled factors).

Dependent samples can be accomplished in other ways as well. Often natural pairs, such as monozygotic twins, are used. Because monozygotic twins have identical genetic material, using such pairs holds all hereditary factors constant. Other natural pairs include litter mates (not often applicable to counseling researchers), marital partners, siblings, and so forth.

The idea of two dependent samples can be expanded to include more than two groups (e.g., two treatment groups and a control group). Typically, the dependency is created by matching or by repeated measures (it is a bit difficult to find enough monozygotic triplets for such a study!). For example, Fitzgerald, Chronister, Forrest, and Brown (2013) were interested in the effectiveness of an employment-focused group counseling intervention—OPTIONS among male inmates. OPTIONS is aimed at enhancing inmates' career exploration, job-search skills, knowledge of career options, goal planning, and identification of resources. The researchers believed that age and release date would affect interventions outcomes. Thus, to ensure equivalency between the treatment intervention and control groups on age and release date, participants were first matched on these two variables before being randomly assigned to the treatment or control group. When more than two participants are matched and assigned to conditions, the design is called a randomized block design. Each group of matched participants is called a block, and the participants within blocks are randomly assigned to conditions. The randomized block design is typically analyzed with a mixed model analysis of variance (see Wampold & Drew, 1990).

In sum, matching is a way to control for a nuisance factor that is believed or known to have an effect on the dependent variable. Dependent sample designs are powerful tools for increasing the power of statistical tests. Properly used, these designs can enable the researcher to accomplish the same purpose with far fewer participants.

One final note: Many times in counseling research, randomly assigning participants to groups is not possible. For example, ethical problems would arise if a researcher tried to randomly assign clients to therapists with different levels of counseling experience, such as beginning practicum, advanced practicum, doctoral-level interns, and senior staff psychologists. If clients were assigned randomly to counselors it is quite likely that a client with complex psychological problems would be assigned to an inexperienced therapist who is ill-equipped to work therapeutically with such a client. In such applied situations, randomization may well introduce more practical problems than it solves experimentally. Sometimes researchers will attempt to show that clients are equivalent (matched) on several dimensions such as age, gender, presenting problem, and personality variables. Matching in such a post hoc fashion can rule out some dimensions in comparing clients, but it is important to realize that many variables, known or unknown, are simply left uncontrolled. Thus, a weakness of such field designs is that unknown variables may confound the relationships among the variables being investigated.

WITHIN-SUBJECTS DESIGNS

The remainder of this chapter examines within-subjects designs. The hallmark of the within-subjects design is that it attempts to minimize error variance due to individual variation by having each participant serve as his or her own control. Similar to the between-groups design, participants are randomly assigned to groups or treatments, and independent variables are manipulated. The unique feature of the within-subjects design is that all participants are exposed to all of the treatment conditions; random assignment involves assigning people to different sequences of treatment.

In this section we first provide an overview of two within-subjects designs: crossovers and counterbalanced crossover designs. We then discuss the strengths and limitations of these within-subjects designs.

Crossover Designs

Suppose a researcher wanted to compare the effects of two treatments (independent variables)—test interpretation of the Strong Interest Inventory (SII) and work genograms—on a dependent variable, vocational clients' career maturity. The researcher could use the within-participants design, as shown in Figure 11.4. Ob_1, Ob_2, and Ob_3 represent different observations—in this case, administration of a career inventory (say, the Strengths Self-Efficacy Scale; Tsai, Chaichanasakul, Zhao, Flores, & Lopez, 2014). Tx_1 represents the test interpretation treatment, and Tx_2 represents the genogram treatment.

FIGURE 11.4 : Crossover Designs

This is called a crossover design; all participants are switched (i.e., crossed over) to another experimental condition, usually halfway through the study. Suppose the researcher conducted this study with 20 vocationally undecided adults as diagrammed. Suppose the researcher found a significantly greater change in career maturity between Ob_2 and Ob_3 than between Ob_1 and Ob_2 ($p < .01$); could he or she conclude that genograms are better at promoting career maturity than test interpretation? This conclusion would be quite tenuous because of the threats to internal validity embedded in this design, such as history (events may have happened to the participants between the administrations), maturation (normal development may have occurred), order effects (i.e., perhaps genogram treatments are more effective if they are presented as a second treatment), or sequence effects (i.e., perhaps the genogram treatment is effective only if it follows and perhaps adds to an SII test interpretation). In point of fact, a major difficulty in the within-subjects design is the possibility of confounding order or sequence effects. Order effects refers to the possibility that the order (i.e., the ordinal position, such as first or third) in which treatments were delivered, rather than the treatment per se, might account for any changes in the development variable. Sequence effects refer to the interaction of the treatments (or experimental conditions) due to their sequential order; that is, treatment Tx_1 may have a different effect when it follows treatment Tx_2 than when it precedes treatment Tx_2.

Counterbalanced Crossover Designs How might the researcher control the sequential order threats to internal validity? One of the primary mechanisms used to control such threats is counterbalancing, which involves "balancing" the order of the conditions. Figure 11.5 is a diagram of a counterbalanced crossover design.

The participants are randomly assigned to two groups: [A] and [B]. Again, Tx_1 and Tx_2 in the diagram represent the two treatments, and the Ob's represent the different observation periods. Ob_{1a} and Ob_{1b} designate a pretesting assessment; Ob_{2a}

FIGURE 11.5 : Counterbalanced Crossover Design

Randomly assigned into two groups [A] and [ctrl]

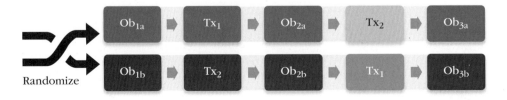

and Ob_{2b} represent an assessment at the crossover point, and Ob_{3a} and Ob_{3b} indicate testing at the end of the experiment. Thus, the groups differ only in the order in which they receive the treatments. In this case, counterbalancing also controls for sequence effects: Tx_1 precedes Tx_2 for group [A], whereas Tx_2 precedes Tx_1 for group [B].

It is important to be aware of two issues with regard to counterbalancing. First, the researcher can now use some simple statistical procedures to determine whether the order of the treatment conditions made any difference vis-à-vis the dependent variables. For example, a simple t test can be conducted on Ob_{2a} versus Ob_{3b} to determine whether treatment Tx_1 resulted in differential effects depending on whether the treatment was administered first or second. A similar t test can be conducted on Ob_{3a} versus Ob_{2b} for treatment Tx_2. These analyses are important not only for the present research, but also so that future researchers can know about order or sequence effects. A second issue is that even if there is an order effect, it can be argued that these effects are "balanced" or equal for both treatments (given the preceding example), and that order effects are therefore controlled.

Piet, Hougaard, Hecksher, and Rosenberg (2010) used a counterbalanced crossover design to examine the effects of group mindfulness-based cognitive therapy and group cognitive-behavioral therapy for young adults with social phobia. Of the 26 participants, 14 were randomly assigned to receive eight sessions of group mindfulness-based cognitive therapy followed by 12 sessions of group cognitive-behavioral therapy. The remaining 12 clients first received group cognitive-behavioral therapy and then mindfulness-based cognitive therapy. Participants' level of social anxiety, anxiety symptoms, and interpersonal problems were assessed (a) prior to treatment, (b) after the first series of treatments, (c) at completion of both treatments, and (d) then followed up 6 and (e) 12 months after treatment. Results revealed that mindfulness-based cognitive therapy achieved moderate-high pre-post effect sizes, and was not significantly different from the cognitive-behavioral therapy. Participants receiving treatments in both sequences continued to improve following the first and second treatment until the 6-month follow-up. Findings from this study suggested mindfulness-based cognitive therapy as an effective treatment along with cognitive-behavioral therapy for young adults with social anxiety.

RESEARCH IN ACTION 11.2

Briefly describe the differences between the two major categories of true experiments: between-groups designs and within-subjects designs. Identify a general research question of your interest and discuss whether it would be more appropriate to use a between-groups design or a within-subjects design. Moreover, are there any differences in what these two designs would address/answer in regard to your research question?

Strengths and Limitations

We will discuss five issues to depict the strengths and weaknesses of within-subjects design that can affect the appropriateness of a within-subjects design for a particular research question. These five issues are (a) experimental control, (b) statistical power, (c) time, (d) order effects, and (e) restriction of certain independent variables.

Experimental Control   The traditional within-subjects design is potentially a powerful design because of its reliance on random assignment of treatments and manipulation of independent variables. The experimenter can often obtain a great deal of experimental control with this design, and the threats to internal validity tend to be low with a counterbalance crossover design. Moreover, the within-subjects design tends to minimize error variance due to normal individual variability by using each participant as his or her own control. The reduction of individual error variance is a noteworthy advantage of the within-subjects design, which merits consideration when the researcher is especially concerned about such error.

Statistical Power   Because each participant receives all levels of the independent variable, there are typically some advantages from a statistical perspective. In general, a researcher can use half the number of participants in a counterbalanced crossover design and still retain the same statistical power as in the between-subjects design (see Kerlinger, 1986, for a more complete statistical discussion of this matter).

Time   Although a within-subjects design can use fewer participants to obtain a level of statistical power similar to a between-groups design, the trade-off is that the within-subjects design takes longer to conduct. Consider a research team who want to compare interpersonal and cognitive-behavioral approaches to the treatment of depression. Suppose they recruit 24 depressed clients. If the team chooses to use a between-groups design, they can randomly assign 12 participants to 12 sessions of interpersonal treatment, and the remaining participants to 12 sessions of cognitive-behavioral treatment. In this design, at the end of 12 weeks the research team has implemented the interventions and has collected the data. If the research team instead uses a within-subjects design with only 12 clients—randomly assigning 6 clients to receive 12 sessions of interpersonal therapy followed by 12 sessions of cognitive therapy, and assigning the remaining 6 participants to receive treatment in the reverse order—the team would need 12 more weeks than for the between-groups design to implement the interventions and collect the data. Thus, sometimes an important consideration is the trade-off between the number of participants and the time required. We would encourage researchers, however, not to be too quick to overlook within-subjects designs only because of the time factor.

Order Effects   As we indicated earlier, a special problem of the within-subjects design is the effects of order. Order effects are threats to internal validity. Even when order effects are controlled, as in the counterbalance crossover design, it is still important to check whether the order of the treatments affected the dependent variable. Sometimes it is assumed that because counterbalancing equalizes any effects due to order, the researcher can ignore such order effects. This strategy, however, does not provide any information about the basic question: Were there any order effects in a particular study? Such information can be useful to future researchers as they design their investigations on a similar topic. Likewise, practitioners may be interested in knowing if the order of treatments makes any difference as they plan to maximize their interventions.

Restriction of Variables   A final consideration in the use of within-subjects designs involves the restriction of certain independent variables. It may not be possible to use certain independent variables in a within-subjects design. It is impossible, for example, to induce both the expectation that a given treatment will be effective and then the subsequent expectation that it will not be effective. Or two treatments may be too incompatible with each other. Kazdin (2003) offered as an example the conflicting approaches of systematic desensitization and flooding. It is important for the researcher considering a within-subjects design to closely examine the effects that multiple treatments may have on one another. Given that each participant receives all treatments, the experimenter must assess whether the combination of multiple treatments can be administered realistically and fairly. Finally, variables that involve some personality, demographic, and physical characteristics may not vary within the same participant in a given experiment. For example, a participant cannot be both a male and female participant, or be a participant from both a rural and an urban community; thus, these variables cannot be examined using within-subjects designs.

It is also important not to dismiss the utility of within-subjects designs if the limitations of these designs initially seem restrictive for a particular study. For example, based on the inherent differences within behavioral and psychodynamic therapy, it could easily be concluded that these two therapy orientations could not be compared within a particular set of participants. However, Stiles, Shapiro, and Firth-Cozens (1988) did use, quite successfully, a within-subjects design comparing eight sessions each of exploratory (interpersonal-psychodynamic) and prescriptive (cognitive-behavior) therapy. Although worries about treatment contamination may be present or even pervasive among counseling researchers, this study challenges us to fairly evaluate the crossover effect and to be creative in our thinking about within-subjects designs.

SUMMARY AND CONCLUSIONS

There are two types of true experiments: between-groups and within-subjects designs. These are true experiments because in both cases there is random assignment of treatments and manipulation of an independent variable. In between-groups designs, the random assignment allocates participants to treatment conditions to create experimental and control groups. In contrast, in within-subjects designs, all participants are exposed to all treatment conditions. Thus, the overall goal of the within-subjects design is to compare the effects of different treatments on each participant. Both designs lend themselves to Kerlinger's MAXMINCON principle. Because randomization of participants is a defining characteristic of both between-groups and within-subjects designs, we discussed participant assignment and group equivalence.

In terms of between-groups designs, we discussed the posttest-only control group design and the pretest-posttest control group design. These experimental designs are clearly powerful designs, because they can rule out many rival hypotheses. Each design controls for all the common threats to internal validity. A key feature of these designs is the random assignment of participants; randomly assigning participants to groups is a major source of control with regard to internal validity. Because control groups are commonly used in these designs, we discussed issues pertaining to different types of control groups, such as no-treatment groups, waiting-list control groups, placebo groups, and matched control groups.

We also described two traditional within-subjects designs, the crossover and counterbalanced crossover designs. Both of these designs make comparisons between two or more groups of participants, but in a different way from the between-groups design. In the crossover design, all participants are switched to another experimental condition, usually halfway through the study. Counterbalancing was introduced within this design as a way of reducing bias due to order effects. We suggested that at least five issues specific to the traditional within-subjects design can affect its utility for examining a particular research question, namely (a) experimental control (particularly with regard to individual participant variation), (b) statistical power, (c) time, (d) order effects, and (e) restriction of certain independent variables. In particular, we encouraged researchers to be creative in the application of traditional within-subjects designs. In short, within-subjects designs offer a powerful means of identifying causal relationships. The advantages of these designs are their ability to reduce both error variance (by using each participant as his or her own control) and the fewer number of participants needed in a particular study.

Clearly, the between-groups and within-subjects designs are useful designs for examining research questions of interest to those in the counseling profession. These designs are flexible and can be made applicable to a wide variety of research problems. However, it is important for the researcher in counseling to evaluate the strengths and limitations of these designs relative to the type of research question being asked and type of participants needed. Given the applied nature of many of our research questions in counseling, the researcher needs to consider carefully a broad range of issues pertaining to external validity to evaluate the utility of the true experimental designs in providing the most-needed information. In addition, many times the random assignment of participants to groups cannot be done because of ethical constraints, such as in a study of the effects of different levels of sexual harassment. We think students should be encouraged to consider the strengths and weaknesses of various designs in relation to the nature of various research questions. In other words, the utility of the design needs to be evaluated in the context of the research question, the existing knowledge bases, and internal and external validity issues.

STIMULUS QUESTIONS

Between-Groups and Within-Subjects Designs

This exercise is designed to promote reflection on between-groups and within-subjects experimental designs. After reading this chapter, write your responses to the following questions. Then discuss your responses with a peer in your class.

1. Talk to faculty and peers about their perceptions of the usefulness of the between-groups and within-subjects designs. What

advantages and disadvantages first come to mind for them? Is there a pattern in the responses that is reflected when others speak of the disadvantages of between-groups and within-subjects designs?

2. Compare the primary strengths and weaknesses of between-groups and within-subjects designs. Could you argue that one of these designs is better than the other?

3. What are the key elements that define true experimental designs?

4. Randomization is a component of true experimental designs. Described how randomization is applied differently for between-groups and within-subjects designs.

5. Make a list of the pros and cons of using a control group. Of all the issues you list, can you pick one that you believe is the most important methodological issue when applying it to a research question of your interest?

6. In the early days of counseling, more between-groups and within-subjects designs were used. Now it is difficult to find good examples of them in our major journals. Why do you think this trend exists, and what do you think it means for the field of counseling?

Quasi-Experimental and Longitudinal Designs: Examining Relationships in Applied Setting

12

Chapter

As discussed in Chapter 11, true experimental designs are very useful in terms of controlling and eliminating many threats to internal validity. One of the hallmarks of a true experimental design is random assignment of subjects to treatments, which allows the researcher to control many of the threats to internal validity. A true experimental design *always* includes random assignment of participants to conditions, manipulation of the independent variable(s), and comparisons between or among groups. For a number of reasons, however, the researcher may not always be able to use a true experimental design.

Much of counseling research happens in natural field settings, which limits the amount of control researchers can have on the design. For example, much sexual violence occurs at the high school level, and yet very few prevention interventions have been reported in this setting. Hillenbrand-Gunn, Heppner, Mauch, and Park (2004) were interested in assessing the impact of a sexual assault prevention intervention in a high school setting. But it is difficult to randomly assign students from different classes into treatment and control groups due to the constraints of the schools, which are often present in field research of this nature. Subsequently, they chose a quasi-experimental design to conduct a three-session intervention with intact high school classes that served as the experimental and control conditions. Briefly, the theoretical framework for the study was social norms theory (Berkowitz, 2003), which maintains that the social influence of one's peers is based more on what one thinks his or her peers do and believe (i.e., perceived norms) than on actual behaviors and real beliefs (i.e., actual norms).

The experimental group participated in a three-session intervention on acquaintance rape that incorporated local social norms. The control group attended their classes as usual. As hypothesized, the participants' ratings of their peers were significantly different (worse) from the peers' ratings of themselves at pretest regarding attitudes toward sexual violence. Furthermore, the experimental group participants' ratings of their peers were significantly more accurate following the intervention, indicating they viewed their peers as less supportive of sexual assault. At posttest, the experimental group demonstrated a significant decrease in rape-supportive attitudes, as compared to the control group, and this decrease was maintained at follow-up four weeks later. Although additional research is needed, this quasi-experimental study was able to provide very useful information about sexual assault prevention in the high schools, and the generalizability of the findings to other midwestern urban high school students would be considered high.

In short, it is often difficult to achieve the conditions of the true experimental design in field settings, especially the requirement of random assignment into groups. Because of this difficulty in much applied research, the quasi-experimental design offers more flexibility. Quasi-experimental designs, like true experimental designs, involve the manipulation of one or more independent variables, but not the random assignment of participants to conditions. With this flexibility, however, quasi-experimental designs also bring some limitations. Nonetheless, with creativity in the use of the designs and appropriate use of controls and statistical procedures, quasi-experimental designs can be very useful for applied researchers.

In this chapter we first illustrate an early quasi-experimental design that provides a historical context for this type of design. Then we discuss some considerations for determining when quasi-experimental designs might be appropriate. We then focus on the two major classes of quasi-experimental designs, the nonequivalent groups designs and the time-series designs. In nonequivalent groups designs, comparisons are made between participants in nonrandomly formed groups. Specifically, we discuss three types of uninterruptible designs, four types of interpretable nonequivalent groups designs, and cohort designs, which are a special case within the broad category of nonequivalent groups designs. Then we discuss the time-series designs, which have as their defining feature multiple observations over time.

HISTORICAL PERSPECTIVE AND OVERVIEW

Quasi-experimental designs were used extensively in the 1950s and 1960s to answer one of the most important and confusing questions that psychotherapy and counseling researchers have grappled with: Does counseling work? To answer this question we need to compare clients who have received counseling to clients who have not. The most rigorous (in terms of internal validity) test of the effects of counseling would involve the random assignment of clients to treatment (receiving counseling) and no-treatment control conditions. The random assignment of clients to a no-treatment condition would in effect constitute the withholding of service, which can, of course, raise ethical considerations for the researcher. To avoid this type of ethical dilemma, early counseling researchers attempted to find other groups of participants with whom to compare the effects of counseling.

Many of the early outcome studies in counseling used quasi-experimental designs. For example, Klingelhofer (1954) was interested in examining the effects of academic advisement on the scholastic performance (grade point average) of students placed on academic probation. He compared three groups of students in this study, all of whom were on academic probation. One group received four one-hour counseling sessions, a second group received one one-hour counseling session, and the third group received no counseling interviews. The students who received one or four hours of counseling were randomly assigned to groups. The students in the control group were drawn from students who had been on academic probation during the preceding year. In essence, Klingelhofer's study had elements of both experimental and quasi-experimental designs. The comparison between the students receiving one or four hours of counseling was a true experiment because there was random assignment of participants to treatments, manipulation of the treatment variable, and a between-groups comparison. The comparison between the students who did and did not receive counseling was a quasi-experimental design because the students were not randomly assigned to conditions. This particular type of quasi-experimental design is called a cohort design. The students who had been on probation the year before the study formed one cohort and the students on probation during the experimental year formed a second cohort. Klingelhofer assumed that the students in the two cohorts were similar because the same rules were used to place students on academic probation both years.

The results of this study did not reveal any differences in subsequent grade point average for students counseled for either one or four sessions. There was, however, a significant difference in grade point average between students who had and had not received counseling. Nonetheless, this result must be interpreted with some caution because pretreatment differences between the students in the two cohorts may have existed due either to some unknown selection factor or to different historical events during their year on probation. Despite these possible limitations, Klingelhofer's study of the effectiveness of one widely used counseling intervention represents a typical quasi-experimental study of counseling in the 1950s and 1960s. The designs are still used today, in part because of the restrictions inherent with randomization.

CONSIDERATIONS FOR SELECTING QUASI-EXPERIMENTAL DESIGNS

Under what circumstances would a quasi-experimental as opposed to a true experimental design be appropriate? We maintain throughout this chapter that selection is a key variable in examining the adequacy and usefulness of a quasi-experimental design. We discuss four reasons that might lead a researcher to choose a quasi-experimental design: (a) cost, (b) selection issues, (c) ethical considerations, and (d) unavailability of appropriate control groups.

Cost

One of the most functional reasons for not conducting a true experimental design is often that of cost. Conducting a true experiment can be quite expensive in terms of time and resources. In true experimental designs, researchers often must pay participants to be part of often two or three treatment groups, along with a control group. Conversely, it is a lot less expensive to evaluate naturally occurring differences in treatment settings, classrooms, or other places where people naturally come together. For example, even in the study of sexual assault prevention provided earlier, if the researchers would have decided to utilize a true experimental design, they would have likely had to obtain a group of 30–40 participants who, after random assignment, would have been willing on their own time to attend a pretest, three intervention sessions, a posttest, and a follow-up one month later. This is a substantial time commitment, and most likely the participants would need to be compensated for their time and involvement. In short, although an experimental design provides a more rigorous design, sometimes the cost is prohibitive. In essence, the researchers may be willing to compromise experimental control in order to conduct the study in the field at a lower cost.

RESEARCH IN ACTION 12.1

Tommy is conducting a study to evaluate the effectiveness of two forms of counseling: cognitive-behavioral treatment (CBT) and interpersonal treatment (IPT). He has four therapists (two for CBT and two for IPT) in his study. Given issues about cost and delays in treatment time, he decides to just assign them to one of the four therapists based on an ecological model (i.e., a rotating system where Therapist 1 is assigned the first client, Therapist 2 the second client, and so on; in addition, therapists are assigned a new client when they have an opening in their schedule). Tommy maintains that this process is "pretty much random" as there is not a specific reason why the clients are assigned to Therapist 1 versus Therapist 4, for example.

Questions

Would this qualify as an experimental design? Why or why not?

What else could Tommy do to enhance the internal validity of the study?

Selection of Participants

The hallmark of experimental designs is randomly assigning participants to various treatment conditions. Ideally, the investigator recruits a pool of participants, and randomly assigns them into the treatment and control groups, which meet at prearranged times. However, a number of issues that arise in field research can make the selection of participants a difficult and complex process. For example, some of the participants might be available to come to a treatment group in the early afternoon, but not in the evening. Such issues of time availability are an important logistical concern in applied research, and often make it more feasible to conduct quasi-experimental investigations within existing group settings such as high school classes, as in the previous example.

In some field settings it would be difficult or even inappropriate to randomly assign participants to an experimental or a control group. For example, an investigator may want to examine the effect of a group session summary (a therapist's written summary of a group session that is mailed to each group member prior to the next session) on session quality and group-member involvement (Yalom, 2005). Group leaders may not agree to randomly assigning clients to groups, because many leaders believe that selecting members to form a compatible mixture is one of the most important decisions a leader makes in order to create an optimal treatment environment in the therapy group. In fact, randomly assigning members may not be what group leaders would consider an effective treatment procedure. The investigator may consequently be restricted to preformed groups. In this case, he or she could use summaries in two preformed groups and not use summaries in two other preformed groups. The researcher could then compare ratings of session quality and member involvement in the groups that did and did not receive the summaries. This design would be a quasi-experimental design because there is manipulation of an independent variable (summary vs. no summary) and a between-conditions comparison, but no random assignment of participants to conditions.

However, this example also illustrates some of the drawbacks of quasi-experimental designs. In this case, the members were selected and the groups composed for a reason (perceived compatibility). If the investigator indeed finds a difference between the groups, one possible explanation is the effect of the independent variable (group summaries), but another equally plausible explanation is selection issues pertaining to the group members. Perhaps the group leaders who led the groups that received the summaries were more effective at composing counseling groups. In that case, the differences between the two conditions may reflect differences in clients, not in the experimental manipulation. In short, sometimes it is actually more appropriate to use existing groups because this enhances the generalizability of the results; conversely, whenever an investigator uses previously established groups (classes in schools, wards in a hospital, or therapy groups), he or she must always be aware that these groups were probably established for some reason, and that differences found between them may have more to do with the selection process than with the experimental manipulation.

Selection may also have a more indirect effect by interacting with other variables (Kazdin, 2003). A selection-by-threat interaction effect occurs when the threats to internal validity operate differently across the treatment conditions. For example, in our group summary example, the group leaders may have used very different selection criteria in establishing their groups. The group leaders in the treatment (receiving summaries) condition may have selected only passive-dependent clients for the group (believing that these clients get the most from a group treatment), whereas the leaders in the control condition may have selected clients with various interpersonal styles (believing that a heterogeneous group leads to a better outcome). If passive-dependent clients mature at a faster rate than do clients with other interpersonal styles, then a selection-maturation interaction might account for any observed differences across conditions. Likewise, history, testing, regression, mortality, or other factors may interact with selection to produce differences across conditions (see Chapter 7). In essence, the investigator must often balance the necessity and feasibility of using existing groups in contrast to the inherent biases built into those preexisting groups.

Ethical Considerations

Some studies focus on participants who are in need of immediate services (like counseling or medical assistance). For example, a researcher might be studying a phenomenon that happens infrequently, such as breast cancer. It may take some time to identify a sufficient number of patients that seek help from a particular agency and to randomly assign them to a group. Consequently, it may raise ethical issues to withhold treatment while waiting for more patients to be randomly assigned into groups. The quasi-experimental designs allow for the use of intact groups who may have already come together in a particular setting. Although randomization may not then be possible, other controls can be designed into the study using the methods we describe in this chapter.

RESEARCH APPLICATION 12.1

Consider the following dilemma: Given that we know that therapy has been empirically supported, is it ethical to continue to use control (no-treatment) groups?

Questions

Under what conditions would it be, or not be, ethical to continue to demonstrate that a new form of counseling is better than not receiving treatment?

Consider taking multiple positions on this dilemma. What support would there be to justify that it is ethical to do so? What would be the counterargument?

To deepen your reflection on question 2, we suggest that you now also consult Chapter 3 on ethics, and identify all of the ethical issues that are relevant to this question.

Unavailability of Appropriate Control Groups

In other circumstances, a researcher may want to investigate the effects of an intervention or treatment when no appropriate control or comparison group is available. In this situation, the researcher can infer whether the intervention or treatment had an effect by comparing observations made before and after the onset of the intervention, typically in a field setting. Such a design, referred to as a time-series design, requires multiple observations over time and the introduction of a treatment at a specified point in time. In other words, in a time-series design the researcher can and does manipulate one or more independent variables, but there is no random assignment to groups or between-group comparisons.

In short, a number of conditions may suggest that a quasi-experimental design may be the most appropriate design. It should be kept in mind, however, that because the researcher has less control in a quasi-experimental design than in an experimental design, the interpretation of the results of these studies has less certainty. In terms of the MAXMINCON principle, researchers using a quasi-experimental design can both maximize differences in the independent variable(s) and minimize error variance due to measurement issues, just as with true experimental designs. However, because there is no random assignment of participants to treatments, they cannot control all of the various threats to internal validity. We suggest throughout this chapter that the usefulness of quasi-experimental designs for advancing knowledge is directly related to how thoroughly the investigator examines and controls for the selection criteria used in forming the initial groupings.

Nonequivalent Groups Designs

In this section we examine a major class of quasi-experimental designs: nonequivalent groups designs. In nonequivalent groups designs, comparisons are made between or among participants in non-randomly formed groups. These groups are referred to as nonequivalent because participants have generally been assigned to a group prior to the research being conducted. Because of this prior group formation, they may differ on several characteristics before the intervention (Kazdin, 2003). For example, a researcher may want to examine the effects of a videotape that provides precounseling information on subsequent counseling dropout rates. He or she may be able to find a counseling agency that uses such a tape and compare the agency's dropout rate with the dropout rate for an agency that does not use this type of tape. Obviously because the clients at the two agencies may be different on a number of variables that may relate to dropout rate (e.g., ethnicity or social class status), the clients in the two agencies represent nonequivalent groups. The usefulness of a nonequivalent groups design is related in part to how much the researcher knows about possible pretreatment differences among participants in the nonequivalent groups.

These types of quasi-experimental designs have also proved beneficial in studying the impact of various training models on counselors in training. For example, Crews and her colleagues (2005) used a nonrandom, pretest-posttest design to study the role of counselor personality traits on counseling performance. Counselors in training were given pretesting to determine their level of self-monitoring (on the Skilled Counseling Scale; SCS) and then self-selected into one of two training conditions, an interpersonal process recall (IPR) condition and a skilled counseling training model (SCTM) condition. The purpose of the study was to determine the impact of two different kinds of training on counselors with differing levels of self-monitoring. The results revealed that there were no statistically significant differences in pretest or posttest scores on the SCS. In addition, both the IPR and SCTM groups improved their scores on the SCS; however, the SCTM group improved significantly more than those counselors in the IPR group.

To examine this design further, we diagram the nonequivalent groups quasi-experimental designs. The symbol Non R represents the nonrandom assignment of participants to groups. As in the previous chapters, X indicates the independent variable or treatment, and O indicates observations of the dependent variable.

Uninterpretable Nonequivalent Groups Designs

We begin our discussion of nonequivalent groups designs with three designs that are virtually uninterpretable because of multiple threats to internal validity. We describe these designs so that the reader can be aware of their shortcomings and have a basis for their comparison with the more-interpretable nonequivalent groups designs. These three uninterpretable designs are (a) the one-group posttest-only design, (b) the posttest-only nonequivalent design comparing multiple active treatments, and (c) the one-group pretest-posttest design.

The one-group posttest-only design can be diagrammed as follows:

$$X_1 \, O_1$$

In this design, observations are made of the dependent variable only after participants have undergone some type of treatment. This design is impossible to interpret because there is no way to infer that any type of change has taken place. In addition, the lack of a control group makes it impossible to investigate the presence of maturational or historical processes.

A posttest-only nonequivalent design can be diagrammed as follows:

$$\text{Non R } X \, O_1$$
$$\text{Non R } \quad O_2$$

In this design, the two groups are formed in a nonrandom manner. The participants in the first group receive the experimental treatment (X) while the participants in the second group do not receive any treatment. Change is measured by comparing the posttests (O_1 and O_2).

It is important to note that the posttest-only nonequivalent design need not compare a treatment with a control group. Two or more active treatments can be compared using this type of design. The following is a diagram of a posttest-only nonequivalent design comparing three active treatments:

$$\text{Non R } X_1 \, O_1$$
$$\text{Non R } X_2 \, O_2$$
$$\text{Non R } X_3 \, O_3$$

Once again, the groups are formed on a nonrandom basis. Treatments (X_1, X_2, and X_3) are administered to the participants in the three groups, and then posttests (O_1, O_2, and O_3) are used to assess the outcomes.

In essence, the posttest-only nonequivalent designs are especially weak because of the difficulty in attributing results to the intervention. The lack of random assignment of participants to groups allows the possibility that the groups may have differed along any of a number of important dimensions prior to treatment. Typically, students are assigned to classes, clients to groups, and residents to living groups based on some rationale, which suggests that the natural groupings we encounter will differ prior to treatment on a few, or in some cases many, dimensions. Thus, one of the problems with the posttest-only nonequivalent designs is the lack of information about any of the possible differences in the groups that exist before treatment.

Consider the following example. Suppose a research team wants to examine the usefulness of an in-class program in alleviating depression in children. They might select two classes of sixth graders in a school and then provide one class with the intervention and not do so in the other class. After one month they assess the students' level of depression. Suppose further that after treatment, the students who received the intervention show less depression. This result may indicate an effect of the treatment, or it may reflect differences between the two classes in their levels of depression before the intervention. Perhaps the principal decided to assign students to classes on the basis of their social skills levels. Research has documented the relationship between social skills and depression (cf. Lewinsohn, Mischel, Chapel, & Barton, 1980). Because there was no pretest, the possible differences in the initial levels of depression were unknown. It is quite possible that the control group actually consisted of students with lower levels of social skills, and subsequently a significantly higher level of depression in the beginning could not be assessed.

The third type of uninterpretable design that we consider is the one-group pretest-posttest design. This design is diagrammed as follows:

$$O_1 \; X \; O_2$$

In this design, pretest observations (O_1) are recorded, a treatment is administered, and posttest observations are made. This design is better than the one-group posttest-only design because by comparing pretest-posttest observations, we can determine if a change occurred. However, the possible cause of this change is still quite ambiguous. For example, the treatment might be responsible for any observed change, but history (the occurrence of other events between pretest and posttest) might also account for the change. Alternatively, if the intervention or treatment was initiated because of a particular problem, then the posttest scores might improve because of statistical regression toward the mean. Another possible explanation for changes in the posttest score is maturation, in which case the change may have nothing to do with the treatment and instead reflects simple growth and development. Without a comparison group, it is impossible to rule out these and other threats to internal validity.

Interpretable Nonequivalent Groups Designs

We now discuss the interpretable equivalent designs, which include (a) the pretest-posttest design, (b) the nonequivalent groups design with a proxy pretest measure, (c) the pretest-posttest nonequivalent groups design with additional pretest, and (d) the reversed-treatment pretest-posttest nonequivalent groups design.

A design that is more useful than the four nonequivalent-groups designs previously is the interpretable pretest-posttest nonequivalent groups design, which is diagrammed as:

$$\text{Non R } O_1 \; X \; O_2$$
$$\text{Non R } O_3 \quad\;\; O_4$$

In this design, participants are nonrandomly assigned to groups and then pretested on the dependent variable. One group then receives the experimental treatment while the other group serves as the comparison (control) group. It is important to note that this design need not involve a treatment-control group comparison; it may involve the comparison of two or more active treatments. The pretest-posttest nonequivalent groups design is a stronger and more interpretable design than the posttest-only nonequivalent groups design because it allows for an examination of some of the inevitable pretreatment differences. For example, the investigator using such a design can assess the similarity of the participants on the dependent variable(s) of interest, and on other variables that may be related to the dependent variable. It is important for the researcher to remember, however, that pretest equivalence on the dependent variable(s) (and on other assessed variables) does not mean equivalence on all dimensions that might be important to the intended change on the dependent variable. A demonstration of pretest equivalence, however, does increase one's confidence in attributing any observed posttest differences between groups to the experimental manipulation rather than to some selection difference. It is also important to note that usually O_1 and O_3 are not exactly equal. In such instances when $O_1 \neq O_3$, the researcher must decide what is "close enough." One way to decide whether the two groups were equivalent at pretesting is to decide beforehand on a difference that is "too large," such as when O_1-O_3 exceeds one standard deviation of O in a normative population. The researcher can then use a statistical test to see whether $O_1 \neq O_3$ is greater than this number. If it is not, then the researcher can conclude that the two groups were equivalent (but just on this one particular measure) at pretesting.

In the pretest-posttest nonequivalent groups design, it is unlikely that observed differences between groups can be attributed to factors such as history, maturation, or testing. However, there can be a selection-by-threat interaction that can pose a threat to internal validity. In other words, an event might affect participants in only one group, or it might affect them differently from participants in the other group(s). For example, because of some selection bias, the participants in one group may mature faster or be more likely to encounter some historical event than those in the other group. Like its experimental equivalent, the pretest-posttest nonequivalent groups design may have problems with external validity because participants in the different groups might react to the intervention(s) based on a sensitizing effect of the pretest. Also, participants in one group may react differently to the pretest than participants in the other group(s). However, the possible bias of pretest sensitization is minor compared to the problem of interpreting the results when there has not been a check on pretreatment equivalence.

Sometimes researchers may not want or be able to pretest the participants in the groups in a nonequivalent groups design. This may happen when they are worried about the possible effects of pretest sensitization, or when they are working with archival data and it is no longer possible to administer a pretest. In this case, the researcher may choose to use a nonequivalent groups design with a proxy pretest measure (a proxy pretest that involves administering a similar but nonidentical dependent variable but that will not sensitize the participants to the treatment intervention). This design is diagrammed as follows:

$$\text{Non R } O_{A1} \text{ X } O_{B2}$$
$$\text{Non R } O_{A1} \qquad O_{B2}$$

The A and B in this design represent two forms of a test or tests designed to measure similar constructs. In this design, groups are formed nonrandomly and a proxy pretest (O_{A1}) is administered to both groups. Later, one group gets the experimental treatment (X), and then both groups are retested with a different posttest (O_{B2}). The viability of this design depends on the ability of the researcher to find a pretest measure (O_{A1}) that relates conceptually and empirically to the posttest (O_{B2}).

For example, researchers may want to examine a new method of counselor training. They find two training programs willing to participate and institute the new method in one program. At the end of the first year, the researcher administers a paper-and-pencil counseling skills test to all students in the two programs and finds that the students in the treatment program scored higher on this test. However, the researcher is worried about possible pretreatment differences in counseling skill level. Suppose the researcher finds that Graduate Record Exam (GRE) scores (which conveniently all students took before starting graduate school) are correlated ($r = .80$) with scores on the paper-and-pencil counseling skills test. (In actuality, the GRE does not predict counseling skills, but suppose it to be the case for this illustration.) In this case, the researcher can use the pretreatment GRE score (O_{A1}) to examine possible pretreatment differences between students in the two programs.

The pretest-posttest nonequivalent groups design can be strengthened by the use of an additional pretest. This design is diagrammed as follows:

$$\text{Non R } O_1 \ O_2 \ X \ O_3$$
$$\text{Non R } O_1 \ O_2 \quad O_3$$

This design is similar to the pretest-posttest nonequivalent groups design except for the addition of a second pretesting to enhance the interpretability of the design. A major threat to the internal validity of a pretest-posttest nonequivalent groups design involves a selection-by-maturation interaction. In other words, the participants in the two groups may be maturing at different rates because of some selection characteristic. The addition of a second pretest allows the researcher to examine this possibility; the difference between O_1 and O_2 for the treatment and control groups can be examined to see if the groups are maturing at different rates and enhances the interpretability of a nonequivalent groups design. A review of the counseling literature, however, suggests that two pretests are rarely, if ever, used. We strongly recommend that researchers contemplating the use of a nonequivalent groups design consider the addition of a second pretest.

We next discuss the reversed-treatment pretest-posttest nonequivalent groups design, which is also rarely used in counseling research. We include a discussion of this design here because it is one of the stronger nonequivalent groups designs. We hope that an understanding of the strengths of this design will encourage its use in counseling research. The design is diagrammed as follows:

$$\text{Non R } O_1 \ X^+ \ O_2$$
$$\text{Non R } O_1 \ X^- \ O_2$$

In this design, X^+ represents a treatment that is expected to influence the posttest (O_2) in one direction, and X^- represents a treatment that is expected to influence the posttest in the opposite direction.

For example, a researcher may want to test the hypothesis that structure is related to productive group development. Certain schools of therapy contend that ambiguity enhances therapy because lack of structure increases anxiety, and anxiety is necessary for productive work to occur. Other schools contend that anxiety interferes with group work and that structure should be used to lessen the amount of anxiety that group members experience. To test this hypothesis, the researcher could obtain pretest and later posttest measures of the quality of group interactions from two groups of clients. One group of clients could be given explicit information about group procedures; it might be hypothesized that this group would experience less anxiety, and thus manifest lower levels of quality interactions. The other group could be given more ambiguous information; it might be hypothesized that this group would experience more anxiety, and this would manifest in higher levels of quality interactions. Posttest scores could be examined to see if the levels of quality of group interactions moved in the predicted directions. It is hard to imagine that two groups of participants would spontaneously mature in different directions. Thus, this design with such hypotheses would greatly reduce a selection ´ maturation threat to internal validity.

The main problem with a reversed-treatment design is an ethical one. For example, it is usually unethical to administer a treatment that would cause participants to become more depressed. Thus, this reversal design may not be appropriate for a number of dependent variables. The researcher wanting to use the reversed-treatment design must, therefore, display a good deal of thought and creativity.

Shadish et al. (2002) discuss several other nonequivalent groups designs (e.g., repeated treatments). Because these designs are so rarely used in counseling research, we believe that a discussion of them is not warranted here. The interested reader is referred to Shadish et al. (2002) for a discussion of the less common designs, as well as an excellent summary of the statistical analysis of nonequivalent groups designs.

RESEARCH IN ACTION 12.2

Try to determine what type of design is being proposed in the following example: Alejandro wants to test the effects of a new approach on training counselors. This approach combines a focus on cognitive complexity with a rigorous examination of decision-making processes of experts. He uses two sections of a basic interviewing skills class as his sample. He does not randomly assign students to the sections, as this would be too difficult and not very practical. One class is held in the morning and the other class is held later in the evening. The morning class typically had younger students, most of whom did not have full-time jobs as compared to the evening class. Alejandro tested the students prior to the semester on decision-making ability and cognitive complexity. He then conducts his training in one class, the evening class, but not the other. He then tests the students again at the end of the semester. Finally, he then tests the students after the end of the year.

Questions

What type of design is this?

What are the advantages of this design?

What are the potential threats to the validity of this study?

What could Neal do to make this study more rigorous?

An Example of a Nonequivalent Groups Design Owen and colleagues (2014) used a nonequivalent groups design with a proxy pretest to examine the effects of two independent variables, client-counselor ethnicity matching and discussion of client perceptions of racial/ethnic microaggressions (i.e., yes, client and counselor discussed the microaggression experience; no, they did not discuss the microaggression experience; and no experience of microaggressions) on the working alliance. Racial/ethnic microaggressions are those subtle, at times ambiguous, negative comments, invalidations, or put-downs regarding one's race or ethnicity (Sue et al., 2007). In addition, the interaction between these two independent variables was tested. Clients were not randomly assigned to counselors nor was the discussion of the microaggression experience. The client-counselor ethnicity match and discussion of the microaggression experience were used to form nonequivalent groups. Owen et al. hypothesized that client-counselor pairs mismatched on ethnic status would share fewer cultural expectations about counseling and may be less likely to form a high-quality working alliance. Moreover, they posited that discussions of microaggressions would be related to having higher quality alliances as compared to those client-counselor dyads who did not discuss the microaggresssion. However, they also believed that those client-counselor dyads who did not experience a microaggression would have even stronger alliances. Lastly, they believed that the ethnic mismatched client-counselor dyads who did not discuss the microaggression would be associated with the lowest alliance ratings.

The data for this study were obtained from 120 racial/ethnic minority clients after counseling was completed at a university counseling center. Two pretest proxy variables were used in the design: the number of sessions and clients' psychological well-being. These proxy variables were assumed to relate to the dependent variable. Specifically, the proxy pretest variables were used as covariates in an analysis. In this manner the author hoped to control several treatment differences that could have affected the analysis of counselor-client match and/or perceptions of racial/ethnic microaggressions. The results of the analysis showed that ethnically mismatch dyads did not significantly differ than matched dyads on the working alliance. However, discussion of microaggressions was significantly related to the client-rated working alliance. Those clients who did not discuss the microaggression experience had lower alliances as compared to those who discussed the microaggression experience or did not experience a microaggression in counseling.

The Owen et al. (2014) study is a good example of the use of a nonequivalent groups design. It was certainly less expensive (in time and money) for Owen et al. to access client perceptions at the end of treatment rather than attempt to follow clients throughout the entire process of counseling. Additionally, it could be unethical to randomize clients to have a discussion of such a negative experience in counseling. Another strength of the study was the use of proxy pretest variables to look for possible selection differences. The major weakness of the study involves the possibility of selection effects. We do not know, for instance, why clients were assigned to particular therapists, or why counselors and clients in some dyads had a discussion of the microaggression experience. In other words, the conditions examined in the study (client-counselor ethnicity match and discussion of microaggression) were formed on some unknown basis that could have affected the results of the study.

Cohort Designs

Cohort designs are a special case of nonequivalent groups designs that utilize adjacent cohort groups that share similar environments. For example, the sixth-grade class at a particular school one year is likely to be similar to the sixth-grade class the following year. In essence, cohort designs allow researchers to make causal inferences because comparability can often be assumed between adjacent cohorts that do or do not receive a treatment (Shadish et al., 2002). However, the compatibility in a cohort design will never be as high as in an experiment with random assignment. Nonetheless, cohort designs have a relative advantage over other types of nonequivalent groups designs because cohorts are more likely to be similar to each other than in typical nonequivalent groups designs.

It is important for the researcher to have as much knowledge as possible about conditions that could affect the cohorts. Cohort designs are strengthened when the researcher can argue conceptually and empirically that the two cohorts did in fact share similar environments, except of course for the treatment. For example, two successive sixth-grade classes at a particular school will likely be similar across two years. However, this would not be the case if, for example, school district lines were redrawn between the two years, or if a new private school opened in the community and attracted many of the wealthier children away from the public school.

Three types of cohort designs have been used in counseling research. The first design, a posttest-only cohort design, is diagrammed as follows:

$$O_1$$
$$- - - - - -$$
$$X\ O_2$$

In this design, the broken line indicates that the two groups are successive cohorts and not nonequivalent groups. The O_1 represents a posttest administered to one cohort, whereas the O_2 represents the same posttest administered to the second cohort. It is important to note that the testing occurs at different times because the cohorts follow each other through the system; however, the posttesting occurs at a similar point in each cohort's progression through the institution.

Slate and Jones (1989) used a posttest-only cohort design to test the effect of a new training method for teaching students to score the Wechsler Intelligence Scale for Children-Revised (WISC-R). One cohort of students took the intelligence testing course during the fall semester, the other cohort during the spring semester. The fall cohort received a standard scoring training procedure, whereas the spring cohort received the new training method. The results indicated that students in the spring as opposed to the fall made fewer scoring errors on the WISC-R. Slate and Jones concluded that the new training method was effective. These authors assumed that the students in the fall and spring cohorts were similar prior to training, and buttressed this assumption by examining several possible sources of pretreatment differences.

For example, they found that the gender composition was similar across the two cohorts and that the students in the two cohorts had similar GRE scores and grade point averages.

A second type of cohort design, a posttest-only cohort design with partitioned treatments, is diagrammed as follows:

$$O_1$$
$$- - - - -$$
$$X_1 \, O_{2a}$$
$$X_2 \, O_{2b}$$

O_1 is the posttest given to the first cohort, X_1 represents the first level of treatment, X_2 represents the second level of treatment, and O_{2b} is a posttest measure given to all members of the second cohort regardless of level of treatment administered. In essence, the posttest-only cohort designs are strengthened by partitioning the treatment, which involves giving different amounts of the treatment to different groups of participants within a cohort.

In the Slate and Jones (1989) study, suppose that some of the students in the second cohort practiced the new scoring procedure for two hours and that the other students in the cohort practiced it for four hours. Slate and Jones could have analyzed the results separately for these two groups of students. If the students who had practiced for four hours (O_3) committed significantly fewer scoring errors than the students who practiced for two hours (O_2), and if the treatment cohort committed fewer errors than the no-treatment cohort, then the assertion of treatment efficacy would be strengthened. Moreover, the results would provide additional information about the amount of training needed. In short, the posttest-only cohort designs can be useful, particularly relative to the posttest-only nonequivalent groups design. Because clients experience various aspects of counseling treatments in different amounts, we urge researchers to use partitioning as a way of strengthening the internal validity of the posttest-only cohort design in counseling research.

The third cohort design that we discuss is the pretreatment-posttreatment cohort design, diagrammed as follows:

$$O_1 \, O_2$$
$$- - - - - - - -$$
$$O_3 \, X \, O_4$$

The first cohort is pretested (O_1) and posttested (O_2), and then the second cohort is pretested (O_3), treated (X), and posttested (O_4). The main advantage of the pretest-posttest cohort design over the posttest-only cohort design is the increased assurance the pretest provides for asserting that the two cohorts were similar prior to the treatment. In addition, the use of the pretest as a covariate in an analysis of covariance provides a stronger statistical test in general. The main disadvantage of this design is that the pretest can constitute a threat to external validity because of pretest sensitization; that is, taking the pretest itself in some way sensitized the participants and caused their scores at posttest to differ. In most cases the advantages of a pretest to examine pretreatment compatibility across groups outweigh the threat to construct validity.

An Example of a Cohort Design   Miller and colleagues (2006) used a quasi-experimental cohort design in comparing feedback-informed therapy for treating 6,424 clients in an employee assistance program. Clients were treated as usual in the first cohort. The clients completed the Outcome Rating Scale prior to each session, which is a measure of psychological distress/well-being (Miller et al., 2003). Clients also completed an alliance measure to assess the quality of the therapeutic relationship. This first cohort was considered the control cohort, and changes from the first session to the last session were considered to be the pretest-posttest. Next, the agency trained the counselors to use feedback with their clients. In doing so, the counselors were encouraged to discuss the progress, or lack thereof, in clients' psychological well-being/distress. Additionally, they were encouraged to discuss the therapeutic relationship.

The baseline assessment lasted for 6 months, the implementation phase also lasted for 6 months, and the continued evaluation phase lasted for 12 months. In essence, there were two distinct cohorts: baseline cohort and implementation/continued evaluation cohort. The baseline cohort demonstrated positive gains, but rather modest in absolute terms (Cohen's $d = .37$). The implementation and continued evaluation cohorts each demonstrated gains that were nearly two times greater than the baseline cohort ($d = .62, .79$). In essence, the findings indicated that participants in all cohorts significantly increased their well-being; however, the implementation and continued evaluation cohorts appeared to have experienced an increased effectiveness. Nonetheless, it is unclear what might have caused this pre-post effect (e.g., maturation, test sensitization), or it could be the training might have had an effect on the outcomes. Consequently, additional research is needed to examine the causal elements of these findings. In short, this study provides a good example of how a cohort model could be implemented in a large-scale manner. In addition, this study provides a great example of how program evaluation of an agency can be implemented (see Chapter 22).

In sum, the Miller et al. (2006) study was well conceived and executed. The authors used natural breaks between no training and training to form cohorts. They have enhanced the design by comprehensively addressing the issue of pretreatment equivalence by comparing the cohorts across multiple measures. In retrospect, they could have used a control group. For instance, they could have recruited clients to not receive the client feedback during the implementation phase. These participants could have been tested during the same time frame as the treatment participants. This type of control could have served to test the temporal confound in examining the results.

TIME-SERIES DESIGNS

The defining characteristic of a time-series design is multiple observations over time. These observations can involve the same participant (e.g., the client's ratings of the working alliance after each counseling session) or similar participants (e.g., monthly totals of clients requesting services at a counseling center). In an interrupted time-series design, a treatment is administered at some point in the series of observations. The point at which the treatment takes place is called an interruption of the series. The logic of the interrupted time-series design involves comparing the observations before and after the treatment or interruption. If the treatment has an effect, there should be a difference in the observations before and after the interruption. Although the logic of comparing pre- and postinterruption observations for evidence of difference is simple and straightforward, the statistical analysis can be complex; see Shadish et al. (2002) for more details.

In this section we concentrate on the logical analysis of interrupted time-series designs. (Chapter 15 discusses time series as applied in single-participant designs.) In the next section we describe two time-series designs with the hope of stimulating counseling researchers to consider these designs in planning their research.

Simple Interrupted Time Series

The most basic time-series design is the simple interrupted time series, diagrammed as follows:

$$O_1\ O_2\ O_3\ O_4\ O_5\ O_6\ X\ O_7\ O_8\ O_9\ O_{10}\ O_{11}\ O_{12}$$

Multiple observations occur both before (O_1–O_6) and after (O_7–O_{12}) the treatment (X) is initiated. The diagram shows an equal number of observations before and after the treatment, but this is not a requirement for the design.

The interrupted time-series design has two advantages over the quasi-experimental designs previously described. First, the time-series design allows the researcher to detect maturational changes that may occur prior to treatment initiation. The researcher does this by looking for changes in the pretreatment observations. If found, these maturational changes can be controlled for in a statistical analysis, allowing a more powerful test of the effect of the treatment. The second advantage of the time-series design is that it also allows for the analysis of seasonal trends. Often, data examined by counseling re-searchers vary systematically over time. For example, more clients seek counseling around holiday periods. It is obviously important to account for this type of systematic variation if a researcher is interested in testing an intervention that affects clients' use of counseling services. The statistical analysis of time-series designs can also control for these types of systematic variations.

Unfortunately, the statistical analysis of interrupted time-series designs can be quite complicated and require considerable expertise (Shadish et al., 2002; Shadish et al., 2013). One of the main problems in analyzing time-series data is dealing with the problem of autocorrelation. Autocorrelation occurs when each score in a series of scores is more similar to the preceding score than it is to the mean score for the series. When scores are autocorrelated, error variance is deflated and a *t* test comparing scores from before and after the interruption is artificially inflated. Therefore, researchers have developed sophisticated statistics to deal with the problems of autocorrelation.

In one example of a simple interrupted time-series design, let's say a counseling center director is concerned about the long waiting list of clients that tends to accrue with the typical academic year. She decides to change the center's primary counseling approach to a time-limited model, and also decides to empirically assess the effects of adopting this time-limited model of counseling on the number of clients on the center's waiting list. The center could initiate the time-limited model in September of one year. She could examine the number of clients on the waiting list each month for the preceding three years and the number of clients on the waiting list during the current year. The analysis of this design would require a comparison of the number of clients on the waiting list prior and subsequent to the initiation of the time-limited model.

Interrupted Time Series with Nonequivalent Dependent Variables

One of the main threats to the internal validity of a simple interrupted time-series design is history. In other words, something other than treatment could affect the researcher's observations. One way to reduce such a threat is to add a second dependent variable. The second time-series design does just that, and is called an interrupted time-series design with nonequivalent dependent variables. This design is diagrammed as follows:

$$O_{A1}\ O_{A2}\ O_{A3}\ O_{A4}\ X\ O_{A5}\ O_{A6}\ O_{A7}\ O_{A8}$$
$$O_{B1}\ O_{B2}\ O_{B3}\ O_{B4}\ X\ O_{B5}\ O_{B6}\ O_{B7}\ O_{B8}$$

In this design, O_A represents one dependent variable and O_B represents a second. Otherwise, the design is identical to the simple interrupted time-series design. If the O_A series shows an interruption at the time of treatment and the O_B series does not, then the internal validity of the treatment effect is enhanced. In other words, it is unlikely (although possible) that history would have an effect on one conceptually related dependent variable but not the other. The important issue in using this design is to select a second dependent variable B that theoretically would not be affected by the treatment.

In the simple interrupted time-series design previously described, the researcher could add a second set of observations—for example, the number of clients requesting services each month. If the number of clients on the waiting list (O_A) shows an interruption at the time that the time-limited model was introduced, but the number of clients requesting services (O_B) does not show a similar interruption, then the director can conclude that the initiation of the time-limited model caused a reduction in the waiting list. It is unlikely that history could cause this effect because history would likely also affect the number of clients requesting services.

A classic interrupted time-series design with nonequivalent dependent variables was conducted by Kivlighan (1990), which examined the effects of live supervision in counselor training. Beginning counselor trainees saw a recruited client for four 50-minute counseling interviews. Advanced counseling doctoral students provided live supervision for the counselor trainees. This supervision involved viewing the counseling interview from behind a one-way mirror, entering the session at some point, commenting on the counseling process, and providing direction for the counselor. The observations in this study consisted of ratings of each of the counselor statements. Trained judges rated each counselor statement on both a cognitive-affective dimension and an immediacy dimension (statements about the client-counselor relationship versus statements outside of the counseling experience). Based on the

FIGURE 12.1 : Counselor Complementarity Before and After Live Supervisions

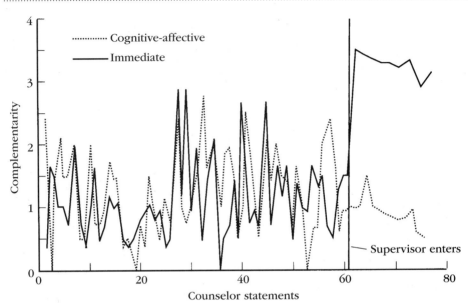

interpersonal training model used, Kivlighan predicted that after the interruption (the supervisor entering the room), the counselor's statements would be less cognitive and more immediate.

Figure 12.1 shows ratings of statements taken from one counselor-client- supervisor triad during the interview. The supervisor intervened between the 60th and 61st counselor statements. A visual inspection of these graphs suggests that the counselor's statements became more immediate and less cognitive after the supervisor's intervention. Based on a statistical analysis of this time series, Kivlighan (1990) concluded that the live supervision interventions influenced the novice counselor to use more affective and immediate statements with clients.

This study illustrates the usefulness of interrupted time-series analysis in studying counseling processes. By using two dependent variables, Kivlighan (1990) strengthened his confidence in the assertion that the observed changes were not due to a history confound. The study could have been further strengthened by replicating this analysis with other counselor-client-supervisor triads, which could enhance the generalizability of the results.

RESEARCH APPLICATION 12.2

Trisha wants to test whether a two-week mindfulness intervention can influence clients' mood, in particular feelings of anxiety. The intervention focuses on relaxation, being aware of one's surroundings and bodily reactions, and controlling one's breathing. She is attempting to do this study with college students and feels like multiple preintervention assessments would be good given the changes in anxiety that can result from testing at midterm and final weeks. She decides to utilize an interrupted time-series design as she thinks that would fit her research question. But Trisha is having trouble getting all of these pieces together, and asks you for assistance.

Questions

First, depict this study using the Os and Xs.

What additional dependent variable would you suggest?

What other confounds could you envision that might affect the results?

How else could she design this study to test her desired question?

Designs Examining Analysis of Concomitance in Time Series

At times, counseling researchers are interested not just in examining the effect of a treatment in a time series, but whether changes in one variable in the time series cause subsequent changes in another variable in the series. In essence, the researcher observes two dependent variables over time. For instance, do changes in the counselor's level of self-disclosure affect the client's level of self-disclosure? This type of analysis, referred to as an analysis of concomitance in time series, is diagrammed as follows:

$$O_{A1} \ O_{A2} \ O_{A3} \ O_{A4} \ X \ O_{A5} \ O_{A6} \ O_{A7} \ O_{A8}$$
$$O_{B1} \ O_{B2} \ O_{B3} \ O_{B4} \ X \ O_{B5} \ O_{B6} \ O_{B7} \ O_{B8}$$

In essence, the researcher observes two dependent variables over time. In this example, the researcher would check to see whether the counselor's level of self-disclosure adds predictability to the client's level of self-disclosure over and above the predictability obtained from patterns in the client's level of self-disclosure. An introduction to the statistical analysis of concomitance in time series can be found in Cook and Campbell (1979).

An Example of a Time-Series Design in Counseling Research

With the advancements in technology, many agencies are able to collect session by session data on their clients' functioning. In doing so, they have a natural time-series design, which can be used to evaluate several interesting questions. For example, Baldwin et al. (2009) used time-series analysis to examine how the rate of change in psychological distress would vary based on the sessions clients attended. Baldwin et al. assessed psychological distress via the Outcome Questionnaire-45 (Lambert et al., 1996) and similar to the Miller et al. study noted previously, clients completed this measure prior to each session. The 4,676 clients were treated a large university counseling center. The primary series of observations consisted of weekly ratings, by clients, of their psychological distress. The primary predictor variable was the total number of sessions attended. The time-series analysis revealed that the rate of change in psychological distress varied by the total number of sessions attended. That is, clients who attended more sessions experienced a slower rate of change as compared to clients who attended fewer sessions. These results indicated that the rate of change is quite variable across clients, and that faster changes occur for those who stay in treatment for fewer sessions. Moreover, some clients need more sessions to make significant improvements.

SUMMARY AND CONCLUSIONS

We believe that quasi-experimental and time-series designs have a place in contemporary counseling research. They are especially useful in examining relationships in applied settings. It is critically important that counseling psychologists and counselors conduct their research with real clients, workers, and students. Although tightly controlled true experimental designs are highly valuable at some stages of research, many of our most important research questions as applied psychologists dictate our data collection in field settings. Experimental designs are often impossible in these settings for a variety of logistical, methodological, and ethical reasons. Especially for findings from studies that do not use real clinical populations or settings, it is important to have replications in a more applied, real-life setting. Studies using quasi-experimental or time-series designs in real settings could be the final point in a series of investigations.

Because there are inherent problems with the interpretation of the results of quasi-experimental and time-series designs, however, researchers must exercise caution. We strongly recommend against the use of posttest-only nonequivalent groups designs in counseling research. As previously discussed, the absence of any way to assess pretreatment equivalence renders the results from a posttest-only nonequivalent groups design virtually uninterpretable. In addition, when using a pretest-posttest nonequivalent design, we recommend that the researcher attend carefully to how the naturally occurring groups were formed; in applied settings,

there is usually some basis on which groupings are made. The more the researcher understands the basis on which the naturally occurring groupings were formed, the better he or she can examine or control for preexisting differences. This can be accomplished by using the selection variable as a covariate in the analysis.

When using the pretest-posttest nonequivalent groups or cohort designs, we recommend that researchers consider using multiple pretest measures or multiple pretesting times to examine pretreatment equivalence. Using multiple measures or measurement periods strengthens the assertion of equivalence of conditions prior to intervention. Also, when using a cohort design the researcher must be vigilant in looking for any differences (other than the experimental manipulation) in what is occurring for participants during the different time periods.

Finally, we believe that counseling researchers have underused time-series designs. These designs can be especially useful in the evaluation of new and innovative programs. Because time-series designs are often used with a single sample from a population, questions concerning their external validity exist. Therefore, researchers should consider replication when they plan their research.

Carefully designed quasi-experiments have the potential for offering critical knowledge of psychological phenomena in naturally occurring settings. Although there are threats to validity inherent in these designs, many of these threats can be controlled by design and statistical techniques.

STIMULUS QUESTIONS

Quasi-Experimental Designs

This exercise is designed to promote reflection on quasi-experimental designs. After reading this chapter, think about your responses to the following questions:

1. Talk to faculty and peers about their perceptions of the usefulness of the quasi-experimental design. What advantages and disadvantages first come to mind for them? Is there a pattern in the type of disadvantages others speak of when they discuss quasi-experimental designs?
2. Why are some quasi-experimental designs uninterpretable? What design elements could make them interpretable?
3. One of the concerns with quasi-experimental designs pertains to using intact groups. What can be done to increase the validity of using intact groups?
4. Identify two research questions you could examine with a quasi-experimental design. What type of quasi-experimental design would you use to examine these questions? Diagram the design using the notation from the chapter.
5. What safeguards would you use to reduce threats to the internal validity of your study?
6. Early in the history of counseling, quasi-experimental designs were used frequently. Now it is more difficult to find good examples of them in the major counseling journals. What factors do you believe have brought about this change?

Quantitative Descriptive Designs: Describing, Explaining, and Predicting Phenomenon

13

Chapter

The goal of science is to describe, explain, and predict; thus, descriptive designs play an important role in describing the existence and establishing the characteristics of a particular phenomenon. As we maintained in Chapter 1, the value of a design is not inherent to the design; rather, the value of a design depends on the state of knowledge in a particular area and the specific questions being addressed. Descriptive designs play a unique and very important function in the process of scientific exploration, especially in the early phases of investigating a phenomenon. With descriptive designs, in contrast to experimental designs, a researcher can quickly and relatively easily describe possible relationships among variables. Descriptive studies can rule out the existence of causal relationships—if no correlation exists between variables, there can be no causal relationship. In addition, descriptive studies are often used to test theoretical conjectures; therefore, having research questions based on theory is critical. Moreover, descriptive studies can suggest possible causal connections among variables that can be examined in a subsequent experimental design.

For example, in the counseling profession, we are often interested in the utilization of counseling services on college campuses, including the types of students that seek treatment (see Nordberg, Hayes, McAleavey, Castonguay, & Locke, 2013). Such information is very useful for developing counseling treatments and prevention programs. Thus, a very important role of our research is to *describe the occurrence* of phenomena of interest. Similarly, we often want to *describe the characteristics* of particular phenomena, like different dimensions of heterosexual knowledge and attitudes regarding lesbian, gay, and bisexual individuals (see Worthington, Dillon, & Becker-Schutte, 2005). Likewise, we often find it useful to *describe the relationship* between two or more variables, such as the relationship among ethnic identity and well-being among African American students (see Whittaker & Neville, 2010). In short, such descriptive information promotes greater understanding of various phenomena, and this knowledge can then be used to increase the effectiveness of a host of counseling interventions. Thus, descriptive designs are very important and useful research strategies of the counseling profession, and consequently are commonly found across counseling journals.

Historically, texts on research design have devoted little attention to descriptive designs. This lack of attention stems partially from what we call the "pure science myth," which holds that the experimental design paradigm was the "correct" or "best" mode of scientific investigation. Moreover, science tends to emphasize the testing and verification of theories (Hoyt & Mallinckrodt, 2012), as well as comparisons among competing theories. However, nearly 30 years ago, Greenberg (1986a) argued that counseling psychology should place greater emphasis on discovery paradigms. He maintained that the empiricist tradition, with its emphasis on the controlled between-groups experiment, was overvalued by counseling researchers. Consequently, too often researchers attempted to manipulate and control variables before enough was known about the phenomenon of interest. Inadequately described phenomena were often subjected to rigid verification, with disappointing results. Before one can test the adequacy of a theory in explaining a phenomenon, one needs a reliable and detailed description of the phenomenon. Clearly, descriptive designs have an important role in the scientific process, which is reflected today in their frequent utilization. Hoyt and Mallinckrodt also noted counseling psychology researchers' growing interest in studying the effects of personal characteristics (e.g., ethnic identity, self-efficacy, attachment styles) and relational attributes (e.g., perceptions of parents, therapeutic alliance), which cannot be experimentally manipulated.

The utility of a descriptive study is directly dependent on the quality of the instruments or assessments used to describe the phenomenon. Moreover, it is impossible to observe all instances of a phenomenon, so instead the researcher carefully studies the phenomenon in a sample drawn from the population of interest. Thus, the reliability and validity of the observations and the generalizability (or external validity) of the sample are two critical issues in descriptive research. At first glance, the MAXMINCON principle that we have emphasized in this text seems antithetical to descriptive research. For example, by exercising experimental control, it might seem that the experimenter would interfere with or change the natural phenomenon he or she was attempting to describe. Indeed, many variables are left uncontrolled in descriptive research, and thus cause-and-effect statements are inappropriate. On the other hand, the investigator can exercise considerable care in making observations so as to minimize measurement errors, which can reduce considerable error variance. Thus, the quality of the observations is the heart of descriptive design. Likewise, the descriptive researcher can exercise experimental control to reduce bias and extraneous variables by using random sampling. Accordingly, in this chapter we emphasize measurement, observation, and sampling as we review the different types of descriptive designs.

The purpose of this chapter is to discuss three major types of quantitative descriptive research: (a) survey or epidemiological research, (b) variable-centered research, and (c) person-centered research. Briefly, epidemiological or survey designs are research strategies designed to characterize the occurrence of behaviors and attitudes in a population. Variable-centered research examines the relationship among variables, whereas person-centered research identifies groups of individuals who share common attributes (Laursen & Hoff, 2006; Muthén & Muthén, 2000).

SURVEY OR EPIDEMIOLOGICAL RESEARCH DESIGNS

Survey research is one of the oldest and most widely used research methods in the social sciences. The use of surveys has been traced to ancient Egypt, and surveys were conducted to assess social conditions in England in the 18th century (Glock, 1967). Today surveys are commonplace, particularly public opinion polls and political surveys.

The basic aim of survey research is to document the nature or frequency of a particular variable (e.g., the incidence and extent of alcohol use) within a certain population (e.g., U.S. college students). Surveys typically use self-reports to identify facts, opinions, attitudes, and behaviors, as well as the relationships among these aspects; data are often collected through questionnaires, mailed surveys, telephone interviews, personal interviews, or online websites. The functions of survey research are to describe, explain, or explore phenomena (Sapsford, 2006). Descriptive research provides basic information about a variable or phenomenon (e.g., the frequency of rape on college campuses). Explanatory research attempts to identify variables (such as beliefs about women, or beliefs about the acceptability of physical aggression) that might explain the occurrence of a phenomenon (such as rape on college campuses). Survey research can also be used to test hypotheses and conjectures (such as factors associated with rape on college campuses).

Survey research has been used to examine the needs of specific student groups. A few examples of survey studies that examined student needs are the mental health needs and use of counseling services of international students (Hyun, Quinn, Madon, & Lustig, 2007) and career counseling needs of mothers in the criminal justice system (Laux et al., 2011). These studies surveyed the needs of participants at one specific time point. Although the findings provide a snapshot of helpful information describing their needs, it does not account for changes that may occur over time.

In addition, survey research is an excellent strategy to address student needs and perception changes over time. For example, a 15-year longitudinal study of career development followed a group of students starting when they were in second grade until five years after completing high school (Helwig, 2008). Different perceptions were compared across time. One of the findings was that the participants perceived the career direction and preparation they received during high school as being less helpful when they looked back five years later compared to when they were still in high school. Using a longitudinal approach provides information about change. To illustrate the cross-sectional and longitudinal comparison through an analogy, cross-sectional survey studies are like taking a photo that provides an image of a particular time point, and longitudinal studies are like filming a video that documents how changes occur over time.

Survey research is not limited to documenting the existence of problems and needs within a population. In fact, a wide range of other types of behavior or variables can be described using this type of approach and group comparisons can be made as well. For example, Lam, Tracz, and Lucy (2013) examined the level of self-efficacy of counselor trainees across different demographic variables. They did not find any significant difference across gender or age-group categories, but did across ethnic groups. Results indicated that Asian and White students reported lower levels of counseling self-efficacy than those of other ethnic groups.

An important contribution of survey research involves studying the patterns, causes, and effects of issues within a certain population, which is referred to as epidemiological research. This type of research method is often used to identify risk factors of certain public health issue within a specific population. A classic example of using epidemiological research is John Snow (known as the father of modern epidemiology) who utilized this approach to stop the spread of clorea (i.e., a small intestine disease that is transmitted through water and food intake). Through survey data, Snow noticed a significantly higher death rate from clorea in a certain area. He then used this information to trace the transmission source to a certain water pump. After using chlorine to clean the water and removing the pump handle, the outbreak was ceased. Thus, findings from epidemiological research can be used to develop preventive interventions accordingly. Following is an example of an epidemiological study, which we will use to illustrate several main issues related to designing survey studies.

An Example of Survey Research

Cook, Alegria, Lin, and Guo's (2009) study used epidemiological research data to examine factors related to the mental health of Latinos. Their goals were to examine variables associated with the length of time in the United States that may predict the probability of psychiatric disorders among Latino immigrants compared with U.S.-born Latinos. Research has been shown that Latino immigrants have better mental health then Latinos born in the United States, and the mental health status of Latinos declines along with their length of time in the United States (Alegría et al., 2008). Moreover, foreign nativity plays a role in the lower level of psychiatric disorders among this population. Thus, this study utilized survey data from the National Latino and Asian American Study (NLAAS) to examine the factors that may be associated with this differential rate of mental health issues among U.S.-born and immigrant Latinos.

The NLAAS consists of data from 2,554 Latinos that were collected from 2002 to 2003 through a nationally representative survey that reflected the U.S. census in terms of gender, age, education, marital status, and geographical distribution. The NLAAS sample included more Latino immigrants and lower income respondents than the census data, which is most likely a result of the census undercounting immigrants and not including undocumented individuals. The data were collected through interviewers administering the NLAAS battery. Cook et al. (2009) found that the explanation for better mental health among Latino immigrants is not simply explained by their immigrant status, but more so by the underlying factors of experiencing lower levels of perceived discrimination and family conflict compared with U.S.-born Latinos. Cook et al. further reasoned that the higher level of perceived discrimination experienced by those who have lived in the United States longer might be associated with them having more valid perceptions of differential treatment and unfairness, as well as more frequent intercultural interactions. In addition, longer time in the United States may diminish the close-knit relationships with family members, which may have previously served as protective factors in their home cultures. Moreover, increased intergenerational conflict with family members may be a result of developing values and norms that more aligned with the U.S. culture over time. In sum, the study serves as an example of using national survey data to explore factors associated with the causes of mental health issues.

Design Issues in Surveys

At least four major activities are included in conducting survey research: (a) developing research questions for a defined population, (b) developing and/or selecting the survey inventories, (c) selecting and developing a data collection method, and (d) analyzing the data. We previously discussed relevant activities related to matching the survey design to the researcher's question in Chapters 5 and 6, and to some extent deriving the sample in Chapter 8, and constructing inventories in Chapter 10. We will discuss selecting inventories and developing the data collection method in Chapter 19. These chapters should all be consulted for relevant activities in developing a survey study.

Research Questions for a Defined Population   The nature of survey research is to provide a description of a certain population from a sample. It involves systematically asking participants standardized questions that are associated with the research questions that the researcher wants to address (Sapsford, 2006). As part of the research question, a population of interest is defined. For example, the NLAAS focused on Latino and Asian Americans with an attempt to include both U.S.-born individuals and immigrants that represented the whole populations of these two racial groups. In terms of the actual design of a survey study, unlike true or quasi-experimental designs, the researcher does not form the actual groups a priori. Although groups may be formed for comparison's sake (e.g.,, U.S.-born individuals vs. immigrants), the survey is often given to the entire identified sample. Even when the researcher decides ahead of time to compare, for example, U.S.-born individuals and immigrants, he or she often finds these participants as they occur in the sample population. However, the NLASS survey purposefully sampled from two groups—Asian Americans and Latinos. Even when this type of purposeful sampling can be done, the researcher cannot assign participants to be in one group or another as can occur in true experimental or quasi-experimental research. Likewise, in survey designs, manipulation of an independent variable is not a requirement, although at times manipulations can be incorporated as part of a survey study. For example, a study may present different sets of questions or information (such as case scenarios where the gender or ethnicity of the key person is manipulated) and compare responses. Likewise, Gallup polls may compare responses to different ways a question is worded.

Survey Inventories   In terms of developing and/or selecting inventories for the survey, we want to emphasize the need to carefully consider the psychometric properties of existing inventories (see Chapter 19). For example, the survey batteries used in the NLAAS were selected from established measures based on strong face validity, internal reliability, and those that have been used among Asian American and Latino populations. However, some studies utilize new items specifically developed for the particular survey study. The procedures for developing new survey items are very important, and a major misconception is that developing new survey items is quick and easy. Readers are encouraged to consult Chapter 10 (Scale Construction) that addresses issues related to survey construction, convenience samples, and cultural issues, as well as steps in developing scales or surveys such as writing items, performing content analysis, and piloting items.

Survey research with diverse populations can present some unique challenges. Ponterotto and Casas (1991) discussed issues that counseling researchers should consider when using a survey design with culturally, linguistically, and/or economically diverse groups. The first issue concerns how to tailor the survey to the particular group under study: Do the respondents understand the questions in the way that the researchers intended? Are any items offensive to people in the group the researcher wants to survey? Do potential respondents understand how to respond to the format? According to Ponterotto and Casas, these questions can be addressed by examining the language and format of potential questions in a pretest conducted on a pilot sample that is representative of the target population. These authors suggest that the survey be pilot tested on a sample that represents about 5% of the target sample to check for readability, completion time, etc. When the pilot test is administered, the respondents should be interviewed to make sure that the questions asked were meaningful, clear, and appropriate for the purpose of the survey. It is important to note that the piloting step should be applied for all surveys, although it is particularly important when studying an understudied population.

A second issue raised by Ponterotto and Casas (1991) involves research with participants who do not speak English. In this case, the researcher must translate potential questions into the participants' native language. For example, due to the attempt to include immigrants in the NLAAS, the surveys were carefully translated to Spanish and Asian languages. Unfortunately, this translation process is neither straightforward nor simple (see Chapter 10, as well as Mallinckrodt & Wang, 2004, and Ægisdóttir, Gerstein, & Çinarbaş, 2008). Briefly, we will highlight two issues here: translation/back-translation and decentering. In back-translation, a bilingual person first translates the original questions into the new language; once this translation is complete, another bilingual person translates the translated questions back into English. Any discrepancies between the original and the back-translated versions of the questions are identified and corrected. Decentering attempts to address the issue of comparable functional and cultural meaning. In decentering, the researcher attempts to ensure that no specific language is the "center" of attention. This decentering is accomplished by having bilingual judges examine both versions of the survey and compare the functional and cultural equivalence of the questions.

Data Collection   As survey research aims to describe a population, data should be systematically collected either from the whole population or a representative sample. Most often, it is more realistic to collect data from a sample as opposed to surveying each individual of the whole population. However, whether the survey sample is representative of the whole population is a critical issue. For example, if we wanted to understand the prevalence of mental illness among Latinos in the United States, the sample should be representative across gender, geographic region, age, nationality of origin, socioeconomic status, etc. Results could be biased if the sampling process overfocused on a group (e.g., those fluent in English), while neglecting others (e.g., non-English speaking immigrants), as results showed that length of time in the United States and immigrant status (which are also linked with English fluency) were associated with the probability of mental health disorders (Alegría et al., 2008). Therefore, the sampling procedure is a critical step in conducting survey studies that examine prevalence rates.

Random sampling is an important issue for survey studies. It would be important that potential participants have equal chance of being invited to participate in the study. However, a number of factors based on the design of the study (e.g., accessibility to online surveys, availability to be interviewed during certain times, voluntary nature) may pose limitations to conducting truly random sampling. This sampling issue was also addressed in greater detail in Chapter 8.

Another approach is using stratified random sampling, which takes into account certain characteristics. This method involves first dividing a population into smaller groups (i.e., strata) based on their shared attributes or characteristics, for example, men and women. Then a sample from each group is extracted based on the proportional size of the group to the whole population. For example, women consisted of 55% of the whole target population. Therefore, in a target sample size of 1,000 participants, 550 women would be randomly selected from the female pool, whereas 450 men would be selected for the male pool. An advantage of using stratified random sampling is that it captures key characteristics that represent the whole population.

The most frequent way of collecting data in survey research is through self-report questionnaires, particularly mailed or online questionnaires. The primary advantage of such surveys is the ease of data collection, particularly when the sample covers a wide geographic area (in which case it would be difficult to collect onsite data). One of the biggest potential disadvantages is the difficulty of getting participants to respond and return the completed questionnaires. For example, often the return rate from a first mailing is only 30%, which raises questions about the external validity of the results. Was there some reason why the majority of the participants did not respond? Would their responses be different from those of the 30% who responded? It is doubtful that one could safely generalize from a 30% return rate of a sample to the target population. Because the return rate is such a critical issue in mail surveys, researchers usually try to make it easy both to complete the questionnaire (by keeping it short) and to submit it (by including a stamped, addressed return envelope in the case of mailing method). Two sets of reminder letters or emails are also usually sent. Typically a follow-up reminder is sent about two or three weeks after the initial mailing, and subsequently two or three weeks later as a final follow-up. Researchers commonly report obtaining around a 30% to 40% return rate from an initial recruitment, and approximately 20% and 10% returns from the two successive follow-ups. Although some published survey research is based on less than a 40% return rate, some researchers recommend at least a 50% return rate as an "adequate" basis for findings (Baddie, 2001).

A popular method of data collection is through an online website. The advantage of such a data collection method is that a broad range of individuals in the target population, from whatever location within the United States or beyond, can complete the questionnaire. Consequently, a researcher can often obtain larger data sets, especially with restricted populations, than through more traditional data collection methods. Conversely, it is difficult to ascertain the representativeness of those participants who complete the online survey. In addition, response rates of online surveys have been found typically lower than those of paper surveys (Shih & Fan, 2008). Moreover, due to the common use of listservs to distribute recruitment emails it is difficult to know who received the recruitment email and among those who actually opened and read the email. Thus, it is almost impossible to estimate the participation rate in this case. Social media has also become a common way to recruit research participants. Through snowballing methods using social media, listservs, and word of mouth, researchers have very little control of who participates in response to the online survey. Therefore, it is essential to screen the data prior to conducting analyses. Including some critical demographic variables to ensure participants fit within the eligible criteria, and using validity check items (e.g., Please simply click "strongly agree" for this item) to see if they carefully read the items are ways that could be helpful for the data screening process.

Not only have using online surveys become a primary way of collecting data, but the use of crowdsourcing has also become increasingly popular and utilized to collect research data. Crowdsourcing is a method of obtaining services (e.g., useful information, ideas, feedback) by soliciting participants from online communities. Mechanical Tuck (MTurk), run by amazon.com, is the most commonly used crowdsourcing service. MTurk is an online labor system that can provide quick, easy, and inexpensive access to research participants who fit researchers' specific criteria of eligibility (Goodman, Cryder, & Cheema, 2013). There have been a few studies that examined the quality of respondents' data provided through MTurk services. For example, MTurk participants have been found in general to provide reliable and consistent responses compared with community and student samples (Goodman et al., 2013). Moreover, clinical and subclinical populations from MTurk have also been found to provide high quality responses (Shapiro, Chandler, & Mueller, 2013). However, MTurk participants were found to be more introverted (Goodman et al., 2013), have lower self-esteem (Goodman et al., 2013), and were more motivated to express distress (Shapiro et al., 2013) compared to other participants. Thus, similar with other online studies, it is important to prescreen MTurk participants so that they fit the key criteria of the study. It is also important to take into account the unique characteristics that MTurk participants have been found to possess and determine whether collecting data through this approach would be appropriate.

Distribution and collection of the survey with minority populations may also present unique challenges. As noted by Ponterotto and Casas (1991), some socioeconomic and/or cultural groups may not trust researchers who reflect the White middle class, and thus be less likely to participate or perhaps be more guarded in their responses. Therefore, obtaining an adequate response rate may be a larger problem with these groups of participants. As recommended by Ponterotto and Casas, it is important to be able to ascertain the reason for a low response rate, and ideally the researcher should attempt to interview a random subsample of respondents and nonrespondents to determine the characteristics that distinguish the respondent and nonrespondent groups.

Data Analysis   The final step entails data analysis. A critical starting point for data analysis is checking the adequacy of the sample. This involves checking how closely the sample resembles the general population along a number of important dimensions. For instance, is the proportion of male and female (or racial/ethnic minorities and Whites, or young and old) respondents in the sample similar to the proportions in the general population? To illustrate, the NLAAS was compared with the census data on various demographic dimensions. Another especially important type of check when conducting longitudinal studies is a comparison of respondents and nonrespondents (e.g., those that dropped out of the study). For example, when using a college population, do respondents and nonrespondents differ by sex, year in school, major, grade point average, etc? Only after this type of sample checking has been done should the data be analyzed and interpreted.

National surveys such as the NLAAS usually include a large set of demographic information and an array of variables representing several constructs. Therefore, many research questions can be examined using the same large data set. For example, if a study included the area code or address of participants, researchers can obtain economic and social data from it—geocoding. Geocoding is using certain geographic coordinates (e.g., address, postal code) to obtain more descriptive information about the particular location (e.g., population, income, racial composition). This approach has been used for research that involves studying demographic information of participants' neighborhood (e.g., medium income, population, minority percentage). Available online tools that can be used for geocoding include one from the Federal Financial Institutions Examination Council (https://geomap.ffiec.gov/FFIEC GeocMap/GeocodeMap1.aspx) as well as another from the U.S. Census Bureau (http://geocoding.geo.census.gov/geocoder/). After entering a certain address, the program will provide associated census demographic data. Thus, this information can then be used to examine neighborhood effects. Of course, each study would have unique research questions that utilize certain variables within the overall data set. For example, the NLASS has resulted in over 50 publications (see publication list on the Center for Multicultural Mental Health Research, 2014 webpage). In short, utilizing existing data from large national data sets is a good way to conduct research studies without the need to collect a new set of data. It would be beneficial to explore existing national data sets that align or intersect with your research interest.

RESEARCH IN ACTION 13.1

Conduct an online search to see if you are able to find large data sets that are available for public use, such as the NLAAS. Explore what types of variables are included in one or two of these data sets. Develop two research questions that could possibly be addressed through these variables.

VARIABLE-CENTERED CORRELATIONAL RESEARCH DESIGNS

Correlational designs are used to examine the relationships between two or more variables. There are many statistical analyses that utilize bivariate or multivariate covariation, including simple correlation, multiple regression, structural equation modeling, test of moderation and mediation, etc. In this section, we will introduce some of the more commonly used variable-centered correlational designs. In Table 13.1, we also list a few commonly used statistical analyses and the corresponding research questions that each analyses tend to address.

Simple Correlations

A simple correlational design examines the relationship between two variables (e.g., depression and social skills), and then uses a statistical analysis (typically a Pearson product moment correlation) to describe their relationship. The correlation coefficient, or r, provides an index of the degree of linear relationship between the variables. Suppose that as one variable (x) increases, so do the scores on the second variable (y); then x and y vary together, or covary, and have a "strong positive relationship." If x scores do not vary with y scores, we typically say there is not a relationship between x and y. The correlation coefficient between two scores can range from $+1.00$ (a very strong positive relationship) to -1.00 (a very strong

TABLE 13.1 Statistical Analyses and Corresponding Research Questions

Statistical Analyses	Questions Addressed
Correlations	The direction and strength of relationship between two variables
Multiple regression	How multiple predictors are related to a criterion variable
Path analysis	How multiple predictors and dependent variables are simultaneously associated in a single model
Structural equation modeling	How multiple predictors and dependent variables are associated in a single model using latent constructs estimated through multiple observed variables
Cluster analysis	How participants can be classified into different groups based on a set of variables
Latent class/profile analysis	How participants can be classified into different latent classes (using probability scores) based on a set of variables
Growth mixture modeling	How participants can be classified into different latent classes based on their profiles on how a variable changes over time
ANOVA	How groups compare on a certain variable

negative relationship). The amount of variance that is shared between two variables is the square of the correlation. Thus, the correlation between x and y might be $+.5$, which means that the amount of variance shared between these two variables is 25% $(.5)^2$. Sometimes in the past (see Cook & Campbell, 1979) these designs were also referred to as passive designs because the researcher neither actively forms groups or conditions through random or nonrandom assignment, nor actively manipulates an independent variable. Following is an example of simple correlations used in a study.

French and Neville (2013) studied sexual coercion among Black and White teenagers and its relationship with psychological and behavioral health. They examined different types of sexual coercion, as well as created an overall (total) index of sexual coercion. Although they investigated several issues in their study, one of the research questions was "Is there a link between type of sexually coercive experience and psychological and behavioral health" (French & Neville, 2013, p. 1198). To address this question, they conducted intercorrelations between sexual coercion experiences and psychological and behavioral health. Results indicated that for Black participants, the overall sexual coercion index and nearly all sexual coercion types (i.e., verbal, substance-facilitated, and physical) were moderately associated with each psychological (i.e., self-esteem, psychological distress) and behavioral (i.e., sexual risk-taking) outcome. The researchers also found that for White participants, all types of coercion had positive correlations with risky sexual behavior ($r = .21$ to $.37$), and the overall sexual coercion index and physical coercion had negative correlations with self-esteem ($r = -.21$ to $-.22$) and positive correlations with psychological distress ($r = .22$ to $.23$). In short, the correlational design aspect of this study allowed French and Neville to describe the degree of relationship between two groups of variables—sexual coercion and psychological and behavioral health among Black and White young women.

We also want to mention a more sophisticated development in the use of correlational designs. Cole, Lazarick, and Howard (1987) maintained that most of the correlational (as well as the experimental) research in counseling has underestimated the relationships among the variables examined because researchers tend to examine only manifest variables—that is, derived scores, usually from an inventory, that are presumed to reflect a person's standing on a construct or latent variable. However, because manifest variables (e.g., the score on the Beck Depression Inventory) contain measurement error, the relationship between two manifest variables is a function of their relationship and the reliability of the measures. Cole et al. described a better method for determining the relationship between the constructs that the manifest variables are presumed to measure.

More specifically, Cole et al. (1987) proposed that the constructs of interest must be assessed by multiple methods, and that confirmatory factor analysis be used to examine the relationship between the constructs, or latent variables. For example, Cole et al. were interested in assessing the relationship between depression and social skills. A simple correlational design could examine the correlation between scores from one depression inventory and one social skills inventory. The authors, however, assessed each of the constructs from four perspectives: self-report, behavioral ratings from researchers, interviews, and ratings from significant others. Cole et al. found an average cross-trait correlation between depression and social skills of $-.25$ across the four measures. When confirmatory factor analysis was used to estimate the relationship between the constructs of depression and social skills, the correlation increased to $-.85$. In essence, rather than accounting for only 6% of the variability of depression using a Pearson product moment correlation $(-.25)^2$, Cole et al. found that social skills accounted for approximately 72% $(-.85)^2$ of this variance using confirmatory factor analysis.

In short, Cole et al. (1987) suggested an important methodological issue with the use of latent as opposed to manifest variables in the analysis of correlational designs. Suffice it to say that although simple correlational designs provide useful information utilizing *variables* (e.g., scores from a depression measure), more sophisticated analyses that use latent variables provide *true estimates of the construct* (e.g., the latent construct of depression) assessed from multiple sources and methods, which minimizes measurement error. This statistical approach of using latent variables can be applied to different types of analyses (e.g., structural equation modeling), which we will later discuss in this chapter. But please note that these types of correlational analyses do not allow for causal explanation.

Multiple Regression

Whereas a correlation identifies the relationship between two variables, most often researchers are interested in describing the relationships among more than two variables. For example, one might ask: If we know the correlation between x and y, would it not be more powerful to include variables a, b, and c (along with x) to study y? Indeed, in many cases it is, and thus multiple regression has become increasingly popular in the counseling literature. We will briefly focus on multiple regression here as a way of increasing our ability to describe the relationships among multiple variables. (For more details, see Cohen & Cohen, 1983; Hair et al., 1987; Wampold & Freund, 1987.)

Multiple regression is a statistical method for studying the separate and collective contributions of one or more predictor variables in the variation of a dependent variable (Wampold & Freund, 1987). In essence, multiple regression can be used to describe how multiple predictor variables are related to a single "dependent" (criterion) variable. Thus, researchers frequently refer to predicting the criterion variable and discuss the extent to which they can accurately predict the criterion. The relationship between a "dependent" variable and a set of multiple "independent" variables is expressed as the multiple correlation coefficient R, which is a measure of how well the predictor scores correspond to the actual scores of dependent variables. The square of the multiple correlation coefficient (R^2) is the proportion of variability of the dependent variable explained by the independent variables. The word *explained* here does not necessarily imply a causal relationship, but rather an association of the dependent variable with variability in the predictor variables (Wampold & Freund, 1987).

We will discuss two basic methods for entering predictor variables in regression equations: simultaneous and hierarchical regression. Because each method serves slightly different purposes and outcomes, it is important for the researcher to be familiar with the strengths and weaknesses of each method (see Wampold & Freund, 1987, for an overview). In *simultaneous regression,* all of the predictor variables are entered concurrently (simultaneously) into the regression equation. Simultaneous regression is most often used when there is no basis for entering any particular predictor variable before any other predictor variable, and the researcher wants to determine the amount of variability of each predictor variable that *uniquely* contributes to the prediction of the criterion variable (after the common variability among the predictor variables has been removed). For instance, Asner-Self and Marotta (2005) used simultaneous regressions to examine the predictors of psychological distress in 68 Central American immigrants who had been exposed to war-related trauma. The authors noted that one of the fastest growing immigrant groups in the United States were people from war torn Central America (Marotta & Garcia, 2003). The authors were particularly interested in examining whether mistrust, identity confusion, and isolation, as results of developmental disruption, would predict symptoms such as depression, anxiety, and posttraumatic stress (PTS). Although a randomized sampling procedure would be preferable, it is difficult to recruit people from this and other immigrant groups for a number of reasons, such as difficulties involving legal status and a host of cross-cultural fears. Therefore, volunteers were recruited via flyers and snowball sampling (Asner-Self & Marotta, 2005). The authors used the three predictors (mistrust, identity confusion, and isolation) in three simultaneous regressions to determine which if any would predict each of the indices of psychological distress (depression, anxiety, and PTS).

The results revealed that the three predictors predicted 32%–51% of the variability of the three distress variables. However, the three predictors were not all equally effective in predicting distress. Although both mistrust and identity confusion were associated with participants' depressive symptoms, identity confusion was a significant predictor of anxiety and PTS, after partialling out the influence of the other predictor variables. Thus, the authors concluded: "The more these Central Americans' sense of identity was in flux, the more likely they were to feel depressed and anxious or to report symptoms related to PTS" (p. 165). This study illustrates how simultaneous regressions can identify which variable is the best predictor of criterion variables. This study also nicely illustrates the need for counselors to be cognizant not only of identity confusion for immigrant groups such as those examined in this study, but also the need to engage in culturally sensitive interventions (Asner-Self & Marotta, 2005).

In *hierarchical regression,* the researcher specifies the order of entry of the predictor variables based on some rationale (e.g., research relevance, causal priority, or theoretical grounds). Hierarchical regression is also used to test moderation and interaction effects, which we will describe in the next section. One might use hierarchical regression if one wants to see if variable *a* (e.g., single-parent family status) adds something above and beyond variable *b* (e.g., SES) in predicting variable *y* (e.g., pathology). For example, single-parent family status might predict a pathology variable. However, if a demographic variable (e.g., SES) is entered first followed by single-parent family status, then single-parent family status no longer significantly predicts the pathology. In this case, maybe it is not the single-parent family status, but rather SES, which is correlated with single-parent family status, that is important in predicting pathology. Following is an example of a study using hierarchical regression.

Piña-Watson, Jimenez, and Ojeda (2014) used the social cognitive theory of well-being (SCTW; Lent, 2004) as a framework to examine the role of career decision self-efficacy, perceived educational barriers, and independent self-construal in predicting life satisfaction beyond the background contextual factors of SES and generational status among Mexican American college women. They conducted a three-step hierarchical linear regression. In Step 1, they examined the predictive role of the demographic variables (i.e., perceived SES and generational status). In Step 2, they added independent self-construal, and in Step 3, they entered the career-related variables (e.g., perceived educational barriers and career decision self-efficacy) into this regression model that predicted life satisfaction among Mexican American college women. In predicting life satisfaction, the multiple R for the two demographic variables was not significant ($R^2 = .02$). When independent self-construal was added, the R^2 increased to .21; these results indicated that independent self-construal added additional predictive variance beyond that accounted for by the demographic variables. In Step 3, when career-related variables were added, the R^2 further increased to .31, indicating that perceived educational barriers and career decision self-efficacy together added an additional 10% predictive variance to life satisfaction beyond the variance accounted for by the variables in the previous two steps. By using a hierarchical model, Piña-Watson and colleagues were able to perform a broader test of the relationship between the predictors of life satisfaction, and demonstrate the important role that self-construal, CDSE, and perceived educational barriers have beyond contextual background factors.

In evaluating the usefulness of multiple regression, it is always important to remember that the results of these types of analyses are based on correlational data. Multiple regression designs use terminology from experimental designs (*dependent variable* and *independent variables*); we prefer the terms *criterion* and *predictor* instead as they seem to be more descriptive on these types of variables. However, even though the variables may be referred to as independent and dependent variables, it is important to note that the results obtained are relational, not causal. Likewise, it is important to note that the choice of a criterion variable and of predictor variables is always arbitrary. In other words, causality cannot be inferred from prediction, and typically, it is not possible to make causal statements with these designs. Multiple regression is suited to describing and predicting the relationship between two or more variables, and is especially useful in examining the incremental as well as total explanatory power of many variables (Hair et al., 1987). Perhaps the main caveats for researchers pertain to inadequate sample sizes (see Wampold & Freund, 1987), and spurious results due to methodological procedures (e.g., a positive correlation between shoe size and reading ability among elementary students, which is actually explained by age—older kids wear larger shoes and read better).

Testing for Moderation and Mediation

As we indicated earlier in this chapter, it is useful to understand when one variable is correlated with a second variable, such as knowing that the client's rating of the working alliance is related to counseling outcomes. However, many times there are more complex relationships among variables that are important for counselors to understand. These more complex relationships not only enhance counselors' understanding, but also advance counseling research and theory. Examining moderating and mediating effects among variables are two common research strategies for understanding more complex relationships among variables (Frazier, Tix, & Barron, 2004).

Mediation and moderation are often confused by psychological researchers, and it is important to distinguish between them (see Baron & Kenny, 1986; Frazier et al., 2004). We will first discuss moderator variables, and then later discuss mediator variables. See Figure 13.1 for a visual illustration. A moderator affects the direction or strength of association between predictor and criterion variables, whereas a mediator links between the predictor and criterion variables.

Moderation   "Questions involving moderators address 'when' or 'for whom' a variable most strongly predicts or causes an outcome variable" (Frazier et al., 2004, p. 116). In essence, a moderator is a variable that affects the direction and/or strength of the relationship between a predictor (independent variable) and a criterion (dependent variable) (Baron & Kenny, 1986). In other words, a moderator changes the relationship between the predictor and criterion variables, and in essence is an interaction between the predictor and moderator variables to predict the criterion variable. Thus a moderator is "nothing more than an interaction" (Frazier et al., p. 116).

FIGURE 13.1   Moderator and Mediator

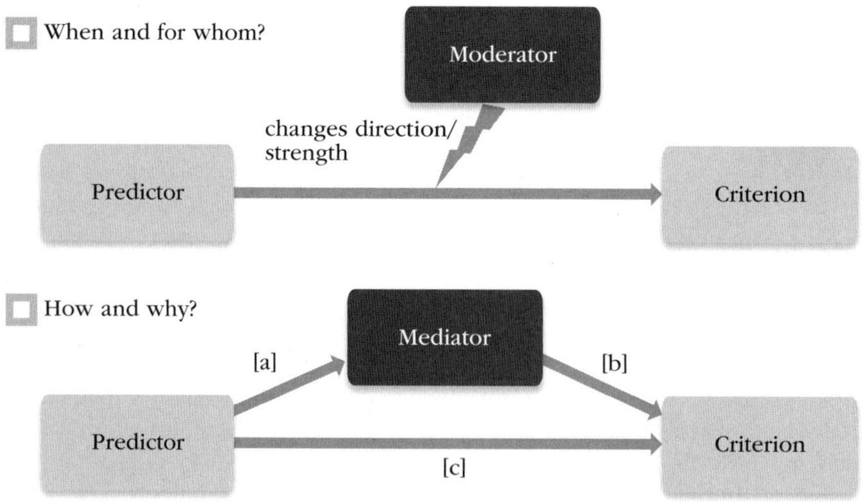

A classic example of a moderator relationship is the stress-buffering hypothesis that has been prominent in social support research. According to this model, social support is predicted to moderate the relationship between negative life events (e.g., death of a spouse) and depression. In this example, negative life events is the predictor variable, social support is the moderator variable, and depression is the criterion variable. Negative life events are theoretically related to depression. However, social support changes this relationship. For people with low levels of social support, the more negative life events a person experiences, the higher her or his levels of depression. However, with higher levels of social support, the relationship between negative life events and depression is altered; when a person has more social support, negative life events do not necessarily result in higher levels of depression. Thus, there is an interaction between negative life events and social support in predicting levels of depression. This example nicely illustrates "for whom" negative life events are associated with higher levels of depression (those with low levels of social support).

Moderators can be either categorical (e.g., sex, type of intervention) or continuous (e.g., amount of social support). The appropriate statistical analysis for testing for moderating effects depends on the categorical or continuous nature of both the moderator variable and the predictor variable. As an example of these analytic procedures, we describe the statistical approach used when the predictor variables are continuous. When both variables are continuous, the potential moderator effect is tested in a hierarchical regression through the interaction effect between the two predictors. In the first step of the regression, both the predictor variables are entered into the regression equation predicting the criterion variable. This first step produces an R^2 representing the amount of variability of the criterion variable that is explained by the predictor variables in combination. In the second step of the regression, the multiplicative product of predictors (or interaction) is entered into the regression equation. After this second step, a new R^2 is obtained; it represents the amount of variability of the criterion variable that is explained by the combination of the predictor variables and their interaction. The difference between the R^2 obtained in the first step of the regression, and the R^2 obtained in the second step, is the amount of variability of the criterion variable that is predicted by the interaction over and above the main effects. If the difference between the R^2 values from the first and second steps of the regression is significant, then there is a moderation effect. For more statistical and design details, see Frazier et al. (2004).

In addition to moderation examples used in true experiments provided in Chapter 11, following is an example from a study examining social connectedness as a moderator of the link between discrimination and posttraumatic stress symptoms in a correlational study.

Carter (2007) proposed the notion of race-based traumatic stress, which has been supported by previous research. Studies have indicated a relationship between perceived ethnic discrimination and posttraumatic stress symptoms in Asian/Asian American, African American, and Mexican American students (Pieterse, Carter, Evans, & Walter, 2010; Flores, Tschann, Dimas, Pasch, & de Groat, 2010). However, Wei, Wang, Heppner, and Du (2012) wanted to identify whether social connectedness would affect the link between discrimination and posttraumatic stress symptoms. In particular, they were interested in examining Chinese international students with bicultural experiences, and investigate whether their social connectedness with the U.S. mainstream society and their social connectedness with their Chinese ethnic community served as protective factors. Wei and her colleagues were interested in examining ways in which the two different cultural forms of social connectedness (with mainstream society and with ethnic community) might differentially moderate or protect against discrimination in predicting posttraumatic stress symptoms. Thus, Wei et al. used hierarchical regression analyses to test the moderation effects. The predictor variable was discrimination. The moderators were the two forms of social connectedness (with mainstream society and with ethnic community), and posttraumatic stress symptoms were the criterion. In addition, Wei et al. wanted to control for participants' level of general stress to highlight the unique posttraumatic stress symptoms. Thus, they first entered general stress (covariate). Then as a second step, they entered discrimination. For the third step, they entered the two forms of social connectedness. In the last step, they added the interactions between social connectedness with mainstream society × discrimination as well as social connectedness with ethnic community × discrimination to determine whether there were interaction effects over and above the first three steps. The results suggested that only one type of social connectedness (with ethnic community) moderated the effects of discrimination on posttraumatic stress symptom above and beyond general stress. Wei et al. found that among Chinese international students, with higher ethnic social connectedness, the strength of the association between perceived racial discrimination and posttraumatic stress symptoms became weaker. In other words, being connected with one's ethnic community protected Chinese international students from the detrimental effect of discrimination to a certain degree.

This study nicely illustrates how the interaction between two variables (in this case social connection and discrimination) can be examined to predict criterion variables (in this case, posttraumatic stress symptoms). Moreover, the results illustrate the importance of examining not only first-order individual relationships between the predictors (i.e., social connectedness, discrimination) and the criterion variables, but also the interaction among the predictors. Finally, the study also illustrates the utility of using more complex regression analyses to identify the specific mechanisms that moderate the negative effects of perceived discrimination, which has direct implications for remedial and preventive interventions with Chinese international students.

Mediation   We will now focus on mediating variables. A mediating variable establishes "how" or "why" one variable predicts or causes a criterion variable (Frazier et al., 2004). That is, a mediator is a variable that explains the relationship between a predictor and the criterion (Baron & Kenny, 1986); more specifically, the mediator is the mechanism through which the predictor influences the criterion variable. This type of research strategy helps counselors to identify the underlying mechanisms that may be important to target in counseling interventions. By knowing why and how changes occur in the process of counseling, counselors will be able to identify the key elements that lead to change and thus optimize the change process (Kazdin, 2009).

For example, cognitive therapy proposes that through the process of changing clients' cognitive thoughts, they gain therapeutic outcomes. In this example, the interventions focus on reframing one's thoughts that leads to cognitive changes, which further leads to therapeutic outcomes. The actual cognitive changes that occur would be a mediator between the intervention and therapeutic outcome in this case.

Figure 13.1 is a modified representation of the path model for mediation presented in Baron and Kenny (1986). This path model depicts three paths or relationships among the three variables. Path [a] depicts the relationship between the predictor variable and the mediator variable; path [b] represents the relationship between the mediator variable and the criterion variable; and path [c] depicts the relationship between the predictor variable and the criterion variable, apart from the mediator. In order to demonstrate that a variable is a mediator, four conditions must be met using Baron and Kenny's classical model: (a) the relationship between the predictor variable and the criterion variable must be statistically significant; (b) the relationship between the predictor variable and the mediator variable must be significant; (c) the relationship between the mediator variable and the criterion variable must be statistically significant; and (d) in a path model that includes all three variables together, the relationship between the predictor and criterion (that was previously significant) is significantly reduced when the mediator is added to the model. If the direct path between the predictor and criterion does not differ from zero when the mediator is added to the model, the strongest demonstration of mediation occurs; this is called a *complete mediator*. If the direct path between the predictor and criterion remains significantly greater than zero after the mediator is added to the model, the mediating variable is called a *partial mediator*. In the classical model to test for mediation, Baron and Kenny recommend that a series of regression models be conducted to test the four conditions listed (for more statistical and design details, see Frazier et al., 2004). However, there are other more advanced methods to test for mediation, such as the bootstrapping method (for more information, see MacKinnon, Lockwood, Hoffman, West, & Sheets, 2002; Mallinckrodt, Abraham, Wei, & Russell, 2006)

We will use an example to illustrate mediating variables in the counseling literature. For example, there is growing empirical evidence of an association between prejudice and discrimination and greater levels of psychological distress with several previously marginalized groups such as African Americans, White women, and lesbian, gay, and bisexual individuals (e.g., Corning, 2002; Moradi & Subich, 2003; Waldo, 1999). However, Moradi and Hasan (2004) noted that there has been a dearth of evidence examining the prejudice stress-distress link with Arab Americans, a group that has been experiencing increasing discrimination. Based on theory and some previous findings, they hypothesized that personal control mediates the relationship between perceived discrimination and both self-esteem and psychological distress in Arab Americans. Their results indicated a relationship between perceived discrimination and psychological distress ($r = .32$). Moreover, they found that a sense of personal control partially mediated perceived discrimination and psychological distress, and fully mediated the relationship with self-esteem. Thus, the loss of control seems to play an important role in underlying the perceived discrimination events leading to decreased self-esteem and increased psychological distress for Arab Americans.

In another example, Wei, Vogel, Ku, and Zakalik (2005) were interested in whether different types of affect regulation might mediate the relationships between attachment styles and psychological distress. More specifically, based on theory and previous research, they hypothesized that (a) the association between attachment anxiety and negative mood or interpersonal problems would be mediated by emotional reactivity (i.e., overreacting to negative feelings) and (b) the association between attachment avoidance and negative mood or interpersonal problems would be mediated by emotional cutoff (i.e., suppressing their negative feelings). Their results supported both hypotheses, and also supported growing evidence suggesting that the link between attachment and distress is not simply a direct relationship, but one involving mediating psychological processes (e.g., Wei, Heppner, & Mallinckrodt, 2003). The results of this study suggest that the anxiety and avoidant attachment styles prefer to use different affect regulation strategies. This study suggests that practitioners can help individuals with anxiety and avoidant attachment styles by recognizing the temporary and long-term positive benefits of using their specific regulation strategies of maladaptive affect.

Parenthetically, Moradi and Hasan (2004) used path analysis whereas Wei et al. (2005) used a statistical analysis called structural equation modeling (SEM), which allowed them to simultaneously examine the direct and indirect effects required for mediational models. The main difference between these two methods is that SEM uses latent variables (utilizing multiple indicators/measures to represent a latent construct); conversely, path analyses uses scores from a single measure to represent the variable. Note that in both studies, the authors provide figures depicting the relationships among the hypothesized variables. (See both articles for more details, as well as Heppner & Heppner, 2004, for more detailed explanations of how to write a results section when using structural equation modeling.)

As noted earlier, the advantages of using latent variables are to derive unbiased estimates for the associations between latent constructs by modeling measurement errors. By allowing multiple measures to be associated with a single latent construct in SEM, this approach enhances measurement accuracy. Figure 13.2 provides a visual illustration of how latent variable (represented in ovals) are derived from multiple sources of observed variables (represented in rectangles). In this example, the research study aims to examine the simultaneous relationships of (a) drinking motives fully mediating the association between personality and alcohol problems, as well as (b) protective behaviors mediating the association between family risks and alcohol problems. (For more detailed information about SEM and best practices, see Martens, 2005; Martens & Haase, 2006.)

Although we provided some examples from studies that use statistical analyses to examine mediating factors, the process of establishing sound evidence that explains the mechanisms of how therapeutic change occurs is sophisticated and often requires a series of studies. Kazdin (2009) provides some guidelines on demonstrating mediators and mechanism for therapeutic change. Seven requirements were proposed: (a) strong association, (b) specificity, (c) consistency, (d) experimental manipulation, (e) time line, (f) gradient, and (g) plausibility or coherence. More specifically, it is important that a clearly specified link between the intervention, mediator, and outcome is tested against plausible constructs and the link is supported by strong associations. Causal relationships should be established through

FIGURE 13.2 Illustration of a SEM Model

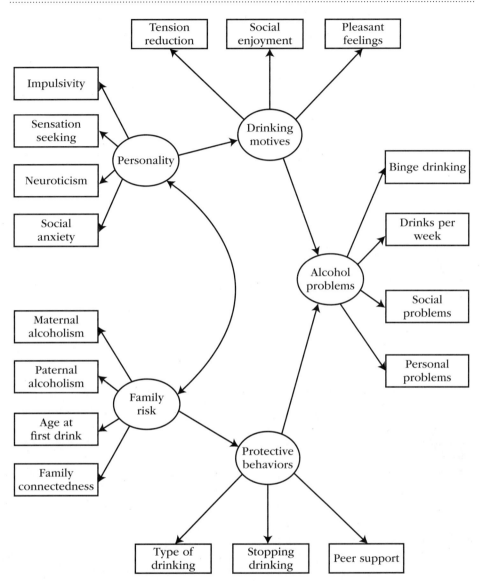

Source: From Martens, M. P. (2005). The use of structural equation modeling in counseling psychology research. *The Counseling Psychologist, 33,* 269–298. doi:10.1177/0011000004272260

experimental manipulation of the mediator, and results should be replicated. The time line demonstrating that the mediator occurs before the outcome changes is important as well as evidence supporting that the strength of the mediator is associated with the outcome magnitude. It is critical to have a coherent and reasonable process that explains the mechanism that can be tested directly. For a more detailed discussion please refer to Kazdin (2009).

RESEARCH IN ACTION 13.2

Using a topic of your own interest, discuss some key predictor and criterion variables that you would be interested in studying. Try to identify some possible moderators and mediators that might explain the mechanisms between a certain predictor and criterion variable. Further discuss why the variables you identified would be categorized as a moderator or mediator.

PERSON-CENTERED RESEARCH DESIGNS

A person-centered approach is particularly useful when analyzing a heterogeneous group of individuals. Frequently, a taxonomic system not only simplifies a data set, but also can have important theoretical implications such as identifying subgroups to address the homogeneity myth. In contrast to person-centered approaches, variable-centered approaches explain aggregated patterns between variables, which can be limited especially in a world in which not everyone is the same. To illustrate, academic challenges in children could be related to various issues (e.g., learning disability, depression, attention deficits, disruptive behavior), and whether a certain intervention is effective would most likely differ across children with different underlying issues. Thus, it would be helpful to identify the different types of underlying issues first (subgroups of children) as opposed to simply examine the effectiveness of a certain intervention with aggregated data from all types of children. Therefore, using person-centered approaches allow researchers to identify groups of people who are similar and different. In addition, comparisons can be made across groups after the different types are identified.

In fact, all sciences start from commonly accepted bases of description and classification. In this section, we will introduce three types of analyses used for person-centered approaches: cluster analysis, latent class/profiles analysis, and growth mixture analysis. We will provide an overview description of each analysis with examples of studies in the counseling field.

Cluster Analysis

Often in counseling we would like to be able to identify natural groupings or subtypes of people, such as clients or counselors. Cluster analysis is frequently used to put people into subgroups, which is quite functional for examining individual differences in counseling research. In essence, cluster analysis is a multivariate statistical method that reduces data by identifying and then classifying similar entities into subgroups (Hair et al., 1987; Hair & Black, 2000). Borgen and Barnett (1987) noted three primary purposes for cluster analysis: exploration (to find a certain structure or set of groupings), confirmation (to test an existing classification, perhaps based on theory), and simplification (to reduce a complex data set into a simpler structure). Cluster analysis can be used to categorize objects (e.g., counselor statements), people (e.g., counseling center clients), or variables (e.g., items on a test) (Borgen & Barnett, 1987).

Cluster analysis is a method based on proximities. Simply put, this analysis calculates the distances as a way to group individuals (or objects, variables) based on how close they are from each other in a metric space. Many of the processes involved in cluster analysis are beyond the scope of this text. Interested readers should consult Hair and Black (2000). Perhaps one of the most critical decisions is to select the appropriate instruments. This decision assumes added importance in cluster analysis because the instruments are the tools for measuring the similarity between objects. Objects can be determined to be similar only in the ways in which they are measured. After data are collected, the researcher proceeds to the statistical procedures involved in cluster analysis.

Two other major decision points in cluster analysis are the number of clusters and the labeling of clusters. The cluster analysis procedure produces a number of possible cluster solutions. The researcher must decide on the best solution for the data set. Although there are some general guidelines (Hair & Black, 2000) available in cluster analysis, the number of clusters retained also involves a subjective decision that should be supported by theory. Once this decision has been made, the researcher makes decisions to name the clusters. To do this, he or she examines the individuals that make up a cluster and identifies an underlying commonality or construct. Obviously, this naming process is subjective, and disagreement about the meaning or interpretation of the cluster can occur. In sum, cluster analysis can be a very powerful classification technique.

In the following paragraphs, we will provide several examples of studies that used cluster analysis as a way to group individuals. These examples not only increase our understanding of individual differences across people, but also provide suggestions for ways counselor and counseling psychologist might develop psychosocial interventions tailored to different people.

Perfectionism has not only been identified as a multidimensional construct with both positive and negative aspects, but different types of perfectionists (neurotic vs. healthy) have also been conceptualized by Hamachek (1978). In other words, there are perfectionists that are adaptive, as well as those that are maladaptive. Normal or adaptive perfectionists have the tendency to set high standards that motivates them to excel (Rice & Slaney, 2002). However, neurotic or maladaptive perfectionists hold rigid adherence to their standards and have a tendency to be overly self-critical in perceiving themselves measuring up short to their standards (Shafran & Mansell, 2001). Utilizing cluster analyses, Rice and Slaney (2002) were able to classify students into adaptive, maladaptive, and nonperfectionists, which mirrored Hamachek's theoretical model. This initial study sparked a line of research examining the different types of perfectionists. For example, Grzegorek, Slaney, Franze, and Rice (2004) sought to replicate a previous cluster analytic study that found three clusters: adaptive, maladaptive, and nonperfectionists. In addition, Grzegorek et al. also examined the relationships between the clusters and other constructs that were predicted based on the conceptualization of perfectionism. Further comparison using ANOVA across the three groups indicated that maladaptive perfectionists had higher scores on self-criticism and depression, and conversely adaptive perfectionists reported higher self-esteem. The Grzegorek et al. study is a good example of testing theory-driven hypotheses based on the conceptualization of the clusters, which also provide estimates of construct validity for the perfectionism scale.

A second example of cluster analysis involves a study by Whittaker and Neville (2010), who classified a sample of 317 Black American college students using the Cross Racial Identity Scale (CRIS; Worrell, Vandiver, Cross, & Fhagen-Smith, 2004). The six CRIS subscales were used as variables in the cluster analysis process, which included Preencounter Assimilation (PA; e.g., "I am not so much a member of a racial group, as I am an American"); Preencounter Miseducation (PM; e.g., "Blacks place more emphasis on having a good time than on hard work"); Preencounter Self-Hatred (PSH; e.g., "Privately, I sometimes have negative feelings about being Black"); Immersion-Emersion Anti-White (IEAW; e.g., "I have a strong feeling of hatred and disdain for all White people"); Internalization Afrocentric (IA; e.g., "I see and think about things from an Afrocentric perspective"); and Internalization Multiculturalists Inclusive (IMCI; e.g., "As a multiculturalist, I am connected to many groups [Hispanic, Asian Americans, Whites, Jews, gay men, lesbians, etc.]). Cluster analysis results yielded a five-cluster solution with clusters labeled Low Race Salience, Multiculturalist, Self-Hatred, Immersion, and Afrocentric based on their profile of the six CRIS subscale scores (see Figure 13.3 for profile examples of Multicultural and Immersion cluster groups).

Following the identification of the five different clusters in Whittaker and Neville's (2010) study, these cluster groups were compared on psychological outcomes through ANOVAs. Three measures were used to assess psychological outcomes: Mental Health Inventory (MHI; Veit & Ware, 1983), Satisfaction With Life Scale (SWLS; Diener, Emmons, Larsen, & Griffin, 1985), and Personal Views Survey III-R (PVS III-R; Maddi & Khoshaba, 2001). Results indicated that students classified in the Multicultural group reported the highest level of psychological well-being on all three measures. In addition, those in the Immersion group reported the lowest level of psychological well-being.

Latent Class/Profile Analysis

In addition to cluster analysis, there are also more advanced statistical approaches that classify individuals using latent modeling analyses. Latent profile and latent class analyses are more advanced statistical approaches (e.g., enhanced accuracy through using probabilities), but serve a similar function as cluster analysis—to identify natural groupings or subtypes of people. Latent class and latent profile analyses are differentiated by the type of variables. When the indicators or variables used to make the classification are continuous, latent profile analysis is used; conversely, when the indicators are categorical, latent class analysis is used. A key advantage of latent class and latent profile analyses are that they calculate the probabilities of each participant belonging to each latent class (e.g., participant [A] having a 93% probability of being in the adaptive perfectionist group, 6% probability of being in the maladaptive perfectionist group, and 1% of being a nonperfectionist) instead of simply grouping individuals into cluster groups

FIGURE 13.3 Sample Profiles Based on CRIS Subscales

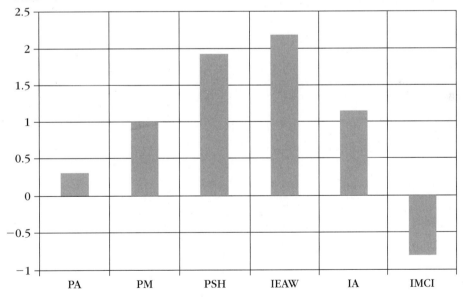

Panel A: Multicultural Cluster

Panel B: Immersion Cluster

Source: From French, B. H., & Neville, H. A. (2013). Sexual coercion among black and white teenagers: Sexual stereotypes and psychobehavioral correlates. *The Counseling Psychologist, 41*(8), 1186–1212. doi:10.1177/0011000012461379.

(e.g., participant [A] being classified as an adaptive perfectionist). This latent approach accounts for the fact that most people do not fit exactly into a certain type, and therefore uses probability scores to provide a more precise estimation of latent classes (i.e., based on probabilities of belonging to each profile group). Latent profile/class analyses also handles missing data in a more sensible way (e.g., using full information maximum likelihood). There are several other advantages of latent profile/class analyses, but due to the scope of this chapter, we will not go into details of this statistical approach. For more information on the statistical approach, please consult Hagenaars and McCutcheon (2002). For more examples of latent profile/class analyses, please see Herman, Trotter, Reinke, and Ialongo (2011), Lopez, Fons-Scheyd, Bush-King, and McDermott (2011), and Villodas, Litrownik, and Roesch (2012).

Growth Mixture Modeling

Classifying individuals can be extended from cross-sectional designs to longitudinal designs. In the previous examples using cluster analysis and latent profile analysis, participants were classified based on their scores on a set of variables that were all measured at one time point. However, participants can also be grouped based on how their scores on a particular variable have changed over a particular period of time. Growth mixture modeling is a statistical analysis that identifies latent subgroups based on how a variable grows/changes over time (Ram & Grimm, 2009). Following we will use a study that examined the longitudinal psychological adjustment process of international students during cross-national transitions as an example.

Wang and his colleagues (2012) conducted a longitudinal study examining psychological distress trajectories of new Chinese international students before and during the first three semesters of their studies in the United States. This study was based on the assumption that not all international students adjust the same over time, and the goal was to identify different adjustment trajectory patterns. Through growth mixture modeling using psychological distress as a variable, Wang et al. identified four groups with distinct trajectories: (a) high levels of psychological distress across four time points (Consistently Distressed, 10%), (b) decreased psychological distress from prearrival to first semester (Relieved, 14%), (c) a sharp peak in psychological distress at the first two semesters (Culture Shocked, 11%), and (d) consistently low psychological distress scores (Well-Adjusted, 65%) (see Figure 13.4). Moreover, various prearrival and postarrival factors were examined to determine which factors predicted these trajectory groups. Overall, results indicated that having higher self-esteem, positive problem-solving appraisal, and lower maladaptive perfectionism prior to studying in the U.S. predicted better adjustment trajectories. In addition, they found that having a balanced array of social support across various sources (i.e., peers from home country, other international students, and American students) during the first semester of studying in the United States was also associated with a better cross-cultural transition. This study provides an example of classifying individuals by the trajectories of psychological distress over time. For more information about the statistical process of growth mixture modeling, please refer to Ram and Grimm (2009) for details.

FIGURE 13.4 | Characteristics of the Four Classes of Psychological Distress Trajectories

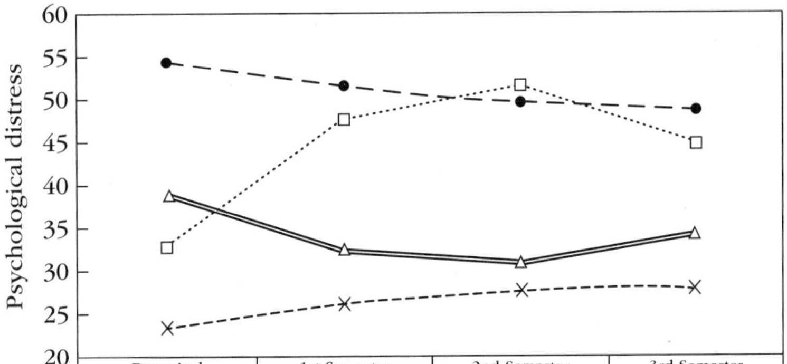

	Prearrival	1st Semester	2nd Semester	3rd Semester
● Consistently Distressed (10%)	54.43	51.51	49.64	48.81
△ Relieved (14%)	38.90	32.43	30.86	34.20
□ Culture Shocked (11%)	32.95	47.65	51.64	44.93
✕ Well-Adjusted (65%)	23.39	26.28	27.79	27.92

Source: From Wang, K. T., Heppner, P. P., Fu, C., Zhao, R., Li, F., & Chuang, C. (2012). Profiles of acculturative adjustment patterns among Chinese international students. *Journal of Counseling Psychology, 59*(3), 424–436. doi:10.1037/a0028532.

SUMMARY AND CONCLUSIONS

This chapter has illustrated a number of descriptive designs, all of which describe variables by making systematic observations, summarizing information, reducing or categorizing information, or providing information about basic relationships among variables. Throughout the chapter we have emphasized that both the reliability and the validity of the variables examined are critical issues in descriptive research and directly affect the internal and external validity of the research.

Survey designs allow the researcher to describe the occurrence and frequency of variables of interest. In these designs the researcher is interested in quantitatively describing the occurrence of a variable in a population. The usefulness of the research results depends to a large extent on the measurements used and the adequacy of the sampling techniques. Researchers should make efforts to use or develop psychometrically sound instruments, choose appropriate sampling techniques, maximize return rates, and include checks between both (a) returners

and nonreturners and (b) characteristics of the sample and parameters of the population.

In descriptive designs, the researcher can examine the relationships between two or more variables. The adequacy of these designs is greatly influenced by the reliability of the measures used in operationalizing the variables of interest. Also, the size of the relationship obtained depends to some extent on the sample size; thus, many multiple regression studies include an adjustment for shrinkage to control for sample size. We hope that more researchers will use latent variables to reduce measurement error when assessing relationships between variables. As for other descriptive designs, sampling considerations and methodological strategies are extremely important in interpreting the results of multiple regression studies. We encourage researchers to use random sampling and/or to replicate their results when using descriptive designs.

Descriptive designs can be used to examine complex relations among variables. Regression analyses allow researchers to examine the effect of multiple predictor variables on a criterion variable. Moreover, regression analyses can be used to examine more complex relations concerning moderation and mediation among variables. Increasingly, counseling researchers are using moderation and mediation analyses to examine complex theoretical models. The same cautions that apply to simple passive designs also apply to the more complex designs.

We would like to offer three suggestions for counseling researchers considering a descriptive design. First, descriptive research should be undertaken from a strong theoretical grounding as much as possible. Researchers would do well to avoid questions such as: How do these sets of variables relate? How do these groups differ? Rather, theory should be used to inform the research in the determination of the variables examined. Second, descriptive designs are strengthened when they contain differential predictions. For example, theory may indicate that a variable (realistic Holland code) might be positively related to one variable (lack of accidents), not related to another (weight), and negatively related to a third (school satisfaction). A study is strengthened when these patterns of relationships are predicted and assessed. Specifically, we recommend that researchers consider examining multiple relationships, especially ones that are predicted to show results in opposite directions. Our third recommendation is that researchers pay particular attention to sample characteristics. Researchers may want to select samples in which various demographic or psychological characteristics are held constant.

For example, researchers wanting to compare "good" versus "poor" counseling sessions in terms of type of therapist response used may want to select only sessions that are temporally close. This type of selection would lessen the chance that the results were influenced by the stage of therapy.

Classification is also an important descriptive step in the scientific endeavor. Cluster analysis and latent class/profile analyses are statistical methodologies that can aid classifying individuals. The groups derived from cluster analysis, as well as the profile classes found in latent class/profile analyses depend on the instruments used and the characteristics of the sample. Therefore, instrument selection and sampling are again important considerations in using these techniques. Factor and cluster solutions should be replicated on separate samples to assure validity. It is also important to validate clusters and profile classes by linking them with other variables. Finally, it is important to note that these procedures involve many decision points, and experts often disagree on criteria for decision making. Thus, the particular methodology or analysis used often affects the results, which suggests the need for further validation.

The designs described in this chapter can be important building blocks in the scientific process. Based on a careful analysis of the current state of knowledge in a given area, the researcher can choose a design that will lead to a progressively better understanding of the content area. When chosen wisely, the descriptive designs can serve the important function of describing phenomena of interest in counseling research.

STIMULUS QUESTIONS

Questions to Test Your Knowledge about Quantitative Descriptive Designs

The purpose of this exercise is to test your understanding of some key issues regarding descriptive designs. Write down your answers to the following questions, and then discuss your responses with a peer in your class.

1. What is the difference between a mediating variable and a moderating variable?

2. There are two main types of regression described in this chapter; what are they and how do they differ?

3. Cluster analyses and latent profile/class analyses have some similarities and some differences; please describe.

4. Think about a possible research question that can be addressed through quantitative descriptive design. Use Table 13.1 to determine which statistical analysis might be most appropriate to use.

5. List three advantages of survey research.

6. The strength of descriptive research is that it allows us to describe phenomena. When might it be possible to use theory to guide the descriptive study, and when is it more helpful not to use theory?

14 Analogue Research: Maximizing Experimental Control
Chapter

This chapter focuses on analogue research in counseling, which is defined as research that is conducted under conditions that resemble or approximate the therapeutic situation. In an effort to follow Kerlinger's MAXMINCON principle, some investigators have sought to reduce bias and extraneous variables by creating tightly controlled conditions that approximate the counseling context. Not surprisingly, analogue research has historically been at the heart of the debate on naturalistic versus experimental approaches to research.

The first section of this chapter provides a brief historical overview of the use of analogue methodology in counseling; the second section provides examples of analogue studies. The third and fourth sections discuss the advantages and disadvantages of this particular methodology. The fifth section proposes that the external validity of analogue research be evaluated by examining variables that depict real-life counseling, most notably those related to the counselor, the client, and the counseling process. The sixth section maintains that the ultimate utility of analogue methodology must be evaluated within the context of current knowledge bases and existing research methodologies used in a particular topic area. The use of analogue methodology in social influence research in counseling is analyzed to demonstrate this point.

HISTORICAL OVERVIEW

Real-life counseling is a tremendously complex process. Clients differ, therapists differ, and counseling is such a highly interactive, emotionally charged, and complex communication process that it is difficult to describe, much less investigate. Over 40 years ago such complexity led Heller (1971) to conclude that the counseling interview, "while an excellent source of research hypotheses, is a poor context for isolating factors responsible for behavior change. The varied complexity of the therapeutic interaction and the inability to specify and control therapeutic operations make it difficult to obtain reliable information concerning exact agents of change" (p. 127). Heller, a strong believer in the scientific method and the use of experimental control, contended that part of the solution to investigating and understanding the complexity within counseling was to exercise the experimental control offered in what he called laboratory research: "The purpose of clinical laboratory research is to determine what factors produce change, under what conditions they operate best, and how they should be combined to produce an effective therapeutic package" (Heller, p. 127).

Basically, a counseling analogue is an experimental simulation of some aspect of the counseling process involving manipulation of some aspects of the counselor, the client, and/or the counseling process. In the past, analogues have been referred to as "miniature therapy" (Goldstein, Heller, & Sechrest, 1966) or as a "simplification strategy" (Bordin, 1965).

Keet (1948) has been credited with one of the first uses of the analogue methodology in psychotherapy research (also see Bordin, 1965; Heller, 1971; Kushner, 1978). Keet used volunteer participants and examined the efficacy of expressive (reflective) versus interpretative therapeutic statements in overcoming previously identified memory blocks on word association tasks. Interpretative statements were found to be more effective. It is interesting to note that even though subsequent research did not replicate Keet's findings (Grummon & Butler, 1953; Merrill, 1952), Bordin observed that "so great is the attractiveness of control and simplification as a research strategy that this failure [to replicate] only spurred further efforts in this direction" (p. 494). In general, however, the use of analogue research has been a relatively recent development within counseling research, a phenomenon Heller attributed to the fact that analogues are rather foreign to psychotherapy because knowledge in the clinical fields has normally been accumulated in the more naturalistic tradition (as, e.g., in the case studies of Freud). Munley (1974) attributed the slow emergence of the analogue to the reluctance of counselors to accept a contrived and highly controlled methodology that might well be too artificial and unrealistic.

Bordin (1965) wrote one of the earliest theoretical critiques of "simplification" (analogue methodology) in counseling research. He appears to have been keenly aware of the strengths and limitations of this methodology. Although the experimental control afforded by the analogue was quickly recognized, some researchers expressed concern about the generalizability or external validity of the results (e.g., Lewin, 1951; Rappaport, 1960). Bordin acknowledged that the criticisms of "simplification" research related primarily to its oversimplification of the phenomenon of interest; to counteract such problems, he proposed three rules for achieving "acceptable simplifications":

1. Start from and keep in central focus the natural phenomenon that aroused the researcher's curiosity.
2. The degree to which a researcher can safely depart from the relevant naturalistic setting is proportional to the amount already known about the phenomenon in question.
3. If not based on prior knowledge, simplification should be accompanied by empirical investigations of the naturalistic phenomenon it simulates.

Researchers initially used analogue methodology in two general lines of research (Heller, 1971). One line of research involved an analysis of therapies to "find their most potent ingredients and the conditions under which each is optimized"

(Heller, pp. 148–149); this approach included analogue studies of systematic desensitization, Rogerian facilitative conditions, and free association.

The second major approach examined the communication process, particularly in terms of the social influence process. This line of research was sparked by the applications of social psychology to counseling, particularly the work of Goldstein, Heller, and Sechrest (1966) and Strong (1968). The late 1960s and early 1970s saw a flurry of analogue studies, primarily examining the effects of counselors' behavior on client perceptions of the counselors' expertness, attractiveness, and trustworthiness. Social influence research "continued unabated" (Borgen, 1984) until the mid-1980s and has been the focus of most of the analogue research in counseling.

There are several different types of analogue studies: (a) video of counseling studies, with counselor behavior as the dependent variable; (b) video of counseling studies, with client behavior as the dependent variable; (c) quasicounseling interview studies (e.g., mock or staged counseling session), with client behavior as the dependent variable; (d) quasicounseling interview studies, with counselor behavior as the dependent variable; and (e) experimental tasks not directly resembling a counseling interview (Munley, 1974). To date, the types of analogues that investigators have used are quite broad, ranging from highly artificial recorded simulations to very realistic live simulations involving multiple sessions.

Despite Bordin's (1965) earlier proposal for "acceptable simplifications," debate over the utility of analogue methodology has persisted. A number of theoretical critiques have addressed the utility of the analogue methodology (see Gelso, 1979; Heller, 1971; Kazdin, 2003). At the center of the controversy is the questionable generalizability of analogue findings. Goldman (1978) summed up the criticisms best by claiming that the "venerated laboratory experiment has been highly overrated as a way to gain understanding of human behavior as it exists in real life. . . . [T]he laboratory has become so 'pure' that it has little or nothing to say about how people function in real life" (p. 8).

Before entering into this debate ourselves, we first provide some recent examples of analogue studies, and then discuss in greater detail the advantages and disadvantages of analogue methodology.

EXAMPLES OF ANALOGUE STUDIES

We will describe three analogue studies to provide more details about how this methodology has been used more recently by investigators. The first study, by Lee et al. (2013), utilized three vignettes to present different client-counselor scenarios to counseling trainees. The second study, by Mohr, Israel, and Sedlacek (2001), used a fictitious intake report to obtain clinical responses from counselors in training. The third study, by Wang and Kim (2010), utilized two types of brief video-analogue sessions demonstrating counseling with and without explicit multicultural competencies expressed by the counselor.

Lee and colleagues (2013) studied counseling trainees' multicultural case conceptualization in a case description of three cases. Specifically, the three cases included:

> (1) a *culture-explicit* case in which an Asian Indian female client explicitly stated that her cultural values conflicted with her desire to divorce her abusive husband, (2) a

culture-implicit case in which an African American male client stated that another student was making derogatory remarks at him (implying, but not explicitly stating, that they were racist), and (3) a *culture-not mentioned* case in which an Asian American female client stated that she had shamed her family because she did not receive an expected promotion at work. (Lee et al., p. 2)

Lee et al. (2013) gathered the data from 61 counseling trainees. They observed each case (randomly ordered) and described their case conceptualization in writing. They utilized a grounded-theory approach (qualitative method, see Chapter 16), to find content themes in the case conceptualizations as well as examining whether these content themes varied across cases. They found both general and multicultural specific themes from the content in trainees' case conceptualizations. Additionally, they found that trainees focused on diversity issues in their conceptualizations when the cases were presented with cultural concerns explicitly or implicitly.

Mohr et al. (2001) investigated the influence of counselors' attitudes toward bisexuality on counselors' clinical responses to a fictitious intake report. Specifically, the independent variable was the counselor's attitude toward bisexuality and the dependent variables were reactions to the client, anticipated reactions to the bisexual client, and psychosocial functioning.

Mohr and his colleagues used one fictitious intake report about a bisexual woman, which was used as a stimulus for each counselor's assessment and response to the client. They summarized the vignette as follows:

> … a two-paragraph fictional scenario summarizing a clinical intake session with a client named Alice, who was a 20-year-old White bisexual woman. … In the scenario, which was set in a university counseling center, the presenting problems included (a) difficulty making a career choice, (b) grief over the end of a 2-year romantic relationship with a woman, (c) a boyfriend who was having difficulty accepting the client's bisexuality. Thus, the predominant clinical issues involved issues with career indecision, negotiating emotional boundaries with parents, and romantic relationships. (Mohr et al., 2001, p. 213)

The data were gathered from 97 counselor trainees in master and doctoral programs. The authors found that attitudes regarding bisexuality were related to counselors' clinical judgments and reactions. Specifically, they found that counselors who had a negative attitude toward bisexuality assessed the function of clients to be low, anticipated biased and judgmental responses to the client, and were more likely to have negative reactions to the client.

Wang and Kim (2010) investigated how counselors' expression of multicultural competencies would be perceived by Asian American college students. They constructed two 15-minute video vignettes as the independent variable, specifically:

> A female European (White) American counselor and a female Asian American client, portrayed by a European (White) American graduate student therapist in a counseling, clinical, and school psychology program and an East Asian American undergraduate research assistant, respectively. In the counseling session, the client tells her counselor about negative interactions she and her family experienced at a restaurant and a hotel. The two video clips showed the counselor implementing either supportive counseling with the additional presence of multicultural skills competencies or supportive counseling without the competencies. For the competencies, we operationalized the seven skills of culturally appropriate intervention strategies into therapist verbal statements.

Examples of these skills include discussing experiences of racism or bias from the vantage of "healthy paranoia," attending to instances of discrimination and being mindful of sociopolitical contexts, and taking responsibility for educating clients on the process of psychological intervention. (Arredondo et al., 1996, p. 396)

The dependent variables were perceived empathetic understanding and the working alliance. They found that students who were assigned to the supportive counseling session with the multicultural competencies rated the counselor higher on the measures of alliance and empathy. These findings suggest that there is an additive effect by including multicultural competencies in session. That is, therapists who infuse multicultural competencies in their work may enhance clients' perceived empathy and strengthen the therapeutic alliance.

RESEARCH IN ACTION 14.1

Now that you have read some examples of analogue research, take some time to reflect on some *variables* within counseling process that you would like to examine in an analogue design. It could be as simple as seeing how participants may view the value of counseling when the counselor is wearing casual clothes or more formal clothes. Remember, the focus here should be on identifying an independent variable that you can manipulate, like the counselor's wardrobe. Also, think about the dependent variable(s) that are of interest to you and connected to the context.

ADVANTAGES OF ANALOGUE RESEARCH

The hallmark of analogue research is control of the experimental situation, primarily by eliminating extraneous variables, controlling confounding variables, and manipulating specified levels of an independent variable. In a counseling situation, many variables pertain to the client and counselor (e.g., personality variables, coping skills, manner of processing information, expectations, and demographic variables), to the counseling process (e.g., counselor interventions and client reactions and disclosures), and to the particular situation (e.g., room decor and arrangement, cost of therapy, and reasons for seeking help). In analogue designs, variables extraneous to the particular research problem can be eliminated or controlled. For example, participants easily can be randomly assigned to treatment conditions, thereby reducing confounds from participant variability. Also, given the technology of today, many online survey tools have the option to post videos and create a randomization schedule for the researcher. Participants also can be selected based on a particular variable (such as locus of control or level of depression), which can be either held constant across treatment conditions or varied to create levels of an independent variable. Therapists' theoretical orientation and interview behaviors can be controlled or even standardized across conditions. In short, analogue research allows for a great deal of situational control by enabling the researcher to manipulate one or more independent variables, to eliminate or hold extraneous variables constant, and to use random assignment.

Along with providing situational control, analogue methodology has the advantage of enabling the experimenter to achieve a high degree of specificity in the operational definitions of a variable. For example, level of counselor self-disclosure could be manipulated to enable examination of, say, three distinct levels of self-disclosure (no self-disclosure, 5 self-disclosures per session, 10 self-disclosures per session). In this sense, analogue methodology often offers greater precision—not only in terms of the variables under examination, but also in terms of experimental procedures. Such increased specificity is a major advantage in isolating specific events or processes in the complex activity that is counseling.

Another advantage of analogue methodology is often the reduction of practical and ethical obstacles in experimentally examining some aspect of the counseling process. Many times, real-world constraints such as financial limits and unavailability of participants can be substantially reduced by using client surrogates in an analogue design. Given that real-life counseling involves clients with real-life problems, stresses, and anxieties, experimental procedures such as randomly assigning clients to placebo groups or to waiting-list control groups can cause problems. Or certain experimental manipulations, such as varying the type of counselor feedback or type of counselor self-disclosure, may pose serious ethical dilemmas when clients with real problems are involved. Creating a situation analogous to counseling or using transcripts, audiotapes, or videotapes of counseling interactions sidesteps ethical problems with manipulations, especially with clients under some kind of duress.

DISADVANTAGES OF ANALOGUE RESEARCH

The major concern about or disadvantage of analogue research pertains to the generalizability of the research findings, or external validity. External validity is of special importance to members of the counseling profession because the primary focus of our work is on real-life, applied counseling with actual clients.

Sometimes the strengths of analogue methodology—experimental control and internal validity—result in rather artificial circumstances. The investigation may be very high in experimental precision but examine events under such artificial and contrived conditions that they no longer resemble actual counseling situations. It can even become unclear whether the research is in fact investigating the counseling process, or instead variables that are so abstract and removed from actual practice that they are irrelevant to real-life counseling. Thus, the most serious concern pertains to whether the results of a particular study can be generalized to actual counseling practice. The power of the experimental controls may result in the loss of external validity, or as Bordin (1965) stated, "oversimplification."

The limitations of analogue methodology often lead to discussions about the relative importance of internal versus external validity. The inexperienced student wants to know which is more important, or which should be the focus of initial research in an area. Although there are reasons to emphasize either internal validity or external validity in undeveloped research areas, we contend that both internal and external validity are needed in all research areas, and that the knowledge accumulated on any one topic should result from research that balances internal and external validity. Given that knowledge on any topic will accrue over time, the issue of which type of validity to examine first is often less important than the larger issue of overall balance.

RESEARCH APPLICATION 14.1

A researcher wants to examine the role of counselor empathy on client reactions (e.g., the degree to which they engage with the counselor in a defensive manner). The researcher comes to you for help. In particular, the researcher wants to use an analogue design, but is worried that counselor empathy will be difficult to convey.

Questions

What strategies could you use to maximize external validity, while maintaining internal validity? Describe the procedure that you would use.

What are the advantages and disadvantages of this approach?

What other research designs could be employed to test this question?

VARIABLES TO CONSIDER IN EVALUATING THE GENERALIZABILITY OF ANALOGUE STUDIES

The basic question concerning analogue research is: To what extent does a particular laboratory experiment resemble actual counseling circumstances? One way to evaluate the external validity of analogue methodology is to consider some of the variables that describe the situation of interest—namely, real-life counseling. We propose that the external validity of analogue research can be evaluated in part by examining the resemblance of the analogue variables to those in real-life counseling. Any given study might vary on these variables and resemble the actual counseling situation to various degrees.

There are many facets of the counseling process, or any interaction, that can be examined via analogue designs. Likely, there are many foundational decision-making processes in both the counselor and client than can be easily tested. There are traits or characteristics of the client or counselor (e.g., gender, race, smiling in session), information provided by the analogue case (e.g., client symptom profiles, counselor use of disclosures), and the interactional or process aspects (e.g., the use of more multiculturally oriented statements), all of which can be examined empirically. How individuals make judgments about viewing these variables can give us some information about how they may approach the situation in real life. Table 14.1 depicts several variables pertaining to the client, the counselor, and the counseling process; each of these variables can be evaluated as having either relatively high, moderate, or low degrees of resemblance to real-life counseling. Rarely are all of the variables relevant for a given study. If, for example, a study focuses primarily on counselor behavior, then evaluating counselor variables would likely be more

TABLE 14.1 : Evaluating the Generalizability of Analogue Methodologies
to Real-Life Counseling

Variables	Relatively High Degree of Resemblance	Moderate Degree of Resemblance	Relatively Low Degree of Resemblance
Client			
Expectation of change	Client expects treatment and change	Person expects experimental treatment	Participant expects course credit or to learn about psychology
Motivation and distress level	Client is distressed enough to seek help at a center	Person is distressed enough to seek relevant academic experiences and psychological experiments	Participant is not distressed and does not seek help; participant has ulterior motivation (such as course credit) other than seeking psychological help and change
Selection of treatment	Client often chooses therapists or type of treatment	Person selects relevant psychological experiments providing treatment	Participant is assigned to treatments and therapists/ interviewers
Presenting problem	Real-life problem typically seen in counseling	Hypothetical problems	None, or some experimental task(s)
Knowledge of problem	Relevant and current concern; high level of information processing and knowledge	Relevant but not pressing concern; moderate level of information processing and knowledge	Irrelevant or new issue; low level of information processing and knowledge
Counselor			
Counselor expectations	Client change	Moderate expectation of client change	Successful role play or interview
Role credibility	High status; appearance is role congruent	Moderate level of status	Absence of status cues; role incongruent
Knowledge bases	Broad range of knowledge about assessments, personality and counseling theories, and the counseling process	Moderate levels of knowledge about assessments, personality and counseling theories, and the counseling process	Low level of knowledge about assessments, personality and counseling theories, and the counseling process
Counseling skill	High levels of procedural skills within the counseling process	Moderate levels of procedural skills within the counseling process	Low levels of procedural skills within the counseling process

(continued)

TABLE 14.1 Evaluating the Generalizability of Analogue Methodologies to Real-Life Counseling *(continued)*

Variables	Relatively High Degree of Resemblance	Moderate Degree of Resemblance	Relatively Low Degree of Resemblance
Motivation level	Highly motivated to provide therapeutic relationship and facilitate change	Moderately motivated to provide therapy; possibly some motivation for experimental change	Not motivated to provide therapy; primary goal is to conduct an interview
Experience level	10 years +	3rd-year doctoral student	1st-year M.A. student
Counseling Process and Setting			
Assessment	Client is carefully diagnosed and goals established	Person may be assessed to determine congruence with treatment goals	Participant is not assessed; goals for specific individual lacking
Interventions	Specifically targeted to client's presenting problems	Relevant to person's problem	Not relevant to participant's concerns or problems
Duration	Several normal-length therapy sessions over time	A few normal-length sessions	A single brief (10 minutes or so) session
Interpersonal interchange	Counselor and client interact and exchange information	Counselor and client/participant interact on restricted topic or in some defined manner	Participant views counseling scenario but does not interact with a counselor
Client reactions	Client processes the counseling experience and reacts in some way to the relevant information	Person reacts to restricted topic or semirelevant topic	Participant views counseling scenario and responds hypothetically
Client change or outcome	Client changes or is different in some way because of the counseling interchange	Person may change in some way, providing the treatment is successful	Participant does not change in any way because the counseling scenario was not personally relevant
Environment	Professional treatment center	Facility that may not offer regular treatment services	Laboratory setting or classroom

important to consider than, say, client variables. For research purposes, it may be useful to increase the specificity of these evaluations by developing Likert-type items to assess each variable. Here we use three rather general categories (low, moderate, and high) for each variable primarily to illustrate varying degrees of resemblance on each dimension. Moreover, variables listed in the table were developed through rational means; empirical research may well identify new variables or rule out some of the variables in this table.

Client Variables

A number of variables pertaining to clients or participants directly relate to the generalizability of research findings to actual counseling practice. We now discuss several client variables that illustrate important aspects of clients seeking counseling and then relate these variables to evaluating the generalizability of a particular study.

There are many examples of how analogue research can be utilized with simple changes to client's demographic information. For instance, researchers have randomized counselors to one of two conditions: (a) a case where the client is a woman or (b) where the client is a man. The case material is identical with this one exception. The instructions are to have the counselors determine a diagnosis. In these studies, women are typically diagnosed with depression, personality disorders at a higher rate than men (Becker & Lamb, 1994; Caplan & Cosgrove, 2004; Potts, Burnam, & Wells, 1991). These analogue studies built the foundation for Owen and colleagues (2010) to develop a measure of microaggressions against women and tested it in a real-life counseling setting. They found that as women reported that their therapist expressed microaggressions against women, their alliance with the therapist was negatively affected as well as their overall therapy outcomes.

Additionally, there are ways to examine clients' presenting concerns or beliefs about their distress via analogue research. In most actual counseling situations, clients experience personal problems and are seeking help or healing from the counselor (Wampold, 2007). These personal problems typically cause anxiety and distress of some sort, as people find themselves "failing" where they want to "succeed" in some way. As people cope with their "current concerns" (Klinger, 1971), they typically engage in a wide range of cognitive, affective, and behavioral trial-and-error processes (Heppner & Krauskopf, 1987). Because these clients typically have thought about their problem and tried a number of possible solutions, they have compiled some kind of knowledge base (whether accurate or inaccurate) pertaining to this problem. Moreover, many people seeking psychological help have expectations about being treated. They often choose a certain therapist based on a recommendation or reputation, and they are motivated to change in some way. In short, typically clients seeking psychological help enter therapy (a) with expectations about change; (b) with expectations about the therapist and treatment; (c) under distress, and thus in a motivated state; (d) with the intention of discussing specific problematic situations; and (e) with a range of information or knowledge about their particular problems. Although there may well be other variables that depict other aspects of clients seeking help, we recommend that researchers evaluating the relevance of analogue methodology begin by considering client variables.

Table 14.1 lists these five client variables and what might constitute relatively high, moderate, and low degrees of resemblance of each to real-life counseling. A relatively high degree of resemblance for client expectations might, for example, entail a client expecting treatment and change, as opposed to a participant simply expecting course credit (low degree of resemblance). Also related to client expectations is the way in which treatment is selected. Clients often choose a type of treatment or counselor based on their presenting problem or a counselor's reputation (high resemblance), rather than being assigned to particular treatments and therapists/interviewers (low resemblance). Distress and motivation levels may also be polarized; a client is distressed enough to seek help at a treatment center (high resemblance), whereas a participant is part of a convenient or captive participant pool and merely seeks course credit (low resemblance) rather than seeking psychological help and change. Perhaps most important, actual clients have both "current concerns" or real problems and a high level of information processing and knowledge about that problem (high resemblance); conversely, participants assigned to a potentially irrelevant task have relatively low knowledge levels about the task and thus represent low resemblance to real-life counseling.

The main point is that several client variables might be considered in evaluating the generalizability of particular analogue methodologies within counseling. Strong and Matross (1973) facetiously referred to typical participants in social influence investigations as "client surrogates." This rather good phrase underscores participant substitution and its many implications, all of which commonly occur in most analogue studies. If an experimenter designs a study in which the participants do not closely resemble actual clients, then the generalizability of the findings to actual clients comes under question.

Counselor Variables

A number of variables pertaining to counselors or interviewers also directly relate to the generalizability of analogue research findings to actual counseling practice. In the ideal therapeutic counseling relationship, the counselor is experienced and has a broad range of knowledge about assessments, personality and counseling theories, and the counseling process in general. In addition, the counselor has high levels of procedural skill—the interpersonal and counseling skills required to in fact be therapeutic with a client. The therapist also is highly motivated to provide a therapeutic relationship, as reflected in establishing Rogerian conditions such as empathy and unconditional positive regard, or perhaps through other ways of establishing a strong working alliance. Thus, the therapist approaches counseling with the expectation that the therapy will be successful, and that the client will change in some desired way(s). Finally, the therapist appears to be a credible professional, an expert and trustworthy person who can provide therapeutic assistance.

Table 14.1 suggests relatively high, moderate, and low degrees of resemblance of six counselor variables to actual counselors. For example, high degrees of resemblance characterize counselors possessing a broad range of relevant knowledge about counseling and high levels of procedural skill. Such counselors have a considerable amount of counseling experience. By contrast, relatively low resemblance to actual therapists characterizes interviewers or inexperienced counselors who lack both essential knowledge about counseling and the skills to actually do counseling. The other variables can also be polarized, so that people resemble actual counselors when they (a) are highly motivated to provide a therapeutic relationship and facilitate change, (b) expect counseling to be successful and the client to change, and (c) appear credible and congruent within a therapeutic role. Conversely, a person having a relatively low resemblance to actual therapists may be characterized as not intending to provide a therapeutic and caring relationship, but rather being motivated solely to conduct an interview. Moreover, often the interviewer reflects an absence of status and credibility cues.

In some historical research in counseling, the counselor variables under examination did not closely resemble the role or behaviors of a typical counselor; several examples are apparent within what is referred to as the social or interpersonal influence area in counseling (see Corrigan, Dell, Lewis, & Schmidt, 1980; Heppner & Claiborn, 1989; Heppner & Dixon, 1981). In the past, researchers have manipulated a broad range of cues associated with perceived counselor expertness, attractiveness, and trustworthiness. One goal of much of this research has been to identify behaviors and cues that enhance the counselor's credibility and subsequent ability to affect the client. A common research strategy has been to examine extreme levels of an independent variable to ascertain whether that particular variable has an effect on client perceptions of the counselor, but all too often the counselor variables have not resembled the role of a typical counselor closely enough.

For example, in attempting to lower the perceived expertness of an interviewer, participants have been told, "We had originally scheduled Dr. _____ to talk with you, but unfortunately he notified us that he wouldn't be able to make it today. In his place we have Mr. _____, a student who unfortunately has had no interviewing experience and has been given only a brief explanation of the purpose of this study. We think he should work out all right, though. Now, if you would step this way . . ." (Strong & Schmidt, 1970, p. 82). Likewise, in some cases the procedural skills of interviewers have been manipulated to produce interviewer behaviors that do not closely resemble those of actual therapists. For example, a counselor portraying an unattractive role "ignored the interviewee when he entered the office, did not smile at him, did not look beyond a few cold glances, leaned away from him, and portrayed disinterest, coldness, and boredom" (Schmidt & Strong, 1971, p. 349).

Gelso (1979) referred to such procedures as "experimental deck stacking" and raised questions about the utility of research on such atypical counselor behaviors. In short, although a considerable amount of information was obtained about events contributing to clients' perceptions of counselor credibility, the generalizability of some of this knowledge to actual counseling practice is questionable because of the relatively low resemblance of the events to actual therapist behaviors. In contrast the counselor's behavior from Wang and Kim (2010) is much more in line with what is to be expected in effective counseling.

In sum, to evaluate the generalizability of analogue research to actual counseling practice, it is important to consider several variables resembling actual counselors' knowledge bases, skills, expectations, and role credibility.

Counseling Process and Setting

We must also consider a set of variables related to the counseling process when evaluating the external validity of analogue research. In a real-life counseling situation, the counselor and client typically meet for a number of sessions, often once per week, extending over several weeks. Typically, the client and his or her presenting problem are carefully diagnosed, and treatment goals as well as intervention strategies are tailored specifically to this particular client. Most important, the counselor and client freely interact and exchange a wealth of information. The client is not a tabula rasa, but instead assimilates the new information into his or her existing conceptual framework and reacts in some way. Indeed, there are several taxonomies to gauge client reactions. These taxonomies could be helpful to analogue researchers in order to more closely approximate an actual counseling setting (see Hill, Helms, Spiegel, & Tichenor, 1988; McCullough et al., 2003; Watson, Schein, & McMullen, 2010, for examples of client reactions taxonomies). In a positive counseling situation, the client changes in some desirable manner, such as learning new behaviors; altering beliefs, attitudes, or feelings; and adapting to environmental demands more effectively. The environmental context for the therapeutic situation is typically a professional treatment center of some sort, a university counseling center, or a community mental health center.

Table 14.1 provides examples of relatively high, moderate, and low degrees of resemblance of seven counseling process variables to actual counseling practice. In terms of assessment and interventions, high resemblance characterizes those situations in which the client is carefully diagnosed and interventions are specifically targeted to the client's problems. Low resemblance involves a lack of assessment, as well as interventions that are not relevant to a participant's concerns or problems. Analogues that resemble the actual therapy process involve multiple 50-minute sessions extended over several weeks (as opposed to one-shot, 10-minute counseling scenarios). In addition, analogues that resemble actual counseling include rather extended interactions between the counselor and client during which a broad range of information is exchanged, as distinct from analogues that do not include live interactions between counselor and client. The analogue also can be evaluated in terms of how much and what kind of information the client processes; high resemblance entails the client's processing the counseling experience repeatedly over time, whereas low resemblance entails the participant's responding to counseling scenarios in a hypothetical and often irrelevant manner. The analogue might also be evaluated in terms of therapeutic outcomes: Did the client change in some desired way? High resemblance involves change of personally relevant behaviors, thoughts, or feelings, whereas low resemblance entails a lack of change on the part of the participant, most likely because the counseling scenario was not personally relevant. Finally, the analogue can be evaluated in terms of the environment or context of the counseling situation. Analogues involving a high resemblance to actual practice take place in a professional environment, such as a treatment or counseling center, whereas an experimental laboratory setting or classroom offers relatively low resemblance.

CREATING ANALOGUE STUDIES THAT MORE CLOSELY RESEMBLE REAL LIFE

Up to now, we have mainly focused on analogue designs that relate to the process of counseling. However, a great deal of research examines factors inhibiting individuals to seek help in general. As such, we would like to provide another example of an analogue study that addresses a noncounseling situation. Hammer and Vogel (2010) examined the effects of adapting a brochure to encourage men to seek help for depression. They examined a brochure, which was part of a large national campaign entitled "Real Men, Real Depression." This campaign highlighted men's personal struggles with depression and how they sought help to address their concerns. For the study, they utilized three brochures: (a) the original brochure for the national campaign, (b) a gender neutral brochure (e.g., "Real People, Real Depression"), and (c) a brochure tailored for men based on the masculinity literature (e.g., which used terms like mental health consultant vs. counselor, and phrases like "attacking the problem"). They randomized 1,397 depressed men who had not sought help for their depression to one of these three conditions. The dependent measures were attitudes about seeking help and self-stigma related to seeking help. The results indicated that the male-sensitive brochure was associated with more positive attitudes about seeking help and lower levels of self-stigma.

This analogue study is particularly noteworthy in that the experimental conditions were imbedded in an actual campaign that could benefit from modified brochure. Additionally, the inclusion criteria, men who were depressed and have not sought help, is important to make the study resemble the target audience in the real world. Although, as Hammer and Vogel (2010) cautioned, the generalizability of the study to extended other men is unclear; moreover it is unclear how many men actually followed through with seeking help.

Evaluating Analogue Utility within an Existing Knowledge Base

Clearly, utility of a particular methodology—in this case, analogue methodology—is contingent upon previous research and the accumulated knowledge bases. There is no doubt that the analogue methodology is powerful and useful. However, when it is by far the most frequently used methodology, the resultant body of knowledge becomes unbalanced and tends to emphasize one methodological approach to the exclusion of others. In short, the utility of the knowledge obtained from the analogue methodology diminishes if this methodology far outweighs other methodologies in a particular research area. Gelso (1979) discussed this issue in terms of paradigm fixation or where an area of research is dominated by one design (e.g., analogue, qualitative, experimental).

When it comes to analogue research, the issue of external generalizability cannot be understated, especially if the particular topic under study has been dominated by the utilization of analogue studies, and very few tests of these finding with real counseling cases.For example, in the past investigators examined the factors that affected counselor's ability to affect change in clients almost totally by using analogue methodologies; unfortunately these results were not upheld when these findings were tested in actual counseling situations (see Heppner & Claiborn, 1989).The ease of doing analogue research can be enticing. Indeed, analogue research is less challenging to conduct in comparison to some other research designs. For instance, it can take years to successfully conduct a counseling outcome study. However, just because analogue research may be easier and less time consuming, these criteria do not make analogue research always result in the best methodological strategy. That is, over time studies, in the field, should progress from analogue designs to testing similar hypotheses in the real world. As noted previously, Owen et al (2010) utilized existing analogue research examining sex biases in counseling, along with other sources of information, to develop a new measure of microaggressions against women in actual counseling sessions. Thus, there should be a progression of testing theoretically meaningful constructs from laboratory studies and both adapting and testing those findings to the real world.

How can you determine whether analogue research is appropriate for your study? Here are some general guidelines/questions to consider:

1. Is there a large literature base in applied settings on your topic? Can additional research using the analogue method significantly increase our knowledge base? Analogue research may be helpful for extending or refining well-established findings in the field. However, there may need to be some caution if the analogue study proposed has been applied in the real world.

2. Would it be unethical to do the study in the real world? For instance, it is likely unethical to randomize clients to conditions where their counselor will say derogatory comments to them. However, in an analogue study, this can be easily manipulated.

3. What resources do you have available? In general, conducting analogue research is less expensive and costly in terms of resources. For instance, many researchers do not have access to examine full-time professional counselors' practice with all of their clients to determine whether there are sex biases in their sessions. However, it may be more feasible to conduct an analogue study to determine whether they perceive sex biases in fictional cases.

In sum, the utility of any given methodology in a particular topic area must be evaluated within the context of existing knowledge bases and prior research methodologies. Studies that consistently use the same methodology create a knowledge base that is vulnerable with regard to the particular disadvantage of that methodology. Moreover, when the overwhelming majority of research in an area derives from the same methodology, the strength and utility of the knowledge base is unclear.

SUMMARY AND CONCLUSIONS

Without a doubt, the analogue methodology can be and often is powerful and useful. In terms of Kerlinger's MAXMINCON principle, analogue research typically allows for a great deal of experimental control to manipulate one or more independent variables, eliminate or hold extraneous variables constant, and use random assignment. The major question surrounding analogue methodology in counseling research pertains to the external validity of the results; sometimes analogue methodology examines circumstances so far removed from actual counseling practice that the research becomes oversimplified and artificial. We propose that the external validity of analogue research can be evaluated in part by examining variables that depict real-life counseling in three categories: (a) the client, (b) the counselor, and (c) the counseling process and setting.

We suggest that analogues fall on a continuum from low to high resemblance to the counseling situation. Given the scarcity of empirical research, the relationship between analogues with various degrees of resemblance to actual counseling is unclear. Nonetheless, as Kerlinger (1986) has indicated, the temptation to incorrectly interpret the results of analogue (laboratory) research as they apply to real-life phenomena is great. When an investigator obtains highly statistically significant results in the laboratory, it is tempting to assume that these results would also be applicable to actual counseling practice. As a general rule, *it is questionable to generalize beyond the conditions or population used in a given study.* Thus, if an investigator is primarily interested in generalizing about clients, counselors, and/or the counseling process, then the analogue methodology must be evaluated with those particular conditions or populations in mind. Depending on the degree of resemblance to actual counseling practice, the investigator may be able to conclude that the analogue results apply to

actual counseling. Again, as a general rule, *relationships found under laboratory conditions must be tested again in the context to which we wish to generalize—typically, actual counseling.*

But does this mean that all analogues should closely resemble the conditions of actual counseling practice? We believe not. In our opinion, a considerable amount of information can be obtained about counseling from tightly controlled analogue studies that do not closely resemble actual counseling. This may well be the case early in a line of research, when relatively little is known about certain variables. For example, researchers have collected a substantial amount of knowledge from tightly controlled analogue studies about events that affect clients' perceptions of counselor expertness, attractiveness, and trustworthiness (see Corrigan et al., 1980; Heppner & Claiborn, 1989).

The extent to which an investigator emphasizes external validity, and perhaps sacrifices internal validity when examining events in counseling, depends on the knowledge base that currently exists in that particular line of research. One argument states that if relatively little is empirically known, the researcher should avoid sacrificing internal validity (cf. Kerlinger, 1986). This reasoning emphasizes the role of internal validity in making scientific advancement. Another argument holds that the powerful analogue methodology can be used to refine knowledge obtained from less internally valid field situations (cf. Gelso, 1979). In this way, the strength of the analogue (precision and experimental control) can be taken full advantage of, and the results may be more readily interpreted within the existing base of knowledge collected in the field. Both lines of reasoning have merit and pertain to a central theme of this book—namely, that the strengths or weaknesses of any particular methodology for a specific research area are related to the existing knowledge base and prior research methods used in that area. In line with Bordin's (1965) recommendation, we suggest that analogue research be combined with empirical investigations conducted in a field setting to create knowledge bases that emphasize both internal and external validity.

STIMULUS QUESTIONS

Analyzing Analogue Studies

This exercise is designed to give you practice in analyzing an analogue study, weighing the advantages and limitations of this research method. We suggest that you pair yourself with a colleague in your class, respond to the following questions individually, and then compare your responses with your colleague's. Pick one of the three recent examples of analogue studies in the second section of this chapter; copy and read that article, and then answer the following questions.

1. One of the advantages of an analogue study is control of the experimental situation. In the study you chose, what independent variable(s) was (were) manipulated by researchers? What extraneous variables were eliminated? Was random assignment used in any way?

2. Another advantage of an analogue study is a high degree of specificity in the operational definition of the dependent variables. What was the operational definition of the dependent variables in this study?

3. What were the main advantages of using an analogue methodology for this study?

4. In order to make the analogue study similar to actual counseling, what did researchers do in this study?

5. What would be some of the possible practical and ethical obstacles that the researchers might well have encountered if they would have tried to examine the same or similar research questions in an actual counseling situation?

6. The major disadvantage of analogue studies is the threats to external validity related to the artificial circumstances of the study. In your view, what factors were the most serious threats to the external validity of the study?

7. Discuss the main conclusions from the study relative to the limitations of the study. What do you believe can be concluded from this study?

Single-Subject Designs: Learning from the Richness of a Sample Size of 1

Studying the individual to understand more about humanity has been a major interest driving students to study counseling and psychology in general. Understanding ourselves and those close to us can be a fascinating endeavor. For example, what makes one individual experience despair while another remains resilient in similar situations? Moreover, single-subject designs are likely the most applicable to counselors in their daily clinical practice as each client presents a single-subject study.

In the past, applied psychologists have sought such answers about an array of individuals by carefully examining single cases, studying a rare psychological phenomenon, or studying an intensive treatment effect with an individual client. However, methodological issues have plagued the development of a scientific analysis of individuals to the point where the study of just one person has sometimes been regarded as unscientific. Error variance, extraneous variables, and numerous sources of bias—major threats to Kerlinger's MAXMINCON principle—have beset researchers using a single subject.

Consequently, many more studies in our scientific journals rely on studying groups rather than single individuals. The field has conducted many more investigations that produce group averages or means as a way to promote understanding of individual behavior. Single-subject designs are not currently utilized extensively in counseling research. For example, a content analysis of the articles published from 1990 to 2001 in the *Journal of Counseling and Development* (*JCD*; Bangert & Baumberger, 2005) revealed only 1% of the articles (two studies) used a single-subject design. As Balkin (editor of *JCD*) noted: "From my perspective, the issue is not that single subject designs is not valued, but rather is simply not utilized... the paradigm of focusing on educational research is not necessarily a good fit for counselors. Counselors do not have abundant access to large, intact groups. Rather, counselors often see individuals and small groups" (personal communication, July 17, 2014). Further as Kazdin (2003) maintained when making valid inferences about human behavior, "there is nothing inherent to the approach that requires groups... findings obtained with groups are not necessarily more generalizable than those obtained with the individual case" (p. 265). Moreover, with the increased availability of different kinds of sophisticated statistical software to analyze single-subject data (e.g., Dennin & Ellis, 2003; Kratochwill & Levin, 2014; Levin & Wampold, 1999; Shadish, Kyse, & Rindskopf, 2013), there are more opportunities to examine a variety of issues within the counselor and client domains that have promise to increase understanding of topics of importance to counseling.

A broad range of scholarship has been very loosely labeled under the term *single-subject designs*. These studies have ranged from loosely controlled anecdotal observations to highly stringent and rigorous experimental designs. This chapter will focus on ways to increase the scientific rigor and validity of investigations that study just one individual such that they can be of maximum benefit to the field. The central thesis of this chapter is that intensive single-subject designs, like other experimental designs, can play an important role in the pursuit of knowledge within the counseling profession. However, important distinctions must be made concerning different types of studies that use a single subject, and concerning the varying amounts of experimental control that are used. This chapter will present a variety of approaches that can be considered single-subject designs. In all cases, single-subject research examines variables that vary within the subject over time. Therefore, single-subject designs involve a longitudinal perspective achieved by repeated observations or measurements of the variable(s). In terms of the type of observations, the data can be quantitative and/or qualitative. Quantitative data can be categorical, ordinal, interval, or ratio. Qualitative data, in contrast, take the form of text derived from interviews with participants. A critical distinguishing feature among the designs pertains to the operation of the independent variable; it can be either manipulated or simply observed. Single-subject designs can also differ in the goal or focus of the research. The goal of the research can focus on either testing or generating hypotheses—in other words, testing a theory or discovering new information.

We will discuss three categories of single-subject designs in this chapter: (a) uncontrolled case studies, (b) intensive single-subject quantitative designs, and (c) single-subject experimental designs. Briefly, the uncontrolled case study typically does not contain systematic observations, but rather contains many uncontrolled variables. A defining feature of intensive single-subject designs are systematic, repeated, and multiple observations of a client, dyad, or group to identify and compare relationships among variables. Even though both the single-subject experimental and the single-subject intensive quantitative designs share a number of similarities and both use quantitative data, the hallmark and distinguishing feature of the single-subject experimental design is the manipulation of the independent variable. Conversely, in the intensive single-subject quantitative designs the independent variable is observed.

The chapter is divided into four major sections. The first section provides a brief historical perspective on the use of single-subject designs within psychology, and particularly within applied psychology. By understanding the historical context, students can better appreciate how this particular design was born and how it has changed as the research methods have become more sophisticated within the field of applied psychology. Second, we differentiate the uncontrolled traditional "case study" from the intensive single-subject design. Unfortunately, there are often misconceptions about single-subject designs, in part based on uncontrolled methodologies, and we want to dispel the myth that all single-subject designs are unscientific and cannot add important information to the counseling literature. It is hoped that this discussion and illustrative examples will not only help students understand important methodological issues in studying individuals, but also promote an understanding of the value and richness of the more rigorous single-subject designs. In the third section, we will focus on single-subject experimental designs (where the independent variable is manipulated). We discuss several defining features of these time-series designs, and then describe and illustrate two different types of designs: AB time series and multiple baselines. In the final section we discuss advantages and limitations of single-subject designs.

A HISTORICAL PERSPECTIVE OF SINGLE-SUBJECT DESIGNS

The study of individual subjects not only has a long history in psychology, but also has played a prominent role in the development of the applied professions. Perhaps the most extensive chronology of the historical sequence of events affecting the development of the single-subject design is to be found in Barlow and Hersen (1984); the interested reader is directed to that source for a more detailed account.

When psychology was initially developing into a science, the first experiments were performed on individual subjects. For example, during an autopsy of a man who had been unable to speak intelligibly, Broca discovered a lesion in the third frontal convolution of the cerebral cortex. The discovery that this area was the speech center of the brain led to the systematic examination of various destroyed brain parts and their relationship to behavior (Barlow & Hersen, 1984). Likewise, Wundt made pioneering advances in perception and sensation by examining specific individuals' introspective experience of light and sound. Ebbinghaus, using a series of repeated measurements, made important advances in learning and memory by examining retention in specific individuals. Both Pavlov's and Skinner's conclusions were gleaned from experiments on single organisms, which subsequently were repeatedly replicated with other organisms. In short, important findings and advances in psychology with wide generalizability have been made from systematic observations of single individuals.

At the beginning of the 20th century, a number of advances facilitating the examination and comparison of groups of subjects were made. The invention of descriptive and inferential statistics not only facilitated group comparisons, but also emphasized a philosophy of comparing the averages of groups rather than studying individuals. Barlow and Hersen (1984) noted that the pioneering work and philosophy of Fisher on inferential statistics was most likely influenced by the fact that Fisher was an agronomist. He was concerned with the farm plots that on average yielded better crops given certain fertilizers, growing conditions, and so forth; individual plants per se were not the focus. In short, as psychology developed in the middle of the 20th century, the methods of inquiry were primarily influenced by statistical techniques such as the analysis of variance.

Meanwhile, in the early 1900s the primary, if not sole, methodology for investigating emotional and behavioral problems within the applied fields of psychiatry, counseling, and clinical psychology was the individual case study. Thus, cases such as Breuer's treatment of Anna O. and Freud's Frau Emmy formed the basis of "scientific" observations, which gradually grew into theories of personality and psychotherapy. These studies of therapeutically successful and unsuccessful cases were not tightly controlled investigations from a methodological standpoint. In addition, the typical practitioner was not well trained in the scientific method of critical thinking, and such practitioners extrapolated from the early case studies in fundamentally erroneous ways.

However, as the fields of counseling and clinical psychology developed in the 1940s and 1950s, more and more clinicians became aware of the inadequacies of the uncontrolled case study (Barlow & Hersen, 1984). Greater methodological sophistication led the applied psychologists to operationalize variables, to adopt the model of between-groups comparisons, and to adopt Fisher's methods of statistical analysis. Armed with these new methodological tools, researchers attempted to document the effectiveness of a wide range of therapeutic techniques, as well as the efficacy of therapy itself. These efforts were most likely fueled by the writing of Hans Eysenck, who repeatedly claimed that the profession did not have very compelling evidence for the effectiveness of therapy (Eysenck, 1952, 1961, 1965). In fact, Eysenck claimed that a client's chance of improving was about the same whether he or she entered therapy or was placed on a waiting list (Eysenck, 1952). Eysenck's charges concerning the lack of empirical support for therapy's effectiveness challenged the very existence of the therapeutic professions.

Although it has taken considerable time, researchers have begun to unravel the evidence concerning the efficacy of therapy. Paul (1967) noted that a global measurement of therapeutic effectiveness was inappropriate because of the overwhelming complexity and number of confounding variables. He suggested that investigators instead examine the question, "What treatment, by whom, is most effective for this individual with that specific problem, and under which set of circumstances?" (p. 111). Others noted that clients were erroneously conceptualized as being similar to each other (the uniformity myth; Kiesler, 1966) rather than as individuals with differences that clearly interact with counseling outcomes. Still other investigators noted that the group comparisons masked important variations across clients, specifically that some clients improved but other clients actually became worse (Truax & Carkhuff, 1967; Truax & Wargo, 1966). In short, although group comparison methods and inferential statistics substantially facilitated research on the effects of psychotherapy, researchers quickly encountered a number of confounding variables that underscored the complexity of the therapeutic experience.

In response to the confusion about and the complexity within the therapeutic process, other methodologies have been subsequently proposed and explored, such as naturalistic studies (Kiesler, 1971), process research (Hoch & Zubin, 1964), and a more intensive, experimental single-subject design (Bergin & Strupp, 1970). On the surface it might seem that the applied professions have come full circle, returning to the study of the individual. This is true only in part; there is considerably more methodological sophistication in scientifically studying an individual subject today than there was during the early part of the 20th century. Indeed, in 2005 the American Psychological Association Council of Representatives adopted a policy on what constitutes empirical-based practice in psychology. This policy included single-subject designs (i.e., systematic case studies, single-case experimental designs).

THE UNCONTROLLED CASE STUDY VERSUS THE INTENSIVE SINGLE-SUBJECT QUANTITATIVE DESIGN

In this section, we will discuss two types of designs—what might best be described as an uncontrolled "case study" as opposed to an intensive single-subject quantitative design. To begin, we will provide some examples of studies that have been conducted in this area. By reading studies done in applied psychology that utilize both of these approaches, we hope to increase understanding of the range of methods as well as to appreciate the richness of data that can be derived from the more elaborate and intensive designs.

In the past, the prototypical design for studying an individual was the uncontrolled case study. "Case study" here refers to a study that simply consists of the following characteristics: observations of an individual client, dyad, or group made under unsystematic and uncontrolled conditions, often in retrospect. Observations may be unplanned and may consist of "recollections" or intermittent records of statements or behaviors that seem to support a particular hypothesis. The lack of experimental control means that it is difficult to exclude many rival hypotheses that might be plausible in explaining the client's behavior, and thus this type of study provides ambiguous information that is difficult to interpret clearly.

Daniels (1976) provides a good historical example of the traditional case study. In his investigation of the effects of thought stopping in treating obsessional thinking, he reported that he found the sequential use of several techniques to be beneficial with clients who wished to control depressing thoughts, obsessive thinking, constant negative rumination, or acute anxiety attacks. The sequential techniques he used consisted of thought stopping (Wolpe, 1969), counting from 10 to 1 (Campbell, 1973), cue-controlled relaxation (Russell & Sipich, 1973), and a modification of covert conditioning. Training consisted of three one-hour sessions to teach the client the various techniques. Daniels reported that these procedures were successful and that clients responded positively to a "sense of control and immediate success" (p. 131). Although this report may be a useful source of ideas for generating hypotheses for future research, the lack of experimental control makes it difficult to interpret the results unambiguously. Clients may have felt compelled in some way to report success, or perhaps the successful effects were temporary and short-lived, or maybe techniques other than thought stopping were responsible for any client changes.

More recently, investigators have used single subjects in counseling research by examining variables much more systematically, intensively, and rigorously. These studies have been designed to much more closely represent our definition of intensive single-subject quantitative design. As you read the following examples, note that they (a) are done in a much more systematic fashion than the case study approach; (b) consist of repeated, multiple observations including multimodal assessment of cognitive, behavioral, and affective variables; (c) were conducted by observing a clearly defined variable; (d) used observations that were planned before the beginning of data collection; (e) allowed for the collection of process and outcome data; and (f) involved comparisons of some sort, which is essential for establishing scientific evidence. Later in this chapter we will discuss how these structural issues are included in different ways within AB designs and multiple-baseline designs; for now just notice these structural elements as we provide some examples of applied research using an intensive single-subject approach.

Gullestad and Wilberg (2011) provide an example of an intensive single-subject quantitative design. They observed one client who met the diagnostic criteria for borderline personality disorder, and obsessive-compulsive personality disorder as well as the criteria for other disorders including bipolar II, social phobia, and eating disorder not-otherwise specified. The client's treatment included 18 weeks of day treatment as well as long-term outpatient treatment. The authors measured both process and outcome data obtained through client report as well as semistructured interviews with the client and counselors. More specifically, measures were used to assess attachment styles; reflective functioning or the ability to reflect upon one's own mental states; psychological distress; and interpersonal functioning. In addition, both the client and counselor gave subjective impressions of treatment effectiveness. Outcome measures, which consisted of the Symptom Checklist-90-Revised (Derogatis, 1983), Circumplex of Interpersonal Problems (Pedersen, 2002), and the Global Assessment of Functioning, were collected immediately after the intake and then repeated at 8, 18, 36, and 54 months (termination). The semistructured interviews occurred at the end of treatment. The primary goal of the study was to describe the link between changes in reflective functioning and changes in psychological distress. With regard to the primary goal: (a) comparisons were made between the pre-treatment statements during the interviews examining reflective functioning to the clients' statements during interviews three years later, (b) changes in symptomology over the course of treatment, and (c) the overall reflections of the client and counselors at the end of treatment.

Outcome measures indicated that treatment was generally positive, but the client reported some increases in her symptomology during the course of treatment. Moreover, the client started at a questionable or low reflective functioning (e.g., nonspecific, general, or superficial reflections of the self), but ended treatment in the ordinary range (e.g., capacity to make sense of internal experiences, but not overly sophisticated).

The study by Gullestad and Wilberg (2011) nicely illustrates an intensive examination of a single subject within a therapeutic context. A great deal of data were systematically collected from multiple sources (client, counselor, raters) and across time. In addition, the objective and subjective data collected from various perspectives allowed comparisons to be made and subsequent conclusions to be drawn based on the convergence of a wide range of information, rather than on a single data point. It is important to note that the generalizability of the conclusions obtained from this single case is unclear, and that replications are needed.

Tasca and colleagues (2011) provide another good example of an intensive single-subject quantitative design with their study of interpersonal processes in psychodynamic-interpersonal (PI) and cognitive-behavioral (CB) group therapies, wherein they examined two groups for the treatment of binge-eating-disordered clients. The authors employed an intensive single-subject quantitative design to compare the groups as a means of increasing scientific knowledge about therapist behaviors in these types of treatments. Similar to Gullestad and Wilberg (2011), this study used multiple measures of process and outcome variables from multiple perspectives (clients and raters). Specifically, information from the clients' perspective was obtained by assessing perceptions of their depressive symptoms and binging episodes over the 16 weeks of treatment via self-report. The sessions were taped and coded based on counselors' interpersonal behaviors (e.g., were they more directive, or giving of autonomy). The authors hypothesized that the PI counselor would be more autonomy-giving to the group members and the CB counselor group would be more directive based on the theoretical underpinnings for these approaches.

Conclusions from this study were that both treatments worked quite well for the clients. In both groups three clients dropped out of treatment, but for those who remained, they decreased their depressive symptoms and reported binge-eating episodes. Moreover, the data indicated that the counselors did indeed enact different interpersonal stances based on their theoretical models, with the PI therapist was more autonomy-giving to the group, while the CB therapist was more directive. Thus, the treatments both worked, and possibly worked in slightly different ways to assist the clients.

Methodologically, the important point here is that conclusions and hypotheses that can direct future research were obtained by examining the convergence of data from multiple sources over time from an intensive single-subject quantitative design. Webb, Campbell, Schwartz, and Sechrest (1966) called this convergence from multiple sources and multiple observations "triangulation." They maintained that multiple independent measures can provide a form of cross-validation.

There are many examples of highly rigorous single-subject quantitative designs that have been published in leading empirical journals. In fact, several journals have specific submission requirements and requests for "evidence-based case studies." For example, the APA journal *Psychotherapy* defines these articles as Evidenced-Based Case Studies. More specifically:

> The goal of these *Evidenced-Based Case Studies* will be to integrate verbatim clinical case material with standardized measures of process and outcome evaluated at different times across treatment. That is, authors should describe clinical vignettes highlighting key interventions and mechanisms of change regarding their specific approach to treatment in the context of empirical scales. At minimum the report should include the assessment (from patient or independent rater perspective, not therapist) of at least two standardized outcome measures, global functioning and target symptom (i.e. depression, anxiety, etc.), as well as one process measure (i.e. therapeutic alliance, session depth, emotional experiencing, etc.) evaluated on at least three separate occasions. Optimally, such a report would include several outcome measures assessing a wide array of functioning such as global functioning, target symptoms (i.e. depression, anxiety, etc.), subjective well-being, interpersonal functioning, social/occupational functioning and measures of personality, as well as relevant process measures evaluated at multiple times across treatment. (http://www.apa.org/pubs/journals/pst/evidence-based-case-study.aspx, retrieved on July 14, 2014)

The opportunities for researchers, especially those who are more clinically inclined, have truly expanded with the opportunity to publish empirical case studies.

Researchers no longer need to rely on informal methods for case studies (e.g., personal recall). Rather, the empirically based case study invites counselors to use brief measures over the course of treatment, such as measures of clients' functioning (e.g., well-being or distress) or more tailored outcomes that are relevant to the client or the treatment approach (see Owen & Imel, 2010, for discussion of measures). Moreover, the empirical case study approach is a great way for students to better understand the impact that they are having with their clients. For example, students can gain important information about how their clients are viewing the process of counseling, and ultimately how their clients perceive the effectiveness of counseling. This feedback process is a clear win-win situation, and ultimately at the heart of infusing science and practice as well as having practice truly inform science.

In sum, this section has provided an overview of both a traditional uncontrolled case study as well as intensive single-subject quantitative designs. We provide this contrast so that the reader can begin to understand the range of methods that are possible with investigations of a single participant. We especially want to promote the use of more elaborate and rigorous single-subject designs.

SINGLE-SUBJECT EXPERIMENTAL DESIGNS

Single-case experimental designs also examine the relationship between two or more variables typically within one or a few subjects. Clearly, the largest single influence in the development of this design has come from researchers working out of an operant conditioning paradigm, using specific target behaviors and clearly identifiable treatment phases in their research. We will demonstrate however, through the use of case illustrations, that this design need not be restricted to this particular theoretical approach. In this section, we first discuss several common features of single-case experimental designs and then describe and illustrate two different types of designs within this category: AB designs and multiple-baseline designs.

Common Features of Single-Subject Experimental Designs

Single-subject experimental designs have a number of common features (Kazdin, 2003) including (a) specification of the treatment goal, (b) repeated measurement of the dependent variable over time, (c) treatment phases, and (d) stability of baseline data.

The first common characteristic of single-subject experimental designs involves the specification of treatment goals. Because single-subject experimental designs were initially developed from an operant conditioning paradigm, most studies have specified behavioral goals, often referred to as "targets" or "target behaviors." In essence, target behaviors are the dependent variables of the investigation. The treatment goal can consist of cognitions, affective reactions, behaviors, physiological responses, or personality characteristics. If systems (groups, families, organizations) are used as the subject of the design, then system characteristics (communication patterns, cohesion, involvement) can be designated as treatment goals.

The second defining feature of single-subject experimental designs is the repeated measurement of the dependent variables over time. For example, in a study where the researcher or counselor is trying to help the client engage in less negative self-blaming thoughts, the measurement might occur on a weekly basis, or daily, or even several times a day. Many times this assessment process starts before the initiation of treatment, in which case it is referred to as a baseline assessment. In this example, the baseline would be the number of negative self-blaming thoughts the subject engaged in before the intervention. Because this assessment process is continuous (or nearly continuous), the researcher can examine the patterns in the dependent variable over time. The independent variable is typically a treatment intervention, often referred to as the intervention. It is important to note that the multiple measurement of the single-subject quantitative design is in stark contrast to other research designs that might collect a single data point before and after an intervention.

The third characteristic of single-subject experimental designs is the inclusion of different treatment phases, each representing a different experimental condition. One method of phase specification is to designate a baseline and a treatment phase. Baseline data are collected before treatment initiation and are used both to describe the current state of functioning and to make predictions about subsequent performance. The second method of defining time periods involves the random assignment of different treatments to different time periods (days, sessions). The basic purpose of changing from one phase to another is to demonstrate change due to the onset of the independent variable or intervention.

The stability of baseline data is also an important feature of most single-subject quantitative designs. Change cannot be detected after the onset of an intervention if the baseline data are unstable—that is, are either increasing, decreasing, or lack consistency. Thus, before the researcher can ascribe causality to an intervention, he or she must obtain an accurate and stable assessment of the dependent variable before the introduction of the intervention. This is especially the case when a baseline versus treatment intervention phase comparison is used.

In this section, we will discuss two major types of designs used in single-subject quantitative designs: AB time-series designs and multiple-baseline designs. We will start with the AB time-series designs, which have many variations; to illustrate the AB time-series design we will discuss three specific designs: AB, ABAB, and randomized AB.

The AB Design   The AB design is basically a two-phase experiment; the A phase is a baseline period, and the B phase is an intervention phase. Typically, multiple measurements or observations are taken during each phase. For example, each phase might be six weeks long, with two observations each week. These multiple observations enable the researcher to ascertain first of all, if the baseline period is stable, which allows a suitable assessment of the subject before the intervention. If the baseline period is unstable (i.e., measurements are accelerating or decelerating), it is often difficult to draw inferences about the effects of the intervention. Multiple observations after the intervention enable a thorough assessment of the effects of the intervention over time. If only one observation per phase were collected, the study would basically be a one-group pretest-posttest design (see Chapter 12), which typically has a number of threats to internal validity. The multiple measurements within an AB design, referred to as a time-series format, provide greater stability over time. The AB design, like the traditional within-subjects design previously discussed, has the subject serve as his or her own control or comparison. Thus, the basic comparison is between the A phase (baseline) and the B phase (intervention) within the same subject. If a researcher measured only the B phase, he or she would have no basis for comparison and would find it impossible to infer any effects due to the intervention.

How does the researcher assess whether change has occurred due to the intervention? Historically, the use of statistical methods to analyze the data generated by single-subject designs has been controversial (Wampold & Freund, 1991). Thus, researchers commonly plotted the raw data on a graph and make inferences from the graph. As you might imagine, such a visual analysis is imprecise and can be unreliable and systematically biased. Consequently, a variety of statistical tests have been proposed for single-subject designs (see Shadish et al., 2013, for review). There are many proposed statistical procedures such as the two standard deviation rule (Gottman, McFall, & Barnett, 1969), the relative frequency procedure (Jayaratne & Levy, 1979), lag analysis (Gottman, 1973, 1979), Markov chain analysis (Lichtenberg & Hummel, 1976; Tracey, 1985), time-series analysis (e.g., Glass, Willson, & Gottman, 1974), randomization tests (e.g., Edgington, 1980, 1982, 1987; Wampold & Worsham, 1986), the split middle technique (White, 1974), and the binomial test (Kratochwill & Levin, 2014). These procedures are meant to increase the validity of the statistical analyses and the observations that can be drawn from this type of data.

More recent statistical applications have utilized multilevel modeling, which is a regression-based statistical procedure that helps address the limitation of traditional regression insofar that the procedure accounts for the interdependencies in scores (e.g., the same person who reports on behavior at multiple occasions; see Shadish et al., 2013). In the case of single-subject designs, there are generally two "levels" in the model. At the first level, there could be repeated observations of the case. Multiple ratings of the client's behavior in each session are a common approach (e.g., the number of times that a client says the phrase "I don't know" in each session). For example, the researcher may be interested in the association between these utterances and the degree to which the therapist responds in a warm versus cold manner (i.e., the DV). In this case, it could be that the number of times a client utters "I don't know" in a session could relate directly to the therapist's response (i.e., warm vs. cold responses). In addition, the second level would be the average observations at each session (i.e., the average number of times a client utters "I don't know" in each session). This second level will help discern whether the average number of utterances of "I don't know" is related to how the counselor reacts *across sessions*. The difference between within a session or between sessions may be important. That is, the within-session effect would address a more immediate counseling process (i.e., the link between client statement and therapist response) and the between-session effect would address a more macro process (i.e., is there an aggregate effect of client statements?). There are other applications of multilevel modeling to case studies. When there is a multiple case study (e.g., comparing two more cases) the first level could be the observation of the clients (e.g., how the client is functioning session by session), and the second level would be the cases.

Although multilevel modeling of single-subject designs can be a flexible modern approach for dealing with complex data, there are limitations. Specifically, statistical power is commonly limited in single-subject designs, so researchers need to consider how many observations they are intending on collecting. Additionally, researchers may want to use other descriptive approaches to help verify their statistical results.

It may be helpful to see an example of this type of AB design in the area of group counseling. The famous group therapist Irvine Yalom (2005) has suggested that an agenda-go-round (in which the therapist asks each member at the beginning of the group session to set an agenda for himself or herself for that session) can be used to improve group cohesion and member involvement. A researcher might examine this suggestion by using an AB design. This could be done by identifying a therapy group, and for the first 10 group sessions measuring the level of cohesion and member involvement in each session. This would be the A phase, or baseline. For the next 10 sessions the researcher could have the group leader use Yalom's agenda-go-round technique and once again measure cohesion and member involvement for each session. This would be the B phase, or intervention. The researcher could compare cohesion and member involvement during the A and B phases to see if the agenda-go-round intervention had an effect. With the rather dramatic changes depicted in the graph of this design in Figure 15.1, it seems that the agenda-go-round intervention did have an effect. This type of obvious difference is not always so apparent in graphic analyses, and thus it is more difficult to ascertain whether the intervention phase actually did have the intended effect.

A problem with this simple AB design is that the researcher cannot eliminate or rule out threats to internal validity from history and maturation as possible explanations for the results. For instance, going back to the example of Yalom's

FIGURE 15.1 AB Design Examining Group Cohesion (Measured on a Five-Point Likert Scale, with 1 = Low Cohesion, 5 = High Cohesion) by Session Number (the Agenda-Go-Round Exercise Was Instituted at Session 11)

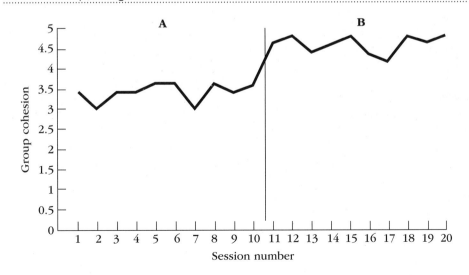

technique, most therapy groups increase in cohesion over time, even without a go-round technique. Thus, although the multiple measurements strengthen this study over the one-group pretest-posttest design, this particular design contains some threats to internal validity. Expansions and refinements of the AB design, including the ABAB design, were developed to circumvent some of these weaknesses.

RESEARCH IN ACTION 15.1

Take a moment to develop your own AB design. What would be the goal of this AB study; that is, what would you like to learn? What would be the target behavior that you would like to change? Remember this could be a behavior, thought, or emotion. How would you measure this target? How many "A" observations would you like to have? What would be the intervention? Finally, how could you study help future counselors?

The ABAB Design In contrast to the AB design, which as we have said is basically a two-phase experiment, the ABAB design is a four-phase experiment, and is also frequently referred to as a reversal design. In essence, the ABAB design examines the effect of a treatment (or independent variable) by either presenting or withdrawing the variable during different phases in an attempt to provide unambiguous evidence of the causal effect of the independent variable. The ABAB design starts with a period of baseline data gathering (A_1) and a treatment phase (B_1), and then it returns to a baseline period (A_2) where the intervention is withdrawn, and then finally a second treatment phase (B_2).

The assumption underlying this reversal is that if the independent variable caused the change in the dependent variable in the B_1 phase, then a removal of the independent variable should return the subject to a level similar to the baseline phase. Moreover, if the reversal in fact results in a return to the baseline, then read ministering the independent variable at B_2 will serve as a replication, further strengthening the inferred causal relationship. If the behavior at A_2 does not revert to the baseline levels, then a causal relationship between the independent and dependent variables cannot be inferred because other (unknown) variables may have been the causal influence. Thus, in the Yalom agenda-setting example given earlier when describing the AB design, an ABAB design would be collected in the following manner: 10 group sessions in which the researcher collected the baseline cohesion and member involvement data (A_1), followed by 10 sessions in which the group leader implemented the agenda-go-round intervention (with continued data collection) (B_1), followed by another 10 group sessions of data collection without the agenda-go-round intervention (A_2), and then a final 10 sessions with the agenda-go-round intervention reinstituted (B_2). Figure 15.2 presents a graph of data collected from this ABAB design. Because group cohesion increased in both B phases, we can infer that the agenda-go-round exercise caused an improvement in group cohesion.

FIGURE 15.2 An ABAB Design Examining Group Cohesion by Session Number (the Agenda-Go-Round Exercise Was Instituted at Session 11, Withdrawn at Session 21, and Reinstituted at Session 31)

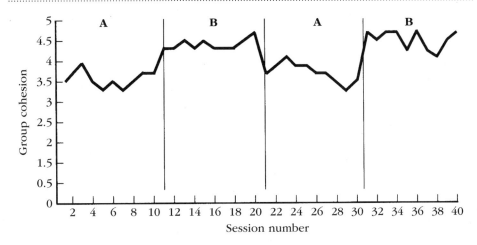

Let's look at another example of the ABAB design to examine the relationship between therapist behavior and client resistance. This study is also a good illustration of programmatic research that uses both descriptive and experimental designs to study a phenomenon. First, using a descriptive research strategy, Patterson and Forgatch (1985) examined the likelihood of client resistance following various types of counselor behavior (e.g., supportive or teaching responses). In essence, they found that client resistance following therapist teaching responses was significantly higher than the clients' baseline resistance. One might guess that this was because the client was feeling talked at or lectured to, and the client may have felt resistance as a result. But because this first study was only descriptive, the authors could not infer that therapist teaching caused client resistance. But this question did provide the researchers with a wonderful question with which to use the ABAB design. Six counselors met with their clients for videotaped sessions. The counselors started with a baseline phase (A$_1$) in which they interacted with their clients without using teaching interventions; this was followed by a treatment phase (B$_1$) in which the counselors increased their use of teaching responses. A second baseline phase followed in which the counselors returned to interacting without the teaching responses (A$_2$). There was then a final treatment phase (B$_2$) in which the counselors once again increased their use of teaching responses. The results of this ABAB study showed that the counselors did give significantly more teaching responses during the two treatment phases, indicating that the experimental manipulation was successful (such a procedural check is referred to as a manipulation check). More important, the clients were more resistant during the treatment phases (B$_1$ and B$_2$). Thus, these data more strongly suggest that therapist teaching behavior caused client resistance.

Although there are many strengths to the ABAB design, it does have three problems that we would like to note. The first problem is a statistical one. Most authors and editors want to report some statistical test that describes the amount of difference between the two phases (A and B; see previous references regarding statistical issues for these designs). When reported, this test is usually a t test or an F test. Both t and F tests, however, assume independent observations, and this is not the case in the ABAB design (Wampold & Freund, 1991). A second problem with the ABAB design is the possible presence of carryover effects (i.e., effects from the manipulation at phase B_1 that affect A_2 or B_2). It could be that the effects of the B_1 intervention are irreversible and cannot be withdrawn. For example, if the dependent variable involves learning or skill acquisition (e.g., study skills such as test-wiseness), it is difficult to reverse these treatments and return the subject to the A_1 level. Obviously, there are many interventions for which treatments are reversible and carryover effects are not present. However, in some ABAB designs, the interventions are not reversible and carryover effects present problems in drawing inferences and in isolating causal relationships. Finally, there are therapeutic situations in which it is undesirable or unethical to reverse the treatment phase, and both the client and counselor may be reluctant to withdraw an effective treatment. These concerns, among others, have led authors (see Edgington, 1987) to call for the use of randomized single-subject experiments or randomized AB designs.

Randomized AB Designs   There are many tests of randomization for single-subject designs (e.g., Houle, 2008; Maggin et al., 2011; Parker, Vannest, & Davis, 2011; Shadish et al., 2013). Even though these statistical tests are beyond the scope of this book, we present one example to introduce readers to the design possibilities within randomized AB designs.

The randomized AB design involves two phases that are repeated in a randomized fashion such that the presence of an A or a B phase at any point in time is dependent on random assignment. For example, the randomized AB design for examining the effects of an agenda-go-round exercise on group cohesion and member involvement might look like this:

	A	A	B	A	B	A	B	B	B	A	B	A	A	B	B	A	B	A	B	A
Session	1	2	3	4	5	6	7	8	9	10	11	12	13	14	15	16	17	18	19	20

In this example, A represents sessions in which the agenda-go-round is not used, and B represents sessions in which this exercise is used. Because the occurrence of A and B phases is random, randomization tests or traditional parametric tests can be used (Edgington, 1980) to compare cohesion and involvement scores for the A and B sessions. This design has a second advantage: It enables the researcher to analyze carryover effects by setting up the following simple 2×2 factorial design.

Phase	Preceded by Phase A	Preceded by Phase B
A	(1) Data from sessions 2, 13	(2) Data from sessions 4, 6, 10, 12, 16, 18, 20
B	(3) Data from sessions 3, 5, 7, 11, 14, 17, 19	(4) Data from sessions 8, 9, 15

Data are assigned to cells based on whether they come from phase A or B and on which phase preceded the phase in question. For example, the first cell in the table contains the data from all phase-A sessions (all sessions without the agenda-go-round) that were preceded by a phase-A session (session without the agenda-go-round). In a like manner, the second cell of the table contains all data from phase-A sessions (without agenda-go-round) that were preceded by a phase-B session (with agenda-go-round). A factorial analysis of variance (ANOVA) using this setup would provide a main effect for phase A versus B, a main effect for preceding phase (preceding A versus preceding B), and an interaction effect for phase ´ preceding phase. The interaction analysis directly tests for carryover effects.

Some final comments about the AB time-series designs seem warranted. First, although we have discussed and illustrated AB designs as having only two (A and B) phases, this need not be the case. A design could contain three (A, B, and C) or more phases. A three-phase design could compare a baseline phase to two different treatments, or it could compare three different levels of an independent variable. The basic logic of the AB design remains the same no matter how many phases are involved—the researcher is attempting to isolate the effects of the independent variable by examining different levels (or trends) across different phases.

Many times AB designs are not considered with particular research projects because of possible ethical concerns. For instance, one may question whether it is appropriate to withdraw a treatment that seems to be having a positive effect on a client. Although this is an excellent question, it is important to note that this is the same dilemma faced by members of the medical profession in the early 1960s in prescribing thalidomide for morning sickness; unfortunately, they decided not to withhold treatment because of the perceived effectiveness of the drug and the results were terrible birth defects. In short, it is important to adequately test the efficacy of our counseling interventions empirically before assuming their effectiveness.

Another concern with AB designs is related to carryover effects of an intervention and the perceived unsuitability of some variables for some theoretical orientations. For example, Gelso (1979) reasoned that one cannot reverse a client's insight (the theoretical effect of an appropriate interpretation), and thus the AB designs would not be well suited for such content. We believe that the AB designs can be successfully applied to a wider range of topics than is typically acknowledged, although the researcher may need to be creative in adapting the AB designs. Doing so can bring the researcher a wealth of data that are highly useful to the practitioner, in addition to generating important research questions in an area.

Multiple-Baseline Designs

The second type of single-subject experimental quantitative design that we will discuss is the multiple-baseline design. The essential feature of this design is that data are recorded on more than one dependent variable, or target behavior, simultaneously. Like the AB designs, there is continual collection of data, but in multiple-baseline designs there are two or more data collection baselines on different dependent measures. The basic assumption is that with several dependent measures, one or more of these variables can serve as controls while the intervention is simultaneously applied to one of the dependent measures. But it is important that the intervention is applied to the different dependent measures at different times. If the intervention is truly the causal agent, there should be change on the dependent variable that was targeted by the intervention, but not on the nontargeted dependent variables. Thus, whereas the ABAB design attempts to identify causal relationships by withdrawing the intervention and reversing the change, the multiple-baseline design attempts to determine causality by identifying changes in some but not all of the multiple dependent measures. One of the problems with the multiple-baseline approach is the possible nonindependence of the dependent variables; thus, when the intervention is targeted at one of the dependent variables but all of the dependent variables change, the cause of the change is unclear (more on this later).

There are three different versions of the multiple-baseline design. The first variation involves collecting data on two or more dependent variables in the same individual. For example, a researcher may want to examine the effects of therapeutic homework assignments on the amount of family communication. To use a multiple-baseline design, he or she would have to identify at least two behaviors to measure family communication, perhaps (a) the amount of time after dinner the parents spend talking, and (b) the amount of time after dinner the parents spend talking with the children. Like the AB designs, the multiple-baseline design starts with a period of baseline assessment. In our example, this would involve daily recordings of interaction time between (a) partners and (b) parents and children. Next, the intervention is targeted at one of these dependent variables; a homework assignment is initiated that is designed to increase interspousal communication. The basic assumption in this example is that the second behavior (amount of communication between parents and children) serves as a control for the first behavior (amount of communication between spouses). If the intervention is causally related to interspousal communication, there should be a change in the amount of time the husband and wife spend communicating, but not in the amount of time the parents spend communicating with the children. As with AB designs, data are collected on these two behaviors for a specified period of time—say, one week. Finally, a homework assignment can be designed to increase parent-child communication. A change in the amount of time spent in parent-child communication would be expected to occur only after the introduction of this intervention. Sometimes three to five different behaviors are identified and targeted over successive time periods to assess the effects of a particular intervention. Continuation of a stable baseline in the behaviors not targeted for intervention (i.e., the controls) indicates the absence of coincidental influences other than the experimental intervention.

The second variation of the multiple-baseline design is to identify the same response across different subjects. Returning to our previous example about agenda setting, a researcher may want to test Yalom's (2005) hypothesis concerning the relationship between the quality of group member agendas and their subsequent involvement in the group. Specifically, Yalom stated that group members will initiate more high-level interactions when the agendas for the group are realistic, interpersonal, and here-and-now oriented. The researcher could begin by making a baseline assessment of each group member's interactions over the first five group sessions. He or she could then begin to train individual group members to set real-istic, interpersonal, and here-and-now agendas. Only one group member would be trained at a time, and the initiation of the training with the individual group members would be staggered; the researcher might train a different member every fifth group session. A change in any individual's quality of group participation would be expected to occur contingent on his or her receiving the agenda training, whereas no change would be expected in those not trained. The basic assumption in this example is that individuals can serve as controls when they have not received the intervention. Data collection is continuous, and only those individuals who have received the intervention are expected to change on the dependent measure. A possible source of contamination in this example is that subjects who have not received training might learn how to set effective agendas by observing their peers who have received training.

The third variation of the multiple-baseline design is to identify a given response for one subject but across different situations. As in all illustrations of the multiple-baseline design, a subject can refer to an individual, a group, a classroom, or a larger unit. Suppose a researcher wants to examine the effects of token reinforcement (the independent variables) on a child interacting with peers (the dependent variable). The amount of interaction with peers could be observed both before and after school on the playground, during a baseline period. The researcher could then begin token reinforcement of prosocial interactions only before school. The researcher would then expect to find a change in the amount of interaction with peers in the morning but not in the afternoon. Later the token reinforcement could be done in the afternoon also, and a consequent change in this baseline would then be expected.

Because the logic of the multiple-baseline design requires that the researcher show changes in one assessed behavior while another assessed behavior remains constant, one of the main concerns in using this type of design is the independence of the dependent variables. If there is a relationship between two or more of the behaviors, then a change in one behavior may well lead to a change in the other. If two behaviors show simultaneous change but only one received the independent variable, then it is impossible to rule out threats to internal validity such as history and maturation. Such unintended changes in baselines seriously jeopardize the strength of the multiple-baseline design and typically produce a study with uninterpretable results.

One way to guard against this complication is to carefully assess the independence of the behaviors, perhaps by correlating the baseline behaviors (Christensen, 1980). Another possible solution is the use of several dependent variables. By increasing the number of baselines, the researcher can guard against the possibility that two of the baselines are dependent on each other.

An example of using a multiple-baseline design was the study by Dennin and Ellis (2003). Briefly, in this study Dennin and Ellis studied the use of self-supervision, which is a systematic process in which an individual works independently directing his or her own professional development. Specifically, they were interested in the impact of these different conditions on trainees' actual use of empathy and meta-phor in their counseling sessions. They assigned four novice female counselors in training to one of three randomized conditions: (a) self-supervision targeting the use of metaphor first and then empathy, (b) self-supervision targeting empathy and then metaphor, or (c) an attention placebo control condition. The researchers collected data over a series of observations and monitored both treatments, empathy and metaphor. The researchers obtained a series of observations across an initial baseline phase and subsequent treatment phases that were targeting different behavior. They continued their data collection period for up to 17 counseling sessions, with each treatment starting at a randomly determined point. The results of their study found that self-supervision helped trainees increase their use of metaphor, but did not result in an increase in empathy.

RESEARCH APPLICATION 15.1

Imagine you are brought in to consult with a teacher who would like to do a multiple-baseline single-subject design study. The teacher would like to examine the effects of a new teaching approach entitled "Motivate." The teacher would like to see if this approach has an effect on students' motivation to learn and performance on a reading test.

Questions

How would you help the teacher define her independent and dependent variables?

How would you observe these targets in a multiple-baseline design?

What could be the limitations of this design?

What could you conclude from this study?

ADVANTAGES AND LIMITATIONS OF SINGLE-SUBJECT DESIGNS

Single-subject designs have a number of advantages and limitations, which we will initially discuss in a rather simple and absolute sense. In weighing these advantages and limitations, it is imperative to distinguish between the utility of the uncontrolled case study on the one hand, and both the intensive single-subject quantitative design and the single-subject experimental quantitative design on the other. In our view, much less can be learned from the uncontrolled case study because of the multitude of rival hypotheses. Conversely, the comparisons and control in the intensive single-subject design and single-subject experimental design provide stronger empirical support and thus lend greater utility to the research design. It is also important to note that the advantages and limitations need to be considered relative to the existing scientific knowledge pertaining to a specific question and the previous research methodologies employed in examining that particular research question.

Advantages of Single-Subject Designs

Lundervold and Belwood (2000) authored an article titled "The Best Kept Secret in Counseling: Single-Case (N = 1) Experimental Designs." They concluded that single-subject designs offer "a scientifically credible means to objectively evaluate practice and conduct clinically relevant research in a practice setting" (p. 92). In this section we discuss some of the strengths and advantages of the single-subject design, specifically as a means of (a) collecting information and ideas and generating hypotheses about the therapeutic process, (b) testing therapeutic techniques, (c) testing new methodologies, (d) studying individuals and rare phenomena, and (e) providing exemplars and counterinstances.

A Means of Collecting Information and Ideas, and Generating Hypotheses about the Therapeutic Process

Although the traditional between-groups design has been useful in examining outcomes in psychotherapy, a prominent difficulty has been the obscuring of individual variations in group averages. The therapeutic process is complex and highly variable. Clients differ from each other in significant ways; they are not uniform (Stiles, 2007). Rather, clients process information about themselves, their experiential worlds, and counseling in idiographic ways, and even differently from one time to the next. The same can be said of counselors; therapists not only differ in important ways from each other, but also are different from one time to another. Thus, in the context of the complex and detailed process of therapy, intensive single-subject methodologies in particular are ideally suited for microscopic analyses and for expanding scientific knowledge. In fact, many years ago Bergin and Strupp (1970) maintained that the intensive single-subject design would be one of the primary strategies to clarify the mechanisms of change within the therapeutic process. Stiles (2007) noted that "An adequate theory has to incorporate the distinct features of each case as well as the common features. If you restrict yourself to the themes that are common across cases, you will overlook the most interesting parts. Each case tells us something new, and new observations are always valuable, whether they confirm previous theory or add something unexpected" (p. 123). Thus, single-subject designs are ideally suited to help advance theory, and capture the unique and at times rare challenges that are commonly faced by counselors.

Both the intensive single-subject design and the single-subject experimental design offer unique opportunities to carefully scrutinize aspects of the therapeutic process in depth. In a way, the single-subject design can allow for a more complete description of what happens in counseling and the mechanisms involved in change. The studies mentioned earlier provided good examples of microscopic analyses of variables involved in the change process. These studies provide important in-depth information that contributes to the scientific knowledge base about counseling and supervision. More specifically, Hill and colleagues (1983) noted that intensive single-subject designs (a) permit a more adequate description of what actually happens between a counselor and client, (b) facilitate more integration of process data with positive or negative outcomes, (c) allow a close examination of the change process in the therapeutic relationship, and (d) allow outcome measures to be tailored to an individual client's problems.

A Means of Testing Therapeutic Techniques   Single-subject designs provide a useful means to test the effects of specific therapeutic techniques. The testing of techniques might happen at several levels: (a) the discovery of a new technique, (b) an intentional examination of a relatively new technique, (c) the application of an established technique to a new population or treatment situation, and (d) an in-depth examination of a well-established technique. Occasionally therapists will discover new techniques through a trial-and-error process with individual clients. Breuer's work with Anna O. resulted in the discovery of a "talking cure" or catharsis. In essence, Breuer found through trial and error that some of Anna's symptoms were relieved or disappeared simply by talking about them (Breuer & Freud, 1955). George Kelley, in part out of boredom with the Freudian interpretations, began fabricating "insights" and "preposterous interpretations," and discovered that often clients could change their lives in important ways if they believed these "alternative constructions of the world" (Monte, 1980, p. 434). Likewise, Rogers abandoned the traditional directive and diagnostically oriented therapeutic style after a dismal therapeutic failure in which a client reentered and redirected therapy by initiating a discussion of her troubled marriage. Rogers discovered that "it is the client who knows what hurts, what direction to go, what problems are crucial, and what experiences have been deeply buried" (Rogers, 1961, pp. 11–12). In short, therapists often stumble onto or create new techniques through their therapeutic work with individual clients. The intentional and consistent examination of new techniques within the informal case study, as well as the more formal single-subject design, can yield useful information about the counseling process. Thus, new observations by the therapist might be informally or formally tested with additional clients to further determine the effectiveness and generalizability of the technique. The single-subject design can also be used effectively to test the application of an established technique with a new problem or a new population. Kazdin (2003) noted that the extension of a given technique to a new problem is really quite common in the literature.

Finally, the single-subject design also lends itself well to an in-depth examination of the effectiveness of a certain technique. For example, a great deal of information could be collected about how a client is processing or reacting to repeated use of a certain technique, such as the Gestalt empty-chair technique, counselor touch, or counselor self-disclosure. Thus, in-depth information could be collected on the use of a specific technique over time.

A Means of Testing Novel Methodologies   The single-subject design is especially well suited to testing novel research methodologies. This design allows the investigator to "experiment" in a way with a new methodology or procedure. The investigator can determine whether a new methodology provides new or more useful information, or whether some aspect of counseling is better understood in some way.

Several investigations by Jack Martin provide excellent examples of testing a different methodological approach by using single-subject designs. Martin has conceptualized counseling through a cognitive mediational paradigm (Martin, 1984), in which he maintained the necessity of examining the cognitive processes of clients.

Martin suggested that the information contained in a client's cognitive structures, and the organization of that information, would have considerable appeal to researchers of counseling outcomes. Using an information-processing perspective, Martin tested a methodology to assess a client's cognitive structures (Martin, 1985). At the end of each session with a client, fictitiously called Carla, he would ask her to relax and then give the first associations to the following words: problem, Bill (fictitious name for her husband), and Carla. As the client mentioned specific word associations, Martin wrote each on a small square. After Carla had responded to the three memory probes, she was asked to arrange the labels on a laminated board using distance and drawing lines to symbolically depict relationships among the words. Martin found that this procedure produced "an incredible amount of data" (p. 558). The pre- to postcounseling diagrams revealed that Carla had acquired important knowledge about battering (the presenting problem) and her options concerning this particular problem (e.g., take advantage of a Women Center's program). Carla's outcomes also reflected important changes in her affective processes, from passive, reactive emotions (such as guilt or shame) to more active emotions (such as hope or anger).

Martin (1985) thus concluded that this particular method of assessing a client's cognitive structures provided very useful data that nicely captured some of the richness and subjective nature of the change process in counseling. Thus, this particular single-subject study provided important information about a new methodological procedure. Given the idiosyncratic nature of the data from this new method, group data would initially be quite overwhelming and not lend itself well to "averaging" across clients. The important point is that the results of Martin's initial study provided empirical support for additional examination of this novel methodology.

A Means of Studying Individual and Rare Phenomena   A major difficulty noted by many applied researchers and practitioners is the obscuring of individual variations and outcomes when subjects are examined in groups and their data are simply "averaged." In fact, trying to think about the "average" or "typical" client is generally not very useful when developing interventions. Clients are seldom homogeneous or "uniform." By contrast, the single-subject design is particularly well suited to describing the idiosyncrasies of individual clients, because of its intensive and often microscopic analyses. Thus, the single-subject design can be considered a useful tool for examining change within a single individual. Single-subject design can be used as a key methodology to isolate specific mechanisms of change as well as advance our understanding of how change occurs, especially when the case does not fit the theory at hand (Stiles, 2007). The case study approach can provide some information as well, but most often it lacks experimental control, which confounds even tentative conclusions.

The single-subject design also lends itself to more qualitative approaches in studying individuals (see Elliott, 2002; Elliott, Fischer, & Rennie, 1999). In this way, the single-subject design can be used to collect data about the "thinking frameworks" of individuals (Edgington, 1987) or higher mental processes (Wundt, 1916). Polkinghorne aptly suggested that human action and decision making, which are central to the therapeutic and counseling processes, appear to be related to a "means-end rationality" or mode of processing information. Heppner and Krauskopf (1987) noted similar thinking processes by using an information-processing model to describe client problem solving in a counseling context. The single-subject design may be particularly well suited for gathering information about (a) how clients process information, (b) the thinking steps or means involved in reaching some end or goal (logically or illogically), (c) an individual's plans and intentions (Heppner & Krauskopf, 1987; Howard, 1985), and (d) how such plans affect the processing of information and subsequent behavior. The complexity of such information processing, at least initially, may be examined more feasibly via a single-subject design. In short, single-subject designs are useful to study complex phenomena, particularly as counselors use some of the more qualitative approaches in examining higher mental processes.

The single-subject design is particularly useful in studying rare phenomena, such as multiple personality. In addition to rare phenomena, the single-subject design can also be used to study relatively low-frequency occurrences, such as male anorexics and college students under unique situational stress (e.g., Middle Eastern students after 9/11). Although a typical university counseling center usually has a very broad range of clients, it is often difficult to study infrequent occurrences in a group comparison format. It is not usually feasible, or ethical, to withhold treatment until enough of these low-occurrence clients seek counseling to enable random assignment of clients to groups, and so forth.

A Means of Providing Exemplars and Counterinstances   The single-subject design can be used to provide exemplars to highlight findings, particularly if these findings run counter to existing beliefs or theories (in which case exemplars become counterinstances). Given that the intensive single-subject and single-subject experimental designs generally provide stronger experimental control, these findings obviously lend themselves better to such highlighting.

More specifically, the findings from a single-subject design can be used to provide data in support of a particular point, argument, or theory. For example, Strupp (1980a, 1980b, 1980c) conducted a series of single-subject studies comparing therapists, each with a successful and unsuccessful case in brief psychodynamic therapy. A wide variety of process and outcome measures were used to examine events related to therapeutic effectiveness. Negative outcomes were related to client characterological problems (as compared to neurotic problems) or counseling countertransference issues. Positive outcomes were related to the client's ability to take advantage of the therapeutic relationship and to work within the therapist's framework. Strupp then used these results to propose that patient variables were more powerful events in assessing therapeutic outcomes, even to the point of overshadowing therapists' attitudes and technical skill. These studies were foundational to common psychodynamic principles found in their treatment manuals.

In sum, there are many advantages to a well-designed and carefully controlled single-subject design. In essence, the single-subject designs can study important phenomena that other designs are less suited to examine in depth.

Limitations of Single-Subject Designs

Although there are a host of limitations to the traditional uncontrolled case study, many of these have been corrected in the two single-subject quantitative designs discussed in the chapter. However, some limitations remain, particularly related to the generalizability of the findings.

As traditionally conceived and conducted, the individual case study almost completely lacks experimental control. Many of Shadish, Cook, and Campbell's (2002) threats to internal validity are present, such as history, maturation, testing, selection, and mortality. In addition, many times "data" are collected in unsystematic and even retrospective ways. After working with a particular client for some time, the therapist may reflect back (sometimes months later) to collect his or her "observations" about the case. Such retrospective analyses most likely involve multiple sources of bias and distortion (e.g., memory loss, memory distortion, subjective impressions, or selective attention), and blur any temporal succession pertaining to causal relationships. Sometimes the "data" also consist of verbal client self-reports collected by the counselor. If the client believes he or she is doing the counselor a favor by completing a questionnaire, data obtained in such a manner may very well be contaminated or biased, most likely by demand characteristics inherent in the situation. Likewise, data may be collected from the client with instruments of unknown reliability or validity, thereby calling into question the adequacy of the data. In short, any of a number of biases of uncontrolled variables can obscure the relationship between the variables under examination and thus obscure interpretation of the findings. Although it *may* be true that variable x affected variable y in some way, it also may be the case that many other variables created the effect on variable y. The upshot of the uncontrolled case study is that there may be several plausible explanations for the observed effect on variable y, thus limiting the scientific value of the study. The uncontrolled case study is a weak source of "data" and at best is suggestive.

By contrast, the intensive single-subject design and the single-subject experimental design typically involve more systematic observations and experimental control. As such they have less limitations than the traditional case study, but some limitations do remain. A major issue in using single-subject designs is the generalizability of the findings to other individuals or situations. Even if one isolates specific relationships among variables, it is unclear whether the results would generalize to other clients with similar concerns or diagnoses (client generality) or whether a particular technique would work in a different setting (setting generality) (see Barlow & Hersen, 1984). Caution must also be used when employing findings from single-subject designs as exemplars or counterinstances. As mentioned previously, in early research relatively uncontrolled case studies were not just overused as exemplars, but also were used as the primary database in the construction of personality theories. Although the generalizability of the findings from single-subject designs must always be questioned, the results can highlight a particular point or cast doubt on previously held beliefs, suggesting that, at a minimum, there are exceptions to the rule or that the rule is somehow incorrect. However, exemplars should not become the only or even primary database relating to a particular phenomenon. Another disadvantage of the intensive single-subject design is that experimenters may find what they expected to find and overlook information that is contrary to their expectations (Stiles, 2007).

SUMMARY AND CONCLUSIONS

The common goal of all counseling research methods is to facilitate an understanding of human behavior. Different methodologies provide different types of data and information about human behavior. Single-subject designs permit an examination of an individual person, dyad, or group. Typically, a practitioner counseling a specific client is less concerned with group averages than with the individual's behavior. It is not sufficient to rely on normative data that suggest a particular intervention strategy works with, say, three out of four clients, and thus simply to rely on probabilities. Single-subject designs, particularly those of an intensive, systematic, or time-series nature, can provide information about the uniqueness of client responses and counselor interventions. However, researchers must be particularly sensitive to various sources of bias and extraneous variables, as well as cautious about generalizing the results from one individual to other individuals or groups.

In this chapter, we discussed three main types of single-subject design, the uncontrolled case study, the intensive single-subject quantitative design, and the single-subject experimental design. A case study refers to a study that consists simply of observations of an individual, dyad, or group that are made under unsystematic and uncontrolled conditions. The intensive single-subject quantitative design typically involves more experimental control and consists of systematic, repeated, and multiple observations of an individual, dyad, or group under experimental conditions designed to identify and compare relationships among variables. Thus, the comparisons and control in the intensive single-subject quantitative design provide stronger empirical support, and thus give it more utility than the case study.

The single-subject experimental designs also examine the relationship between two or more variables, typically within one or a few subjects, and involve considerable levels of experimental control. These designs are characterized by specific treatment goals, numerous and repeated measurements of the dependent variable, and the inclusion of different phases or periods of time (each representing a different experimental condition such as a baseline phase or an intervention phase). The basic purpose of changing from one phase to another is to demonstrate change, presumably due to the onset of the independent variable or intervention.

Two major types of single-subject experimental designs are the AB time-series designs (AB, ABAB, randomized AB) and multiple-baseline designs. We maintain that the time-series designs are not only appropriate for behavioral researchers, but also can be fruitfully employed within other theoretical orientations.

We firmly believe that both the intensive single-subject quantitative design and the single-subject experimental designs can be powerful methodologies to increase understanding of counseling and the counseling process. These designs can be used for (a) collecting information and ideas, and generating hypotheses about the therapeutic process; (b) testing therapeutic techniques; (c) testing new methodologies; (d) studying individuals and rare phenomena; and (e) providing exemplars and counterinstances. However, limitations imposed by threats to both internal and external validity must be clearly examined and considered. Bergin and Strupp (1970) initially predicted that the single-subject design would be one of the primary strategies used to clarify the process of counseling; this remains to be demonstrated. Nonetheless, because we strongly believe in the potential of this methodology, our first recommendation is to use the more rigorous single-subject designs more frequently in counseling research. These designs can be especially rich in providing more holistic data of both a content and process nature.

A number of the examples cited in this chapter were intentionally drawn from group counseling. One of the main obstacles in group counseling research is sample size. Many times in group counseling research, the variable of interest is a group-level variable such as cohesion. Often, however, researchers use individual scores, such as each subject's attraction to the group, so they can increase the size of the groups in a between-groups design. Researchers could circumvent this sample-size problem by using more single-subject experimental time-series designs. Accordingly, our second recommendation is an increased use of single-subject experimental designs in group (and family) research. This recommendation could also help address a second problem in group research—that most group counseling studies use analogue groups of very short duration. Time-series designs allow the researcher to study the group as an entity and to use real client groups without having to line up a prohibitively large number of subjects.

Our third recommendation is the increased use of randomized designs in AB time-series research. Randomized designs offer additional complexity and flexibility, and enable the researcher to examine for the presence of carryover effects between treatments. In addition, randomized designs permit the use of powerful parametric statistical analyses. Editors are often reluctant to publish studies that do not have statistical comparisons, and readers rely on these statistical comparisons as a way of comparing studies for AB time-series designs; parametric statistical tests can only be performed appropriately when A and B phases are randomly assigned.

A final methodological consideration in discussing the use of the single-subject methodology is the type of data or knowledge currently available on a particular research question. For example, Desmet and colleagues (2013) examined how many psychoanalytical single-subject studies were published from 1995 to 2011. Single-case studies in this area are common and important given the length of treatment (e.g., can be over one year) and the importance placed on these designs in this community. Of the 445 articles they located, the majority (88%) did not use any systematic qualitative or quantitative methods. However, there was a larger push in recent years to do so. The movement toward more systematic methods potentially illustrates the natural movement from the less known, simple observation, to more complex understanding of the processes involved in psychoanalytical counseling. The point is that merely ascertaining the advantages and limitations of the single-subject design is not enough; researchers must also weigh these advantages and limitations relative to the applicable existing scientific knowledge base and the types of designs used in past research.

STIMULUS QUESTIONS

Single-Subject Designs

This exercise is designed to help promote reflection on single-subject designs. After reading this chapter, think about your responses to the following questions.

1. Some students have told us that their training programs "do not allow" single-subject designs for a thesis or dissertation. Why do you think that is the case? If you were a person who wanted to conduct an

intensive single-subject design for your own thesis or dissertation, what arguments would you use to convince your training program of their validity?

2. In the history of counseling, there have been a number of uncontrolled case studies. Now it is more difficult to find examples of these designs in our major journals. What factors do you believe have brought about this change in thinking and the reduced use of the uncontrolled case studies?

3. Think about the topics you feel passionate about in your own scholarly work and practice. Identify three research questions that would lend themselves well to some sort of a single-subject quantitative design. How would you design a study using an intensive single-subject design for this topic?

4. One of the concerns with single-subject design is the issue of generalizability. What can be done to increase the level of external validity or generalizability with such designs?

5. Talk to faculty and peers about their perceptions of the usefulness of the single-subject designs. What advantages and disadvantages first come to mind for them?

Qualitative Research: Complexities and Richness from Digging Deeper

With Yu-Wei Wang

A central concept of the research designs discussed in previous chapters is that psychological constructs can be measured at the individual level and that understanding can be obtained by averaging these measurements over many persons. The participants respond to questions that in turn yield numbers that the researcher uses to form an understanding that is applicable to others. Participants may be subjected to various treatments or other manipulations, may complete inventories or instruments, and may interact with the researcher; all such actions, however, are used in the service of examining the relationship among the constructs assessed. Although we can learn much about counseling from the quantitative measurement of persons involved in the endeavor, as counselors well understand, the individual meaning that people attribute to their activities and experiences are critically important.

Qualitative research involves understanding the complexity of people's lives by examining individual perspectives in context. Qualitative research methodology, as opposed to quantitative methods, is a radically different way to approach knowing and understanding. This methodology emphasizes the importance of context in helping us understand a phenomenon of interest. In particular, qualitative methodology stresses the process in which individuals create and give meanings to their social experience and lived realities.

This chapter will provide a discussion of qualitative research methods and designs. First, the definition of qualitative research and key myths and facts about qualitative research will be presented. Next, we make the case for the usefulness of qualitative methods within counseling and counseling psychology research. Then we describe the five phases of qualitative inquiry as offered by Denzin and Lincoln (2011). As we describe each phase, we review key elements of the research process.

WHAT IS QUALITATIVE RESEARCH?

Qualitative research is a method of inquiry that cuts across disciplines and philosophical traditions. It has a long and complex history with roots in sociology and anthropology, and its precise definitions vary by traditions and disciplines (for a detailed description, see Denzin & Lincoln, 2011). Regardless of specific tradition or discipline, however, most qualitative researchers agree that qualitative methods of inquiry emphasize the importance of context in helping us to understand a phenomenon of interest. Denzin and Lincoln (2011) defined qualitative research in this way:

> Qualitative research is a situated activity that locates the observer in the world. Qualitative research consists of a set of interpretive, material practices that make the world visible. These practices transform the world. They turn the world into a series of representations, including field notes, interviews, conversations, photographs, recordings, and memos to the self. At this level, qualitative research involves an interpretive, naturalistic approach to the world. This means that qualitative researchers study things in their natural settings, attempting to make sense of or interpret phenomena in terms of the meanings people bring to them. (p. 3)

In other words, qualitative researchers are devoted to understanding the specifics of particular cases and embedding their research findings in an ever-changing world. Influenced by the interpretivist-constructivist tradition, qualitative researchers believe that objective reality can never be fully understood or discovered, and there are many possible ways of looking at realities.

Qualitative researchers seek to capture the individual's point of view through the use of multiple strategies such as interviews and observations. As such, emic (i.e., categories emerge from the perspective of the participants) and idiographic (i.e., knowledge about one or a very small group of participants) perspectives are utilized. This view differs from etic (i.e., the researcher purports particular categories or expectations) and nomothetic (i.e., generalizations are made from a larger group to individuals) perspectives that are commonly associated with quantitative research. In other words, qualitative researchers do not aim to discover and describe universal principles by quantifying the observed phenomena or using experimental methods and statistical tests to verify or falsify a priori hypothesis. Instead, qualitative researchers begin the research process with research questions rather than proposed hypotheses and utilize research tools in order to better understand the phenomenon of interest (Nelson, Treichler, & Grossberg, 1992). They value rich descriptions of the phenomenon under analysis and attempt to represent an individual's lived experience through writing and interpretations.

Similar to quantitative research, the questions that qualitative researchers ask their participants and the methods that they utilize to observe certain phenomena are "filtered" through the researchers' lenses of knowledge, language, values, and worldviews. Denzin and Lincoln (1998) described qualitative research as "an interactive process" shaped by the researcher's "personal history, biography, gender, social class, race and ethnicity, and those of the people in the settings" (p. 4). Qualitative researchers acknowledge ("bracket") their assumptions about the study by taking field notes, writing reflexive journals, and informing the readers as to what their "filters" are. The lived experiences of the research participants are what qualitative researchers focus on, and the researchers are the instruments in this discovery process who hold their expectations and hunches about the phenomenon under study in abeyance (Rennie, 2000).

The discovery orientation of the qualitative approach helps researchers focus on the context where the phenomenon is situated and makes the findings more applicable for people's everyday lives in various cultures. Qualitative inquiry allows researchers to study the local interactions in counseling settings and their meanings for counselors and clients.

MYTHS AND FACTS ABOUT QUALITATIVE RESEARCH

Due to insufficient understanding of the definition and characteristics of qualitative research, there are several common myths about this form of inquiry. Anecdotal stories passed among training programs suggest that qualitative research is less rigorous and less scientific than quantitative research. This perspective, in our opinions, contributes to these myths and to implicit or explicit messages to students and junior faculty to avoid pursuing qualitative research.

The first common myth is the tendency to equate "qualitative data" with "qualitative research." In other words, there is a mistaken belief that qualitative research consists only of asking people open-ended questions and analyzing participants' answers. Second, it is not uncommon for individuals to assume that only one method of qualitative inquiry exists and that all qualitative research uses the same methods. As will be discussed throughout this chapter, there are over 20 different approaches to qualitative inquiry, and the qualitative research process (including the type of data collected) varies depending upon the approach. In fact, the complexities associated with truly understanding the details of each of these approaches likely contribute to a tendency (or perhaps, a wish) for people to assume that only one method exists. Indeed, one method would greatly simplify the research process.

Third, there is a misguided belief that qualitative research should be used only in areas where we do not have enough information to conduct quantitative studies. This perspective overlooks the ways in which qualitative research can be used to add to the depth and breadth of our understanding about phenomena as outlined in Chapter 6. For example, Morrow (2007) highlighted the value of qualitative methods in exploring variables that are not easily identifiable or that have not yet been identified, explaining phenomenon when theories do not yet exist, contributing to theory building and extension, and expanding knowledge that will inform the formulation of interventions.

Finally, as a student, you might feel inclined to adopt a qualitative approach because you feel uncomfortable with statistics or believe that it is *easier* to conduct qualitative research than it is to conduct quantitative research. In fact, we have heard qualitative research referred to by colleagues as nothing more than "good journalism." This perspective neglects the fact that conducting qualitative research actually requires time-intensive processes, rigorous efforts, and introspection. Indeed, qualitative research necessitates that the researchers listen to other people's stories, and retell them or reconstruct the stories with the participants. As such, qualitative research is incredibly complex, and time and labor intensive. In his explanation of expectations for qualitative researchers, Creswell (1998) maintained that qualitative researchers should be willing to:

1. Commit to extensive time in the field;
2. Engage in the complex, time-consuming process of data analysis—the ambitious task of sorting through large amounts of data, and reducing them to a few themes or categories;

3. Write long passages, because the evidence must substantiate claims and the writer needs to show multiple perspectives; and

4. Participate in a form of social and human science research that does not have firm guidelines or specific procedures and is evolving and changing constantly. (pp. 16–17)

In other words, although some qualitative research procedures may not be as clearly delineated as quantitative research procedures, researchers must acquire highly specialized knowledge and demonstrate rigor in their work. Undertaking a qualitative study with limited knowledge of qualitative methods or skills to allow for a rigorous study is deeply concerning to those of us who value these methods and their place within our research. This is due, in part, to the number of researchers who assume that the collection of qualitative data and arbitrary analysis of that data will suffice; such assumptions are not accurate!

Students who are interested in conducting a qualitative study are encouraged to reflect on the following factors before deciding to conduct that study: (a) the fit between the research question and qualitative methodology; (b) the extent of their knowledge on the fundamental paradigms and methods of qualitative inquiry, and the corresponding level of skills gained from appropriate coursework and research apprenticeship; (c) whether they have adequate support from advisors and/or research mentors who are knowledgeable about qualitative methodology; (d) the existing knowledge bases and types of research designs previously used; and (e) their readiness to conduct a rigorous, qualitative investigation. These elements are worthy of considerable reflection and are essential in conducting quality research.

QUALITATIVE METHODS AND COUNSELING RESEARCH

Within counseling and counseling psychology, qualitative research has an interesting history. Qualitative methods were commonly used by some of the notable historical figures in developmental psychology (e.g., Erikson and Piaget) and psychotherapy research (e.g., Horney and Freud). Yet, qualitative methods were largely abandoned as the disciplines of counseling and counseling psychology adhered to the mounting pressure to increase scientific rigor, utilized more experimental designs, and conducted research that used sophisticated statistical analysis borrowed from the physical sciences (see Morrow, 2007, for a historical review). Indeed, some authors have highlighted the limited use of qualitative methods within the counseling literature. For example, based upon their content reviews of major journals, Berríos and Lucca (2006) and Ponterotto and colleagues (2008) found that qualitative research represented fewer than 20% of empirical studies published in the 1990s and 2000s. Further Ponterotto's 2005a review of counseling psychology training programs revealed that only 10% required coursework in qualitative research. Lack of training, in combination with the myths just described, may contribute to fewer researchers utilizing qualitative methods or ensuring rigor in their use of qualitative methods. Moreover, some (e.g., Eisenhard & Jurow, 2011) have argued that students learn qualitative research best by being a part of a qualitative research team and experiencing the entire process of a qualitative study.

Despite this history, many (e.g., Hill et al., 2005; Morrow et al., 2012; Ponterotto, 2005b, 2010) have called for counselors and counseling psychologists to recognize the value of qualitative methods in research. Because of qualitative research's emphasis on understanding context and the discovery orientation inherent in qualitative approaches, some authors (e.g., Morrow, 2007; Ponterotto, 2010; Yeh & Inman, 2007) have maintained that qualitative methods are particularly suited for counseling research. In particular, qualitative methods have been highlighted for their usefulness in research that explores multicultural topics, bridges the science-practice gap, and is accessible to practitioners and to the public.

Ponterotto (2010) suggested several benefits of using qualitative methods in particular for multicultural research. For example, he maintained that qualitative research necessitates that empathy be fostered on the part of the researcher as the researcher seeks to understand participants' lived experiences. Qualitative researchers also typically develop close connections to their own and participants' emotional reactions as they become immersed in personal and intimate details shared by the participants. In combination, close connections and fostering empathy may minimize some of the power differentials between the researchers and participants, which may subsequently facilitate a more accurate understanding of the phenomenon of interest and decrease the potential that researchers will further marginalize or stereotype participants or their communities when disseminating study findings. In addition, he suggested that qualitative methods of inquiry may be more comfortable for participants who are members of diverse and collectivistic cultures who may otherwise experience discomfort related to completing surveys or experimental research, particularly given the historical missteps of some research with underrepresented groups (see Trimble & Fisher, 2006, for a review).

Qualitative methods also have been posited to be particularly relevant to counseling and psychotherapy research. For example, reviewing qualitative materials (e.g., session recordings or transcripts) may facilitate a deeper understating of the interactions that occur in psychotherapy. Gathering data from clients and therapists via interviews offers another promising means by which researchers can better understand the meaning and experience of psychotherapy among clients and practitioners. In addition, Morrow (2007) posited that the narrative mode by which qualitative findings are presented may be more accessible to practicing clinicians or the lay public. As such, she suggested that qualitative research may be a useful mechanism to bridge the science and practice gap (Morrow, 2007).

PHASES OF THE QUALITATIVE RESEARCH PROCESS

In this section, we overview five phases to conducting qualitative investigations. These phases were identified by Denzin and Lincoln (2011) to guide qualitative researchers in the completion of an investigation (see Table 16.1 for an overview of the phases). Although there are many different qualitative strategies of inquiry, these five phases apply to all of the qualitative strategies of inquiry. There are critical tasks that the researcher must consider within each phase; it is important to note that the phases are not intended to be linear, but rather iterative. For example, even though

TABLE 16.1 Qualitative Research Phases and Associated Tasks

Phase of Qualitative Research	Primary Tasks
Phase 1: The Researcher as a Multicultural Subject	Identify the social location of the researcher(s)
	Reflect upon one's assumptions and biases germane to the research question and topic area
	Record biases, assumptions, and values throughout all stages of the research process through memo writing
Phase 2: Theoretical (or Interpretive) Paradigms and Perspectives	Identify philosophical assumptions and values associated with a chosen paradigm
	Select paradigm to guide the investigation
Phase 3: Strategies of Inquiry and Interpretive Paradigms	Select a particular strategy of inquiry and interpretive paradigm
	Review features specific to the selected paradigm to guide the design of each stage of the research study
Phase 4: Methods of Data Collection and Analysis	Determine how data will be gathered (observations, interviews, existing materials)
	Determine data coding and analyses as associated with the selected strategy of inquiry and interpretive paradigm
Phase 5: The Art, Practices, and Politics of Interpretation and Evaluation	Determine the interpretive approach as guided by the selected strategy of inquiry and interpretive paradigm
	Consider the artistic and political implications associated with interpretations offered
	Carefully evaluate the research process

evaluation is listed in Phase 5, researchers should be attending to evaluative elements throughout the development of a study, and all study phases, to ensure quality and rigor. In the subsections that follow, we describe the primary tasks associated with each phase.

Phase 1: The Researcher as a Multicultural Subject

A core assumption of qualitative research is that the researcher is an individual whose influence on the research is inextricably connected to each phase. Qualitative researchers recognize that science cannot be value-free and instead seek to identify and utilize the social location of the researcher, or "self" (Yeh & Inman, 2007), throughout the research process. Qualitative researchers recognize that their specific contexts are shaped by their personal histories and identities (e.g., class, gender, racial, and ethnic cultural perspectives: Denzin & Lincoln, 1998; Yeh & Inman, 2007), and in this way, the researcher's worldview (or context) affects all aspects of the study.

The identity of the researcher interacts with that of the research participants and shapes the study. Terms such as self-awareness (Creswell, 1998) and reflexivity (Morrow, 2005) are used to describe this process. In other words, there is an interactive process that takes place between the researcher and the participants. This process is continuously informed by the context and identities of the researcher (e.g., race, social class, gender identity, and expression), by the context and identities of the participants (e.g., religion, nation of origin, age), and by the setting. For example, qualitative researchers explicitly acknowledge that the research questions asked and the methods utilized to observe certain phenomena are filtered through the qualitative researchers' knowledge, language, values, and worldviews.

In order for this interactive process to occur, researchers are expected to engage in a thorough process of reflectivity and to openly acknowledge their positions, including in the written manuscript. As such, subjectivity (rather than objectivity) is assumed and embraced. Qualitative researchers cannot be separated from their work and are expected to acquire an understanding of how worldview (including their biases and beliefs) can influence the work. This process requires time and energy in a manner distinct from quantitative research. In the following example, one of us (Thompson) summarized her experience of this process related to working on the project described in Thompson, Cole, and Nitzarim (2012).

RESEARCH IN ACTION 16.1

Since I can remember, I have valued the importance of context and understanding the lens through which I and others see the world. This is certainly a key factor that drew me to the discipline of counseling psychology. The process is also one in which I regularly engage through supervision of my clinical work, consultation with peers, and evaluation of the questions that inform my pursuit of research topics. Yet, I was surprised by the intellectual and emotional reactions that emerged as I embarked on the qualitative research process. For example, in my research teams with graduate students in my department, I now needed to share my personal biases and assumptions explicitly and open myself to my team members' questioning my reactions (in other words, my "stuff"). Given the nature of our study (Thompson, Cole, & Nitzarim, 2012), which explored the experiences of clients who identified as low income in psychotherapy, our conversations as a team included moments in which we laughed together, disagreed with one another, and shared together a deep emotional connection to our participants and their stories. The intensity of the process was clear throughout the countless hours that we met to analyze and interpret data through our team meetings. It was, at times, emotionally exhausting and at times, deeply exhilarating. When it came time for writing the manuscript for publication, a new set of reactions emerged. Just when we had gained comfort with sharing with one another and challenging each other's biases, we were asked to explain this process, and our biases, to an undefined audience. Although we each had our own levels of comfort/discomfort with broadly sharing personal information, we appreciated the fact that putting this information out there in a published manuscript meant that it would be out there for all to see. Doing so elicited new emotional and intellectual reactions, including fears about misrepresenting our experiences or that of our participants.

Phase 2: Theoretical (or Interpretive) Paradigms and Perspectives

In Chapter 1, we described four paradigms that bear on the research process. Readers are encouraged to review that chapter again to be familiar with the philosophical foundations of scientific inquiry. At the most fundamental level, a paradigm is a "basic set of beliefs that guides action" (Guba, 1990, p. 17). Morrow, Castañeda-Sound, and Abrams (2012) offered the following definition of paradigm:

> An umbrella containing the researcher's views of reality, how knowledge is acquired, the values that guide the research, the methods used to conduct the research, and the language used to communicate the research processes and findings. (p. 95)

As such, a paradigm is comprised of a variety of assumptions and values of the researcher. The assumption that the researcher is a multicultural subject at Phase 1, therefore, is one component. A second is the particular paradigm's associated values and assumptions. These include:

- ontological (view of nature and nature of reality),
- epistemological (beliefs about the process by which reality is known and perspective on the relevance of the relationship between researcher and participant),
- axiological (perspectives on the role and place of values in research),
- rhetorical structure (choice of language used to present research findings),
- methodology (utilization of specific research processes and procedures), and
- methodological assumptions (beliefs about how we gain knowledge).

In general, qualitative approaches assume *relativist ontology* (i.e., that there are multiple realities that are socially and individually constructed) and *transactional epistemology* (i.e., that the knower and the known are inextricably intertwined), as well as *interpretive methodology* by which findings emerge from the data (Guba & Lincoln, 1998). These common assumptions, therefore, imply that the qualitative researcher values perceptions as representing the reality of each person's lived experiences (i.e., the researcher and the participants) and assumes that these perceptions lead to each person's knowledge. As such, a goal of the researcher is to use analytic methods in order to make meanings that are directly connected each person's experience.

It is essential that qualitative researchers understand the different paradigms and strategies of inquiry prior to embarking on a research project. The paradigm and methodology are determined by the approach to inquiry selected by the researcher. Each strategy of inquiry used to guide qualitative research has somewhat different philosophical underpinnings (see Ponterotto, 2005b, for an excellent discussion about locating the strategies of inquiry within research paradigms).

Researchers should be clear about the differences among various strategies of inquiry (as discussed in Phase 3 that follows) in order to make informed decisions regarding which qualitative approaches to use and when to use them (Creswell, 1998), and subsequently design studies according to the guidelines of the chosen strategy. The rationale of using a specific paradigm and strategy of inquiry should be presented and the relationship between the paradigms/ strategies of inquiry and purposes/research questions of the studies should be explicated. Strategy selection and methodology (as will be reviewed in the next sections) should be anchored in the chosen paradigm. As such, this phase cannot be overlooked. Although it is possible that a researcher may choose to draw from multiple paradigms, Morrow (2007) warned that researchers must make this choice carefully and intentionally from the start of a project. This is particularly important because paradigm selection determines the standards by which the research will be evaluated.

It is not uncommon for students to feel lost in wading through these paradigms and their associated beliefs and practices. Yet, carefully articulating one's intended core beliefs and course of the study from the start is essential to ensure solid qualitative research. In some ways, we liken this process to that of a theoretical orientation used to guide interventions with clients in counseling. The decisions made at this phase of the research process should provide the roadmap for the entire study and should guide your decisions at each step of the way. Just as trainees are expected to describe a coherent theoretical orientation that guides their case conceptualization and treatment planning, qualitative researchers are expected to clearly identify the paradigm and associated strategy of inquiry that guides their research process. This process requires time and intentionality from the inception of a study. In the following example, one of us (Thompson) summarizes her experience of this process based upon her reflection of the process when completing the project that was described in Thompson, Nitzarim, Her, and Dahling's (2013) manuscript.

RESEARCH IN ACTION 16.2

Prior to embarking upon our investigation of undergraduate students' experiences of the vicarious unemployment of a caregiver (Thompson, Nitzarim, Her, & Dahling, 2013), my research team and I met to dialogue about what we wanted to know from the study. In these conversations, we discussed such topics as what do we want to know about this group, why do we think that this knowledge is important, what biases and assumptions will we bring with us to this study, and how do we view the nature of reality among our anticipated participants. From these conversations, we agreed that we wanted to understand the experience of vicarious unemployment though the eyes of the participant. We wanted to choose an approach that would allow us to capture their lived experiences through their assumptions, values, beliefs, and emotions. We believed that using a constructivist lens would best facilitate this process. Because we each had some prior familiarity with this topic (based upon personal experiences in our own families and/or prior scholarly interests), we also wanted to explicitly acknowledge our role as instruments in the research process. Further, we were interested in identifying the emergence of an interconnected storyline so as to allow for divergent experiences across participants and to be able to capture the nuances of their experiences. We, therefore, chose grounded theory with a reliance upon a constructivist lens to guide each stage of our project.

Phase 3: Strategies of Inquiry and Interpretive Paradigms

The third phase of qualitative research is comprised of several components that mutually inform one another and shape subsequent phases. Denzin and Lincoln (2012) described this phase as the research design phase. They described design, or the purpose of the study, as "a flexible set of guidelines that connect theoretical paradigms, first, to strategies of inquiry and, second, to methods for collecting empirical material" (Denzin & Lincoln, 2012, p. 14). In other words, strategies of inquiry include the skills, assumptions, and practices of the researcher that are utilized to inform the process by which the researcher links a paradigm with data collection, analysis, and interpretation.

There are at least 20 qualitative strategies of inquiry across disciplines and each has distinct purposes and methods. Just as points of contention exist between qualitative and quantitative researchers, tensions exist among qualitative researchers who advocate one qualitative strategy over another (interested readers may consult Erickson, 2011, for a review of this tension). In the final section of this chapter, "Four Examples of Qualitative Research Strategies of Inquiry," we will summarize four strategies of qualitative inquiry that are commonly used in the counseling and counseling psychology literature: grounded theory, phenomenology, consensual qualitative research, and participatory action research/community-based participatory research. As you will note when reading that section, each of these strategies of inquiry has a slightly different set of assumptions, skills, and practices that the qualitative researcher is expected to follow. We provide exemplar studies to describe the common features of each of the four strategies. Moreover, the selection of a specific strategy has important implications for Phases 4 and 5 of the qualitative research process.

Each specific type of inquiry offers somewhat different information that can be used to answer research questions. Regardless of the specific strategy of inquiry selected, qualitative research provides an opportunity to gather incredibly rich information that is critically important in creating a very strong scientific foundation to the counseling and counseling psychology literature.

Phase 4: Methods of Data Collection and Analysis

Qualitative data are generally gathered from a limited and purposefully selected group of participants or materials germane to the research question. Although there are notable differences across paradigms and strategies of inquiry selected (as reviewed previously), there are a few tasks associated with data gathering, analyses, and presentation that are considered to be common across qualitative designs. In the following sections, we review steps associated with data gathering, coding, and analysis that are considered to be common across designs.

Data Gathering   Researchers are expected to clarify the type of data that will be gathered in accordance with paradigm and strategy of inquiry selection. Although there are many ways to collect data in qualitative research, we discuss three primary sources: observations, interviews, and existing materials. Wolcott (1992) refers to these sources in the active voice as *experiencing*, *enquiring*, and *examining*, respectively, which provides a glimpse of the qualitative researcher's state of mind in these three activities.

Observations   Observations are obtained by a trained observer who is present and involved in the phenomenon of interest and who makes reports of her or his observations. There are several advantages of observations in qualitative research. First, because observers can experience firsthand the transactions among persons in the field, they need not rely on retrospective reports of the participants, which could be clouded by the participants' involvement in the situation. In the vernacular, observations take place "where the action is." Second, by being close to the phenomenon, observers can feel, as well as understand, the situation. The emotion present in any situation is likely to be attenuated as time passes; the oft-spoken expression, "You had to be there [to understand]" aptly summarizes this advantage of observations. Moreover, informants may not be willing or able to talk about sensitive material, may not be aware of important events, or may consider important transactions to be routine. Third, deep involvement in the process over time will allow researchers to develop conceptualizations that can be examined subsequently. In contrast to quantitative research, investigators will not have a conjecture a priori that will be confirmed or disconfirmed according to all qualitative approaches (except for CQR, which does allow for categories to be identified by the research team a priori). Qualitative researchers may, over the course of the study, come to identify themes based on the observations of the participants and to relate those themes to each other, but such themes and their relations grow out of observation. This inductive process is the basis of some methods of qualitative research, such as grounded theory.

Degree of Involvement of Observers   Qualitative observers traditionally have followed the dictum of nonintervention (Adler & Adler, 1994), which holds that the observer does not influence the phenomenon, but acts as a recorder of events. The observer neither asks the participants questions, nor poses problems to be solved, nor suggests solutions to dilemmas. Observers can be described by their degree of involvement in the context being observed. Historically, the involvement of the observer ranged from complete observer, to observer-as-participant, to participant-as-observer, to complete participant (Gold, 1958). The complete observer is entirely outside the context and would most likely be undetected by the participants. This role of the researcher is common to ethnographic research approaches and may include observations of behaviors that occur in a public space. For example, an ethnographic researcher who is interested in understanding political protests would likely be regularly present in the public spaces related to the protests, but would be unknown to any particular individual as a researcher.

The observer-as-participant is known to the participants, but is clearly identified as a researcher and does not cross over to membership in the group being observed or to friendship. An example might include a researcher who is conducting an ethnographic study of a local YWCA in order to understand its after-school program in the life of youth. In this case, the researcher-as-participant would be known to youth because of that individual's regular presence, but researchers would not interact with the youth or program staff.

In both the observer-as-participant and participant-as-observer contexts, observations are used to gain a better understanding of the naturalistic context. In modern conceptualizations of qualitative research, the unique contribution of participants-as-observers is their insider perspective: as participants-as-observers, they can experience what the other participants are experiencing, gaining an understanding of the context in ways that nonparticipant observers cannot. Participants-as-observers sometimes fill roles within the group, although "without fully committing themselves to members' values and goals" (Adler & Adler, 1994, p. 380). Many studies of schools have involved participants-as-observers who, in roles such as teachers or coaches (see, e.g., Adler & Adler, 1991), become important people in the lives of the participants.

The final observational role is the complete participant, in which the investigator is a full-fledged member of the group before the research begins. Monographs are examples of qualitative products created by complete participants in an activity. In an example from psychotherapy, Freud took the role of complete participant in his description of his cases. The degree to which one becomes a participant obviously depends on the phenomenon being studied. As Patton (1987) noted, one cannot become chemically addicted in order to become a participant in drug treatment programs, although one could be involved in such programs in ancillary ways (e.g., as a staff member).

Whatever the role of the observer, the "challenge is to combine participation and observation so as to become capable of understanding the experience as an insider while describing the experience for outsiders" (Patton, 1987, p. 75). The tension between participant and observer is ever present and again emphasizes the necessity of research teams, which can process this tension and use it to produce an informative product.

Methods of Observations Obtaining data through observations involves several steps. In the first step, the observer must select the phenomenon and its setting. Care must be taken in making this selection. It is important that the setting be appropriate given the goals of the investigation and to select settings strategically so that the data are meaningful. For example, instead of choosing a representative (i.e., average) psychotherapist to study intensively, a qualitative researcher may be more interested in studying therapists identified as successful, powerful, charismatic, or even unsuccessful.

The second step involves training investigators to be skilled and careful observers. Observers must be taught to attend to detail, to separate the mundane from the important, to write highly descriptive field notes, to be sufficiently knowledgeable to make sense of the context, and to be open to reconciling observations with those of other research team members.

The third step is to gain access to the context being studied. Gaining access, of course, varies greatly, depending on the nature of the study. Observing public behavior involves no special arrangements other than finding a suitable vantage point, but investigations that involve potential risk to participants (e.g., undocumented workers or students who risk deportation if identified) require much energy to gain consent from participants, to minimize potential risks for participants, and to carefully consider other ethical and legal issues at hand (see Chapter 3 for more information). Trust is often one key to gaining entrée to a group and researchers are encouraged to carefully consider the personal, contextual, and ethical implications of becoming engaged in such investigations.

The fourth step involves deciding the time and duration of observations. At the outset, the observations are relatively unfocused and the researcher is getting the "lay of the land," and thus the duration of observation is as important as the time of the observation. Generally, observations should be taken at various times so as not to miss something particular to a certain time. For example, a study of work climate should involve observations from all shifts and during various days of the week. Clearly, the focus of the study should guide the researcher. For example, a researcher interested in how people from various disciplines negotiate their roles in multidisciplinary settings will want to observe instances in which the disciplines work together (e.g., in staff meetings or multidisciplinary work groups). As the research progresses, the data will suggest ways that the observers can focus their attention. For example, if a theme that begins to emerge from the work climate study is the different ways in which individuals approach conflict, the researchers will want to arrange observations during times when conflict is most likely to surface (e.g., near impending deadlines).

The fifth and final step is to collect the data. Most frequently observational data are the researcher's field notes (memos) taken during or immediately after the observations. Field notes are descriptions of everything relevant to understanding the phenomenon. Because relevance is not always clear in the beginning, initially field notes are likely to contain everything that happened. The novice observer will feel overwhelmed, but it should be recognized that almost anything missed will be repeated over and over again. As the observations become more focused, so will the field notes. Using the work climate study example, if it is observed that one group is superior in multidisciplinary work, the observations may be focused on how this is established as new members join the group; the field notes would similarly be focused on the process of transmitting power to incoming persons.

Field notes should contain basic descriptions of the setting—time, physical setting, persons present, the purpose of activity, and so forth—as well as complete descriptions of the interactions among the participants. Patton (1987) provides a good contrast between vague, generalized notes and detailed, concrete notes:

Research Application: Writing Field Notes

Vague field notes:	The new client was uneasy waiting for her intake interview.
Detailed field notes:	At first the client sat very stiffly on the chair next to the receptionist's desk. She picked up a magazine and let the pages flutter through her fingers very quickly without really looking at any of the pages. She set the magazine down, looked at her watch, pulled her skirt down, and picked up the magazine again. This time she didn't look at the magazine. She set it back down, took out a cigarette and began smoking. She would watch the receptionist out of the corner of her eye, and then look down at the magazine, and back up at the two or three other people waiting in the room. Her eyes moved from people to the magazine to the cigarette to the people to the magazine in rapid succession. She avoided eye contact. When her name was finally called she jumped like she was startled. (p. 93)

Source: Patton (1987, p. 93)

The latter description is more complete and involves little inference on the part of the observer, whereas the vague description both involves the inference that the client was uneasy and lacks data to enable confirmation of this inference at a later time. People's conversations should be recorded as close to verbatim as possible. Audiotapes can be used to supplement field notes if possible. Field notes should contain the observer's interpretations of events, but these interpretations should be so labeled to distinguish them from descriptions. Field notes might also contain working hypotheses, suggestions for interviewers, and so forth.

Undoubtedly, observations and field notes are influenced by the personal constructions of the observers. Multiple observers cross-checking their descriptions and their interpretations are vital for the integrity of observations, because trained observers may see a situation very differently. Acknowledging and honoring these perspectives is part and parcel of qualitative research.

Interviews   An interview is a social interaction (Davies & Dodd, 2002) that occurs between a participant (or group of participants) and the researcher. Although counselors and counseling psychologists are trained to ask questions, it is important to remember that "research interviewing has different goals and requires different skills" (Polkinghorne, 2005, p. 143). Although the goals of qualitative interviewing will depend on the type of qualitative research conducted, a generic goal is to

TABLE 16.2 : Types of Qualitative Interview Questions

Type	Examples
Background	Tell me about your background.
	Tell me about your work experiences at this agency.
Behavioral	If I had been with you during a typical day, what would I observe you doing?
	Describe a typical day with your family.
Opinion or belief	What do you usually do when this situation happens?
	What is your opinion about the recent decision to use untrained assistants?
	What do you believe is the best way to provide service to these clients?
Feeling questions	How do you feel about the decision to reduce the number of counselors in the agency?
Knowledge questions	How do you know when to terminate?
	How do clients get assigned to counselors?
Sensory questions	Describe for me the waiting room at your counselor's office.
	When you go to the principal's office after being tardy, what do you see?
Experiential	What is it like to be a counselor at this agency?
	Describe for me your experience of being in counseling for the first time.

understand the experience of the participant; therapeutic actions should be avoided. Patton (1987) described a typology of qualitative research questions. Using this typology, we offer some examples of questions (see Table 16.2).

Interviewing is the predominant mode of obtaining data in qualitative research in counseling and counseling psychology, and has been deemed to be one of the most difficult and advanced skills to master (Fassinger, 2005; Hill et al., 2005; Polkinghorne, 2005). DiCicco-Bloom and Crabtree (2006) and Sands, Bourjolly, and Roer-Strier (2007) discussed qualitative interviewing in depth. In particular, the procedures for conducting focus group interviews can be found in Kamberelis and Dimitriadis (2011).

Neophyte qualitative researchers are, therefore, encouraged to build their skills in this area. Within most strategies of inquiry that utilize interview data, researchers are expected to develop relationships with participants. Indeed, Yeh and Inman (2007) argued that collaboration is a necessary component of qualitative design, even though its emphasis varies by the specific design. Establishing relationships with research participants has implications for data collection (i.e., the richness of the data) and interpretation (i.e., the adequacy with which the research is able to base interpretations in the data).

Qualitative interviews can take a variety of forms (determined, in large part by the paradigm and approach to inquiry selected, as reviewed in Phase 3), and can range in terms of objectives and style. Regardless of interview format, there are a number of steps that are involved in conducting interviews. We now briefly examine the various steps in conducting qualitative interviews, adapted from Fontana and Frey (2000). These include gaining entrance into the community, understanding the language and culture of the interviewees, determining how best to present oneself to participants, identifying the interviewees, establishing rapport with interviewees, deciding how data will be collected (e.g., recording), and completing the interview(s).

The first step is to gain entrée to the setting in a way similar to gaining entrée for observations described previously. The second step involves preparing to understand the language and the culture of the interviewees. A qualitative investigator strives to have participants express their experiences in their own language. To achieve that goal, the questions should be understandable and nonoffensive to participants. Also, the interviewer must instantly understand what the interviewee means by various idioms and expressions so that appropriate follow-up questions can be asked. This knowledge is acquired from previous experience and diligent preparation, and can be refined over the course of interviews. For example, in a research project that seeks to understand the intergenerational transmission of social class information within a family, the researchers needed to take care to understand how adolescents were interpreting this construct and to use language that was pertinent to their understanding in interview questions. Also, it is often helpful (and important) to seek feedback on the interview protocol from experts who are familiar with the phenomenon under study or by conducting a pilot interview prior to actual data collection.

The third step is to make a decision about self-presentation. Whereas quantitative researchers present themselves as objective scientists, qualitative researchers can choose among various self-presentations. For example, a researcher might present herself to women who have experienced domestic violence as a feminist as well as a researcher. Basically, the issue here is the degree to which the researchers should share of themselves and how it would affect the participants' willingness to share their stories or personal accounts.

The fourth step is to identify the interviewees. One way to think about this is to considerhow to identify *key informants,* or individuals whose perceptions are particularly important for understanding the context being studied. Of course, the key informants will likely be unknown to the investigator initially, but as knowledge is gained, their identity will emerge. Key informants are often those who have a different experience than the norm, who are willing to divulge sensitive information, and so forth. In some cases, key informants may not be directly involved in the phenomenon being studied. For example, the support staff in a mental health clinic could provide important information relative to counseling at the agency, even though they neither deliver nor receive treatment. In quantitative research the emphasis is on representative samples, but in qualitative research the goal is to obtain a depth of understanding, and thus the choice of interviewees is a crucial process. Indeed, this is key to reaching theoretical saturation (later described in the section "Grounded Theory").

The fifth step is to establish rapport with each interviewee, a process that is beneficial for two reasons. First, rapport leads to trust, which in turn leads to honest and descriptive responses. Second, an empathic stance enables the interviewer to better understand the interviewee's responses. Interviewers must take care, however, that the natural affinity that goes hand in hand with empathy does not cloud their assessment of the situation.

The sixth and final step is to decide how the interview data will be collected. If done unobtrusively, interviews should be recorded and subsequently transcribed for analysis. In any case, field notes should be taken (note that the comments regarding field notes for observations apply here as well). Important information is contained in the nonverbal responses of the interviewees, and in the setting and its surroundings. Therefore, certain critical data may be missing when interviews are conducted over the phone or via email.

Types of Interviews   There are three common formats of interview questions utilized: structured interviews, unstructured interviews, and semistructured interviews. In a structured interview, the questions and the order in which they are asked are determined a priori. Moreover, responses are classified into categories or are quantified according to some protocol that also is developed a priori. The interviewer develops rapport with the respondent but takes a neutral stance in that he or she does not show either approval or disapproval of responses and does not follow up on unusual, interesting, or uninformative responses. The advantage of structured interviews is that they are standardized across respondents and minimize variations. However, they have limited usefulness in qualitative research because they (a) shape data to conform to structures that emanated from the investigator's previously held beliefs about the phenomenon, (b) use a standard language across respondents (rather than questions customized to the language of particular respondents), and (c) restrict affective components of responses (Fontana & Frey, 1994). Although technically not an interview, the questions can be printed and administered to participants, which is similar to a questionnaire except that the responses are not constrained in any way.

On the other end of the continuum, unstructured interviews provide latitude to explore the responses of participants and to adapt questions for respondents. Qualitative researchers often use unstructured interviews to collect data, and the responses would not be quantified. The type of question asked in qualitative research is shaped by the type of research conducted; thus, ethnographers approach this endeavor differently from grounded theorists (for example). Because the questions are not determined a priori, the interviewer has great latitude to explore the phenomenon and ask probing questions to get a more complete description. The respondents are encouraged to use their own language to describe their experiences; however, the interviewers must take care not to shape the responses by covertly reinforcing certain types of responses (e.g.,following up only on responses that fit the researchers' assumptions). As Polkinghorne (2005) suggested, "although the produced account is affected by the researcher, it is important that the participant remain the author of the description" (p. 143). Also, in the case when more than one researcher is conducting interviews, interviewers need to discuss how each person's personal styles may influence the participants' responses and subsequent analytic results. Furthermore, note that data from unstructured interviews take a lot more time to collect and organize. Researchers usually need to do follow-up interviews because new insights about the phenomenon (and thus, additional questions) may emerge as more participants are interviewed.

Semistructured interviews offer a balance between structured and unstructured interviews. Specifically, researchers may use semistructured interviews to provide some consistency across interviews while also allowing the respondents ample opportunity for offering richer and more personalized responses. Semistructured interviews require the use of an interview protocol that is the same for all participants and also uses a discovery-oriented approach to qualitative interviewing that includes a list of questions that is permitted to adapt with each participant and as new insights emerge throughout the course of the study. The challenge of utilizing the semistructured format lies in the decision of how much structure should be imposed on the interview process. In addition, as with unstructured interviews, the interviewer must be careful to consider when follow-up questions or probes are used so as not to unintentionally steer the direction of the interview according to preconceived notions or researcher expectations. The example interview questions identified Table 16.2 are exemplars of the types of questions that may be used in semistructured interviews. Examples of probes include prompts such as "Can you tell me more about that?" and "When you described that experience, you used the word ____. Can you tell me what you meant by that?"

It is important to note that all interviews do not take place in a one-to-one context (i.e.,one interviewer with one interviewee). Group interviews are another interview format that allow for the researcher to collect different information. In group interviews, sometimes called focus groups, more than one person is interviewed simultaneously. Madriz (2000) describes a focus group as "a collective rather than an individualistic research method that focuses on the multivocality of participants' attitudes, experiences, and beliefs" (p. 836). Particularly exciting possibilities exist for focus groups, a modality that evolved from marketing research related to reactions to products, advertisements, and services (for a brief history of the development of the focus group method, see Morgan, 1988, or Madriz, 2000.) In marketing research, the members of a focus group are strangers, but applications to qualitative research suggest possibilities for using intact groups, such as the staff of a job placement agency. The goal of a focus group is to obtain the participants' opinions, not to reach a consensus or reconcile opposing views; the expression of different opinions is informative. Typically, the participants in a focus group are relatively homogeneous and are asked to reflect on a particular issue. The economy of using group interviews is self-evident. An additional advantage of the group format is the interaction among the respondents, which can provide richer information as various members of the group provide more details, disagree on points, and reconcile differences of opinions. Having participants respond in a social context is thought to provide honest and responsible comments. However, the interviewer needs to ensure that minority opinions are allowed expression, given the natural tendency for such opinions to be suppressed (Madriz, 2000). A good illustration of this method was provided by Maguire and her colleagues (2008), who used focus groups to explore the vocational experiences of people with HIV/AIDS.

Existing Materials   Existing materials are written text and artifacts, which can inform qualitative research in ways that observations and interviews cannot. Such materials are essential to any historical study for which direct observations or interviews are impossible. Written documents are of two types, official records and personal documents (Lincoln & Guba, 1985). Official documents include government reports, licenses, contracts, news articles, and so forth. Personal documents include diaries, letters, email, literature, field notes, and so forth. Artifacts include material and electronic traces, such as buildings, art, posters, and nontextual computer files—essentially any disturbance of the natural environment created by people. The goal is to use these materials to provide a richer understanding of the phenomena being examined.

Two types of existing material that have been utilized are the psychotherapy session and client records. Specifically, psychotherapy researchers may review client sessions via a verbal recording (i.e., a tape recording) or as text (i.e., a transcript) or may examine the contents of client records. Researchers may rely upon such information to code and analyze questions regarding a variety of questions, such as client progress or client-therapist interactions.

Of the three sources of qualitative data discussed (observations, interviews, and existing materials), existing materials are, in our opinion, the most underutilized within the counseling and counseling psychology literature. These materials can be particularly valuable, and also pose challenges for the researcher with regard to interpretation of the text or artifact. For example, when reviewing historical materials, the researcher is constrained by the material at hand and may be limited in an ability to collect additional information.

Data Coding and Analyses   McCracken (1988) summarized the goal of all qualitative analysis as determining the patterns, themes, relationships, and assumptions that inform the participants' experience related to the topic. Coding is a method used across a number of qualitative research paradigms and strategies of inquiry. Most qualitative inquiry approaches rely upon data coding in order to tease apart the data and begin to identify themes in the data. In other words, coding is used to "fracture" (Strauss, 1987, p. 29) the data in order to identity patterns, themes, or categories that are grounded in the data. The actual process of data coding (e.g., timing for data coding, steps to coding), however, differs by qualitative approach as reviewed previously in Phase 3. Regardless of the specific process of coding, however, most approaches use coding to allow themes and relationships to emerge from the data. Themes are recurrent patterns in data that represent a concept, whereas relationships are the interconnections among the themes.

Analysis of participant data typically begins as an inductive process as the researcher works to understand the meanings of the data and then transitions to a deductive process as existing data are compared with new data that surface throughout the data collection process. This cycle is often referred to as recursive, iterative, abductive, fluid, or circular, and it allows the research process (as well as the interview questions, themselves, in some strategies of inquiry) to flexibly adapt over time based upon emerging data. Yeh and Inman (2007) defined this as circularity, or the process by which "the complexity, depth, and comprehensiveness of qualitative research as it emerges from its connectedness across researcher, method, analysis, and developing theory" (p. 384).

Qualitative research relies upon a variety of materials, and it is common for researchers to utilize a variety of types of data in a given study. For example, bracketing of researcher biases, field notes, memoing, interviews, and existing artifacts may all be used in order to assist the researcher in better understanding the subject matter at hand and making the phenomena more visible in some way. In other words, these data provide "layers of analysis" (Creswell, 1998, p. 36) that are used for interpretation. Because of this, Denzin and Lincoln (2011) described a popular image of a qualitative researcher as a "bricoleur, quilt maker, or a person who assembles images into montages" (p. 4). They suggested that qualitative researchers use data from a variety of sources to construct scenes upon which interpretations are made. As such, varying perspectives, experiences, voices, and sources of data are woven together to facilitate interpretation.

Phase 5: The Art, Practices, and Politics of Interpretation and Evaluation

The final, or fifth, phase of qualitative research, according to Denzin and Lincoln (2011), involves data interpretation and presentation. This phase asks the researcher to carefully interpret the data and present it in accordance with careful consideration of the implications of the findings. It also includes attention to the various criteria used to evaluate qualitative findings.

Interpretation   As is the case for the collection and analysis of qualitative data, the interpretation and presentation of qualitative data depend on the paradigm and particular qualitative approach to inquiry utilized. Wolcott (1994) suggested that interpretation, in its most general sense, is aimed at extracting meaning and identifying context. Interpretations of the data often hinge on the extent to which they are based in the data (Denzin & Lincoln, 2011) and to which the researcher is able to answer the questions "how?" or "what?" (Creswell, 1998).

Rather than providing a theory of a specific phenomenon by discussing and relating themes in the data, interpretation addresses more global issues, such as "What is the role of race and ethnicity in American society?" and "How do cultural factors affect conceptions of mental health and treatment?" Wolcott noted that "at the interpretive extreme, a researcher-as-writer may seem merely to swoop down into the field for a descriptive morsel or two and then retreat once again to the lofty heights of theory or speculation" (p. 11) and that interpretation "is well suited to mark a threshold in thinking and writing at which the researcher transcends tactual data and cautious analyses and begins to probe into what is to be made of them" (p. 36). Interpretation requires an ability to synthesize information in an effort to communicate the implications of the findings, or in essence, the bigger picture to readers. Clearly, novice researchers need to acquire more training and experiences in order to master these types of higher level skills.

Thick description (Geertz, 1973) is often cited as the most basic means of presenting qualitative findings. Essentially, a thick description is an untouched and thorough presentation of the data (i.e., a direct quote from a participant). The researcher may write some introductory and transitory material, but the presentation principally consists of lengthy excerpts from interviews, field notes, and existing materials (text and/or descriptions of artifacts).

The consumers of thick descriptions have the raw data, which for the most part have not been altered by the investigator. In this way, "the data speak for themselves" and provide a rich account of what happened. Of course, the process of observing, interviewing, collecting materials, and deciding what to describe filters what is available to consumers. Thick descriptions are closer to the phenomenon being studied than are any other means, qualitative or quantitative.

Despite the primary advantage that the data are minimally filtered, there are some disadvantages to fully relying upon thick descriptions. True descriptions are too lengthy for journal articles, and many important thick descriptions languish as lengthy dissertations or unpublished reports. Another disadvantage is that the thick descriptions may be unfocused and uninteresting. When describing this critique, Wolcott (1994) put it this way:

> Readers are likely to get the idea that the researcher has been unable to sort out (or unwilling to throw away) data and has simply passed the task along. ... [D]ata that do not 'speak' to the person who gathered and reported them are not likely to strike up a conversation with subsequent readers either. (pp. 13–14)

A goal of qualitative interpretation is that the story, as told by the participants and as interpreted by the investigator, will be fascinating enough to hold the interest of readers.

Rarely are qualitative investigators able to present all data verbatim in a thick description, and thus they must use various strategies to present a condensed but still relatively complete description. As discussed earlier in this chapter, the methods of condensing and presenting the data vary in accordance with the strategies of inquiry adopted. Regardless, the investigator has the critical task of deciding what must go, and there are few guidelines. Crucial decisions about data should be made through a process that acknowledges the investigators' suppositions. Moreover, the process involved in examining these suppositions and making sense of the data in the context of these suppositions should be a prominent part of the presentation so that readers can understand how the descriptions were distilled to a reasonable length.

When interpreting the data, the qualitative researcher is expected to attend to potential implications of the findings. Denzin and Lincoln (2011) described the process as "both artistic and political" (p. 15). As such, they urged qualitative researchers to carefully evaluate their processes and do what they can to guard against potential negative implications resulting from the interpretations. As discussed in Chapter 3, we are required as researchers to consider the legal and ethical implications of our findings so as to protect from negative or erroneous interpretations by readers who may not be familiar with scientific research or academic publishing, or qualitative research in general. For example, researchers must take care in presenting the limitations to a given investigation. Given the richness of data gathered through qualitative approaches and the power of the participants' stories as recounted by the researcher, it might be easy for a person unfamiliar with scientific research to assume that the findings from an investigation can be applied to a large population of individuals even though the actual sample relied upon a relatively small number of participants—or in the case of a case study, a single participant.

Evaluation The final or fifth phase of the research process also includes an emphasis on evaluation of the research. Questions related to evidence or rigor within qualitative research have long been considered controversial (e.g., Denzin, 2009). In response to questions raised about the credibility of qualitative research, Hill and colleagues (1997) moved toward establishing evaluative procedures that draw from postpositivist paradigms, whereas others (e.g., Morrow, 2005) have encouraged qualitative researchers to hold to their values for evidence associated with their study and paradigmatic methodology (e.g., Denzin, 2009). Indeed, Denzin speculated about the dangers of adopting a gold standard by which qualitative research is evaluated. He stated:

> We live in a depressing historical moment, violent spaces, unending wars against persons of color, repression, the falsification of evidence, the collapse of critical, democratic discourse, repressive neo-liberalism, disguised as dispassionate objectivity prevails. Global efforts to impose a new orthodoxy on critical social science inquiry must be resisted, a hegemonic politics of evidence cannot be allowed. Too much is at stake. (p. 155)

Nonetheless, questions related to standards of quality have been a topic of much attention. A variety of terms are utilized to describe evaluation within the context of qualitative research. These include rigor, reliability, validity, credibility, trustworthiness, fairness, authenticity, attentiveness, engagement, awareness, and carefulness (e.g., Davies & Dodd, 2002; Morrow, 2005). Most qualitative researchers, therefore, assume that ethics are inherently connected to evaluations of rigor and to the process by which research is conducted (Davies & Dodd, 2002). Davies and Dodd described rigor in this way:

> We want our qualitative research to be reliable but not in the sense of reliability over time and across contexts. Rather, we aim for a reliability in our data based on consistency and care in the application of research practices, which are reflected in the visibility of research practices, and a reliability in our analysis and conclusions, reflected in an open account that remains mindful of the partiality and limits of our research findings. (p. 280)

Standards of trustworthiness, rigor, and credibility vary by paradigm, so it is essential that researchers and reviewers understand and evaluate qualitative studies accordingly. Nevertheless, some authors have argued that common elements cut across paradigms and strategies of inquiry. For example, Morrow (2005) suggested that there are four domains of trustworthiness that transcend paradigms: (a) social validity, (b) subjectivity and self-reflexivity, (c) adequacy of the data, and (d) adequacy of the interpretations. We describe each of these domains next.

Social Validity Social validity is the social value of qualitative research (Morrow, 2005). This refers to the notion that qualitative research is evaluated based upon the extent that it has implications of value to other researchers, practitioners, and the public (Tracy, 2010). Tracy (2010, p. 849) put it this way:

> Good qualitative research is like a crystal, with various facets representing the aims, needs, and desires of various stakeholders including participants, the academy, society, lay public, policy makers, and last, but certainly not least, the researcher. (Ellingson, 2008)

Qualitative research that is based in a critical theory paradigm takes this domain of trustworthiness one step further and argues that research also must be evaluated on the basis of consequential validity (Lather, 1993), or the extent to which the research provides an impetus for societal change.

Subjectivity and Self-Reflexivity   Subjectivity and self-reflexivity are considered to be core to qualitative research and comprise the second domain used to establish trustworthiness (Morrow, 2005). Self-reflexivity is a practice used to explore researcher biases and the method by which to best address those biases (Morrow, 2005; Rennie, 2004).

The exact components of this process vary by strategy of inquiry but all share an emphasis on researchers acknowledging and bracketing their biases. The aim of this bracketing, however, differs across strategy of inquiry. For example, typically CQR relies upon auditors or judges in order to provide checks on the data so as to guard against researcher influences on the data and move toward objectivity, whereas phenomenology relies heavily on memoing throughout the research process in order to appropriately integrate the values, beliefs, and assumptions of the researcher and explicate the analysis. Member checks (i.e., asking participants to review the data or the researcher's interpretation of the data in order to provide the feedback; Guba & Lincoln, 1998) and method triangulation (e.g., using one research team comprised of individuals inside the cultural group of the participants and one comprised of individuals outside the cultural group of the participants to provide checks and balances related to research team bias; Denzin, 1978) are other methods that may be used in order to address researcher biases in data analysis and interpretation.

Adequacy of the Data   Third, trustworthiness can be evaluated by the adequacy of the data (Morrow, 2005). In other words, rich and complex findings require sufficient data. It is not enough to assume that completing interviews with 10 participants will yield adequate data to offer interpretations. Instead, researchers must take care to ensure that their data are appropriately rich in order to capture the nuance in a given experience or phenomenon.

A variety of factors impact the adequacy of the data and may be used as indicators for the researcher. These include issues related to the sample and interviews themselves, such as sample size, the quality and depth of the interview data, redundancy in the data, and whether theoretical saturation has been reached. This may include deliberate attempts on the part of the researcher to seek out unexpected findings, discrepant evidence, and disconfirming examples to ensure that the data are appropriately rich and the interpretations adequately nuanced. In addition, adequacy of the data can be evaluated via the use of multiple points of evidence and data triangulation from a variety of data sources (e.g., interviews, field notes, member checks, self-reflective journals, participant observations, and other artifacts).

Adequacy of the Interpretation   Finally, qualitative research is evaluated based upon the adequacy of interpretation (Morrow, 2005). As noted previously, adequacy of interpretation refers to the extent to which interpretations are authentically and consistently grounded in the data. This requires that researchers become immersed in the data, have a well-defined and articulated analytic strategy, and present findings in a manner that balances thick description (e.g., participant words) with researcher interpretation. As highlighted throughout this chapter, researchers are expected to be aware of the extent to which they may impose their own perspectives or biases on the interpretations and must closely listen to participants in order to adequately understand their experiences.

Tracy (2010) identified eight criteria by which to evaluate qualitative research. These eight criteria overlap with many of those proposed by Morrow (2005), and include worthy topic, rich rigor, sincerity, credibility, resonance, significant contribution, ethics, and meaningful coherence. These criteria, and questions to assist readers in evaluating each, are listed in Table 16.3. At the time of writing of this chapter, Division 5 of the American Psychological Association had assembled a Task Force

TABLE 16.3 Research Application: Evaluating Qualitative Research

Criteria by Which to Evaluate Qualitative Research	Question(s) to Guide
Worthy topic	Is this research relevant, timely, significant, and interesting?
Rich rigor	Does the study utilize sufficient, abundant, appropriate, and complex theoretical constructs? Does the study utilize data and time in the field? Are the samples and contexts appropriate to the study aims? Does the study appropriately engage in data collection and analysis in accordance with paradigms and strategies of inquiry?
Sincerity	Does the study integrate self-reflexivity and transparency regarding methods, recruitment, ethics, and challenges?
Credibility	Is the research marked by thick description, triangulation or crystallization, and member reflections?
Resonance	Does the research influence, affect, or move a reader via transferable findings, generalizability, and evocative representation?
Significant contribution	Does the research contribute conceptually/theoretically, practically, morally, methodologically, and/or heuristically?
Ethical	Does the research consider procedural ethics associated with human subjects research? Does the study consider situational and culturally specific ethics, relational ethics, and exiting ethics (or the process by which researchers share the results so as to avoid unjust or unintended consequences)?
Meaningful coherence	Does the study achieve what it purports and use methods and procedures that match its aims? Does the study meaningfully interconnect literature, research questions, findings, and interpretations?

Source: Table adapted from Tracy, 2010, p. 840

on the Publication of Qualitative Research. The recommendations that emerge from this Task Force are likely to have important implications for the design and publication of future qualitative research.

FOUR EXAMPLES OF QUALITATIVE RESEARCH STRATEGIES OF INQUIRY

In this section, we want to introduce readers to different types of qualitative research in order to provide an overview of qualitative research strategies. As noted previously in Phase 3, there are more than 20 different strategies for how investigators approach conducting qualitative research. In this section, we will introduce you to only four types of qualitative inquiry strategies used in counseling and counseling psychology. We will not only describe these four methods of inquiry, but also illustrate different components of each of these four methods by providing specific illustrations from recent publications. In this way, we hope that readers will start to understand different ways that qualitative research can provide critically important scientific knowledge about phenomenon of interest to counselors and counseling psychologists. In addition, we hope that readers will understand that there are many different inquiry strategies that qualitative researchers can utilize to examine topics of interest, and that there is no one best way to conceptualize a qualitative study. Rather, the selected inquiry strategy should be informed by the research question of interest.

Specifically, in this section, we summarize three strategies of qualitative inquiry that are most commonly cited within counseling and counseling psychology research: grounded theory (GT), phenomenology, and consensual qualitative research (CQR). In addition, we summarize participatory action research (PAR)/community-based participatory research (CBPR) as a strategy of inquiry that has been gaining increased attention within counseling and counseling psychology literature. A complete description of each of these approaches (or the numerous other approaches to qualitative inquiry) is admittedly beyond the scope of this chapter, so our intent is to situate each approach in its associated paradigm and to describe the primary features. Readers who are interested in a particular approach should review its specific methodological literature. In each section that follows, we briefly describe the core features among the four strategies of inquiry (i.e., GT, phenomenology, CQR, and PAR/CBPR) and highlight these features with an exemplar manuscript. Note that the exemplars cited are good examples of qualitative research, but are not the "only correct" way to conduct qualitative inquiry. While a detailed review of the studies themselves is beyond the purposes of this chapter, we refer readers to specific sections of the manuscripts in order to illustrate how the primary features associated with each approach are depicted in a published study.

Grounded Theory

This section provides the definition and purpose of the GT approach. Then, its primary features will be discussed: (a) memo writing or memoing, (b) constant comparative method, (c) theoretical sampling, and (d) the emerging theory that is grounded in data.

GT methods have gained increased popularity among researchers across various disciplines over the past two decades (see Fassinger, 2005; Rennie, Watson & Monteiro, 2002). Indeed, these approaches have been named "the most influential paradigm for qualitative research in the social sciences today" (Denzin, 1997, as cited in Patton, 2002, p. 487). The GT approach also has been described as the most commonly used design within the counseling literature (Morse et al., 2009).

GT was developed by Glaser and Strauss (1967) in an attempt to challenge the dominant trend of "excessive reliance on the quantitative testing of hypotheses derived from a small number of grant (totalizing) theories, typically through numerical survey and other statistical approaches" (Henwood & Pidgeon, 2003, p. 132). The GT approach is rooted in sociology and the tradition of symbolic interactionism. It is appropriate for studying "the local interactions and meanings as related to the social context in which they actually occur" (Pidgeon, 1996, p. 75). As such, scholars (e.g., Fassinger, 2005; Morrow, 2007) have maintained that it is particularly attractive to counseling researchers.

Since GT's inception, a number of authors, including Glaser and Strauss, have expanded and extended GT to include the integration of explicit constructivist components and pragmatist perspectives (e.g., Strauss & Corbin, 1990). Indeed, GT has a complicated history in that it has been associated with seemingly discrepant philosophical views, including realism (a direct reflection of the data), interpretivism (multiple realities exist and each are valid), and constructivism (meaning is constructed via symbolic interactionism and believing that values are socially constructed; Guba & Lincoln, 1994; Henwood & Pidgeon, 2003). Some of this history emerged as a result of Glaser and Strauss diverging in their advocated approach to GT. Strauss (e.g., Strauss & Corbin, 1990, 1998) began to emphasize the use of particular coding practices (i.e., open coding, axial coding, and selective coding) in order to specify the properties and dimensions of categories and organize the emerging theory. Glaser (1992), on the other hand, stressed the importance of a constant comparative method and theoretical memoing in generating a theoretical model and openly criticized Strauss as abandoning the inductive and discovery-oriented approach (Charmaz, 2006). Charmaz (2006), who studied with both Glaser and Strauss, later offered a constructivist GT approach that bridges these perspectives by offering a research method that provides structure while permitting paradigmatic flexibility.

These divergent perspectives often perplex novice researchers. Readers are encouraged to consult the key literature for more information about specific GT methods before embarking on a GT study. Nonetheless, there are some commonalities across various GT approaches that will be described next: (a) memo writing or memoing, (b) constant comparative method, (c) theoretical sampling, and (d) the emerging theory that is grounded in data. Readers are encouraged to review the exemplar study (Thompson, Cole, & Nitzarim, 2012) in order to elucidate these features. This study used GT to explore the experience of social class in the psychotherapy room among 16 participants who self-identified as low income and who had attended at least six sessions of psychotherapy within six months of the interview.

Memo Writing or Memoing   Throughout all stages of the research process, GT emphasizes the *process* of data collection in an attempt to ensure the trustworthiness of the data. Trustworthiness of the data was described previously. Specifically, researchers are expected to make preliminary and ongoing analytic notes about personal assumptions and biases, reactions to interviews and codes, and other ideas through the process of memoing. Memo writing provides a space for researchers to record "hunches; comments on new samples to be checked out; explanations of modifications to categories; emerging theoretical reflections; and links to the literature" (Pidgeon & Henwood, 1996, p. 95). Disagreement exists among grounded theorists with regard to how much or little a researcher should be immersed in the literature on the research question prior to the study, but all agree that researchers must enter with an open mind after setting acknowledging assumptions and biases.

Charmaz (2000) described memo writing in this way:

> Memo writing is the intermediate step between coding and the first draft of the completed analysis. ... It can help us to define leads for collecting data—both for further initial coding and later theoretical sampling. Through memo writing, we elaborate processes, assumptions, and actions that are subsumed under our codes. (p. 517)

Pidgeon and Henwood (1996) also warned that researchers should "write a memo as soon as the thought has occurred, for, if left unrecorded, it is likely to be forgotten" (p. 95). In sum, memo writing serves as an instrumental mechanism for the constant comparative practice (reviewed next) and facilitates the theoretical sampling and theory development processes that will be described in the subsequent sections. Thompson et al. (2012) described their use of memo writing in three places in the manuscript. First, in the context of describing themselves as researchers (p. 210):

> The study was conducted in a collaborative format in which all three researchers were involved in each component of the project. Given the focus within GT of researchers as instruments (Glaser & Strauss, 1967), potential researcher bias was considered. The list of these biases included: (a) knowledge of the therapeutic process and a value for the importance of common factors in the therapist-client relationship, (b) cultural assumptions and biases regarding low income clients, (c) personal SES identity and awareness related to this identity as described below, and (d) criticisms of the psychotherapy literature for ignoring issues related to poverty and social class as a unique cultural identity.
>
> The first author is a 32-year old assistant professor at a large Midwestern university. Growing up in a lower-middle class family situated within a more privileged community, she oscillated between being surrounded at school by those from more privileged backgrounds and at "home" by her extended family members who were primarily lower class. The second researcher is a Caucasian 30-year old, third year doctoral student who grew up in a low income urban center with a single mother until adolescence, at which point she moved to a homogeneous middle class suburb. The third author is a 25-year old, second year doctoral student who grew up in a middle class home. As a child, she attended a private Jewish school where most of her peers were middle-upper to upper class. Her father was often unemployed or between jobs and thus, she experienced feeling different or less privileged than her peers. Throughout data analysis, each researcher was involved in the local political movement related to employee unions that has resulted in decreased medical and mental health service to low income individuals in this region.

Second, they described their memoing in their description of the development of interview protocol (p. 211):

> A core set of open-ended questions was developed at the outset of the study to guide data collection and was based on the literature reviewed previously. Consistent with GT (Charmaz, 2006), the interview questions and probes evolved as data emerged and the need for clarification of new subject matter became relevant after coding was completed following each interview (See Appendix A for a final list of all questions). The three authors comprised the interviewers for this study, and each had previously engaged in qualitative research projects, attended trainings, and/or completed classes in qualitative methodology. The first author, a licensed psychologist, supervised all interviews. At the conclusion of each interview, the interviewer completed field notes indicating nonverbal observations during the interview, potential biases that emerged, perceived rapport with the participant, and other significant interview characteristics in order to include nuanced findings in addition to the audio recordings (Creswell, 2007). Interviews were transcribed verbatim.

And third, they depicted their memoing in their presentation of the data analysis process (p. 210):

> Several data analysis techniques and checks were utilized to maintain quality and rigor. First, we individually coded each interview transcript. The transcripts were then reviewed until the team agreed upon, or added codes, to satisfy all emerging ideas. Second, we met with an expert qualitative researcher, who acted as an auditor, twice during the coding process. The auditor was used to limit or control for bias, offer "investigator triangulation" (Denzin, 2008, p. 17), and put forward alternative perspectives on the data analysis. Our auditor reviewed transcripts, interview questions, and emerging themes and presented feedback to us in order to represent an impartial analysis of the data. The auditor affirmed that the emerging themes accurately represented the transcript data. After discussions, revisiting transcripts, and reflection of the emerging findings, there were no issues of discrepancy between the auditor and the researchers. Third, we attempted to use member checks in order to enhance the reliability of data. All participants received a copy of the results and had an opportunity to offer feedback or suggestions to the researchers. No participant contacted the researchers with feedback regarding the results. Finally, the research team maintained a detailed audit trail that included meeting notes and discussions about biases and implications. Field notes were referenced during data analysis to create a trustworthy and authentic theoretical framework. (Lincoln & Guba, 1985)

Constant Comparative Method   Most approaches to GT utilize the constant comparative method to develop an increasingly complex understanding of the data. Theory development occurs as the researcher continuously compares new data to data gathered early in the process, data to codes, codes to categories, and categories back to data. The constant comparative method, often considered a hallmark of GT research, consists of four stages: (a) comparing incidents (or exemplars) applicable to each category, (b) integrating categories and their properties, (c) delimiting the theory, and (d) writing the theory (Glaser & Strauss, 1967). It is worth noting that although one stage leads to another, some earlier stages will continue operating simultaneously until the termination of the data analysis.

Glaser and Strauss (1967) developed the constant comparative method to generate "many categories, properties, and hypotheses about general problems" and to formulate a theory that is grounded in the data (p. 104). Pidgeon and Henwood (1996) emphasized the importance of documenting this analytical process fully, which helps to track the procedures and helps the researchers become aware of their implicit, a priori assumptions. Pidgeon and Henwood described the analytic process using the flowchart shown in Figure 16.1.

Consistent with the depiction in Figure 16.1, this data collection and analytic procedure was described as a "zigzag" process by Creswell (1998), "out to the field to gather information, analyze the data, back to the field to gather more information, analyze the data, and so forth" (p. 57). In other words, data collection and data analysis are not discrete stages. This method sets GT apart from content/thematic analysis, which employs reliability and validity as criteria and uses "the counting of instances within a predefined set of mutually exclusive and jointly exhaustive categories" (see Pidgeon, 1996, p. 78).

Grounded theory research is often characterized by rigorous data analysis procedures that include three phases of coding: open, axial, and selective (Strauss & Corbin, 1990). Thompson et al. (2012) described their data analysis process in detail (p. 211) as follows:

> Data analysis was conducted via the methods described by Glaser and Strauss (1967) and later expanded by Charmaz (2006). The interviews were coded in three phases, which led to the emergence of core themes through an interconnected storyline. The initial phase (open coding) occurred following the completion of each interview and included a low level of abstraction in which all members of the research team named concepts very close

FIGURE 16.1 : The Grounded Theory Approach

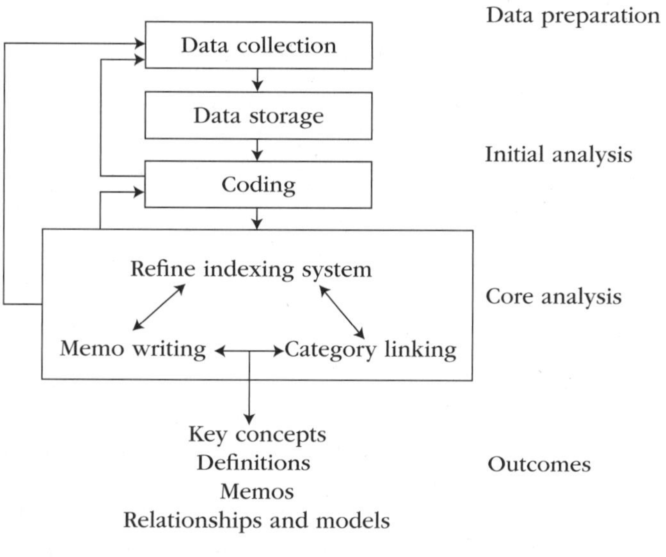

Source: Adapted from Pidgeon & Henwood, 1996.

to the interviewees' own words. Interviews were coded using a line-by-line level of analysis in which individual responses were coded into more concise statements. Each author independently completed the open-coding process and then came together to share her codes, reflect upon implicit meanings of the emerging statements, and examine how the units of meaning were similar or different from one another.

In the axial phase, the line-by-line codes were placed into higher order categories (Glaser & Strauss, 1967). Data were grouped and arranged on the basis of parallels and theoretical connections across transcripts. We remained open to new findings as they emerged across all 16 transcripts, avoided forcing data into larger categories (as recommended by Glaser, 1978), and included all opinions rather than debating to consensus. According to GT methodology, the first two phases of coding were completed after the interviews were transcribed so that the line-by-line coding from prior interviews was used to focus the axial coding for subsequent interviews. This process culminated in the construction of 70 distinct codes across the 16 transcripts.

The third phase (selective coding) represents the highest level of data abstraction and involves synthesizing and integrating the axial codes so that they can be incorporated into theory (Glaser & Strauss, 1967). During this phase, we considered the list of codes in its entirety, revisited participants' incidents within codes, and began extrapolating the main themes that brought together the relationships and connections within the data. This process of selective coding began when it was apparent that new and unique themes within the data were no longer emerging (which coincided with the time when the final three transcripts were being coded).

Next, we independently grouped together the 70 codes into themes that captured the essence of the codes and came together to share findings and to identify the emergent theoretical model. Throughout each phase of the coding process, we moved toward higher points of abstraction and nearer to the development of a theory, and analysis shifted between levels of abstraction. This flexibility is especially important when one is considering whether theoretical saturation has been met. (Charmaz, 2006; Strauss & Corbin, 1998)

Theoretical Sampling Theoretical sampling characterizes the ongoing analytic process in the field and is a theory-driven method of sampling. It helps researchers target new data that might facilitate the emergence of a theory after the initial analysis of the data at hand. It is used by grounded theorists to select a sample of individuals to study based on their contribution to the development of the theory. Often, sampling begins with a relatively homogeneous sample of individuals who are similar and have experience with the research question. As data collection proceeds and the categories emerge, the researcher seeks a heterogeneous sample to explicate the conditions under which the emerging categories hold true (Creswell, 1998). Theoretical saturation occurs when "the new data fit into the categories already devised" (Charmaz, 2000, p. 520), thereby marking the end of data collection.

The data sources of grounded theory research include a combination of data types (e.g., archival/textual materials, participant observation, autobiographies, and journals). Data analysis begins upon data collection and allows the research process to be flexible and emergent (Morrow & Smith, 2000). For example, interview questions may emerge through the process of data collection as new information is uncovered by participants that moves the research into new directions. Theoretical sampling suggests that the researcher uses the existing data and emerging analysis in order to identify what is not yet known. In this way, theoretical sampling differs from the sampling method used in quantitative research, in which researchers are expected to obtain a representative sample in order to enhance generalizability of the research findings.

Emerging Theory Is Grounded in the Data   Morrow and colleagues (2012) described theory in the context of GT as "a conceptual model" (p. 101) and Charmaz (2006) suggested that it "assumes emergent, multiple realities; indeterminacy; facts and values as linked; trust as provisional; and social life as processual" (p. 126). In other words, ideas and themes emerge from the data and are presumed to offer insight into reality. Throughout the research process, grounded theorists develop analytic interpretations of the data to focus further data collection, which is subsequently used to inform and refine the emerging theory. In this way, the research process is interactive and requires a relationship between the researchers and participants that leads to the discovery of meaning.

Grounded theorists maintain that theories should be derived from the data. Unlike quantitative researchers, grounded theorists neither test an existing theory nor try to fit their data into preconceived concepts. Instead, all of the theoretical concepts should be derived from the data analysis and account for the variation in the studied phenomenon. This process allows the theoretical framework to emerge through the aforementioned constant comparative practice, memo writing, and theoretical sampling processes (Charmaz, 2000).

Thompson et al. (2012) described this process in their articulation of their data analysis process previously and presented their emerging theoretical framework in a figure (p. 212) designed to capture the dynamic process by which social class is experienced within psychotherapy. Figure 16.2 is used to illustrate the process that

FIGURE 16.2 : The Dynamic Process by Which Low-Income Clients Experience Social Class within Psychotherapy

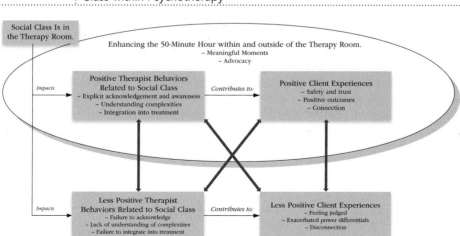

is detailed throughout the results section using participants' words. The authors summarized the figure in this way:

> All participants noted the salience of social class in the therapy room, which was per-ceived to affect their experiences in psychotherapy. Most participants described positive experiences in psychotherapy (i.e., feelings of safety and trust within the therapeutic relationship, perceived positive therapy outcomes, and connection to their therapist). Therapists' explicit acknowledgment of social class complexities and the incorporation of social class-related content into treatment contributed to positive experiences. In con-trast, social class differences contributed to less positive experiences in psychotherapy for some (i.e., feeling judged by their therapist, perceiving exacerbated power differences between the therapist and the participant, and feeling disconnected from the therapist). Specific therapist behaviors were perceived to contribute to these less positive experi-ences, such as failures on the part of the therapist to acknowledge social class differences, to communicate an understanding of the complexities related to being low income, and to integrate social class into treatment. All participants described an appreciation for their therapist's willingness to enhance the traditional 50-min therapy hour. Meaning-ful moments and acts of advocacy by the therapist were perceived to facilitate positive experiences in therapy regardless of specific therapist behaviors. (p. 212)

Phenomenology

The purpose of phenomenology is "to produce an exhaustive description of the phenomena of everyday experience, thus arriving at an understanding of the essen-tial structures of the 'thing itself,' the phenomenon" (McLeod, 2001, p. 38). Phenom-enology is a discovery-oriented qualitative approach with roots in constructivism and in the work of Edmund Husserl in phenomenological philosophy. In the follow-ing paragraphs, the historical development of the phenomenological approach and its major principles will be introduced along with an exemplary study.

Phenomenology has its roots in the work of Edmund Husserl on phenom-enological philosophy. Since then, social scientists (e.g., Giorgi, Moustakas, and Polkinghorne) have followed its tenets and transferred Husserl's work from philosophy to psychological or sociological research. Over the past decades, dif-ferent approaches to phenomenology were developed (e.g., empirical/psychological phenomenology, hermeneutic phenomenology, existential phenomenology, social phenomenology, reflective/ transcendental phenomenology, and dialogical phe-nomenology; see Creswell, 1998, for a review). A review of the phenomenological movement in psychology and a comparison between phenomenological research and other qualitative methods can be found in Wertz (2005).

Despite the multiple phenomenological approaches, most phenomenological researchers rely upon a few guidelines to inform their work. These guidelines were summarized by Creswell (1998) into five areas: (a) philosophical perspec-tives and epoché, (b) research questions and lived experiences, (c) criterion-based sampling, (d) phenomenological data analysis, and (e) essential, invariant structure (or essence) of the lived experience. These five areas will be described as follows.

Philosophical Perspectives and Epoché Researchers who intend to adopt the phe-nomenological approach should have a thorough understanding of the underlying philosophy because its philosophical assumptions greatly influence the formulation of research questions and inquiry techniques (Creswell, 1998; McLeod, 2001). Before embarking upon a phenomenological study, researchers are expected to set aside any and all feelings, assumptions, preexisting scientific knowledge, and judgments about the phenomenon in order to have a fresh and untainted perspective. Indeed, in describing phenomenology, Wertz (2005) argued that "scientific knowledge begins with a fresh and unbiased description of its subject matter" (p. 167). The researcher must document this process in detail. This strategy was termed epoché by Husserl, who suggested that phenomenological researchers bracket and question all of their assumptions. This process is intended to reveal new and meaningful understanding that transcends the extant knowledge about a particular phenomenon (McLeod, 2001). In phenomenological research, this is an ongoing process and is written into the results.

A study conducted by Røseth, Binder, and Malt (2013) will be used to illustrate the phenomenological approach. Their research aimed to understand the "comprehensive phenomenological understanding of depression in women" (p. 155). The authors indicated that although past research had focused on gender differences in depression, and that some qualitative research had described the cultural construction of gendered depression, studies examining the "essential meaning structure of depression as experienced by women" (p. 155) had not been previously conducted.

Røseth and colleagues (2013) explicitly described their reliance upon Husserl's (1962) work to ground their investigation. The authors described in considerable detail their philosophical perspective and epoché on pages 155–157 of the manuscript. They also illustrated their reliance upon understanding themselves as cultural beings as related to the research process.

Research Questions and Lived Experiences   The key subject matter studied by phenomenological researchers is the lived world of human beings (i.e., "the life-world manifests itself as a structural whole that is socially shared and yet apprehended by individuals through their own perspectives"; Wertz, 2005, p. 169). The research questions for a phenomenological study are developed to provide a mechanism by which to understand the everyday lived experiences of individuals and to explore what those experiences mean to the individuals (Creswell, 1998). Data are typically generated via research participants offering written or verbal responses to "a descriptive task with instructions" (Wertz, 2005, p. 171) or an open-ended interview, respectively. Data collected via interviews generally use global questions in an effort to capture the essence of participants' experience related to the phenomenon of interest. The aim is simply to describe the essence (and not to construct meaning, develop theory, or make interpretations).

Criterion-Based Sampling   Criterion-based sampling is used in a phenomenological study to select participants who meet two criteria. First, participants must have experienced the phenomenon under study. Second, participants must be able to articulate their lived experiences (Creswell, 1998). A key task for the researcher is to identify prospective participants who have experienced the phenomenon. Similar to the grounded theory approach, there is no absolute number of participants needed for a phenomenological study. Yet, in assessing the adequacy of the sample size, the following criteria were proposed by Wertz (2005): "deliberation and critical reflection considering the research problem, the life-world position of the participant(s), the quality of the data, and the value of emergent findings with regard to research goals" (p. 171).

Røseth and colleagues (2013) used their criteria when determining their sample. These authors described the criteria they used to select participants in this way:

> We unsystematically recruited women from two psychiatric outpatient clinics and from two local GP practices in two areas in Norway. Eligible women were asked to participate in the study by their GP or therapist. Women who agreed to participate were contacted for further assessment. We included only women who satisfied the diagnostic criteria for major depression disorder (MDD) according to the diagnostic and statistical manual of mental disorders, DSM-IV-TR (American Psychiatric Association [APA], 1994). Within these limits we selected women with diverse experiences of MDD. Thus, we made a purposive selection to insure collecting rich data on the phenomenon (Polkinghorne, 2005). (p. 157)

In addition, a "thick" (detailed) description of the participants (e.g., their relationship status and psychiatric history) was provided in the article.

Phenomenological Data Analysis   Husserl developed the procedure of intentional analysis to guide data analysis. According to Wertz (2005), intentional analysis "begins with a situation just as it has been experienced—with all its various meanings" and requires the researcher to "reflectively explicate the experiential processes through which the situation is lived," thereby producing "knowledge of human situations, their meaning, and the processes that generate those meanings" (p. 169). Intentional analysis is carried out through the use of epoché and through the researcher's development of an empathic understanding of the participants' lived experiences. Meaning units from participant data are highlighted and grouped into themes in order to provide a written description of the essence of participants' experiences.

In the analytic process, the researcher constantly "focuses on relations between different parts of the situation and the psychological processes that subtend it while attempting to gain explicit knowledge of how each constituent contributes to the organization of the structure as a whole" (Wertz, 2005, p. 172). Yet, phenomenological researchers who follow the different traditions mentioned earlier have proposed different analytic techniques (McLeod, 2001). Researchers need to decide which tradition to follow when conducting their analyses and clearly state the steps of the analytic method in their research methodology section.

In their manuscript, Røseth and colleagues (2013) utilized interviews as the data collection method for this study. Each of the three participants was interviewed twice, the interviews were audiotaped, and subsequently transcribed verbatim. The authors followed Giorgi's descriptive phenomenological method (1970, 2009) and explicitly delineated the phenomenological analytic approach utilized in their study:

> We started by adopting the phenomenological attitude, to bracket our preconceptions about the phenomenon and withhold the existential claim (Husserl, 1913/1962). Within

the phenomenological attitude, we analyzed the interviews in four logical steps: First we read the entire transcript of each interview several times to get a sense of the whole. Secondly, for each interview we divided the transcript into meaning units by being sensitive to and marking shifts in the psychological meaning of what was said. Thirdly, we transformed each meaning unit into psychologically sensitive language, where the more general meaning was identified by imaginative variation. During imaginative variation we probed the descriptions, trying out different levels of categorizations and thereby teasing out invariant meanings that can encompass facts from several individuals. In our analysis we read between the lines and teased out the coherence between explicit and implicit meanings in the descriptions. In the fourth and final step we synthesized the transformed meaning units of all the descriptions of the three participants into an essential meaning structure. However, we did not conduct the analysis in a strictly linear fashion; it was a dynamic process where we moved back and forth between steps until the final essential meaning structure was described. (p. 158)

Essence of the Lived Experience   Phenomenological researchers use the intuition of essence or eidetic reduction to understand the essence of the phenomenon under study and to achieve psychological reduction. Husserl developed a procedure, free imaginative variation, in order to guide phenomenological researchers in this effort. Free imaginative variation "starts with a concrete example of the phenomenon of which one wishes to grasp the essence and imaginatively varies it in every possible way in order to distinguish essential features from those that are accidental or incidental" (Wertz, 2005, p. 168). Throughout analysis, the researcher is expected to examine a phenomenon from all possible angles in order to understand the essence of the phenomenon and the exceptions to this essence. The exhaustive descriptions of the phenomenon of interest are then constructed through extracting the significant statements from participant data, formulating meanings, and clustering themes of the original data (Creswell, 1998). The exhaustive descriptions are used to provide the readers with an understanding of the essence of the lived experiences and represent a unifying structure of a phenomenon.

Røseth and colleagues (2013) used their analysis to identify an essential meaning structure that emerged from the data. They described this as:

A mission, initially embarked on with hope and emotional investment, has backfired and is now experienced as a major source of distress that the subject feels unable to abandon. Feeling trapped in this negative situation over an extended period of time, she finds herself lacking the necessary personal resources to resolve the situation. She is strongly affected by the perceived disapproval of others concerning her situation, which throws her into ambivalence, doubt and excessive worry. She is deeply sensitive to others' feelings and judgments, temporarily invalidating or subordinating her own feelings and judgments. Feelings of excessive responsibility are coupled with feelings of shame and guilt, which can be traced back to negative experiences in her past. Despite the experience of hopelessness about changing the distressing situation, she feels deeply responsible for the emotional well-being of others. Her mission is to succeed in her goal, to satisfy others' demands and to relieve her intense feelings of shame and guilt. However, this is achieved by ignoring her own distressing and negative embodied emotions. Consequently these neglected negative emotions grow awry and are experienced as forced down upon her in increasingly unexpected and frightening ways: feelings of sickness, fatigue, sadness, panic attacks or inner restlessness, which also deprive her of sleep. Gradually she becomes less able to fulfill the responsibilities that she has claimed or accepted, thus adding to her burden of shame and guilt. Deep inside the feeling of unfairness about her situation frustrates her and negatively affects her relationship with others, which again produces more feelings of guilt. Eventually she experiences a breakdown as she is forcefully submerged in her emotional body. (p. 159)

The authors then move into describing the six interrelated essential meaning constituents in order to further explicate the Gestalt of the essential meaning structure. Throughout their description of the six constituents: (a) entrapment in a mission; (b) sensitivity to others' distress and negative judgment; (c) the present constraint of past guilt and shame; (d) ignoring embodied emotions; (e) feelings of injustice and anger; and (f) submerging in a threatening alienated emotional body—the breaking point. The authors provided a rich description of the themes with the participants' narratives. One of these constituents was described as follows:

Entrapment in a mission. The women had initially made a choice to embark on a personal mission, which gradually developed into a very stressful situation in which they felt trapped. Despite the negativity and stress, they found themselves unable to give up their mission. Rather, their sense of failure induced more guilt, which spurred the women to work even harder to succeed in their 'mission,' giving beyond their resources.

"Christine" had just reunited with the father of her child and she was very committed to the relationship. Shortly after they moved back together, her partner and his family underwent a serious crisis. Christine unexpectedly finds herself trapped in their traumatic and negative life circumstances and she grieves the loss of a "new beginning" with her partner. "It's obviously a big challenge getting together again, and then we have to go through a crisis like this." Her personal mission is to avoid separation, and live through the traumatic situation with her partner and his parents. "If I'm going to be strong and be a part of it, and kind of manage to support him and his family, we'll have to talk together all the time." "I have to get some input about what's going on." She feels responsible for their emotional well-being and believes that she is the only one who can help them. "And the fact that we're sort of the ones closest to them and we're the closest relatives, andalmost the only relatives they let come so close, if you see what I mean?" The situation feels hopeless as she experiences herself as being without the means to help her partner and his family, and thereby also herself.

For the last five to six years "Eve" has worked excessively to succeed with her company, which two years ago was expanded to a corporate company. Her mission was to be successful and not let herself and the co-owners of the company down. Feeling deeply responsible for the project, she took on work that should have been done by others. But the intensive work also had the effect of tem`porarily moving her conscious focus from her troubling thoughts. The co-owners communicated to the public that the business was a success, but she felt unsure whether the company lacked the financial resources needed to succeed. She realized at some point that the financial insecurity was too great for her to take responsibility for, and to live with; subsequently she decided to terminate the business, against the will of the co-owners. Thus, in addition to the stress connected to overworking, she now also felt that she had failed and consequently faced the perceived negative feelings and judgments of others.

"Josephine" made an authentic choice to discontinue a socially approved project, i.e. studying, in favor of a less approved project, i.e. working in a department store. However, the disapproval from others induced anxiety, doubt, and ambivalence concerning her choice. Her mission was to work hard and satisfy the job demands in order to achieve others' approval and to relieve guilt. Her hard work rapidly made her move ahead to a leading position, making her coworkers become her employees. The originally authentically chosen project, working in a department store, slowly turned into a negative and stressful 'prison,' which she felt unable to handle successfully. (pp. 160–161)

In the discussion section, the authors presented a rich and extensive dialogue of the essential meaning structure along with phenomenological and contemporary literature. The rich description about the three women's' experiences with depression provided new knowledge about a phenomenon that was understudied. The authors conclude this dialogue with the following summary of their work:

> The contribution of this study to the field is to focus on how the emotional body serves to clarify the role of emotions and extreme sensitivity in depression. The literature abounds with theories and hypotheses alleging that it is women's emotionality and hypersensitivity that render them more vulnerable to the diagnosis than men. In vogue theories of depression, for example, highlight dysfunctional emotional regulation in depression. Our analysis reveals that guilt and shame occupy center stage in the emotional drama, and that emotions are bodily based. The women in our study overwork or over-involve themselves in a personal mission about which they have a deep commitment. Faced with negativity within the social arena, which they judge as unfair, their natural, pre-morbid sensitivity to others decays into a cauldron of distressful emotions that paradoxically both disconnects them from others yet highlights them, and estranges them from their bodies which swallows them up. Put differently, they neglect and ignore their distressed emotional bodies, which they view as a source of weakness. Gradually, their emotional body goes awry and becomes an obstacle. Ultimately the women are forced to submerge in their alienated and threatening emotional body; they succumb to depression. (p. 175)

The authors' detailed illustrations of the method, analysis results, and their reasoning help the reader understand how their interpretations were derived from the data. More exemplars of phenomenological studies can be found in Wertz (2005), McLeod (2001), and the *Journal of Phenomenological Psychology*.

Consensual Qualitative Research

Consensual qualitative research (CQR) is a systematic way of examining the representativeness of results across cases through the process of reaching consensus among multiple researchers. It is a relatively new form of inquiry that was developed by counseling psychologists (Hill, Thompson, & Williams, 1997). In the sections that follow, we describe CQR's development, delineate its paradigmatic roots, and summarize primary procedures inherent in the research process.

In their development of CQR, Hill and her colleagues (1997) borrowed principles from grounded theory (Glaser & Strauss, 1967; Strauss & Corbin, 1990), comprehensive process analysis (Elliott, 1989), phenomenological approaches (Giorgi, 1970, 1985, as cited in Hill et al., 1997), and feminist theories (e.g., Fine, 1992; Harding, 1991, as cited in Hill et al., 1997). While CQR shares common premises with each of these approaches, it is also distinct in several ways (see Hill et al. 1997; Hoshmand, 1997, for a review). Hoshmand noted that in the initial guidelines for CQR, Hill and colleagues (1997) "did not articulate the implicit philosophical perspective on which the communal processes of CQR are based" (p. 601).

As such, CQR has been described as a "generic" qualitative approach (McLeod, 2001, p. 147). In 2005, Hill and her colleagues attempted to locate CQR's philosophical stance in order to link the gaps among the ontology, epistemology, and methodology. The cited goal of developing CQR was to develop a design that was easy to use and rigorous in analysis (Hill et al., 2005). As such, CQR is described as being based in a postpositivism paradigm in that it relies upon quasistatistics or numerical classification of results or a constructivist-interpretive paradigm given its assumption that there are multiple perspectives of reality and that it is up to the research team to identify meaning from those perspectives.

Qualitative researchers who choose to adopt this strategy of inquiry are strongly encouraged to locate the paradigm on which they base their research. For example, in an exemplary study conducted by Wang and Heppner (2011), the authors described the paradigm for their CQR study on the experiences of Taiwanese survivors who suffered from childhood sexual abuse.

> The current study was grounded on a feminist paradigm, and the consensual qualitative research method (CQR; Hill et al., 2005; Hill, Thompson, & Williams, 1997) was utilized as the strategy of inquiry. In general, qualitative paradigms assume relativist ontology (i.e., multiple realities that are socially and individually constructed), transactional epistemology (i.e., intertwined relationship between the knower and the known), and dialogic/interpretive methodology (i.e., knowledge is constructed through the interactions and dialogues between the participants and researchers; Guba & Lincoln, 1998). The current study is based on a feminist paradigm that emphasizes reduction of gender inequality, empowerment of women and other marginalized groups through research and social advocacy, understanding of the meso-system knitting the link between societal/institutional forces (macrosystem) and human activities (microsystem), and critical reflection on the influence of sociopolitical contexts and researchers' own group membership on the research process (Maguire, 1987; Olesen, 2000). Qualitative feminist researchers bring their professional skills to the study and consider themselves as both the researcher and the learner, who make efforts to understand the participants' perspectives (Renzetti, 1997).
>
> Further, we used the CQR method (Hill et al., 2005, 1997) to implement the collaborative focus of the feminist paradigm. CQR and feminist theories both emphasize unconstrained methods of reaching consensus through open dialogue, collaboration among researchers to come to a shared understanding of the phenomenon, recognition of power differentials that may influence the consensual process, and treating the participants as experts of their experiences (Hill et al., 1997; Hoshmand, 1997). Consistent with recommendations by Durham (2002), a sensitive practitioner research methodology (e.g., interviewing and antioppressive research practice) was employed to examine the impact of CSA in this study. CSA survivors were encouraged to participate in a dialogue on an issue that concerned them, with both the researchers and participants collectively contributing to the success of this project. (Wang & Heppner, 2011, p. 396)

Although CQR has become one of the most commonly used qualitative research designs in counseling psychology, it is relatively unused outside of the discipline. Unlike GT, phenomenology, and postmodern approaches, CQR outlines specific expectations that researchers must carefully follow across four domains. These four domains include: (a) researchers, researcher biases, and training of the research team; (b) participant selection; (c) interview (data collection) and transcription; and (d) data analytic procedure. Each of these is depicted in Table 16.4 and will be described in the sections that follow.

TABLE 16.4 : Recommendations for Using CQR

Consideration	Recommendation
Consensus process	1. Researchers should openly discuss their feelings and disagreements. 2. When there are disagreements among the researchers about the interviews, everyone should listen to the tape of the interview.
Biases	1. Report demographics and feelings/reactions to topic in the methods section. 2. Discuss the influence of biases in the limitations section. 3. Openly discuss biases among the research team throughout the process. 4. Journal reviewers need to be aware that biases are a natural part of any research, including CQR.
The research team	1. Either set or rotating primary teams are acceptable. 2. All team members must become deeply immersed in all of the data. 3. At least three people should comprise the primary team. 4. The educational level of team members should match the abstractness of the topic. 5. Team members with more designated power should not claim "expert status." 6. Power issues should be addressed openly. 7. Rotate the order of who talks first to reduce undue influence.
Training team members	1. Prior to training, read Hill et al. (1997), the present article, and exemplar studies. 2. Consult with an expert if having difficulty learning the method. 3. Describe training procedures in the methods section.
Sample	1. Randomly select participants from a carefully identified homogeneous population. 2. Choose participants who are very knowledgeable about the phenomenon. 3. Recruit 8 to 15 participants if one or two interviews are used.
Interviews	1. Review the literature and talk to experts to develop the interview protocol. 2. Include about 8–10 scripted open-ended questions per hour. 3. Allow for follow-up probes to learn more about the individual's experience. 4. Conduct several pilot interviews to aid in revising the interview protocol. 5. Train new interviewers 6. Ideally, each interviewee should be interviewed at least twice.
Data collection	1. Match the data collection format to the data desired and the needs of the study. 2. Record reactions to interviews; review tape before subsequent interviews.
Domains	1. Develop the domains from the transcripts or a "start list." 2. The entire primary team codes the data into domains in the first several cases; the remaining coding can be done by one researcher and reviewed by the team.

(*continued*)

TABLE 16.4 : Recommendations for Using CQR *(continued)*

Consideration	Recommendation
Core ideas	1. Use the participant's words; avoid interpretive analysis. 2. The entire primary team develops the core ideas for the first several cases; the remaining core ideas can be done by one researcher and reviewed by the team, or the entire primary team can work together to code the domains and construct the core ideas.
Cross-analysis	1. Use frequency labels to characterize data: *General* applies to all or all but 1 case; *typical* applies to more than half up to the cutoff for general; *variant* applies to 2 cases up to the cutoff for typical. When more than 15 cases are included, *rare* applies to 2–3 cases. Findings applying to single cases are placed in a miscellaneous category and not included in results/tables. 2. When comparing subsamples, results are *different* if they vary by at least two frequency categories (e.g., general vs. variant). 3. Continually refer to the raw data in making interpretations. 4. Continue revising the cross-analyses until elegant and parsimonious. 5. If there are mostly variant or rare categories or a lot of miscellaneous items, revise the cross-analysis (e.g., combine categories, subdivide the sample, or collect more data). 6. Get feedback from others about the cross-analysis.
Auditing	1. Either internal or external auditors are appropriate for the domains and core ideas, but at least one external auditor is desirable for the cross-analysis. 2. For inexperienced researchers, it is helpful for the auditor to examine revisions until he or she is confident that the data are characterized accurately. 3. Auditors should also be involved in reviewing the interview protocol.
Stability check	The stability check (i.e., holding out two cases from the initial cross-analysis), as proposed by Hill et al. (1997), can be eliminated, but other evidence of trustworthiness should be presented.
Charting the results	Charting or other visual approaches for depicting findings (e.g., "webs" or organizational diagrams of categories) could be helpful.
Writing the results and discussion section	1. At least the general and typical categories should be fully described in the results section, although all categories in the cross-analysis should be included in a table. 2. Either quotes or core ideas can be used to illustrate the results. 3. Case examples are useful for illustrating results across domains. 4. In the discussion section, pull together results in a meaningful way and develop theory.
Participant's review	Give transcripts of interviews and write-up of results to participants.

Note: CQR = consensual qualitative research

Source: Adapted from Hill et al., 2005

Researchers, Researcher Biases, and Training of the Research Team Hill and colleagues (1997) stressed the importance of clearly describing the researchers because the data analysis of CQR relies upon the consensual process of the research team members. Researchers need to explicitly consider the various possibilities of team composition and be careful in selecting team members. Team selection should be made after accounting for possible power differences among the group members, types of expertise, and the level of commitment needed from each team member. Before the data collection and the analytic processes begin, researchers must receive appropriate training in conducting interviews and in data analysis. It is also crucial that all of the researchers bracket (i.e., set aside) their biases so that data can be approached from a fresh perspective and to ensure that the data be allowed to "speak" for itself. The intended goal of researchers engaging in self-reflection is to allow readers an opportunity to "evaluate the findings with this knowledge in mind" (Hill et al., 2005, p. 197).

The research conducted by Wang and Heppner (2011) serves as a good exemplar of CQR. The researchers aimed to understand the coping and recovery processes of Taiwanese childhood sexual abuse (CSA) survivors in a Chinese sociocultural context. In their manuscript, the authors clearly portrayed the backgrounds and experiences of the researchers composing the CQR team.

> **Researchers-as-instruments.** The first author is a Taiwanese/Chinese woman, fluent in both Chinese and English, who conducted all of the interviews in Mandarin with one of the research assistants present (except for one participant who requested to be interviewed only by the first author because she felt "too embarrassed" about her CSA experience). The second author is a European American man who has over 30 years of involvement in both the men's and women's movement in the United States. He consulted on all phases of this study. The first author had several years of training and experience working with CSA survivors and has published articles using the qualitative research methodology. She recruited 26 undergraduate or graduate students in counseling/clinical psychology in Taiwan to join the research team. The team was composed of four groups of research assistants: a data collection team (15 women and one man), an interview/transcription team (eight women), a data analysis team (three women), and an auditing team (six women). Some of the team members were involved in more than one group. All but one team member (an auditor) lived in Taiwan at the time of the study. The data collection team members distributed research flyers around Taiwan and on various websites. The interview/transcription team members observed one or two interviews, took field notes, and transcribed the interview(s) that they observed. The first author and two other Taiwanese women (one undergraduate student in a counseling psychology program in Taiwan and one counselor who held a master's degree in clinical psychology from a U.S. university and was working in Taiwan as a clinician at the time of the study) formed the analysis team for the present study. In addition, two counseling psychologists (European Americans, one male and one female) with expertise in coping and sexual violence served as the consultants to the data analysis process.

Wang and Heppner (2011) also described the training that all research team members received. They took specific steps to decrease the effects of researchers' assumptions on the data analysis results and to monitor the group dynamics (e.g., documenting their observations and reflections in their field notes and reflexive journals, discussing their assumptions about potential findings prior to the actual data collection).

Participant Selection   Consensual qualitative research utilizes a criterion-based sampling method, and the criteria of selecting the participants must be clearly stated. This method ensures that the participants have had some depth of experience with the phenomenon of interest and can provide meaningful information for the purpose of the study. Usually, 8 to 15 cases are studied intensively when using CQR because (a) this sample size, albeit small, usually provides a sufficient number of cases for the researchers to examine variability and consistencies across cases; and (b) additional cases typically add minimal new information (Hill et al., 1997).

For example, Wang and Heppner (2011) described their process for recruiting and interviewing participants. They interviewed 10 Taiwanese women who saw the research flyers and contacted the researchers. The participants self-identified as being sexually abused as children, with varying ages (20–39 years old), educational levels (from undergraduate education to master's degree), and majors (i.e., psychology, counseling, nursing, social welfare/work, rehabilitation, English, and philosophy). The onset age of sexual abuse varied (from 3 to 12 years of age); so did the duration of abuse (from once to 9 years). The majority of the perpetrators were family relatives, while the rest of them were acquaintances.

Interview (Data Collection) and Transcription   Usually in CQR studies, data are collected via open-ended, semistructured interviews with individuals that are comprised of 8–10 questions for a one-hour interview (Hill et al., 2005). An interview protocol can be developed based on literature review, conversations with the population of interest, and researchers' personal reflections (Hill et al., 2005). Pilot interviews are conducted in order to evaluate the adequacy of the interview protocol (at least two pilot interviews are recommended by Hill and colleagues). The actual interviews could be conducted over the phone or face to face. Although less common, it is also possible within CQR to utilize surveys or an email exchange to collect data (see Hill et al., 2005). Immediately following the interviews, the interviewer(s) should record memos (e.g., impression of the interviewee, comments about the flow of the session) that later may be used to facilitate data analysis. Once the interview is completed, it should be transcribed verbatim with identifying information omitted and unnecessary nonlanguage utterances ("um," "ah") and fillers ("you know") deleted.

For example, Wang and Heppner (2011) developed a semistructured interview protocol for the purpose of their study. One of the authors (Wang) developed the protocol on the basis of the literature and her reflections. The interview protocol was reviewed by the research team and counselors/psychologists who worked with CSA survivors in Taiwan. It was also piloted with one CSA survivor and modified based on the pilot interviewee's feedback. The pilot interview was used to examine the appropriateness and relevance of the interview questions from the participant's perspective and to uncover any important concepts that were unexpected by the researchers. All of the interviews were conducted face to face. Interviews were subsequently transcribed verbatim, and each transcript was checked by the participants for accuracy. In the manuscript, the interview procedure was presented in great detail, and examples of interview questions were provided.

Data Analytic Procedures   Hill and colleagues (1997) delineated a step-by-step data analytic procedure that was recently revisited (Hill, 2012). They recommended that data analysis consist of six sequential stages. These include (a) identify domains, (b) summarize core ideas, (c) construct categories from the cross-analysis, (d) audit the analysis results, (e) check the stability of the results, and (f) chart the findings.

Data analysis begins with a "start list" of domains gathered from the literature, from the data, or from a combination of the prior literature and interview data. These domains are used to code the data. Next, core ideas are identified that express participants' words. At this point, the research team uses cross-analysis to examine the core ideas across cases that are clustered into categories whose frequency is identified across the sample according to whether they are general, typical, or variant. Throughout the data analysis process, CQR requires that the research team debate to consensus. This process "relies on mutual respect, equal involvement, and shared power" (Hill et al., 1997, p. 523). Discussion of biases among the research team is required throughout data analysis so as to ensure that analysis is not negatively affected. Auditors or judges (both internal and external to the team) provide detailed feedback, and external auditors are particularly valued as a mechanism to bring a fresh perspective to the data set. Hill et al. (2005) recommended that researchers save two cases from prior stages of analysis in order to provide a stability check. These two cases are used as a check to ensure that the data from the cases fit into the categories identified in the prior stages of analysis and that data saturation is reached. Finally, the results are charted in order to visually present the findings according to their frequency across the sample. Hill (2012) urged researchers to chart results via tables or "webs" (i.e., organizational diagrams) as a method by which to present information efficiently and to facilitate the reader's ability to understand how the data are connected.

Following the CQR guidelines, the analysis team members in Wang and Heppner's (2011) study coded the data independently and convened to form consensus on the domains, core ideas, and categories through cross-analyses. Six auditors reviewed the work of the data analysis team, and the auditors' feedback was subsequently discussed and incorporated into the final results by the team members. Findings from this study were charted and summarized in Table 16.5 and in Figure 16.3, according to CQR recommendations.

Overall, the participants in Wang and Heppner (2011) study described their postabuse coping and recovery processes. In particular, the participants explained how certain Chinese sociocultural context and values influenced their appraisals of self and the traumatic event(s), others' perceptions of and attitudes towards them, as well as their coping mechanisms and outcomes. Categories, which emerged from the data, were discussed and illustrated with direct quotes from participants. Following is the description of one of the domains with categories and quotes.

> *Appraisals of self and others.* Two general categories emerged within this domain. First, all participants reported that they had developed a *negative evaluation of themselves* after the abuse. Regardless of the severity of sexual abuse, participants reported that they felt their bodies were physically damaged. Even though they were children at the time of the actual abuse, participants also talked about at some point developing a fear of losing

TABLE 16.5 Clusters, Domains, Categories, and Frequencies

Cluster I: CSA Stress

1. CSA Events
   a. Degree of sexual exposure (G)
   b. Trust violation (G)
   c. Physical/verbal coercion and denigrating messages (T)

2. Relational Context
   a. Pre- and postevent family relationships (G)
   b. Pre- and postevent nonfamilial interpersonal relationships (G)
   c. Postevent romantic relationships (G)

Cluster II: Problem Appraisal

1. Appraisals of Self and Others
   a. Negative self-evaluation (G)
   b. Negative evaluation of others and relationships (G)

2. Appraisals Related to the Sociocultural Context
   a. Gender specific stress related to virginity, chastity, and gender role expectations (G)
   b. Inadequate and/or incorrect sex education from parents and schools (G)
   c. Stress related to traditional family values (G)
   d. Stigma and cultural myths related to CSA (G)
   e. Negative portraits of CSA in the media (T)
   f. Frustration with and lack of support from the legislations (T)
   g. Generational differences in attitudes towards CSA (T)
   h. Inadequate public and social resources for CSA survivors (V)
   i. Inadequate professional resources and stigma related to seeking professional help (V)
   j. Socioeconomic status of CSA survivors (V)
   k. Geographical differences in attitudes toward CSA (V)

Cluster III: Coping Strategies and Outcomes

1. Constructive Coping Strategies with Effective Long-Term Outcomes
   a. Empowering others (G)
   b. Cognitive processing and positive self-reinforcement (G)
   c. Positive cognitive reframing and acceptance (T)
   d. Promoting positive emotions or physical exercise (T)

2. Avoidance/Distraction Coping Strategies with Short-Term Relief but Ineffective Long-Term Outcomes
   a. Short-term self-concealment (G)
   b. Tension-reduction or distraction-coping activities with no immediate self-harming consequences (G)
   c. Denial (G)
   d. Fantasy/wishful thinking (T)
   e. Avoiding or distancing themselves from environmental stimuli (T)

3. Destructive Coping Strategies with Ineffective Short-Term and Long-Term Outcomes
   a. Enduring one's pain and long-term self-concealment (T)
   b. Intentional self-sabotaging behaviors (T)
   c. Tension reduction or distraction coping strategies with immediate self-harming consequences (T)

4. Help Seeking with Effective Outcomes
   a. Self-disclosing the event to or sought help from mental health professionals (G)
   b. Self-disclosing the event to or sought help from family (V)
   c. Participating in religious or spiritual activities (V)
   d. Self-disclosing the event to or sought help from friends (V)
   e. Self-disclosing the event to or sought help from romantic partner(s) (V)
   f. Self-disclosing the event to or sought help from non-mental health professionals (V)

TABLE 16.5 : Clusters, Domains, Categories, and Frequencies *(continued)*

Cluster III: Coping Strategies and Outcomes (Continued)

5. Help-Seeking with Ineffective Outcomes
    a. Self-disclosing the event to or sought help from family (G)
    b. Self-disclosing the event to or sought help from mental health professionals (T)
    c. Self-disclosing the event to or sought help from romantic partner(s) (T)
    d. Participating in religious or spiritual activities (V)
    e. Self-disclosing the event to or sought help from non-mental health professionals (V)

Cluster IV: Psychosocial Adjustment

1. Negative Adjustment Outcomes
    a. Symptomatic manifestations (general posttraumatic reactions and sexual difficulties) (G)
    b. Self-deprecation (G)
    c. Interpersonal difficulties (G)
    d. Anger and fear towards perpetrators (G)

2. Positive Adjustment Outcomes
    a. Self-validation and empowerment (G)
    b. Positive relationships and support (G)
    c. Symptom reduction and resolution (T)

Note: G = general (9–10 cases), T = typical (6–8 cases), V = variant (2–5 cases)

Source: Table adapted from Wang and Heppner (2011, p. 339)

FIGURE 16.3 : Transactional and Ecological Model of Coping (TEMoC)

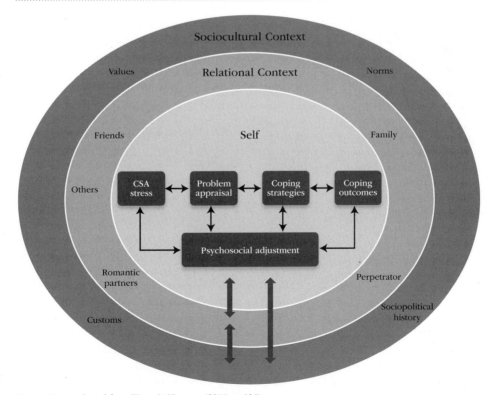

Source: Figure adapted from Wang & Heppner (2011, p. 404)

their virginity or of becoming pregnant. Many of the participants blamed themselves for the abuse. For example, one participant felt that she was a "coward" for not disclosing the sexual abuse, thereby feeling that she was colluding with the perpetrators to "commit a crime." Another woman reported feeling ashamed and angry with herself after the abuse happened and described how the CSA incident was connected to her negative self-evaluation, coping styles, and adjustment:

> All of the problems I have dealt with since childhood were all connected together. ... [Because of the sexual abuse] I felt scared, ashamed, resentful, and then tried to gain power and release tension by engaging in compulsive sexual behavior ... [All of these problems] really bothered me and I spent so much time and energy to deal with every problem at various stages of my development. ... I tried to think why [my uncle abused me] and then I became even angrier with myself ... [I thought I was abused because] I was too cute ... I was too compliant ... stupid. ... I don't know whether or not there will be a day when I could feel that I am fully recovered from the sexual abuse. ... As a child, I often thought of myself as an ugly, broken doll ... a broken mechanical product. (Wang & Heppner, 2011, p. 400)

In this way, Wang and Heppner (2011) followed CQR procedures that suggest that researchers use quotes from the interviews or core ideas to illustrate each category (e.g., Hill et al., 2005). Further, they used the tables and figure as visual representations of the results in order to help the readers understand the relationships among categories.

Participatory Action Research (PAR)/Community-Based Participatory Research (CBPR)

There are a few research approaches that are considered to be housed within a critical theory or critical-ideological paradigm that have become increasingly prevalent within counseling and counseling psychology literature. PAR and CBPR are two such approaches; both are informed by critical theory and constructivism. These approaches infuse value for democratic participation into research design and may best be considered *approaches to* research (rather than a design) that value doing research *with* rather than *on* individuals or communities. Indeed, in both PAR and CBPR approaches, participants are considered coresearchers who provide input into each stage of the research process.

Both PAR and CBPR operate from the belief that the research process is a mechanism of social change (Schwandt, 2001), and the goal is to work toward empowerment for research participants and their communities. Increased empowerment, in turn, is anticipated to allow participants emancipation from oppression. The origin of these approaches is often traced to Freire's (1970) work related to literacy in Brazil.

In summarizing the PAR process, Kidd and Kral (2005) stated "you get people affected by a problem together, figure out what is going on as a group, and then do something about it" (p. 187). Research questions emerge from dialogue that prompts social action in the form of a research project. Meaning is constructed between the researcher and the target population, and members of the target population become research collaborators who play an integral role in all stages of data collection and analysis (Kidd & Kral, 2005).

Importantly, CBPR and PAR research may draw from different paradigms at different stages of the work. For example, in its early stages of project identification, the researcher(s) spend considerable time developing relationships with community members. Over time, a research question emerges from the conversation. In this way, the researcher and community partners utilize a *constructivist* and *critical-ideological* lens to identify the question. Depending upon the nature of the question and the methods used to carry out the study, the actual data collection and analysis process may rely upon quantitative as well as qualitative methods. Throughout the process, however, the partners rely upon continuous conversation using a *constructivist* and *critical-ideological* lens to make meaning of the data and determine pathways for moving forward to effect change at community and policy levels.

Self-reflection on the part of the researcher is absolutely critical. The researcher is proactive and interactive within the community throughout the duration of the project, and the social justice values of the researcher explicitly direct inquiry. The researcher's role in the community is intentionally designed to be time sensitive, given that the research belongs to the community and the researcher works to develop self-sufficiency among the stakeholders to move the work forward into the future.

Because of the time intensive and complex nature involved in action-oriented research, using only one study as an exemplar can be challenging as this type of research often extends over several years, and any manuscript may focus on one part of the study or its findings. As such, we utilized Vásquez, Minkler, and Shepard's (2006) description of a CBPR study, called the Earth Crew Study, as a case study to illustrate the various stages relevant in CBPR research. This case study offers the readers an opportunity to understand the ability of such approaches to, over time, impact not only research, but also policies that directly relate to individuals and communities. Vásquez and colleagues (2006) described the Earth Crew Study, which was a collaborative project between WE ACT (a nonprofit organization in northern Manhattan whose goal is to "advance environmental health policy, public health, and quality of life." p. 103) and the Columbia Children's Center for Environmental Health. The inception of the Earth Crew Study began as a result of a conversation with a community partner who questioned the impact of pollution on the health and well-being of a specific community. Through partnership with researchers, the community and academic partners developed a study that would include paid community youth interns as stakeholders. The purpose of the study was to investigate sidewalk concentrations of diesel exhaust particles resulting from emissions in a community that is known to be culturally diverse and to have disproportionate rates of disability, asthma, and premature death (Vásquez et al.). Researchers worked at four different sites within the community. The researchers at each site provided mentoring and specific study-related training to the paid youth partners. These paid youth interns assisted in data collection by wearing backpacks with air monitors (Vásquez et al.). Consistent with CBPR, throughout the research process, colearning was expected to occur and did occur. Vásquez and colleagues summarized a particular example of this colearning in this way:

> An academic researcher thus described how in one instance, input from community members caused him to rethink the placement of ambient monitors. Community members questioned the outside researchers' decision to place air monitors solely on school rooftops, suggesting that they instead be placed outside the windows where the children breathe. As this academic partner commented,

> Sometimes as scientists we make assumptions and don't rethink assumptions to see how they fit in a natural situation. I think community people, because they are looking at it from a fresh perspective, will question the assumptions in a way that actually improves the science. It may tailor things to the situation in a way we would not have thought of.

> In sum, the participation of community partners in identifying research questions and offering advice on study design and the extensive involvement of WE ACT Earth Crew youth in implementing the study appeared to contribute substantially to the research component of this CBPR project. (p. 104)

Consistent with CBPR, the researchers and community partners did not stop at the analysis of the data and initial publication of the research findings (Vásquez et al., 2006). Instead, they sought ways to effect change at a policy level that would have real implications for the community and its members. Vásquez and colleagues (2006) described the "frustration" (p. 105) inherent in pursuing such change efforts. These authors described this in more detail on pages 105–107 of the manuscript. In their description, Vásquez, Minkler, and Shepard (2006) stated: "Policymaking proceeds nonlinearly and is embedded within changing sociohistorical contexts" (p. 105). The authors described several steps that the project stakeholders pursued to enact changes at the policy level, one of which was to file a complaint against the federal Department of Transportation.

In their discussion, Vásquez and colleagues (2006) highlighted a number of successes that have resulted from the Earth Crew Study (e.g., empirical findings continue to be cited in research, buses in the area were converted to "clean diesel," permanent community-based air monitoring was initiated in the community). The authors also described some of the factors that were identified as contributing to the success of the project, including:

> WE ACT's strong community base, the scientific credibility of the partnership's research, strong policy alliances, and the careful background work and strategic planning in which WE ACT engaged. The relationship of mutual trust and respect between partners and the community partner's effective use of the mass media also appeared to have contributed to the visibility and impact of the WE ACT partnership and its policy change efforts. (p. 108)

In addition, Vásquez et al. (2006) reviewed some of the challenges inherent in CBPR or other action-based research approaches. For example, the authors described the tensions that commonly arise in the use of community-based research approaches between credible science and community action. To manage this tension in the Earth Crew Study, colearning was emphasized and valued throughout all stages. For example, structured workshops and informal conversations among all partners were underscored throughout. Vásquez and colleagues cited the time spent prior to the outset of the study to develop the relationship and to come to agreement on the variety of questions and issues pertaining to the study as an important factor that likely contributed to the success in this project. For example, one of the academic partners from this study noted: "It requires a lot of effort and energy. If you are going to do it, do it fully ..." (p. 108).

Given the time commitment required when conducting community-based action research, there is a need to consider the equitable distribution of resources among all stakeholders at all stages of the project. For the Earth Crew Study, one way in which attention to distribution of resources was actualized was via writing and receiving a federal grant. WE ACT (the community agency) was the primary grantee (Vásquez et al., 2006). In addition, any community-based action research approach requires that the researchers and all project stakeholders actively and routinely consider the potential risks for all stakeholders. In the case of the Earth Crew Study, the filing of the complaint ultimately led to a number of positive outcomes (e.g., quarterly meetings with the diesel leadership team and community residents). Vásquez and colleagues noted that all project stakeholders were responsible for considering and carefully weighing the potential risks of such action for all involved (e.g., the community, WE ACT as an agency, the academic partners, and the youth) prior to embarking on such action.

SUMMARY AND CONCLUSIONS

In this chapter, we discussed the definition and underlying paradigms of qualitative research. The key myths and facts regarding qualitative methodology were also explored. Occasionally, we have encountered students who have undertaken qualitative research under the misguided notion that qualitative research is easier or less technical than quantitative research. Rigorous qualitative research certainly is different from quantitative research, but selecting this approach will lead to disappointment if the primary motivation is the avoidance of work or numbers. Qualitative research is time consuming and thought provoking. Be prepared to stay up late thinking about the meaning of field notes or transcripts, attempting to make sense of intrinsically ambiguous data, and writing, writing, writing.

This chapter has only scratched the surface of qualitative research. Volumes have been written about this subject, and one could devote an entire textbook to learning about only one particular strategy of qualitative inquiry. In this chapter, we sought to provide the reader an appreciation of qualitative research, an overview of four strategies of inquiry, general methods, guidelines for evaluating the rigor of qualitative research design, and references for those who want to pursue the topic in greater depth.

Finally, we recommend that students seek out ongoing qualitative research teams and volunteer to participate. As suggested by McLeod (2001), we believe that the *personal qualities* of qualitative researchers (e.g., integrity, perseverance, and willingness and ability to struggle with ambiguity), rather than the *methodology* per se, have a greater impact on the potential contribution of the studies. The experience of conducting a qualitative research apprenticeship with veteran qualitative researchers not only can hone a person's methodological skills, but also can help to facilitate the development of these notable personal qualities.

STIMULUS QUESTIONS

Analyzing Three Qualitative Studies

The following exercises are designed to help readers become familiar with the qualitative methodology and various strategies of inquiry.

1. Identify four published articles that utilized grounded theory, phenomenology, consensual qualitative research, or participatory action research/community-based participatory research approach in the following journals: *Grounded Theory Review, Journal of Phenomenological Psychology, Journal of Counseling Psychology,* and *Qualitative Psychology.* Review these

articles and respond to the following questions for each of the four articles:

a. How did the authors situate their study in a particular paradigm (philosophical tradition)?

b. How did the paradigm selected by the authors fit the conclusion of the literature review, the research question(s), the intended purpose(s), and the strategy of inquiry?

c. Which strategy of inquiry was adopted? Write down the corresponding data collection method and analytic procedure utilized by the authors.

d. How did the authors provide a "thick description" of the participants, the context, and their own perspectives about the phenomenon under investigation?

e. How did the authors present their findings and their interpretations of the results?

f. What methods did the authors utilize to establish the trustworthiness of their research?

2. After responding to the previous questions for all four articles, compare and contrast your answers. Then, select a topic of interest and a strategy of inquiry that may help to answer your research questions. Design a study using this particular strategy. Locate and read a number of publications that would help you gain more knowledge about this type of qualitative approach. Record the appropriate paradigm, research method and design, analytic procedure, and expected outcomes.

Mixed Methods Designs:
17 When Qualitative
Chapter and Quantitative Designs Meet

As the name suggests, mixed methods research refers to the use of both qualitative and quantitative strategies in a single research study (e.g., Creswell, 2011; Greene, Caracelli, & Graham, 1989; Teddlie & Tashakkori, 2011). In this way, mixed methods designs capitalize on the strengths of qualitative and quantitative designs and minimize the weaknesses associated with each approach. They allow the researcher the opportunity to utilize data collection, analysis, and interpretation strategies traditionally utilized by only qualitative or quantitative approaches.

Although mixed methods designs are relatively new in comparison to strictly quantitative or qualitative designs, they may be particularly well suited for use in counseling and counseling psychology research. Our orientation and training as scientists and practitioners highlights our tendency to rely upon both numerical data and qualitative data on a regular basis. As we have discussed throughout this book, mental health practitioners are expected to be present in the room with the client in a way that we are deeply attuned to the client's individualized and unique experiences. At the same time, we are expected to ensure that our therapeutic interventions are informed by the scientific literature. In many ways, mixed methods designs are likely to appeal to our inclinations as scientists and practitioners to understand phenomenon and individuals at deep and nuanced levels as well as at more "objective" levels.

This chapter will provide a discussion of mixed methods research. First, the definition of mixed methods research and key characteristics of the mixed methods researcher will be presented. Next we describe some of the benefits and challenges in utilizing mixed methods designs. Then we identify some of the reasons that researchers may choose to use mixed methods designs within counseling and counseling psychology research. Finally, we describe the five phases of mixed methods research. In this description, we include key elements of the research process. We conclude the chapter by offering an overview of two recent examples of mixed methods research in the counseling and counseling psychology literature.

DEFINING MIXED METHODS RESEARCH

Mixed methods research has been referred to as the "third methodological movement" (Tashakkori & Teddlie, 2003, p. 5) following quantitative and then qualitative methods. Although conversations about mixing methods in research dates back to the late 1950s, it was not until the late 1980s that researchers began to formally describe mixed methods research (see Creswell, 2011, for a review). During this time, scholars from a variety of disciplines (e.g., sociology, management, nursing, education) were wrestling with the questions of whether, and how, to combine qualitative and quantitative methods (Creswell & Plano Clark, 2011). Through these conversations, authors began to delineate practical suggestions for how quantitative and qualitative methods might be combined, and attended to the potential benefits and challenges of mixing methods.

In the past four decades, a number of definitions of mixed methods research have been offered. These definitions vary in their emphasis on methods, philosophy, and design (e.g., Greene, Caracelli, & Graham, 1989; Johnson, Onwuegbuzie, & Turner, 2007; Greene, 2007; Patton, 1990; Tashakkori & Creswell, 2007). Patton (1990) described mixed methods as putting "flesh on the bones of quantitative results, bringing the results to life through in-depth case elaboration" (Patton, 1990, p. 132). In another definition, Hammersley (1996) emphasized the role of methodological eclecticism in which researchers incorporate both qualitative and quantitative methods "…on the ground that this promises to cancel out the respective weaknesses of each method" (p. 167).

Teddlie and Tashakkori later (2011) extended the attention toward methodological eclecticism by emphasizing qualities of the researcher and the importance of attending to the research question when considering the use of mixed methods designs. They offered this definition:

> For us, *Methodological eclecticism* involves *selecting and then synergistically integrating the most appropriate techniques from a myriad of Qual, Quan, and mixed methods* in order to more thoroughly investigate a topic of interest. A researcher employing methodological eclecticism is a *connoisseur of methods* who knowledgeably (and often intuitively) selects the best techniques available to answer research questions that frequently evolve during the course of an investigation. (p. 286, italics original)

As such, Teddlie and Tashakkori emphasized characteristics of the researchers and the usefulness of mixed methods research to provide both breadth and depth of understanding as well as corroboration across data sources.

Creswell and Plano Clark (2011) extended the emphasis on mixed methods researchers outlining what they consider to be core characteristics of the mixed methods researcher. They described the mixed methods researcher as a person who:

- Collects and analyzes persuasively and rigorously both qualitative and quantitative data (based on research questions);

- Mixes (or integrates or links) the two forms of data concurrently by combining them (or merging them) sequentially by having one build on the other or embedding them within the other;
- Gives priority to one or to both forms of data (in terms of what the research emphasizes);
- Uses these procedures in a single study or in multiple phases of a program of study;
- Frames these procedures within philosophical worldviews and theoretical lenses; and
- Combines the procedures into specific research designs that direct the plan for conducting the study (p. 5).

Utilizing mixed methods designs, therefore, requires that researchers have a diverse set of skills and knowledge of both qualitative and quantitative design, analysis, and interpretation techniques.

BENEFITS AND CHALLENGES ASSOCIATED WITH MIXED METHODS DESIGNS

Mixed methods research requires researchers to design studies that are complex and draw upon multiple philosophies. As such, these designs offer a number of advantages to the researcher. They also pose unique challenges. In the following sections, we overview some of the benefits and challenges to utilizing mixed methods designs in counseling and counseling psychology research.

Benefits of Conducting Mixed Methods Research

There are several benefits to using mixed methods designs. As noted previously, mixing methods allows a study to be strengthened in a number of ways. Using both quantitative and qualitative approaches ensures that researchers have greater evidence to address a research question of interest than if the researcher were restricted to only qualitative or only quantitative research designs. For example, the ability to draw from both qualitative and quantitative data allows researchers to triangulate data. As described in Chapter 16, triangulation refers to the process by which data from one source is checked against, and combined with, data from another source. Using more than one method to address a research question strengthens our ability to understand the phenomenon under investigation and allows us to ask research questions that have greater breadth and depth. Mixed methods research has the advantage of appealing to a broad audience, including those who may otherwise find either quantitative or qualitative methods less accessible.

Moreover, utilizing mixed methods research designs helps to protect against biases or flaws inherent in the reliance upon only one design. Specifically, quantitative designs may provide findings that are more generalizable and higher in internal validity. Qualitative designs allow the researchers to explore a question in depth and with nuance. Mixed methods designs do both. In this way, mixed methods research offers researchers a mechanism by which to offset weaknesses inherent in using strictly qualitative or strictly quantitative designs. For example, mono-method bias and mono-operational bias can be reduced and various forms of validity can be strengthened (see Chapter 7 for a review).

Further, the use of mixed methods designs has been purported to be particularly valuable when used in an effort to increase the cultural appropriateness of our research. For example, we might learn from qualitative interviews that particular questions or constructs do not apply to individuals who are members of specific cultural groups. In addition, as described in Chapter 16, qualitative methods can be utilized to serve as a starting point by which researchers can understand the nature of particular phenomenon specific to cultural groups. Utilizing mixed methods designs would subsequently allow the researcher to extend these initial findings by using them to generate specific hypotheses that can be tested via quantitative data collection and analysis.

Some authors (e.g., Creswell & Plano Clark, 2011) also have suggested that mixed methods research has the benefit of being more practical for researchers than strict adherence to qualitative or quantitative only designs. In other words, mixed methods designs allow researchers to make use of the variety of research methods (e.g., design, data collection techniques, data analysis) available rather than restricting a researcher to the use of only quantitative or only qualitative methods. Researchers then often have greater flexibility to collect and analyze various types of data that may, in combination, allow the researcher to most adequately respond to the research question.

Mixed methods research, therefore, also may offer a bridge that fosters connections and collaborations across individual researchers. Researchers with expertise in particular elements of design or data analysis may come together to ask research questions from a broader lens. Some authors (e.g., Hanson et al., 2005) have suggested that team approaches be used to conduct mixed methods research so that researchers with different expertise can contribute to the study. In this way, researchers who otherwise may not have worked together can come together to strengthen knowledge, to contribute to research that has greater depth, and to collaborate on studies that appeal to a wide audience.

Challenges in Conducting Mixed Methods Research

Mixed methods research designs also present unique challenges that researchers must consider when contemplating the use of such a design. These challenges primarily rest in the extent of knowledge required by the researcher, logistical factors that make mixed methods research difficult, publication or dissemination considerations, and financial and time investment required when utilizing a mixed methods design. We will briefly review each of these challenges.

As we have discussed throughout this book, quantitative and qualitative research requires different skill sets. For example, qualitative researchers need to be skilled in gaining an in-depth and nuanced understanding of a particular research question from a narrow set of data, and then integrate these data. Quantitative researchers, on the other hand, need to be skilled in designing large-scale studies that have strong internal validity so as to allow the researcher to draw inferences based upon analysis of collected data. A mixed methods researcher, therefore, needs to be skilled in both approaches (particularly if the individual researcher is not working as a part of a research team). Developing expertise in both quantitative and qualitative research design takes time, which can be challenging for beginning researchers.

Conducting mixed methods research also presents some logistical challenges. First, mixed methods designs require a greater investment in time than a research study that is strictly qualitative or quantitative in nature (i.e., a researcher must complete steps associated with both the qualitative and the quantitative designs). The time intensive nature of such designs has implications for individual researchers as well as for financial requirements needed in order to complete the research project. For example, graduate students and young scholars who have external demands to complete projects in specified time periods because of degree completion requirements or tenure requirements (respectively) may feel less inclined to embark upon a mixed methods study given the likely time demands that such a design might require. In addition, mixed methods designs often require a greater investment of financial resources.

Given the complexities inherent in designing and conducting a mixed methods investigation, we recommend that researchers carefully consider the particular research question, and whether a mixed methods design is needed in order to address that question. In practical terms, researchers also are encouraged to ask themselves a variety of questions prior to embarking on a mixed methods study. Although this list is certainly not exhaustive, some of these questions are listed in Table 17.1.

TABLE 17.1 Research Application: Practical Questions to Consider Prior to Embarking on a Mixed Methods Research Study

Question	(✓)
Do I have access to the financial resources needed in order to facilitate participant recruitment?	
Do I have the time required to complete data collection for both research foci (i.e., qualitative and quantitative)?	
Do I have the skills required in order to complete data collection for both research foci?	
Do I have the skills required in order to complete data analysis and interpretation for both research foci?	
Do I have the time or resources needed in order to transcribe, code, and gather qualitative data?	
Do I have access to software program(s) and familiarity with the software needed to analyze the data for both research foci?	
Do I have access to collaborators or other study personnel who will assist with the research processes required?	

Finally, a researcher may wish to consider logistical issues related to dissemination of mixed methods research. The page restrictions of most journals may make publication of true mixed methods research studies challenging. As discussed later in this chapter, authors must describe all relevant details of both the qualitative and quantitative portions of the study. Although manuscript outlets that have more friendly guidelines for mixed methods research are increasing in popularity and some journals are dedicated exclusively to the publication of mixed methods research (e.g., *Journal of Mixed Methods Research*), the publication process for mixed methods studies poses unique challenges that researchers may wish to consider.

In summary, we suggest that researchers who are considering the use of a mixed methods design do so while considering the benefits and challenges associated with the design. We encourage researchers to carefully weigh the benefits of the design with the realities. As discussed in Chapter 6, the use of mixed methods should be tied clearly to the research question and after carefully considering the rationale for using such a method.

WHEN TO USE MIXED METHODS RESEARCH DESIGNS

Given the strengths and challenges associated with conducting mixed methods research, it is critical that researchers carefully determine whether a mixed methods design is most appropriate to address a particular research question. Several authors have described the variety of reasons that a researcher may consider using a mixed methods design (e.g., Creswell & Plano Clark, 2011; Greene, Caracelli, & Graham, 1989; Teddlie & Tashakkori, 2011). As described in the sections that follow, mixed methods are used to initiate, develop, and refine our ability to address new and emerging areas of research, as well as to deepen our understanding of phenomenon of interest.

To Initiate, Develop, and Refine the Ability to Address Emerging Research Questions

In Chapter 16, we described the usefulness of qualitative methods to explore research questions that are new or to develop an initial understanding of poorly understood areas of inquiry. Researchers may, therefore, elect to use qualitative methods in order to explore a phenomenon of interest. After this initial knowledge is gained, a researcher may follow with a quantitative study in order to examine relationships or test hypotheses gathered from the qualitative investigation. In this way, the researcher is able to apply the knowledge gleaned from the qualitative data to the selection of variables to be defined and tested with a larger sample, thereby increasing generalizability. In this way, mixed methods designs allow researchers the opportunity to *use one data source to inform the development of a second data source*. In other words, when utilizing mixed methods designs, researchers are able to make use of the variety of sources of data that are needed in order to address a particular research question in greater depth.

Mixed methods designs may be used to *bolster a study* by embedding, or nesting, a second study into a primary study. This allows the researcher to better understand a particular component of the research process. For example, researchers may realize that they may lack knowledge about the cultural context surrounding a population of interest. The researchers may, therefore, choose to embed a preliminary qualitative design with members of the cultural group of interest into their larger intervention research design. In the qualitative portion of the design, the researchers might sensitively interview prospective participants regarding a range of issues, including study recruitment materials or incentives in order to learn the most appropriate and culturally relevant practices for potential participants. Once the researchers have learned from the participants, they could develop recruitment, incentive, and an intervention protocol that would be most likely to elicit not only participant involvement but also ensure culturally appropriate practices in the intervention phase of the research.

To Complement, Extend, or Expand Knowledge

In our introduction to this chapter, we noted that qualitative and quantitative designs have unique strengths and limitations. Mixed methods designs provide a mechanism by which researchers can *offset the inadequacies of one design with the strengths of the other*, thereby offering a more nuanced perspective of the research question(s) at hand. Mixed methods research designs provide more complete evidence for the research question in that they provide both breadth and depth.

Mixed methods research designs are useful as a mechanism by which to *deepen results from an initial set of data*. Such research designs may be used when additional data are required in order to offer an explanation for the findings. For example, researchers who are interested in understanding the level of financial strain among individuals who are unemployed might design a quantitative study in order to assess a large group of individuals' levels of financial strain using a variety of standardized measures, and to test specific research hypotheses examining the relationship of individual and environmental factors (e.g., neighborhood poverty, neighborhood violence) to levels of financial strain. Although findings from this study would allow the researcher to make inferences about the relationship of unemployment and environmental characteristics to levels of financial strain, they would not allow the researcher to understand specific factors that may impact this relationship. Collecting qualitative interviews with a subsample of the original sample may allow the researcher to ask more detailed questions in order to better understand individuals' experiences of financial strain and to help elaborate upon or explain the results generated from the quantitative data.

Mixed methods designs also may be particularly useful for *expanding knowledge* when included as a part of longitudinal research designs (as described in Chapter 12) and program evaluation (see Chapter 22). These two designs may utilize mixed methods over time across the duration of the study or project. This information may be gathered simultaneously (e.g., different types of data are collected at the same time over the course of the study or evaluation) or sequentially (e.g., different types of data are collected at different points of time over the course of the study or evaluation). In such designs, the assumption is that the research questions of interest and study purpose(s) are best addressed over time, and via multiple methods of data collection. For example, a 20-year investigation that is designed to understand the relative impact of a community-based program developed to enhance social skills among children living in a particular neighborhood, may likely benefit from the collection of both quantitative and qualitative data.

Specifically, researchers might utilize quantitative data collection (e.g., survey data, school attendance, and performance indicators) in order to first test specific research hypotheses relative to the intended outcomes of the intervention. These researchers also might utilize qualitative data (e.g., face-to-face interviews with participants in the program at a number of points in time) in order to understand the specific intervention components that may be perceived by participants to have lasting impact, as well as to understand other life experiences that are important to the individuals.

In summary, there are a number of instances in which researchers may utilize mixed methods research designs in order to address a research question. The utilization of mixed methods allows researchers opportunities to initiate and refine new and emerging areas of research, and particularly, to deepen our understanding of phenomena of interest.

PHASES FOR CONDUCTING MIXED METHODS RESEARCH

In this section we overview five phases to conducting mixed methods investigations (see Creswell & Plano Clark, 2011; Hanson et al., 2005; Morrow et al., 2012). We summarize these phases in hopes that they might serve as a guide to researchers who are considering the use of mixed methods (see Table 17.2 for an overview of the phases). There are critical tasks that the researcher must consider within each phase. It is important to note that the phases are not intended to be linear, but likely will

TABLE 17.2 : Phases for Conducting Mixed Methods Research

Phase of Mixed Methods Research	Primary Tasks
Phase 1: Identify the research problem, question, and purpose.	Identify research topic of interest.
	Identify research question(s).
Phase 2: Articulate the rationale for using mixed methods.	Determine appropriateness of using mixed methods.
Phase 3: Determine the paradigm that will guide the study.	Examine the appropriateness of various paradigms as utilized in mixed methods research.
	Articulate the paradigm that will undergird the study.
Phase 4: Determine the mixed methods design.	Identify elements of design as relative to qualitative and quantitative research strands: • Timing • Priority • Degree of interaction • Plan for mixing the data
Phase 5: Evaluate the study and prepare for dissemination.	Carefully evaluate the research process.
	Ensure that all major elements of design and study procedures are carefully outlined.

be iterative. In other words, even though evaluation activities are listed in Phase 5, researchers should be attending to evaluative elements throughout all phases of a study in order to ensure quality and rigor. In the subsections that follow, we describe the primary tasks associated with each phase.

Phase 1: Identify the Research Problem, Question, and Purpose

It is essential that researchers carefully consider the research problem, research question(s), and the purpose(s) of the research project prior to embarking upon a mixed methods investigation. Researchers might question if both the qualitative and quantitative designs are needed at this time (e.g., will conducting two sets of analyses significantly add new knowledge to the findings?). Given the complexities, resources, and skills required in order to conduct a mixed methods investigation, it is particularly important for researchers to carefully weigh the benefits and costs to conducting a mixed methods investigation.

Phase 2: Articulate the Rationale for Using Mixed Methods

After the research question(s) and study purpose(s) have been identified, a researcher will need to determine and articulate her or his rationale for choosing a mixed methods design. Despite the many advantages to using a mixed methods approach, researchers are encouraged to carefully consider whether mixing methods is appropriate and to remember that "not all situations justify the use of mixed methods" (Creswell & Plano Clark, p. 7).

Most often, mixed methods designs are fixed designs, or designs that indicate a plan for the use of mixed methods from study inception. In these designs, researchers will have clearly identified the need for mixing methods prior to embarking on the investigation. Another type of mixed methods design is referred to as an emergent design, or one in which the need to use a second method is not known from study inception but rather emerges over the course of the research; in such cases the researchers recognize that the initial source of data (and associated design) was insufficient for addressing their research question and need for additional data (Morse & Niehaus, 2009).

Within counseling and counseling psychology, there are a number of research questions that may warrant the use of a mixed methods design (as opposed to relying upon a quantitative-only or qualitative-only design). In Table 17.3 we offer some sample research questions and associated rationale for selecting a mixed methods design.

Phase 3: Determine the Paradigm That Will Guide the Study

As has been described in prior chapters (e.g., Chapter 1, Chapter 16), researchers are encouraged to consider the worldview and paradigm that will undergird their investigation. When conducting mixed methods research, this process is equally important. This phase can be a bit more involved when using mixed methods designs given the need to articulate the manner in which the qualitative and quantitative designs (and their associated worldviews) will be integrated.

TABLE 17.3 Research Application: Sample Research Questions and Rationale for Selecting Mixed Methods Design

Research Question	Brief Rationale for Mixed Methods Design
Do individuals who are undocumented immigrants living in the United States respond to questions regarding mental health similarly via standardized mental health assessments as they do via in-person interviews?	Data from qualitative and quantitative sources will provide a richer and more nuanced understanding of the appropriateness of using standardized mental health assessments within this population.
How would a particular psychotherapy treatment best be adapted to meet the needs of women who identify as Muslim and live in the United States?	Qualitative interviews with individuals from the target population could be conducted pretreatment in order to better understand the needs of the women, and subsequently, the focus of the qualitative study may be refined accordingly.
What specific factors from a career development intervention program designed to increase self-efficacy for computer skills among grade school girls contribute to increased levels of self-efficacy for computer skills following the intervention?	Qualitative interviews could be conducted postintervention in order to understand the factors to which the participants attributed change in self-efficacy for computer skills following the intervention.

It also should be noted that there is some disagreement among scholars within the literature surrounding the appropriateness of mixing methods. While a full review of the historical debate regarding the integration of worldviews associated with mixed methods research is beyond the scope of this book, we do want to highlight that questions have been raised about the extent to which qualitative and quantitative research can or should be mixed. In brief, one perspective notes that because qualitative and quantitative approaches are housed in two distinct paradigms (constructivist or postmodern and postpositivist, respectively), they are fundamentally incompatible. Scholars with the alternate perspective note that such a division is exaggerated and that the critique is unfounded. The interested reader is referred to Creswell (2011), Creswell and Plano Clark (2011), and Tashakkori and Teddlie (2003) for an in-depth review of some of the historical and contemporary controversies related to mixing qualitative and quantitative research methods.

We do not wish to convince the reader of the merits of one position over the other. Instead, we want to suggest that any researcher who intends to utilize mixed methods designs familiarize oneself with this literature and carefully articulate the philosophical foundations and paradigms that undergird the intended mixed methods design. When choosing to embark upon a mixed methods study, it is important to clarify one's position regarding how the paradigms will be integrated. Although there is not one "correct" paradigmatic framework used as a guide for all mixed methods research, many researchers have adopted a pragmatist paradigm to guide the use of a mixed methods design. In short, pragmatism is a worldview that ascribes to the following assumptions as detailed by Creswell and Plano Clark (2011):

Assumptions of Mixed Methods Researchers

- A belief in the existence of both singular and multiple realities and world-views (ontology)
- A belief that the researcher and the participants in the research have a relationship that is housed in "what works" in order to best address the research question(s) at hand (epistemology)
- A belief that values have multiple roles in the research process (axiology)
- A belief that researchers have both biased and unbiased perspectives that interact and intersect within the research process at various stages (axiology)
- A belief that combining or mixing methods best allows the researchers to address their particular research question, and that such integration allows for data to be triangulated (methodology) (adapted from Creswell & Plano Clark, 2011, p. 42)

Pragmatists believe that the research question should drive the selection of the methods and that the selection of methods (qualitative and quantitative) is based upon the research question (Tashakkori & Teddlie, 2003). In this way, pragmatists advocate that the "…forced-choice dichotomy between postpositivism and constructivism should be abandoned" (Creswell & Plano Clark, 2011, p. 44).

Phase 4: Determine the Mixed Methods Design

Phase 4 is a complex phase that entails multiple decisions specific to the study design. In this phase, the researcher considers such issues as the timing, priority, degree of interaction, and plan for mixing the qualitative and quantitative foci of the research. We provide an overview of some of the decisions that the mixed methods researcher will make related to design in the paragraphs that follow.

First, researchers must consider the degree of interaction between the qualitative and quantitative foci of their research. In a mixed methods study, the two foci can interact or be independent from one another. When the two foci interact, data collection or data analysis for the qualitative and quantitative foci of the study occur simultaneously. When the two foci are independent from one another, the data collection and analysis occurs separately for the two strands.

Second, researchers must consider the priority or amount of emphasis that will be placed on each research foci. The two foci (qualitative and quantitative) can be determined to have equal priority or unequal priority. If, for example, the study is designed such that the primary focus and efforts relate to the quantitative portion of the research, that study would be said to have prioritized the quantitative foci. In such a case, qualitative data might be collected and analyzed in an effort to confirm or further explain the findings, but the primary emphasis would be on the quantitative data and its interpretation.

Third, researchers specify the timing of the quantitative and qualitative foci. In some designs, the data collection for the qualitative and quantitative foci occurs simultaneously. In a concurrent design, qualitative and quantitative data are simultaneously collected. For example, a researcher might collect qualitative data via in-person interviews with participants when they come to the lab to participate in an intervention study.

In a sequential design, one focus will follow a second focus and the two are relatively independent from one another. For example, a researcher may expand a qualitative study by collecting quantitative data on a separate sample to extend the results from the qualitative data. In a multiphase sequential design, studies utilize both concurrent and sequential elements of design across the duration of an entire study. These are generally large-scale projects that rely upon multiple stages of data collection over an extended period of time (such as in a longitudinal research design or program evaluation). Within each stage, data may be collected concurrently or sequentially.

Fourth, researchers specify the point of interface for the qualitative and quantitative foci. In other words, this is the stage of integration between the qualitative and quantitative foci and refers to the process by which the foci will be mixed, integrated, and combined (Morse & Niehaus, 2009). In some designs, quantitative and qualitative data will be collected, analyzed, and interpreted as separate components. In other designs, qualitative and quantitative data are mixed throughout data collection, analysis, and interpretation. This point of interface can occur at four levels: data interpretation, data analysis, data collection, or design.

At the data interpretation interface level, the qualitative and quantitative foci interface only during interpretation, or at the final step of the research process. For example, after the researcher has analyzed and drawn conclusions from the qualitative and quantitative data, the researcher will offer interpretations related to the integration of the two sets of results. These integrated interpretations are typically then summarized and stated in the discussion section of a manuscript or research report.

At the data analysis interface level, data from the two foci are collected and analyzed separately, but then mixed or merged using a strategy by which the researcher combines the two foci and analyzes the data. For example, a researcher might further the analysis of two independent sets of results by relating them to one another and synthesizing the information. Alternatively, data can be transformed (e.g., qualitative data can be transformed into themes that can be coded for quantitative analysis) and then analyzed. Historically, most mixed methods studies have considered the quantitative and qualitative data to be analyzed and interpreted independently. More recently, however, there is an emerging trend toward data analysis that allows for data from qualitative and quantitative data to be integrated and analyzed (Teddlie & Tashakkori, 2011). Bazeley (2003) explained this process in this way:

> Software programs … offer … the capacity of qualitative data analysis (QDA) software to incorporate quantitative data into a qualitative analysis, and to transform qualitative coding and matrices developed from qualitative coding into a format which allows statistical analysis… the "fusing" of analysis then takes the researcher beyond blending of different sources to the place where the same sources are used in different but interdependent ways in order to more fully understand the topic at hand. (p. 385)

In other words, data from the quantitative and qualitative foci are fused and analyzed, thereby permitting the data to interface at the analysis level.

At the data collection level of interface, results from one set of data create the connection to the second study. Specifically, the results from the first set of data are used to guide the development of the research questions, data collection procedures, and design of the second study. For example, qualitative results collected via a series of interviews may be analyzed and interpreted. These results may subsequently be used to shape the research questions and hypotheses for the second quantitative study and the subsequent collection of quantitative data.

Finally, the two strands may interface at the design level. In such cases, the qualitative and quantitative foci are embedded during study design. As we described earlier in this chapter, there are several possible ways in which designs can be mixed. For example, supplemental qualitative data could be embedded within a larger quantitative design. In addition, qualitative data could be collected along with survey data.

Given the complexities inherent in mixed methods designs and the varying ways in which designs can be mixed, it may be useful to visually depict the mixed methods design. Specifically, Creswell and Plano Clark (2011) recommended that authors include a diagram, flowchart, or table in manuscripts that depict the various steps included in the study as well as the timing of the various elements. Examples are included in Table 17.4 and Figure 17.1.

Phase 5: Evaluate the Study and Prepare for Dissemination

Mixed methods researchers are encouraged to carefully evaluate throughout each phase of the research process. In essence, the phases are not considered to be linear and researchers should attend to questions related to evaluation and dissemination at each phase of the research process. To evaluate rigor in the context of mixed methods designs, researchers also must be aware of what constitutes rigor in both quantitative and qualitative designs. Thus, researchers who are interested in mixed methods designs are encouraged to first develop expertise in quantitative designs and in qualitative designs. Alternatively, researchers may cultivate research teams in which they are able to work collaboratively with other individuals who have complimentary expertise and ability to carefully evaluate the quantitative and qualitative foci of their research.

Creswell and Plano Clark (2011) provided the checklist shown in Table 17.5 to guide the evaluation of mixed methods research, to which we offer a few other

FIGURE 17.1 Sample Flowchart of Study Activities for a Sequential Mixed Methods Design

TABLE 17.4 Sample Timeline of Study Activities for a Two-Year Multiphase Mixed Methods Design

Timeline of Activities	Year 1			Year 2		
	Fall	Spring	Summer	Fall	Spring	Summer
Development						
Identification of psychometrically supported quantitative measures	X					
Development of interview questions	X					
Development of intervention (curriculum, procedures, recruitment processes)		X	X			
Baseline						
Baseline assessment (collect and analyze quantitative data)			X			
Interview 1 (collect and analyze qualitative data)			X			
Analyze qualitative data and triangulate with quantitative data				X		
Intervention						
Implement Intervention				X		
Postintervention						
Follow-up quantitative data collection and analysis					X	
Interview 2 and analysis					X	
Triangulation of quantitative and qualitative data						X
Dissemination						X

TABLE 17.5   Research Application: Checklist for Reviewing Mixed Methods Research

Question	(✓)

Do the authors indicate (identify) the topic of the study?

Do the authors note the philosophical and/or theoretical foundations to the study?

Do the authors identify the study's purpose(s) or aim(s)?

Do the authors describe each component of the qualitative foci?
  Data collection procedures
  Sample and sampling procedures
  Data analysis procedures

Do the authors describe each component of the quantitative focus of the study?
  Data collection procedures
  Sample and sampling procedures
  Data analysis procedures

Do the authors provide a clear rationale for collecting both qualitative and quantitative data?

Do the authors articulate the prioritization of the qualitative and quantitative data?
  Equal
  Unequal
  Qualitative prioritized
  Quantitative prioritized

Do the authors explain the timing of the quantitative and qualitative data?
  Concurrent
  Sequential
  Multiphase combination

Do the authors determine the point at which qualitative and quantitative data interfaced?
  Design level
  Data collection level
  Data analysis level
  Data interpretation level

Do the authors describe how the two qualitative and quantitative foci were mixed and contributed to interpretation?

Did the authors explain the overall design?

Did the authors include a diagram depicting the overall study design and flow of study activities?

Source: Adapted from Creswell & Plano Clark, 2011, p. 114

words for consistency with our chapter. We encourage readers to use this checklist when in the process of developing and implementing a mixed methods study.

EXAMPLES OF MIXED METHODS RESEARCH IN COUNSELING AND COUNSELING PSYCHOLOGY

In this section we introduce readers to two examples of mixed methods research in the counseling and counseling psychology literature. We use two recent publications to illustrate different components of mixed methods research (i.e., Green, Barkham, Kellett, & Saxon, 2014; Wöhrmann, Deller, & Wang, 2014). In this way, we hope that readers will further understand different ways that mixed methods research designs can provide critically important scientific knowledge about phenomenon of interest to counselors and counseling psychologists. In addition, we hope that readers will understand that there are many different strategies that mixed methods researchers can utilize to examine topics of interest, and that there is no one best way to conceptualize or design a mixed methods study. Rather, the selected design should be informed by the research question of interest. Readers are encouraged to review the following exemplar studies for further details regarding each stage of the research process and the full description of its use.

Green and colleagues (2014) utilized a mixed methods design to examine therapist effects in the treatment of self-help interventions based in cognitive behavioral therapy. Specifically, these authors investigated therapist effects after controlling for pretreatment severity across a sample of 1,122 patients and 21 psychological well-being practitioners in Northern England. The authors used a cross-sectional design that examined outcome data (i.e., depression and anxiety symptomology) from patients along with therapist self-assessments of ego strength, intuition, and resilience to examine effects and interviews with therapists and supervisors on patient outcomes.

For the quantitative focus of the research, multilevel modeling was used to analyze the percentage of variance that was associated with therapist effects in patient outcomes. Results indicated that 9% of the variance in patient outcomes were associated with therapist effects (Green et al., 2014). These data were then used to identify the most and least effective therapists, and to group the therapists into upper and lower quartiles based upon levels of effectiveness. In addition, survey data were collected from the therapists and supervisors who were asked to complete standardized instruments that assessed the constructs of interest to the researchers: resilience, organizational skills, knowledge, and ego strength. The researchers used these data to examine the extent to which more and less effective therapists were clustered in terms of self-rated resilience, ego strength, and intuition.

For the qualitative focus of the research, Green and colleagues (2014) collected interview data from the therapists as well as from supervisors in order to further understand factors that contribute to better patient outcomes and to therapist effectiveness. Qualitative analysis followed procedures of template analysis (TA: King, 1998) whereby prior codes that were expected to emerge from the data were identified a priori. The authors detailed their analysis process, consistent with steps described in Chapter 16. Specifically, the authors developed higher and lower order themes in the therapist effectiveness quartiles from therapists and supervisors in order to identify themes that differentiate more and less effective therapists.

Qualitative data from supervisor accounts offered corroborative evidence of the finding that therapist resilience, organization, and knowledge contributed to greater effectiveness. Although we will not review all of the findings from this study here, we do want to note a specific example to demonstrate the manner in which the qualitative and quantitative data were triangulated. Specifically, supervisors described more effective therapists as those who remained open to learning and discussing challenges in treatment, thereby offering supportive evidence to the finding from the quantitative data that indicated that therapist resilience is related to level of effectiveness.

Taken together, this study utilized a mixed methods design that prioritized the quantitative focus. Qualitative data from supervisors and therapists were used to further describe and triangulate the results from the quantitative data analysis. Further, these authors used a sequential design in which the researchers utilized existing quantitative outcome data and then followed with qualitative interviews. The qualitative and quantitative data were mixed at the level of data analysis. In particular, the researchers analyzed the quantitative and qualitative data together in their interpretation of study results.

In another study, Wöhrmann, Deller, and Wang (2014) used a mixed methods design to explore the benefits and facilitating factors related to older adults' postretirement work planning processes. Specifically, the authors were interested in understanding the relationships among postretirement career intention, postretirement career outcome expectations, and environmental factors. Given the relative dearth of data related to the positive expectations, or of factors that contribute to these expectations among older workers, the study was initiated with the qualitative focus.

The authors collected qualitative data from a sample of 22 adult employees of an aerospace company in Germany. Fourteen older workers and eight subject matter experts (i.e., individuals who were employed in an administrative role in the same company) participated in 45-minute interviews regarding their postretirement work planning expectations and processes. The interviews were recorded and transcribed. The authors analyzed the interview data using content analysis, consistent with steps described in Chapter 16. Results from the qualitative data indicated the emergence of five categories of benefits of postretirement work: financial, generativity, meaningful occupation, mental and physical fitness, and social integration (although the generativity aspect was not mentioned by the subject matter experts). Further, results revealed three facilitating factors to postretirement work: individual capability to continue working, job opportunity, and social approval.

Wöhrmann and colleagues (2014) used the results from the content analysis of the qualitative interviews and combined them with the theoretical underpinnings outlined in social cognitive career theory (SCCT: Lent, Brown, and Hackett, 1994) to inform the quantitative foci of the study. Specifically, they quantitatively tested the expected benefits, or positive outcome expectation, regarding postretirement work as well as the three categories of factors that facilitated an intention to engage in postretirement work in one's career. Two hundred and twelve adult workers in the same aerospace company as was used to comprise the qualitative sample completed a series of measures to tap the constructs of interest. All of these measures were designed on the basis of the qualitative interview results to assess constructs such as outcome expectations (i.e., positive expectations regarding postretirement work), job opportunities postretirement, and social approval. Results from hierarchical multiple regression analyses demonstrated that the constructs that emerged in the qualitative interviews (e.g., outcome expectations and facilitating factors) were significantly and positively related to postretirement career intention in the quantitative analyses.

Taken together, this study utilized a sequential design in which the qualitative focus occurred prior to the quantitative focus. The qualitative and quantitative foci interfaced at the design level and the quantitative foci built directly from the results of the qualitative data. Specifically, the researchers used the findings from the qualitative interviews to inform the development of items that were used to measure the constructs of interest in the subsequent quantitative foci of the study.

SUMMARY AND CONCLUSIONS

In this chapter we discussed the definition and key characteristics of mixed methods research. Central to the definition of mixed methods is the acknowledgement that the research will draw upon both qualitative and quantitative data. Because of this, the mixed methods researcher must possess expertise in both qualitative and quantitative research methods. Alternatively, the researcher can work as part of a larger collaborative team in which researchers have varying skills and knowledge in research design.

Mixed methods research designs allow researchers to approach research questions with both breadth and depth. As such, these designs allow the researcher to acquire deeper levels of knowledge related to their research questions that have the potential to appeal to wide audiences. At the same time, these designs are complex and often time consuming. Students considering mixed methods research designs are encouraged to think carefully about the feasibility of completing such projects and may benefit from doing so via a collaborative team approach.

STIMULUS QUESTIONS

Analyzing Mixed Methods Studies and Designing a Mixed Methods Study

1. Identify two published articles that utilized a mixed methods approach. Review these two articles and respond to the questions outlined in Table 17.5 in this chapter for the two articles.
2. Design an original research study that would require the use of mixed methods.
   a. Be sure to describe the rationale for why a mixed methods approach is necessary.

   b. For the quantitative components of your design, clearly state the theoretical grounding for your study, your proposed hypothesis(es), and your research design (including outline of procedures and analysis).
   c. For the qualitative components of your design, be sure to describe your research questions and procedures. Describe which qualitative approach will guide your method and the reasons to support the use of this approach.

Part 4

METHODOLOGICAL ISSUES

18

Chapter

The Independent Variable: The Drivers of the Study

One of the primary goals of the research endeavor is to establish a causal relationship between the independent and dependent variables. After researchers have identified a research question, they take the critical step of selecting or designing these variables. This chapter focuses on issues pertaining to independent variables or the variable that is assumed to affect the outcome of the study, while Chapter 19 focuses on dependent variables or the outcomes of the study.

Selection, design, and evaluation of the independent variable are crucial in establishing and interpreting causal relations in a study. If the independent variable is poorly designed, the researcher's effort will be unrewarding—either the expected effect will not be found or the results will be ambiguous or meaningless. Poorly designed independent variables create unwanted bias and extraneous variables, which are clear threats to Kerlinger's MAXMINCON principle.

This chapter discusses four issues related to the development and selection of independent variables. The first section discusses operationalizing the independent variable. But even when a researcher has carefully designed an independent variable, there is no assurance that the experimental manipulation will achieve its purpose, and thus the second section describes methods to check or verify the manipulation of the independent variable, often called manipulation checks. The third section focuses on interpreting the results of a study, whether the manipulation of the independent variable was successful or unsuccessful.

Thus, the first section focuses on issues pertaining to the independent variable that are relevant before an experiment begins, the second section on issues during an experiment, and the third section on issues after an experiment has been conducted. In the final section of the chapter we discuss independent variables that are not amenable to manipulation, which we define as status variables.

Prior to operationalizing the independent variable (IV), it is important to recognize that the IV can include both manipulated variables and status variables. In brief, manipulated IVs are those in which the research can assign to the participant. For example, a researcher may want to randomize clients to Treatment A or Treatment B to test the effectiveness of these treatments on psychological well-being. Thus, the IV is Treatment (with two conditions, A and B) and it is directly manipulated by the researcher. In contrast, status variables include those in which the researcher cannot manipulate. For example, a researcher may want to examine whether a treatment for depression is differentially effective based on gender identity (i.e., men, women, transgender men, transgender women, gender queer). Accordingly, sex (with five levels, men, women, transgender men, transgender women, and gender queer) is the IV, but the researcher cannot "assign" clients to their gender identity.

OPERATIONALIZING THE INDEPENDENT VARIABLE

Before an experiment begins, four concerns with regard to operationalizing the independent variable are particularly important to the researcher: (a) determining the conditions or levels of the independent variable, (b) adequately reflecting the constructs designated as the cause in the research question, (c) limiting differences between conditions, and (d) establishing the salience of differences in conditions.

Determining Conditions

In counseling research, the typical independent variable consists of several conditions. In the between-groups designs discussed in Chapter 11, the emphasis is on independent variables with two conditions: treatment and no treatment (i.e., a control group). However, an independent variable can contain any number of conditions. For example, a treatment study can examine three treatments as well as a no-treatment condition (i.e., four conditions in all). Or a treatment group may be contrasted with a placebo control group and a no-treatment control group (i.e., a total of three conditions). Of course, the independent variable is not restricted to psychological treatments. For instance, Lee et al. (2013) examined counselors' multicultural case conceptualization ability based on three conditions (or three different clinical cases vignettes) that differed on the degree to which cultural factors were implicitly mentioned, explicitly mentioned, or not mentioned. The authors wanted to know whether trainees' responses to these cases (i.e., how they include multicultural aspects in their case conceptualization) would differ based on the clients' mention of their cultural identity. The ability to manipulate the degree to which the cases included cultural factors allowed casual inferences to be made. In this chapter, independent variables are discussed generally; Chapter 20 contains a presentation of treatment outcome designs in which the independent variable is used to establish the efficacy of treatments (i.e., at least one of the conditions is a treatment).

Two notes need to be made about our discussion of conditions. First, we will use the term *conditions* to indicate the groups that constitute the independent variable (IV). Other researchers commonly use other terms interchangeably such as, *levels of the independent variable, groups, categories,* and *treatments.* Second, we have conceptualized the independent variable as a categorical variable—that is, each condition is discrete (e.g., a participant is either assigned to Treatment A or Treatment B). For instance, participants may be assigned to receive either cognitive-behavioral treatment or psychodynamic treatment for depression. Alternatively, in a psychotherapy treatment study, the independent variable might be the amount of homework assigned.

Consider the following description of a study and determine what the IV is and also the conditions that constitute the IV (also analyze whether this study would be ethical; see Chapter 3):

RESEARCH IN ACTION 18.1

Shawna wanted to see whether her teaching method was a good approach for teaching multicultural counseling class. She developed two sets of lecture slides, one that included her method for teaching multicultural counseling, which included lessons on "therapists exploring their cultural identity" and "identifying cultural markers in session." The other set of slides did not include these lessons; rather they focused on the history of multicultural counseling. She examined students' scores on the final exam and self-reported multicultural competencies (e.g., knowledge, skills, and awareness) to determine if her teaching method was successful.

The most important point is, in experimental designs, the conditions of the independent variable are determined by the researcher. This determination is often referred to as the experimental manipulation, because the researcher essentially manipulates the independent variable to determine what effect it has on the dependent variable. In this way, the independent variable is related to the cause, and the dependent variable is related to the effect.

Adequately Reflecting the Constructs of Interest

It is important that the independent variable be designed to reflect the construct(s) designated as causal in the research question. That is to say, the independent variable should be adequately defined or operationalized (see Chapter 5). For example, if the researcher would like to know whether *cognitive-behavioral treatment* is more effective than *no treatment* for participants who are diagnosed with social anxiety, then it would be important to adequately define what *cognitive-behavioral treatment* is as well as define what *no treatment* actually is. Although the answer to these questions may seem obvious, defining these constructs in theory is different than what they can look like in the real world (see Baardseth et al., 2012). Extending this example, if some participants in the *no-treatment* condition received medication for their social anxiety, but did not receive *cognitive-behavioral treatment,* would they truly qualify as receiving no treatment? Simply, if the causal construct is inadequately defined, alternative explanations for the results can be offered; these alternatives are potential confounds. In this chapter we indicate how problems associated with potential confounds can be minimized or eliminated.

To illustrate the importance of adequately reflecting the construct designated as causal, consider a study conducted by Peeters et al. (2013) who examined the effects of cognitive-behavioral treatment (CBT), interpersonal treatment (IPT), CBT+antidepressant medication, and IPT+antidepressant medication for participants who were seeking treatment for depression. Clients were able to select their treatment of choice, which was intended to help generalize to routine clinical care settings. The therapists were encouraged to adhere to the manualized treatments (e.g., IPT or CBT), however, the therapists delivery of the treatment was not monitored. The results demonstrated that all treatments were effective and they were all similarly effective in reducing depressive symptomology. To provide a better test of the independent variable (IPT, CBT, IPT+meds, CBT+meds), it might have been useful to monitor the counseling sessions to gauge whether the counselors were actually providing CBT or IPT, as well as to monitor the degree to which clients were adhering to their medication protocols. Adherence is an important concept in randomized clinical trials. That is, the IV in these studies is treatment, and thus it is important to know whether the treatment was conducted in a way that is consistent with the treatment manual. Consequently, if the treatment was delivered according to the treatment manual, then we have some assurance that the independent variable was actually implemented as planned as opposed to if the therapists were not monitored or delivered the treatment with little regard for the manual.

Often constructs represented by an independent variable are operationalized by selecting various exemplars of the construct or by using various stimuli (sometimes called stimulus sampling). Generally, there are two considerations when selecting exemplars or stimuli. First, variability among the stimuli increases the generalizability of the results. This principle can be understood by examining the case where only one stimulus or exemplar is used. Suppose that a researcher is interested in the effects of self-disclosure on counseling process and decides that, in order to standardize the independent variable in the study, every counselor should use exactly the same self-disclosure. When the researcher concludes that self-disclosure affects the counseling process, the study is open to the criticism that the result is restricted to the idiosyncratic nature of the particular self-disclosure used in the study. It would be advisable for this researcher to have the counselor use a variety of self-disclosures, as was the case in a study of self-disclosure discussed later in this chapter (Kim et al., 2003). An additional example of the failure to address the issue of stimulus sampling is Burkard and Knox's (2004) study of the effects of counselor color-blind attitudes (or believing that racial/ethnic differences do not exist) on empathy. Each participant received *one* vignette that varied on two dimensions: client race (European American or African American) and whether the counselor believed that the client is experiencing distress because of discrimination or depression (i.e., causal attribution). However, all respondents only received one vignette (e.g., all participants who received the European American client with the causal attribution of discrimination received the same vignette). Thus, the result that therapist level of color blindness was inversely related to capacity for empathy may have been specific to the particular vignettes used in this study; the study would have been improved by using several variations of each vignette.

The second issue is that the exemplars and stimuli should be representative of the universe of such exemplars and stimuli as they exist in the natural world. This idea stems from the work of Egon Brunswick, and is sometimes referred to as ecological validity (see Dhami, Hertwig, & Hoffrage, 2004). Again, there is a tension, this time between experimental control and ecological considerations. To the extent that the self-disclosures were similar to self-disclosures typically used in counseling and were delivered in the therapeutic context (i.e., in an actual case rather than in a one-session mock session), the conclusions would be more generalizable to actual counseling situations. However, this increase in generalizability results in a threat to internal validity, because one is less able to attribute differences to isolated differences in the independent variable. Illustrating this tension, Dhami et al. (2004) demonstrated that many conclusions about cognitive decision tasks obtained in laboratory studies do not hold in studies that attended to issues of representativeness of actual decision tasks. These tensions were discussed further where analogue research is covered in Chapter 14.

Limiting Differences between Conditions

The conditions selected for the independent variable should differ only along the dimension of interest. If the conditions are allowed to differ on other dimensions, the additional dimensions may confound the results. To illustrate this principle, consider the seminal study of perceived credibility of White American and Latinos/as as counselors as a function of counseling style and acculturation (Ponce & Atkinson, 1989). Although several independent variables were considered in a factorial design in this study, we focus here on the independent variable related to ethnicity of the counselor. Although there are many possible ways to operationalize ethnicity of the counselor, in this study ethnicity was manipulated by showing the participants photographs of the counselor and by using written introductions. In one condition, participants saw a photograph of a Mexican American counselor, and the introduction used surnames and birthplaces that reflected Mexican American ethnicity (e.g., *Chavez* and *Mexico,* respectively). In the other condition, participants saw a photograph of a European American counselor, and the introduction used surnames and birthplaces that reflected European American ethnicity (for example, *Sanders* and *Canada,* respectively). Clearly, this arrangement operationalizes ethnicity of the counselor; the question is whether the two conditions differed on any other dimension. Because Ponce and Atkinson chose to use photographs, there exists the possibility that the Mexican American and European American counselors in the photographs also differed in personal attractiveness, which would provide an alternative explanation for the results pertaining to this independent variable. That is, higher ratings given to Mexican American counselors by the Mexican American participants may be due to either the counselor's ethnicity or to the counselor's personal attractiveness. Fortunately, Ponce and Atkinson were aware of this potential confound and controlled for it by ensuring that the counselors in the photographs were comparable with regard to personal attractiveness (and with regard to age, another possible confound).

As in the stimulus sampling methods described previously, before research is conducted, potential confounds should be considered. It is not always possible to eliminate confounds, but identifying them before the study begins can enable the researcher to add features that minimize such confounds (e.g., with manipulation checks, discussed later in this chapter). It is distressing to discover a major confound after the data are collected when some prior thought could have led to a modification of the study that ruled it out.

Consider the following example:

RESEARCH APPLICATION 18.1

Sam would like to test whether emotion-focused therapy (EFT) is better than cognitive-behavioral therapy (CBT) for couples. Sam is able to recruit 20 counselors who are experts in EFT and 20 counselors who are experts in CBT. She is also able to recruit 200 couples, where she randomly assigns them to the treatments: EFT versus CBT. She assesses each couple on relationship satisfaction prior to treatment as well as at session 5, 10, and at the end of the 20 sessions of treatment. She also records every session and has coders (trained graduate students) rate each session to ensure that the counselors are actually doing EFT or CBT. After halfway through the study she realizes that 15 counselors (5 EFT and 10 CBT) are not adhering to their respective treatments (e.g., the counselors are doing other treatments than EFT or CBT). Moreover, there are 4 counselors who are having much better outcomes than the other counselors, and unfortunately 3 counselors are having much worse outcomes.

Questions

What are the potential confounds to the study?

What could have Sam done about it? Would training or screening of the counselors helped?

Some troublesome confounds are unique to treatment studies. For example, the counselor who is providing the treatment can be a confound if the focus of the study is on the specific treatment. Although it may seem odd that counselors would be considered a confound, there is substantial evidence to suggest that counselors differ in their effectiveness (i.e., some counselors are better than others; Baldwin & Imel, 2013). Thus, if a researcher would like to test whether Treatment A is more effective than Treatment B, then a potential confound to the study could be if some of counselors in one condition are more effective than counselors in the other treatment. Ruling out counselor confounds could be accomplished by holding the counselors constant across treatments; that is, the same counselors would administer all treatments. However, some counselors may be more skilled with one treatment than with another, or counselors may have some allegiance to one treatment or the other, and so forth. Hence, the superiority of a treatment may not be due to the treatment at all, but instead to the skill or allegiance of the counselor.

One alternative is to have experts in a particular treatment administer it, but this strategy introduces possible confounds related to experience and training and limits generalizability. Another possibility is to select relatively untrained counselors (e.g., graduate students in counseling), randomly assign them to treatments, and then give them equal training in their respective treatments. Of course, this reduces the external validity of the study because the results are then generalizable only to inexperienced therapists. Counselor or therapist effects are discussed further in Chapter 20.

Establishing the Salience of Differences in Conditions

The difference between the conditions on the desired dimension should be salient—that is, noticeable—to the participants. For example, Ponce and Atkinson (1989) could have used only the surname and birthplace of the counselor to operationalize ethnicity, which would have eliminated the personal attractiveness confound and made the research simpler. However, they included the photograph to increase the salience of ethnicity because without it, it would have been easy for the participants to read the half-page introduction (which focused more on the client) without attending to the counselor's surname and birthplace.

Although it appears that salience on the important dimension of the independent variable is vital to a study's validity, there are dangers when the salience is too great. If the participants can infer the research hypothesis from the study's procedures, then there is the possibility that responses will be biased. Transparent salience creates a situation in which the participant may react to the experimental situation (as opposed to the intended manipulation), a threat to construct validity mentioned in Chapter 7. Often the inference about the hypothesis is based on the research's stated (to the participant) purpose and various procedures, as well as on the salience of the experimental manipulation. Presumably, participants who guess the research hypothesis may respond in ways that please the researcher and thus confirm the research hypothesis.

The saliency of the independent variable can also result in a *reactivity* to the experiment, especially for some participants. For example, consider the following example:

RESEARCH IN ACTION 18.2

Pendum is doing his dissertation examining the association communication quality between supervisors and advisors in doctoral programs. He randomizes participants to one of two conditions; where one is an advisor yelling at the student and the other condition the student and advisor are having a nice supportive conversation related to the strengths of the student and the student's future. He then sends his recruitment to students who he knows that have had a difficult relationship with their advisor.

Clearly, Pendum decided to amplify the effects of his study by highlighting polar opposite conditions, coupled with a purposeful recruitment strategy—participants who might have been more reactive to the conditions.

In sum, conditions of independent variables should vary on the intended dimension but not on other dimensions, and the intended dimension should reflect the research question of interest. Furthermore, differences between experimental conditions on the intended dimension should be salient, but not transparent; participants within a condition should be aware of the critical component of the condition but should not be able to infer the research hypothesis. Of course, making decisions between salience and transparency is difficult and one of the skills that experienced researchers acquire.

MANIPULATION CHECKS

Even when great care has been taken to define and operationalize the independent variable, there is no assurance that the experimental manipulation will achieve its purpose. It is possible for the researcher to misjudge the salience of the independent variable. To verify that a manipulation has been adequately designed, it is often advisable to check the characteristics of the manipulation. The goal of manipulation checks is to show one or more of the following: (a) that conditions vary on the intended dimension, (b) that conditions do not vary on other dimensions, and (c) that the conditions are implemented in the intended fashion.

To determine whether the conditions vary on the intended dimension, judgments of characteristics related to the dimension should differ across conditions. This determination can be made in a number of ways. First, inquiries can be made of the participants themselves. For example, Wang and Kim (2010) in a study of the effects of counselor multicultural competencies manipulated by having participants watch 15-minute videos of a counseling session. In one condition, the counselor's comments were primarily supportive of the client's negative interactions with family members. In the other condition, the counselor's comments were also supportive but included multicultural skills. The manipulation check was accomplished by having participants rate seven items on a six-point scale as to whether the counselor's comments were phrased with multicultural skills (or not). For example, they asked participants, "In the session I viewed, the counselor helped the client determine whether the 'problem' stemmed from racism or people's biases so that she wouldn't blame herself too much and offered to intervene with the restaurant on the client's behalf." (p. 396). As anticipated, there were significant differences between the conditions on the manipulation check scales, providing evidence that the manipulation was indeed salient to the participants.

Another means to assess differences on the intended dimension is to have independent raters (persons other than the participants or the experimenters) judge the experimental materials. These independent raters could be either naïve individuals (those untrained in counseling) or experts. In the ethnicity-of-counselor study discussed previously, Ponce and Atkinson (1989) also varied counselor style (directive vs. nondirective). Graduate students in counseling psychology rated the dialogue of the sessions, and the intended differences in directiveness were found, lending support for the adequacy of the independent variable.

Independent raters and the participants can also be used to establish that the conditions do not vary on dimensions other than the intended one. Recall that

Ponce and Atkinson's (1989) use of photographs of the counselors introduced a possible confound related to the counselors' personal attractiveness. To control for this threat, undergraduates rated the attractiveness of several European Americans and Mexican Americans in photographs, and the photographs used in the study were matched on the dimension of personal attractiveness.

A laudatory study that featured the various considerations relative to the independent variable discussed earlier was conducted by Kim et al. (2003). The authors investigated whether counselor self-disclosure and Asian American client cultural values affected the counseling process. In this study, counselor self-disclosure was manipulated by forming two conditions, one in which counselors did not self-disclose and another in which they did. After counselors received training in self-disclosure, clients were randomly assigned to counselors and counselor-client dyads were assigned to conditions; that is, counselors were told to self-disclose to some clients and to refrain from self-disclosing to other clients. Clearly, this is a manipulation that needs to be checked to determine the following: (a) Did counselors follow the directions to self-disclose and to refrain from self-disclosing? (b) Were the sessions comparable with the exception of the self-disclosure? and (c) Were the self-disclosures salient to the clients? With regard to disclosure, observers were used to record each self-disclosure, and it was found that the sessions in the self-disclosure condition contained many self-disclosures ($M = 6.39$ per session) whereas the sessions in the no self-disclosure condition contained few ($M = .13$). Furthermore, the sessions for the two conditions did not differ in terms of client ratings of session quality, therapeutic relationship, counselor credibility, and counselor empathy. Finally, to check for salience, clients were asked to rate the degree to which the counselor self-disclosed; it was found that clients in the self-disclosure condition reported more counselor self-disclosure than did clients in the control condition. Moreover, Kim et al. allowed counselors to use several types of disclosures and tested the effects of the various types, thus ensuring that the conclusions were not restricted to one type of disclosure. Kim et al. carefully designed the independent variable and built in ways to assess critical aspects of the manipulation—fortunately, the checks demonstrated that the manipulation was successful.

In treatment studies it is important that the treatments be delivered to participants in the intended fashion. In a seminal study, Jacobson et al. (1996) tested the components of cognitive-behavioral treatment for depression. One condition consisted of counselors utilizing only behavioral activation. The second condition also included behavioral activation but added challenges to automatic thoughts, and the last condition was the full cognitive-behavioral treatment, which added increased attention to changing core schemas. The researchers had coders rate sessions in the early, middle, and late phases for these specific treatment components (i.e., behavioral activation, challenging automatic thoughts, focus on core schemas). As anticipated the different conditions varied on these components assisting the researchers to better understand the casual relationship of treatment on client outcomes. Interestingly, the researchers did not find any significant differences between the treatments in client outcomes. When the saliency of a manipulation is in doubt, checks provide a means of verifying the researcher's claim that the conditions differ on the intended dimension only. Whether or not manipulation checks are worth the extra time and effort required to implement them is a determination that can be made only in the context of a particular research study. Further issues related to manipulation checks in the context of outcome studies are discussed in Chapter 20.

INTERPRETING RESULTS

The purpose of an experimental design is to establish a causal relationship between the independent and dependent variables. Thus far we have discussed topics related to design of the independent variable and to checking on the manipulation. Equally important is interpreting the results of an experiment, which provide much of the information upon which inferences are based. In this section we discuss various problems in interpreting statistically significant and statistically nonsignificant results with regard to the independent variable.

Statistically Significant Results

Statistical significance indicates that the results for each of the conditions are sufficiently different, and consequently the null hypothesis of no differences is rejected. That is to say, there appears to be a true difference among conditions. For example, in a comparative treatment study, a statistically significant result indicates that some treatments were more effective than others, and thus the omnibus null hypothesis of no differences among treatments is rejected.

Although it might appear that statistically significant results are easy to interpret, there is much room for confusion. As we discussed earlier, the results may be due to a confound; that is, there may be another explanation for the results other than the intended one. In a treatment study, the effectiveness of the therapist may be a confound. Even though the researcher attempts to design independent variables in such a way that there are few plausible confounds, no experiment is perfect, and several confounds may remain. Although manipulation checks can be used to rule out remaining alternatives, checks can also introduce confusion.

RESEARCH IN ACTION 18.3

Hammon wanted to test the role of counselors' interpretations on client outcomes (changes in client symptom distress). She instructed one set of counselors to not provide any interpretations and the other set of counselors to interpret as clinically appropriate. There were independent raters who coded each session. They found that the counselors in the no-interpretation condition provided approximately one interpretation per session, whereas the interpretation condition provided five. Hammon did not find any statistical differences between the conditions and concluded that interpretations are not an effective intervention in counseling. Another plausible conclusion could be that providing at least one interpretation per session is sufficient.

One of the most confusing instances occurs when the manipulation check fails to indicate that the conditions varied on the intended dimension, yet statistically significant differences on the dependent variable were found. This outcome is ambiguous because there are at least three explanations for the results. First, the results of the check may have been misleading; the failure to find that the conditions varied may be due to Type II error, inadequate measures, or poor procedures. A second explanation for a failed manipulation check but observed differences on the dependent variable may be related to the presence of a confound: The manipulation check was accurate (i.e., the conditions did not vary on the intended dimension), but the conditions varied on some other dimension. Even if the researcher checked other dimensions and found no differences, it is not possible to check all confounds. A third possibility is that the statistically significant results were in error (i.e., Type I error). Clearly, statistically significant results in the presence of failed manipulation checks are difficult to interpret.

It would seem that the best situation is when the results are statistically significant and the manipulation check shows that the conditions differed on the desired dimension. But even here ambiguities may exist. A manipulation check can be reactive, and thus significant results may be due to the demand characteristics of checking the manipulation and not to the independent variable. More specifically, asking the participants about the experimental manipulation may have sensitized them to many aspects of the study, and their responses on the dependent measures may have been due to this sensitization. For example, Davis et al. (under review) randomized racial/ethnic minority clients to recall a difficult time in their therapy sessions due to (a) general offense conditions: strains or ruptures in the therapeutic relationship, or (b) microaggression offense conditions: strains or ruptures in the therapeutic relationship due to microaggressions regarding their gender or race (or subtle discriminatory statements). The manipulation checks were two single items to assess whether the participants in both conditions believed that the strain or rupture was related to their gender and/or race. However, by asking this question to the participants in the general offense condition may have influenced their subsequent responses, via priming them to reflect on issues based on gender and/or race.

To minimize reactivity, the researcher should consider administering the check after the dependent measure (of course, then the check may be influenced by the dependent measure), making the check indirect rather than transparent, and using unobtrusive measures (see Chapter 19). It is worth repeating that successfully checking the manipulation to determine that the conditions varied on the intended dimension does not rule out confounds, for it is entirely possible that the conditions varied on other dimensions as well. Nevertheless, interpretation is least ambiguous when the check was successful and the expected differences among conditions were found.

Statistically Nonsignificant Results

From a philosophy of science perspective, null results are very informative. Nevertheless, nonsignificant results can be due to a number of factors other than the lack of a true effect, including inadequate statistical power (e.g., not having sufficient number of participants to find a significant effect, if one indeed exists), insensitive instruments, violated assumptions of statistical tests, careless procedures, and bias. We can also add poorly designed independent variables to this list. Showing that the experimental manipulation successfully differentiated the conditions increases the importance of nonsignificant findings; that is, if the conditions were indeed found to be distinct as expected but the results did not produce the expected pattern, then evidence begins to accumulate that the hypothesized causal relationship is not present. The Jacobson et al. study of cognitive-behavioral counseling did not produce the expected differences between treatments; without the manipulation check it would have been easy to attribute the null results to lack of salience of differences in conditions (i.e., all the treatments were the same).

Nonsignificant findings can also accompany unsuccessful manipulation checks, as occurs when the check indicates that the conditions did not differ on the intended dimension, and the expected differences on the dependent variable are not found. This circumstance suggests the distinct possibility that poor design of the independent variable was responsible for the nonsignificant findings; consequently, the importance of the null findings for the field of counseling is mitigated.

STATUS VARIABLES

In this chapter we have emphasized the fact that the nature of the independent variable is determined by the researcher. By designing the independent variable in some particular way, the researcher attempts to examine its effect on the dependent variable. We have used the word *manipulation* to characterize this deliberate process. As mentioned previously, a study may contain more than one independent variable, in which case the effects of independent variables are typically examined in a factorial design. For example, Ponce and Atkinson (1989) manipulated both counselor ethnicity (European American or Mexican American) and counselor style (directive and nondirective) in a 2 × 2 factorial design.

Counseling researchers are often interested in variables that are not amenable to manipulation, due either to ethical constraints or to logical impossibilities. It is not ethically permissible to assign participants to a partner abuse condition, nor is it possible to assign participants to a gender condition. We define all participant-related variables that cannot be assigned as *status variables*. Examples include personality variables (e.g., locus of control), socioeconomic variables (such as education), gender, and ethnicity. Although many researchers label these variables as independent variables, the distinction between status variables and independent variables is critical to understanding the types of conclusions that can be drawn from these two types of variables.

Independent variables are manipulated and the effect on the dependent variable is subsequently assessed; if everything goes well, a *causal relationship* is established. In contrast, status variables cannot be manipulated, and statistical tests involving them detect *associations*. For example, Owen, Fincham, and Moore (2011) examined whether college students engaged in casual sex over the course of a semester and examined the differences between those who did and those who did not on changes in depressive symptoms. Because Owen et al. were not able to randomly assign participants to engaging in casual sex or not (i.e., manipulate the independent variable), it would not be proper to assert that casual sex caused changes in depressive symptoms. The causal relation could be in the opposite direction; for example, depressive symptoms may be the cause of casual sex behaviors for college students. Or a third variable (e.g., loneliness) could be the cause of both depressive symptoms and engaging in casual sex behaviors.

An important point must be made about the statistical analysis of status variables: Even though the analysis of status variables is often identical to that of independent variables, it is more difficult to make causal inferences because status variables are not manipulated (Shadish et al., 2002). It is the design, not the analysis, that determines the inferential status of the study (cf. Cohen, 1968; Wampold & Freund, 1987). For example, Owen et al. (2011) conducted a linear regression with engaging in casual sex as the independent variables (casual sex or not); because engaging in casual sex was not manipulated, it cannot be said that casual sex was the cause of differences in the dependent variables.

It is not unusual to include both independent variables that are manipulated and status variables (that are not manipulated) in the same study. For example, Kim et al. (2003) included adherence to Asian cultural values as a status variable as well as the manipulated self-disclosure independent variable. Frequently, research hypotheses are directed toward an interaction of an independent variable with a status variable; studies that address the question of which treatments work best with which clients are of this type.

We do not make the distinction between independent variables and status variables so that one type can be considered first class and the other inferior. The important point is that independent variables are manipulated so that causal inferences can be made directly. This is not to say that causality can never be attributed to some status variables. However, inferences in this case are made in a much different (and more difficult) manner. Consider the research on smoking and health. Smoking behavior cannot be ethically manipulated; for example, participants cannot be assigned to smoking and nonsmoking conditions. Even though there is little ambiguity about the fact that smoking is the cause of a number of diseases (cf. Holland, 1986), this causal relationship was established by animal studies, epidemiological surveys, cross-cultural studies, retrospective comparisons, and the like. Because smoking cannot be an independent variable, the American Tobacco Institute is correct when it states that there has not been *one* study that has established scientifically that smoking is the cause of any disease; however, the causal relation has been firmly established over *many* studies. The first step in this process was to establish that a relationship exists between smoking and disease; then, alternative explanations were ruled out. We return to status variables in the context of sampling in Chapter 8.

Confusing interpretations of studies are sometimes made because independent and status variables are not differentiated. A perusal of research articles in counseling demonstrates that status variables are often called independent variables. Nomenclature is not the issue here; there is little harm when the term *independent variable* is used inclusively. However, attributing causality without justification is an error that should be avoided assiduously. Causality is the strongest claim that can be made about relations between constructs, and one should always carefully examine the basis of causal attributions.

SUMMARY AND CONCLUSIONS

If causal attributions about the relation between constructs in counseling research are to be made correctly, the independent variable must be adequately designed. As we discussed in Chapters 5 and 6, the first step in this process is to state the research question clearly so that the manipulation of the independent variable can adequately operationalize the cause of an effect. Once the critical dimension has been identified, the researcher must design the independent variable such that the conditions vary on the intended dimension, but not on other dimensions. When the conditions vary on a dimension other than the intended dimension, a confound is said to exist, and it is not possible to ascertain whether the construct of interest or the confound is the cause of an effect. Furthermore, the intended differences among the conditions of the independent variable must be salient, so that they have an effect on participants, but not so vivid as to become transparent to participants, in which case their responses may be affected. If the independent variable does indeed vary on the intended dimension and is salient to the participants, then between-group variance is maximized. Furthermore, avoiding confounds gives the researcher more control. Clearly, the independent variable is a critical component of Kerlinger's MAXMINCON principle.

To demonstrate that the experimental manipulation accomplishes what the researcher intended, it is often advisable to check the manipulation. The goal of manipulation checks is to show that the conditions vary on the intended dimension, that the conditions do not vary on other dimensions, and/or that treatments are implemented in the intended

fashion. Manipulation checks typically are made by having either participants in the experiment or independent raters judge various aspects of the conditions of the independent variable. However, even when manipulation checks are used, the results of an experiment can be confusing. For example, ambiguity results when statistically significant differences are found among groups on the dependent variable but the manipulation check reveals that the conditions did not vary on the intended dimension. When the manipulation check is successful and there are statistically significant differences on the dependent variable, causal attributions are most plausible, although the researcher needs to make sure that the manipulation check was not reactive.

In many counseling studies, status variables are included in the design and analysis. Status variables are variables that cannot be manipulated by the researcher, such as personality variables, socioeconomic variables, gender, and ethnicity. Although the analysis of status variables may be identical to the analysis of true independent variables, the inferences that can be made are much different. When status variables are used, statistical tests detect associations rather than causal relations.

Clearly, design of the independent variable is a critical step in research. It is not unusual for researchers to have confidence in their manipulations only to discover after the data have been collected that a threatening confound was present. It is best always to be one's own greatest critic, and attempt to think of every possible problem with the independent variable before a study is conducted.

STIMULUS QUESTIONS

Independent Variables

1. Find three studies in your area of interest. For each study, identify the independent variable. For each independent variable, state the various levels of the independent variable and indicate whether they are experimentally manipulated or are status variables.

2. Suppose a researcher is interested in editorial reactions to manuscripts on oppositional defiant children, where the research manuscripts differ on the basis of the ethnicity of the children (European American vs. African American) and the attribution for the cause of the children's difficulties (external, such as poor family conditions, vs. internal, such as poor impulse control). Describe how you would design a study to operationalize the independent variable.

3. Find a study in which a manipulation check was successfully used and one in which the failure to use a manipulation check led to a major threat to validity of the conclusions. Describe how the use of the manipulation check improved the validity in the first study. For the second study, design a manipulation check that could have been used.

4. Suppose a researcher compared the efficacy of two treatments for depression and found that one treatment was superior to another. Discuss possible threats to this conclusion that could result from the manner in which the independent variable was designed.

The Dependent Variable: Skillfully Measuring Intended Outcomes

The purpose of the dependent variable (sometimes called the dependent measure) is to measure the construct that is hypothesized to be the effect (referred to as the effect construct; see Chapter 7). Thus, selecting or designing dependent variables and the methods of data collection are critical activities for the researcher. Glancing at most journal articles, you will see one subsection of the methods section entitled "Measures" and contains a brief description of and some psychometric information about the dependent and independent variables used in the study. It is paramount to select the best dependent variables. So, how best is it to start this process? Here are some questions to get the process started: What outcomes should be evident if the independent variable has the anticipated casual effect on the participants? What outcomes are primary (i.e., most likely to occur based on theory) and what outcomes are secondary (i.e., less likely to occur based on theory, but still relevant)? Why were these particular variables included and others excluded? Clearly, researchers cannot assess every outcome that they would like, so some exclusions needs to be made. However, these exclusions do affect the types of conclusions that can be inferred from the study. Caution must be exercised in this process because the choice of dependent variables can be critical to the merits of the research. Consider the following example:

RESEARCH APPLICATION 19.1

Tim, a counseling researcher, is studying the effects of interpersonal counseling as compared to dance therapy for the treatment of social phobia. Thus, his independent variable is treatment and there are two conditions (interpersonal counseling and dance therapy). He is carefully considering several dependent variables and decides the following variables will be a balanced way of assessing at outcomes, including general distress measure, verbal communication skills, and dance ability. After he analyzed the results, he found no difference between interpersonal therapy and dance therapy on the general psychological distress measure, but found that those in dance therapy had better dance ability at the end of the study as compared to those who received interpersonal therapy. Yet, those who received interpersonal counseling had better verbal communication skills.

Questions

Do you feel that Tim was justified in his selection of dependent variables? Why or Why not?

What other dependent measures might you want encouraged Tim to select?

The conclusions of Tim's study could be dramatically different if he used only one dependent measure. For instance, if he was to only use the general psychological distress measure, the conclusions may be that both treatments are equally effective. However, there were treatment specific outcomes that differed between the conditions. Given that these outcomes are predictable based on the theoretical framework of the treatment, it would be important to consider these outcomes.

Moreover, how the dependent variable is assessed can be another important consideration. For example, a mother's report may be used to assess her children's behavior, but her ratings of her children's behavior may be affected more by her own psychopathology than by the children's actual behavior (Webster-Stratton, 1988). Likewise, the reported outcome of psychotherapy and counseling can differ depending on whether the effects are judged by clients, therapists, or independent raters (McDonagh, et al., 2005; Orlinsky, Grawe, & Parks, 1994). Investigations with poorly chosen or poorly designed dependent variables will at best be uninformative or uninterpretable, and at worst be erroneous and misleading. Conversely, creatively designing a set of dependent variables might reveal new information that adds greatly to the knowledge base in a particular area.

In the first half of this chapter, we discuss considerations in choosing or designing dependent variables. The essential issue is selecting dependent variables that are adequate operationalizations of the effect constructs in the research question of interest. In the second half of the chapter, we discuss methods of data collection for dependent variables. In that section we classify and discuss seven nonexclusive methods of data collection that are useful in counseling research. The essential point is that because each method of data collection has different advantages and disadvantages, the task of the informed researcher is to collect data in a method that provides the type of information most relevant to the research question.

OPERATIONALIZING THE DEPENDENT VARIABLE

Selecting dependent variables that are adequate operationalizations of the effect constructs in the research question is a critical step in research. The dependent variables must be designed or selected to reflect the constructs embodied in the research question. This section focuses on three issues related to the design and/or selection of dependent variables. First, we examine the psychometric properties of the variables; we discuss reliability and validity as considerations in understanding the degree to which a construct is properly operationalized. Second, because the researcher must take care to ensure that the dependent variables do not react with the treatment in some way, we briefly discuss the role of reactivity of the dependent variable within the experimental context. Third, we discuss several procedural issues that can potentially affect participants' responses to the dependent variable, such as total administration time of dependent variables, order of presentation, and the reading level of the instruments.

A clear research question is critical to the proper choice or design of a dependent variable, as we emphasized in Chapter 5. It is important that the dependent variables be designed to reflect the construct designated as the effect or outcome of the independent variable. For example, in a treatment study of anxiety, it should be mentioned whether the treatment is expected to affect state anxiety (i.e., time or situation specific), trait anxiety (i.e., consistent across time/situations), or both. If the target construct is not easily differentiated from related constructs, the research question (and related discussion) should explicitly indicate how it differs. Once the relations among constructs are hypothesized and the constructs differentiated from each other, the researcher's task is to choose or design dependent variables that appropriately operationalize the construct that is expected to change as a function of manipulation of the independent variable.

PSYCHOMETRIC ISSUES

One important question about the operationalization of a construct involves the psychometric properties of the dependent variable. Researchers need to know to what extent the dependent variables they have selected to operationalize a construct are reliable and valid. If the estimates of reliability and validity are poor, then the operationalization of the construct is likely to be inadequate. Although entire volumes have been devoted to psychometrics, we will review the rudiments nontechnically here because they are critical to understanding the degree to which a construct is properly operationalized, and how this affects the validity of research. The skilled researcher needs to have a strong background in psychometrics and broad knowledge of the psychometric properties of the variables used in a study.

Reliability

To be informative, scores on the dependent measure need to vary among a study's participants. If everyone obtained the same score on a measure, nothing can be learned about the individuals; however, when participants' scores are different, we begin to learn something about how the participants differ. For example, a researcher wants to know whether teaching a multicultural class whether using lectures only or experiential exercises are better for learning outcomes. The researcher assigns students to one of two sections, lectures only or experiential exercises. At the end of the semester, all students received As. Thus, it could be that both ways of teaching (lecture only or experiential exercises) are equally effective or the grading process could be flawed. It is hoped that differences between two scores are due to true differences in the level of the characteristic of interest; that is, variance in scores should reflect variance in the respondents. Unfortunately, the variance among scores may also be due to various types of error. To understand reliability, we must understand that the variances in scores obtained in any context are due to several factors.

The first vital factor accounting for variance in scores is related to the central construct being measured. In test theory, the *primary assumption* is that for each individual a true score exists that reflects the actual level of the construct of interest for each individual. The degree to which obtained scores reflect the true scores for individuals is the reliability of the scores. Thus, there is a *theoretical true score* and an *observed score*. For example, there is theoretically a construct referred to as intelligence, and when intelligence tests are administered we obtain an observation (i.e., the score on the intelligence test). More technically, reliability is the variance in scores that is due to true differences among the individuals. If an instrument produces generally reliable scores, then participants who possess more of a given construct will obtain higher scores on the variable (or lower, depending on how the variable is scaled). For example, on a scale designed to measure depression, a participant with a high score on the scale presumably is in fact truly depressed (and more depressed than someone who has a lower score). Nevertheless, as we will see, some of the variance in most scores obtained from instruments is due to factors other than differences in the true scores.

Typically, the reliability coefficient of scores for variable X is denoted by the symbol r_{xx}. A coefficient of r_{xx} that equals .80 indicates that 80% of the variance in the scores is due to true differences, and that 20% is due to other factors. (Note that this coefficient is not squared to obtain variance accounted for, as is the case for a Pearson correlation coefficient.)

With regard to reliability, we first examine several sources of error in measurements: random response error, specific error, transient error, interrater disagreement, scoring and recording errors, and compounding. Then we discuss how to interpret reliability estimates and how to estimate reliability (i.e., the variance due to true scores). Finally, we discuss how reliability affects the relationship among measured variables.

Random Response Error

Any response that a participant makes will contain error. The most obvious example of these errors occurs in response to written items in a paper-and-pencil instrument or an online survey, but random response error occurs in measurements of all kinds. One participant may read the word "ever" as "never" and respond accordingly; another participant may be distracted by a noise during testing and mark a response to the wrong item; a third participant might forget which end of the rating scale is "disagree" and which is "agree"; or a fourth participant may not be reading any of the questions and just indicate any response to get through the survey.

Although later in the text we discuss ways to calculate error due to random responses, a few important points need to be made here. First, the assessment of almost all meaningful characteristics of individuals and situations contains random response error. Simply asking participants "What is your gender?" can result in a random response error rate of about 5% (i.e., it has a reliability of coefficient of .95). With regard to measuring more ambiguous characteristics than gender or age, performance tests (such as intelligence tests) typically have the lowest random response error rates (namely, reliabilities in the neighborhood of .90). Measurements of other characteristics, such as personality traits or therapist skill level, generally have larger random response error rates.

A second point is that instruments typically contain many items measuring various aspects of the same trait/quality so that a single random response to one item will not unduly affect the total score. Indeed, the purpose of having multiple items is to better capture the various aspects of any given construct. For instance, there are many aspects of depression (e.g., feeling sad, loss of energy) and as such there should be multiple items in a depression measure to capture these facets. Given items of the same trait/quality, instruments with more items will be more reliable than instruments with fewer items. Consider a 15-item scale with reliability of .84. It can be shown mathematically (with the Spearman-Brown formula) that randomly selecting seven items to compose the scale would produce a reliability of .70. As such, it is important to consider how many items are needed to have a reliable assessment of the trait/quality in question. More global traits/qualities will likely need more items to capture the true score; whereas more specific traits/qualities likely need fewer items (Clark & Watson, 1995; Owen, Rhoades, Stanley, & Markman, 2011). For example, how many items would it take to measure how happy individuals are in their romantic relationship? This is a general attitude about the totality of the individual's romantic relationship; thus, it might include items related to how well the partners communicate, how committed they are to the future of the relationship, the degree of trust in the relationship, and so on. However, if a researcher wanted to measure communication quality (one facet of overall relationship satisfaction), it is likely that fewer items would be needed.

Although researchers are aware of this problem, occasionally they believe some phenomenon to be so straightforward that a single item is sufficient. For example, it is all too common to see global evaluations of satisfaction, such as "On a scale of 1 to 100, how satisfied were you with this experience?" In such cases, researchers can pay dearly in terms of low reliabilities.

Specific Error

Specific error is error produced by something unique to the instrument that is different than what the researcher intended. For example, in an instrument designed to measure depression, the questions may be phrased in such a way that participants are well aware that responses to the questions vary in degree of social desirability; in such cases, participants' responses are determined to some extent by the degree to which they wish to appear socially desirable (a legitimate construct in itself), as well as to the degree to which they are depressed. Specific error is a confound because scores on this instrument measure both depression and social desirability.

Transient Error

Transient errors occur when a researcher is measuring a trait/quality at a single point in time in such a way that the conditions at that time affect the measurement of the trait. Consider the measurement of depression, the manifestation of which can be affected by transient mood states: A depressed college student's responses to a depression inventory, for example, would be affected by receiving a failing grade on an examination in the hour preceding the assessment; other participants' responses would be similarly affected by moods created by recent events.

Transient errors can be induced by administering tests in a particular order. In this way, it is the response to a stimulus that can be affected by the research design. For example, an instrument used to assess anxiety may in fact create in participants an anxious mood, which in turn would affect scores on a subsequent instrument, producing artifactual scores on the second instrument. These transient effects create error that is unrelated to true scores.

Consider the following example and determine what type of errors are being expressed:

RESEARCH APPLICATION 19.2

A researcher would like to examine multicultural competencies of beginning counselors, and as such the researcher examines novice counselors' treatment of only one client. The clients are asked to rate their counselors on a scale of 10 items that assess client perceptions of therapists' multicultural competencies, including items such as "My counselor is effective in helping me, because of his/her/their multicultural competencies." Clients are given this measure after their second session of treatment.

Questions

Are there sources of random response error? If so, what data supports your conclusion?

Are there sources of specific response error? If so, what data supports your conclusion?

Are there sources of transient error? If so, what data supports your conclusion?

Interrater Disagreement

In counseling research, raters are often used to obtain assessments. Consider a study of the antisocial behavior of school children involving naturalistic observations of the children's conduct in the school setting. Although raters of the children's conduct would be trained to adhere to some coding system, some of the variance in the observers' rating may be due to the observer rather than the behavior (e.g., some raters are more sensitive to negative behaviors). If ratings reflect the actual behavior and not idiosyncrasies of the observer, then we would expect the observers' ratings to agree. In any observational study, adequate agreement among raters is required. For example, Melby, Hoyt, and Bryant (2003) demonstrated that rater race may account for significant variance in rater bias. Furthermore, race-related bias may not decrease with training. The authors suggest these findings may indicate that certain interpretations of target behavior are culturally mediated.

It should be noted that interrater agreement is necessary, but not sufficient, for reliable assessments. If the observers rate an individual's behavior at a single time, then transient error remains problematic. Schmidt and Hunter (1996) described a study (McDaniel, Whetzel, Schmidt, & Maurer, 1994) that found that the correlation between raters of a common job interview was .81, but the correlation between raters of the same applicant in different interviews was only .52, demonstrating the magnitude of transient error. Specific error may also occur because the rating system is sensitive to some construct other than the targeted construct. For example, raters in the antisocial behavior example who are sensitive to personal appearance may rate unkempt participants as more antisocial, regardless of behavior, which would then add error variance to antisocial ratings. Moreover, observers can agree and still be off the mark. Continuing the antisocial behavior example, several observers may initially be sensitive to every antisocial behavior (as when a student bumps into another student intentionally), but as they are exposed to more egregious behavior (students striking other students or threatening others with weapons) they may become desensitized to and consequently ignore less objectionable behavior, all the while maintaining rater agreement. This is called *observer drift*.

Scoring and Recording Errors

Errors in assessment can be created by researchers through scoring and recording errors, which are any errors created in any way by manipulating the data in the process from scoring a protocol to preparing the data for statistical analysis. For example, a researcher may be entering the item depression scores into a spreadsheet, and the scores were rated by participants on a scale ranging from 1 to 7. But, instead of putting a "7" for a score the researcher erroneously keys in "77." These errors, which function as random response error (and technically could be classified as such) obscure true score variance. Outliers in data may result from such errors (e.g., a 77 could easily be an outlier if the actual range of scores should be within 1 and 7). Researchers are encouraged to treat their data carefully to minimize such errors, although scoring and recording errors are usually minor in comparison to the previously discussed errors.

Compounding Errors

The errors we have mentioned can be compounded to form an assessment with abysmal reliability. Consider the worst-case scenario: Several observers, each observing one participant, rate some characteristic only a single time in response to a single stimulus using a one-item, pencil-and-paper rating instrument, and then record the response, which later will be entered into the computer. This is exactly the case when a practicum instructor is asked to rate, on a scale of 1 to 100, the skill level of a practicum student with a particular client in a particular session. This operational-ization of counseling skill introduces many sources of error. First, there is unknown variance among the practicum instructors. They likely have very different implicit criteria that underlie their judgment of skill; interrater reliability is unknown and indeterminate because multiple raters of the same participant were not used. Second, only a single, ambiguous item was used to assess the construct. Third, the skill level displayed in a single session is subject to transient errors due to the characteristics of the client, to the presence of particular factors that affect the success of the session (e.g., the mood of student and client), and to other factors. Finally, opportunities for scoring and recording errors were not minimized. Although we are unlikely to encounter a case this extreme, awareness of the various sources of error can help researchers avoid the problems discussed here. In this example, it would have been much better to have more than one rater rate all of the students, over several ses-sions with several clients, using an instrument that contained multiple items related to skill that was scored via computer.

Interpreting Reliability Estimates

Determining the reliability of a research instrument involves many considerations. First, any reliability coefficient is an estimate of the true reliability, in the same way that a mean of a sample is an estimate of the population mean. A common error in describing the reliability of a measure is to suggest that the measure is reliable (e.g., the ABC inventory is a reliable measure), or that the measure is reliable with certain participants (e.g., college students, women, rugby players). A more accurate state-ment would be that the reliability properties are associated with the observations in any given study (e.g., the ABC inventory demonstrated a reliability estimate of .80 in this study). Thus, the context of the study needs to be considered. For example, a test written in English, intended to be used with those with a high school educa-tion or greater, may not produce reliable estimates for recent non-English speaking immigrants to the United States, especially if they are younger (e.g., middle school students). Later in this section we describe various methods for calculating reliabil-ity coefficients, but it should be kept in mind that these coefficients are estimates that vary across samples.

Second, reliability reflects variance due to true scores, but it does not indicate what the true scores are measuring. A set of scores that are reliable may be measur-ing something quite different than what was postulated; for example, a personality measure may be measuring social desirability rather than the targeted construct. Developers of scales often attach names to them that indicate some construct (for example, the ABC Scale of Social Skills), but adequate reliability does not establish that the instrument actually measures that construct (in this instance, social skills). It is *validity*, which will be discussed later in this chapter, that is concerned with whether the construct being measured is the construct of interest.

Third, reliability is based on the scores and not on the instrument from which they were derived. The scores have certain properties that are derived from the characteristics of the instrument. A vital consequence of this distinction is that reliability estimates are restricted to the types of participants on whom, and the conditions under which, the psychometric study was conducted. An instrument may perform adequately for one type of participant but not for another type, or under one set of conditions but not under others. For example, an anxiety measure that yields adequate reliability estimates with undergraduates when administered in a classroom may be completely useless for measuring the anxiety of agoraphobics in a clinical setting. Put another way, the instrument may be very sensitive to midrange differences in anxiety but insensitive at the upper range. This is called a *ceiling effect*; the agoraphobics may have scored at or near the maximum end of the scale, and thus their scores were not reflective of true differences in anxiety. Of course, this problem may also be manifest at the bottom of the range, creating a *floor effect*. Reliability is also dependent on characteristics of the participants, such as reading ability and age. An instrument may yield adequate reliability for college students but not for high school dropouts because of random error created by the latter's difficulty in reading the items. Moreover, instruments may contain items that have different meanings to different cultures, and it should not be assumed that reliability estimates are transferable. The implication of this discussion is that researchers should choose instruments that are sensitive in the range of scores anticipated and the type of participants used in the study. Such a choice requires a careful reading of the psychometric studies conducted on various instruments. Alternatively, the reliability of the scores actually obtained in a study could be estimated; typically this is impractical because large numbers of participants are needed for such studies (typically in excess of 300; cf. Nunnally, 1978) and because reliability estimates are affected by mean differences obtained for the various conditions of the independent variable.

Benchmarks for Evaluating Reliability

In the end, researchers would like to know: How high should reliability be? Some sources indicate that reliability estimates in excess of .70 are sufficient (e.g., Clark & Watson, 1995; Nunnally, 1978). Certainly, all things being equal, the instrument that yielded the highest reliability should be chosen over other instruments. However, there are often other issues to consider. For instance, for more global measures the estimates are likely to be lower than for measures that have a more specific focus (Clark & Watson, 1995). The type of reliability is also an important consideration (e.g., test-retest reliability, cronbach alpha; see following). Other factors need to be considered, including validity, time required to complete the instrument, and costs (topics to be discussed later in this chapter). Thus, in instances when a construct is elusive, reliability of .70 may be adequate. Keep in mind, however, that reliability of .70 means that 30% of the variance of the scores on the dependent variable is due to error. Certainly, reliability indexes below .50 contain serious psychometric problems that limit the utility of the instrument. However, it is important to note that low reliability estimates do not make results appear in a random or haphazard manner. Rather, they affect the likelihood of finding a significant result, if one truly exists. Thus, to maximize the chance of actually finding a true effect, it is important to select measures that are likely to perform in a reliable manner for the sample under study. Consider the following example:

RESEARCH APPLICATION 19.3

Fred wanted to examine how an existing treatment for anxiety, called anti-nerves treatment (ANT), would perform with adolescents. He designs a study to compare ANT to naturally occurring treatment (e.g., treatment that is not adjusted or informed by the researcher). Currently, ANT has only been utilized with adults and Fred has experience conducting adult ANT treatment studies. He decides to select measures for his study that he typically uses with adults. At the end of the study, he finds that there is no difference between ANT and the naturally occurring treatment. However, his primary measure of anxiety only had a reliability coefficient of .60. Nonetheless, Fred concludes that ANT is not an effective treatment for anxiety with adolescents.

Questions

Is this a fair conclusion?

How much error variance is there in the dependent measure?

Conversely, if there were a significant difference between ANT and the naturally occurring treatment, and Fred concluded that ANT was an effective treatment of anxiety in adolescents, would the reliability of the anxiety measure affect the conclusions?

Calculating Estimates of Reliability

There are many ways to estimate the reliability of scores, each of which is sensitive to one or more of the errors previously discussed. The various coefficients will be briefly discussed here; for additional detail the reader is referred to psychometric texts. Primarily, you will see *internal consistency coefficients, test-retest correlations, and interrater agreement coefficients* as estimates of reliability.

Internal consistency refers to the homogeneity of the items. If the various items of an instrument are measuring the same construct, then scores on the items will tend to covary; that is, someone who has a high level of the construct (e.g., is anxious) will tend to answer all the items in one direction (assuming the items are all keyed in the same direction), whereas someone who has a low level of the construct (e.g., is not anxious) will tend to answer all the items in the other direction. When scores for the various items are highly intercorrelated, internal consistency is high. There are several ways to calculate this internal consistency. The most common metric is coefficient alpha (sometimes referred to as Chronbach's alpha after Lee Chronbach who developed this statistic in 1951). Simply, coefficient alpha is based on the average interitem correlations and the number of items on the measure. As such, as the number of items or the average interitem correlations increase, so will the coefficient alpha. There is a limit to the impact of adding more items; at some point the increase of coefficient alpha is likely not worth the additional time it will take participants to complete more items. One occasionally sees reliability estimated with the Kuder-Richardson 20 formula, which is a special case of coefficient alpha used when items are scored dichotomously (i.e., when each item has two possible outcomes, such as correct and incorrect). Additionally, the split-half test is another measure of internal consistency, but it is rarely used. Briefly, this score is derived by correlating one half of the items with the score derived from the other half of the items. This correlation (corrected for the fact that it is derived from tests half as long) is called the split-half reliability coefficient. Because this coefficient is dependent on the particular split, a better estimate is derived using the formula for the coefficient alpha, which is equal to the mean of all the possible split-half coefficients.

Although measures of internal consistency are widely used, they are not sensitive to specific and transient errors. For example, a measure of extroversion may reflect (to some degree) transient mood states, or a measure of counseling skill may be specific to a particular client. Scores on extroversion or counseling skill may be internally consistent but contain variance due to extraneous specific or transitory sources.

Indexes that take into account measurements taken at different times or made in response to different stimuli are sensitive to transient effects. The most common such index is the *test-retest correlation*. If a construct is expected to remain stable over a period of time, and if the instrument is not subject to transient or random response errors, then test-retest correlations should be high. If internal consistency is high, but the test-retest coefficient is relatively low and the construct is expected to be stable over that period of time, then the scores reflect transient effects. A similar index can be used to assess transient effects due to different stimuli. If a measure of counseling skill is internally consistent with one client, but the correlation of the skill measure with two different clients is low, then one can conclude that the skill measure is not adequate to measure general counseling competence because it is measuring something related to specific clients (e.g., Imel et al., 2011; Owen & Hilsenroth, 2014). Of course, test-retest coefficients are inappropriate if the construct being measured is not expected to remain constant.

One problem with the test-retest coefficient is that it overestimates reliability because it is not sensitive to specific error. If something unique is measured by an instrument, then this unique characteristic would be measured on the second administration of this instrument as well. One way to address this problem is to use parallel forms at the two times. Correlations between parallel forms of an instrument at two different times (or in response to two different stimuli) help identify random response, specific, and transient errors.

Lastly, if ratings are used, indexes of *interrater agreement* are necessary. Essentially, multiple raters are needed so that their level of agreement can be calculated. Although there are many ways to measure interrater agreement, most methods simply index agreement between the raters and do not take into account random response, specific, or transient errors, as discussed previously. Even if raters are responding randomly, they will agree occasionally merely by chance, and consequently any measure of interrater agreement should be corrected for chance agreements.

Effects of Unreliability on Relationships among Variables

We have made much of the fact that instruments should yield reliable measures in order to be useful in counseling research. We now illustrate, through some examples, the pernicious effects of unreliability. Consider two constructs, A and B, and two measures of the constructs, X and Y, respectively. Suppose that all of the sources of error (internal inconsistency, transient errors, and so forth) for these two constructs are equal to about 30%; that is, $r_{xx} = .70$ and $r_{yy} = .70$. Now suppose that the researcher claims that the two constructs are distinct because X and Y are highly, but not perfectly, correlated—say, $r_{xy} = .70$. In this example, the researcher is claiming that two constructs exist, A and B, and that interpretations can be made about those constructs from the variables X and Y, respectively. Thus, X is a measure of A and Y is a measure of B. But it should be kept in mind that the correlation of .70 is the correlation of the measures X and Y, not the correlation of the constructs A and B. Because the error in each of the measures cannot be systematically related (i.e., it is random error), the obtained correlation of the measures is less than the correlation of the constructs, and we say that the correlation of the constructs has been attenuated by the unreliability of the measures.

Classical test theory provides a formula for correcting for the attenuation:

$$r_{AB} = r_{xy}/\sqrt{r_{xx}\, r_{yy}}$$

Put into words, the correlation between the constructs is equal to the obtained correlation between the measures divided by the square root of the product of the reliabilities of the measures. In our example immediately before, the correlation between the constructs would be:

$$r_{AB} = 0.70/\sqrt{(0.70)(0.70)} = 1.00$$

That is, the correlation between the constructs is perfect, and the only differences between the scores on X and Y are due to random error; thus, any interpretations involving two distinct constructs would be in error.

The point of this example is that even if two constructs are perfectly correlated, the obtained correlation will be dramatically attenuated by unreliability. (Note that we have not discussed the effect of sampling error, which could also dramatically affect the obtained correlation.) This is not an artificial example; many subscales of instruments are correlated in the neighborhood of .70, with reliabilities in the neighborhood of .70. Thus, when correlations are this high, it could suggest that these subscales could be measuring the same construct, rather than distinct constructs; more extensive work is needed to better understand how the measures are unique (see, e.g., Drinane, Owen, Adelson, & Rolodfa, 2014). Or alternatively, the two constructs covary to the point of being essentially the same. Now consider the following example, which illustrates how unreliability can make it almost impossible to obtain expected results in a study.

RESEARCH IN ACTION 19.1

Suppose that a researcher is interested in the relation between the skills of counselors in training and counseling outcome. The generic skill of the beginning counselors is rated by the practicum instructor on a single-item scale anchored by "Very skilled—top 5% of all practicum students" and "Very unskilled—lowest 5% of all practicum students." Suppose that a single measure of outcome was used—for example, a measure of depression. Now also suppose that the researcher is very fortunate to sample all of the students in a large program, say $N = 30$. What are the chances that the researcher will detect a true relationship between skill and outcome? As we will see in the following, the probability is low. As we discussed earlier, the reliability of skill ratings, especially on a single-item instrument, is probably extremely low; for this example, suppose that the reliability of such ratings is generously assigned a value of .50. Suppose also that the measure of depression is fairly reliable—say, $r_{yy} = .80$. Furthermore, suppose that about 20% of the variance in outcome is due to the counselor's skill (a reasonable estimate, given that variance in outcome is also due to initial severity, treatment administered, motivation for therapy, social support of client, and so forth). If 20% of the variance in outcome is due to skill, then the population correlation between the constructs of skill and outcome would be .45 (i.e., variance accounted for is the square of the correlation coefficient; $.45 \times .45 = .2025$ or 20%). However, this correlation is attenuated by the unreliability of the measures of the constructs; using the attenuation formula shown previously, the correlation is reduced to .28. The power to detect a population correlation of .28 with 30 participants is about .35; that is, the probability of rejecting the null hypothesis of no relationship between skills and outcome is .35 when the true correlation is .28. Said another way, about 65% ($1 - .35 = 65$) of the times this study would be executed, the researcher would conclude that there was no relationship between therapist skill and outcome, despite the fact that the true relationship between skill and outcome is strong! This is obviously a disturbing result, because it will likely be concluded that the skills of practicum students are unrelated to outcome, when this is not the case.

In Chapter 7, we discussed threats to the statistical conclusion validity of a study due to unreliability of measures and low power; the previous example is a graphic illustration of these effects. The central point here is because of the unreliability of the measures the obtained relation between measures of constructs may be very different than the actual or true relationship between constructs. Accordingly, researchers would be wise to select measures with a history of demonstrating high reliability estimates.

Although the preceding example involved correlations, the same principles apply to experimental designs. The reliability of the dependent variable, and the degree to which the independent variable faithfully and saliently represents the intended differences between conditions, reduces the size of the effect as well as reduces the power of the statistical test of differences among groups. Any conclusion that a

treatment resulted in no differences in outcome may be due to the low power resulting from unreliability rather than the treatment. Accordingly, when any statistical
relation is represented, one must be very clear about whether one is discussing variables (measures of constructs) or constructs.

There are also more advanced and complex issues when it comes to psychometric properties of scales that we did not cover. Readers who are interested in more
information about item response theory, a different way to examine the viability of
items on a scale, should refer to Embretson and Reise (2000) or DeMars (2010).
Additionally, the field has developed ways to understand how reliability is related
to other similar concepts, such as generalizability theory (see Brennan, 2001). We
encourage readers who to explore these concepts after mastery of the foundational
psychometric principles.

RESEARCH APPLICATION 19.4

Summary Check of Reliability

We have covered a lot of information regarding reliability. Take a moment to reflect
on the various key terms/constructs described.

1. What is (a) random response error, (b) specific error, (c) transient error,
   (d) reporting error, (e) interrater disagreement error, and (f) compound error?
2. What is (a) coefficient alpha, (b) interrater agreement, and (c) test-retest
   correlation?
3. What is a ceiling and floor effect? How can they occur?
4. If a reliability estimate (alpha) is .80, then how much error variance is there
   in the measure?
5. How can unreliability affect the results of studies?

VALIDITY

Of the many types of validity, the most important type for research purposes is
construct validity—the degree to which the scores reflect the desired construct
rather than some other construct. Clearly, unreliable scores cannot have construct
validity because they are due mostly to random error. Nevertheless, as mentioned
previously, reliable scores may reflect one or more constructs other than the one
specified. Specifically, scores may be quite reliable but lack construct validity. Determining construct validity, although complicated and indirect, is vital to the integrity
of a study.

There are several ways to determine construct validity. We will walk through the
steps of developing a measure to give you a better understanding of the process and
so that you can better evaluate measures in your reading and studies. First, researchers typically generate a large set of items based on several sources of information
(e.g., theoretical foundation, their knowledge of the field, conversations with those

in the target population, suggestions of experts). These items should represent various aspects of the trait/quality that they intend to capture. These items are then typically evaluated with those who have expertise in the field to ensure that the items truly capture the trait/quality in question. This process for what is typically referred to as *content validity*; that is, the content of the items has been approved, or sanctioned by experts in the field on the particular topic (e.g., multicultural competencies). Parenthetically, several items are typically removed and/or reworded in the vetting process by the experts.

After the items have been vetted, the items are administered to a sample from the target population. Next, construct validity can be established through a statistical procedure called factor analysis (Tinsley & Tinsley, 1987), a data reduction procedure that examines the factors that underlie a set of items (e.g., multicultural competencies). If the set of variables is the scores on a variety of tests, then factor analysis can be used to detect a small number of factors that account for the variance in the scores—for example, if a researcher develops 100 items for a new measure of depression for adult men after doing focus groups with adult men. After vetting the items through experts, only 50 items remained. Then the researcher administered the 50 items to 500 men in the local community and conducted an exploratory factor analysis. Items that measure the same construct will be grouped together in the sense that they will correlate highly (load on) a single factor. The factors are then interpreted as constructs. During this process, some items are removed from the measure as they may not "fit" into a factor. Two factors emerged: one factor reflected sullen or low energy (labeled Sullen and Low) and the other factor reflected agitation and irritation (labeled Agitated and Irritated), two aspects of depression. After this process, ideally, researchers administer the measure to a different sample from the target population and conduct a confirmatory factor analysis (Kline, 2010). In essence, a confirmatory factor analysis examines whether the factor structure established by the exploratory factor analysis would be maintained or confirmed in a second sample. If the same factor structure is replicated, the researcher has a little more assurance that the factor structure is stable (see Kline, 2010, for more details).

Finally, after the factor(s) of the measure have been established, then researchers examine the relation between scores on the instrument and scores on other instruments intended to measure the same and other constructs. Clearly, there should be a high correlation between instruments that measure the same construct. If these expected correlations are found, then *convergent validity* is said to exist. Measures of different constructs should not be highly correlated, although a moderate correlation can be tolerated and may even be expected. Nevertheless, the correlation of measures of different constructs should be smaller than correlations of measures of the same construct; if this pattern is found, *discriminant validity* is said to exist.

There are some cautionary notes about this process. Theoretical foundation is key to the development of a measure. Theory can be informative in the creation of the items as well as in the selection of the factors and which items to retain on the factors. However, sometimes factor analysis is used to develop scales. That is, a set of items is subjected to a factor analysis, items are segregated by their loadings on factors, descriptors are assigned to factors, and subscale scores are calculated based on the segregation (e.g., the score for the subscale that corresponds to Factor 1 is formed by summing the scores for those items that load on Factor 1). Although this process can be useful, it is not a substitute for theoretically informed decisions. Specifically, there are three problems with an over reliance on factor analysis: (a) The method is atheoretical and may lead to factors that have little psychological basis and are driven by the data; (b) even if the factor analysis uses a method that produces independent factors, the subscale scores likely will be highly correlated, because items load to some degree on all factors; and (c) the reliability of single items or factors with low number of items is low, and thus the results of factor analyses are often unstable.

The preceding discussion of factor analysis and the potential for subscales raise an issue about whether one should use the total score of an instrument or its subscale scores. The choice is exclusive; that is, one should never use both the total score and one or more of the subscale scores in the same analysis, because they are dependent and will result in nonexistent or meaningless solutions in statistical analyses. The decision to use subscale scores or total scores is primarily related to the hypotheses of the study, but it is partially related to psychometrics as well. If the hypotheses of the study reference the general construct (e.g., global evaluation of the counselor), then one should either use the total score or combine the subscale scores, rather than performing analyses on each separate subscale. However, if the hypotheses specify relationships for the constructs of the various subscales, then one should analyze the subscales separately (Huberty & Morris, 1989). For example, Rhoades et al. (2010) examined how four related aspects of romantic commitment were associated with the likelihood of breaking up. Specifically, they examined dedication (e.g., desire for long-term vision of the relationship, strong couple identity), felt constraints (e.g., feeling stuck), material constraints (e.g., living together, joint bank account), and perceived constraints (e.g., concern for partner welfare) as predictors of breakup status over an eight-month time frame. Because they speculated that each of these factors would uniquely relate to breakup status, they did not combine the subscales. Interestingly, all four subscales did predict breakup status, after controlling for the other scales (i.e., felt constraint, dedication, material constraint, and perceived constraint). Finally, subscale scores should never be used if there is not persuasive evidence that they are measuring distinct constructs, a point on which we will elaborate subsequently.

MULTIPLE MEASURES OF A CONSTRUCT TO IMPROVE CONSTRUCT VALIDITY

The use of multiple dependent variables is often recommended (Shadish, Cook, & Campbell, 2002; Kazdin, 2003). No one variable can adequately operationalize a construct because, as was discussed previously, some of the variance in this variable is due to other constructs (specific variance) and some is due to error. Using several variables can more adequately represent the construct because one variable will be sensitive to aspects of the construct absent in other variables. The overlap of these variables reflects the essence of the construct, as represented in Figure 19.1.

FIGURE 19.1 ⋮ Use of Multiple Variables to Operationalize a Construct

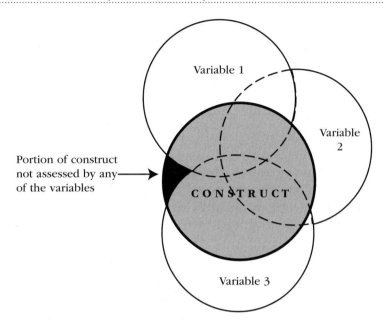

Another reason for including multiple measures is the expectation that different constructs produce different outcomes. In an important historical exemplar, McNamara and Horan (1986) investigated how behavioral and cognitive treatments affected behavioral and cognitive manifestations of depression. The cognitive battery contained the Automatic Thoughts Questionnaire, the Cognitive Scale, and the Recalled Cognitions exercises. The behavioral battery included the Pleasant Events Schedule, the Behavioral Scale, and Observer-Evaluated Social Skills ratings. They found that the cognitive treatments clearly reduced cognitive manifestations of depression with some generalization to behavioral measures, whereas the behavioral treatments appeared to have little effect on either the cognitive or the behavioral measures. Although this example is noteworthy, generally, counseling studies find that treatments do affect symptom measures similarly.

Multiple measures of constructs can also be used to avoid the attenuation of correlations between constructs and can account for method variance. The next two sections discuss the intricacies involved in using multiple measures to form latent variables or a general variable that is based on several observed measures, which represent constructs better than any single variable can.

We have discussed how unreliability attenuates measures of association, such as correlations. Multiple measures of a construct can be used to detect relationships among constructs that are untainted by unreliability. We now show how structural equation modeling can be used to detect the relationships among constructs after controlling for measurement error. Structural equation modeling is a statistical method that examines the relationship among constructs (sometimes called latent variables or traits) by using several observed measures to operationalize the construct (see Brown, 2015; Enders, 2001; Kline, 2010).

RESEARCH IN ACTION 19.2

The statistical method is complex, and only a conceptual presentation is included here. The example we consider here is provided by Cole (1987). Cole examined two important constructs—depression and anxiety— from Tanaka-Matsumi and Kameoka's study (1986).

Tanaka-Matsumi and Kameoka administered three commonly used measures of depression and six commonly used measures of anxiety; the correlations among these measures are presented in Table 19.1. Several observations can be made from this table. First, it appears that the measures of the same construct are moderately high, showing some convergent validity (correlations for depression measures ranged from .54 to .68; however, the correlations for the anxiety measures were wider in range, from .32 to .79). The constructs of anxiety and depression seem to be related because the obtained correlations among measures of depression and anxiety ranged from .33 to .74. However, we must keep in mind that all the correlations in this table were attenuated by unreliability. Structural equation modeling provides a means of estimating the correlation of the constructs of depression and anxiety, taking this unreliability into account.

The results of the structural equation modeling are presented in Figure 19.2. First note the arrows from the ellipse "Depression" to ZungD, BDI, and DACL (observed variables in rectangles), which indicate that the construct (or latent variable) of

TABLE 19.1 Correlations of Depression and Anxiety Measures*

	Depression				Anxiety				
	ZungD	BDI	DACL	ZungA	SAI	TAI	MAS	EHE	EHS
ZungD	1.00								
BDI	0.68	1.00							
DACL	0.54	0.60	1.00						
ZungA	0.71	0.67	0.48	1.00					
SAI	0.61	0.60	0.66	0.60	1.00				
TAI	0.74	0.73	0.61	0.69	0.66	1.00			
MAS	0.67	0.71	0.50	0.72	0.53	0.79	1.00		
EHE	0.39	0.42	0.33	0.47	0.37	0.48	0.49	1.00	
EHS	0.40	0.40	0.36	0.41	0.32	0.53	0.52	0.60	1.00

*ZungD = Zung Self-Rating Depression Scale; BDI = Beck Depression Inventory; DACL = Depression Adjective Checklist; ZungA = Zung State Anxiety Measure; SAI = State Anxiety Inventory; TAI = Trait Anxiety Inventory; MAS = Manifest Anxiety Scale; EHE = Endler-Hunt Examination Anxiety; EHS = Endler-Hunt Speech Anxiety.

Source: Tanaka-Matsumi, J., & Kameoka, V. A. (1986). Reliabilities and concurrent validities of popular self-report measures of depression, anxiety, and social desirability. *Journal of Consulting and Clinical Psychology, 54,* 328–333.

FIGURE 19.2 : Multiple Measures of Depression and Anxiety

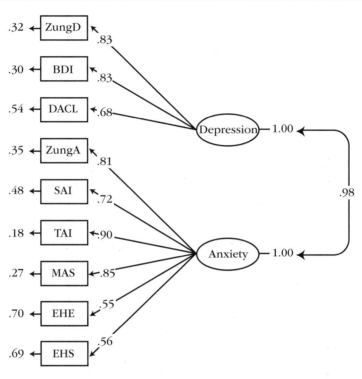

depression loads on these three instruments. This is akin to factor loadings in exploratory factor analysis; here the instrument loadings are .83, .83, and .68, respectively. The latent variable "Depression" is a statistical entity representing the construct operationalized by the three measures of depression. This latent variable represents the construct depression measured without error, because in a sense it is the variance that the three measures have in common, excluding specific or error variance. This procedure statistically accomplished what is pictured in Figure 19.1 (i.e., it uses the common variance among measures to produce a variable that represents the construct). Similarly, the construct of anxiety (the ellipse "Anxiety") is the statistically developed measurement of the construct of anxiety from the six observed measures, with factor loadings ranging from .55 to .90.

   The correlation of the constructs of depression and anxiety is then estimated from the latent variables of anxiety and depression. The curved double arrow between "Depression" and "Anxiety" represents this correlation, which was calculated to be .98. This number indicates the estimate of the correlation of the constructs of depression and anxiety, as measured by the three measures of depression and the six measures of anxiety, which is .98. This correlation is not attenuated by unreliability.

   The conclusion here is that, at least as measured by these commonly used instruments, the constructs of depression and anxiety are not distinct, but overlap a great deal with each other. If these nine measures were used in an outcome study, it would only make sense to talk about the effect of treatment on the aggregate of the measures because these constructs as operationalized in this study are not distinct. Thus, it would be misleading to talk about the relative effectiveness of one treatment on one of the constructs but not the other (e.g., to say that Treatment A is more appropriate for the treatment of depression). It would be even more problematic to perform individual tests on the nine measures and make conclusions about individual measures, as the data indicates they are measuring the same construct. Moreover, conducting nine statistical tests dramatically increases the probability of obtaining a statistically significant result by chance alone. With nine variables, the probability of obtaining at least one significant result by chance is approximately .40, dramatically higher than is desired to make valid conclusions (Hays, 1988).

One last issue to consider in the previous example. Although it has been shown that latent variables can be used to calculate correlations that are not attenuated by unreliability, these correlations may be inflated by the fact that measures use the same method of data collection. In the next section we show how this method variance can also be removed.

REMOVING METHOD VARIANCE

In the previous example, all of the measures of anxiety and depression were pencil-and-paper measures. As discussed in Chapter 7, construct validity can be enhanced by utilizing different methods of assessment. It may well be that something in these instruments affects participants' responses, but is unrelated to either depression or anxiety. One possibility is trait negativity, a general tendency to evaluate oneself negatively on all dimensions; these respondents would appear to be more depressed and more anxious than is truly the case. Still another possibility is a transient mood state that might affect responses to the instruments. Students attending the testing session just after receiving grades on their midterm examinations may experience transient feelings (either positive or negative) induced by the results of the exam. Because only one assessment method was used, these possibilities are likely to affect responses to all instruments similarly, increasing the correlations among them. Variance common to all measures using the same method is called method variance. Method variance inflates relationships among variables; that is, the relationship between two measures is due not only to a conceptual relationship in the constructs of interest, but also to a relationship in how the constructs were measured. Whereas unreliability attenuates correlations, method variance inflates correlations, as the following example demonstrates.

In this next example, we will present a fictitious example to illustrate another multitrait-multimethod approach to understanding convergent and discriminant validity. Table 19.2 displays the multitrait-multimethod correlation matrix in which two traits, A and B, are measured with three different methods, forming six measured variables, A1, A2, and A3 (Trait A measured using the three methods) and B1, B2, and B3

TABLE 19.2 Correlations of Two Traits Measured Using Three Methods

| | Trait A | | | Trait B | | |
| | Method 1 | Method 2 | Method 3 | Method 1 | Method 2 | Method 3 |
	A1	A2	A3	B1	B2	B3
A1	1.00					
A2	0.64	1.00				
A3	0.57	0.60	1.00			
B1	0.72	0.54	0.46	1.00		
B2	0.39	0.78	0.46	0.56	1.00	
B3	0.35	0.43	0.75	0.54	0.55	1.00

(Trait B measured using the three methods). In this fabricated example, the correlations correspond to the convergent and discriminant validity presented in Table 19.1. Notice that the correlations of the same trait with different methods are relatively high (.57 to .64 for Trait A and .54 to .56 for Trait B), and the correlations between different traits using different methods are relatively low (.35 to .54). However, as described earlier, correlations of different traits using the same method are inflated by method variance, and are relatively high (.72 to .78). Furthermore, assume that all the correlations are attenuated by unreliability. From this matrix, we want to estimate the correlation between Traits A and B to determine whether they are independent, related but distinct, or essentially the same. To this end, we again use structural equation modeling.

The first structural equation model, shown in Figure 19.3, examines the correlation of the latent traits in the same manner as we did for depression and

FIGURE 19.3 Multiple Measures of Trait A and Trait B

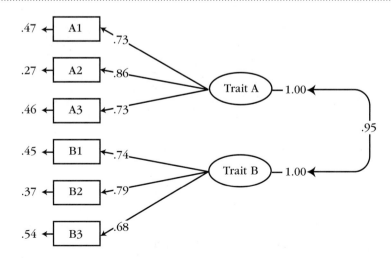

anxiety. (Structural equation modeling provides model fit indexes that assess the adequacy of measurement. Although not discussed here, these fit indexes should be examined to determine whether the constructs are being measured well.) It appears that both Trait A and Trait B are measured well because the loadings on the observed variables (observed variables are those that are assessed directly) are high, suggesting convergent validity. Moreover, the two traits are highly correlated (namely, .95), indicating that Trait A and Trait B likely are not distinct.

However, it should be kept in mind, that the three correlations that estimate the relationship between different traits measured with the same method were inflated by method variance. Structural equation modeling can reflect this method variance by calculating correlations of the same method across traits, shown by the two-headed arrows in Figure 19.4 (essentially, paths have been added to the model to take method variance into account). The correlations .25, .32, and .37 in the figure reflect the method variance for methods 1, 2, and 3, respectively. As expected, the correlation between the traits dropped from .95 to .76 when the method variance was included in the analyses (or model), indicating that the traits are distinct, although not independent.

Method variance appears often in counseling research when various aspects of counseling are rated from the same perspective. For example, if the supervisor rates both cultural competence of the counselor and therapeutic progress of the client, then the correlation between the cultural competence and outcome is influenced in part by the rating perspective by the same person (i.e., the supervisor). If the supervisor has a generally favorable attitude toward the counselor, then that supervisor may tend to rate all aspects of the counselor and the client as positive.

FIGURE 19.4 Multiple Measures of Trait A and Trait B Accounting for Method Variance (Correlated Errors)

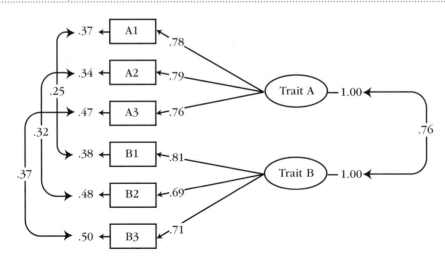

RESEARCH APPLICATION 19.5

Multiple Measures: Final Considerations

The previous sections can be summarized by the following seven points:

1. A single scale or instrument should be understood as that, only one representation of a construct. As such, one scale limits the conclusions that can be drawn from the study.
2. The correlation between two constructs is attenuated by unreliability.
3. Unreliability makes it more difficult to detect true effects (should any be present) because of reduced statistical power. However, it does not make spurious results appear.
4. The correlation between two measures using the same method of assessment is inflated by method variance.
5. Preferably, multiple measures using multiple methods should be used to operationalize a construct.
6. Typically, interpretations of relationships should be made at the construct level, for seldom are we interested in the measures per se. In other words, researchers are likely more interested in the construct of depression as compared to the items of "feeling low" and "loss of pleasure." It is important for researchers to be aware of the effects of unreliability and method variance and that the unreliability of measures and method variance can greatly affect the conclusions drawn from a study.

REACTIVITY

The dependent variable should be sensitive to some characteristic of the participant, but the assessment process itself should not affect the characteristic directly; that is, the dependent measure should indicate how the participant functions normally. Sometimes, something about obtaining scores on the dependent measure alters the situation so that "false" readings are obtained. Variables that affect the characteristics of the participants they are intended to measure are said to be *reactive*. For example, a test-anxious participant may report increased anxiety on a self-report instrument because completing the instrument is like taking a test; an aggressive child may display less aggressive behavior when being observed by an adult than at other times; a person may smoke less when asked to record the number of cigarettes smoked; a counseling trainee may demonstrate more culturally sensitive behaviors because he or she is aware of being observed. Clearly, the reactive nature of dependent variables must be considered in designing research; again, knowledge of the substantive area is vital. For example, psychotherapy typically shows larger effect for reactive measures as compared to nonreactive measures (Minami et al., 2009). Later in this chapter we discuss unobtrusive measures, which are designed to be nonreactive.

PROCEDURAL CONSIDERATIONS

A number of procedural issues must be considered when selecting or designing the dependent variable. Often, the time involved with the assessment is critical to the success of the study. Participants will be reluctant to volunteer for studies that demand a long time to complete forms and instruments, or if they do volunteer, they may respond carelessly to items (which increases error), especially toward the end of a long assessment period. As mentioned previously, the readability of instruments is critical to their psychometric performance. Often the manuals of published tests contain references to the reading level required. Alternatively, the researcher can use one of the relatively easy-to-use methods for determining readability, included in many computer document processing applications (e.g., Microsoft Word).

The order of the administration of instruments can have an effect on responses; one instrument may sensitize or otherwise influence responses on another instrument. An instrument that draws attention to a participant's own pathology (e.g., the Minnesota Multiphasic Personality Inventory) may well affect how the participant rates other measures (e.g., the counselor on the Real Relationship Inventory; Gelso, 2011). Order is also important when the same instrument is administered repeatedly. Performance at a given time may be due to previous responding (a testing effect) rather than to the characteristic being assessed. For instance, on an intelligence test, participants may acquire knowledge about specific questions or tasks (such as picture completion) that improves performance, even though intelligence remains unchanged. When repeated measures are used in a study, use of alternative forms is desirable if testing effects are anticipated. Alternative forms enable the researcher to give a pretest and a posttest without having to use the identical instrument.

RESEARCH APPLICATION 19.6

Juanita is looking to examine the effects of discrimination on women's ability to solve math and science questions. In her study, she randomly assigns women to one of two conditions. In the first condition, the participants complete a measure of discrimination, with questions asking about the types, frequency, and intensity of discriminatory actions they have experienced over the past year. She then administers a set of general math and science questions. In the second condition, she reverses the order of the stimuli. She finds that women in the first condition scored lower on the math and science questions as compared to the women in the second condition.

Questions

What are the strengths of this procedural approach?

What are the limitations?

What could she do to further rule out the order effects of her study?

Note: For more information on stereotype effects, see Nguyen & Ryan, 2008, for review.

Students often ask questions about what to include when describing the psychometric properties of an inventory for something like a Methods section of their thesis, dissertation, or journal article. Although all of the above conceptual issues are essential considerations in the design of research, when describing the psychometric properties of a particular instrument that will be used, authors typically provide a description of the inventory, roughly in the following order:

1. Description of measure itself
   a. Instruescriptioment name
   b. Acronym
   c. Author(s)
   d. Key references
   e. A brief description of the construct the instrument measures
   f. Self-report, behavioral observation, interview, or other
   g. Number of items and examples of items
   h. Type of items (e.g., Likert items)
   i. Factors or subscales, and their definitions
   j. Indication of the direction of scoring, and what a high score means
2. Validity estimates
   a. Convergent and discriminant validity
   b. Samples on which measure was validated
3. Reliability estimates
   a. Cronbach's alpha coefficients
   b. Test-retest (if applicable)
   c. Reliability is a property of the scores resulting from a particular administration of a test, so researchers should report reliability estimates for the current data set.

Readers are encouraged to consult Heppner and Heppner (2004) for specific written examples of instruments.

METHODS OF DATA COLLECTION

Given that the basic purpose of the dependent variable is to measure the effect or outcome of the independent variable, an essential aspect of any discussion of dependent variables involves collecting data vis-à-vis the dependent variable. To this point we have emphasized the use of instruments in data collection. Nevertheless, there are a number of other methods to collect data relevant to the dependent variable. We will discuss seven nonexclusive methods of data collection that are relevant in counseling: (a) self-reports, (b) ratings of other persons and events, (c) behavioral observations, (d) physiological indexes, (e) interviews, (f) projective techniques, and (g) unobtrusive measures.

There are other ways to categorize methods; for instance, measures can be divided into objective versus subjective methods. Whenever relevant, these other methods of classification are discussed. Note also that these seven data collection methods may sometimes overlap; the interview method also is a form of self-report, and ratings of other people are sometimes behavioral measures. The main point is that there is a broad range of data collection methods, each of which has its respective advantages and disadvantages. Finally, each method of data collection should be evaluated in terms of its congruence with the research question, psychometric properties, relation to other methods used in the study, reactivity, and so forth.

Self-Reports

In self-report measures, the participant assesses the degree to which some characteristic is present or to which some behavior has occurred. The self-report may be accomplished by responding to items in an inventory, completing a log, or keeping a journal. Generally, the assumption is made that the report accurately reflects the true state of affairs—that participants respond honestly and accurately. In this section we discuss advantages, disadvantages, types of inventories, and scoring formats for self-report inventories.

Advantages of Self-Reports   Although they take many forms, self-reports have some general advantages that make them the most popular assessment device in counseling research. First, they are relatively easy to administer. Most self-report inventories, tests, or questionnaires used in counseling research can be administered to a group of participants, providing economy of time. Even when administered individually, self-report measures typically do not require special expertise on the part of the administrator; for example, clients can be given complete inventories on computers or tablets prior to each session (see, e.g., Lambert, 2012). Similarly, most self-report inventories are relatively simple to use and require little training of the participant.

Another advantage of self-reports is that they can be used to access phenomena that otherwise would be extremely difficult or impossible to measure. Self-reports can assess private cognitions and feelings, behavior in private settings (e.g., sexual behavior), and future plans. In addition, participants can be asked to report about cognitions, feelings, and behaviors in hypothetical situations. Consider the following examples. Counselors could be asked to report how they would respond to a sexual advance by a client or trainees might be asked to respond to how they would react to a culturally insensitive remark made by a supervisor, both situations that would be unethical to arrange experimentally.

Self-reports also are advantageous because they are compatible with phenomenological views of counseling and psychotherapy. According to the phenomenological perspective, the thoughts and feelings of a client are of paramount importance, and self-reports of such constructs as happiness, marital satisfaction, and anxiety are more important than other indicants of these constructs, such as therapist ratings of client change, behavioral observations, physiological measures, or other measures that use a locus other than the self. For example, even though anxiety can be assessed physiologically, the distress caused by anxiety states is the debilitating factor for clients, and their self-report of anxiety is essential to understanding this phenomenon.

Disadvantages of Self-Reports   The most obvious, and the most troublesome, disadvantage of self-reports is that they are vulnerable to distortions (intentional or unintentional) by the participant. For a variety of reasons, the participant may consciously or unconsciously respond in a way that yields a score that reflects a response bias rather than the construct being measured. For example, participants may guess the hypothesis of the study and respond in a way that they think will confirm the researcher's conjecture. They may respond to questions in a manner that makes them look good or socially desirable. For example, therapists may complete a measure of multicultural competencies in a way that suggests they are culturally competent to avoid appearing biased (see Worthington et al., 2007). Additionally, some participants in counseling research may respond in a way that makes them appear more distressed than is truly the case (e.g., in order to receive services).

Some inventories are constructed to minimize such distortions. For example, the Minnesota Multiphasic Personality Inventory-2 (MMPI-2) contains four scales to assess the attitude of the participant. Two scales (L and K) measure whether the participant is trying to look better than is actually the case, one scale (F) measures deviate response sets, and one scale (the "?" scale) indicates the number of questions unanswered, which may indicate the participant's resistance to the test, confusion, or insufficient time to complete the test (Graham, 1990). To avoid participant bias, the Edwards Personality Preference Schedule is constructed so that the two choices for each item are equivalent with regard to social desirability (Sax, 1989).

Another disadvantage of self-report measures is that the participant may not be aware of the characteristic being measured. For example, a test-anxious participant may deny that he or she is anxious and attribute poor performance to inadequate preparation. Self-report measures must assume that participants have sufficient insight into their experience such that they are able to convey information about it to others through conscious terms.

A final disadvantage of self-report measures is the flip side of the advantage related to the congruence between a phenomenological perspective and self-reports: Self-reports are less valued by some theoretical perspectives. For example, self-reports tend to be of minimal importance to staunch behaviorists. In spite of the disadvantages of self-reports, a listing of the dependent variables used in counseling research clearly indicates that the self-report is the most frequently used dependent measure.

The increasing availability of internet access for many individuals has led to the internet being an increasingly viable research tool. The use of self-report scales adapted for online data collection may facilitate the investigation of research questions that might have previously been logistically unfeasible or impractical (e.g., obtaining self-report data from a geographically diverse sample of counselors in training) and may have a number of other pragmatic advantages (e.g., reductions in missing data, reduced errors in data entry). The use of internet technology provides an easy way for respondents to complete surveys. An additional practical advantage of internet data collection is that data may be directly imported into a statistical software package, rather than being entered by hand (Strickland et al., 2003).

The disadvantages of self-report measurement may be exacerbated in the context of internet data collection. The first and most obvious disadvantage is that research utilizing online data collection is necessarily restricted to participants with access to computers. This may or may not be an important consideration depending on the research question (e.g., most counselor trainees will likely have access to the internet), but should nevertheless be considered (e.g., potential participants from low socio-economic status backgrounds and without access to a computer will be selected against, thus biasing the sample). Additionally, without ever meeting the participants, researchers utilizing the internet for data collection are entrusting that the person who is completing the measure is actually who they say they are (not to mention only completing the survey once and in a state of mind that is ideal for purposes of the study). Researchers should recall that results cannot be generalized beyond the sample studied. In this case, the interpretation of most web-based studies should be limited to those individuals with computer access who would be able to complete the study online (Crowston et al., 2012; Strickland et al., 2003).

In terms of validity and reliability, the main question the researcher must contend with is whether the internet is an appropriate vehicle for collecting the data of interest. As we have noted earlier, reliability estimates are a product of the setting and the manner in which an instrument is used (not the instrument itself). Therefore, it cannot be assumed that simply because a paper-and-pencil self-report measure demonstrated adequate psychometric properties previously that it will do so in an internet modality. The change to electronic administration introduces another source of variability and increases the need for researchers who utilize traditional paper-and-pencil tests in a web-based format to report the psychometric properties of the current administration (Crowston et al., 2012; Strickland et al., 2003).

Ratings of Other Persons and Events

Counseling research often relies on ratings made of other persons or of events. The procedures here are similar to those for self-reports, except that respondents rate characteristics of the participant or the event. Often the respondents are experts, and their judgment is assumed to reflect accurately characteristics of the person or event. For example, in treatment studies, the therapist or a significant other could rate the degree of dysfunction or improvement of a client. A perusal of the literature in counseling reveals that direct rating of participants is seldom used and when they are they are typically done by therapists or external raters who are coding a counseling session.

Ratings of other persons and events share many of the advantages of self-reports, particularly their ease of administration and flexibility. When raters are experts, their judgments are particularly valuable because they are made with a rich background and deep understanding. Experienced counselors' judgments take into account years of experience with many types of clients. Another advantage is that many rating scales have proven psychometric properties under various conditions or being rated by various individuals (counselor, client, external observer).

The primary problem with ratings of other persons and events is that the ratings may be systematically biased. This is especially a problem when the raters are aware of the hypotheses and cognizant of the conditions to which participants belong. If counselors are raters who also are involved in the experimental treatment, they may rate the progress of clients higher because they have an interest in the outcome of the study. If at all possible, raters should be blind to as many factors of the experiment as possible. When interpreting ratings of events (or of other persons, for that matter), researchers must be careful to separate the variance due to differences in the event from the variance due to the raters themselves. In doing so, researchers can evaluate the interrater agreement as discussed previously. Ultimately, it is most advantageous to utilize multiple methods (e.g., self-report, other-report) to gather information about a dependent measure.

Behavioral Observations

Behavioral measures are derived from observations of overt behavior, most typically reported by a trained observer. Behavioral psychology has emphasized the importance of overt behavior and deemphasized intrapsychic phenomena. Accordingly, observing and recording behavior is the key component of applied behavior analyses (see the *Journal of Applied Behavior Analysis* for examples of this type of research). Essentially, behavioral observations are the same as ratings of other persons or events, except that behavioral measures focus on overt, observable behavior and presumably do not rely on inferences by raters. For example, a trained observer could count how many times a client raises their hand in a psychoeducational group.

As is the case with other modalities of assessment, behavioral assessment encompasses a wide variety of methods (see Barlow, 1981; Mash & Terdal, 1988, for historical perspective). Generally, behavioral assessment requires an operational definition of the behaviors of interest, direct observation of participants' behavior, recording of occurrences of the targeted behavior, and some presentation or summarization of the data.

The general advantages of behavioral observations are that they are direct and objective measures. Although there can be systematic biases in the observation and recording of overt behavior, behavioral measurements are not typically as subject to the personal biases inherent in self-reports. Another advantage of behavioral measures is that participants can be assessed in various environments. Studies have repeatedly shown that behavior is situation specific; behavioral measures can be used to assess functioning in several situations. Finally, for many dysfunctions the behavior itself is problematic (e.g., stuttering, social skills deficits, sexual dysfunction, physical avoidance, substance abuse) and thus warrants specific attention.

Among the disadvantages of behavioral observations is that problems and concerns of clients frequently do not center around readily observable behavior. Marital satisfaction is a construct that is difficult to operationalize behaviorally (although there are many behavioral correlates of marital satisfaction). The central question, as with any operationalization, is whether the behavior chosen reflects the construct of interest. Another disadvantage of behavioral observations is related to representativeness.

A presumption of behavioral assessment is that the behavior sampled is representative of behavior at other times. However, for a number of reasons, this may not be the case. For instance, nonrepresentativeness can occur when behavior is recorded at fixed but unusual times (e.g., classroom behavior on Friday afternoons). In addition, the reactivity that results when participants are aware that they are being observed leads to observations that may not be representative.

Issues related to reliability are problematic for behavioral assessment. An observer's decision that a particular behavior occurred may be idiosyncratic to that observer. In the context of behavioral assessment, these reliability issues are judged by calculating indexes of agreement; that is, how well do observers agree about the occurrence of targeted behavior?

Even if overt behavior is of paramount importance, it may not be possible or practicable to observe the behavior. Observation of sexual behavior, for instance, is typically precluded. Other behaviors are difficult to observe and are sometimes assessed in contrived situations. In counseling research, the behavior of a counselor often is assessed using confederate clients who appear to manifest some type of problem. Of course, the representativeness of behavior in contrived situations must be considered as well as the ethical implications of these designs (see Chapter 3).

Behavioral observations have been used successfully in counseling and supervision process research. In the usual paradigm, the interactions between counselor and client (or supervisor and trainee) are recorded and coded as a stream of behaviors. A number of coding systems have been developed or adapted for this use (see, e.g., Friedlander et al., 2006; Hill et al., 1983; Hilsenroth, 2007). The sequence of behaviors is used to derive measures that can be used to characterize the nature of the counseling or supervision interaction. The simplest measure is the frequency of behaviors. For example, Leubcke et al. (in press) utilized Hill et al.'s coding system of therapists' interventions to examine the type of counselor interventions that were utilized for couples who were experiencing varying levels of commitment to their relationship over the course of couple counseling. Yet simple frequencies are not sensitive to the probabilistic relation between behaviors. More sophisticated methods can be used to ascertain whether the frequency of a behavior of one participant (e.g., the client) increases the likelihood of some behavior in another participant (e.g., the counselor).

Physiological Indexes

Biological responses of participants (e.g., FMRI, heart rate, cortisol levels) can often be used to infer psychological states. Many psychological phenomena have physiological correlates that can be used as dependent variables. In fact, physiological responses often can be thought of as direct measures of a construct. For example, whereas self-reports of anxiety can be biased by a number of factors, measures of physiological arousal can be made directly and are often presumed to be free of bias. However, although physiological arousal is a focus in the theoretical conceptualization of anxiety, the relation between physiological states and psychological phenomena is not as straightforward as was anticipated in the early years of this research. Moreover, physiological measures are expensive, require special expertise, may be reactive, and may be subject to error due to a number of mechanical and electronic factors (such as electrical interference). As a result, physiological measures are infrequently used in counseling research. However, the proliferation of increasingly sophisticated physiological measurement techniques holds great promise for counseling psychology and may be an area of increasing focus for the next generation of counseling researchers. For example, numerous researchers have begun to investigate the neurobiological correlates of psychotherapy response (e.g., Goldapple, Segal, & Garson, 2004). Counseling researchers are well positioned to bring a level of expertise in regards to measuring counseling process and outcome that has been lacking in these studies thus far.

Interviews

Interviews are a straightforward means of obtaining information from participants. In Chapter 16 we discussed using interviews in qualitative research. Essentially, the process of using interviews to obtain data on a dependent variable is similar, except that the goal is to quantify some construct. In everyday life, interviewing is a pervasive activity; we simply ask people to supply information. Interviews typically involve an interpersonal interaction between the interviewer and the interviewee or participant. Kerlinger (1986) advocated using personal interviews because of the greater control and depth of information that can be obtained. The depth of information most often results from carefully planning and developing the interview schedule.

Personal interviews allow flexibility in questionnaire design; the interviewer can provide explanations (and thus reduce participant confusion), make decisions during the interview about the adequacy of a particular response (and probe if necessary), and evaluate the motivation of the participant. The flexibility of the personal interview can be a real advantage if the topic is complex and if participants are unaware of their psychological processes; interviewer probing can then be extremely beneficial and add considerable depth to the information obtained. Babbie (2001) also observed that personal interviews that are properly executed typically achieve a completion rate of at least 80%–85% of the participants targeted. Even though interviews rely on the self-report of the participant, the human interaction with the interviewer provides another facet to the self-report.

Interviews, however, are costly in terms of money and time. If the topics are sensitive (e.g., sexual behavior), then participants may be more reluctant to divulge information than if they were allowed to respond to an anonymous questionnaire. It is also important in quantitative research to standardize procedures across interviews to avoid introducing confounding variables due to different interviewer behavior or biases. Often considerable training is needed to standardize procedures (general greeting, introduction of the interview schedule, methods of recording exact responses, manner of asking questions, responses to participants' questions, handling of unusual participant behavior, and termination of the interview).

The telephone interview consists of a trained interviewer asking a participant a series of questions over the telephone. This method is usually quick and inexpensive (financially). Moreover, the telephone method reduces the amount of evaluative information that the interviewer can observe about the participant. As with other personal interviews, an interview schedule must be developed, but an additional consideration is the generally lower responsiveness of telephone participants. Moreover, telephone interview measures need to be psychometrically evaluated. That is, researchers should not assume that the psychometric properties (e.g., reliability) from a survey will be similar when administered over the telephone.

Projective Techniques

Although seldom utilized in counseling research, projective techniques are another way to collect data. The rationale behind projective techniques is that participants' responses to ambiguous stimuli will reveal some facet of their personality. The Thematic Apperception Test (which uses ambiguous drawings) and the Rorschach (which uses inkblots) are probably the two most well-known projective tests. However, a wide variety of possibilities exist, including drawing pictures, writing essays, completing sentences, playing with dolls, word association tests, and so forth. The assumption is that because the method is indirect, participants will not censor themselves. In turn, participants' responses are indirect measures and need to be interpreted in some way. Scoring of projective tests is typically subjective, although there are some very objective systems for scoring them, such as the Exner system for scoring Rorschach responses (Exner, 1974).

Historically, projective techniques have been associated with psychodynamic approaches to understanding human behavior. One of the most troublesome aspects of these techniques is that their scoring is subject to systematic biases that tend to confirm preconceived (but incorrect) conceptions about people (for historical example see Chapman & Chapman, 1969). Furthermore, the connection between underlying personality characteristics and overt behavior is tenuous. Moreover, the amount of time that it can take to administer and score each test can be daunting (e.g., 2 to 5 hours, and then some).

Unobtrusive Measures

To eliminate reactivity, it is often possible to collect data on participants without their awareness of this process. Measures used in such a way that participants are unaware of the assessment procedure, known as unobtrusive measures, have been described in some detail by Webb, Campbell, Schwartz, and Sechrest (1966). It may be possible to observe participants without their knowledge in naturalistic settings, to observe participants in contrived situations (e.g., with a confederate), to collect data from archives or other sources (such as school records), or to examine physical traces (such as garbage or graffiti). Most psychologists are extremely interested in sources of unobtrusive data. How often do people observe others in public and make interpretations of their behavior?

Of course, the most conspicuous advantage of unobtrusive measures is that they are by definition nonreactive. Because participants are not aware that data are being collected, they do not alter their responses for a variety of reasons (e.g., impression management). For example, grade point averages obtained from the registrar will be more accurate than those obtained from participants' self-reports. Still, there are a number of limitations to unobtrusive measures. Certain types of unobtrusive measures are unethical. For instance, disclosure of personal information by public agencies without the participant's permission is forbidden. Another limitation is that unobtrusive measures are often difficult and/or expensive to obtain. In addition, once the data are obtained, interpretation or classification is often needed; a study of graffiti might involve classifying the graffiti as sexual, drug related, violent, and so forth.

Although use of unobtrusive measures is not widespread in counseling research, the literature contains a number of studies that have used such measures. Heesacker, Elliott, and Howe (1988), in a study relating Holland code to job satisfaction and productivity, assessed a number of variables unobtrusively. Productivity data were obtained through the payroll office by multiplying the units produced by the value of the unit; absenteeism rates were obtained from the payroll office; data on injuries on the job were obtained from examining health insurance claims; and demographic information was gleaned from employment applications. Stice et al. (2004) examined the association between participants' self-report of dietary restraint, or the degree to which they restrain their eating or attempt to control their caloric intake, to an unobtrusive measure of restraint. Specifically, they weighed a plate of food (e.g., cookies) before and after the study to determine how much the participants were able to restrain their intake. They found that participants' self-report was generally not strongly correlated with the unobtrusive measure.

RESEARCH APPLICATION 19.7

Imagine you are attempting to research the association between couples' relationship satisfaction and their interactions with their in-laws. Based on the different ways described previously regarding how to collect data, explain at least four ways that you might approach collecting data on the main constructs in this study: (a) interactions with in-laws and (b) relationship satisfaction. What issues related to reliability and validity may be particularly important to consider for each of these methods?

SUMMARY AND CONCLUSIONS

The basic purpose of the dependent variable is to measure the effect or outcome of the manipulation of the independent variable. We discussed several issues that relate to operationalizing the construct that represents the effect of some cause.

Once the construct has been defined, the psychometric properties of the dependent variable vis-à-vis the construct should be established. Reliability and validity are the primary psychometric considerations. *Reliability* refers to the proportion of variance in the dependent variable that is due to true differences among participants.

The remaining variance is error. To be useful, a dependent variable must have adequate reliability. Although there are several types of validity, the one most germane to research design is *construct validity*, the degree to which scores reflect the desired construct rather than some other construct. Establishing construct validity is complicated and indirect, but nevertheless vital to the integrity of a study. Construct validity can be investigated in a number of ways, including recent applications of structural equation modeling. Commonly, a single dependent variable is unable to adequately operationalize a construct; multiple dependent variables are often recommended. The hope is that each variable reflects some aspect of the construct of interest, and that together they measure the essence of the construct. In any study, the researcher must be cognizant of both the attenuation of true relationships due to unreliability and the inflation of true relationships due to method variance. However, the dependent variables are designed or chosen such that they do not react with the treatment.

There are many methods of collecting data related to dependent variables, each of which has its advantages and disadvantages. The most widely used measure in counseling research is the self-report. The sine qua non of the self-report is that each participant makes his or her own observations or reports. The advantages of self-reports are that they are relatively easy to administer, can access areas that otherwise would be impossible or difficult to measure (such as sexual behavior), and are compatible with phenomenological views of counseling. The most conspicuous problem with self-reports is that they are vulnerable to distortions by the participant. However, participants may not be consciously aware of the construct being measured, and self-reports are incompatible with several theoretical approaches to counseling (e.g., behavioral approaches). Self-report instruments may either be published, by professional publishers or in the literature, or be tailor-made for a specific study, and they can be written in a number of formats.

Less frequently used dependent measures include ratings of other persons and events, behavioral measures, physiological indexes, interviews, projective techniques, and unobtrusive measures. Ratings of other persons and events are useful because experts or participants can be used to judge important aspects of counseling, such as the counseling interview itself. Behavioral measures reflect overt behavior and thus are not subject to the distortions that can plague self-reports and ratings of other persons and events; furthermore, they are compatible with behavioral approaches to counseling, even though they may be incompatible with other approaches (such as psychodynamic approaches). Physiological responses can be used to infer psychological states because many psychological phenomena (e.g., anxiety) have physiological correlates; however, due to lack of reliability, significant expense, and other problems, physiological indexes are infrequently used in counseling research. Interviews are advantageous because much information can be obtained quickly and because the interviewer can pose follow-up questions, but they are relatively expensive, depend on the skill of the interviewer, and can be biased. Projective techniques, which use ambiguous stimuli to reveal some facet of personality, can be useful to uncover unconscious aspects of the personality. Unobtrusive measures are designed to eliminate reactivity because the participant is unaware that any measurement is being conducted.

Given the multitude of data collection methods, the task of the informed researcher is to collect data with a method that provides the type of information that is most relevant to the research question.

Obviously, the selection of the dependent variable and the method of data collection require considerable forethought and examination of the research literature. Moreover, these tasks often require creative thinking to tailor measurements to the constructs of interest. Unfortunately, sometimes researchers spend very little time in selecting dependent variables, and weak and disappointing findings often result. We firmly believe that careful deliberation and consultation with colleagues can greatly facilitate the selection of dependent variables and enhance the overall quality of research in counseling.

STIMULUS QUESTIONS

The Dependent Variable

1. Randomly select four recent counseling research articles. Classify the dependent measures according to the method of data collection (self-report, ratings of others or events, behavioral observation, physiological indices, interviews, projectives, or unobtrusive measures). Discuss the adequacy of the method used to capture the nature of the construct in question.

2. Select a commonly used measure in your area of interest. Research the development and validation of the measure and discuss the adequacy of the measure for the purpose it was intended.

3. As discussed in this chapter, the nature of the sample on which a measure was normed is important. Consider measures commonly used in outcome research (e.g., the Beck Depression Inventory, the Brief Symptom Inventory, the Outcome Questionnaire) and characterize the samples on which the measure was normed and validated.

4. Suppose a researcher is interested in the construct of cultural competence and wishes to avoid self-report measures. Indicate how the researcher could use raters for this purpose. What issues would be considered?

20
Chapter

Counseling Outcome Research: Does Counseling Work?

Does counseling really work? Is therapy effective? Can couples assessment and feedback improve relationships? Is cognitive-relaxation coping skills training more effective than social skills training in reducing anger expression of early adolescents? Can the addition of brief group therapy to an academic assistance program improve the academic and social functioning of low-achieving elementary school students? Does helping group clients set realistic, interpersonal, and here-and-now agendas enhance group participation and client outcome? These and many similar research questions are questions about counseling outcome.

Typically, outcome research attempts to address the question of counseling efficacy by comparing a treatment group to a control group or by comparing different treatments. Outcome research—which is not a category of research designs per se, but rather a specific focus within counseling research—is predominantly conducted using true experimental or quasi-experimental designs, but all designs discussed in this book can be and have been applied to the study of counseling outcomes. The counseling researcher must address a number of methodological issues, which constitute the major focus of this chapter.

By way of introduction to outcome research, we initially discuss how outcome questions have captivated counseling researchers since the beginning of the profession. In addition, we briefly examine how methodological critiques of outcome research have occupied a central role in researchers' thinking about evaluating counseling. Next we describe the different types of strategies used to conduct outcome research and provide recent examples of each of these strategies. The subsequent section focuses on four methodological issues in outcome research: (a) selecting the appropriate comparison group (i.e., inclusion and exclusion criteria), (b) assessing treatment integrity, (c) measuring outcomes and change, and (d) therapist effects. Additionally, throughout the chapter we summarize literature that questions some of the fundamental assumptions underlying counseling outcome research.

EARLY OUTCOME RESEARCH IN COUNSELING

At the beginning of research in counseling it was evident that outcome research was prominent and valued. Indeed, the first article in the first issue of the *Journal of Counseling Psychology* (Forgy & Black, 1954) was a three-year follow-up assessment of 100 Stanford students counseled with either "client-centered permissive counseling procedures and materials" or "highly structured counselor-centered procedures" (p. 1). In the original study, the 100 students were counseled by one of three counselors, each of whom used each counseling method (i.e., therapists were crossed with treatment; see the issues involved with therapist effects that are discussed in the section on methodological issues). At the end of treatment, satisfaction data suggested that the students were more satisfied with the client-centered procedures. However, at the follow-up, Forgy and Black found no differences in client satisfaction between the type of counseling (client-centered vs. counselor-centered) or among the counselors. They did detect, however, a significant interaction between counselor and type of treatment: One of the three counselors had more satisfied clients when he used the counselor-centered methods, whereas the other two counselors had more satisfied clients when they used the client-centered methods.

In another early study, Rogers (1954) was interested in comparing two different counseling techniques: a "test-centered" and a "self-evaluation" method of test interpretation. The major differences in the two methods were the amount of client participation in the interview and the relative concentration on nontest data. Rogers conducted all the test interpretation interviews, alternating between the two methods of test interpretation. The outcome measure in this study was a "self-understanding score," which represented the match between the student's self-assessment and the counselor's assessment of the student. Rogers used an integrity check to assess whether the two types of test interpretation interviews were conducted properly. Specifically, he and a second counselor listened to audiotapes of 20 sessions (10 tapes from each method of test interpretation) and classified each discussion unit (a counselor-client exchange regarding a given topic). Based on these tape ratings, Rogers concluded that the "test-centered" and "self-evaluation" methods had the expected differences in session content and process. An analysis of changes in self-understanding revealed that both methods of test interpretation led to increases in self-understanding, but no difference in overall counseling effectiveness. Rogers did, however, identify an interaction between students' level of intelligence and the type of test interpretation used: More-intelligent students had gains in self-understanding with either method of test interpretation, whereas less intelligent students showed gains in self-understanding only when the "self-evaluation" method of test interpretation was used.

By today's standards, the outcome measures and statistical analyses used in Forgy and Black (1954) and Rogers (1954) are rather primitive. Still, a clear continuity is evident between the questions and research design strategies used in 1954 and today. Researchers remain interested in testing the efficacy of treatments. As well, the results of these and the other early studies foreshadowed predominant patterns of results with regard to the small or nonexistent differences in outcomes among different treatment types (Wampold & Imel, 2015) and the presence of differences among therapists (Baldwin & Imel, 2013). Early outcome researchers attended to many important methodological issues, including assessing how faithfully the proposed treatments were delivered and assessing therapist effects and their influence on outcomes. In addition, the differential effects of the type of test interpretation session for clients with different levels of intelligence is an example of client characteristics that moderate treatment outcome, a reminder that treatment effectiveness may not be uniform (what Kiesler, 1966, initially referred to as the uniformity myth).

Treatment effectiveness has received a tremendous amount of attention in the past 40 years (for a partial listing, see Bergin & Garfield, 1971, 1994; Garfield, 1993; Garfield & Bergin, 1978, 1986; Hollon, 1996; Howard, Moras, Brill, Martinovich, & Lutz, 1996; Jacobson & Christensen, 1996; 2013; Lambert & Bergin, 1993; Lambert, Christensen, & Dejulio, 1983; Rachman & Wilson, 1980; Strupp & Howard, 1993; Vandenbos, 1996; Wampold & Imel, 2015). Clearly, determining the effectiveness of the treatments counselors use is fundamental to the field as, after all, counseling is most centrally involved with the delivery of services to people—logically, counseling researchers are charged with ensuring that such services are indeed benefiting these people.

It was not always accepted that counseling and psychotherapy were effective. One of the most important challenges came from Hans Eysenck (1952, 1960, 1969), who asserted that little empirical evidence supported the effectiveness of psychotherapy. Eysenck's critique influenced a number of researchers to examine the outcome question; over the years, more and more knowledge has been created using ever more sophisticated research methodologies. In a landmark study, Smith and Glass (1977) published a meta-analytic review of all controlled research in counseling and psychotherapy that, although controversial at the time, established that counseling and psychotherapy interventions were remarkably effective (see Smith, Glass, & Miller, 1980; Wampold, 2013; Wampold & Imel, 2015).

It is important not only to know that treatments work, but also to answer Gordon Paul's (1967) important question: "What treatment, by whom, is most effective for this individual with that specific problem, under which set of circumstances, and how does it come about?" (p. 111; see also Kiesler, 1966). Other researchers, suggesting that much valuable information is lost when researchers only test pretest to posttest change, have argued for the need to examine important events from session to session and within sessions. (See Chapter 21 for more details on counseling process research.)

STRATEGIES FOR CONDUCTING OUTCOME RESEARCH

In this chapter, seven types of outcome research strategies are discussed: (a) the treatment package strategy, (b) the dismantling strategy, (c) the additive strategy, (d) the parametric strategy, (e) the comparative outcome strategy, (f) the common factor control group design, and (g) the moderation design. We now describe each strategy and provide an illustrative example from the counseling literature.

The Treatment Package Strategy

The most fundamental question that outcome research can address is whether a treatment or intervention has an effect. For example, does dialectical behavior therapy (DBT; Salsman & Linehan, 2006) lead to a decrease in self-injurious behavior in individuals diagnosed with borderline personality disorder (BPD)? In one study on this subject, researchers randomized 50 females diagnosed with BPD to an inpatient DBT treatment program or to a wait-list/community referral control. Results indicated that DBT led to significant decreases in a majority of clinically relevant variables including self-harm relative to the wait-list/community treatment control (Bohus et al., 2004).

This type of effectiveness question is addressed by the *treatment package strategy,* in which the researcher compares a treatment, in its entirety, to some control condition, usually a condition where the participants do not receive any treatment (e.g., a no-treatment or wait-list control). In this way, the following question can be answered: Is the treatment, as a package, more efficacious than no treatment? In such a design, ideally, the only difference between the two conditions is the treatment—one group of participants receives the treatment and the other does not, so that differences found at the end of the study can be attributed to the treatment.

We now discuss the logic of the no-treatment control and the design of the control group in more detail. The basics of this design were introduced in Chapter 6. Randomly assigning clients to the two groups, treatment and control, is supposed to assure that the groups are comparable in all respects; that is, any differences between the two groups, for any variable (e.g., initial severity of the disorder, age, ethnicity, or ego strength), measured or not, that exist before treatment are due to chance and not any systematic factor. In order to estimate how effective the treatment is, the objective is to compare the difference in mental health status (i.e., the dependent variables) between those who received treatment and those who did not. Therefore, the typical strategy in treatment package studies is to administer the treatment to one group and to provide no intervention to the other group. The assumption is that any differences between the groups at the end of the study were due to treatment.

RESEARCH APPLICATION 20.1

One of the keys for these types of studies to work properly is *randomization*. Randomization does not assure that the groups are equal on every variable. Test yourself in this randomization drill. Flip a coin 10 times and record the outcomes (i.e., heads or tails). Based on randomization principles, there should be 5 heads and 5 tails. Now, flip the coin 50 more times, recording the outcomes still. You should see that the more times you flip a coin the likelihood of getting a 50–50 split (or close), in this example, should go up. Randomization does however ensure that whatever differences occur, they have occurred by chance and not because of a systematic bias.

There are several issues inherent in the treatment package design. One is that it is assumed that a difference in the groups at the end of treatment, should a difference be found, was due to the efficacy of the treatment. However, as discussed often in this book, such a difference may be due to chance. This is, of course, a problem encountered in any experimental design and one that is addressed by the statistical test. That is, one sets an alpha level that is tolerable; for example, if alpha was set at .05, then the probability of falsely claiming that the treatment works (i.e., rejecting the null hypothesis) would be less than 5 out of 100.

A second issue relates to the assumption that mental health status at the end of treatment of the no-treatment control group is truly representative of how clients would fare without treatment. If the treatment is for a mental disorder (e.g., depression), then a no-treatment group is intended to represent the natural history of the disorder (i.e., the course of the disorder without any intervention). An issue here is that the experimental situation attenuates the validity of this assumption. Suppose that the study is examining a treatment for depression, and those who are enrolled in the study are eager to avail themselves of the latest treatment. Some clients, when notified that they have been assigned to the no-treatment group, will become demoralized: "Story of my life—I never have any good luck. Even when I enroll in a study I get the short end of the stick." Other clients may seek treatment elsewhere. In these ways, the status of the control group clients might not represent how they would have fared had they never heard of and enrolled in the experimental protocol.

A third issue is an ethical one. If viable treatments are available for a particular disorder, then withholding a treatment from control group clients is problematic. One solution is to promise that, should the treatment being studied be found to be effective, it will be made available to the clients at the end of the study. Typically, novel treatments being studied are not generally available, and clients in the control group are informed that they are being placed on a waiting list for the treatment, in which case the control condition is labeled "wait-list control group." However, the mental health status of those on the wait lists should be monitored so if serious sequelae of the disorder should arise, such as suicidal behavior of depressed clients, appropriate action can be taken. The benefits to society that accrue from comparing a treatment to a no-treatment control group should always be weighed against the risks of withholding treatment. However, it could be argued that until a treatment for a disorder has been established as effective, not providing a treatment does not disadvantage a client.

The Dismantling Strategy

If several research studies have shown that a treatment package is effective, a researcher may want to determine which components of the multicomponent intervention are necessary and which are superfluous. In other words, the outcome question is: What are the active/effective components of the treatment? This design attempts to take apart the treatments to identify the critical components, and thus aptly has been labeled as a "dismantling" study. In a study using the dismantling strategy, the researcher compares the treatment package to the treatment package with one or more of the critical components removed.

Perhaps the best example of a dismantling study is Jacobson et al.'s (1996) study of cognitive therapy (CT) (Beck, Rush, Shaw, & Emery, 1979). Although Beck et al. are explicit in their claim that the alteration of core cognitive schemas drives the effectiveness of CT, the treatment contains numerous components that may be responsible for treatment efficacy. If the hypothesis is that alteration of core schemas is crucial to the effectiveness of CT, then the full package of CT should be significantly more effective than a treatment without the purported critical components. In order to test the mechanisms involved in the efficacy of CT, Jacobson et al. used a three-group pretest-posttest experimental design. The first treatment contained the full package of CT (i.e., containing all its components). The second treatment contained both the behavioral activation (BA) and automatic thought components of CT, but no therapeutic actions related to altering core schemas. The third treatment contained only the BA component (i.e., no therapeutic actions related to reducing automatic thoughts or changing core schemas). All therapists were well trained and adhered to treatment protocols (see the section on methodological issues in this chapter for a discussion of adherence in outcome research). Despite an admitted researcher bias toward CT, results indicated no differences in the efficacy of the three treatments at termination or at six-month follow-up, suggesting that the cognitive components are not critical for the success of cognitive therapy for depression (see Wampold & Imel, 2015).

The Additive Strategy

The additive strategy is used to determine whether adding some component to treatment already demonstrably shown to be effective adds to the benefits of the treatment. Research examining whether a particular component, when added to an established intervention, enhances treatment effectiveness is considered the *additive strategy* (Bell et al., 2013). In the prototypic additive design, one group of participants receives the standard treatment regime and another group of participants receives the adjunctive component in addition to the standard treatment.

For example, Foa and Rauch (2004) compared exposure therapy (ET) to exposure therapy plus cognitive restructuring (ETC) in the treatment of female assault survivors with chronic posttraumatic stress disorder (PTSD). This study was designed to test the hypothesis that the addition of a cognitive component would augment the efficacy of exposure procedures. The researchers also measured trauma-related thoughts (as measured by the Post-Traumatic Cognitions Inventory (PTCI); Foa, Ehlers, Clark, Tolin, & Orsillo, 1999), hypothesizing that ETC would have a more pronounced impact on this measure than ET alone. Although the decrease of trauma-related thoughts was related to symptom improvement, no treatment differences were observed on this measure.

The Parametric Strategy

In using the parametric strategy, counseling researchers try to identify changes in *treatment parameters* that are related to the effectiveness of a treatment. The term *parameter* refers to the quantities of aspects contained in a treatment rather than whether or not a component of treatment is present. For example, a parametric study of homework assignments would attempt to identify the optimal number of homework assignments, whereas a component design (e.g., a dismantling design) would attempt to determine whether homework was necessary or not. Thus, a study using the parametric strategy compares two or more treatments that differ in the quantity of the component.

Turner, Valtierra, Talken, Miller, and DeAnda (1996) provide an interesting example of a parametric strategy, in which they hypothesized 50-minute counseling sessions would be more effective than 30-minute counseling sessions. The authors used a two-group pretest-posttest design to test their hypothesis. The 94 college students who came to the counseling center and volunteered to participate in the study were randomly assigned to receive either eight 50-minute sessions or eight 30-minute sessions. A 2 (treatment group; 50-minute session vs. 30-minute session) × 2 (time; pretest vs. posttest) repeated measures analysis of variance (ANOVA) was used to analyze data from the College Adjustment Scales (Anton & Reed, 1991). The analysis of the College Adjustment Scales data revealed a significant main effect for time, but no significant main effect for treatment and no significant interaction effect for treatment time. The analysis of separate Client Satisfaction Questionnaire (Attkisson & Zwick, 1982) data also revealed no significant effect for treatment group. Turner et al. (1996) concluded that their study "found weekly 30-minute sessions to be as effective as 50-minute sessions when using a brief therapy model with young adult, college students" (p. 231).

The "Common Factor" Control Group

One of the issues inherent in the treatment package design is that it is not possible, if it is found that the treatment is effective, to determine which components of the study are responsible for the benefits. The dismantling, additive, and parametric strategies are designed to shed some light on this important issue. However, these strategies are designed to isolate one or a few critical components that might be related to positive outcomes attained by clients. One of the debates in psychotherapy is whether the benefits produced by treatment are due to the specific ingredients in treatments or whether the benefits are due to the factors common to all treatments. For example, are the benefits of cognitive-behavioral treatment for depression due to the therapist's specific strategies to reduce irrational thoughts and change core schemas (specific ingredients) or are they due to the relationship with an empathic healer, the provision of a treatment rationale, agreement about tasks and goals, and other factors common to all or most treatments intended to be therapeutic? Modern medicine faces a similar issue in attempts to demonstrate that the active ingredients of a medication are responsible for the benefits and not hope, expectation, or other psychological factors. In medicine, the effects of the psychological factors are often called placebo effects.

The "gold standard" for establishing the efficacy of drugs is to compare a pill with active ingredients to a placebo (sugar) pill in a randomized double-blinded design. Double blind refers to the conditions that render both the recipient of the pill and the administrator of the pill "blind" to whether it is the pill with the active medication or a pill with inert ingredients (i.e., the placebo). (Actually, the best design is a triple blind in which evaluators are also blind to treatment administered.) To maintain the blind, the active medication and the placebo must be indistinguishable so that no cues are given to the patient or the administrator that the pill is active or a placebo. If the design is successful, any superiority of the drug over and above the placebo is due to the effects of the active ingredients and not due to hope, expectation, or receipt of an explanation. In this case, the "specificity" of the drug is established because the benefits of the drug are due, in part, to the specific ingredients. Medical researchers are not interested in whether the placebo pill is superior to no treatment (i.e., the existence of a placebo effect) (see Wampold, Minami, Tierney, Baskin, & Bhati, 2005).

In 1956, Rosenthal and Frank suggested that psychotherapy borrow the randomized placebo control group design for the study of psychotherapy to control for the factors that are common to all treatments, such as the relationship. The logic of the placebo control group in psychotherapy is that it contains all these common factors but none of the specific factors of the treatment. For example, if the researcher was testing a cognitive-behavioral treatment for a particular disorder, the placebo control would have no ingredients related to cognitive-behavioral treatments (such as behavioral activation, reality testing, changing core schemas, and so forth) but would likely involve a compassionate and caring therapist who responded empathically to the client (Wampold & Imel, 2015; Wampold et al., 2005). Often these control groups are referred to as "alternative treatments," "supportive counseling," or "common-factor controls," the latter to indicate that they control for the common factors. The term *placebo control* is not often used in psychotherapy research any longer; Wampold and Imel (2015) refer to these type of controls as pseudo-placebos, the reason for which will be clear as the problems with such designs are discussed.

First, clearly psychotherapy trials cannot be double-blinded. The therapists providing the treatment are always aware of whether they are providing the "real" treatment or the "sham" treatment (the term *sham* is often used in medical studies to denote the placebo). Moreover, critical common factors are not present in such a control group. For example, the provision of a cogent rationale is common to all treatments, but is typically absent in common factor controls (see Wampold & Imel, 2015). Nevertheless, the common factor control group design is often used in psychotherapy research.

In one such study, Markowitz, Kocsis, Bleiberg, Christos, and Sacks (2005) compared the effect of interpersonal psychotherapy (IPT), Sertraline, and brief supportive psychotherapy (BSP) in the treatment of individuals diagnosed with dysthymia, a disorder that has been traditionally understudied. Although a nonspecific control, the authors indicated that BSP was by no means a nontreatment because therapists were well trained and motivated. Results did not support the superiority of IPT over BSP in reducing depressive symptoms. The authors indicated that their control treatment may have been "too active" and that well-trained therapists with a motivated supervisor who performed BSP may have obscured any treatment differences. In retrospect, Markowitz and colleagues contend that in this case BSP may be considered an active treatment. This example illustrates the numerous difficulties involved in interpreting results from common factors control group designs (see Baskin, Tierney, Minami, & Wampold, 2003).

RESEARCH APPLICATION 20.2

The challenge: Try to create a nonspecific control treatment. What elements would you include in the treatment? What would you exclude? For example, would you include the use of homework assignments? How about instructing therapists to reflect feelings of their clients? Simply, what are the active mechanisms of client change? Do you think it is truly possible to have a nonspecific control treatment? Why or why not?

The Comparative Outcome Strategy

The comparative outcome strategy is used to determine the relative effectiveness of two or more treatments. Sometimes the strategy can be used to identify which of two established treatments is more effective. Other times it can be used to determine whether a new treatment, which is perhaps less costly or complex, is as effective as an established treatment. Essentially, the design involves comparing two or more treatments that are intended to be therapeutic for a particular disorder. Of course, the researchers may also choose to use another type of control group, such as a no-treatment control group, in addition to the two (or more) treatments being studied. In this latter case, two research questions would be addressed: (a) which of the treatments intended to be therapeutic is superior, and (b) are the treatments superior to no treatment? It should be emphasized, however, that a no-treatment control group is not needed to answer the first of these two questions. Again, a central principle of outcome research is that the question to be answered determines which groups are chosen to constitute the independent variable.

Care must be taken to ensure that the comparison between the treatments of a comparative outcome study is fair. For example, if one treatment lasts 12 sessions and the other treatment lasts only 6 sessions, the dose of treatment becomes a confound. It is relatively easy to think of numerous potential confounds, but perhaps the most important one is the skill and allegiance of the therapist. It has been shown that the allegiance of the researcher to a particular treatment has a large effect on the outcome of the study (e.g., Luborsky et al., 1999; Munder et al., 2011, 2012, 2013; Wampold & Imel, 2015).

Although the causes of researcher allegiance effects are difficult to discern, there is some evidence to suggest that it is because the therapist's allegiance to and enthusiasm for the treatment being advocated by the researcher are greater than for the alternative treatment (Wampold & Imel, 2015). It is also important that the therapists delivering the various treatments are equally skilled (this issue is considered in more detail when therapist issues are discussed in the section on methodological issues). In any event, care must be taken to ensure that the comparison is fair. The fact that researcher allegiance is such a strong predictor of the effects produced in such designs is *prima fascie* evidence for bias in the design of comparative outcome studies.

In a comparative design, Clarkin et al. (2007) compared the effectiveness of psychodynamic psychotherapy, with a focus on transference (PD), dialectical behavior therapy (DBT), and supportive psychotherapy (SP) in the treatment of clients diagnosed with borderline personality disorder. All therapists were well trained and technically adherent. The study's authors had a stronger allegiance to the PD treatment, as one of the authors created the specific form of treatment utilized in the study. In this trial, results indicated that all treatments were effective at decreasing depressive symptoms, anxiety, global functioning, and social adjustment. However, DBT and PD were superior to SP in reducing suicidality. Only PD was associated with changes in anger and irritability relative to DBT and SP. The authors state that all of these structured treatments are useful approaches in the treatment of clients with borderline personality disorder. They further suggest that there are likely different pathways to helping clients change. Yet, they do note that the differences in the primary outcome seemed to vantage DBT and PD, which may highlight some unique differences in the treatments.

Although there might be many reasons for the lack of differences between treatments, such a state of affairs raises questions about "why" therapy works. For instance, counseling is effective, and there are multiple treatments that are effective. Thus, it could be that these counseling approaches achieve good outcomes through different mechanisms, or that there are common factors that underlie all of these approaches. Addressing why counseling works will be addressed in more detail in Chapter 21 (process chapter). However, "who" therapy works best for is also another important consideration.

The Moderation Design

In the designs considered to this point, the independent variable has consisted of various treatments and controls. Accordingly, conclusions are restricted to statements about the treatments vis-à-vis the types of clients being treated. However, these designs do not address the question raised by Paul (1967) about which treatments work with which types of clients. In the moderation design, the researcher attempts to answer this question by examining the relative effectiveness of treatments for various types of clients, settings, or contexts (Kazdin, 2007, 2009). For example, Beutler et al. (2011) contend that resistant clients do better with unstructured treatments, whereas nonresistant clients do better with structured treatments. Such contentions suggest factorial designs and interaction effects (see Chapters 11 and 12). They conducted a meta-analysis of 12 studies, which included 1,102 clients that examined this exact question. In support of their hypothesis, they found that clients who were lower in resistance responded better to more directive types of treatment. Additionally, as expected, those clients who exhibited more resistance did better when the treatments were nondirective.

Hembree, Street, Riggs, and Foa (2004) provide an example of a study that used this strategy. Hembree and colleagues examined predictors of response in 73 female assault victims diagnosed with chronic PTSD. The researchers hypothesized that certain trauma-related variables (e.g., childhood trauma, trauma severity, type of assault) would predict response to CBT for PTSD. Results indicated that a history of childhood trauma resulted in greater PTSD severity posttreatment. The authors concluded that prior experience of trauma interferes with the ability to process and cope with later traumatic experiences.

RESEARCH APPLICATION 20.3

Now that we have reviewed the major designs in counseling outcome research, take a moment to reflect on the differences and similarities. In doing so, try to create a study utilizing at least two of the designs. For instance, if you wanted to test whether assigning homework to a client was effective, what designs could you use? What would be the IV and DV in your study? Practically speaking, how could you recruit clients for your study? Would your recruitment efforts bias your results? Who would be your therapists? How many clients would you want to have, realistically?

METHODOLOGICAL ISSUES IN CONDUCTING OUTCOME RESEARCH

In this section we will discuss four methodological issues that researchers undertaking an outcome study must address: (a) inclusion and exclusion criteria, (b) assessing treatment integrity, (c) measurement of change, and (d) consideration of counselor effects.

Inclusion and Exclusion Criteria

One decision that must be made in outcome research is related to the inclusion and exclusion criteria relative to the participants of the study. Of course, inclusion and exclusion criteria should be determined, to the extent possible, by the research question. However, there will also be pragmatic, ethical, and design issues to be considered; many of the issues here have been discussed in Chapter 3, but will briefly be discussed here as they pertain particularly to outcome research.

We illustrate inclusion and exclusion criteria by considering a researcher who has developed a new treatment for adults with depression. Logically, the nature of the research dictates that participants be adults with depression. The researcher could operationalize this in various ways: DSM diagnosis of, say, major depressive disorder or score above a cut point on a depression inventory. Certain types of patients may also be excluded so that the conclusions are made with regard to depressed patients and not patients with other disorders (i.e., rule out comorbidities). For example, such trials typically exclude clients with psychosis, substance abuse, suicidal ideation or attempts, and certain personality disorders (see Shadish, Matt, Navarro, & Phillips, 2000). Moreover, clients concurrently taking psychotropic medication are also excluded so as not to confound psychotherapy and drug effects. For ethical, clinical, and research purposes, suicidal clients are often excluded. These exclusionary criteria result in fewer threats to validity, but at the expense of generalizability; that is, the clients seen in a trial with fairly stringent inclusion and exclusion criteria may not be similar to the population of depressed clients. (For a discussion of the representativeness of clients in clinical trials, see Norcross, Beutler, & Levant, 2006; Westen, Novotny, & Thompson-Brenner, 2004).

Clearly, the researcher wants to balance the validity of conclusions with regard to whether differences noted among groups are due to treatment (internal validity) with the representativeness of the sample to patients seen in practice (external validity). This is an example of the tension between various types of validity; such tensions are inherent in the design of research in applied psychology, as discussed elsewhere in this book.

Assessing Treatment Integrity: Adherence, Competence, and Differentiation

As discussed in Chapter 7, one of the components of construct validity is that the independent variable be properly defined, specified, and operationalized.

In treatment studies, the independent variable is constituted by the various treatment conditions and control groups that are employed by the researcher. In the various designs discussed in the previous section, issues relative to the validity of the control group were discussed. However, it is important to ensure that the treatment delivered to clients in the treatment conditions is a valid representation of the treatment purported to be studied. If the treatments are not valid representations of the purported treatment being studied, then the validity of the study could be criticized (i.e., a lack of efficacy could be due to the treatment itself or to a failure to implement the treatment competently).

For example, Doss et al. (2005) compared traditional behavioral couple therapy (TBCT) with integrative behavioral couple therapy (IBCT). They were interested in the mechanisms of change in these forms of therapy. In order to do so they assessed both measures of relationship satisfaction, communication, behavioral change, and emotional acceptance four times throughout the course of therapy. The authors found that both treatments resulted in positive effects on relationship satisfaction. However, they also found that TBCT was related to early *changes* in target behaviors; whereas IBCT was associated with great *acceptance* of target behaviors over the course of therapy. Given that the authors were able to train counselors to deliver treatments with sufficient attention to the nuances in the treatments, these results were able to be detected.

Bhar and Beck (2009) examined the degree to which studies that compared psychodynamic and cognitive behavioral were conducted adequately in terms of counselor adherence and competence. That is, they examined the degree to which these studies the researchers monitored if the treatments were conducted in a way that ensured the counselors adhered to the therapeutic principles of psychodynamic and cognitive-behavioral treatments, respectively, as well as delivered the treatment competently. They concluded that 67% of the studies did not meet an adequate level of monitoring treatment adherence (or the degree to which the counselors actually did the treatment), and 67% of the studies also did not adequately monitor whether the counselors were competent in their delivery of the treatments. These issues raise questions about the independent variable in these studies (also see Perepletchikova, 2009).

There are several steps to developing and deploying an adequately valid treatment, including (a) specifying the treatment, (b) training the therapists to adequately deliver the treatment, and (c) checking whether the treatment was delivered as intended. The degree to which these steps are completed successfully is often referred to as *treatment integrity* or *treatment fidelity*.

One of the advances related to specifying the treatment has been the development of treatment manuals. A treatment manual, according to Luborsky and Barber (1993), contains three components: (a) a description of the principles and techniques that characterize the particular treatment, (b) detailed examples of how and when to apply these principles and techniques, and (c) a scale to determine how closely a specific session or treatment conforms (adherence measure) to the principles and techniques described in the manual. Luborsky and Barber traced the advent of treatment manuals to Kelerman and Neu's (1976) unpublished manual describing an interpersonal approach for treating depression; the best known manual is the *Cognitive Behavioral Treatment of Depression* (Beck, Rush, Shaw, & Emery, 1979).

The treatment manuals developed to date involve far more precise specification of the experimental treatment. Still, treatment manuals in and of themselves do not guarantee that the treatment in any particular study is delivered as the researcher intended. *Adherence measures* attempt to assess the degree of match between the intended treatment (as described in the manual) and the treatment actually delivered in a study. Although at least rudimentary treatment manuals have existed for some 30 years, in the late 1980s researchers began to develop adherence measures that are associated with specific treatment manuals (see Waltz et al., 1993). One adherence measure that has been used in several counseling studies is Butler, Henry, and Strupp's (1992) Vanderbilt Therapeutic Strategies Scale. Developed to measure adherence to Strupp and Binder's (1984) treatment manual, *Psychotherapy in a New Key,* the Vanderbilt Therapeutic Strategies Scale consists of two scales, labeled Psychodynamic Interviewing Style (with 12 items) and Time-Limited Dynamic Psychotherapy (TLDP) Specific Strategies (with 9 items). Trained observers typically watch a videotape or listen to an audiotape of a counseling session and then use the Vanderbilt Therapeutic Strategies Scale to indicate the degree to which each of the 21 items was descriptive of what the therapist had observed.

By using scales like the Vanderbilt Therapeutic Strategies Scale, researchers can begin to obtain an assessment of how well the treatment implemented in a study matches the treatment described in the manual. Measuring adherence, however, is not completely straightforward. One unresolved issue concerns who should perform the ratings of adherence. Some authors propose that ratings of adherence are best done by experienced clinicians who are "experts" in the treatment model being rated (see, e.g., Luborsky & Barber, 1993); other authors contend that clients can use treatment adherence measures to report on counselor session behavior (see, e.g., Owen, Hilsenroth, & Rodolfa, 2013); still others maintain that the counselor's supervisor is in the best position to assess adherence (see, e.g., DeRubeis, Hollon, Evans, & Bemis, 1982; Hilsenroth, 2007); and finally some claim trained laypersons (e.g., undergraduates) can accomplish the task (Baucom et al., 2012). In any event, researchers will need to design procedures to ensure that therapists are delivering the treatments as intended by the manual.

It is probably not sufficient to rate adherence without also examining the quality of treatment implementation. Counselors may follow all of the principles outlined in the manual and perform all of the associated techniques, but they might not apply the principles and techniques skillfully. Waltz et al. (1993; see also Barber & Crits-Christoph, 1996) use the term *competence* to refer to the skillful application of principles and techniques to such things as the correctness and appropriate timing of an interpretation or the correct identification of cognitive distortions. As with adherence, it is not absolutely clear who should determine the competence of the counselor. The conventional wisdom is that only experienced clinicians who are experts in a particular treatment can accurately rate how competently that treatment was delivered (Waltz et al., 1993). Yet, both adherence and competence ratings have been called into question as both have little to no relationship with treatment outcomes (Webb et al., 2010). Rather, researchers have suggested that the relationship between adherence and outcome is likely more complex, based on other factors like the therapeutic relationship (e.g., Barber et al., 2006; Owen & Hilsenroth,

2011, 2014). Additionally, Stiles (2009) mentioned that the notion of adherence is likely a misnomer as therapists will likely be responsive to their clients' needs, regardless of the proscribed treatment manual.

When conducting a comparative outcome study, the researcher should establish not only that the therapists adhered to the manual and competently delivered the treatment, but also that the treatments delivered were noticeably different (Wampold & Imel, 2015). Kazdin (1996) defined *differentiation* as "whether two or more treatments differed from each other along critical dimensions that are central to their execution" (p. 416). If, for example, a researcher wanted to compare the relative effectiveness of Strupp and Binder's (1984) time-limited dynamic psychotherapy (TLDP) and Beck et al.'s (1979) cognitive therapy for the treatment of depression, she or he must show that the two treatments, as delivered, differed along the critical dimensions that distinguish the two theories. Specifically, the TLDP manual and the associated Vanderbilt Therapeutic Strategies Scale specify that the counselor identifying a maladaptive interpersonal cycle is a critical component of the model. Therefore, the researcher should expect the counselors who use the TLDP model to rate high on this component of the Vanderbilt Therapeutic Strategies Scale; conversely, the counselors who use the cognitive therapy model would be expected to rate low on this component of the Vanderbilt Therapeutic Strategies Scale.

This example suggests that differentiation can often be assessed by applying the adherence scales from two different approaches to treatments from both approaches. To demonstrate differentiation, a treatment session must rate highly on its treatment adherence measure and have low ratings on the adherence measure from the other treatment (see Waltz et al., 1993; Hilsenroth, 2007).

In another example, Trepka et al. (2004) measured counselor competence in a study of cognitive therapy for treatment of depression. They found that counselors' competence in delivering cognitive therapy was not significantly associated with counseling outcomes; however, the effects were in the positive direction, suggesting that counselor competence in cognitive treatment might be a positive indicator of outcomes.

To summarize, the assessment of treatment integrity involves a complex and multidimensional process. First, the treatment must be explicitly specified in a treatment manual so that counselors can know how to deliver the treatment and so that future researchers can replicate the treatment. Next, the researcher must demonstrate that the treatment as delivered adhered to the specifications of the manual and was delivered in a competent manner. Finally, in comparative outcome, dismantling, constructive, or parametric studies the researcher must also show that the treatments compared differed along the crucial dimensions studied.

Measuring Change

As noted by Francis et al. (1991), measuring and analyzing change plays a central role in many areas of study, but especially when trying to identify counseling outcomes. There is a voluminous literature dealing with the measurement of change (see Baldwin et al., 2009; Stulz et al., 2010, for counseling outcome examples). Although we cannot review this entire literature here, three areas have particular relevance to counseling researchers: (a) clinical versus statistical significance, (b) hypothesis testing, and (c) growth curve analysis. In the following subsections we discuss how each of these issues relates to the conduct of counseling outcome research.

Clinical versus Statistical Significance

A number of authors have argued that statistical significance is not a good indicator of treatment effectiveness. Lambert and Hill (1994) asserted that a well-designed outcome study can achieve statistically significant differences between treatment groups without producing real-life differences in enhanced functioning. For example, even though a date rape prevention program may result in a small but statistically significant decrease in rape myth acceptance when compared to a no-treatment control group, it is not clear that this small change makes any difference in the likelihood that one of the program's participants will commit a date rape. To address these types of practical issues, Jacobson, Follette, and Revenstorf (1984) and Jacobson and Truax (1991) introduced methods for calculating clinical significance.

As initially defined by Jacobson and Truax (1991), *clinical significance* is the degree to which an individual client improves after treatment. Two criteria are used to define improvement or recovery for a particular client. First, to be labeled as recovered, a participant's posttest score on a particular measure (e.g., Inventory of Interpersonal Problems) must fall within a functional (as opposed to a dysfunctional) distribution of scores, given that the participant's pretest score on the particular measure fell within a dysfunctional distribution of scores. The second criterion for determining improvement is labeled the *reliable change index,* in which the pretest to posttest difference observed for a client is greater than the change that would be expected due to chance alone. The formula used to calculate the reliable change index is:

$$(\text{Pretest} - \text{Posttest})/\text{Standard Error of Measurement}$$

A score greater than 1 on this index indicates that there was more change from pretest to posttest than the measurement error in the instrument. Using these criteria, an individual participant in a treatment study is considered to have improved if her or his posttest score is in the functional distribution and her or his reliable change index is greater than 1. In a study calculating clinical significance for a treatment group versus control group design, the researcher would compare the percentage of participants in the treatment group who had improved versus the percentage of participants in the control group who had improved.

Reese et al. (2009) utilized the reliable change criteria proposed by Jacobson and Truax (1991) to evaluate the outcomes of a client-feedback study. They conducted two studies with 74 clients in each study. They were randomized to a feedback condition or treatment as usual. The feedback condition consisted of the client and therapist systematically monitoring and discussing treatment progress and the working alliance throughout the course of counseling. The outcome measure was the Outcome Rating Scale (Miller & Duncan, 2000). In the first study 80.0% of the clients in the feedback condition reported reliable change as compared to 54.2% in the treatment as usual. In the second study, 66.7% of the clients in the feedback condition demonstrated reliable change as compared to 41.4% of clients in the treatment as usual condition. Additionally, they found that those clients in the feedback condition experienced reliable change sooner in counseling as compared to clients in the treatment as usual. Thus, clients in the feedback condition experienced more reliable change and did so at a quicker rate than those in the treatment as usual condition.

Tingey, Lambert, Burlingame, and Hansen (1996) presented an extension of Jacobson and colleagues' method for calculating clinically significant change. At the heart of this new method is an expanded definition: Tingey et al. defined clinically significant change as "movement from one socially relevant sample to another based on the impact factor selected, rather than (moving) from a 'dysfunctional' to a 'functional' distribution as proposed by Jacobson and Revenstorf (1988)" (p. 111). Tingey et al. proposed that multiple samples be used to form a continuum, and that a client's pretest-posttest movement (or lack of movement) along this continuum be used to identify clinically significant change.

According to Tingey et al. (1996), five steps are involved in establishing such a continuum:

> 1) selecting a specifying factor that is defined by a reliable outcome instrument; 2) identifying an impact factor (a behavior relevant to society that covaries with different levels of the specifying factor); 3) determining the statistical distinctiveness of these socially relevant samples; 4) calculating RCI's (Reliable Change Indices) for all possible sample pairs; and 5) calculating cutoff points between adjacent sample pairs along the continuum. (Tingey et al., 1996, p. 114)

For example, for Step 1, Tingey et al. used the SCL-90-R (Derogatis, 1983) as the specifying factor. According to these authors, one important factor related to the SCL-90-R is the type of psychological treatment a person receives, because more symptomatic clients generally receive more intensive treatment (e.g., inpatient vs. outpatient services). Consequently, for Step 2 they identified four samples of people who differed in the intensity of psychological treatment they were receiving: (a) asymptomatic (a specially collected healthy sample), (b) mildly symptomatic (unscreened community adults), (c) moderately symptomatic (people receiving outpatient counseling), and (d) severely symptomatic (people receiving inpatient counseling). Next, for Step c, Tingey et al. utilized *t* and *d* tests to ascertain whether the four identified samples were in fact distinct. In this example, their tests showed the four samples to be distinct. RCIs were calculated for the 10 possible pairs of samples (Step d). Finally, the authors established cut points and confidence intervals for each pair of adjacent samples; these cutoff points represent the point at which a score is more likely to be in one distribution as opposed to the adjacent distribution.

One of the most exciting features of Tingey et al.'s (1996) approach is that any researcher who uses the SCL-90-R as a pretest-posttest measure can use the information provided in the article to calculate the amount of clinically significant change for each individual client in her or his study. Lambert and his colleagues (Condon & Lambert, 1994; Grundy & Lambert, 1994b; Lambert et al., 2004; Seggar & Lambert, 1994) have used this method of defining clinical significance with several other well-validated psychometric instruments (State-Trait Anxiety Inventory, Auchenbach Child Behavior Checklist, Outcome Questionnaire-45, and Beck Depression Inventory). In addition, clinicians can use the information to ascertain whether their clients are making clinically significant change.

RESEARCH APPLICATION 20.4

To illustrate how this information can be useful, let's consider an example using a measure of psychological well-being. Specifically, Blais et al. (1999) created the Schwartz Outcome Scale-10 (SOS-10). This is a 10-item measure of psychological well-being. They conducted studies to determine the *clinical cutoff score* that differentiated between clinical samples and nonclinical samples—specifically, the scores on the measure range from 0 to 60 (with higher scores indicating better well-being). The clinical cutoff score is 41 and reliable change index is 8 points. Thus, for a client who started therapy at 21 and changes over the course of therapy to a score of 51 would indicate that the client has experienced both reliable change (change of 30 points is well over the 8 points) and clinically significant change or a movement from distressed to nondistressed (the final score is above the clinical cutoff score of 41). For further illustration of this measure see Owen and Imel (2010) for a review of this measure and other brief clinically meaningful measures.

The idea of calculating clinically significant change is very appealing. Clearly, counseling researchers would like to know that their treatment interventions are making a real difference. Even though it would be very useful if the profession had a specified standard for determining the clinical significance of a study's results, the measurement of clinical significance has not been widely embraced by counseling researchers. Few studies published in counseling-related journals have yet provided calculations of clinically significant change, perhaps because this method is not without psychometric problems. In order to determine whether a score is in a functional or a dysfunctional distribution, the researcher must have good psychometric information about a test. At the very least, the test must have been administered to one population clinically defined as dysfunctional, and to another clinically defined as normal. For more sophisticated analyses of clinical change, several different population groups must be identified. For example, Tingey et al. (1996) identified four different samples (asymptomatic, and mildly, moderately, and severely disturbed on the SCL-90-R) in their analysis of clinically significant change. Unfortunately, for many measures used in psychotherapy outcome research, this type of normative data is not readily available. Even when a measure has been used with different samples, the adequacy of the sampling procedure is often questionable.

Therefore, a great deal of additional psychometric work must be done before the assessment of clinical significance can become a standard practice in most counseling outcome studies. Nonetheless, we contend that calculations of the clinical significance of change should be used more widely than currently occurs in counseling research. For example, the population of students that seeks help at a career counseling center is probably more undecided about a career than a population of students in general; although not labeled as dysfunctional, the career center population is one normative group that could be used in a study examining the clinical significance of a career exploration intervention.

Measuring Outcomes and Change   Measuring outcome and estimating change over the course of therapy involve tricky issues that statisticians and methodologists have struggled to address. Often, strategic choices make little difference, but there are instances when adoption of a certain statistical model can drastically influence the conclusions that are made about psychotherapy (see, e.g., Elkin, Falconnier, Martinovich, & Mahoney, 2006; Kim, Wampold, & Bolt, 2006; Wampold & Bolt, 2006, for an example of debates about models and the conclusions they produce). Thus, great care must be taken in choosing statistical models, and the researcher should be familiar enough with the data to ensure that results are indeed reflections of the data and not artifacts from inappropriate statistical models. In this section, we briefly review several options.

The simplest method, and a logically defensible one, of measuring the outcome of any of the designs discussed in this chapter is to use only the posttest measure and perform some type of analysis of variance on these measures to test the omnibus hypothesis that the groups vary on the posttest. If clients were randomly assigned to treatment groups and/or controls, and the experiment was well designed in other respects, then differences among groups at the posttest are due either to the treatment or to random sources (i.e., error variance). The analysis of variance results in a test of the null hypothesis that is valid. If the null is rejected, and, say, it is concluded that Treatment A is superior to Treatment B and alpha was set at .05, then there are less than 5 chances out of 100 that differences as large as those observed were due to chance. In a no-treatment comparison, if client outcomes at posttest of Treatment A are found to exceed the outcomes of clients receiving no treatment (e.g., a wait-list control) at the .05 level, then it can be concluded that Treatment A provides some benefits to the clients vis-à-vis the natural course of the disorder.

Using posttest scores often raises the (uninformed) objection that it is impossible to know whether patients improved over the course of therapy. The superiority of Treatment A over a no-treatment control group may be due to the fact that the clients in Treatment A, as a group, displayed no change (posttest scores would have been equal to the pretest scores, had they been assessed) but that those in the no-treatment group deteriorated. Some would claim that the posttest-only design cannot detect this pattern of results and thus one cannot determine whether Treatment A actually helped clients. Moreover, with posttest-only designs the calculation of clinically significant change cannot be determined.

Notwithstanding the discussion about not logically needing a pretest score, there are several reasons for collecting a pretest score (again, see Chapter 11). First, the pretest score is often used to make decisions about inclusion (i.e., is the score above the cutoff for this disorder?). Second, the pretest score is typically correlated with the posttest score (i.e., much of the variance in the final score of any participant is accounted for by the pretest score), and thus the pretest score can be used in a way that increases the power of the statistical test by reducing unexplained variance (i.e., error variance). In other words, the pretest score can be used as a covariate in the analysis. Third, despite the problems with interpreting pretest to posttest scores, as a descriptive statistic, it can be useful to have an indication of the progress of clients. For example, a pretest score is needed to determine clinically significant change. Additionally, the pretest score can be used to calculate a residualized change score.

A description of the statistical theory that forms the bases of these three methods and the relative advantages and disadvantages of the methods is beyond the scope of this text (see Keller, 2004; Willett, 1997; Willett & Sayer, 1994). For these reasons, outcome studies typically involve collection of pretest scores.

The most stringent method with which to measure client progress in any intervention is to collect data over time. Measuring client functioning solely at pretest and posttest restricts knowledge of client functioning to two points—at the beginning of therapy and at the end of therapy. More sophisticated methods, often called growth curve modeling, can be used to investigate therapeutic effects if multiple measurements across the course of therapy are collected. In a linear growth curve model there are two primary components of interest: the *intercept*, which typically denotes the average score of the participants at the beginning of therapy, although the intercept can be changed to be any time point, and the *slope*, which describes the rate of change over time. The rate of change may be linear or curvilinear (e.g., accelerating change).

To illustrate these patterns we created Figure 20.1. In this figure, we illustrate the scores on a measure of psychological well-being (possible range 0 to 20) from two different studies. For both studies let's assume there were 50 clients who were treated for depression. As you can see at Session 1, the clients in Study 1 had, on average, an initial score of 7, whereas the clients in Study 2 had an average score of 10. The slope or growth in scores for the clients in Study 1 were linear, suggesting that for each session there was approximately a 1-point growth in psychological well-being. In contrast, the growth for the clients in Study 2 demonstrated a quadratic growth (or log-linear), wherein there was an initial growth in psychological well-being; however, around Session 5 the growth essential leveled off.

FIGURE 20.1 : Measuring Change in Counseling

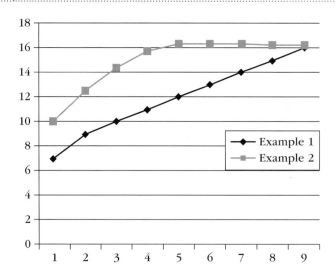

Note: Example 1 = trajectory of change for participants in Study 1. Example 2 = trajectory of change participants in Study 2.

Statistical methods that use multiple measurements are able to estimate the rate and nature of change rather than simply estimating the amount of change, increase the power of statistical tests, handle missing data points, and model other important aspects of therapy (such as therapist effects—see the following section). For example, Owen et al. (in press) examined how clients changed over the course of therapy. In a sample of 10,854 clients they found three groups of clients who had different patterns of change over the course of therapy. Notably, one group (5% of the clients in the study) reported a notable increase in symptomology in the initial sessions, and then rebounded as therapy continued. The second group (19% of the clients in the study) reported a slow and steady increase over the course of treatment. The largest group (75% of clients in the study) reported improvements early in treatment followed by a plateau of functioning when another notable improvement in functioning was demonstrated. Interested readers should consult Raudenbush and Bryk (2002), Hox (2010), Snijders and Bosker (2012) for more in-depth reading on multilevel modeling and modeling change over time.

Counselor Effects

Wampold and Bhati (2004) examined the history of psychotherapy and clinical trials and noted that many important aspects of psychotherapy have been omitted in current theory and research. One of the important omissions is the therapist. Because the randomized control group design was originally used in the fields of education, agriculture, and medicine, the provider of service was thought to be unimportant. Education was interested in which programs were effective; relatively unimportant were the teachers, primarily women, who were thought to be interchangeable. Agriculture was focused on fertilizers, seed varieties, and irrigation and not on the farmer. Finally, medicine, attempting to distance itself from charismatic healers such as Mesmer, emphasized the potency of medicines and purposefully ignored physician effects. Psychotherapy research, borrowing the randomized design, similarly ignored the provider of service—that is, the therapists. Indeed, apparently there are no clinical trials of psychotherapy that have considered therapist effects in the primary analyses of the data (Wampold & Bhati, 2004). Unfortunately, ignoring therapists (or groups in group-based treatments; see Baldwin, Murray, & Shadish, 2005) has deleterious effects on conclusions that are made in outcome research (see Wampold & Imel, 2015, for an extensive discussion of these issues).

The essential issue with regard to therapist effects is that it seems reasonable to believe that therapists vary in the outcomes they attain with clients. That is to say, some therapists may consistently produce better outcomes with their clients than do others. Indeed, it appears that this is true. Based on reanalyses of existing data sets and analyses of outcomes in practice settings, it appears that between 3% and 8% of the variance in outcomes is due to therapists (Baldwin & Imel, 2013; Wampold & Imel, 2015; Wampold & Brown, 2005), which when compared to other sources of variability in outcomes, including what treatment the client receives, is extraordinarily large (e.g., the particular treatment that is administered accounts for less than 1%; Wampold, 2001). This variability also appears to extend to psychiatrists in pharmacotherapy trials (McKay, Imel, & Wampold, 2006). Therapist variability suggests a new definition of competence: Competent counselors are those who produce better than average outcomes. This definition stands in contrast to that discussed earlier, which involved ratings of competence by observers.

There are two reasons to examine counselor effects in any study of counseling interventions. The first reason is rather obvious—therapist effects are interesting and informative in their own right. If much of the variability in outcomes in a study is explained by differences among counselors, then it can be concluded that the therapist is an important factor—this is particularly interesting when counselor effects are much larger than treatment effects and as large as any other effects, such as the alliance (see Laska, Gurman, & Wampold, 2014; Norcross, Beutler, & Levant, 2006). The second reason to examine counselor effects in any treatment study is that ignoring counselor effects inflates estimates of treatment effects (Owen, Drinane, Idigo, & Valentine, in press; Wampold & Imel, 2015; Wampold & Serlin, 2000). Essentially, in analysis of variance, the estimate of between-group variability is due in part to counselor effects as well as treatment effects (see Wampold & Serlin, 2000). Conceptually this makes sense—if counselors indeed are an important determinant of outcomes, then the choice of therapists for a treatment in a particular study will determine, in part, the outcomes produced. Suppose that therapists are randomly selected to administer Treatment A and Treatment B and suppose, by chance, that the therapists chosen to deliver Treatment A were superior to those chosen to deliver Treatment B; then it will appear that Treatment A is superior to Treatment B even if the two treatments are equally effective. This is not an easy phenomenon to grasp (similar in that respect to regression toward the mean) but it is extremely important. If therapist effects are present and ignored, then the likelihood that a researcher will falsely conclude that a treatment is more effective than another is relatively large, and any estimate of treatment differences will be inflated. The size of those errors are presented and discussed by Wampold and Serlin (2000).

In comparative treatment studies, two designs are possible: crossed and nested. In the crossed design, therapists deliver all treatments. For example, in the Reese et al. (2009) study mentioned above, therapists provided the treatment as usual as well as utilized client feedback. The crossed design has the advantage that the general skill of the counselor is balanced. However, problems arise if the counselors have more allegiance to or skill in delivering one of the treatments. In the nested design, counselors deliver one of the treatments only (i.e., the therapists are nested within treatment). Ideally, the counselors delivering a particular treatment would have allegiance to and skill in delivering the respective treatment and allegiance and skill would be balanced. A commendable effort to balance allegiance and skill was shown by Watson et al. (2003), who compared cognitive-behavioral treatment and process experiential treatment for depression. The counselors for each treatment were adherents to their respective treatment and then were trained by internationally recognized experts in this treatment.

Appropriately including counselors in the design and analysis of outcome research is more complex than simply ignoring them. However, the extra effort is needed to correctly estimate treatment effects, and it has the potential to detect counselor effects should they exist. Generally it is recommended that counselors be considered a random factor in the model; that is, counselors are assumed to be randomly selected from the population of counselors. Of course this is rarely done, but the issues are comparable to the ones created by the fact that we do not randomly select study participants from a population of participants (see Chapter 8 and Serlin, Wampold, & Levin, 2003). In the nested design, the analysis would be a mixed model in which the treatments are considered to be fixed (i.e., not drawn from a population of treatments) and the counselors are a random factor (Wampold & Serlin, 2000). In a balanced design, the analysis would be a relatively simple mixed model analysis of variance; when the number of clients per therapist and the number of therapists per treatment varies, it is recommended that a multilevel model (sometimes called a hierarchical linear model) analysis be conducted (Raudenbush & Bryk, 2002; Hox, 2010; Snijders & Bosker, 2012).

SUMMARY AND CONCLUSIONS

Counseling researchers often address questions related to counseling outcome. This chapter described several different strategies for addressing outcome questions and provided counseling examples for each. Each strategy answers a different research question; researchers are advised to select the strategy that is appropriate to the goals of the investigation. In addition, a number of methodological issues important for researchers planning a counseling outcome study were discussed. These issues, which involve inclusion and exclusion criteria, treatment integrity, measuring outcomes and change, and therapist effects, have to be considered so that valid conclusions are made from outcome research.

A chapter on outcome research was included in this book because of its importance in answering questions that are central to the field of counseling: Are the interventions we use more effective than no treatment? Are some treatments more effective than other treatments? Are some treatments more effective with certain clients under certain circumstances? Are the benefits of treatments due to the specific therapeutic ingredients? Although there are complex issues involved in outcome research, such research must be undertaken and undertaken well to answer these questions.

STIMULUS QUESTIONS

Three Exercises to Enhance Students' Understanding of Outcome Research

1. Suppose that you have developed a new treatment for a particular disorder or problem. Discuss how you would design a series of outcome studies to establish that this treatment is the treatment of choice. What steps would need to be taken before the first study was undertaken? What precautions would need to be instituted

to protect the research from threats to validity?

2. Find three outcome studies. Describe the design of each and classify them into one of the types of outcome research discussed in this chapter. Discuss the degree to which each study handled the issues presented in this chapter appropriately.

3. Find several outcome studies and discuss how allegiance was handled in each study.

Process Research: The How's and Why's That Make Counseling Work

21
Chapter

Every counselor has reflected on what happens in the course of counseling. Beginning counselors often ask supervisors about ways of establishing a working alliance, how to confront clients, or how to use various counseling interventions, such as the Gestalt empty chair technique. Moreover, counselors realize that all clients are not alike, and that it is important to consider how to establish a working alliance with very different clients. All these counseling topics are related to aspects of the counseling process in some way and have been the focus of considerable research. Such research can be exciting, as the researchers attempt to discover "how counseling works."

This chapter provides a general introduction to the research methods that are typically utilized in counseling process research, and in doing so, we will highlight some exemplar studies. Moreover, we will discuss issues that are salient in designing counseling process studies. Process research is not a category of research design per se; rather, it is a specific area of focus within counseling research. That is, there are a variety of research designs used to conduct process research, including descriptive, single-subject, qualitative, quasi-experimental, time-series, and experimental designs.

There are four major sections to this chapter. In the first section we define process research in general terms and provide a snapshot of early process research. The second section focuses on various methodological issues in the design of process studies. The third section focuses on major research designs typically utilized in counseling process research as well as highlighting some current exemplar studies. The last section focuses on some final thoughts regarding analytical considerations when designing studies.

DEFINING COUNSELING PROCESS RESEARCH

Counseling process research explores the events that occur within the therapeutic encounter, typically examining variables such as therapist and client overt and covert thoughts, feelings, and behaviors, as well as therapist-client interactions during treatment (Crits-Christoph, Connolly Gibbons, & Mukbergee, 2013;

Hill & Williams, 2000). In contrast, counseling outcome research typically concerns itself with the immediate and/or long-term changes in clients' functioning (Lambert, 2013). Although these definitions seem straightforward, the conceptualization of the process and the outcome of counseling often overlap. For example, some researchers have described session outcomes as "little o's (or outcomes)" and counseling outcomes at the end of treatment as "big O's (or Outcomes)" (Greenberg, 1986; Lambert, 2013). However, session outcomes can also be described as a counseling process leading to overall counseling outcomes.

More specifically, there are three major types of counseling process research: (a) studies that examine a specific process alone (e.g., what typifies counselor empathetic responses), (b) studies that examine the relationship between counseling processes to other counseling processes (e.g., how counselors' use of cognitive behavior techniques are associated with client-rated working alliance), and (c) studies that examine the relationship between counseling processes and counseling outcomes (e.g., are counselors' use of cognitive behavioral techniques associated with counseling outcomes?). In this chapter, we will describe a variety of studies that embody one of these three approaches to counseling processes.

Over 60 years of research has identified a very wide range of variables that are important to the counseling process (Crits-Christoph et al., 2013; Orlinsky & Howard, 1978; Orlinsky et al., 1994, 2004). The large number of variables identified has led numerous researchers to organize the variables into some sort of classification system. Although there are disadvantages and advantages to the various classification systems, we present one system here. A classic system, developed by Clara Hill (1991), listed the following seven types of behaviors that have been examined within the process area, which are enumerated in increasing levels of complexity; the first types are more observable and discrete, whereas the latter tend to involve more abstract behaviors that occur over longer periods of time:

1. Ancillary behaviors such as speech quality, or nonverbal behaviors such as the body posture of the counselor
2. Verbal behaviors, such as therapist self-disclosure, interpretation, and confrontation
3. Covert behaviors, such as therapist intentions "to support" or "to challenge"
4. Content, which examines the topics of discussion and typically focuses on client behaviors
5. Strategies, which focus on therapist techniques such as identifying maladaptive cognitions or challenging client defenses
6. Interpersonal manner, such as therapist involvement, empathy, and congruence
7. The therapeutic relationship, such as the working alliance and control of the topic of discussion

As seen here, there are differences in the focus and content of the process variables, all of which can be rated by clients, counselors, or judges. Likewise, the term *process* has been used to describe very different units of measurement, from very small units involving microprocesses (e.g., gaze shifts) to session processes (e.g., repair of the working alliance) over the course of an hour or even months (see, e.g., Elliott, 1991; Imel et al., 2011; Owen, Tao, Imel, Wampold, & Rodolfa, 2014; Muran et al., 2009; Safran & Muran, 2000). We will describe how some of these areas can be examined within the various research designs. But first we will provide a historical framework of the early days of process research.

Early Process Research

An examination of the first volume of the *Journal of Counseling Psychology (JCP)* attests to the early roots of counseling process research. Not only has process research per se been an important theme within counseling research, but also many of the topics and questions studied today have their roots in research published in 1954 in the first volume of *JCP*. Current research, however, is more sophisticated methodologically and conceptually because of technical advances in both of these areas. In this section we compare and contrast the focus of early researchers with those of current process researchers.

Let's consider three studies published in the first volume of *JCP*. Dipboye (1954) was interested in examining differences in counselor style among different content areas of discussion. This researcher used nine mutually exclusive categories to examine counselor style—questions about content, questions about feelings, responses to content, responses to feelings, interpretation of content, interpretation of feelings, suggestions about content, suggestions about feelings, and giving information. These categories bear remarkable similarity to the six categories of response modes (questions, advisements, information, reflection, interpretation, and self-disclosure) that Elliott et al. (1987) found to underlie a variety of response mode systems. Dipboye's content categories included test discussion, interpersonal relations, family relations, educational and vocational problems and planning, self-reference, and study skills. Dipboye found that four of the six counselors he examined changed their style of interaction when different content areas were being addressed. Unfortunately, he did not examine which styles were related to which content areas.

The second process study published in Volume 1 of *JCP* involved an examination of counselor directiveness. Danskin and Robinson (1954) examined counselor directiveness by rating the amount of "lead" in a counselor statement. They defined "lead" as (a) "the extent to which the content of the counselor's remark seems to be ahead of the content of the client's last remark," and (b) "the degree of pressure or definiteness in the counselor's remark that is apparently used to bring about client acceptance of the expressed idea" (p. 79). They found that counselor lead was related to the type of problem being discussed. They found that the counselor used more leading statements with clients who had a "skills" problem than with clients who had an "adjustment" problem.

A third study (Berg, 1954) examined differences between two groups of clients (those whose presenting problems either were or were not sexually related) in nonverbal behavior displayed during counseling interviews. Based on psychoanalytic theory, Berg tabulated the following classes of gestures, which were thought to represent sexual symbolism: rotating and sliding, clasping or wrapping, insertion, pressing, and licking and biting. Although the categories of coding nonverbal behavior seem quite different today, there is still a continuity of this line of research (see, e.g., Hill & Stephany, 1990). Berg found, contrary to his hypothesis, that both groups of clients made a relatively high number of sexually suggestive gestures. Thus, the content or the presenting concern bore little relationship to the type or number of nonverbal gestures exhibited.

There are important differences between these early studies and more recent process research. Two of the most striking differences involve the emphasis on content in the counseling interview and the link between process and outcome. In two of the studies from Volume 1 of *JCP*, the content of the counseling interview was an important defining focus. As mentioned earlier, Dipboye (1954) categorized segments of counseling interviews as representing one of six content categories. Likewise, Danskin and Robinson (1954) used four categories to classify the content of their counseling interviews. Such emphasis on content is representative of the focus that content received in much of the early research, which is now primarily done via qualitative process studies today. Moreover, in process studies today there is more focus on client perceptions of the process (e.g., the alliance; Horvath et al., 2011) as well as on overall ratings of session quality or techniques (e.g., Hilsenroth, 2007).

A second point of discontinuity concerns the process-outcome link. Early counseling research tended to focus solely on either client outcome or counseling process; the early studies did not attempt to link the process variables with some measure of outcome. For example, Danskin and Robinson (1954) did not know whether more-leading questions were more productive than less-leading interviews in addressing skill problems. Within the last 30 years, however, studies have emphasized linking process to outcome (Crits-Christoph et al., 2013). For example, Owen, Tao, and Rodolfa (2010) found female clients' perceptions of gender-based microaggressions in sessions were associated with lower client-rated alliance scores (another process measure) and client-rated counseling outcomes. However, there are still some studies that highlight counseling process only.

METHODOLOGICAL ISSUES IN PROCESS RESEARCH

Although counseling process research can be very exciting, it can also be tedious, and the number of methodological details and the volume of data can be overwhelming. The many details and the complexity can translate into more opportunities for problems to arise. In this section, we focus on several major methodological issues that typically face the process researcher: Where to start? What to measure? Whose perspective? How much to measure?

Where to Start

One of the first steps is to choose the general topic or focus of the process research (see Chapter 5). Hill underscored the importance of developing a good research question and hypothesis:

> This has been a particularly difficult problem in the process area, perhaps because of the overwhelming nature of the multitude of variables in counseling which can be examined. What seems to have happened in the past is that researchers have responded with

a flight into detail, creating an obsessive's nightmare for themselves and their readers. Researchers tend to painstakingly describe, categorize, and develop measures but rarely are these put into a context of what they mean for counseling or theory. Further, there has been a tendency to study easy variables that can be measured reliably because of clear operational definitions rather than those which might have more clinical relevance. (Hill, 1982, p. 10)

It is common for researchers to develop research ideas as they engage in actual counseling, perhaps by reviewing a tape of a counseling session, or in discussions with a supervisor or supervisee. It is critical to go well beyond the initial identification of the idea and to spend considerable time reviewing relevant literature. In doing so, the act of writing typically facilitates the process of identifying the topic, operationalizing variables, and thinking through procedural details.

An equally important issue pertains to the context or setting in which the study is to be conducted; typically, researchers decide to what degree the study will be conducted in an actual counseling session or analogue (see Chapter 14). This issue basically concerns the levels of internal and external validity that the researcher deems most important to best answer the relevant research questions. If the researcher wants a great deal of internal validity (and typically to be able to manipulate one or more independent variables), an analogue setting might be advisable (see Chapter 14). However, if external validity (or generalizability) is very important, then a study conducted in more of an actual counseling setting may be advisable. The decision between an analogue and actual counseling setting is not a categorical either/or decision, but rather one that involves a continuum. Some analogue designs emphasize internal validity more than others, and some actual counseling designs incorporate analogue methods to create quasinaturalistic settings (see Chapter 12). In the final analysis, the decision regarding the type of context or setting is thus a matter of the degree to which the research will be conducted in a context that maximizes either internal or external validity.

Another key design issue is whether to use a quantitative or qualitative approach (see Chapter 16). It is critical to carefully contemplate both the type of research questions of interest and the type of data that will best answer those questions at this time. For example, despite an abundant literature on reducing client resistance, there has been very little research on either willingness to work through interpersonal difficulties in family therapy or a family's level of engagement/disengagement. Because of the lack of empirical data, Friedlander et al. (1994) used a qualitative, discovery-oriented approach to examine events related to successful, sustained engagement in family therapy. Moreover, they were able to develop a conceptual model of successful, sustained engagement based on their qualitative analysis. This work latter informed an observer-based measure of systemic alliance in couple and family therapy (Friedlander et al., 2006).

What to Measure?

Once a general research topic has been identified, a subsequent issue concerns the aspect of the counseling process to examine. At the most basic level, researchers must decide whether they want to examine aspects of the individual participants' behaviors or aspects of the developing relationship or system. Process research focuses on either a participant (counselor or client), the relationship, or some combination thereof. *Ultimately, theory should guide our decisions regarding what to study and what to measure.*

In group and family counseling, the clients are obviously multiple individuals, and the counselor dimension often involves a measurement of the activities of cocounselors. In individual counseling, the relationship involves how the client and counselor work together. In group and family process research, this relationship dimension is usually referred to as the group (cohesion, norms) or family (closeness, involvement) process. We will discuss issues pertaining to what to measure specifically with regard to individual participants and the client-counselor relationship.

Suppose that a researcher, Dr. B. Famous, decides to conduct a process study that examines the counselor's behavior. But there are many counselor behaviors: what the counselor said, how the counselor said it (e.g., emphatically or angrily), how often the counselor said it, when the counselor said it, and so on. So the insightful Dr. Famous knows it is necessary to consider specific types of counselor behaviors that might be examined. Elliott's (1991) four focal points of the communication process—content (what is said), action (what is done), style (how it is said or done), and quality (how well it is said or done)—could be used to clarify the focus study. Likewise, Hill's (1991) classification scheme (described earlier in this chapter) could be used to think about "what type of behaviors" Dr. Famous might want to examine.

Suppose as well that Dr. Famous was especially keenly interested in counselor intentions; how might she measure that? One strategy might be to make some type of measurement after each counselor statement, but such a measurement would involve many "microscopic" assessments for each interview hour. Another strategy might be to ask counselors to reflect on their overall intentions during a counseling session, which would be a more global type of assessment.

Process researchers must decide at what level they are going to measure the aspects of the process. Greenberg (1986a) suggested that three levels of analysis be used in examining the counseling process: speech acts, episodes, and the relationship. In counseling process research, *speech acts* refers to the microanalysis of statement-by-statement transactions, *episodes* refers to a coherent thematic section of counseling, and the *relationship* refers to the ongoing counselor-client relationship over multiple sessions. Greenberg nicely elucidated the need to examine the notion of different levels of measurement within process research, from the microscopic (statement by statement) to the more global or general. He also suggested that process measurements be context sensitive, such as within a relationship.

At the end of the day, process researchers should be reminded that there have been a vast amount of process variables examined over the past 60 plus years. Thus, researchers should develop a clear definition of the process variable in question and do a diligent search of the literature to determine if there are established measures or ways of examining the variable in question. Yet, we caution researchers to allow ways of the past to ultimately dictate the measurement of counseling processes. As described in the following, there are new technological developments that are changing the ways we examine counseling processes, such as counselor-client speech patterns (e.g., vocal synchrony; Imel et al., 2014). Again, researchers should rely on theory to be a guide on how to approach measurement.

Whose Perspective?

Another major question that process researchers must address is: From whose perspective should the counseling process be evaluated? A considerable amount of evidence suggests that client, counselor, and observer perspectives on the counseling process may offer quite diverse views of what happens in counseling. For example, Fuertes et al. (2006) examined the correlation between clients' perspectives of their therapists' multicultural competencies and therapists' perspectives of their own multicultural competencies. They found a correlation estimate of $r = -.03$, suggesting very little correspondence between clients and therapists (also see Eugster & Wampold, 1996). It is important to note that convergence might be the result of utilizing different assessment methods. For example, a client self-rating may be different than external observers who are coding part of a session.

Different relationships among the three perspectives have been found in research that has examined the working alliance. A notable historical example comes by Tichenor and Hill (1989) who suggested that clients, counselors, and observers have different views of the working relationship (correlations among the three perspectives averaged $r = -.02$). Other research, however, found that both client and counselor ratings of the working alliance are related to client outcome, suggesting that even though different perspectives of the working alliance may measure different constructs, each of them is important (see Horvath et al., 2011).

Less discrepancy among raters from the three perspectives may occur when concrete and observable behaviors are assessed. The more subjective the process variable is (especially if the assessment pertains to the raters' perceptions of conditions), the greater the difference among various raters is likely to be. When researchers want to examine more subjective process variables, they should obtain ratings from multiple perspectives. In this way, researchers can empirically examine the degree of relationship among the perspectives on the particular variable of interest and determine if the different perspectives add useful information. Put another way, the combination of client, counselor, and observer perspectives on, say, the working alliance may be a better predictor of counseling outcome than any single perspective. Accordingly, we encourage researchers to think carefully about the different perspectives when they are developing their research questions.

Lastly, it is also important to consider what type of information is being assessed based on perspective. For example, Hook et al. (2013) developed a client-rated measure of counselors' cultural humility. Thus, clients' perspectives of counselors' cultural humility was being assessed and was defined as:

> *Cultural humility* involves the ability to maintain an interpersonal stance that is other-oriented (or open to the other) in relation to aspects of cultural identity that are most important to the client. Cultural humility is especially apparent when a therapist is able express respect and a lack of superiority even when cultural differences threaten to weaken the therapy alliance. Culturally humble therapists rarely assume competence (i.e., letting prior experience and even expertise lead to overconfidence) for working with clients just based on their prior experience working with a particular group. Rather, therapists who are more culturally humble approach clients with respectful openness and work collaboratively with clients to understand the unique intersection of clients' various aspects of identities and how that affects the developing therapy alliance. (p. 354)

Based on this definition, Hook et al. concluded that counselors are not likely in a good position to comment on their own level of cultural humility. That is, would truly humble counselors report that they are very humble? Accordingly, process variables, like cultural humility or multicultural competencies are best measured by clients or external observers.

How Much to Measure?

If you were doing a process study, would it be sufficient to collect data from one session, or should you collect from multiple sessions? If you are using measures that assess statement-by-statement variables (e.g., counselor intentions), should you collect data from the whole counseling session, or perhaps from only the first (or last) 15 minutes of the session? Although it seems desirable to collect a lot of data from multiple sessions, which would increase the external validity or generalizability of the findings, such a strategy quickly results in an overwhelming amount of data. Process researchers must decide how much of a session or how many sessions to use in their analyses. There are mixed perspectives on this issue, but by in large researchers should frame what is needed based on the research question at hand.

The question of whether to use sample session segments seems to depend on the type of research question and the nature of the design. Certainly, investigators must be alert to individual differences across clients, particularly across very different diagnostic groups. Moreover, some differences in counselor behavior seem likely over time. Accordingly, researchers might choose to include both individual differences and time intervals in their research questions. If these variables are not desired in the research questions, then the researcher could decide to control these variables to reduce potential confounds.

When it comes to coding session-level data, such as counselor techniques or family alliances, some coding systems require coders to review the entire session (e.g., Friedlander et al., 2006; Hilsenroth, 2007). Additionally, for single-subject designs more intensive coding of multiple full sessions may be advantageous (see Friedlander et al., 1988). Following we highlight a qualitative study of a single case to illustrate this point. If more macroassessments of a session or interaction are desired then less data might be usable (e.g., 10% of a session). For example, within the couple and family literature, the use of "thin slices" (e.g., coding 3 minutes of interaction) can be quite predictive of behavior, such as infidelity (see Lambert, Mulder, & Fincham, 2014). The key question that researchers should ask themselves is whether the sample of observations from whatever session(s)/interaction(s) is truly representative of the actual behavior/interaction. For instance, if a researcher examines 2 minutes of a session and concludes that the client-counselor seemed disconnected, but the rest of the session was characterized by supportive client-counselor interactions, then this coding segment would not be very generalizable or representative of what actually occurred in the session.

The issue of generalizability of observations is important to consider when measuring even more macroprocesses, such as the working alliance. For example, client-rated working alliance is typically rated at the end of a session and reflects the overall level of collaboration, engagement, and agreement on the goals for treatment, the process to meet those goals, as well as the relational bond between the counselor and client (see Bordin, 1979; Horvath et al., 2011). Historically, studies examining the association between the alliance and outcome relied on one session rating (typically, early in the treatment process, like the third session). However, Crits-Christoph et al. (2011) applied generalizability theory to examine whether one session of alliance ratings are truly reflective of other sessions (see Wasserman, Levy, & Loken, 2009, for further discussion of generalizability theory). Specifically, Crits-Christoph et al. (2011) noted: "Thus, the generalizability coefficient can tell you whether scores from one session are stable, given any session-to-session variability on the alliance, in measuring individual alliance differences between patients" (p. 269). In their study, they concluded that at least four sessions of the alliance were needed to develop a dependable alliance for clients. We will return to this issue again when we discuss time-series counseling process designs.

Now that we have covered some of the basic questions to get counseling process research set up, we will now turn to some commonly utilized research designs for counseling process research as well as highlight some process studies. In doing so, we will also discuss some other pressing issues in counseling process research, such as therapist effects.

RESEARCH APPLICATION 21.1

As you think about designing a study, here are some questions to guide your thinking:

1. What is your research question? Why is this counseling process important to understand?
2. What is the definition of the counseling process variable you want to study? How have other researchers defined this process variable?
3. How would you measure this process variable? Whose perspective would you need to answer your research question (e.g., client, counselor, external observer)? What are the pros and cons of having this person (or these people) rate the process variable?
4. How often will you measure the counseling process variable (e.g., each session, once). What are the pros and cons of measuring this process variable this often?
5. What is your outcome variable? What is the rationale for your outcome variable to be linked to the proposed counseling process variable?

Based on what you have learned so far, try to outline a counseling process study following these questions.

RESEARCH DESIGNS IN PROCESS RESEARCH

It is important to reiterate that process research is not a category of research design. Many of the methodological considerations pertaining to the selection of the research topic (see Chapter 5), independent or predictor variables (Chapter 18), dependent or criterion variables (Chapter 19), quantitative descriptive studies (Chapter 13), qualitative designs (Chapter 16), population issues (Chapter 8), multicultural issues (Chapter 9), and experimenter/participant bias (Chapter 23) apply to conducting counseling process research. In this section we highlight common methodological approaches typically utilized in counseling process research. We will focus on quantitative approaches (primarily experimental, correlational, and time-series designs), and then we will describe qualitative approaches to examining counseling process research. But first, selecting the correct research design starts with the research question.

Quantitative Counseling Process Designs

Experimental Counseling Process Designs There are several popular quantitative designs for counseling process research. We will first focus on experimental designs (also see Chapter 11), which are characterized by active manipulation of the independent variable and randomization of clients to the levels of the independent variables. Before we move on too far, it is important to note that most process variables are not viable candidates for experimental designs. For example, it is not realistic to conduct an experimental study where therapists either are empathic or are not empathic. Such a study would not be very realistic as therapists naturally convey empathy in various ways. Simply, the lack of inclusion of some process elements (e.g., empathy, alliance, open-ended questions) is simply not feasible as these processes are part and parcel of what counseling is. Additionally, it is important to consider the ethical implications of conducting experimental designs where some element of treatment is withheld (or added), such as empathy. In these situations, other research designs are likely a better option. Nonetheless, it is feasible to conduct experimental studies with some process variables.

Let's consider the following example of a researcher, Janet, who following Hill's categorization system (mentioned previously) wanted to examine counselor verbal behaviors. In this case, she wanted to examine the association between counselors' self-disclosure on counseling outcomes. Thus, prior to the study, Janet needed to first define the independent and dependent variables. She defined counselor self-disclosures as counselors sharing their personal reactions regarding the client or client-counselor interactions (also see Hill & Knox, 2002. Additionally, like many counseling outcome studies, she decided to use client self-report of psychological functioning (e.g., well-being, symptoms) as the dependent variable. She found a commonly utilized measure of psychological functioning (e.g., Behavioral Health Measure; see Kopta & Lowry, 2002) to operationalize the dependent variable. This measure has demonstrated strong psychometric properties with similar samples as the one Janet utilized in her study.

Next, Janet selected her counselors; in this case she utilized four master-level licensed professional counselors. She conducted a brief training with all four counselors to orient them to the study and trained them to utilize counselor self-disclosures. During this training she also tested the counselors via role-play demonstrations to be sure that they were able to use self-disclosure in a competent manner. Janet relied on two trained coders to review the role-play demonstrations and rate the counselors' performance on a scale of counselor self-disclosure competency (she developed this measure herself with the assistance of her coders). The scale consisted of five items, which were rated on a 5-point scale (ranging from 0 = not at all competent, 3 = competent, to 5 = very competent). The counselors needed to perform at 3 or higher on each item of the scale to be approved for the study. Fortunately, the training coupled with counselors' natural ability resulted in high competency ratings, as they all scored 4's or 5's on each item.

Next, Janet randomly assigned 40 clients (10 clients per counselor) to one of two conditions. In one condition, the counselors were instructed to use self-disclose 5 times per session. In the other condition, the counselors were instructed to not self-disclose at all. Thus, the independent variable, counselor self-disclosure, has two levels (5 discloses per session vs. no disclosures). Clients were randomized within the counselor's caseload. That is, each counselor performed both conditions; or five clients within each counselor's caseload were in the self-disclose condition and the other five clients within each counselor's caseload were in the no self-disclosure condition. Janet utilized a random number generator for each counselor to help ensure that each randomization will be conducted appropriately (see www.randomizer.org for an online example of a random number generator).

Janet decided to let the counselors do treatment as they would normally, with the exception of counselor self-disclosures. She also videotaped each session and had the same raters who reviewed the counselors in the training examine each session to ensure that counselors performed the conditions as instructed (e.g., self-disclosed 5 times in the self-disclosure condition, and did not self-disclose in the other condition). In this case, Janet was very fortunate. Only one client in the no counselor self-disclosure condition received on average 3 counselor self-disclosures per session. Janet decided to remove this case from the final analysis to ensure that the no counselor self-disclosure condition will be reflective of the intent of the study.

At the end of the study, she decided to examine whether the two conditions differed on clients' psychological functioning. She did so by conducting an ANCOVA, wherein clients' psychological functioning score at the end of treatment was the dependent variable, the counselor self-disclosure conditions was the independent variable, and clients' psychological functioning score at the start of treatment was the covariate.

There are also some complex issues in designs like this. First, in this example, the clients were randomized to one of the two conditions; however, the counselors were not. Rather, counselors performed treatment within both conditions and clients were randomized within counselor's caseload. On the one hand, counselors served as their control, which resulted in the two conditions being equally influenced by counselors' ability. On the other hand, since counselors were in both conditions there may have been influenced by Janet to favor the self-disclosure condition (Janet was hypothesizing that the counselor self-disclosure condition would be superior to the control condition). This is a type of researcher allegiance bias (see Chapter 23). Second, there could be some concerns about the external validity of the study. That is, it may be artificial for counselors to self-disclose 5 times per session or to instruct counselors to not self-disclose. It could be that counselor self-disclosure is a process that is best to not control, but rather may happen naturally. Third, not all counselor self-disclosures are equal in impact or depth. For example, a counselor who self-discloses that he/she/they have children may have a different impact than a counselor who self-discloses that he/she/they experienced sexual trauma while growing up. Accordingly, it can be difficult to truly "control" or "manipulate" the independent variable in some process research.

Let's now consider a great actual example of experimental counseling process research from Høglend et al.'s (2006, 2011) study on transference interpretations in psychodynamic treatment. The independent variable, transference interpretations, was defined by the following techniques:

> (a) The therapist was to address transactions in the patient–therapist relationship; (b) the therapist was to encourage exploration of thoughts and feelings about the therapy and therapist including repercussions on the transference by high therapist activity; (c) the therapist was to encourage the patient to discuss how he or she believed the therapist might feel or think about him or her; (d) the therapist was to include himself or herself explicitly in interpretive linking of dynamic elements (conflicts), direct manifestations of transference, and also allusions to the transference; and (e) the therapist was to interpret repetitive interpersonal patterns (including genetic interpretations) and link these patterns to transactions between the patient and the therapist. The first three techniques are not interpretations per se, but preparatory interventions. In contrast, in the comparison group, the therapist consistently focused on interpersonal relationships outside of therapy as the basis for similar interventions (extratransference work) and did not link these patterns to the interaction between the patient and the therapist. (Høglend et al., 2011, p. 699)

The independent variable consisted of two conditions. The first condition consisted of 52 clients who received low to moderate transference interpretations during their psychodynamic therapy, and the second conditions consisted of 48 clients who received psychodynamic therapy that did not have transference interpretations. The clients were randomized to one of the two conditions, and were treated by one of seven therapists, based on the therapist availability in their caseload (i.e., when a therapist has an opening in his or her caseload to treat a new client). As such, clients were randomized to condition, but not therapist. Additionally, it was not assured that therapists treated a similar number of clients in each condition (i.e., some therapists treated as few as 10 clients, whereas other therapists treated up to 17 clients).

The researchers also utilized a manipulation check (see Chapter 11) by having raters who did not know which condition they were observing code four or five videos for each client in the study (the mean number of sessions attended was 34). They rated the sessions for the use of transference interpretations on a scale ranging from 0 (not at all used), 2 (moderately used) to 4 (very much used). In the transference interpretation condition there was a moderate amount of transference interpretations (mean = 1.70, standard deviation = .70). In the comparison group, there was a very few (almost no) transference interpretations utilized (mean = .10, standard deviation = .20). By examining the use (or lack thereof) of transference interpretations, along with the clear difference between the two conditions provides more credence in the independent variable being a key mechanism of change.

The dependent variables in this study included four measures of psychological functioning, including interpersonal functioning and symptom change. They found no significant differences on any of their dependent variables by the end of treatment. However, they found an interesting difference in counseling outcomes based on a pretreatment measure that they believed might play a role. More specifically, they administered a measure of quality of object relations, which assesses a history of mature interpersonal relationships. Those clients who reported a low quality of object relations tended to have better outcomes when they were in the transference interpretation condition as compared to clients who also had low quality of object relations but were in the no-transference interpretation condition. These results point to the importance of examining counseling processes within the context of who is receiving the process. That is, some counseling processes are not likely to affect all clients in the same manner. Indeed, Høglend et al. (2006) could have concluded that transference interpretations did very little to aid treatment outcomes, if they did not consider important client factors along with transference interpretations.

RESEARCH APPLICATION 21.2

Think about a counseling process variable that you would like to test. There are many process variables that are likely of interest to you, but for this exercise just select one. The goal here is design an experimental study: (a) define your process variable; (b) describe how you would measure your process variable (e.g., whose perspective, how often); (c) describe the necessary conditions (e.g., types of treatment) needed to test your process variable; (d) describe how you would randomize the clients (or counselors) to the conditions; (e) define your outcome variable, and why it should be related to the process variable; and (f) describe what ethical concerns could arise from your study.

As mentioned previously, experimental counseling process studies are not very common. This is largely due to the difficulty of actually manipulating the independent variable, such as empathy or alliance. Accordingly, correlational designs are one of the most commonly utilized designs in counseling process research.

Correlational Counseling Process Designs

The classic counseling process-outcome correlational design consists of (a) measuring clients' psychological functioning prior to the start of treatment and at the end of treatment (i.e., pretreatment to posttreatment change equals counseling outcomes), (b) measuring the counseling process during the course of treatment (e.g., at Session 3), and (c) correlating the counseling process with the counseling outcome (i.e., correlating the counseling process with the end of the treatment ratings of client psychological functioning, after controlling for the precounseling ratings of client psychological functioning). For example, Lo Coco et al. (2011) examined the association between client and therapist ratings of the real relationship and counseling outcomes. The real relationship is a facet of the therapeutic relationship and is defined as "the personal relationship existing between two or more people reflected in the degree to which each is genuine with the other and perceives and experiences the other in ways that befit the other" (Gelso, 2009, pp. 254–255). Fifty clients rated their perceptions of the real relationship at third session and also completed a measure of psychological functioning at pretreatment and posttreatment. Therapists also completed a measure of the real relationship. The authors found clients' ratings of the real relationship significantly predicted counseling outcomes, but the same was not true for therapist ratings of the real relationship. That is, clients' ratings (but not therapists' ratings) of the real relationship predicted counseling outcomes at the end of treatment. This is a good example of how utilizing multiple raters of the counseling process can lead to different conclusions.

As mentioned previously, not all counseling process studies correlate a process measure with counseling outcomes. For example, Mallinckrodt, Porter, and Kivilighan (2005) examined the association among several client factors and counseling process variables. In particular, they were interested in the association between clients' attachment to their counselor and the working alliance. Client attachment styles were based on the general models of adult attachment theory and were defined as:

> (a) *Secure*—clients perceive their therapist as a comforting presence who is responsive, sensitive, and emotionally available; (b) *Avoidant–Fearful*—clients are reluctant to make personal disclosures, feel threatened or humiliated in sessions, and suspect that their therapist is disapproving and likely to be rejecting if displeased; and (c) *Preoccupied–Merger*—clients long for more contact and to be "at one" with their therapist, wish to expand the relationship beyond the bounds of therapy, and wish to be their therapist's "favorite" client. (p. 87)

The authors assessed these counseling process variables between Sessions 4 and 9 for the majority of the clients in the two samples ($n = 38$, $n = 44$) they collected data. They found very high correlations between secure attachment to the counselor and the working alliance (Sample 1, $r = .69$, Sample 2, $r = .84$). The correlations for avoidant-fearful attachment to the counselor and the working alliance were not as strong, but still large sized effects, and logically in the opposite direction from the correlation for secure attachment and the working alliance (Sample 1, $r = -.62$, Sample 2, $r = -.56$). The last subscale, preoccupied-merger attachment demonstrated the lowest and nonsignificant correlation with the working alliance (Sample 1, $r = -.13$, Sample 2, $r = .12$). These associations suggest that the working alliance and clients' secure attachment to their counselor are quite similar almost to the point of redundancy (see Chapter 18 for attenuation formulas). However, the other attachment subscales demonstrated less connection to the working alliance, especially preoccupied/merger subscale. This latter association between preoccupied/merger-alliance suggests that clients may desire to have a stronger connection with their counselor, but may not be capable of doing so (or at least perceive that to be case). The avoidant-fearful attachment-alliance correlation suggests that those who are less willing to engage with their counselor also perceive that the alliance (e.g., engaging in the process of therapy collaboratively) is strained.

Although correlational counseling process designs may seem simple, they can grow in complexity as we consider the impact of counselors in the counseling process. In particular, in most studies, counselors treat more than one client (as this mirrors everyday practice). This provides a great opportunity for counseling process researchers. Specifically, researchers can test whether clients of the same therapist have a similar experience (as evidenced by similar scores on a process measure, such as the working alliance inventory). In this way, we would expect that clients of the same counselor would have similar, yet different, experiences with their counselor; however, we would not expect that clients of the same counselor to be as consistent as external observers who are rating the exact same session (see following for further discussion of multilevel modeling).

Moreover, one of the basic assumptions in most statistical analyses is that the observations of one participant are independent of the observations of the other participants. Given that clients of the same counselor are more likely to have a similar experience, as compared to clients of a different counselor, then researchers need to identify a way to deal with this dilemma. To better illustrate this point, Figure 21.1 displays three counselors who each treated 10 clients. Counselor 1 had good outcomes with 8 of the 10 clients (i.e., he or she reported clinically significant change by the end of treatment). Counselor 2 had good outcomes with half of the clients. Counselor 3 was less effective and only had 2 of 10 clients report clinically significant change. What this example demonstrates is that who the counselor is can be an important consideration when designing studies as the experience of the clients are clearly impacted by the counselor they were assigned. Although this example is purposively extreme, the research on therapist effects clearly demonstrates that some therapists are better than others in facilitating positive counseling outcomes as well as executing various counseling processes (see Baldwin & Imel, 2013; Owen, 2013).

FIGURE 21.1 Client and Counselor Interdependency

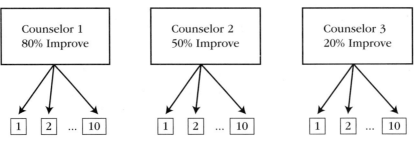

Note: Each counselor treated 10 clients. Counselor 1 had 8 out of 10 clients improve, whereas Counselor 2 had 5 out of 10 clients improve, and counselor 3 had 2 out of 10 clients improve.

As a more concrete example of how counselors can impact a study, Baldwin, Wampold, and Imel (2007) disentangled the counselor and client contribution to the correlation between client-rated alliance and counseling outcome. That is, the alliance-outcome correlation includes multiple contributions. For example, some clients may be more able or willing to form collaborative bonds with their counselor as compared to other clients. Additionally, some counselors may be better able to facilitate a high quality alliance across a range of clients as compared to other counselors. Of course, there could be an interaction between clients and counselors; wherein some counselors may be better able to form better alliances with those clients who generally are more capable of forming those alliance (see DeRubeis et al., 2005, for further discussion).

In a sample of 331 clients and 80 counselors, Baldwin et al. (2007) tested whether counselors' aggregate alliance score was related to client outcomes to determine whether those therapists who generally had better alliances with their clients also had better outcomes. This aggregate score was essentially the mean working alliance for each counselor based on the ratings of the therapist's clients—that is, the aggregate alliance is an indicator of the counselors' ability to form working alliances with a range of clients. If the mean alliance across clients is high, then the counselor is able to form a strong alliance across a range of clients, as compared, say, with a therapist with a relatively low mean alliance. They also examined the association between clients' ratings of alliance to counseling outcomes as compared to the other clients of the same counselor. This second estimate provides a counselor-specific comparison—clients of the same counselor are compared to one another. Thus, the data in this study has two levels: (a) counselor level and (b) client level. This makes intuitive sense to separate these levels, as counselors can have a specific impact on outcomes and so can clients.

Similar to the Lo Coco et al. (2011) study, Baldwin et al. (2007) assessed clients' psychological distress at pre- and postcounseling and they assessed clients' perspectives of the working alliance at Session 3 or 4. If Baldwin et al. (2007) were to not separate these two estimates, their findings would have been consistent with previous studies. That is, they found a partial correlation between client-rated alliance and counseling outcomes was $r = -.21$, after adjusting for precounseling distress. The negative correlation was due to the outcome measure, as it was a measure of psychological distress (where lower scores indicate less distress). This finding is slightly lower, but not too far off, than the average estimate of 190 independent studies, $r = .28$ (Horvath et al., 2011). Given this, they would have concluded that clients who rated their alliance with their counselor higher at Session 3 had better counseling outcomes. However, the results were a bit more complicated than this simple conclusion.

Specifically, they found that counselors who on average were better able to form strong alliances with their clients also had clients who had better outcomes as compared to other counselors. Said in a different way, counselors who were rated as having stronger alliances at third session, on average, had clients with better outcomes by the end of treatment. Thus, client ratings of their counselor were important as it differentiated between those counselors who were best at facilitating strong alliance and outcomes. However, as seen in Figure 21.2, clients' ratings of

FIGURE 21.2 Therapist Effects the Association between Alliance and Outcome

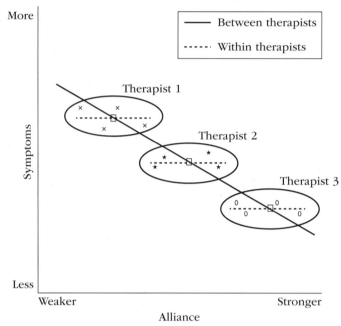

Source: Baldwin et al., 2007

the alliance were not associated with better outcomes as compared to other clients of the same counselor. This association is represented by the horizontal regression lines within each counselor's caseload in the figure. In other words, differences in alliances within a counselor's caseload were not related to outcome. Thus, it is the counselor's contribution to the alliance, rather than the client's contribution, that is related to outcome. Consequently, this study demonstrated an important lesson regarding the alliance-outcome association, namely that counselors have a large role in facilitating and maintaining high quality alliances, which ultimately impacts counseling outcomes. The more general point is that a process variable, whether alliance, empathy, or skill level, is due to both client and counselor contributions. The total correlation of the process variable and outcome may be due to either the counselor's contribution or to the client's contribution.

One area of the counseling process that has received more attention as a process variable is counselors' adherence to the treatment method. Adherence describes the degree to which counselor-client dyads participate in a specified approach (Sharpless & Barber, 2009; Waltz et al. 1993; Webb, DeRubeis, & Barber, 2010). Adherence is an important counseling process as Imel and Wampold (2008) noted: "If a specific ingredient offered in a treatment is critical to the success of the treatment, the degree to which the therapist adheres to the treatment protocol should be related to the outcome" (p. 253). In randomized clinical trials, the independent variable is the treatment provided; thus, adherence to the treatment manual is critical to ensure that the independent variable is truly in the control of the researcher. In contrast to medication where a dose can be specified, counseling is likely more variable. Thus, adherence speaks to whether the treatment is delivered in a uniformed manner (e.g., each client receives the same treatment) and is done in a specified manner (e.g., the treatment is conducted in a way that is specific to particular treatment protocols). If adherence is not consistent, then it raises questions to whether the independent variable is really what it is purported to be. Historically, researchers utilized manipulation-check measures to assess whether counselors were actually employing the treatment in a manner that is consistent with the original intention (e.g., is cognitive therapy being performed in a manner that is consistent with the treatment manual?). Now these types of measures are utilized to assess what techniques and how consistently these techniques are being implemented in treatment protocols.

As seen in the Høglend et al. (2006) study, high levels of adherence can be achieved; however, it becomes more challenging when the independent variable is not just one technique. For example, Imel et al. (2011) examined the counselors' adherence to the use of motivational enhancement therapy (MET) techniques. They examined whether the counselors adhered to the MET manual in a sample of 79 clients who were treated by 12 counselors. The clients attended three sessions of MET for substance use concerns. Independent raters coded the counseling sessions to ensure that counselors adhered to MET. If adherence to MET was high, then they should have found consistency across clients who were treated by the same counselor, as well as consistency across counselors in their use of MET. Yet, they found that counselors were quite variable in their adherence to the MET manual, such that counselors do not deliver the same treatment to clients within their caseload. In particular, some counselors were very inconsistent in their use of MET as compared to other counselors.

This study provides a very useful reminder that the independent variable in many counseling outcome experimental designs may not be as controlled as once thought. That is, if the counselors were not delivering the treatment in a consistent way, what were they doing? This level of variability may be a sign of flexibility and responsiveness to clients' needs (see Owen & Hilsenroth, 2014). However, it calls into question whether randomized clinical trials, which purport to control the independent variable (i.e., the treatment process), are truly valid.

As mentioned previously, technology is advancing the ways in which we can examine microprocesses in psychotherapy. Historically, researchers would examine the degree to which clients and counselors moved in their chairs to be an indicator of restlessness (i.e., anxiety) and potential countertransference. However, as biological and cognitive models of psychology have advanced, so have the ways in which researchers have examined microcounseling processes. For example, Imel et al. (2014) examined vocal synchrony (based on the symmetry of fundamental frequency levels) between counselors and clients. They did so to determine whether vocal synchrony would be able to discern those sessions where external raters coded the session as high or low in counselor empathy. They defined vocal aspects by "mean fundamental frequency" which is a measure of the "vibration created by the vocal folds in the throat and corresponds to the lowest harmonic produced during speech" (Kappas, Hess, & Scherer, 1991, p. 147). Clearly, the technology to assess this level of vocal quality requires expertise; however, these ratings are likely more precise and have their foundation in basic science. Indeed, Imel et al. (2014) found that high levels of counselor empathy were linked to counselor-client vocal synchrony, which seems to suggest that there are important nuances in the ways that counselors communicate with clients as compared to the content of their words in a session.

Longitudinal Counseling Process Designs

Should counselors utilize exploratory questions before they offer interpretations? Do changes in the working alliance in the early phase of treatment relate to counseling outcomes later on? Should counselors be mindful of the timing of implementing certain techniques? These are the type of questions that can be addressed with time-series counseling process studies. Indeed, counseling processes unfold over time in a way where counselors and clients find the best fit of explorative, supportive, and challenging interventions to facilitate change. Thus, the timing of interventions can be important to consider (see Crits-Christoph & Connelley, 2003). Yet, interventions are nestled within a therapeutic relationship (see Barber et al., 2008; Owen & Hilsenroth, 2011). Accordingly, it is important to examine any counseling process within the context of therapeutic relationship elements that also evolves over time. Clearly, all of these moving parts add to the complexity of time-series designs (e.g., as the therapeutic relationship develops, how does that influence counselors' use of techniques?). Consequently, process researchers should be mindful of the counseling processes necessary and sufficient for achieving positive counseling outcomes *over the course of the treatment process.*

At the same time, not all changes in counseling are linear. For example, the working alliance may not be best captured in one session, or the average of four sessions. Rather, for some client-counselor dyads there are ebbs and flows of the alliance (i.e., rupture-repair), wherein some sessions the client and counselor are on the same page, and in other sessions they are on different pages (see Safran & Muran, 2000; Stiles et al., 2004). Given the multitude of variations within the counseling processes, how should one proceed?

Time-series designs can take many forms in counseling process research. Commonly, time-series designs examine whether a process variable changes over time (and whether those changes are associated with counseling outcomes; see Chapter 20 for discussion of linear and quadratic change). For example, researchers could examine whether client ratings of the alliance vary across the course of treatment, and if these changes are signs of positive outcomes or not. In the example mentioned previously, Baldwin et al. (2007) only assessed clients' perspectives of the alliance at Session 3. But obtaining more alliance assessment from other sessions could have provided additional information about the ways in which the alliance changes (or providing evidence that the alliance is rather stable).

For example, Owen et al. (in press) examined 2,990 military adolescents who were treated by 98 counselors for issues related to substance use, or risk factors for substance use (i.e., preventive efforts). They examined how the working alliance changed over the first seven sessions and whether these changes were associated with counseling outcomes. Similar to Baldwin et al. (2007), they separated the client and counselor contributions to the association between changes in the working alliance and counseling outcomes. They found that clients who reported growth in their working alliance had better outcomes as compared to other clients. Counselors who on average had clients who demonstrated growth in their working alliance scores also had clients with better outcomes. These results suggest that counselors should examine the degree to which youth clients' working alliance ratings are improving in the early phases of therapy in an effort to better ensure positive treatment outcomes. In contrast, Owen et al. also compared whether a single session of the working alliance (e.g., measuring the working alliance at Session 5) would produce a similar correlation with counseling outcomes as compared to the association between changes in the working alliance over the first seven sessions and counseling outcomes. The changes in the working alliance explained nearly 10% of the variance in counseling outcomes; whereas the single session of the working alliance only accounted for approximately 4% of the variance in counseling outcomes.

RESEARCH IN ACTION 21.1

As discussed in Chapter 12, time-series designs can be used to determine whether the introduction of a new process could influence counseling outcomes. Consider the following example: a researcher wants to examine whether the use of homework assignments (specifically, watching one movie a week) will affect couples' relationship happiness over the course of counseling. The researcher proposes to continue to monitor couples' relationship happiness over the course of counseling. The researcher decides to assign this homework starting in Session 5.

Questions

What type of time series-design is this?

What is the independent variable?

What is the dependent variable?

What are the limitations of this design?

What alterations to this design could be done to increase claims of causality?

Qualitative Counseling Process Designs

Qualitative designs are frequently utilized to better understand counseling processes. As discussed in Chapter 16, there are many different approaches to conduct qualitative research (e.g., CQR, grounded theory). The use of qualitative methods can help illuminate more specifically the experiences of clients or counselors. For example, Hill et al. (2008) examined the process of immediacy, or comments about how the counselor feels about the client, or comments regarding what is occurring between the client and counselor in the moment. Although she utilized a mixed methods approach, for this illustration we will focus on the qualitative aspects of their study.

Specifically, Hill et al. (2008) utilized consensual qualitative research (CQR) to analyze the case of one client. The research team transcribed and watched each of the 17 sessions between a White heterosexual, 55-year-old male counselor and an African American lesbian, 29-year-old female client. The research team stopped the tape and came to consensus about their responses to four questions: "(a) Who initiated the immediacy? (b) What type of immediacy was it? (c) What were the effects of immediacy? and (d) Why was immediacy used?" (p. 302). Utilizing this methodology, they concluded that seven most commonly utilized immediacy interventions "enabled the therapist and client to negotiate the relationship, helped the client express her immediate feelings to the therapist, helped the client open up to deeper exploration of concerns, and provided the client with a corrective relational experience" (p. 298).

This is a great example of how qualitative research can be utilized to deepen our understanding of a clinical process. Although this example only included one case, most qualitative research involves in-depth interviews/analysis of multiple clients, albeit with fewer participants than most quantitative studies.

Research Design Meets Data Analysis

Now that we have reviewed four common research designs for counseling process research, we will turn our attention to some of the core methodological issues that are common across these designs. Suppose that in carefully designing a process study you have identified specific variables within several focused research questions that interest you. You have also deliberated on what to measure and from whose perspective, and you have decided how much to measure. Now another major issue looms—how to analyze the process data? Although it is tempting to wait until you have collected the data, we strongly recommend that you think carefully about how you will analyze the data *before* they are collected. As researchers think through various issues related to data analysis, they may realize that more participants are needed, or that the data need to be collected more frequently. Thus, it is important to think through the issues related to data analysis while designing a process study; rather than post hoc, and when it may be impossible to then collect additional data, which would greatly strengthen the study.

The data analysis might involve a wide range of activities, depending on the nature of the data (see Hill & Lambert, 2004). Qualitative data might require non-parametric statistics, or perhaps categorizing data in the form of events by independent judges (see Chapter 16). Quantitative data might involve a range of statistical procedures, such as analysis of variance and correlations, or more complex designs such as sequential analysis and multilevel modeling. Because process researchers typically have a lot of data (maybe even over 11,000 data points!), the data will need to be summarized or reduced in a way that still allows appropriate analysis. Although this book is not a book on data analysis, we will briefly discuss statistical strategies to analyze quantitative data in counseling process research.

There are many approaches to analyzing process research data. However, we will only discuss various methods as they relate to the research design. At the most basic level, researchers could use a bivariate correlation to assess the association between process variables and counseling outcomes (or other process variables). As mentioned previously, Mallinckrodt et al. (2005) found a bivariate correlation of .84 between clients' secure attachment to therapist and clients' perspective of the working alliance. As the saying goes, correlation does not equal causation; thus, this finding could suggest that those clients who report a more secure attachment with their counselors are better able to form higher quality alliances. Alternatively, those clients who report higher quality alliances are more likely to develop secure attachment with their therapists.

Similar to bivariate correlations, a *t* test (for two groups) or ANOVA (for three or more groups) can test whether there are differences on a variable. Returning to Janet's study (mentioned in the beginning of this chapter) of counselor self-disclosure, she had an independent variable that had two conditions (5 self-disclosures vs. no self-disclosures). Thus, if she wanted to examine clients' psychological functioning at the end of treatment, then she could utilize a *t* test to determine whether the scores in the two conditions were different from one another. If she wanted to control for the variance of other variables, then she could conduct an ANCOVA. For example, she allowed the counselors to conduct treatment in the way they normally would have, with the notable exception of the use of counselor self-disclosures. Accordingly, she might want to control for the effects of number of sessions attended to help rule out this confound using an ANCOVA.

An alternative way of examining the relationship between counselor behavior and client response is time-series analysis (which is also referred to as sequential or autoregressive analyses; also see Wampold & Kim, 1989), a set of statistical techniques that examine the mutual influence of counselor and client behaviors. For example, sequential analysis can be used to examine the likelihood of a client response (e.g., self-disclosure) given a prior counselor response (e.g., interpretation). At a more sophisticated level, sequential analyses can examine issues such as control and power (i.e., is the counselor's response made more predictable by knowing the client's preceding response, or vice versa?).

One example of the use of time-series analysis with the working alliance and counseling outcome data is from Zilcha-Mano et al. (2014). The main question they wanted to examine was whether the working alliance was the result of improvements in psychological functioning (i.e., I feel engaged in counseling because I am feeling better) or whether the working alliance resulted in better psychological functioning (i.e., I am feeling better because I am engaged in my counseling). This is a classic question of what came first, the chicken or the egg.

Zilcha-Mano et al. (2014) assessed clients' perspectives of the working alliance and their psychological functioning every session. As seen in Figure 21.3, they approached this analysis by examining the immediate association between the working alliance and psychological functioning from session to session. More specifically, in Part I of their model, they predicted clients' current sessions depression score by using the clients' previous session depression score and the working alliance score. For example, clients' second session working alliance and depression scores would predict their third session *working alliance* scores. Then, clients' third session working alliance and depression scores would predict fourth session *working alliance* scores, and so on. In Part II of the model, they predicted clients'

FIGURE 21.3 Autoregressive Cross-Lagged Model

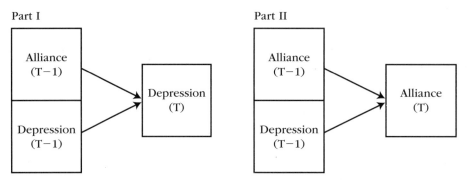

Note: T = time, T − 1 = time − 1 session. For example, clients' second session alliance and depression scores would predict their third session alliance scores. Then, clients' third session alliance and depression scores would predict fourth session alliance scores, and so on.

current session working alliance by clients' previous session working alliance score and depression score. For example, clients' second session working alliance and depression scores would predict their third session *depression* scores. Then, clients' third session working alliance and depression scores would predict fourth session *depression* scores, and so on for each subsequent session. They found that previous session working alliance scores and depression scores were significant predictors of next session depression scores (Part II of the model). However, only previous session working alliance scores were a significant predictor of subsequent session working alliance scores (Part I of the model). Simply, clients' perspective of the working alliance aids in the prediction of their psychological functioning; however, clients' psychological functioning adds little to the prediction of the quality of the working alliance. In sum, time-series analyses can be very useful to identify the influence of multiple process variables on counseling outcomes.

Another critical statistical issue that confronts many counseling process researchers involves the analysis of process variables collected over time. Growth modeling, also known as growth curve analysis, offers a powerful alternative method for analyzing repeated assessments of counseling process data (see Chapter 20 for example of growth curve modeling). For example, if a linear growth model is used in group counseling research, each group will have (a) an intercept term that represents that group's process score (e.g., level of cohesion) at a particular time, and (b) a slope term that represents the linear change in the group's process score (e.g., cohesion) over time.

From a research design perspective, it is important to understand a priori how many time points one needs to estimate the growth they anticipate. For example, if a researcher would like to determine whether the alliance changes in a curvilinear manner (e.g., perhaps starting with positive linear growth for the first three sessions, then decline for the next three sessions, then rebound with linear growth for the next three), then the researcher will need to have at least nine time points of data collection. There are also some concerns when fitting a growth model. We will provide a fictitious example of a client who reported his/her/their

FIGURE 21.4 Change in Alliance Scores Over Time

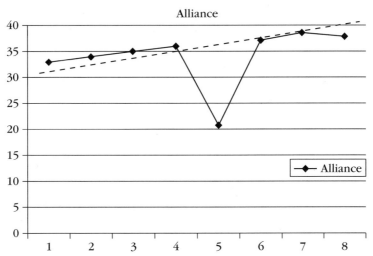

Note: This graph displays the alliance score of one client over the course of 8 sessions. The possible alliance score ranges from 0 to 40. The dashed line represents the estimated growth in alliance if a linear growth pattern was estimated. The solid line represents the actual scores.

working alliance scores for the first eight sessions of counseling (see Figure 21.4). As seen in the figure, this client's working alliance score was generally positive, and grew in a linear manner. This linear growth is denoted by a dashed line. Said differently, if a researcher attempted to fit this data to a linear growth model, then it is highly likely that this would be supported (e.g., the model would be statistically significant or the predicted model would correspond nicely to the observed data). However, this client reported a drop in the working alliance at Session 5, which rebounded by Session 6. This pattern could be a sign of a rupture in the working alliance that was repaired (see Safran & Muran, 2000, for discussion of rupture-repair cycles). If the researcher only examined linear growth, this deviation would not have been captured. Yet, this deviation could be quite meaningful from a clinical and research standpoint. For example, it could be that the rupture-repair cycle is the key marker of successful outcomes as compared to slow linear growth in alliance scores. Accordingly, it is important for researchers to screen their data prior to running growth models. Most importantly, time-series designs can be a very useful way to identify how *changes* over the course of counseling are related to outcomes.

Another common issue in counseling studies is the issue of nested data. For example, in the Baldwin et al. (2007) study that we discussed earlier, there were two levels of data (clients who were nested within their counselors). In terms of research design, this creates two levels of data, both of which need to be considered in terms of statistical power. For example, if a researcher were interested in therapists' aggregate working alliance quality, as in the Baldwin et al. example, then the researcher would need a sufficient number of therapists. Although the number of therapists is one consideration, there also should be a consideration of how many clients per therapist. For example, therapists' aggregate working alliance ability is based on the mean alliance score from their clients. Thus, if therapists only treated two clients each, then therapists' aggregate working alliance ability score might not be as representative as if therapists treated 25 clients each. Statistical power is an important consideration in all studies, as sometimes true differences exist, but the differences are difficult to find with smaller samples. Thus, increasing the sample size allows a greater likelihood of finding the difference, if it truly exists. For a full discussion of multilevel modeling (and statistical power) in counseling and psychotherapy, see Adelson and Owen (2012).

SUMMARY AND CONCLUSIONS

This chapter provided a general introduction to counseling process research, or investigations that examine events that occur within the therapeutic encounter. Researchers have examined a very wide range of activities, such as therapist self-disclosure, client reactions, the working alliance, perceived therapist empathy, client openness, and various interventions (e.g., interpretations). In the first part of the chapter, we discussed Hill's (1991) scheme for classifying the various behaviors within process research, which consists of the following seven types of behaviors: (a) ancillary behaviors, (b) verbal behaviors, (c) covert behaviors, (d) content, (e) strategies, (f) interpersonal manner, and (g) the therapeutic relationship. The discovery of new knowledge pertaining to these categories of counseling process research can be exhilarating.

Most of the counseling process research over the years has focused on individual counseling with European American participants; however, there is a growth in studies with minority clients. Although much has been learned about the counseling process in the past 50 years, many basic research questions relative to various ethnic and nonethnic minority populations remain.

We also highlighted methodological and measurement issues that are particularly relevant for counseling process researchers: (a) what to study, (b) what to measure, (c) whose perspective, (d) how much to measure, and (e) coding and analysis considerations. We maintained that it is very important for researchers to be very careful in selecting behaviors to examine in process research; examination of various classification schemes (see, e.g., Elliott, 1991; Hill, 1991) might help guide researchers. In addition, it is important to consider at what level the researcher wants to examine the behaviors, from statement-by-statement speech acts to more global levels. Research clearly documents that the counseling process differs across various perspectives, such as from the client, counselor, or observer perspective. We encourage researchers to carefully think about the different perspectives in developing research questions, and if appropriate, to examine the counseling process from multiple perspectives.

In determining how much to measure, it is critical to think through the research questions very carefully; it may be useful to include individual differences or time intervals in the research questions. With group designs, sampling a part of several sessions will likely yield acceptable results, whereas single-subject designs may need to examine the entire session without sampling. Finally, in terms of analyzing the data, we highlighted common design consideration for data analysis. We are very fortunate to have learned so much about counseling process over the past 60 years and clearly there is much more to learn.

STIMULUS QUESTIONS

An Exercise to Analyze Two Counseling Process Studies

The following exercise is designed to help readers not only to become more aware of the intricacies of counseling process research, but also to become more aware of different types of counseling process methods.

First, identify two published articles that investigated the counseling process. One article should employ quantitative methods and the second qualitative methods. Study these two articles, and then respond to the following questions. In addition, if you want, ask a peer to join you in this exercise; independently respond to the questions for the same two articles, and then discuss and compare your responses.

1. What constructs or variables were investigated in each article?
2. How were the constructs or variables for each of these two articles measured or assessed?
3. How adequately do you think the constructs/variables were measured or assessed?
4. From whose perspective was the counseling process examined?
5. What were the pros and cons of examining the counseling process from these perspectives?
6. What were the pros and cons of the quantitative and the qualitative methodologies used across the two articles?
7. What conclusions were drawn from each article about the counseling process?
8. What limitations do you see about the conclusions from each study?
9. What would be some exciting "next best studies" to follow each of the two process articles?
10. What types of methodologies would you use to conduct those studies, and why?

Program Evaluation: Applying Science and Practice to Real Life

With Matrese Benkofske and Clyde C. Heppner

The focus of this book is on research design, its application in the counseling profession, and the conditions needed to conduct quality research. Turning to a slightly different topic, this chapter describes program evaluation—what it is, how it is similar to and differs from counseling research, and how it is used within counseling settings. The chapter describes in considerable detail the phases of program evaluation. The first step is to define program evaluation.

PROGRAM EVALUATION DESCRIBED

Program evaluation and research share a number of similarities and have key differences. Whereas researchers are typically most interested in enhancing the profession's knowledge base, such as comparing the efficacy of two particular treatments, program evaluators are most interested in the effectiveness of a particular program for a particular group of people. To illustrate some of the primary features of program evaluation, and how it differs from research, we will start with an example. Suppose that an evaluator has been contracted to provide a program evaluation for a program designed to strengthen family relationships via psychoeducation and group counseling.

Program evaluators ideally want to be involved while programs are being designed. For example, if an evaluator is contracted to evaluate a program that is going to be implemented in a particular community, that evaluator would want to be involved during planning meetings. Through this involvement, the evaluator might learn that the community and neighborhood citizenry want the counselors to come from the community so that they would be sensitive to the families' cultural differences and needs. However, this could have both positive and negative effects on the program's outcomes: If counselors are culturally sensitive, program recipients may be more likely to disclose to them so that real progress can occur, but the families may be so familiar with the counselors that they feel uncomfortable talking with a "friend" about their parenting style. By being present during the planning meetings and knowing the community's requirement of selecting only local counselors, an evaluator could be sure to include "level of familiarity between counselor and client" as a variable in the project.

By being involved during the planning stage, evaluators also learn more about how the particular counseling treatment was chosen. Perhaps it was the only counseling treatment considered or perhaps several counseling treatments were identified, and this particular treatment was judged by the community's counseling professionals as most likely to be most effective with families living in this particular community given its characteristics (e.g., a high rate of poverty and racial disparities in high school graduation rates). In short, for program evaluators, knowing how a particular counseling treatment was chosen and what outcomes it can be expected to deliver has a direct impact on the choice of outcome measures. It then becomes an evaluator's responsibility to determine if there is a match among the treatment, the anticipated outcomes, and the outcome measures.

After the program has begun, the evaluator typically carefully monitors the data collection procedures to ensure that the evaluation measures (e.g., the measures that will be used to provide outcome information to the evaluator) are administered prior to the first counseling session. In addition, the evaluator periodically checks the family's file to record each time a family attends counseling and to ensure that the family completes the evaluation measures each month. During these visits the evaluator also makes various observations, including: How are families treated when they enter the center for counseling? Are the administrative staff friendly and welcoming, or disinterested and rude? This information may be needed if the evaluator finds a very high or a very low dropout rate at the program's end.

While at the center, the evaluator may also note who the clients are and whether they represent the targeted population. For example, if the program is designed to address the needs of family functioning, are all members of the family present for counseling? Perhaps the program evaluator should bring up in focus group discussions how important it is to have all family members involved in counseling and how the family and the ultimate success of counseling were affected when some family members did not participate in counseling. The evaluator might also raise the same issue with the counselors.

In addition to making periodic visits to the counseling site, the evaluator might also include home visits to observe the families before, during, and after the counseling sessions. Prior to these visits, the evaluator has worked with the counselors and program administrators to create a list of behaviors that would indicate that a family needs counseling in parenting skills and that the counseling has improved the family's interactions. After being pilot tested and then refined, this list would serve as an additional measure of change within each family.

By being actively involved in the program from conception to implementation, evaluators are in a position to (a) identify problems with the data collection procedures to minimize the risk of losing valuable data, (b) collect data to evaluate program effectiveness, (c) formulate and then test hypotheses that arise as the program matures, (d) document changes in the program's implementation over time, (e) give possible explanations for unanticipated results, and (f) document unanticipated positive outcomes. For the sake of this example, suppose that no significant difference in family functioning was detected upon review of all collected data at the end of the program. By being actively involved in the program, the program evaluator might, through a review of his or her field notes, be able to identify reasons for the lack of significant change in family functioning and assist in modifications of the program before implementing it again at the same or another site.

Or suppose instead that the evaluator identified significant differences in family functioning over time, but through discussions with the program recipients and observations at the treatment center, the evaluator ascertained that because the program was housed within a community center, the families also availed themselves of social services other than counseling. In that case, to say that the improvement in family functioning was due solely to the counseling program would be erroneous. Without being engaged in many aspects of the program, the program evaluator might incorrectly ascribe the effects to the counseling treatments alone.

By looking at this project from a program evaluator's perspective, several distinctions between research and program evaluation become evident. Whereas the goals of research are primarily to enhance the profession's knowledge base, the program evaluator's goal is to evaluate the effectiveness of a particular program with a defined group of participants. The researcher develops specific hypotheses and emphasizes internal and/or external validity; the program evaluator typically collects a wide range of data to determine whether an intervention was effective, and to formulate other hypotheses about the causes and effects that explain the outcomes. Whereas both researchers and evaluators carefully select assessment measures a priori, the program evaluator also collects a wide range of additional data as the program unfolds. Program evaluators are expected to use both their knowledge of research methods (as reviewed throughout the book) as well as observational methods developed and refined by anthropologists or cost/benefit analyses used in the business sector. Indeed, several authors (e.g., Committee on Prevention of Mental Disorders, 1994; Hage et al., 2007) have warned that researchers need to be competent in every aspect of the research process prior to embarking on research that includes program evaluation. Because program evaluation requires an extensive investment in time and resources and has the potential to impact large groups of individuals, it is essential that program evaluators are knowledgeable about research design, measurement, and analysis.

Program evaluation is utilized across disciplines. Evaluators have a wide range of professional experiences, content-related expertise, preferred data collection methodologies, formal training, and professional viewpoints. Program evaluation is often described as a process for judging the worth of a program relative to other alternatives, based on defensible, previously defined criteria (Scriven, 1980). Put another way, program evaluation is undertaken when a program's decision makers, recipients, funders, and/or managers want to determine whether a program is effective, to what degree, under what conditions, at what financial or social costs, and with what intentional or unintentional outcomes.

Perhaps because of its roots in education and testing, early program evaluations focused almost exclusively on measures of program recipients' progress after exposure to a program. For example, programs were developed to assess the mastery of life skills after participating in a program designed to increase those skills or to examine self-esteem increases among children who attended a particular after school program. Yet, as we saw in the previous example, much more than just the program's intended outcomes must be measured during an evaluation of a program. The environment, the population, the political climate, the needs of the community where the program is being implemented, the beliefs of program administrators as to the targeted population's needs, and many other factors (including previously unanticipated factors) play an integral role in defining the program and must be included in the evaluation of the program.

Program evaluation also has been conceptualized within the fields of counseling and counseling psychology as a mechanism to promote prevention (e.g., Albee, 2000; Hage et al., 2007; Romano, Koch, & Wong, 2012). Authors (e.g., Albee, 2000; Hage et al., 2007; Kiselica, 2001) have broadly defined prevention to include an emphasis on risk reduction, wellness, and social justice. As such, engagement in program evaluation aligns well with the counseling profession's emphasis on social justice, multiculturalism, and development in general.

Practitioners and scholars have used both program development and evaluation to address important social justice issues relevant to our field. For example, programs have been developed and evaluated to address such topics as personal and academic effectiveness with multiethnic youth (e.g., Cohen, Garcia, Apfel, & Master, 2006; Cohen, Garcia, Purdie-Vaughns, Apfel, & Brzustoski, 2009; Rivera-Mosquera, Phillips, Castelino, Martin, & Dobran, 2007; Vera et al., 2007), bullying (Espelage & Swearer, 2003; Newman-Carlson & Horne, 2004), and suicide prevention (e.g., May, Serna, Hurt, & DeBruyn, 2005). Yet, many counseling students are not often trained in the practice of program evaluation (e.g., Blustein, Goodyear, Perry, & Cypers, 2005; Hage et al., 2007; Matthews & Skowron, 2004). In this chapter, we describe the phases of program evaluation in an effort to highlight the importance of these activities and offer a starting place for training in these skills.

PHASES OF PROGRAM EVALUATION

The steps for conducting a program evaluation do not always follow a routine set of procedures. In essence, what an evaluation looks like—what aspects of a program it examines, what data are collected, and how its results are used—depends largely on what stage in the program the evaluation occurs. Typically people often think of doing an evaluation at the end of a program, and often this is when it in fact occurs, but as suggested previously, an evaluation can (and most often should) occur at one or a combination of four stages of a program: during conceptualization, design, implementation, or upon completion (Rossi & Freeman, 1999).

Starting with the framework presented by Herman, Morris, and Fitz-Gibbon (1987), an evaluator undertakes four phases of program evaluation, applicable at any stage of a program: (a) setting the boundaries of the evaluation, (b) selecting appropriate evaluation methods, (c) collecting and analyzing information, and

(d) reporting the findings. Within each of these four phases are specific steps, which we examine in the following sections.

Phase 1: Setting the Evaluation's Boundaries

This first phase entails (a) determining the purposes of the evaluation, (b) collecting background information about the program, (c) writing a description of the program and then ascertaining whether the evaluator's understanding matches that of others associated with the program, (d) making a preliminary agreement as to what the evaluation may include, and (e) coming to a final agreement concerning the program evaluator's role, and the specific services and final products the evaluator will provide. This same agreement also describes the resources available to the evaluator and a preliminary estimate of the costs associated with the evaluation.

During this initial phase, it is crucial that the evaluator understands the program, its mission, its scope, and its magnitude. The clearer the evaluator is as to what the program is designed to do, the less likely unforeseen issues will pop up after the evaluation's budget, time line, and methodology have been set. Much of the information about the program can be obtained by meeting with the program manager, but it is also wise to meet with others associated with the program—funders, program advocates, and perhaps even opponents—to get a broad view of the mission and scope of the program. The evaluator might request written summaries of the program to provide an initial understanding before these meetings.

The evaluator must define the population of interest at this phase of program evaluation. Sometimes, conducting a needs assessment is useful to allow the evaluator to obtain a clear sense of the needs of various stakeholders (e.g., funders, organizational staff, and the community). This phase also involves identifying and developing clear objectives for the program. The objectives must be measurable, ideally based upon theory, and supported by research evidence (Vera & Reese, 2000). Theory is used to guide an evaluator's understanding of the etiology of the problem, the anticipated mechanism of change, cultural components, and the best methods to address specific problems (Nation et al., 2003). Grounding one's work in theory and prior research guards against the potential for unintended negative consequences (Hage et al., 2007).

The programming must be culturally sensitive to the target population. This might include a need to focus on norms within the local community, cultural beliefs, and practices. If a program is perceived to be irrelevant to potential participants, participants are unlikely to participate or to maintain participation over time. One mechanism to help improve relevance is to include participants in the planning and implementation processes so as to ensure that needs are being recognized and addressed (Nation et al., 2003).

Utilizing the considerations in the preceding paragraphs (e.g., cultural sensitivity), we suggest the following questions to assist the evaluator in understanding the purpose of the program, the anticipated outcomes of the program, and the expected accomplishments of the program:

Research Application: Key Questions and Associated Rationale to Guide
Program Evaluation

Key Questions	Rationale
What are the program's objectives, and how will this program be implemented to address these objectives?	Knowledge of the program objectives is essential in order to link what the program was designed to accomplish and the measurable behaviors observed in the evaluation.
What will this program involve? How long will the program last? How many sessions will a participant typically attend? What type of techniques (e.g., intervention methods, evaluation methods) will be used?	This information helps the evaluator to shape the evaluation, the time line, and the types of statistics (nonparametric or parametric) used in the analyses.
What types of effects do program planners anticipate? When should these effects be measurable? Does the program manager anticipate long-term benefits of the program? What type of evidence would the program manager need to claim that the program's mission has been met?	Information about these questions enables the evaluator to tailor the evaluation methods to the informational needs of stakeholders and program planners alike.
Has anyone written a proposal for funding? Are any program requirements tied to program funding (e.g., including a segment of a special population as program recipients, paying program providers, or using some specific treatment in the program)? If, for example, the women's center on campus provided a portion of the program's funding, they may require the program to address issues identified by women students, such as child care availability for a few hours while attending class rather than paying for an entire day.	These kinds of stipulations can have dramatic implications on the evaluation design, and it is better to know this before the evaluation has been set in motion.
What is the funding level for the program, and how much has been set aside for the evaluation process?	A guideline used at times is that the funding for the evaluation should constitute approximately 10% of the cost of the program. This helps to prevent a very small project from having a far too expansive evaluation, and vice versa. Designers of programs often severely underestimate the cost of conducting a program evaluation.

(continued)

Research Application: Key Questions and Associated Rationale to Guide
Program Evaluation *(continued)*

Key Questions	Rationale
What are the program manager's expectations for the evaluation? Does the program manager have a preferred data collection strategy? What role will the evaluator play?	Some agencies have staff members capable of helping with data collection, which reduces the billing cost of the evaluation. In some cases, the program manager expects the evaluator to be highly visible throughout the program's direction. Knowing what the program manager feels comfortable with in terms of evaluator exposure helps in planning the evaluation.
Why is an evaluation of the program being undertaken? Do the funders require it? Have the outcome measures and the sampling procedures been predetermined?	Knowing the reasoning behind the evaluation enables the evaluator to tailor the evaluation to the needs of the program manager and stakeholders. For example, if the funders of the evaluation have clearly stated their objective, they typically expect measurable, and scientifically rigorous data to be collected in order to be considered for continued funding. Because of this, the evaluation will be different from one designed to help program implementers better serve and understand their clients.
What resources are available to the evaluator? Will staff help with data collection? Are interns or clerical help available? What types of records (e.g., medical, financial, academic) are available to the evaluator?	Knowing what resources are readily available enables the evaluator to select data sources that provide reliable and easily accessible, understandable data.

Among the many purposes of these questions, first and foremost the evaluator seeks to understand what the program is designed to do, what people associated with the program expect it to accomplish, and what outcomes or results are anticipated. The evaluator uses the answers to these questions to begin formulating a strategy for carrying out the evaluation. Moreover, the evaluator is trying to understand what aspects of the evaluation have already been arranged or agreed upon, and what aspects are yet to be determined.

Evaluators then work closely with program staff to select the intended delivery method of the program and of the evaluation. This decision also must be informed by prior research and theory. In other words, we need to know "what works with whom and under what circumstances." Cultural components, including the values of the intended population, assumptions inherent in the content or process of the chosen interventions, and cultural adaptations of existing interventions, must be considered when selecting the intended delivery method (Hage et al., 2007).

Nation et al. (2003) indicated that programs that include skill-based components and implement various teaching methods are most effective. For example, in developing programming related to decreasing binge drinking among college students, one must consider skills that are relevant to be targeted in the intervention such as assertiveness training, effective communication, and drinking refusal. Skills may be taught via use of a variety of methods (e.g., experiential learning, verbal learning) that are perceived to be meaningful, personal, and applicable.

Experienced evaluators also try to ascertain whether a request for an evaluation is sincere, or an attempt to "rubber stamp" a program as being a quality program. Novice evaluators, especially eager ones, often find themselves entangled in such situations. Our advice: Do not get involved. It may lead to the reputation that the evaluator will take any work, regardless of its merit. All evaluators wish they had never undertaken certain projects because they did not conduct the type of evaluation they had envisioned. Evaluators can use the following questions to determine whether they want to agree to an evaluation: Are there sufficient time and resources to conduct the evaluation? Do I have the needed resources, background knowledge, and time to commit to the evaluation? Typically, an evaluator need not be a content expert—that is, an expert in antibullying or binge drinking—to conduct the evaluation, but some program managers also rely on the evaluator to judge the worthiness of the treatment. If this is the case, and the evaluator is not an expert in the topic area, is there sufficient funding to hire a content expert, or will the program evaluator take on that role, too?

Evaluators cannot expect all of these questions to be answered fully. Not all programs are precisely defined, and many of these questions may not be answerable, especially during the initial planning. Although this leaves a lot of gray area for constant negotiation between the evaluator and the program designers, we suggest that evaluators come to a program during its planning phase because that allows them to integrate the evaluation's data collection procedures into the day-to-day operations of the program, rather than coming in after the program has begun. In the latter case, the data collection procedures become "add-ons" that are often viewed by already overworked staff as optional, as time fillers, or, worse yet, as mindless paperwork. But by asking these questions during the negotiations, the program evaluator is in a position to make an informed decision about whether or not to agree to conduct the evaluation.

During the initial meetings and throughout the evaluation process, the evaluator must develop the ability to listen to his or her intuition, "gut instincts," or "inner voice." Program evaluation is probably three-quarters science and one-quarter art. The art of program evaluation involves listening to and then coming to trust one's own intuition. Even though being a competent researcher, possessing above-average written and oral skills, and exhibiting excellent organizational skills will make for an above-average program evaluator, the ability to hear and then trust intuition is required for entering the ranks of the expert. A good program evaluator often carries a notebook for keeping notes of meetings, interactions, and observations—and to jot down impressions and insights as well. Even though many of these notes and insights are never acted upon, some of them—especially those that keep reappearing—become working hypotheses for further investigation and study. Keeping a log of these impressions, insights, and hunches, and reviewing them from time to time, can take an evaluation from a regurgitation of facts to a more complete understanding of a program, including its benefits and its deficits.

At the end of this first phase, an evaluator should have a good understanding of the program's objectives, how it will be implemented, the outcomes it is intended to accomplish, and a preliminary understanding of what the program designers anticipate the evaluation might entail. To help crystallize this understanding, the evaluator writes a description of the program, which has three purposes. First, by documenting on paper what he or she understands about the program, the evaluator can often identify loosely defined concepts or unanswered questions. Second, the evaluator should share this document with others in the program, as a reality check. Discussing points of disagreement often helps program designers identify and clarify fuzzy aspects of the program. Finally, this document can serve as the first section of the program report: the program description. The evaluator should include with the description a short memo stating that he or she has agreed to proceed with the evaluation, assuming that a final agreement can be reached concerning the cost and methodology of the evaluation. This memo can serve as an informal agreement until a more detailed one can be drafted.

Phase 2: Selecting Appropriate Evaluation Methods

During the second phase of the evaluation process, the focus moves from a description of the program and its objectives to the evaluation—how it will measure or provide information about the program's effects. One of the most difficult parts of conducting an evaluation is keeping the goals of the program evaluation in focus—concentrating on the primary goals of the evaluation that are important, and not being sidetracked by interesting but unimportant side issues. Taking specific steps to keep the program goals in focus is a crucial but sometimes forgotten task. The results of such an omission include wasting valuable time and resources collecting data on unimportant aspects of the program; causing anxiety, frustration, and tension between the evaluator and stakeholders as they sort out what is supposed to be included in the evaluation; missing opportunities to collect important data; and perhaps even entirely missing the aim/goals of the evaluation, such that the subsequent results are deemed useless. Every evaluator likely has, at one time or another, failed to adequately plan for an evaluation and has suffered the frustration, professional embarrassment, and perhaps even panic associated with scrambling to fill in gaps in the evaluation as the final report comes due. Enough forces and factors can often create a great deal of confusion—political posturing, incompetent program staff, belligerent program recipients, and funding cuts—potentially lurk around some evaluations to derail the program and its evaluation; this confusion does not need to be intensified by a poorly focused evaluation. The following seven steps are the key tasks in creating a focused evaluation.

Research Application: Seven Steps to Guide a Focused Evaluation

Steps	Evidence to Support That the Step Has Been Met
1. Solicit input from stakeholders and identify program goals.	
2. Design a plan for examining program implementation to achieve program goals.	
3. Design a plan for evaluating program progress toward program goals.	
4. Create a consolidated data collection plan to assess progress toward program goals.	
5. Plan the data analyses to examine program goals.	
6. Estimate the financial and time costs of the evaluation needed to meet program goals.	
7. Come to a final agreement about services, costs, and responsibilities with relevant stakeholders needed to reach program goals.	

Each task, along with relevant questions for the program evaluator to consider and examples, is described in detail in the sections that follow.

Step 1: Solicit Input from Stakeholders and Identify Program Goals   The process of creating the evaluation's focus/goals begins with face-to-face meetings with the program managers, funders, and others who have some special interest in the program. Note that this list does not include only those people responsible for carrying out the program.

This step is the first one in helping to foster both greater clarity in the program goals as well as greater investment and commitment by stakeholders. By believing in the evaluation process and then personally committing time to clarify/understand their goals, design the evaluation, periodically review the evaluation process, and perhaps even collect some data, stakeholders often can more clearly see their concerns about the program being addressed. When they become fully involved in the evaluation of the program, stakeholders often are more likely to feel that funds for the evaluation will result in helpful feedback, that data need to be faithfully collected, and that the evaluation's results will be successfully incorporated into the next cycle of the program.

Getting stakeholders actively involved in the evaluation process is one of the most counterintuitive steps of evaluation. Beginning evaluators often approach evaluation like research, setting down a protocol for collecting data, implementing it, and then analyzing the results. Allowing others to help shape the protocol, to suggest data-collection methods, and to help interpret the findings seems to fly in the face of scientific objectivity! Experience with involving stakeholders leads most evaluators to the following observations. First, stakeholders often take a very objective perspective, even when they are deeply committed to the program. They tend to quickly understand that using suspect evaluation methods jeopardizes the evaluation and the implementation of the evaluation's results. Rather than being too lax, stakeholders often favor the most objective and stringent methods available. Second, with even minimal guidance from the evaluator, stakeholders often create the type of evaluation the evaluator had originally envisioned. Third, evaluators should remember that they are soliciting input from the stakeholders, not turning the entire evaluation over to them. Ultimately it is the evaluator, not the stakeholders, who must make final decisions about the evaluation protocol. Fourth, choosing to involve stakeholders should not be mere "lip service," but rather a commitment to weigh the opinions of the stakeholders. Anything less can jeopardize the evaluation because it is the stakeholders who ultimately make the final decisions about the utility of the program.

Including stakeholders in the initial planning meetings allows the evaluator to include data collection strategies that meet the stakeholders' need for information when determining a program's worth. Inclusion helps to decrease the temptation of some stakeholders to claim that the evaluation was flawed, especially if the program does not fair well in the final report.

It is important, however, not to be disheartened if stakeholders seem less interested in becoming involved in the program evaluation planning process. In these cases, it is helpful to actively solicit the opinions and suggestions of stakeholders. The key word here is *actively*; it may take more than one formal invitation of marginal stakeholders, plus a well-placed phone call from the evaluator, during which the importance of the stakeholder's participation is emphasized. Another strategy for garnering stakeholder input is for the same individuals to be involved in both the initial planning of the program and the planning of the evaluation, assuming that this group also includes people who will be using the program.

At the least, the evaluation plan, once prepared in first draft, should be presented publicly through existing meetings typically attended by program administrators/ staff, recipients, and/or the general public. For example, if one were evaluating a counseling program for stress reduction, the evaluation plan could be presented to governing bodies involved in funding the counseling center. For other programs, this public body may be the PTA of a school program, the city council (for a city-sponsored program), or a steering committee for campus programs. It is very important that the input of such meetings be incorporated into the evaluation plan; this is not the time to force a plan without an adequate discussion or to solicit input only to dismiss it. If evaluators seek input from stakeholders, it is their responsibility to consider suggestions and input seriously. The evaluator should revisit the goals of the program when determining the appropriate evaluation procedures. A few questions may help to guide the evaluator while generating the evaluation:

1. What aspects of the program should be evaluated?
2. Will the whole program be evaluated or only newly added components?
3. At what point in the program will the evaluation begin, and when will it end?
4. Will it focus on the conceptualization stage, the design stage, or the implementation stage of the program?
5. Is the program sufficiently mature for the evaluator to expect any measurable efficacy?

By reflecting on these questions while formulating the evaluation plan, the evaluator is more likely to keep the evaluation in line with the goals of the program evaluation.

Moreover, by keeping the program's time frame and maturity in mind while designing the evaluation, it is more likely that the evaluation will be appropriate for the program.

This is also the time that the evaluator heeds the specific questions to be answered during the evaluation. Conducting an evaluation with only the very general questions, "Is this program worthwhile?" or "Has this program been successful?" is not sufficient and violates the first standard of program evaluation. The need for utility, or the first standard of program evaluation (Joint Committee on Standards for Educational Evaluation, 1994) requires the evaluation to answer the questions of interest (i.e., address their goals) of the stakeholders.

These initial meetings present good opportunities for the evaluator to better understand the needs and interests of the primary stakeholders, and their relationships with one another. During the meetings the evaluator should pay attention to how people are interacting with one another. Some questions to consider include:

1. Are there factions within various groups? If so, how does these factions affect the stated that goals of the program evaluation?
2. How deep are these divisions, and on what are they based?
3. How large of an effect will these factions have on the evaluation process, and on the reception of the evaluation results?
4. How are differing points of view dealt with in this group?
5. Are viewpoints in opposition to the key stakeholders' allowed to surface and be fully considered, or are they quickly dismissed? (If the latter occurs, the evaluator should steer the conversation back to the overlooked viewpoint, perhaps by saying, "I'd like to come back to a point just made. Could you elaborate on …")

It is the evaluator's responsibility to ensure that the concerns raised at meetings represent not just the opinions of the vocal, but also those of potentially disenfranchised, underrepresented, or overlooked stakeholders.

Throughout these initial meetings, the evaluator is typically considered by the program managers and other stakeholders to be an "expert" (and sometimes whose words are taken as fact). Thus, it is important that evaluators allow others to speak and to facilitate the discussion process. If the evaluator becomes too vocal, the evaluation can quickly become one devised by the evaluator, not the one envisioned by stakeholders.

Step 2: Design a Plan for Examining Program Implementation to Achieve Program Goals   After the evaluator understands the goals that the stakeholders would like the evaluation to address, evaluators often create two plans for data collection, each with a slightly different focus. The first plan, which we cover in this section, addresses collecting evidence of what the program actually did or how it was actually implemented. The second plan (described in the next section) presents a data collection strategy for measuring the effectiveness of the program. Both of these plans require the evaluator to work back and forth among the set of evaluation goals/questions proposed by the stakeholders, the limited resources such as funds and time, and commonly accepted data collection methods. Perhaps the easiest

TABLE 22.1 An Example of an Evaluation Planning Matrix for a Workshop

Evaluation Questions	Sources of Information	Needed Resources	Data Collection Methodology	Time Line	Data Analyses
How is the information presented in workshop?	Workshop; workshop's presenters	Planning documents	Structured observations; workshop planning documents	Throughout the duration of workshop	Descriptive statistics
Did the workshop meet the needs of attendees?	Workshop participants' journals; survey of attendees	Journals for a sample of attendees; possibly some payment for completion; printed surveys	Journals; survey	Journals to be returned at last workshop; survey to be administered at final workshop	Qualitative data

way to begin is to create a matrix like that shown in Table 22.1. For each evaluation question, five categories are examined: (a) sources of information, (b) needed resources, (c) data collection methodology, (d) time line, and (e) data analyses.

In short, when assessing the implementation of a program, the program evaluator needs to carefully consider what a program actually did and how it was implemented. Although it may seem obvious, the importance of this cannot be overlooked, as highlighted in the following example.

RESEARCH IN ACTION 22.1

Consider this example. A program evaluator is contracted to evaluate the implementation of a peer mentoring program through a campus LGBTQ Center on a college campus. In order for the program evaluator to determine whether the program was a success, the evaluator would need to know that a peer mentoring program was implemented, what the program involved, who participated, and how well it met its participants' needs. These are measures of program implementation.

It may seem obvious to state that only after the evaluator knew that the mentoring program occurred would it make sense to judge its merits. However, it is important not to assume that what is supposed to happen in fact happened, or that the unexpected never occurred.

Every program evaluator has numerous examples of a disparity between what the program was intended to be, and what it in fact turned out to be. Although there are numerous examples of a program failing because some of its components were omitted, other programs succeed in unintended ways as highlighted in the following example.

RESEARCH IN ACTION 22.2

Consider the example of a program designed to help students with physical disabilities who attended a large, midwestern university. The Student Services Center's goal was to improve the study skills of these students, both through skill building workshops (e.g., test-taking strategies, mnemonics) and by providing them cutting-edge technology to facilitate the access of information (e.g., large-print computer monitors for students with poor vision, or a voice-activated word processor for quadriplegic and paraplegic students). These services were made available to students, and some students were quite successful because of the training. However, conversations with the students revealed that the two most important, beneficial aspects of the program were having a place to come between classes, where they could interact with other students with physical disabilities, and knowing that there were people who could assist them in more mundane activities such as buttoning a coat, fixing eyeglasses, or coming to get them if their wheelchairs became inoperable. It was these services that enabled them to be full-time students on a large college campus.

Observational methodology is the most common way to determine whether the program took place and the form it took during implementation. One form of observation requires the observer to be detached from the activity, and typically the observations sample the program's activities in a structured fashion.

RESEARCH IN ACTION 22.3

Consider this example. A community center wishes to offer a program intended to prepare individuals who are transitioning from incarceration to the community. The program is structured to include six, 60-minute workshops that present information related to searching for jobs, applying for jobs, and enhancing support during the transition.

Structured observations for this program would require the evaluator to observe the workshops for a specified amount of time—for example, 25 times for five-minute intervals over the course of the six hour-long workshops. In each of the five-minute intervals, the evaluator would mark on a standardized code sheet what is taking place in the workshop. If one of the goals of a program is to use real examples from life as the vehicle for presenting information (rather than relying on a theoretical, lecture-style presentation) then a structured observation would, among other things, monitor how the presenters provided the information during one-minute segments. Potential categories of presenting information might be (a) statements of fact, (b) presentations of examples, (c) questions and answers,

(d) other, and (e) no presentation of information. Having more than one observer reliably code human behavior in discrete categories can be difficult at times, so pilot-testing these forms before formally collecting the data is time well spent. Fitzpatrick, Sanders, and Worthen (2004) is a good reference for learning how to construct and pilot-test observation forms and analyze structured observation data.

Another commonly used observation methodology is participant observation, which requires the observer to actually become involved in the process, typically as a program participant (Patton, 2002). Participant observation is much less structured and more qualitative (as described in Chapter 16), and it requires the observer to take notes throughout the course of the activity or as soon after the activity as possible. Readers wanting more information about participant observation methodologies are referred to Patton (2002). Whereas structured observations are designed to capture the quantity of activities that occurred, participant observations are especially useful when descriptions of the mood preceding, during, and following an activity are also desired.

Even though structured observations and participant observations provide two different data sets and typically answer different questions, it is not uncommon to use both observation methods during an evaluation (although not simultaneously!). Assessing program activities through periods of both structured and participant observations provides a rich data set. The program evaluator asked to evaluate the stress-reduction program may begin with participant observations. The evaluator might attend the first few workshops, describing the structure of these workshops, the extent to which the participants actually practice stress-reduction techniques, and how she or he felt during these workshops. During these observations, the evaluator might, in turn, create some potential hypotheses about the program, such as: "Discussions about stressors are often brought up by participants but not addressed by the counselor" or "These stress-reduction techniques sound easy here in class, but I don't think I would practice them outside of this workshop. My life is just too hectic to take the time." These hypotheses, as well as impressions, observations, and other hypotheses, can then be used to create questions for participant surveys or they can be followed up through a structured observation.

Although observational methods are especially useful in evaluating a program's implementation, other methods may be useful as well. Program records such as activity logs, sign-in sheets, and individual client records (with permission) can provide a useful paper trail as to what activities occurred during a program.

RESEARCH IN ACTION 22.4

Consider this example. A program evaluation is conducted to assess whether a program that intends to connect program participants to community support programs (i.e., medical attention, food resources, or child care classes) was effective.

In order to evaluate the effectiveness of this goal of the program, a program evaluator may review a random sample of the family records. These same records may even indicate whether the participants sought these sources of assistance, and the extent to which these services were provided to the participants. Other times, however, the participant may have to be asked directly what services he or she was referred to and what services he or she actually experienced. There can, of course, be a difference between the number of participants referred to a community resource and the number of participants who ultimately receive services.

As we indicated earlier, as the evaluation process unfolds, an evaluator can easily drift from the goal of the evaluation. For example, an evaluator might find it interesting to ask *why participants referred to services never follow through* with them. Was it because they were referred to the wrong service agency, or they did not qualify for the particular service, or they never went to the initial appointment due to a lack of transportation or child care, or they do not trust social services agencies and refused to go? Although it may indeed be very functional, the program evaluator must first focus on the goal of the evaluation, and then determine whether new questions are within the scope of the goals of the evaluation.

Step 3: Design a Plan for Evaluating Program Progress toward Program Goals   The evaluation must not only examine how the program was implemented, but also ascertain whether the anticipated effects of the program are evident, and (if the program has not reached completion) whether the program is on track to achieve the stated program goals. As with monitoring program implementation, program documents and observations can be used to measure a program's goals as well as their progress related to their anticipated outcomes. In addition, satisfaction surveys, focus groups, self-report logs or journals, and content testing may be useful. We discuss each of these methods next.

Surveys are a fairly easy and inexpensive method to collect information about a program's effects on participants. Traditional surveys have several advantages that often make them the method of choice when soliciting information from program participants. Surveys can be used to track participant characteristics over time (e.g., a symptom inventory administered after each program session), to monitor overall functioning before the start of the program and at the completion of the program (e.g., pretest and posttest design), and to document participant self-reported behaviors (e.g., did the person follow up with the referral).

It is also important to consider the limitations of using surveys, as well as ensuring the cultural appropriateness of their use with intended participants. For example, the program evaluator needs to assess the population asked to complete the survey. If, for example, literacy is an issue for this population, then the evaluator may wish to use an oral interview administered either individually or in a group setting. If a pretest-posttest design is to be used, are the program participants easily located, or would tracking these individuals to collect the posttest program information be difficult? Is the information easily conveyed in a singular response, or is further clarification needed before a full understanding is possible?

Written surveys should not be the data collection method of choice when detailed written responses are needed; people typically will not complete numerous open-ended questions, and generally the responses are never more than a sentence or two. Situations that limit the usefulness of survey methodologies are often present in social programs.

RESEARCH IN ACTION 22.5

Consider this example. An agency hired to conduct evaluations of three independent programs had difficulties with all three surveys of program participants. The data for families in public housing were lost because of major difficulties in collecting the posttest program data; in the middle of the year-long program, the public housing units were renovated, thereby scattering the program's families across the city, and very few of the displaced families returned to the public housing units or provided a forwarding address. The evaluation of another program, again located in a public housing facility, required housing residents to respond to a written survey concerning aspects of their community they would like to change. Only after the data were analyzed did the evaluator, unable to see a consistent pattern of responses, realize that many of the respondents were illiterate and had randomly marked responses on the questionnaire! The third evaluation required the program staff to help program recipients complete a survey after completing a four-week course, but before receiving services. The evaluator assumed that this was occurring but learned only after the program had ended that staff seldom had program recipients complete the survey before beginning the program; almost none of the respondents had both pretest and posttest program surveys

---

Other methods, such as focus groups or interviews, can be used to collect in-depth data from participants regarding a program's intended outcomes. Focus group methodology relies on the interaction of people as they discuss a common experience or viewpoint. Because the data are always qualitative and reflect people's experiences, thoughts, ideas, and impressions, this method is basically a self-report of how the program affected participants. As discussed in Chapter 16, qualitative data gathered from interviews or focus groups can provide rich descriptors regarding individuals' experiences. These data may be appropriate to gather when the evaluator is interested in gaining a more nuanced understanding of people's experiences, thoughts, ideas, and impressions of the program. Focus groups may also be used with program staff to gain additional perspectives regarding program concerns, benefits, and worth. Some specific skills are needed for conducting a successful focus group; see Kamberelis and Dimitriadis (2011) and Krueger and Casey (2000) for excellent discussions of focus group methodology as it applies to the social sciences.

Self-report logs or journals are another method used to assess participant and staff reactions to a program, or to record the frequency of specific behaviors. Self-report logs are typically in a checklist format and ask the respondent to periodically record the frequency of the behavior under study whereas journals generally ask participants to provide more narrative descriptions of the behavior. Using self-report logs and journaling methods can provide specific data about behaviors *as they occur* rather than the broader statements about behaviors and feelings collected via surveys at discrete points in time, or that rely upon participant recollections from prior days, weeks, or months.

RESEARCH IN ACTION 22.6

Consider this example. If you are evaluating the ability of a stress-reduction program to reduce stress, you might ask program participants to carry a small notebook. Every time they feel stressed they would jot down the stressor, their initial reaction to it, and a description of how this behavior increased, decreased, or had no effect on the stress they were feeling. If you as program evaluator also wanted to collect quantitative data, you could generate a mutually exclusive list for each of the categories (stressor, behavior, and consequences) and ask participants to check one item in each category. A more complex log might involve collecting information about the conditions surrounding the stressful event, the duration of the stressful feelings, and the time of day the stressor occurred.

Content testing, on the other hand, evaluates program participants' knowledge about a topic. Course exams are a form of content testing. This type of data is useful when distinct facts or information is being conveyed through the program. For example, participants in the stress-reduction program might be asked to respond to questions that assess their knowledge of the content taught through the program (e.g., stress-reduction techniques, physiological symptoms associated with stress). Content testing can be administered in a pretest and posttest format in an effort to assess the acquisition of knowledge before and after the program. Content testing can also be used to determine respondents' familiarity with specific topics so as to inform program content or to classify respondents into various groups (e.g., high, medium, and low) to be used in subsequent analysis.

Step 4: Create a Consolidated Data Collection Plan to Assess Progress toward Program Goals   It is sometimes easy to become lost in the "forest" of data, and consequently have too much data in one area … and alternatively, no data in another. After considering all data collection options, we suggest a matrix to identify the evaluation question and the various methods that will be used to answer each question. Using the example of program evaluation designed to evaluate a sexual assault bystander intervention program, we will describe the first column of the matrix.

Research Application: Example Matrix to Guide Identification of Program
Evaluation Questions and Methods

	Evaluation Question Example: Does the program teach bystander intervention skills?	Evaluation Question 1	Evaluation Question 2	Evaluation Question 3
Method 1	*Two observers trained to observe and code content discussed during sessions*			
Method 2	*Two reviewers examine workshop curriculum and handouts for content*			
Method 3 ...	*Participants rate knowledge of bystander intervention techniques before and after workshop*			

In this way, evaluators rely upon data triangulation, as discussed in Chapter 16. Multiple methods, multiple data sources, and more than one data collector or observer over time provide the most robust assessment of a program's effectiveness. Such a strategy also reduces the reliance on any particular source. Just as a medical diagnosis seems more reliable when it comes from several different physicians, so too is the judgment of a program's worth more valid when based on several sorts of data.

Step 5: Plan the Data Analyses to Examine Program Goals   The final column in the matrix of evaluation questions and data collection methods in Table 22.1 is "data analyses." As discussed in previous chapters, there are a variety of methods for analyzing data and the evaluator must have a clear sense of the appropriateness of a given analysis based upon the data collected. For example, some questions used to guide this process are as follows:

1. Will subscores be calculated, or will frequencies for each item be calculated?
2. Will a respondent's survey data be correlated with workshop attendance, and if so, is there a way to match these two sources of data, through either a name or a code?
3. What statistical analysis will be performed on the data, and are the data in a form that allows the analysis to occur without extensive manipulation?
4. If the data are qualitative, how will the data be analyzed?
5. Will there be case studies or a summary of findings?

Time spent planning for the data analyses (whether the data are qualitative, quantitative, or archival) saves considerable time when conducting the data analyses. Extensive planning can also prevent fatal data collection errors from occurring, such as collecting pretest and posttest data only to find that there is no way to link the data because identifying names or codes were not included on the survey instrument.

Step 6: Estimate the Financial and Time Costs of the Evaluation Needed to Meet Program Goals   This step is often difficult and requires the evaluator to carefully consider all elements of the program evaluation. Careful attention to this stage, however, is essential. As has been discussed throughout this book, there are a number of factors that affect the time and resources required in designing and implementing a research study. In the same way, there are a variety of factors that must be considered when conducting a program evaluation.

Creating a budget for an evaluation is similar to creating a budget justification used within a grant proposal. Although there are no hard and fast rules, some common strategies have been suggested. First, determine the fixed costs. These are the costs of which evaluators often have little control, including but not limited to postage, consultant time, overhead costs (heat, electricity, phone), printing, test and instrument purchase, and supplies or equipment needed to complete the project. When determining these fixed costs, it can be helpful to calculate the "per unit" cost for each of these items. Specifically, printing costs should be "per page," and overhead costs might be calculated "per month." Similarly, "person-hours" also are typically calculated on a weekly or monthly basis. Per person costs should include all expenses associated with individuals, such as benefits, income tax, and social security tax that routinely are charged for a person's employment.

Next, evaluators can begin to create the actual budget. The exact level of detail and layout of the budget depend on funders' needs, forms required by the evaluator's own organization, and the evaluator's level of experience. This process can be quite complex, especially for a large evaluation. It can be made less daunting by creating a detailed list of specific tasks needed to complete each component of the program evaluation. For example, for a survey, the evaluator would estimate the costs for each step needed to move the survey from creation to data interpretation. Experience makes this process easier; knowing some of the areas that can cause problems allows the evaluator to allocate sufficient resources within the budget. It is rare when an evaluator says, "I overestimated the amount of time this project would take" or "I have more resources than I know what to do with!"

Although this process can seem tedious, the more detailed this list of tasks is, the less likely it is that the evaluator will underestimate the time associated with each task or underestimate the needed resources. Clearly, the more information the evaluator can add to this list, the better estimate the evaluator will make. Some details result from specific decisions, such as how many surveys will be given out and how they will be distributed and returned. Other details emerge as a result of consulting with others. For example, the evaluator would want to know that the bus company charges by person or by the hour when calculating the projected expenses for participant transportation. Staff working within the particular program being evaluated can sometimes be very good resources for information relating to the participants, such as participant transportation costs.

Finally, assign a timeline to each component. Each component should be broken into its individual tasks, and then estimates of time to complete each task and the subsequent cost for that task should be made. Through this process, the evaluator will have created a budget with a built-in time line. This time line can then be transferred into a variety of software apps and programs that can be shared across relevant stakeholders, funders, and staff.

Research Application: Matrix to Guide Estimation of Budget and Timeline

Budget Item	Description	Estimated Cost	Intended Time Line
Fixed Cost 1			
Fixed Cost 2			
Fixed Cost 3 ...			
Project Task 1			
Project Task 2			
Project Task 3 ...			
Total Cost			

Step 7: Come to a final Agreement about Services, Costs, and Responsibilities with Relevant Stakeholders Needed to Reach Program Goals   After outlining the data collection procedures and creating a time line and budget to encompass these activities, the program evaluator typically submits the materials for final approval to the agency commissioning the program evaluation. The precise documents submitted will vary somewhat based upon the procedures specified by the funder(s) and organization(s), but generally contain the following:

1. A document that provides an overview of what will and will not be covered in the evaluation process, how and to whom the data will be reported, the cost of the evaluation, and the terms for payment. This document, sometimes known as a letter of agreement or contract, should be succinct. It serves as an overview of the entire evaluation process and should be signed by both the program evaluator and a representative of the agency commissioning the program evaluation.
2. A document that identifies the following for each component of the program evaluation: a brief rationale, the data that will be collected, the procedures for collecting the data, the person(s) responsible for given tasks, the roles and responsibilities of assistants, the time line, and the costs.
3. A current vita or resume of the program evaluator.

Modifications to these documents throughout the evaluation process are common, particularly for longer-term programs. For example, there may be some back and forth before the documents are signed to reach a final agreement on the details specified in the documents. These documents also may be modified after the evaluation has begun. All modifications need to be documented in writing and signed by the program evaluator and a representative of the agency commissioning the program evaluation. These documents can be invaluable should disputes arise concerning any component.

Phase 3: Collecting and Analyzing Information

All of the steps we have described up to this point occur *before* one piece of data has been collected. With careful planning, effective promotion of the program, and clear documentation, collecting and analyzing the information and then reporting the findings are rather straightforward. Proper planning and good record keeping will also allow the evaluator to know exactly what data need to be collected, when and by whom the data will be collected, and how the data will be analyzed and interpreted. This also allows the evaluator to judge whether collecting additional data would be beneficial, whether funds allow for following up on a newly presented data collection opportunity, and how any follow-up data will fit into the overall evaluation. In essence, the work up to this point has been to create a road map that will be used to keep the evaluation on track once data collection is underway. After the evaluation has been completed, this road map will also guide decisions about the format, content, and style of the evaluation report.

The role that the evaluator has specified and negotiated during Phase 2 determines how actively involved he or she is in the day-to-day data collection process. The evaluator may assume the role of data manager rather than data collector if the program is large and will be replicated at several sites or if site employees will collect a majority of the data to keep the cost of the evaluation down. At other times the evaluator serves as the principal data collector. Regardless, *ultimately the evaluator is responsible for the data, their integrity, their validity, and their timely collection.* Several steps, therefore, must be undertaken to ensure that the data are clean, as error-free as possible, unbiased, and collected on time and within budget.

First, every data collection procedure should undergo pilot testing. This requires thoroughly training any data collectors or site personnel concerning how the data are to be collected. Implementing actual face-to-face training with several opportunities for role playing and questions can eliminate many points of confusion. For example, if a questionnaire is to be administered, data collectors should practice administering it; if observations are to be made, practice sessions should occur until all data collectors observe the same situation and collect exactly the same data 90% to 95% of the time. If such coding reliability does not happen within a reasonable amount of time, the evaluator should consider simplifying the observation form or replacing some observers.

In instances where the evaluator is not the principal data collector, the second step is to establish and implement a checks-and-balances system to evaluate the data being collected. For example, the evaluator would want to know the answer to a variety of questions, such as:

1. Are the surveys filled out correctly and completely?
2. Are pretests being given to clients before the first counseling session?
3. Are files complete enough so that clients can be tracked for a six-month follow-up interview?

The evaluator should never assume that the data are being collected as instructed; periodic monitoring of the data collection process is essential, as illustrated in the following example.

RESEARCH IN ACTION 22.7

Consider this example. An inexperienced evaluator once failed to check on a data collector because this particular collector had been working with the evaluation group for a couple of years before working for the evaluator. You can imagine the evaluator's horror, dismay, and embarrassment when, while visiting the program site, she was asked when the data collector was going to observe the program; she had just looked over the data supposedly collected from that site the previous week! The combination of that and similar experiences has led the evaluator to hang above her desk the following sign, which summarizes her philosophy about data collection, "If you haven't seen it, heard it, touched it, smelled it, rolled in it, felt it, and tasted it, you don't know it."

Periodic checks of the program site, both announced and unannounced, are essential for monitoring the program and helping to keep the data clean.

As we mentioned earlier, it is essential to have a strong commitment (i.e., buy in) from all program stakeholders (staff, funders, participants). Staff must be well trained and the evaluator must make intentional efforts to foster positive morale and to increase team cohesiveness. Providing formative and summative feedback throughout the process of program evaluation helps to foster team effectiveness and efficiency (Nation et al., 2003).

The task of checking the data does not end once they arrive on the evaluator's desk. For example, data entry must be checked for accuracy and to ensure that specified procedures for data entry and data cleaning (e.g., eliminating out-of-range scores) have been followed. Once all of the data have been collected and prepared for analyses (i.e., quantitative data have been entered into a spreadsheet or statistical analysis package, field notes have been typed into case notes, tapes of focus groups have been transcribed), then the evaluator is now ready to conduct the data analysis. We divide data analysis into two distinct steps: primary analyses and secondary analyses.

Primary Data Analyses   The first analyses, called primary analyses, are similar to those presented in the results sections of empirical articles as described in Chapter 4. For program evaluation, it can be useful to analyze the data from each component of the evaluation in isolation from other data. For example, the results of the inventory measuring participant endorsement of depressive symptoms are presented independently from the descriptions of the intervention prepared by the participant-observer. In other words, each component has its own methods, results, and summary sections.

There are several advantages to analyzing and interpreting each data component in isolation from the other components. First, these primary data reports are excellent vehicles for periodically presenting data to stakeholders. They can offer stakeholders preliminary indication of some of the findings, thereby preparing stakeholders for the final report. Second, they prevent the data from becoming backlogged. Third, primary data reports help the evaluator see holes in the data or areas that need additional examination. Programs are fluid entities; despite the best planning, changes in the program, failed data collection procedures, or ambiguous results sometimes require the evaluator to augment planned data sources. By analyzing the data as they come in, the evaluator may have enough time to develop a plan for collecting additional data before the program has ended. Finally, conducting a primary data analysis also expedites the secondary data analyses, as we discuss next.

Secondary Data Analyses   Secondary data analysis ties together the primary analyses to describe a component of the program. Because multiple sources of data are used, the program evaluator must reexamine each of the primary analyses to determine where findings support one another and where there are discrepancies. This is illustrated in the following example.

RESEARCH IN ACTION 22.8

Consider the example of a program evaluator assessing the effectiveness of a program designed to teach mindfulness. The evaluator will consider multiple data sources when answering the question, "Did the mindfulness program provide program participants with strategies they could implement?" For example, the evaluator would look at the participant responses to survey items (which would have already been summarized into frequencies and percentages in the primary analyses) that asked respondents how often they used a particular mindfulness technique, as well as examine journals kept by the respondents and the field notes taken during the participant observations. If program participants said they used a specific meditation technique frequently, was this a technique that was emphasized in the workshops? At the same time, if "deep breathing" was a technique emphasized during training but did not appear in the participants' journals, was this because the participants did not understand the importance of breath awareness, or because it was not presented clearly enough in the program to be useful?

The evaluator in this example would use the multiple sources of data in order to more fully assess the effectiveness of the mindfulness program. In other words, access to data from participant surveys, participant journals, and observation, in combination, will allow the evaluator to more fully understand whether the program met its intended goals.

The multiplicity of data requires some method for weaving together these sources. For example, the evaluator begins with the program's goals and objectives and examines the primary data reports to see how the results of each data collection component support or refute the supposition that the program met its goals. The evaluator then weaves together the data from each component into an integrated whole. Using the meditation program example above, some questions to guide the evaluator in this process might include:

1. What evidence is there that participants who have taken part in the mindfulness program have learned several new skills?
2. Did items on the questionnaire given in the workshop address this question?
3. What did respondents say in focus groups when asked if they learned new skills?
4. According to the field notes of the participant-observer, were participants introduced to "several" skills?
5. If another goal of the mindfulness program was to have respondents feel better able to handle stressful situations, what evidence either supports or refutes this claim of the program?
6. If program attendees kept journals, do they contain evidence that attendees implemented mindfulness over time?

In this way, the secondary analysis moves back and forth among stated program goals and objectives to data sources. Reducing the data via primary data analyses in Step 1 allows the evaluator to utilize results from the primary analyses in order to expedite secondary analyses. The secondary analysis—this moving back and forth from the program's objectives to the evidence and the weaving together of the individual pieces of data into a holistic picture—*is* program evaluation. Combined with recommendations and comparisons to similar programs, the secondary analysis creates the evaluation of the program. A program evaluator should never leave the interpretation of the evaluation to the stakeholders. It is the program evaluator's role to pull the pieces together and to clearly state what she or he means in terms of the program's implementation, anticipated outcomes, implications for the successful conduct of this or future programs, and limitations.

When evaluating a program, the evaluator should also attend to components that will allow the program to be revised and replicated. As such, the evaluator must consider potential mechanisms that will allow one to follow participants over time, identify factors or characteristics that impact outcomes, and assess issues related to program implementation that impacted success (Catalano et al., 2002). In this way, it is important to evaluate not just whether the program was effective, but also which specific elements of a program contributed to its effectiveness. In addition, it is important to evaluate the potential negative implications of the program on the individual or community (Caplan & Caplan, 1994) in order to guide further development and demonstrate worth.

Phase 4: Reporting the Evaluation's Findings and Disseminating the Report

The fourth phase of program evaluation involves writing and disseminating the final report. A good evaluation report, according to Fitzpatrick, Sanders, and Worthen (2004), contains the following nine sections:

1. An executive summary;
2. An introduction to the report stating the evaluation's purpose, the audience for whom the report was intended, any needed disclaimers of limitations, and an overview of the report contents;

3. A section that describes the focus of the evaluation and the program under evaluation;
4. An overview of the evaluation procedures;
5. A presentation of the evaluation results (the primary and secondary analyses);
6. The conclusions;
7. Recommendations;
8. Responses to the report (if any);
9. Appendices, including the detailed evaluation plan, copies of instruments, and detailed analyses (the primary analyses).

Several references provide the reader detailed information about each of these sections (e.g., Fitzpatrick, Sanders, & Worthen, 2004; Patton, 1997). Many of these sections are similar to the components of a research report as described in Chapter 23; however, a research report and a program evaluation final report also differ in important ways. Unlike a research report intended for publication in an academic outlet, a program evaluation final report is written to be consumed by stakeholders, funders, organizational staff, and community members. As such, the reports should be written succinctly and at a level that is accessible to individuals unfamiliar with research design or psychological or counseling literature. In addition, two elements of the final report are likely to be new to researchers: the executive summary and the recommendations sections. These two sections are critical and the sections that are the most likely to be read by people who come into contact with the report. We describe these sections next. Then we describe considerations related to dissemination of the report.

Writing the Executive Summary   Evaluators are encouraged to carefully attend to the style of this section. To illustrate this point, Fitzpatrick, Sanders, and Worthen (2004) described an experience in evaluating a statewide "controversial program" for which three separate reports were prepared for review by stakeholders: (a) the full report containing all of the technical detail of how the evaluation was conducted, (b) a medium-size summary of major interpretations drawn from the data, and (c) a brief executive summary. These authors noted that the availability of the reports was widely disseminated via newspaper postings and that only one person ever requested the full report, 40 people requested the midsize report, and 400 people requested the executive summary. These authors concluded by highlighting the fact that brief reports are more likely to be consumed by a broader audience than lengthy and overly detailed reports.

Given the potential broad reach of the executive summary, evaluators must take care in its preparation. We suggest the following guidelines to assist novice evaluators in preparing the executive summary. The executive summary should (a) be no more than three pages in length, (b) provide the reader an overview of the goals of the program, and (c) indicate the services provided, the outcomes anticipated, and the extent to which these objectives were met. An executive summary should stand on its own; it should contain enough detail so that a person can grasp the program, its purpose, and its impact.

Writing Recommendations   Although writing the recommendations for improvement is perhaps the most important part of the evaluation process, it is daunting, especially for people new to program evaluation. Even experienced evaluators can have doubts. The solution is not to write the recommendations in isolation. Evaluators should work closely with stakeholders during all stages of program evaluation, including the report- and recommendation-writing stage.

One strategy is to present the final report minus the recommendations to stakeholders prior to offering recommendations. After stakeholders have had an opportunity to digest the contents of the final report—and stakeholders will do this at different levels of intensity—the evaluator could schedule a meeting at which the evaluator facilitates a group conversation designed to collectively generate recommendations based on the final report. As the stakeholders write recommendations, the evaluator notes the differences from his or her own prewritten recommendations. The evaluator also may need to draw the group's attention to points not yet brought into the discussion. By using this method of including stakeholders in writing the recommendations, two important goals are achieved. First, stakeholders are reminded that program evaluation is not something that happens to them and their program, but instead is a collaborative discussion in which several perspectives shape the final recommendations. Second, the evaluation report and the subsequent recommendations are not viewed as being the sole property of the evaluator but rather as reflecting the thoughts of several professionals closely related to the program.

Utilizing the experience of stakeholders to help formulate the recommendations can be very beneficial, but a successful meeting does not occur without proper planning. First, because it is likely that many stakeholders assembled have not read the report prior to the meeting, the evaluator should provide a brief overview of the evaluation findings. Moreover, the evaluator should have a list of recommendations she or he feels are absolutely crucial for inclusion and should ensure their inclusion in the discussion. A block of uninterrupted time must be set aside for this meeting. No one has ever complained if a meeting does not fill the whole block of time, but trying to hurry through the discussion can leave stakeholders feeling that ideas have been forced upon them. The evaluator should be the keeper of the agenda and move the meeting along at a reasonable pace, allowing for discussion but preventing it from straying from the stated purpose. Finally, it is extremely important to invite the full range of stakeholders to this meeting, *including those with dissenting views,* and everyone invited should be notified as to who else will be in attendance. The evaluator should act as a facilitator, encouraging people to express their opinions within the constraints of the program. This meeting is not the vehicle for settling long-standing disagreements.

Recommendations include both the positive and negative aspects of the program as it was implemented and the subsequent outcomes. The strengths of the program are generally listed first, separate from the weaknesses (sometimes called the limitations) of the program. Careful wording of the recommendation section of the report is crucial; the goal is to write recommendations that adequately describe the strengths and limitations of the program without being overly critical or mired in detail. One strategy to accomplish this goal is to focus on the future. For example, a program might answer questions such as:

1. What aspects of the program would be absolutely critical for success next time?
2. What are the key, beneficial features of the program that need to be incorporated into future programs?

3. What parts of the program were not implemented as anticipated, and what does this mean for future replications of the program?
4. What is missing from the current program that, if included in future years, would make it stronger?
5. What can be done to strengthen the program in future replications?

Some evaluators simply list recommendations; others include a short rationale that describes the formulation of the conclusions drawn in the report.

Disseminating the Report   Prior to signing a letter of agreement, decisions about who owns the data and to whom the written findings are disseminated are negotiated. The evaluator and program administrators should come to an understanding about how many copies of the final report are needed, the number of presentations the evaluator is expected to make, and how the evaluation results should be disseminated. Even when working with agencies that are bound by the Public Information Act (which makes the report automatically available to anyone who requests a copy), it is important to identify the spokesperson for the evaluation and communicating the results or findings, as well is to articulate the limitations for using the evaluation data and the subsequent report.

Dissemination of the report is a critical step as outlined in the *Program Evaluation Standards* (Joint Committee on Standards for Educational Evaluation, 1994). Consider the following examples. Suppose the local newspaper chooses to print only that portion of an evaluation that outlines a controversial program's weaknesses, or suppose the program administrator requests from the evaluator an updated summary but then forwards to a federal funding agency only those portions of the evaluator's report that favor the program. In both cases, the evaluator and the program administrator could have taken steps to prevent or minimize the effect of these actions. In the *Program Evaluation Standards,* the "formal parties [in this case, the evaluator and program administrator] should ensure that the full set of evaluation findings along with pertinent limitations are made accessible to the persons affected by the evaluation, and any others with expressed legal rights to receive the results" (Propriety Standard 6). Both the evaluator and the program administrator are responsible for monitoring the release and use of the evaluation. In the second situation, it was the evaluator's responsibility to require the program administrator to provide a copy of the summary prior to releasing it to the funding agency. An evaluator should *never* give up editing responsibility to others; editing, summarizing, or releasing portions of an evaluation should remain exclusively in the evaluator's direct control.

Concluding the Evaluation

Finally, program evaluators are expected to create an evaluation trail and to conduct a metaevaluation. An evaluation trail is a file that outlines the steps taken during the evaluation, beginning with a copy of the letter of agreement. All original data, including completed surveys, field notes, copies of transcribed tapes, and data files, should be organized, labeled, and included. Also needed are any internal review board documents, signed consent forms, and financial records outlining how money for the evaluation was spent. Finally, a clean copy of the final report, including any appendices, should be placed in this file. This evaluation trail should stand as an archival record of when and how the evaluation was completed and should contain all original documents associated with the evaluation.

The last step in the evaluation process encourages growth and reflection by the evaluator. After each evaluation, the program evaluator should take some time to reflect on the evaluation process. This should include noting what went well and what aspects of the evaluation could have been completed more efficiently, professionally, or rigorously. Some evaluators keep a professional journal in which they keep a record of the pitfalls and triumphs of each evaluation. When completed honestly and reviewed periodically, these journals can assist evaluators in identifying recurring themes that need to be addressed. They also can serve as personal histories of evaluators' growth and accumulating experience.

SUMMARY AND CONCLUSIONS

This chapter introduced program evaluation and described how it differs from and is similar to research as covered in other chapters in this book. We also discussed the four phases of program evaluation. Although program evaluation uses many of the same data collection methods as are used in empirical research, the scope of a program evaluation is often much broader than that of empirical research.

Evaluations of social programs examine not only the effects of the program (outcomes), but also the program's implementation (process). An examination of how the program is implemented often reveals the reasons a program met or failed to meet specified outcomes. Documenting the factors that limit and enhance the program as it was administered can help to strengthen the program or similar programs in the future. A defining feature of program evaluation is the use of and interpretation of *triangulated* data—data collected from more than one source, at more than one setting, using more than one data collection methodology. By using data triangulation, program evaluators increase the validity of the evaluation's findings.

This chapter described four phases of program evaluation. An evaluator begins the process by setting the boundaries of the evaluation. A crucial step in this phase involves

allowing all stakeholders to have a voice in the scope of the evaluation to ensure that the evaluation's findings are fair and unbiased. Linking the program's goals and objectives to specific evaluation questions also enhances utility.

After setting the boundaries of the evaluation, the second phase involves selecting appropriate evaluation methods. The selection of the methodology depends on the information needs of the evaluation audience; the time, personnel, and financial resources available to the evaluator; and the constraints of the program. During this phase the program evaluator also plans how the data will be collected and prepared for analyses, and trains the program staff to ensure reliable collection.

The third phase entails the actual collection and analyses of the data. The evaluator pilot-tests all newly created or modified instruments and observation forms, monitors data collection by program staff or evaluation staff, and ensures that agreements of anonymity and/or confidentiality are upheld. Primary data analyses are conducted and reported in a manner similar to those conducted in empirical research. Secondary analyses examine the various primary data analyses to focus the findings on specific evaluation questions.

The fourth phase of evaluating a program requires the evaluator to report the findings of the evaluation. The evaluator and client should agree upon methods of dissemination, report deadlines, and types of reports to be created. All evaluation reports should contain sections that describe (a) the program, (b) the evaluation process, (c) the data collection procedures, and (d) the results and findings of the evaluation. In addition, all reports should contain an executive summary and a list of recommendations that include the positive aspects of the program as well as the areas that may need improvement.

STIMULUS QUESTIONS

An Exercise in Program Evaluation

You have been asked to evaluate a week-long, overnight camping experience for girls ages 7 to 14. Use this example when answering the following questions:

1. What sources of information will you use to describe the program and understand its mission and goals?
2. Outline a couple of evaluation questions you might pose during the implementation phase of the program.
3. How would the evaluation questions change if the evaluation were conducted during the conceptualization phase of the program?
4. Who are the possible stakeholders for your program? Are there any silent stakeholders? Are there any disenfranchised stakeholders?
5. The second phase in the evaluation of a program involves outlining data collection steps and time lines. What is the relevance of this procedure?
6. What data collection strategies will you use?
7. What might be some of the advantages and disadvantages of using participant observation in your evaluation?
8. What does it mean to "triangulate the data sources"?
9. When does primary data analysis occur, and why is it important in the evaluation of a program?
10. What is secondary data analysis, and how does it differ from primary data analysis?
11. What are some of the advantages of involving the stakeholders when writing the evaluation recommendations?
12. What is an "evaluation trail," and what does it include?
13. How do research and program evaluation differ?

23 Chapter

Bias: Error Variances from Investigators, Experimenters, and Participants

When a researcher designs a study, he or she seeks to examine the relationships among specified variables. One of the most crucial tasks that confronts the researcher is to control the extraneous variables or reduce the error variance (serious threats to Kerlinger's MAXMINCON principle) that may influence the relationships among the study's experimental variables of interest. Most often, when the extraneous variables or sources of measurement error are known, they are relatively easy to control; the problem is that in designing most studies, it is difficult, if not impossible, to identify all of the possible extraneous variables and error variance.

The purpose of this chapter is to identify potential sources of bias in participants, investigators, and experimenters of particular relevance to researchers in counseling. By the term *bias,* we mean the systematic introduction of extraneous variables that may distort or disguise the relationships among the experimental variables. Whereas *error variance* (or "noise" or "static") refers to variance due to random events, *bias* refers to the creation of differential effects between groups or subgroups of participants due to some systematic kinds of errors. These biases can either be in the forms of implicit or explicit attitudes and behaviors (Dovidio, Kawakami, & Gaertner, 2002). Explicit biases are those that are deliberative and well considered; in contrast, implicit biases are those that are more complex, ambivalent, and often unconscious.

In this chapter, *investigator* refers to the person who designs the study, and *experimenter* refers to the person who executes the investigation. The first section of this chapter examines investigator and experimenter bias, particularly with regard to (a) experimenter attributes, (b) investigator and experimenter expectancies, and (c) experimental procedures. The second section of this chapter examines participant bias, particularly with regard to (a) demand characteristics, (b) participant characteristics, and (c) introspective abilities. Throughout both sections we use the example from Research Application 23.1 (same example as Research Application 7.1 used in Chapter 7), as well as those from previous research efforts to clarify different types of bias. Moreover, in discussing the various sources of bias, we also discuss some strategies for controlling or minimizing these variables.

RESEARCH APPLICATION 23.1

Suppose that a researcher suspects that cognitive treatments of social anxiety have had only limited success because the interventions do not generalize to behavioral situations. The researcher hypothesizes that in vivo behavioral exercises added to cognitive therapy will improve the efficacy of the therapy. In vivo behavioral exercises are operationalized carefully by designing homework that involves a progressive set of situations in which clients first smile at a stranger, later engage strangers in a short conversation, and finally arrange a social encounter. Social anxiety is operationalized by having the participants report on the (fictitious) ABC Anxiety Test to measure the level of anxiety that they experienced after talking with a stranger that the researcher arranged for them to meet (called a confederate). The independent variable is manipulated by randomly assigning the participants to one of two conditions: cognitive therapy alone or cognitive therapy plus in vivo behavioral exercises. Further suppose that 40 participants are randomly chosen from people who (a) answered an advertisement for a program to treat social anxiety, and (b) were assessed by the researcher in a clinical interview to be socially anxious. After the 10-week program, anxiety was assessed with the ABC Test; a statistical test indicates that there was a reliable difference between the groups in the hypothesized direction. That is, the mean level of anxiety, as indicated on the ABC Test, is lower for the group that received the in vivo exercises, and this difference has a low probability of occurring by chance

   Pleased with these results, the researcher concludes that (a) a true relation exists between the independent variable and the dependent variable (i.e., participants who receive in vivo exercises in addition to cognitive therapy have lower scores on the ABC Test than participants who receive cognitive therapy only), (b) the manipulation of the independent variable was indeed the cause of the difference in scores (i.e., the exercises were the cause of the lower anxiety scores), (c) in vivo behavioral exercises increase the effectiveness of the cognitive treatment of social anxiety, and (d) the results are applicable to socially anxious participants generally (and not just to the participants in this particular study). These conclusions, or more specifically these inferences, seem reasonable in this case; however, there are always flaws in any research, and it is appropriate to keep in mind that one or more of these inferences may be incorrect.

Question

Can you think of any possible biases in this study that would raise questions about the validity of the conclusions?

INVESTIGATOR AND EXPERIMENTER BIAS

In an ideal world, an investigator is an objective, unbiased seeker of truth who engages in a systematic, scientific enterprise and is able to remain an impartial, passive observer throughout. In this way, the researcher does not contaminate the research in any way, but rather is an unbiased observer of some phenomenon, and subsequently a reporter of the truth. We know, however, that investigators do not conduct research in such an unbiased manner. Moreover, we know that experimenters who execute investigations may consciously or unconsciously affect the results of their studies. Instead, researchers have opinions, beliefs, and values that may unconsciously (or even consciously) compromise their objectivity, sometimes in very subtle ways.

Researchers' values and cultural biases are inherent in their assumptions concerning participants, research hypotheses, data analysis strategies, and conclusions. Thus, culturally encapsulated researchers may unknowingly make a number of decisions that might introduce a number of systematic biases in their research. In essence, it is important for investigators and experimenters to be cognizant of their cultural stereotypes and preconceived notions, particularly with cultural groups that are less familiar to the researcher. For example, Erickson and Al-Timimi (2001) suggested that because Arab Americans are one of the most misunderstood ethnic groups in the United States and often face discrimination (Ahmed, 2010), thus, certain biases may be elicited within our research. Moreover, these biases can be explicit (intentional and overt discrimination) or implicit (more complex, ambivalent, and likely unconscious prejudice) (Dovidio, Gaertner, Kawakami, & Hodson, 2002). In short, biases in various forms have impact on research findings.

Although in this chapter we will focus on biases that are more directly associated with the design of research studies, implicit biases cannot be overlooked. Researchers are raised and trained in sexist, racist, homophobic, xenophobic environments, and thus have implicit biases that could affect the research conducted regardless of their own race, gender, etc. Our worldview can be a huge source of bias. Investigator and experimenter implicit and explicit biases pertaining to biological sex, race, ethnicity, sexual orientation, age, and physical disability might inadvertently affect participants' responses, either negatively or positively. For example, a highly educated investigator who is insensitive to social class issues and makes prejudicial comments might systematically bias the recruitment of participants. In another case, racial bias can influence the interaction and communication between the experimenter and participants (see Dovidio et al., 2002). In addition, implicit biases might inhibit comparison studies that examine racial or gender differences. Moreover, implicit biases might appear in the form of avoidance and result in a lack of research on certain groups of people. In other words, implicit attitudes can also affect the research studies that people do, as well as choose not to do. Another example pertains to having implicit biases toward a certain religious group. Even though researchers with this kind of bias might not conduct studies discrediting the people with the particular religion, they might simply choose to avoid studying this group. Most importantly, if a profession as a whole neglects a certain group, there will be a lack of important knowledge in the literature pertaining to that specific group. In short, implicit biases may not only result in distorted findings for particular studies, but could also have a substantial impact on the profession as a whole if certain topics are *not* examined.

The story of Clever Hans nicely illustrates the effects of a subtle experimental bias associated with implementing a study. Hans was a horse around the turn of the twentieth century that reliably computed various arithmetic problems, identified musical intervals, and had a working knowledge of German. His owner, Herr Wilhelm von Osten, would ask Hans all kinds of questions; Hans would tap numbers out with his hoof or gesture with his head toward objects. Hans passed a number of tests with various local citizens and professionals, much to everyone's amazement—until, that is, a young psychologist, Oskar Pfungst, came along. Pfungst discovered that Hans could reliably answer questions (i.e., nine times out of ten) only when the interrogator knew the correct answers, but his performance dropped to one out of ten if the interrogator was ignorant of the answer. As it turned out, Hans had not learned math, or music, or the German language, but rather had learned to read subtle cues in the interrogator's posture, breathing, and facial expressions (Pfungst, 1911). Research in the 1980s revealed that laboratory animals can learn to read a wide variety of subtle behavioral cues in trainers that give away the intended answer.

In short, not only investigators and experimenters can be the source of implicit biases, but also other factors such as extraneous variables and error variance may very well bias the results of a study. We next discuss three major types of bias: experimenter attributes, investigator and experimenter expectancies, and experimental design and procedures (see Table 23.1). In addition, we offer some strategies for reducing such biases.

TABLE 23.1 Investigator and Experimenter Biases and Strategies to Minimize Biases

Bias Type	Bias Description	Strategies to Minimize Bias
Experimenter attributes	Biological (e.g., age, gender, race) and interpersonal characteristics (e.g., friendliness, previous contact)	• Use multiple experimenters • Analyze whether differences across experimenters exist • Specify characteristics of experimenters • Refrain from overgeneralizing results
Investigator/ experimenter expectancies	Unintentional expectancy effect (e.g., head nods, smiles, glances, subtle comments, enthusiasm)	• Keep experimenters (partially) blind • Assess the accuracy of experimenter expectancies • Monitor experimenter involvement
Experimental design and procedures	Design aspects of the study and various interactions with participants (e.g., recruitment, greeting, obtaining informed consent, administering research, reminding)	• Make comparisons with best practices rather than control groups or less credible treatments • Explicitly describe experimental procedures • Standardize procedures • Reiterate basic procedures • Train experimenters • Maintain close contact with experiment personnel • Check experimenter performance and combat experimental fatigue • Diversity training for experiment personnel

Experimenter Attributes

Experimenter attributes are primarily biological and interpersonal characteristics of the experimenter that may cause differential responses in participants. Examples include the experimenter's age, gender, race/ethnicity, physical appearance, and interpersonal style. For example, some participants might respond more honestly to a female researcher investigating sexual harassment than to a male. Likewise, a 50-year-old experimenter might inhibit younger participants, but facilitate disclosure for older participants. In another case, the experimenter's interpersonal style (say, unfriendly and dominant) might interact with the independent variable (e.g., expertness cues), such that some participants feel uncomfortable or even threatened during the experiment. Race and ethnicity can also influence bias in a study's results if a participant has preconceptions or stereotypes about the experimenter's racial or ethnic group. Another potential biasing characteristic pertains to previous contact between the experimenter and participants. Some participants may feel that having some prior knowledge about an experimenter would make it easier for them to respond, whereas others may feel much less likely to disclose personal information.

In short, a wide range of experimenter characteristics might influence some or all participants to respond differentially in a particular experiment, thereby confounding its results. In fact, several writers (see Kazdin, 2003) have reported empirical investigations that document that experimenter characteristics can affect responses given by participants on various tasks, such as self-report inventories, projective tests, laboratory tasks, and measures of intelligence (see Strickland & Suben, 2012). To illustrate, studies have found that the racial attitudes of African Americans were associated with whether they preferred having a counselor of the same race (Ferguson, Leach, Levy, Nicholson, & Johnson, 2008) and some African American clients tend to rate White counselors as less proficient and credible (Watkins & Terrell, 1988). Therefore, characteristics of experimenters (e.g., race of counselors) can influence how participants perceive the effect of counseling in research studies.

In short, experimenter attributes can create threats to validity. Using Research Application 23.1 presented earlier in the chapter as an example, imagine the investigator, who is a professor, has reason to believe that including an in vivo component in the intervention would be more effective in treating social anxiety. The professor designs a study in which two bright, advanced graduate students serve as experimenters to conduct the interventions, each lasting 10 weeks. Each student conducts one of the treatment groups. Suppose a broad array of extraneous participant variables are controlled (e.g., age, sex, and personality traits), the treatments are carefully matched, and random assignment of clients is used. Suppose also that the results clearly favor the treatment that included in vivo exercises. However, the results of the treatment groups cannot be separated from the different experimenter attributes and their potential biases. That is, if different experimenters are used to administer different treatments, it would be difficult to determine whether the results are due to the different treatments, the different experimenters, or an interaction between the two. In reality, it may be that the two experimenters' attributes did not affect clients differentially, but we have no way of determining whether this is the case.

Experimenter attributes can also threaten the external validity or generalizability of a study by interacting in some way with the independent variable. For example, it could be that the results of a study would generalize only to therapists with certain characteristics, such as androgynous men, feminist therapists, or African American therapists. Imagine the following modifications to the fictitious example just mentioned. Suppose that the investigator uses two female therapists in their thirties with excellent interpersonal skills to provide the intervention for both groups. Within the cognitive therapy treatment, a major therapeutic intervention involves establishing a collaborative working relationship with the clients. Would these obtained results generalize to other female therapists who may not have excellent interpersonal skills, or to male therapists? Although this can be seen as a generalizability issue (see Chapter 7 for a more detailed discussion on external validity), but if the intent is to generalize the findings from this study to all female therapists, then this becomes a bias issue. Even though this is obviously an empirical question, it is useful because it highlights how experimenter attributes might interact with independent variables and possibly limit the generalizability of specific findings.

Among the many strategies that investigators can use to reduce the possible effects of experimenter attributes are the following:

- *Avoid using a single experimenter* for different levels of the independent variable if at all possible, because this clearly confounds the study's construct validity with experimenter attributes. Whenever possible, use two or more experimenters for each level of the independent variable.
- If two or more experimenters are used for each level of the independent variable, statistically *analyze the data for differences across experimenters* to determine whether any differences could be related to experimenter attributes such as gender. Often this is done as a preliminary data analysis to rule out possible confounding variables related to experimenter attributes. For example, one should examine whether counselors' attributes differentially affected the dependent variables first before proceeding with the main statistical analyses.
- Because there are currently so many unknowns concerning the effects of experimenter attributes, it would be useful for investigators to *specify the characteristics of therapists used in treatment interventions*. Perhaps over time patterns pertaining to certain therapist characteristics might emerge, such as interpersonal style. Kazdin (2003) suggested that investigators analyze their data for experimenter characteristics (gender), which might provide a useful knowledge base over time.
- Authors should explicitly *examine the generalizability of their data in terms of experimenter attributes*, and qualify the conclusions in their discussions accordingly. For example, if researchers used only male therapists, then the discussion of the results should focus on male therapists, and not on therapists in general. Gender is a particularly important variable in counseling research.

Investigator and Experimenter Expectancies

Investigator and experimenter expectancies are beliefs and desires about either how the participant should perform or how the study should turn out. Kazdin (2003) noted that the effect of these expectancies has been referred to as an unintentional expectancy effect, because even though the investigator and experimenter may not intentionally try to influence the participant, they actually do so unconsciously through a range of verbal and nonverbal behaviors (such as head nods, smiles, glances, or subtle comments). Such bias obviously introduces confounding variables, as illustrated in the Clever Hans story.

Robert Rosenthal, one of the first to investigate this topic in the early 1960s, found that investigator and experimenter expectancies directly influenced how participants performed in the in-person interactions during the research administration process (see Rosenthal, 1966). More recently, scholars have focused more on how biases may occur due to experimenters having the tendency to design studies to yield their preferred results (e.g., Munder, Brütsch, Leonhart, Gerger, & Barth, 2013; Munder, Flückiger, Gerger, Wampold, & Barth, 2012; Strickland & Suben, 2012). In this section, we will discuss how biases could occur during the administration process, and biases related to design aspects will be addressed in the following section.

Both positive and negative expectancies can occur in many different ways. Investigator and experimenter bias can affect participants or clients at any stage of an investigation, such as during participant recruitment, during data collection, or after treatment interventions. Using Research Application 23.1 as an example, the experimenters may subtly or not so subtly promote the effectiveness of one intervention over others. To illustrate, there could be the possibility that the experimenters in the study unintentionally and nonverbally conveyed to the participants who received in vivo exercises in addition to cognitive therapy that their treatment should be very effective. In other words, their levels of enthusiasm may be different when administering the study to the two groups. Thus, participants in that intervention group could have somewhat felt the need to report progress through the self-reported ABC Test. Therefore, part of the reason for the significant results showing the advantages of the in vivo exercises could have likely been biased due to experimenter expectations.

Sometimes the desire to be effective even leads experimenters serving as therapists to break protocol and engage in activities outside of normal therapeutic or experimental procedures. For example, in one study that examined the counseling process, a relatively inexperienced therapist was found engaging in a friendly conversation with the client immediately after the counseling session, during which time the client was completing surveys evaluating the counseling session and the counselor! This type of interaction could certainly influence participants to give more favorable responses.

Investigator and experimenter bias also can influence clients in a negative way. For example, if an experimenter is not very motivated or interested in conducting a study, the lack of enthusiasm can very well affect client recruitment and willingness to participate. Halfhearted efforts by experimenters, especially research assistants, can result in halfhearted responses by clients. Biases resulting from lack of experimenter motivation can be a particular problem with doctoral dissertations, notably when the author asks a friend to assume total responsibility for certain aspects of a study (such as recruitment, data collection, or monitoring data flow); even most "good friends" will not be as motivated as the researcher, especially as problems arise and frustrations mount. Sometimes inexperienced investigators feel shy or guilty about asking clients to participate in a study, but telling clients three or four times in an apologetic tone that they do not have to participate is not especially persuasive. Another probable source of bias can arise during the administration of inventories to participants or clients; a busy counseling center receptionist, for example, might be tired at the end of each working day, given the added demands of the research, and verbally or nonverbally convey impatience to the final clients.

In summary, there are many opportunities for investigator and experimenter bias to contaminate the results of a study. Experimenter and investigator expectancies can bias participants whenever anyone involved in conducting the study interacts with participants, which can bias the results to favor one treatment over another, or can affect the generalizability of findings. Thus, experimenter and investigator expectancies can affect both construct and external validity in similar ways to those discussed with respect to experimenter attributes.

Some strategies to lessen the effects of investigator and experimenter expectancies include the following:

- Perhaps the most common strategy to offset experimenter biases is to keep *experimenters "blind"* as to the purpose of the study. Thus, for example, an investigator who is comparing the effectiveness of two treatment approaches would not communicate to the experimenters serving as therapists the specific purposes and hypotheses of the study, thereby reducing the probability that the therapists will unintentionally influence participants in the hypothesized direction. In fact, the investigator may want to keep anyone involved in the study who has contact with participants (e.g., receptionists, therapists, or assistants who collect data from participants) blind as to the specific purpose of the study.

- Because keeping various personnel blind is more difficult in some studies than others, the investigator may need to *resort to a partial-blind strategy.* For example, it would be very difficult to keep therapists blind as they administer a cognitive-behavioral group treatment for bulimics that will be compared with a placebo nondirective discussion group. In such cases, the investigator might try to keep the therapists as blind as possible, and especially with regard to the specific hypotheses and variables involved in the study. Another strategy is to restrict the amount of contact the partial-blind therapists have with participants; therapists might administer the treatments only and not be involved in participant selection, data collection, and debriefing. In short, even when one can achieve only a partial-blind situation, the goal is to keep the experimental personnel as blind as possible to the purpose of the study.

- Because experimenter expectancies can affect participant responses, another strategy is for investigators to *assess the accuracy of experimenter expectancies.* For instance, an investigator may assess whether experimenters correctly surmise the purpose of the study, or even the general hypotheses. If experimenters have accurately pieced together the purpose of the investigation, the potential bias from experimenter expectancies is generally much higher than if the experimenters have not adequately discerned the nature of the study. Although experimenters might still bias participants in subtle ways even when kept blind about the purpose of a study, the probability that participants will be biased toward the hypotheses is reduced. In short, assessing experimenter expectancies allows for both an evaluation of the degree to which experimenters have been kept blind and an assessment of the accuracy of their expectancies.

- *Use strategies for decreasing negative experimenter bias due to halfhearted efforts.* Given our experience, which suggests that no one will do the same quality of work as the researcher most directly affected, investigators should try to avoid conducting a study in absentia; if it is absolutely impossible to avoid such a predicament, researchers should regularly converse with their collaborators and make repeated on-site visits.

Experimental Design and Procedures

In this section, we will discuss issues related to the study design and procedural implementation. As discussed in the previous section, research could be biased due to investigator and experimenter expectations while administrating research experiments. Moreover, expectations during the research design process could also bias results of studies through design aspects. An important influencing factor is researcher allegiance, which refers to the preference of the researcher for a certain treatment to be effective (Luborsky et al., 1999).

In general, researcher allegiances have been operationalized through indices such as whether the researchers developed, advocated for, or contributed to the treatment model, how much they have published articles supporting the treatment, and whether they reviewed previous evidence and made hypotheses in favor of the treatment (Munder, Gereger, Trelle, & Barth, 2011). Several meta-analyses have found researcher allegiances to have substantial associations with outcome (e.g., Miller, Wampold, & Varherly, 2008; Spielmans, Gatlin, & McFall, 2010). That is, outcome effects for the preferred treatment are larger in studies with stronger researcher allegiances. In addition, researcher allegiances have also been found to be causal factors that threaten the validity of outcome comparison studies with moderate effect sizes (Munder, Brütsch, Leonhart, Gerger, & Barth, 2013; Munder, Flückiger, Gerger, Wampold, & Barth, 2012). Moreover, researcher allegiances may also impact how a study is designed. For example, the researcher may compare the advocated treatment with a weak or intentionally ineffective treatment, which has been described as "intent-to-fail conditions" (Westen & Bradley, 2005, p. 267).

Through a meta-analytic study, Munder et al. (2011) found methodological quality to buffer the association between research allegiance and outcome. In other words, when the research study is designed with stronger methodological quality the link between research allegiance and outcome was weaker. In addition, differences between the conceptual qualities of the treatments compared (a form of methodological quality) were also found to mediate the effect of researcher allegiance on outcome. To have solid methodological designs is a critical factor. It is important for researchers to be aware of their preferences and motivation for conducting their studies, and therefore be cautious of designing studies in a way that would bias towards their preferred results.

In addition to concerns around using control groups or less credible alternative treatments in outcome comparison studies, biases can also occur in the way stimuli are designed even when there are no face-to-face interactions between the researcher and participants. For example, Strickland and Suben (2012) conducted a study to examine this potential bias. They randomly assigned undergraduate experimenters to receive two different hypotheses about folk intuitions of consciousness. One group (feeling condition) was given the hypothesis that people would be more acceptable to the feeling mental state ascription than the nonfeeling mental state ascription, whereas the other group (nonfeeling condition) was provided with the opposite hypothesis. The undergraduate experimenters were then asked to help design experimental stimuli based on their hypotheses for a study using Amazon's Mechanical Turk (online data collection), in which consisted no face-to-face interactions between the experimenters and participants. Results indicated that for those given the nonfeeling hypothesis 10 out of 10 experimenters produced results supporting it, whereas for those provided with the feeling hypothesis, only 5 out of 9 experimenters yielded the same result as the other group. The findings from this study clearly indicate that experimenter bias can occur through the design process of a study.

Once investigators have carefully designed and developed a study, operationalized constructs, identified variables, and controlled as many extraneous variables as possible, they usually attempt to conduct the experimental procedure in a constant and consistent manner. A typical study involves a wide range of experimental procedures—recruiting participants, greeting participants, obtaining informed consent, administering instructions, providing a rationale, administering interventions, recording observations, reminding participants about returning questionnaires, interviewing participants, administering questionnaires, and debriefing; imprecision or inconsistencies in the manner in which the experimental procedures are conducted can therefore be a major source of bias and contamination. Procedural imprecision occurs when the activities, tasks, and instructions of an experiment are not specifically defined. As a result, experimenters might treat participants differently because they are unclear exactly how to conduct the experiment in specific situations. Thus, experimenters introduce bias (or error variance, if it occurs randomly) into an experiment due to experimental procedures.

Again, using Research Application 23.1 as an example, the training given to the experimenters should be clearly specified, and the specific ways the experimenters are to interact with participants should be clearly delineated as well. How should the experimenters greet the participants at the beginning? Should they engage in small talk before and after the study? Are the experimenters supposed to actually provide information about the purpose of the study? If so, what kind of information? How should they respond if participants probe for more detailed information? This example indicates only some of the ways that if the investigator does not specifically delineate what the experimenters should and should not do, it is very likely that a wide variability in activities will occur across the different experimenters administrating the study. Moreover, the lack of delineation of experimenter responsibilities increases the probability of systematic biases, such as preferential treatment for more talkative participants, for same-gender or opposite-gender participants, or for students who appear more socially anxious during the study.

Even if an investigator has carefully specified the procedures for a particular study, variability across experimenters can occur for a number of reasons, of which we discuss three: fatigue, experimenter drift, and noncompliance. An experimenter who becomes fatigued over time, resulting in different performances across participants, can be a particular problem if experimenters engage in an intensive activity, such as interviewing several participants or clients in a short period of time. An experimenter may also gradually and unconsciously alter his or her performance over time (experimenter drift); this is of special concern if an experimenter is involved in repetitive tasks over time. Or an experimenter may fail to comply with the exact experimental procedures over time, perhaps because of a lack of awareness of the importance of some procedures. For example, toward the end of a data collection process in one study, an experimenter began to estimate a timed task to "about the nearest minute," obviously an imprecise procedure! In another study designed to compare the effects of two therapists, a researcher was chagrined to find one counselor complying with the normal 50-minute sessions while the other counselor, trying very hard to do well, conducted therapy sessions for as long as 70 minutes each! In short, even when procedures are carefully specified, experimenter variability can still occur.

At least three problems are associated with procedural imprecision. First, as suggested in the preceding example, experimenters most likely vary among themselves in addition to introducing systematic biases over time. Thus, not only is there a good chance that each experimenter would engage in quite different activities in their role, it also is likely that they would act differently from one student to another, thereby adding a confounding variable to the study.

Second, if the procedures are unclear, the investigator does not know what actually occurred. It may be unclear whether the independent variable was administered consistently, or whether other variables might have intervened (recall the discussions of construct validity in Chapter 7 and independent variables in Chapter 18). If significant results are found, it is not clear whether they are to be attributed to the independent variable or to other variables. Or if a participant responds negatively in a survey, it is unknown as to whether this is the participant's true response or if he or she responded negatively due to frustration, such as completing the survey in a loud environment. In short, if investigators do not know what was done in an experiment, their conclusions are confounded, and it is difficult, if not impossible, to discuss the study's results with much precision.

A third problem of procedural imprecision pertains to the statistical issue of introducing error variance or "noise" into the data due to experimenter variability. Statistically speaking, the variability due to the experimenter increases the within-group variability, making it more difficult to find an effect due to the independent variable (assuming such an effect actually exists). Thus, the independent variable must be more potent to offset the increased within-group variability due to imprecisions around how experimenters implement the study.

The following strategies can be useful in reducing bias due to experimental designs and procedures:

- It is important for researchers to be cognizant of their own preferences of how they hope the results would come out. Oftentimes, how studies are designed is implicitly or explicitly influenced by researcher allegiance. To counter the issue of making comparisons with control groups or alternative treatments that are designed to fail, it is highly suggested to make comparisons with treatment modalities that have been empirically identified as best practices, if possible (Westen & Bradley, 2005).

- Perhaps the most basic strategy is to *carefully describe and make explicit the experimental procedures* involved in a particular study. Putting the procedures in writing both organizes the investigator's thoughts and communicates precise procedures for personnel involved in conducting the study. If experimenters are to make specific statements, it is important that they be delivered verbatim and smoothly. Especially for complex or extended therapeutic interventions, it is often useful to write detailed training manuals that identify and document the specific interventions of treatment (see Lorencatto, West, Seymour, & Michie, 2013). Such manuals are helpful both in training experimenters and for communicating to other investigators the content of a particular intervention.

- In another common strategy, investigators *attempt to standardize the procedures* through some type of structure or even automation. For example, an investigator interested in studying the effects of counselor self-disclosure might encounter some difficulties in examining similar types of self-disclosures from different therapists across different clients. However, video or audio recordings portraying counselor self-disclosures can be developed and shown to participants, so that each participant sees or hears identical counselor self-disclosures (see Yeh & Hayes, 2011, for such an example). Another common example of standardization is to develop a structured interview so that experimenters ask the same questions in the same order using exactly the same words. Other examples of standardization include formulating verbatim statements for experimenters or receptionists, providing participants written instructions for completing tasks or inventories, developing a specific order for participants to complete instruments, and using structured forms to facilitate the observation and recording of data. The intent of all these examples is to enhance consistency throughout various aspects of a study by standardizing or providing structure for various procedures.

- Given that misunderstandings and different assumptions can lead to important differences in experimenter procedures (e.g., duration of counseling sessions), it can be useful to *reiterate basic experimental procedures with all personnel*, before a study begins and at various times throughout the study.

- Investigators can often improve standardization if they *train experimenters*. Such training includes specific instructions to experimenters about their experimental tasks and interventions, as well as role playing, feedback, and skill-acquisition exercises. One way to standardize experimenter behavior is to carefully train experimenters to behave exactly in the manner desired. If at all possible, all experimenters should be trained simultaneously to ensure they will receive identical information. Training typically involves attention to and suggested guidelines for anticipated procedural problems or participants' reactions. Ideally, experimenters will have consistent responses to difficult questions (e.g., "How did you get my name?") or ways of responding to infrequent but difficult situations (such as strong negative emotional reactions of clients, including crying or pleas for additional help).

- Another strategy for reducing problems related to experimenter procedures is to *maintain close contact with all the personnel involved with the study.* Close monitoring of experimenters' experiences with their assigned tasks, especially when the research is just getting under way, often reveals unexpected problems that may require small changes in the protocol or procedures. In addition, actively encouraging experimenters to report problems, ask questions, and identify errors leads to useful feedback and opens lines of communication. Whereas novice investigators may erroneously believe that they can sit back and relax once the experiment starts, veteran researchers spend a considerable amount of time vigilantly monitoring and troubleshooting to ascertain whether the study is proceeding as planned.

- Investigators have developed various strategies that *check experimenters' performance and combat experimental fatigue.* Most of these strategies are in essence manipulation checks. For example, Kazdin (2003) reported on the use of confederate participants to check on the experimenter. The confederates were randomly assigned to the various experimental conditions and provided feedback to the investigator about the adequacy of the experimenter's performance. Sometimes merely informing experimenters that confederate participants will be used is enough incentive to maintain performance standards. Likewise, researchers can use audio recordings or direct observations of structured interviews or counseling sessions to evaluate experimenters' performance. For example, when Hogg and Deffenbacher (1988) compared cognitive and interpersonal-process group therapy in the treatment of depression, as a check on the adequacy of the experimental manipulation they trained undergraduates to identify components of cognitive or behavioral treatments. After the undergraduates listened to the therapy sessions, they were highly proficient (96%) in correctly identifying the type of treatment. Hogg and Deffenbacher concluded that because raters who did not know the details of the experiment were able to discriminate audiotapes of different types of treatment with accuracy and certainty, the therapists were reliably following treatment guidelines. Another strategy is to discuss the potential problem of experimenter fatigue with the experimenters and then enlist their help in finding solutions to this problem.

- As a general strategy, it is a good idea to *have researchers participate in a wide range of diversity training activities* to enhance their awareness, sensitivity, and skills pertaining to a wide range of diverse issues, such as racism, sexism, and homophobia (see Pedersen, Draguns, Lonner, & Trimble, 2008; Ponterotto, Casas, Suzuki, & Alexander, 2001; Sue, 2003).

RESEARCH IN ACTION 23.1

Are there particular research topics in which your values and beliefs could more easily result in cultural biases?

PARTICIPANT BIAS

Returning again to our ideal world, the perfect participant is an honest, naive person who comes to an experiment without any preconceived notions, willingly accepts instructions, and is motivated to respond in as truthful and helpful a way as possible (Christensen, 1980). Such participants would not be afraid to be seen in a negative light and would be willing to disclose personal information concerning their innermost secrets. Likewise, within counseling, ideal clients would openly discuss their experiences in counseling, the problems they have been unable to solve on their own, the reasons they chose to enter counseling, their perceptions of their counselor, and the ways in which they have changed. Moreover, ideal participants would be aware of both their subjective experiences and the world around them, and thus they could reliably describe their internal and external worlds.

Unfortunately, we know that participants often come to psychological experiments with preconceived notions, sometimes even resenting their participation in a research study. For example, a meta-analysis study suggests that clients overall prefer a therapist of the same race (Cabral & Smith, 2011). As Christensen (1980) observed, participants entering a psychological experiment are not passive organisms just waiting to respond to the independent variable; instead they bring with them a host of opinions, preferences, fears, motivations, abilities, and psychological defenses that may or may not affect how they respond in different experiments.

We discuss three major sources of participant bias—demand characteristics, participant characteristics, and participants' abilities to report their experiences—and again we offer some strategies for guarding against such confounding variables (see Table 23.2).

Demand Characteristics

One major source of participant bias pertains to what is commonly referred to as demand characteristics, which are cues within an experiment that may influence participants to respond in a particular way apart from the independent variable. Demand characteristics may or may not be consistent with an experimenter's expectancies; they often include events other than the experimenter's expectancies. Examples of demand characteristics include instructions on a personal problems questionnaire that give the impression that most college students do not have personal problems, a receptionist's nonverbal behaviors that seem intended to make potential participants feel guilty if they do not complete a questionnaire, or an experimenter's apologetic nonverbal cues toward participants in the control group.

Demand characteristics are typically subtle influences or pressures, although sometimes they are not so subtle. Using Research Application 23.1 as an example again, imagine that the research participants in the in vivo exercise group were specifically asked a question such as "How much do you think the in vivo exercises helped decrease your anxiety?" It would likely probe them to come up with reasons of how helpful the in vivo exercises were along with added expectations that their anxiety levels should have decreased. The researchers would likely have obtained more unbiased

TABLE 23.2 | Participant Biases and Strategies to Minimize

Bias Type	Bias Description	Strategies to Minimize Bias
Demand characteristics	Subtle cues within an experiment that may influence how participants respond (e.g., questionnaire instructions, receptionists' nonverbal behaviors)	• Conduct pilot trials to identify possible issues • Conduct postexperimental inquiry to identify unwanted influences
Participant characteristics	Self-presentation style, motivation level, intellectual skills, psychological defense, worldview	• Keep participants blind to research purpose • Assess and adjust for social desirability • Minimize concerns about confidentiality • Highlight importance of the study • Present research in adequate reading level for participants • Utilize "spot check" items
Participants' ability to report their experiences	Difficulty with accurately describing mental process in ambiguous situations (e.g., varying processes to access emotions, inaccurate attribution of behavior)	• Attend to participants' ability to report their cognitive and affective processes • Incorporate other assessment methods (e.g., physiological indicators)

information on the helpfulness of the in vivo exercises if the question were asked as "Which aspects of the interventions were helpful; and which ones were not?" Demand characteristics can occur at any point during an experiment, such as in recruiting participants, during interactions with any personnel involved with the experiment, during the completion of inventories or experimental tasks, and in debriefing.

Demand characteristics operating within a particular study are often difficult to identify. Even though investigators' intentions are to be objective and conduct a rigorous study, they may be unaware that the specific instructions on an inventory might influence some participants to withhold personal information. Likewise, very minor comments in recruiting participants may mask the effects of the independent variable. For example, consider the story of a group of researchers interested in the effects of breaches of confidentiality on participants' perceptions of counselor trustworthiness. In the pilot study, the researchers were shocked to find that blatant breaches of confidentiality within a counseling analogue did not seem to affect how participants rated the counselor on trustworthiness. For example, even if the counselor began an interview by commenting on the previous participant, saying something like, "Did you see that person who just left? Boy, he has some serious problems!" the second participant still rated the counselor as quite trustworthy. Close examination of all of the experimental procedures revealed that when participants were initially contacted, they were asked if they would be willing to participate in a counseling study in which they would talk with a "highly competent professional counselor, a person who is well liked and has a very positive reputation with students on campus." Additional piloting of participants revealed that omitting this emphasis on prestige in the introduction resulted in more accurate perceptions of the counselor's behaviors. In sum, demand characteristics operating on participants are often subtle and unintentional.

Participant Characteristics

Not all participants respond in the same way to different experimental tasks and procedures, or even to demand characteristics mentioned earlier in the chapter. Some participants may respond more than others to subtle cues or pressures. A broad range of participant characteristics may affect how participants respond not only to demand characteristics, but also on a broader level to the experimental situation. We now briefly discuss five participant characteristics that may bias participants' responses: self-presentation style, motivation level, intellectual skills, psychological defenses, and worldview.

Self-Presentation Style   A theme among participant motives in psychological experiments is positive self-presentation, a desire to present themselves in a positive light (Krumpal, 2013). Some participants may begin to feel threatened if they believe their performance is inadequate or their responses are "wrong"; other participants may be reluctant to disclose negative information about themselves or others, especially if they feel that the investigator will be able to connect their responses to their name in some way. For example, participants may feel uncomfortable sharing their true perceptions because of not knowing who might see their responses.

Likewise, participants may feel compelled to respond in socially desirable ways, such as reporting positive outcomes from counseling (e.g., improvement in social anxiety in Research Application 23.1) or liking their therapist. Social desirability is sometimes a difficult issue when investigating topics that require socially undesirable responses, such as premature termination of counseling. Former clients may feel reticent to report negative perceptions of the counselor, particularly if they believe that their comments will be disclosed to or cause trouble for the counselor.

Participants with a strong desire to present themselves in a positive manner may be more susceptible to being influenced by demand characteristics. Such participants may use demand characteristics to identify the types of responses that make them appear most positively. In short, participants who want to present themselves well may try, either consciously or unconsciously, to be the "good participant" and respond in a way they believe is consistent with the experimenter's desires or wishes. Interested readers might examine Friedlander and Schwartz (1985) for a theory of self-presentation in counseling.

Motivation Level   The participant's motivation level can also be a source of bias. Sometimes participants in psychological experiments really do not want at some level to put forth much energy in the study. For a variety of reasons, participants might feel apprehensive about the experimental conditions, apathetic about the experimental tasks, angry about being in a control group, or simply tired. As a result, participants may fail to appear for a scheduled appointment, give halfhearted responses or, worse yet, give random responses.

Some clients in counseling research may be motivated to "help" their counselor. Thus, in studies that evaluate some aspect of the counselor, clients who feel very grateful or even indebted to the therapist may be motivated to give glowing responses to "help" their counselor.

Intellectual Skills   Sometimes bias is introduced into a study because participants do not have adequate intellectual skills, such as reading or writing ability. One investigator at a midwestern college was surprised to learn from interviews that some of the participants had difficulty reading the assessment inventories; this was after she had collected data on three self-report inventories! Another investigator gave four self-report inventories, commonly used with college students, to rural midwestern farmers and learned that such intellectual activities constituted a very demanding task for this group, who required considerably more time to complete the forms. Yet another investigator found that a group of inpatient alcoholics experienced a great deal of difficulty in completing a commonly used instrument on college campuses; after defining many words in the items, he learned that the average reading level for this group was below the sixth grade. Moreover, using Research Application 23.1 as an example, some clients with lower intellectual capacities might have difficulties comprehending aspects of cognitive therapy, such as why their beliefs are irrational. In short, the intellectual skills of the participants can bias the results of a study and thus require some consideration.

Psychological Defenses   Sometimes bias is introduced into a study because of some participants' psychological defenses. For example, even though some men feel sexually aroused when viewing a violent rape film, it is difficult for most of them to admit such sexual arousal even to themselves, much less to others. Thus, some participants may feel threatened by their responses to certain material and may deny or repress their true feelings.

At other times some participants may feel defensive or paranoid about revealing their feelings or thoughts about sensitive topics (e.g., sexual orientation, race relations, or feelings of inadequacy or embarrassment). Again, using Research Application 23.1 as an example, a gay client might worry about expressing feeling more socially anxious around other men compared to women, fearing the researcher might uncover his sexual orientation. Likewise, participants such as prison inmates may be suspicious of any experimenter and withhold or temper their responses because of perceived danger. In short, bias may be introduced into a study because participants perceive some real or imaginary threat, which consciously or unconsciously tempers their responses.

Worldview   Sometimes bias can be introduced into a study because of the worldview of the participants. Worldview pertains to a complex constellation of beliefs, values, and assumptions about people, relationships, nature, time, and activities in our world (Ibrahim & Owen, 1994); in essence, worldview represents the lens through which we view the world (Ivey, Ivey, & Simek-Morgan, 1997). As such, the participants' beliefs, values, and assumptions constitute a certain way of perceiving events, a bias (also see Ibrahim, Roysircar-Sodowsky, & Ohnishi, 2001). The participants' worldview may sometimes affect the results of a study. Using Research Application 23.1 to illustrate, participants from a Western culture that value being expressive and extraverted may have more difficulties admitting their social anxiety compared to participants from an Asian culture that place less emphasis on being assertive, but rather value modesty and conformity. In another example, some East Asians tend to frequently endorse the middle or center points of the scale (Chen, Lee, & Stevenson, 1995; Chia, Allred, & Jerzak, 1997; Gibbons, Hamby, & Dennis, 1997). This tendency is connected to the Confucian value, the doctrine of the mean (*zhong yong*) that encourages individuals not to stand out. This cultural value may reflect Asians' avoidance of being extreme in their responses, which could influence results when making cross-cultural comparison between Asians and other groups.

Participants' Ability to Report Their Experiences

A topic with a great deal of relevance for counselors is clients' ability to accurately report their internal experiences. (This discussion extends the previous discussion in Chapter 19 on self-report inventories.) Self-report is one of the most common and easiest ways to gather information about participants' emotional states (Diener, 2000). However, individuals do not always consistently and accurately report their emotions in the same way. Robinson and Clore (2002) proposed four different ways people access knowledge about their emotions: (a) through their feelings directly (experiential knowledge), (b) by retrieving specific aspects of past events (episodic memory), (c) by beliefs of how they would feel under a certain situation (situation-specific belief), and (d) by beliefs of how they would feel in general (identity-related belief). Through each different method of access to knowledge, individuals may provide potentially different responses about their emotions. And as time passes by, pieces of information are gradually lost. Therefore, oftentimes when people are unable to utilize experiential knowledge (e.g., actually reexperiencing the feelings of being discriminated), they turn to episodic knowledge (e.g., putting pieces of contextual information together about the last incident of being discriminated). When episodic knowledge is used, biases can occur depending on the certain aspects that are retrieved about the incident (e.g., which could be feeling fearful when called a derogatory term, feeling insulted when reflecting shortly after the incident, or feeling shameful afterward due to internalized racism); one might only remember certain parts of the experience and have forgotten others. Also, when memories are vague, individuals might simply express how they believe they would feel toward a specific situation or in general (e.g., anger). Moreover, participants may also have greater difficulty describing their mental processes when the situation is ambiguous, such as when participants are unaware of the stimuli that trigger their cognitive responses. Again using Research Application 23.1 as an example, some participants with social anxiety might have a difficult time identifying their level of social anxiety because that has been how they felt in social settings for a period of time. Thus, also incorporating other indicators such as measuring physiological responses could provide more objective information.

An early experiment conducted by Maier (1931) nicely depicts participants' inability to connect causal elements in ambiguous situations. Maier used the "string problem," in which participants were given the goal of holding two cords (one in each hand) hanging some 10 feet apart from the ceiling of a room that also contained various objects. Some of the participants, after some trial and error, would tie an object onto one of the cords, swing it like a pendulum, walk over and grab the other cord with one hand, and catch the swinging cord with the other hand. Voilà, the solution! If participants were unsuccessful in finding a solution, Maier, who had been wandering around the room, would walk by the cords and swing one of them into motion. Some of these participants then would subsequently pick up some object, tie it to the end of the cord, swing the cord like a pendulum, and shortly thereafter solve the problem. But when Maier asked these participants how they had arrived at the solution, he got answers such as "It just dawned on me" or "I just realized the cord would swing if I fastened a weight to it." In short, most of Maier's participants could not accurately report the causal events involved in their cognitive and affective processing. Other research in experimental information processing also suggests that participants have difficulty explaining the causal chain of events in their cognitive processes, particularly with the passage of time (Ericsson & Simon, 1984).

The ability to accurately report one's experiences should be carefully considered when counseling researchers attempt to examine clients' cognitive processes, especially within the often-ambiguous situation we call counseling. For example, why clients changed or what influenced them to change in the course of counseling may be a very difficult question for them to answer accurately and reliably. Likewise, as one researcher learned, asking clients how they decided to seek help at a counseling center resulted in a very broad range of responses—some of them incomprehensible! In short, counseling researchers in particular must carefully consider the type of information that can be accurately and reliably obtained about clients' mental processes, particularly retrospectively. Researchers may well ask clients to tell them more than the clients can know, and thus clients may provide misleading self-reports.

Strategies for Reducing Participant Bias

Investigators can use several strategies to reduce participant bias:

- Perhaps the most commonly used strategy to reduce participant bias due to the "good participant" role is to *keep participants blind or naive to the real purpose of the study,* which makes it more difficult for participants to consciously or unconsciously conform in ways similar to the predicted hypotheses. Participants are kept blind by withholding information not only about the hypotheses of the study, but sometimes even about the purpose of the study as well. When both participants and the experimenter are kept blind, as discussed in the previous section, the study is called *double blind.* Because the double-blind procedure tends to reduce both experimenter and participant bias, it is often recommended in counseling research.
- To reduce bias due to participants' desire to present themselves in a positive light, a general strategy is to *reduce the threat associated with the experiment.*

Thus, instructions on a questionnaire may explicitly state that "there are no right or wrong answers" and that "this inventory is not a test." The actual title of an inventory might also be altered if it is found to arouse anxiety or introduce demand characteristics. In addition, some researchers attempt to reduce threat by explicitly normalizing typical participant fears. For example, in a study of the coping process, participants might be told that it is normal to have unresolved personal problems, and that in fact "everyone has them."

- Participants' level of *responding to the research in socially desirable ways can also be assessed* using measures of social desirability. For example, the Marlowe-Crowne Social Desirability Scale (1982) is a commonly used scale to assess the level of social desirability scores in a particular study and to control for its effects through statistical analyses. However, there have been debates on whether correcting for social desirability enhances the validity of the study. Social desirability biases are not always undesirable and whether to control for them needs discretion (Fisher & Katz, 2000). Factors to consider would be how strongly are the variables associated with social desirability and whether impression management is part of what the researcher wants to incorporate along with the other variables when addressing their research question. In sum, the main question is: Would the validity of the study be enhanced or decreased by removing social desirability? For a more detailed discussion, please refer to Fisher and Katz (2000).

- Several procedures can be used to *increase participants' honesty and reduce participants' fears about confidentiality.* First and foremost, researchers often make honest and direct statements about their desire or need to obtain honest responses to increase the profession's understanding of a phenomenon. In addition, researchers typically communicate to participants that their responses will be strictly confidential, and then they explain the mechanisms for safeguarding confidentiality (e.g., coding). Moreover, in research using groups of participants, it is often helpful for participants to know that the researcher is interested in how whole groups of participants respond to the items, rather than specific individuals. Sometimes participants are asked to omit their name from their questionnaires, thereby maintaining anonymity. To ensure confidentiality when a researcher needs to collect data on several occasions and then compare a given participant's responses over time, participants can be asked to supply a code name in lieu of their actual name, or to generate an alias or develop a code based on some combination of numbers related to their birth dates, age, social security number, or the like. With today's technology, some programs have the function of tracking participants without indicating their identity. However, for online surveys the issue of confidentiality and anonymity are more complicated as certain information can be traced (Couper, 2000). For example, Buchanan and Hvizdak (2009) provided a number of strategies for protecting confidentiality and anonymity with online surveys, such as (a) having a clear idea of where the survey tool company stores the data and what happens to the data after the study has been completed, (b) ensuring that the survey company does not sell the data to third parties, (c) work with local institutional IT departments to ensure security, (d) provide information about the data collection site when recruiting participants, (e) inform participants that there are no completely secure interactions online, and (f) ensure that the data and participant identifiers are kept on separate servers. For more detailed information and strategies, please see Buchanan and Hvizdak's article.

- Often researchers will *make appeals to participants to increase their motivation level*. For example, participants can be briefly told the importance of the research and its possible outcomes (e.g., honest responses to the questionnaires will clarify changes or growth within supervision, or learning about one's experience as an Asian American will provide information about potential ethnic-related stressors). In exchange, researchers sometimes promise to provide participants with the results of the study, particularly if the study is of a survey nature.

- To identify potential demand characteristics, a strategy would be to *conduct pilot tests prior to administrating the study*. It would be helpful to closely simulate the actual study as much as possible, and then ask for feedback from those that participated to test out the procedures. Areas to gain feedback would include how the experience was like for those piloting, what factors influenced how they felt, thought, and responded during the study, their perceptions of the goals of the study and how that impacted their responses, as well as other issues that they encountered during the process. These pilot tests could provide information to minimize identified demand characteristics. However, there would certainly be other demand characteristics that were not identified prior to the study, and would need to be assessed after the study.

- Sometimes researchers concerned about demand characteristics and participant bias *conduct a postexperimental inquiry*. After the experiment the experimenter assesses potential participant bias by asking participants questions about their understanding of the purpose of the experiment, about their beliefs concerning how the experimenter wanted them to respond, and about any problems they encountered. Such a postexperimental inquiry might consist of a brief questionnaire (with perhaps follow-up inquiries of those participants who identified the true purpose of a study or those who felt pressured in some way) or be conducted via direct interviewing. Because direct interviewing can introduce demand characteristics in and of itself, it may best be done by someone who has not previously interacted with the participants. Even though there is considerable value in postexperimental inquiries, they have their limits: If participants have been biased by some demand characteristic but are totally unaware of any such influence, postexperimental inquiry will not reveal such participant bias.

- In addition to withholding information about the purpose of a study, a researcher can *reduce participant bias through disguise or deception*. The purpose of a study can be disguised by giving participants information that leads them to believe that a particular study is investigating some other research topic. Such strategies, however, carry important ethical considerations (see Chapter 3), and should be followed by a debriefing after the study. For example, participants about to take part in an attitude-change study might be told that they are being asked to evaluate whether the university should institute final oral exams for all undergraduates. Likewise, a study involving client perceptions of counselors might be framed in terms of evaluating the adequacy of the counseling center's service delivery.

- In counseling research that uses undergraduate students who participate to fulfill a class requirement, lack of student motivation or apathy can be a serious source of bias. One strategy to counter this bias is to *perform "spot checks" on participants' performance.* For example, a question can be inserted in the middle of a questionnaire telling participants that this is a validity-check item and asking them to simply "leave this item blank" or "select 'strongly agree'"; participants who do not follow such simple instructions are then removed from the study.
- With regard to intellectual skills, researchers can and should *evaluate the reading level of all reading materials (e.g., instruments, informed consent)* used in a study and match them to the sample. The reading level of materials can be easily assessed using a readability statistics function in Microsoft Word. Information about the sample can be obtained from personnel in the corresponding agencies or from colleagues familiar with the participants of interest.
- Researchers in counseling must *be attentive to participants' ability to report their cognitive and affective processes.* One strategy is to develop questionnaires based on cognitive processes that are most readily accessible to participants. Another is providing participants additional information to facilitate accurate reporting of the more ambiguous cognitive and affective processes, such as by enabling video or audio replay or by using interpersonal process recall (Kagan, 1975).

SUMMARY AND CONCLUSIONS

This chapter identified potential sources of bias in participants, experimenters, and investigators that might disguise or cloud the relationships between the experimental variables of interest; such biases are major threats to Kerlinger's MAXMINCON principle. The less controlled are the conditions of an experiment, the more various biases are likely to create error variance or extraneous variables. More error variance makes it more difficult to identify systematic variance due to the independent variables in question; the introduction of extraneous variables makes it difficult to isolate the variables responsible for change. Thus, participant, experimenter, and investigator biases introduce extraneous variables that may distort or disguise the relationships among the experimental variables.

This chapter discussed investigator and experimenter biases that may well affect the results of a study. We discussed three major types of experimenter bias: experimenter attributes, investigator and experimenter expectancies, and experimental design and procedures. We also discussed three major sources of participant bias—demand characteristics, participant characteristics, and participants' abilities to report their experiences—and described several strategies for controlling or minimizing such biases.

Participant, investigator, and experimenter biases represent serious problems for the counseling researcher. These sources of bias can quickly reduce the results of many long hours spent developing and conducting a study into a pile of meaningless information. The veteran researcher remains vigilant of various sources of bias and constantly monitors the study to detect any biases that might have crept in. Bias is a particularly important issue for counseling researchers because much of our research is conducted in applied settings, where fewer experimental controls are available and thus more sources of bias are potentially operative.

Because minimizing and eliminating bias is a matter of degree, and because the researcher is often uncertain whether various sources of bias are operative, it is useful to qualify the results of one's research (typically done in the discussion section) concerning the possible sources of bias that might have been operative. An increasingly common research strategy is for investigators to statistically test for the existence of various biases and confounds through a series of preliminary analyses. Cheng, Tsui, and Lam's study (2014) provides an example of using such preliminary analyses. They examined the demographic and outcome variables at baseline to detect differences between the experimental and control groups. Such statistical procedures are recommended, as are frank discussions of other possible sources of bias that were untested.

Finally, although the chapter mostly focuses on biases related to design and administrative aspects of research studies, implicit biases cannot be overlooked. Our worldviews as researchers can have substantial impact on the results of research studies that we conduct. Our implicit attitudes as a profession can also influence the research that we choose to do, or not do, which can have a substantial impact on the field as a whole

STIMULUS QUESTIONS

Reflections on Bias

It is often very difficult to clearly identify the myriad of biases that threaten the validity of a study. The purpose of this exercise is to reflect on a wide range of biases with the goal of becoming more aware and sensitive to biases that threaten the validity of a study.

1. Briefly discuss how your values and beliefs could result in cultural biases when conducting a research study.
2. In considering your research interests, which of your personal attributes could cause differential responses in participants?
3. List four ways you could most significantly reduce biases related to the experimental procedures in the type of research topics you are considering.
4. Identify potential demand characteristics in the research topics you are considering.
5. Discuss how the participants' worldviews might create some confounding biases in the type of research topics you are considering.
6. In what ways could participants' need for self-presentation, or saving face, affect the results of your research?
7. Discuss the most important things you have learned about investigator, experimenter, and participant bias in scholarly research.

References

Academy of Psychological Clinical Science. (2014). APCS Mission page. Retrieved December 18, 2014, from https://www.acadpsychclinicalscience.org/mission.html

Addis, M. E., Hatgis, C., Krasnow, A. D., Jacob, K., Bourne, L., & Mansfield, A. (2004). Effectiveness of cognitive-behavioral treatment for panic disorder versus treatment as usual in a managed care setting. *Journal of Consulting and Clinical Psychology, 72*, 625–635. Retrieved from http://dx.doi.org/10.1037/0022-006X.72.4.625

Adelson, J., & Owen, J. (2012). Bringing the psychotherapist back: Basic concepts regarding the examination of therapist effects using multilevel modeling. *Psychotherapy, 49*, 152–162.

Adler, N. E., Epel, E., Castellazzo, G., & Ickovics, J. (2000). Relationship of subjective and objective social status with psychological and physiological functioning: Preliminary data in healthy white women. *Health Psychology, 19*(6), 586–592.

Adler, P. A., & Adler, P. (1991). *Backboards and blackboards.* New York: Columbia University Press.

Adler, P. A., & Adler, P. (1994). Observational techniques. In N. K. Denzin & Y. S. Lincoln (Eds.), *Handbook of qualitative research* (pp. 377–392). Thousand Oaks, CA: Sage.

Ægisdóttir, S., Gerstein, L. H., & Çinarbaş, D. C. (2008). Methodological issues in cross-cultural counseling research: Equivalence, bias, and translations. *The Counseling Psychologist, 36*(2), 188–219. Retrieved from http://dx.doi.org/10.1177/0011000007305384

Ahmed, A. M. (2010). Muslim discrimination: Evidence from two lost-letter experiments. *Journal of Applied Social Psychology, 40*(4), 888–898. doi:10.1111/j.1559-1816.2010.00602.x

Albee, G. W. (2000). Commentary on prevention and counseling psychology. *The Counseling Psychologist, 28*(6), 845–853. doi:10.1177/0011000000286006

Alegría, M., Canino, G., Shrout, P. E., Woo, M., Duan, N., Vila, D., & …Meng, X. (2008). Prevalence of mental illness in immigrant and non-immigrant U.S. Latino groups. *The American Journal of Psychiatry, 165*(3), 359–369. doi:10.1176/appi.ajp.2007.07040704

Alexander, C. H., & Suzuki, L. A. (2001). Measurement of multicultural constructs: Integration and research directions. In J. G. Ponterotto, J. M. Casas, L. A. Suzuki, & C. M. Alexander (Eds.), *Handbook of multicultural counseling* (2nd ed., pp. 499–505). Thousand Oaks, CA: Sage.

American Counseling Association. (2014). *Code of ethics.* Alexandria, VA: Author.

American Educational Research Association, American Psychological Association, & National Council on Measurement in Education. (2014). *Standards for educational and psychological testing.* Washington, DC: American Educational Research Association.

American Psychiatric Association. (1994). DSM-IV. *Diagnostic and statistical manual of mental disorders* (4th ed.). Washington, DC: American Psychiatric Association.

American Psychological Association, APA Presidential Task Force on Evidence-Based Practice (2006). Evidence-based practice in psychology. *American Psychologist, 61*(4), 271–285. doi:10.1037/0003-066X.61.4.271

American Psychological Association. (1983). *Publication manual of the American Psychological Association* (3rd ed.). Washington, DC: Author.

American Psychological Association. (1994). *Publication manual of the American Psychological Association* (4th ed.). Washington, DC: Author.

American Psychological Association. (2002). *Ethical principles of psychologists and code of conduct.* Washington, DC: Author. doi:10.1037/e305322003-001

American Psychological Association. (2003). Guidelines on multicultural education, training, research, practice, and organizational change for psychologists. *American Psychologist, 58*, 377–402. doi:2003-06802-00610. 1037/0003-066X.58.5.377. Retrieved from http://dx.doi.org.ezproxy.library.wisc.edu/10.1037/0003-066X.58.5.377

American Psychological Association. (2004). *Resolution on culture and gender awareness in international psychology.* Washington, DC: Author. doi:10.1037/e590742010-004

American Psychological Association. (2005). Evidence-based practice in psychology. APA Presidential Task Force on Evidence-Based Practice. *American Psychologist, 61*, 271–285.

American Psychological Association. (2006). *Report of the Task Force on the Implementation of the Multicultural*

Guidelines. Washington, DC: Author. Retrieved from www.apa.org/pi

American Psychological Association. (2007). Task Force on Socioeconomic Status. *Report of the APA task force on socioeconomic status*. Washington, DC: American Psychological Association. doi:10.1037/e582962010-001

American Psychological Association. (2010a). *Publication manual of the American Psychological Association* (6th ed.). Washington, DC: Author.

American Psychological Association. (2010b, June). *Ethical principles of psychologists and code of conduct* (original published 2002, amended June 1, 2010). Retrieved from http://www.apa.org/ethics/code/index.aspx

Anders Ericsson, K. (2008). Deliberate practice and acquisition of expert performance: A general overview. *Academic Emergency Medicine, 15*(11), 988–994.

Anton, W. D., & Reed, J. R. (1991). *College adjustment scales*. Odessa, FL: Psychological Assessment Resources.

Armento, M. E., McNulty, J. K., & Hopko, D. R. (2012). Behavioral activation of religious behaviors (BARB): Randomized trial with depressed college students. *Psychology of Religion and Spirituality, 4*, 206–222. Retrieved from http://dx.doi.org/10.1037/a0026405

Arnett, J. J. (2008). The neglected 95%: Why American psychology needs to become less American. *American Psychologist, 63*(7), 602–614. doi:10.1037/0003-066X.63.7.602

Arredondo, P., Toporek, M. S., Brown, S., Jones, J., Locke, D. C., Sanchez, J. & Stadler, H. (1996). Operationalization of the Multicultural Counseling Competencies. Alexandria, VA: AMCD. doi: 10.1002/j.2161-1912.1996.tb00288.x

Asner-Self, K. K., & Marotta, S. A. (2005). Developmental indices among Central American immigrants exposed to war related trauma: Clinical implications for counselors. *Journal of Counseling and Development, 83*, 162–171. doi:10.1002/j.1556-6678.2005.tb00593.x

Atkinson, D. (Ed.). (2004). *Counseling American minorities*. Boston: McGraw-Hill.

Atkinson, D., & Hackett, G. (2004). *Counseling diverse populations*. Boston:: McGraw-Hill.

Attkisson, C. C., & Zwick, R. (1982). The Client Satisfaction Questionnaire: Psychometric properties and correlations with service utilization and psychotherapy outcome. *Evaluation and Program Planning, 6*, 299–314.

August, R. A. (2011). Women's later life career development: Looking through the lens of the kaleidoscope career model. *Journal of Career Development, 38*(3), 208–236. doi:10.1177/0894845310362221

Awad, G. H., & Cokley, K. O. (2009). Designing and interpreting quantitative research in multicultural counseling. In J. G. Ponterotto, J. M. Casas, L. A. Suzuki, C. M. Alexander, (Eds.), *Handbook of multicultural counseling* (3rd ed., pp. 385–396). Thousand Oaks, CA: Sage.

Azibo, D. A. (1988). Understanding the proper and improper usage of the comparative research framework. *Journal of Black Psychology, 15*, 81–91.

Baardseth, T. P., Goldberg, S. B., Pace, B. T., Wislocki, A. P., Frost, N. D., Siddiqui, J. R., et al. (2012).

Cognitive–behavioral therapy versus other therapies: Redux. *Clinical Psychology Review, 33*, 395–405. doi: 10.1016/j.cpr.2013.01.004

Babbie, E. (2001). *The practice of social research* (9th ed.). Belmont, CA: Wadsworth/Thomson Learning.

Baker, D. B., & Benjamin, L. J. (2000). The affirmation of the scientist-practitioner: A look back at Boulder. *American Psychologist, 55*(2), 241–247. Retrieved from http://dx.doi.org/10.1037/0003-066X.55.2.241

Baker, T. B., McFall, R. M., & Shoham, V. (2008). Current status and future prospects of clinical psychology: Toward a scientifically principled approach to mental and behavioral health care. *Psychological Science in the Public Interest, 9*(2), 67–103. doi:10.1111/j.1539-6053.2009.01036.x

Baldwin, S. A., Berkeljon, A., Atkins, D. C., Olsen, J. A., & Nielsen, S. L. (2009). Rates of change in naturalistic psychotherapy: Contrasting dose-effect and good-enough level models of change. *Journal of Consulting and Clinical Psychology, 77*, 203–211. doi: 10.1037/a0015235

Baldwin, S.A., & Imel, Z. E. (2013). Counselor effects. In M. J. Lambert (Ed.), *Bergin and Garfield's handbook of psychotherapy and behavior change* (6th ed.). New York: Wiley.

Baldwin, S. A., & Imel, Z. E. (2013). Therapist effects: Findings and methods. *Bergin and Garfield's handbook of psychotherapy and behavior change*, 258–297. New York: Wiley.

Baldwin, S. A., Murray, D. M., & Shadish, W. R. (2005). Empirically supported treatments or type I errors? Problems with the analysis of data from group-administered treatments. *Journal of Consulting and Clinical Psychology, 73*, 924–935. doi: 10.1037/0022-006X.73.5.924

Baldwin, S. A., Wampold, B. E., & Imel, Z. E. (2007). Untangling the alliance-outcome correlation: Exploring the relative importance of therapist and patient variability in the alliance. *Journal of Consulting and Clinical Psychology, 75*(6), 842–852. doi: 10.1037/0022-006X.75.6.842

Bangert, A. W., & Baumberger, J. P. (2005). Research designs and statistical techniques used in the *Journal of Counseling and Development*, 1990–2001. *Journal of Counseling and Development, 83*, 480–487. doi: 10.1002/j.1556-6678.2005.tb00369.x

Barber, J. P., & Crits-Christoph, P. (1996). Development of a therapist adherence competence rating scale for supportive-expressive dynamic psychotherapy: A preliminary report. *Psychotherapy Research, 6*, 79–92. doi: 10.1080/10503309612331331608

Barber, J. P., Gallop, R., Crits-Christoph, P., Barrett, M. S., Klostermann, S., McCarthy, K. S., & Sharpless, B. A. (2008). The role of the alliance and techniques in predicting outcome of supportive-expressive dynamic therapy for cocaine-dependence. *Psychoanalysis Psychology, 25*, 461–482.

Barber, J. P., Gallop, R., Crits-Christoph, P., Frank, A., Thase, M. E., Weiss, R. D., et al., (2006). The role of therapist adherence, therapist competence, and alliance in predicting outcome of individual drug counseling: Results from the National Institute Drug Abuse Collaborative Cocaine Treatment Study.

Psychotherapy Research, 16, 229–240. doi: 10.1080/ 10503300500288951

Barkham, M., & Mellor-Clark, J. (2000). Rigour and relevance: Practice-based evidence in the psychological therapies. In N. Rowland & S. Goss (Eds.). Evidence-based counselling and psychological therapies: Research and applications (pp.127–144). London: Routledge.

Barlow, D. H. (2004). Psychological treatments. *American Psychologist, 59,* 869–878. Retrieved from http:// dx.doi.org/10.1037/0003-066X.59.9.869

Barlow, D. H. (Ed.). (1981). *Behavioral assessment of adult disorders.* New York: Guilford Press.

Barlow, D. H., & Hersen, M. (1984). *Single case experimental designs: Strategies for studying behavior change* (2nd ed.). New York: Pergamon Press.

Baron, R. M., & Kenny, D. A. (1986). The moderator-mediator variable distinction in social psychological research: Conceptual, strategic, and statistical considerations. *Journal of Personality and Social Psychology, 51,* 1173–1182. doi:10.1037/0022-3514.51.6.1173

Baskin, T. W., Tierney, S. C., Minami, T., & Wampold, B. E. (2003). Establishing specificity in psychotherapy: A meta-analysis of structural equivalence of placebo controls. *Journal of Consulting and Clinical Psychology, 71,* 973–979. doi: 10.1037/0022-006X.71.6.973

Baucom, K. J. W., Baucom, B. R., & Christensen, A. (2012, June 18). Do the naïve know best? The predictive power of naïve ratings of couple interactions. *Psychological Assessment.* Advance online publication. doi: 10.1037/a0028680

Baumrind, D. (1976). *Nature and definition of informed consent in research involving deception.* Background paper prepared for the National Commission for the Protection of Human Subjects of Biomedical and Behavioral Research. Washington, DC: Department of Health, Education, and Welfare.

Bazeley, P. (2003). Computerized data analysis for mixed methods research. In A. Tashakkori & C. Teddlie (Eds.), *Handbook of mixed methods in social and behavioral research* (pp. 385–422). Thousand Oaks, CA: Sage.

Beauchamp, T. L., & Childress, J. F. (2001). *Principles of biomedical ethics* (5th ed.). New York: Oxford University Press.

Beck, A. T., Rush, A. J., Shaw, B. F., & Emery, G. (1979). *Cognitive therapy of depression.* New York: Guilford Press.

Beck, A.T., Ward, C. H., Mendelson, M., Mock, J., & Erbaugh, J. (1961). An inventory for measuring depression. *Archives of General Psychiatry, 4*(6), 561–571. doi:10.1001/archpsyc.1961.01710120031004.

Becker, D., & Lamb, S. (1994). Sex bias in the diagnosis of borderline personality disorder and posttraumatic stress disorder. *Professional Psychology, 25,* 55–61. doi: 10.1037/0735-7028.25.1.55

Bell, E. C., Marcus, D. K., & Goodlad, J. K. (2013, May 20). Are the parts as good as the whole? A meta-analysis of component treatment studies. *Journal of Consulting and Clinical Psychology.* Advance online publication. doi: 10.1037/a0033004

Bem, D. J. (2003). Writing a review article for Psychological Bulletin. In A. E. Kazdin (Ed.), *Methodological issues*

and strategies in clinical research (3rd ed., pp. 859–873). Washington, DC: American Psychological Association. doi: 10.1037/0033-2909.118.2.172

Benjamin, L. J., & Baker, D. B. (2003). Walter Van Dyke Bingham: Portrait of an industrial psychologist. In G. A. Kimble & M. Wertheimer (Eds.), *Portraits of pioneers in psychology* (Vol. V, pp. 141–157). Washington, DC; Mahwah, NJ: American Psychological Association.

Bentler, P. M., & Chou, C. P. (1987). Practical issues in structural modeling. *Sociological Methods and Research, 16,* 78–117. Retrieved from http:// dx.doi.org/10.1177/0049124187016001004

Berg, I. A. (1954). Ideomotor response set: Symbolic sexual gesture in the counseling interview. *Journal of Counseling Psychology, 1,* 180–183.

Bergin, A. E., & Garfield, S. L. (Eds.). (1971). *Handbook of psychotherapy and behavior change.* New York: Wiley.

Bergin, A. E., & Garfield, S. L. (Eds.). (1994). *Handbook of psychotherapy and behavior change.* New York: Wiley.

Bergin, A. E., & Strupp, H. H. (1970). New directions in psychotherapy research. *Journal of Abnormal Psychology, 76,* 13–26. doi: 10.1037/h0029634

Berkowitz, A. D. (2003). Applications of Social Norms Theory to other health and social justice issues. In H. W. Perkins (Ed.), *The social norms approach to preventing school and college substance abuse.* San Francisco: Jossey-Bass.

Bernal, G., & Scharró-del-Río, M. R. (2001). Are empirically supported treatments valid for ethnic minorities? Toward an alternative approach for treatment research. *Cultural Diversity and Ethnic Minority Psychology, 7,* 328–342. doi:10.1037/1099-9809.7.4.328

Bernal, G., Cumba-Aviles, E., & Rodriguez-Quintana, N. (2014). Methodological challenges in research with ethnic, racial, and ethnocultural groups. In F. T. L. Leong (Editor-in-Chief), *APA handbook of multicultural psychology, Vol. 1: Theory and research* (pp. 105–124). Washington, DC: American Psychological Association. doi:10.1037/14189-006

Berríos, R., & Lucca, N. (2006). Qualitative methodology in counseling research: Recent contributions and challenges for a new century. *Journal of Counseling and Development, 84*(2), 174–186. doi:10.1002/ j.1556-6678.2006.tb00393.x

Betancourt, H., & Lopez, S. R. (1993). The study of culture, ethnicity, and race in American psychology. *American Psychologist, 48,* 629–637. doi:10.1037/ 0003-066X.48.6.629

Betz, N., & Fitzgerald, L. (1987). *The career psychology of women.* New York: Academic Press.

Beutler, L. E., Harwood, T. M., Michelson, A., Song, X., & Holman, J. (2011). *Psychotherapy relationships that work: Evidence-based responsiveness* (2nd ed.). New York: Oxford University Press. doi: 10.1093/ acprof:oso/9780199737208.003.0013

Bhar, S. S., & Beck, A. T. (2009). Treatment integrity of studies that compare short-term psychodynamic psychotherapy with cognitive-behavior therapy. *Clinical Psychology: Science and Practice, 16*(3), 370–378. doi: 10.1111/j.1468-2850.2009.01176.x.

Bishop, R. M., & Bieschke, K. J. (1998). Applying social cognitive theory to interest in research among counseling psychology doctoral students: A path analysis. *Journal of Counseling Psychology, 45*(2), 182–188. doi:10.1037/0022-0167.45.2.182

Blais, M. A., Lenderking, W. R., Baer, L., deLorell, A., Peets, K., Leahy, L., & Burns, C. (1999). Development and initial validation of a brief mental health outcome measure. *Journal of Personality Assessment,73,* 359–373. doi: 10.1207/S15327752JPA7303_5

Blustein, D. L., Goodyear, R. K., Perry, J. C., & Cypers, S. (2005). The shifting sands of counseling psychology programs? Institutional contexts: An environmental scan and revitalizing strategies. *The Counseling Psychologist, 33*(5), 610–634. doi:10.1177/0011000005277820

Bohart, A. C., & Tallman, K. (1999). *How clients make therapy work: The process of active self-healing.* Washington, DC: American Psychological Association.

Bohus, M., Haaf, B., Simms, T., Limberger, M. F., Schmahl, C., Unckel, C., Lieb, K., & Linehan, M. M. (2004). Effectiveness of inpatient dialectical behavioral therapy for borderline personality disorder: A controlled trial. *Behaviour Research and Therapy, 42,* 487–499. doi: 10.1016/S0005-7967(03)00174-8

Boice, R. (1989). Procrastination, busyness and bingeing. *Behaviour Research and Therapy, 27*(6), 605–611. doi:10.1016/0005-7967(89)90144-7

Bordin, E. S. (1965). Simplification as a strategy for research in psychotherapy. *Journal of Consulting Psychology, 29*(6), 495–503. doi:10.1037/h0022760

Bordin, E. S. (1979). The generalizability of the psychoanalytic concept of working alliance. *Psychotherapy: Theory, Research and Practice, 16,* 252–260.

Borgen, F. H. (1984). Counseling psychology. *Annual Review of Psychology, 35,* 579–604. doi: 10.1146/annurev.ps.35.020184.003051

Borgen, F. H., & Barnett, D. C. (1987). Applying cluster analysis in counseling psychology research. *Journal of Counseling Psychology, 34,* 456–468. doi:10.1037/0022-0167.34.4.456

Bracht, G. H., & Glass, V. V. (1968). The external validity of experiments. *American Educational Research Journal, 5,* 437–474. doi:10.3102/00028312005004437

Bradley, J. V. (1968). *Distribution-free statistical tests.* Englewood Cliffs, NJ: Prentice-Hall.

Brandon, D.T., Isaac, L.A., & LaVeist, T.A. (2005). The legacy of Tuskegee and trust in medical care: Is Tuskegee responsible for race differences in mistrust of medical care? *Journal of the National Medical Association, 97*(7), 951–956.

Brennan, K. A., Clark, C. L., & Shaver, P. R. (1998). Self-report measurement of adult attachment: An integrative overview. In J. A. Simpson & W. S. Rholes (Eds.), *Attachment theory and close relationships* (pp. 46–76). New York: Guilford Press.

Brennan, R. L., (2001). Generalizability theory. New York: Springer. doi:10.1007/978-1-4757-3456-0

Breuer, J., & Freud, S. (1955). Studies on hysteria. In J. Strachey (Ed. and Trans.), *The standard edition of the complete psychological works of Sigmund Freud* (Vol. 2). London: Hogarth Press. (Original work published 1893–1895.)

Bridgewater, C. A., Bornstein, P. H., & Walkenbach, J. (1981). Ethical issues and the assignment of publication credit. *American Psychologist, 36,* 524–525. doi: 10.1037/0003-066X.36.5.524

Broad, W., & Wade, N. (1982). *Betrayers of the truth.* New York: Simon & Schuster.

Brown, S. D., Lent, R. W., Ryan, N. E., & McPartland, E. B. (1996). Self-efficacy as an intervening mechanism between research training environments and scholarly productivity: A theoretical and methodological extension. *The Counseling Psychologist, 24,* 535–544. Retrieved from http://dx.doi.org/10.1177/0011000096243012

Brown, T. A. (2006). *Confirmatory factor analysis for applied research.* New York: Guilford Press.

Brown, T. A. (2015). *Confirmatory factor analysis for applied research* (2nd ed.). New York: Guilford Press.

Buchanan, E. A., & Hvizdak, E. E. (2009). Online survey tools: Ethical and methodological concerns of human research ethics committees. *Journal of Empirical Research on Human Research Ethics, 4*(2), 37–48. doi: 10.1525/jer.2009.4.2.37

Buchler, J. (Ed.). (1955). *Philosophical writings of Peirce.* New York: Dover.

Buki, L. P., & Selem, M. (2012). Health disparities: Issues and opportunities for counseling psychologists. In N. A. Fouad, J. A. Carter, & L. M. Subich (Eds.), *APA handbook of counseling psychology,* Vol. 2: Practice, interventions, and applications (pp. 235–251). Washington, DC: American Psychological Association. doi:10.1037/13755-010

Burkard, A. W., & Knox, S. (2004). Effect of therapist color-blindness on empathy and attributions in cross-cultural counseling. *Journal of Counseling Psychology, 51,* 387–397. doi: 10.1037/0022-0167.51.4.387

Burlew, A. K. (2003). Research with ethnic minorities: Conceptual, methodological, and analytical issues. In G. Bernal. J. E. Trimble, A. K. Burlew, & F. T. L. Leong (Eds.), *Handbook of racial and ethnic minority psychology* (pp. 179–197). Thousand Oaks, CA: Sage. doi:10.4135/9781412976008.n9

Butler, S. F., Henry, W. P., & Strupp, H. H. (1992). *Measuring adherence and skill in time-limited dynamic psychotherapy.* Unpublished manuscript, Vanderbilt University.

Byrne, B. M. (2014). Recent statistical advances. In F. T. L. Leong (Editor-in-Chief), *APA handbook of multicultural psychology, Vol. 1: Theory and research* (pp. 125–140). Washington, DC: American Psychological Association.

Byrne, B. M., & Watkins, D. (2003). The issue of measurement invariance revisited. *Journal of Cross-Cultural Psychology, 34,* 155–175. doi:10.1177/0022022102250225

Cabral, R. R., & Smith, T. B. (2011). Racial/ethnic matching of clients and therapists in mental health services: A meta-analytic review of preferences, perceptions, and outcomes. *Journal of Counseling Psychology, 58*(4), 537–554. doi:10.1037/a0025266

Campbell, D. T., & Stanley, J. C. (1963). *Experimental and quasi-experimental designs for research.* Chicago: Rand McNally.

Campbell, L. M., III. (1973). A variation of thought stopping in a twelve-year-old boy: A case report. *Journal of Behavior Therapy and Experimental Psychiatry, 4,* 69–70. doi: 10.1016/0005-7916(73)90043-8

Caplan, G., & Caplan, R. B. (1994). The need for quality control in primary prevention. *The Journal of Primary Prevention, 15*(1), 15–29. doi:10.1007/BF02196344

Caplan, P. J., & Cosgrove, L. (Eds.). (2004). *Bias in psychiatric diagnosis.* Northvale, NJ: Jason Aronson.

Carr, A. G., & Caskie, G. L. (2010). A path analysis of social problem-solving as a predictor of white racial identity. *Journal of College Student Development, 51*(6), 622–636. doi:10.1353/csd.2010.0024

Carter, L. I., Mollen, D., & Smith, N. G. (2014). Locus of control, minority stress, and psychological distress among lesbian, gay, and bisexual individuals. *Journal of Counseling Psychology, 61*(1), 169–175. doi:10.1037/a0034593

Carter, R. (1995). *The influence of race and racial identity in psychotherapy: Toward a racially inclusive model.* New York: Wiley.

Carter, R. T. (2007). Racism and psychological and emotional injury: Recognizing and assessing race-based traumatic stress. *The Counseling Psychologist, 35,* 13–105. doi:10.1177/0011000006292033

Chang, D. F., & Yoon, P. (2011). Ethnic minority clients' perceptions of the significance of race in cross-racial therapy relationships. *Psychotherapy Research, 21*(5), 567–582. doi:10.1080/10503307.2011.592549

Chao, R., Wei, M., Good, G. E., & Flores, L. Y. (2011). Race/ethnicity, color-blind racial attitudes, and multicultural counseling competence: The moderating effects of multicultural counseling training. *Journal of Counseling Psychology, 58*(1), 72–82. doi:10.1037/a0022091

Chapman, L. J., & Chapman, J. P. (1969). Illusory correlations as an obstacle to the use of valid psychodiagnostic tests. *Journal of Abnormal Psychology, 74,* 271–280. doi: 10.1037/h0027592

Charmaz, K. (2000). Grounded theory: Objectivist and constructivist methods. In N. K. Denzin & Y. S. Lincoln (Eds.), *Handbook of qualitative research* (2nd ed., pp. 509–536). Thousand Oaks, CA: Sage.

Charmaz, K. (2006). *Constructing grounded theory: A practical guide through qualitative analysis.* Thousand Oaks, CA: Sage.

Chavez-Korell, S., & Torres, L. (2014). Perceived stress and depressive symptoms among Latino adults: The moderating role of ethnic identity cluster patterns. *The Counseling Psychologist, 42*(2), 230–254. doi:10.1177/0011000013477905

Chen, C., Lee, S-Y., & Stevenson, H. W. (1995). Response style and cross-cultural comparisons of rating scales among East Asian and North American students. *Psychological Science, 6,* 170–175. doi:10.1111/j.1467-9280.1995.tb00327.x

Cheng, C., Lau, H.-P. B., & Chan, M.-P. S. (2014). Coping flexibility and psychological adjustment to stressful life changes: A meta-analytic review. *Psychological Bulletin.* Advance online publication. doi:10.1037/a0037913

Cheng, S., Tsui, P., & Lam, J. M. (2014). Improving mental health in health care practitioners: Randomized controlled trial of a gratitude intervention. *Journal of Consulting and Clinical Psychology, 83,* 177–186. doi:10.1037/a0037895

Cheng, S. K., Chong, G. H., & Wong, C. W. (1999). Chinese Frost Multidimensional Perfectionism Scale: A validation and prediction of self-esteem and psychological distress. *Journal of Clinical Psychology, 55,* 1051–1061. doi:10.1002/(SICI)1097-4679(199909)55:9<1051::AID-JCLP3>3.0.CO;2-1

Chia, R. C., Allred, L. J., & Jerzak, P. A. (1997). Attitudes toward women in Taiwan and China: Current status, problems, and suggestions for future research. *Psychology of Women Quarterly, 21,* 137–150. doi:10.1111/j.1471-6402.1997.tb00105.x

Choi, K. H., Buskey, W., & Johnson, B. (2010). Evaluation of counseling outcomes at a university counseling center: The impact of clinically significant change on problem resolution and academic functioning. *Journal of Counseling Psychology, 57,* 297–303. Retrieved from http://dx.doi.org/10.1037/a0020029

Christensen, L. B. (1980). *Experimental methodology* (2nd ed.). Boston: Allyn & Bacon.

Chung, Y. B., & Katayama, M. (1996). Assessment of sexual orientation in lesbian/gay/bisexual studies. *Journal of Homosexuality, 30*(4), 49–62. doi:10.1300/J082v30n04_03

Chwalisz, K. (2003). Evidence-based practice: A framework for twenty-first-century scientist-practitioner training. *The Counseling Psychologist, 31*(5), 497–528. doi:10.1177/0011000003256347

Claiborn, C. D. (1985). Harold B. Pepinsky: A life of science and practice. *Journal of Counseling and Development, 64,* 5–13. Retrieved from http://dx.doi.org/10.1002/j.1556-6676.1985.tb00994.x

Claiborn, C. D. (1987). Science and practice: Reconsidering the Pepinskys. *Journal of Counseling and Development, 65,* 286–288. Retrieved from http://dx.doi.org/10.1002/j.1556-6676.1987.tb01286.x

Clark, L. A., & Watson, D. (1995). Constructing validity: Basic issues in objective scale development. *Psychological Assessment, 7*(3), 309–319. doi: 10.1037/1040-3590.7.3.309

Clarkin, J. F., Levy, K. N., Lenzenweger, M. F., & Kernberg, O. F. (2007). Evaluating three treatments for borderline personality disorder: A multiwave study, 922–928. *The American Journal of Psychiatry, 164,* 6.

Cohen, G. L., Garcia, J., Apfel, N., & Master, A. (2006). Reducing the racial achievement gap: A social psychological intervention. *Science, 313*(5791), 1307–1310. doi:10.1126/science.1128317

Cohen, G. L., Garcia, J., Purdie-Vaughns, V., Apfel, N., & Brzustoski, P. (2009). Recursive processes in self-affirmation: Intervening to close the minority achievement gap. *Science, 324*(5925), 400–403. doi:10.1126/science.1170769

Cohen, J. (1968). Multiple regression as a general data-analytic strategy. *Psychological Bulletin, 70*, 426–443. doi: 10.1037/h0026714

Cohen, J. (1988). *Statistical power analysis for the behavioral sciences* (2nd ed.). Hillsdale, NJ: Lawrence Erlbaum.

Cohen, J., & Cohen, P. (1983). *Applied multiple regression/correlation analysis for the behavioral sciences* (2nd ed.). Hillsdale, NJ: Erlbaum. doi:10.1037/0022-0167.34.3.315

Cohen, M. R., & Nagel, E. (1934). *An introduction to logic and scientific method*. New York: Harcourt, Brace & Company.

Cohen, R. J., Swerdlik, M. E., & Phillips, S. M. (1996). *Psychological testing and assessment: An introduction to tests and measurement*. Mountain View, CA: Mayfield.

Cokley, K. (2004). The use of race and ethnicity constructs in psychological practice: A review. In R. Carter (Ed.), *Handbook of racial cultural psychology and counseling* (Vol. 2, pp. 249–261). Hoboken, NJ: Wiley.

Cokley, K. O., & Awad, G. H. (2013). In defense of quantitative methods: Using the "master's tools" to promote social justice. *Journal for Social Action in Counseling and Psychology, 5*, 26–41.

Cole, D. A. (1987). The utility of confirmatory factor analysis in test validation research. *Journal of Consulting and Clinical Psychology, 55*, 584–594. doi: 10.1037/0022-006X.55.4.584

Cole, D. A., Lazarick, D. L., & Howard, G. S. (1987). Construct validity and the relation between depression and social skill. *Journal of Counseling Psychology, 34*, 315–321.

Coleman, H. L. K., Wampold, B. E., & Casali, S. L. (1995). Ethnic minorities' ratings of ethnically similar and European American counselors: A meta-analysis. *Journal of Counseling Psychology, 42*, 55–64. doi:10.1037/0022-0167.42.1.55

Committee on Prevention of Mental Disorders. (1994). *Reducing risks for mental disorders: Frontiers for preventive intervention research*. Washington, DC: National Academies Press, Institute of Medicine.

Condon, K. M., & Lambert, M. J. (1994, June). *Assessing clinical significance: Application to the State-Trait Anxiety Inventory*. Paper presented at the annual meeting of the Society for Psychotherapy Research, York, England.

Constantine, M. G., Quintana, S. M., Leung, S. A., & Phelps, R. E. (1995). Survey of the professional needs of division 17's ethnic and racial minority psychologists. *The Counseling Psychologist, 23*, 546–561. doi:10.1177/0011000095233011

Cook, B., Alegría, M., Lin, J. Y., & Guo, J. (2009). Pathways and correlates connecting Latinos' mental health with exposure to the United States. *American Journal of Public Health, 99*(12), 2247–2254. doi:10.2105/AJPH.2008.137091

Cook, T. D., & Campbell, D. T. (1979). *Quasi-experimentation: Design and analysis issues for field settings*. Boston: Houghton Mifflin.

Cooper, Z., Doll, H., Bailey-Straebler, S., Kluczniok, D., Murphy, R., O'Connor, M. E., & Fairburn, C. G. (2015). The development of an online measure of therapist competence. *Behaviour Research and Therapy. 64*, 43-48. doi:10.1016/j.brat.2014.11.007

Corning, A. F. (2002). Self-esteem as a moderator between perceived discrimination and psychological distress among women. *Journal of Counseling Psychology, 49*, 117–126. doi:10.1037/0022-0167.49.1.117

Corrigan, J. D., Dell, D. M., Lewis, K. N., & Schmidt, L. D. (1980). Counseling as a social influence process: A review [monograph]. *Journal of Counseling Psychology, 27*, 395–441. doi: 10.1037/0022-0167.27.4.395

Couper, M. P. (2000). Review. Web surveys: A review of issues and approaches. *Public Opinion Quarterly, 64*, 464–494. doi:10.1086/318641

Cournoyer, R. J., & Mahalik, J. R. (1995). Cross-sectional study of gender role conflict examining college-aged and middle-aged men. *Journal of Counseling Psychology, 42*, 11–19. doi:10.1037/0022-0167.42.1.11

Cramer, R. J., Miller, A. K., Amacker, A. M., & Burks, A. C. (2013). Openness, right-wing authoritarianism, and antigay prejudice in college students: A meditational model. *Journal of Counseling Psychology, 60*, 64–71. doi:10.1037/a0031090

Creswell, J. W. (1994). *Research design: Qualitative and quantitative approaches*. Thousand Oaks, CA: Sage.

Creswell, J. W. (1998). *Qualitative inquiry and research design: Choosing among five traditions*. Thousand Oaks, CA: Sage.

Creswell, J. W. (2007). *Qualitative inquiry and research design: Choosing among five approaches* (2nd ed.). Thousand Oaks, CA: Sage.

Creswell, J. W. (2011). Controversies in mixed methods research. In N. K. Denzin & Y. S. Lincoln (Eds.). *The Sage handbook of qualitative research* (pp. 269–283). Thousand Oaks, CA: Sage.

Creswell, J. W., & Plano Clark, V. L. (2011). *Designing and conducting mixed methods research* (2nd ed.). Thousand Oaks, CA: Sage.

Crews, J., Smith, M. R., Smaby, M. H., Maddux, C. D., Torres-Rivera, E., Casey, J. A., & Urbani, S. (2005). Self-monitoring and counseling skills-based versus Interpersonal Process Recall Training. *Journal of Counseling and Development, 83*, 78–85. doi: 10.1002/j.1556-6678.2005.tb00582.x

Crits-Christoph, P., & Connolly Gibbons, M. B. (2003). Research developments on the therapeutic alliance in psychodynamic psychotherapy. *Psychoanalytic Inquiry, 23*(2), 332–349. doi: 10.1080/07351692309349036

Crits-Christoph, P., Connolly Gibbons, M. B., & Mukberjee, D. (2013). Psychotherapy process outcome research. In M. J. Lambert (Ed.), *Handbook of psychotherapy and behavioral change* (6th ed., pp. 298–340). Hoboken, NJ: Wiley.

Crits-Christoph, P., Connolly Gibbons, M. B., Hamilton, J., Ring-Kurtz, S., & Gallop, R. (2011). The dependability of alliance assessments: The alliance-outcome correlation is larger than you might think. *Journal of Consulting and Clinical Psychology, 79*(3), 267–278. doi: 10.1037/a0023668

Cross, W. E. (1978). The Cross and Thomas models of psychological nigrescence. *Journal of Black Psychology, 5*(1), 13–19. doi:10.1177/009579847800500102

Cross, W. E., & Vandiver, B. J. (2001). Nigrescence theory and measurement: Introducing the cross racial identity scale (CRIS). In J. G. Ponterotto, J. M. Casas, L. A. Suzuki, & C. A. Alexander (Eds.), *Handbook of multicultural counseling* (2nd ed., pp. 425–456). Thousand Oaks, CA: Sage.

Crowston, K., Wei K., Howison J., & Wiggins A. (2012). Free/Libre Open Source Software Development: What we know and what we do not know. *ACM Computing Surveys. 44.*

Cuijpers, P., Driessen, E., Hollon, S. D., van Oppen, P., Barth, J., & Andersson, G. (2012). The efficacy of non-directive supportive therapy for adult depression: A meta-analysis. *Clinical Psychology Review, 32*, 280–291. doi: 10.1016/j.cpr.2012.01.003

Currah, P., & Minter, S. (2000). *Transgender equality: A handbook for activists and policymakers*. Washington, DC: National Gay and Lesbian Task Force.

Cvetokovich, A. (2013). *Depression: A public feeling*. Durham, N.C.: Duke University Press.

Daniels, L. K. (1976). An extension of thought stopping in the treatment of obsessional thinking. *Behavior Therapy, 7*, 131. doi: 10.1016/S0005-7894(76)80231-6

Danskin, D. G., & Robinson, F. P. (1954). Differences in "degree of lead" among experienced counselors. *Journal of Counseling Psychology, 1*, 78–83.

David, E. J. R., Okazaki, S., & Giroux, D. (2014). A set of guiding principles to advance multicultural psychology and its major concepts. In F. T. L. Leong (Editor-in-Chief), *APA handbook of multicultural psychology, Vol. 1: Theory and research* (pp. 85–104). Washington, DC: American Psychological Association. doi:10.1037/14189-005

Davies, D., & Dodd, J. (2002). Qualitative research and the question of rigor. *Qualitative Health Research, 12*(2), 279–289. doi:10.1177/104973230201200211

Davis, D. E., DeBlaere, C., Brubaker, K., Owen, J., & Jordan, T. (under review). Microaggressions in counseling: Cultural humility mediates the relationship between negative affect and counseling outcomes.

Dawis, R. V. (2000). Scale construction and psychometric considerations. In H. E. A. Tinsley & S. D. Brown (Eds.), *Handbook of applied multivariate statistics and mathematical modeling* (pp. 65–94). San Diego: Academic Press. doi:10.1016/B978-012691360-6/50004-5

de Groot, A. D. (1969). *Methodology: Foundations of inference and research in the behavioral sciences*. The Hague: Mouton.

Del Re, A. C., Flückiger, C., Horvath, A. O., Symonds, D., & Wampold, B. E. (2012). Therapist effects in the therapeutic alliance–outcome relationship: A restricted-maximum likelihood meta-analysis. *Clinical Psychology Review, 32*(7), 642–649. doi:10.1016/j.cpr.2012.07.002

Delgado-Romero, E. A., Galván, N., & Maschino, P. (2005). Race and ethnicity in empirical counseling and counseling psychology research: A 10-year review. *The Counseling Psychologist, 33*, 419–448. Retrieved from http://dx.doi.org/10.1177/0011000004268637

DeMars, C. (2010). *Item response theory*. New York: Oxford University Press.

Dennin, M. K., & Ellis, M. V. (2003). Effects of a method of self-supervision for counselor trainees. *Journal of Counseling Psychology, 50*, 69–83. doi: 10.1037/0022-0167.50.1.69

Denzin, N. K. (1978). *The research act: A theoretical introduction to sociological methods*. New York: McGraw-Hill.

Denzin, N. K. (1997). Contingency, biography, and structure: On the history of the Society for the Study of Symbolic Interaction. *Symbolic Interaction, 20*(2), 107–113. doi:10.1525/si.1997.20.2.107

Denzin, N. K. (2008). Drawn to Yellowstone. *Qualitative Research, 8*(4), 451–472. doi:10.1177/1468794108093895

Denzin, N. K. (2009). The elephant in the living room: Or extending the conversation about the politics of evidence. *Qualitative Research, 9*(2), 139–160. doi:10.1177/1468794108098034

Denzin, N. K., & Lincoln, Y. S. (2011). Introduction: The discipline and practice of qualitative research (pp. 1–26). In N. Denzin & Y. Lincoln (Eds.), *The SAGE handbook of qualitative research* (4th ed). Thousand Oaks: Sage.

Denzin, N. K., & Lincoln, Y. S. (Eds.). (1998). *The landscape of qualitative research: Theories and issues*. Thousand Oaks, CA: Sage. doi: 10.1111/j.1365-2648.2005.03538_2.x

Denzin, N. K., & Lincoln, Y. S. (Eds.). (2011). *The SAGE handbook of qualitative research*. Thousand Oaks, CA: Sage.

Derogatis, L. R. (1983). *SCL-90-R administration, scoring and procedures manual*. Towson, MD: Clinical Psychiatric Research.

DeRubeis, R. J., Brotman, M. A., & Gibbons, C. J. (2005). A conceptual and methodological analysis of the non-specifics argument. *Clinical Psychology: Science and Practice, 12*, 174–183.

DeRubeis, R. J., Hollon, S. E., Evans, M. D., & Bemis, K. M. (1982). Can psychotherapies for depression be discriminated? A systematic investigation of cognitive therapy and interpersonal therapy. *Journal of Consulting and Clinical Psychology, 50*, 744–756. doi: 10.1037/0022-006X.50.5.744

Desmet, M., Willemsen, J., & Inslegers, R. (2013). Psychoanalytic single cases published in ISI-ranked journals. The construction of an online archive. *Psychotherapy and Psychosomatics, 82*, 120–121. doi: 10.1159/000342019

DeVellis, R. F. (2012). *Scale development: Theory and applications* (Vol. 26). Thousand Oaks, CA: Sage.

Dhami, M. K., Hertwig, R., & Hoffrage, U. (2004). The role of representative design in an ecological approach to cognition. *Psychological Bulletin, 130*, 959–988. doi: 10.1037/0033-2909.130.6.959

DiCicco-Bloom, B., & Crabtree, B. F. (2006). The qualitative research interview. *Medical Education, 40*(4), 314–321. doi: 10.1111/j.1365-2929.2006.02418.x

Diemer, M. A., & Ali, S. R. (2009). Integrating social class into vocational psychology: Theory and practice implications. *Journal of Career Assessment, 17*, 247–265. doi:10.1177/1069072708330462

Diemer, M. A., Mistry, R. S., Wadsworth, M. E., López, I., & Reimers, F. (2013). Best practices in conceptualizing and measuring social class in psychological research. *Analyses of Social Issues and Public Policy (ASAP), 13*, 77–113. doi:10.1111/asap.12001

Diener, E. (2000). Subjective well-being: The science of happiness and a proposal for a national index. *American Psychologist, 55*, 34–43. doi:10.1037/0003-066X.55.1.34

Diener, E., & Crandall, R. (1978). *Ethics in social and behavioral research*. Chicago: University of Chicago Press.

Diener, E., Emmons, R. A., Larsen, R. J., & Griffin, S. (1985). The Satisfaction With Life Scale. *Journal of Personality Assessment, 49*(1), 71–75. doi:10.1207/s15327752jpa4901_13

Dillman, D. A. (2000). *Mail and Internet surveys: The tailored design method* (2nd ed.). New York: Wiley.

Dipboye, W. J. (1954). Analysis of counselor style by discussion units. *Journal of Counseling Psychology, 1*, 21–26.

DiPrima, A. J., Ashby, J. S., Gnilka, P. B., & Noble, C. L. (2011). Family relationships and perfectionism in middle-school students. *Psychology in the Schools, 48*(8), 815–827. doi:10.1002/pits.20594

Dixon, W. A. (1989). *Self-appraised problem solving ability, stress, and suicide ideation in a college population* (unpublished master's thesis, University of Missouri, Columbia).

Dong, N., & Maynard, R. (2013). PowerUp! A tool for calculating minimum detectable effect sizes and minimum required sample sizes for experimental and quasi-experimental design studies. *Journal of Research on Educational Effectiveness, 6*, 24–67. Retrieved from http://dx.doi.org/10.1080/19345747.2012.673143

Donoghue, K., Patton, R., Phillips, T., Deluca, P., & Drummond, C. (2014). The effectiveness of electronic screening and brief intervention for reducing levels of alcohol consumption: A systematic review and meta-analysis. *Journal of Medical Internet Research, 16*(6), 3–22. doi:10.2196/jmir.3193

Doss, B. D., Thum, Y. M., Sevier, M., Atkins, D. C., & Christensen, A. (2005). Improving relationships: Mechanisms of change in couple therapy. *Journal of Consulting and Clinical Psychology, 73*, 624–633. doi:10.1037/0022-006X.73.4.624

Dovidio, J. F., Gaertner, S. L., Kawakami, K., & Hodson, G. (2002). Why can't we just get along? Interpersonal biases and interracial distrust. *Cultural Diversity and Ethnic Minority Psychology, 8*, 88–102. doi:10.1037/1099-9809.8.2.88

Dovidio, J. F., Kawakami, K., & Gaertner, S. L. (2002). Implicit and explicit prejudice and interracial interaction. *Journal of Personality and Social Psychology, 82*, 62–68. doi:10.1037/0022-3514.82.1.62

Drew, C. F. (1980). *Introduction to designing and conducting research* (2nd ed.). St. Louis, MO: Mosby.

Drinane, J. M., Owen, J., Adelson, J. L., & Rodolfa, E. (2014). Multicultural competencies: What are we measuring? *Psychotherapy Research. Psychotherapy Research*, advanced publication on-line. Doi: 10.1080/10503307.2014.983581

Duckitt, J. (2001). A dual-process cognitive-motivational theory of ideology and prejudice. In M. P. Zanna (Ed.), *Advances in experimental social psychology* (Vol. 33, pp. 41–113). New York: Academic Press. doi:10.1016/S0065-2601(01)80004-6

Duckitt, J., & Sibley, C. G. (2009). A dual-process motivational model of ideology, politics, and prejudice. *Psychological Inquiry, 20*, 98–109. doi:10.1080/10478400903028540

Duncan, G. J., & Magnuson, K. A. (2003). Off with Hollingshead: Socioeconomic resources, parenting, and child development. In M. H. Bornstein, R. H. Bradley, M. H. Bornstein, & R. H. Bradley (Eds.), *Socioeconomic status, parenting, and child development* (pp. 83–106). Mahwah, NJ: Lawrence Erlbaum.

Edgington, E. (1982). Nonparametric tests for single-subject multiple schedule experiments. *Behavioral Assessment, 4*, 83–91.

Edgington, E. S. (1980). *Randomization tests*. New York: Marcel Dekker.

Edgington, E. S. (1987). Randomized single-subject experiments and statistical tests. *Journal of Counseling Psychology, 34*, 437–442.

Eisenhard, M., & Jurow, A. S. (2011. Teaching qualitative research. In N. K. Denzin & Y. S. Lincoln (Eds.) *The SAGE handbook of qualitative research* (pp. 699–714). Thousand Oaks, CA: Sage.

Elion, A. A., Wang, K. T., Slaney, R. B., & French, B. H. (2012). Perfectionism in African American students: Relationship to racial identity, GPA, self-esteem, and depression. *Cultural Diversity and Ethnic Minority Psychology, 18*(2), 118–127. doi:10.1037/a0026491

Elkin, I., Falconnier, L. Martinovich, Z., & Mahoney, C. (2006). Therapist effects in the National Institute of Mental Health Treatment of Depression Collaborative Research Program. *Psychotherapy Research, 16*, 144–160. doi: 10.1080/10503300500268540

Elkin, I., Shea, M. T., & Watkins, J. T. (1989). National Institute of Mental Health Treatment of Depression Collaborative Research Program: General effectiveness of treatments. *Archives of General Psychiatry, 46*, 971–982. Retrieved from http://dx.doi.org/10.1001/archpsyc.1989.01810110013002

Ellingson, L. L. (2008). *Engaging crystallization in qualitative research*. Thousand Oaks, CA: Sage.

Elliott, E. (1989). Comprehensive process analysis: Understanding the change process in significant therapy events. In M. J. Packer & R. B. Addison (Eds.), *Entering the circle: Hermeneutic investigation in psychology* (pp. 165–184). Albany, NY: State University of New York Press.

Elliott, R. (1985). Helpful and nonhelpful events in brief counseling interviews: An empirical taxonomy. *Journal of Counseling Psychology, 32*, 307–322. doi:10.1037/0022-0167.32.3.307

Elliott, R. (1991). Five dimensions of therapy process. *Psychotherapy Research, 1*, 92–103.

Elliott, R. (2002). Hermeneutic single-case efficacy design. *Psychotherapy Research, 12*, 1–21. doi: 10.1080/713869614

Elliott, R., Fischer, C., & Rennie, D. (1999). Evolving guidelines for publication of qualitative research studies in psychology and related fields. *British Journal of Clinical Psychology, 38,* 215– 229. doi: 10.1348/014466599162782

Elliott, R., Hill, C. E., Stiles, W. B., Friedlander, M. L., Mahrer, A. R., & Margison, F. R. (1987). Primary therapist response modes: Comparison of six rating systems. *Journal of Consulting and Clinical Psychology, 55,* 218–223.

Ellis, M. V., Ladany, N., Krengel, M., & Schult, D. (1996). Clinical supervision research from 1981 to 1993: A methodological critique. *Journal of Counseling Psychology, 43,* 35–50. doi:10.1037/0022-0167.43.1.35

Embretson, S. E., & Reise, S. P. (2000). *Item response theory for psychologists.* Hillsdale, NJ: Lawrence Erlbaum.

Enders, C. K. (2001). A primer on maximum likelihood algorithms available for use with missing data. *Structural Equation Modeling, 8,* 128–141. doi: 10.1207/S15328007SEM0801_7

Erickson, C. D., & Al-Timimi, N. R. (2001). Providing mental health services to Arab Americans: Recommendations and considerations. *Cultural Diversity and Ethnic Minority Psychology, 7,* 308–327. doi:10.1037/1099-9809.7.4.308

Erickson, F. (2011). A history of qualitative inquiry in social and educational research. In N. K. Denzin & Y. S. Lincoln (Eds.) *The SAGE handbook of qualitative research* (pp. 43–60). Thousand Oaks, CA: Sage.

Ericsson, K. A., & Simon, H. A. (1984). *Protocol analysis: Verbal reports as data.* Cambridge, MA: MIT Press. doi:10.1037/0022-0167.32.4.483

Espelage, D. L., & Swearer, S. M. (2003). Research on school bullying and victimization: What have we learned and where do we go from here? *School Psychology Review, 32*(3), 365–383.

Eugster, S. L., & Wampold, B. E. (1996). Systematic effects of participant role on evaluation of the psychotherapy session. *Journal of Consulting and Clinical Psychology, 64,* 1020–1028. Retrieved from http://dx.doi.org/10.1037/0022-006X.64.5.1020

Exner, J. E., Jr. (1974). *The Rorschach: A comprehensive system* (Vol. 1). New York: Wiley.

Eysenck, H. J. (1952). The effects of psychotherapy: An evaluation. *Journal of Consulting Psychology, 16,* 319–324. doi: 10.1037/h0063633

Eysenck, H. J. (1960). *Behavior therapy and the neuroses.* Oxford: Pergamon Press.

Eysenck, H. J. (1961). The effects of psychotherapy. In H. J. Eysenck (Ed.), *Handbook of abnormal psychology* (pp. 697–725). New York: Basic Books.

Eysenck, H. J. (1965). The effects of psychotherapy. *International Journal of Psychology, 1,* 97–178.

Eysenck, H. J. (1969). *The effects of psychotherapy.* New York: Science House.

Farmer, H. S., Wardrop, J. L., Anderson, M. Z., & Risinger, R. (1995). Women's career choices: Focus on science, math, and technology careers. *Journal of Counseling Psychology, 42,* 155–170. doi:10.1037/0022-0167.42.2.155

Fassinger, R. (1990). Causal models of career choice in two samples of college women. *Journal of Vocational Behavior, 36,* 225–248. doi:10.1016/0001-8791(90)90029-2

Fassinger, R. E. (2005). Paradigms, praxis, problems, and promise: Grounded theory in counseling psychology research. *Journal of Counseling Psychology, 52*(2), 156–166. doi: 10.1037/0022-0167.52.2.156

Faul, F., Erdfelder, E., Lang, A.-G., & Buchner, A. (2007). G*Power 3: A flexible statistical power analysis program for the social, behavioral, and biomedical sciences. *Behavior Research Methods, 39,* 175–191. Retrieved from http://dx.doi.org/10.3758/BF03193146

Ferguson, T. M., Leach, M. M., Levy, J. J., Nicholson, B. C., & Johnson, J. D. (2008). Influences on counselor race preferences: Distinguishing Black racial attitudes from Black racial identity. *Journal of Multicultural Counseling and Development, 36*(2), 66–76. doi:10.1002/j.2161-1912.2008.tb00071.x

Fine, M. (1992). *Disruptive voices: The possibilities of feminist research.* Ann Arbor, MI: University of Michigan Press.

Fisher, R. J., & Katz, J. E. (2000). Social-desirability bias and the validity of self-reported values. *Psychology and Marketing, 17*(2), 105–120. doi:10.1002/(SICI)1520-6793(200002)17:2<105::AID-MAR3>3.0.CO;2-9

Fitzgerald, E. L., Chronister, K. M., Forrest, L., & Brown, L. (2013). OPTIONS for preparing inmates for community reentry: An employment preparation intervention. *The Counseling Psychologist, 41*(7), 990–1010. doi:10.1177/0011000012462367

Fitzpatrick, J. L., Sanders, J. R., & Worthen, B. R. (2004). *Program evaluation: Alternative approaches and practical guidelines.* Boston: Pearson/Allyn & Bacon.

Flores, E., Tschann, J. M., Dimas, J. M., Pasch, L. A., & de Groat, C. L. (2010). Perceived racial/ethnic discrimination, posttraumatic stress systems, and health risk behaviors among Mexican American adolescents. *Journal of Counseling Psychology, 57,* 264–273. doi:10.1037/a0020026

Flückiger, C., Del Re, A. C., Wampold, B. E., Symonds, D., & Horvath, A. O. (2012). How central is the alliance in psychotherapy? A multilevel longitudinal meta-analysis. *Journal of Counseling Psychology, 59*(1), 10–17. doi:10.1037/a0025749

Foa, E. B., Ehlers, A., Clark, D. M., Tolin, D. F., & Orsillo, S. M. (1999). The Posttraumatic Cognitions Inventory (PTCI): Development and validation. *Psychological Assessment, 11,* 303–314. doi:10.1037/1040-3590.11.3.303

Foa, E. B., & Rauch, S. A. (2004). Cognitive changes during prolonged exposure versus prolonged exposure plus cognitive restructuring in female assault survivors with posttraumatic stress disorder. *Journal of Consulting and Clinical Psychology, 72,* 879–884. doi: 10.1037/0022-006X.72.5.879

Fontana, A., & Frey, J. H. (1994). Interviewing: The art of science. In N. K. Denzin & Y. S. Lincoln (Eds.), *Handbook of qualitative research* (pp. 361–376). Thousand Oaks, CA: Sage.

Fontana, A., & Frey, J. H. (2000). The interviewing: From structured questions to negotiated text. In N. K. Denzin & Y. S. Lincoln (Eds.), *Handbook of qualitative research* (2nd ed., pp. 645–672). Thousand Oaks, CA: Sage.

Ford, D. H. (1984). Reexamining guiding assumptions: Theoretical and methodological implications. *Journal of Counseling Psychology, 31*(4), 461–466. doi:10.1037/0022-0167.31.4.461

Forgy, E. W., & Black, J. D. (1954). A follow-up after three years of clients counseled by two methods. *Journal of Counseling Psychology, 1*, 1–8. doi: 10.1037/h0061454

Forster, M. (2000). Hard problems in the philosophy of science: Idealisation and commensurability. In R. Nola & H. Sankey (Eds.), *Australasian studies in history and philosophy of science: After Popper, Kuhn, and Feyerabend. Recent issues in theories of scientific method* (Vol. 15, pp. 231–250). Dordrecht, Holland: Kluwer Academic.

Fouad, N. A. (2002). Cross-cultural differences in vocational interests: Between-group differences on the Strong Interest Inventory. *Journal of Counseling Psychology, 49*, 283–289. Retrieved from http://dx.doi.org/10.1037/0022-0167.49.3.282

Fouad, N. A., & Brown, M. T. (2000). Role of race and social class in development: Implications for counseling psychology. In S. D. Brown, R. W. Lent, S. D. Brown, & R. W. Lent (Eds.), *Handbook of counseling psychology* (3rd ed., pp. 379–408). Hoboken, NJ: Wiley.

Fouad, N. A., Carter, J. A., & Subich, L. M. (2012). *APA handbook of counseling psychology, Vol. 1: Theories, research, and methods*. Washington, DC: American Psychological Association. doi:10.1037/13754-000

Fouad, N., Fitzpatrick, M., & Liu, J. P. (2011). Persistence of women in engineering careers: A qualitative study of current and former female engineers. *Journal of Women and Minorities in Science and Engineering, 17*, 69–96. doi: 10.1615/JWomenMinorScienEng.v17.i1.60

Francis, D. J., Fletcher, J. M., Stuebing, K. K., Davidson, K. C., & Thompson, N. M. (1991). Analysis of change: Modeling individual growth. *Journal of Consulting and Clinical Psychology, 59*, 27–37. doi: 10.1037/0022-006X.59.1.27

Frazier, P. A., Tix, A. P., & Barron, K. E. (2004). Testing moderator and mediator effects in counseling psychology research. *Journal of Counseling Psychology, 51*, 115–134. doi:10.1037/0022-0167.51.2.157

Freire, P. (1970). *Cultural action for freedom* (p. 46). Harvard Educational Review.

Fremont, S., & Anderson, W. P. (1986). What client behaviors make counselors angry? An exploratory study. *Journal of Counseling and Development, 65*, 67–70. doi:10.1002/j.1556-6676.1986.tb01233.x

French, B. H., & Neville, H. A. (2013). Sexual coercion among black and white teenagers: Sexual stereotypes and psychobehavioral correlates. *The Counseling Psychologist, 41*(8), 1186–1212. doi:10.1177/0011000012461379

Fretz, B. R. (1982). Perspective and definitions. *The Counseling Psychologist, 10*, 15–19. http://dx.doi.org/10.1177/0011000082102004

Friedlander, M. L., Ellis, M. V., Siegel, S. M., Raymond, L., Haase, R. F., & Highlen, P. S. (1988). Generalizing from segments to sessions: Should it be done? *Journal of Counseling Psychology, 35*, 243–250.

Friedlander, M. L., Escudero, V., & Heatherington, L. (2006). *Therapeutic alliances with couples and families: An empirically-informed guide to practice*. Washington, DC: American Psychological Association.

Friedlander, M. L., Escudero, V., Heatherington, L., & Diamond, G. M. (2011). Alliance in couple and family therapy. *Psychotherapy, 48*(1), 25–33. doi:10.1037/a0022060

Friedlander, M. L., Ecudero, V., Horvath, A. O., Heatherington, L., Cabero, A., & Martens, M. P. (2006). System for observing family therapy alliances: A tool for research and practice. *Journal of Counseling Psychology, 53*(2), 214–224. doi: 0.1037/0022-0167.53.2.214

Friedlander, M. L., Heatherington, L., Johnson, B., & Showron, E. A. (1994). Sustaining engagement: A change event in family therapy. *Journal of Counseling Psychology, 41*, 438–448.

Friedlander, M. L., & Schwartz, G. S. (1985). Toward a theory of self-presentation in counseling and psychotherapy. *Journal of Counseling Psychology, 32*, 483–501.

Frost, R. O., Marten, P. A., Lahart, C., & Rosenblate, R. (1990). The dimensions of perfectionism. *Cognitive Therapy and Research, 14*, 449–468. doi:10.1007/BF01172967

Fuertes, J. N., Stracuzzi, T. I., Hersh, M., Bennett, J., Scheinholtz, J., Mislowack, A., et al. (2006). Therapist multicultural competency: A study of therapy dyads. *Psychotherapy, 43*(4), 480–490.

Fukuyama, M. (1990). Taking a universal approach to multicultural counseling. *Counselor Education and Supervision, 30*, 6–17. doi:10.1002/j.1556-6978.1990.tb01174.x

Furman, R., & Kinn, J. T. (2012). *Practical tips for publishing scholarly articles: Writing and publishing in the helping professions* (2nd ed.). Chicago, IL: Lyceum Books.

Furnham, A., & Procter, E. (1988). *The multi-dimensional Just World Belief Scale*. [Mimeograph] London: London University.

Gambrill, E. (1990). *Critical thinking in clinical practice*. San Francisco: Jossey-Bass.

Gambrill, E. (2005). *Critical thinking in clinical practice: Improving the quality of judgments and decisions* (2nd ed.). Hoboken, NJ: Wiley.

Gambrill, E. (2012). *Critical thinking in clinical practice: Improving the quality of judgments and decisions* (3rd ed). Hoboken, NJ: Wiley.

Garb, H. N. (1998). Studying the clinician: Judgment research and psychological assessment. Washington, DC: American Psychological Association. doi:10.1037/10299-002

Garfield, S. L. (1993). Major issues in psychotherapy research. In D. K. Freedheim (Ed.), *History *of psychotherapy* (pp. 335–360). Washington, DC: American Psychological Association.

Garfield, S. L., & Bergin, A. E. (Eds.). (1978). *Handbook of psychotherapy and behavior change* (2nd ed.). New York: Wiley.

Garfield, S. L., & Bergin, A. E. (Eds.). (1986). *Handbook of psychotherapy and behavior change* (3rd ed.). New York: Wiley.

Geertz, C. (1973). *The interpretation of cultures: Selected essays* (Vol. 5019). New York: Basic Books.

Gelso, C., & Fretz, B. (2001). *Counseling psychology* (2nd ed.). Belmont, CA: Wadsworth.

Gelso, C. J. (1979). Research in counseling: Methodological and professional issues. *The Counseling Psychologist, 8*, 7–35. Retrieved from http://dx.doi.org/10.1177/001100007900800303

Gelso, C. J. (2009). The real relationship in a postmodern world: Theoretical and empirical explorations. *Psychotherapy Research, 19*, 253–264.

Gelso, C. J. (2011). *The real relationship in psychotherapy: The hidden foundation of change*. Washington, DC: American Psychological Association.

Gelso, C. J., Baumann, E. C., Chui, H. T., & Savela, A. E. (2013). The making of a scientist–psychotherapist: The research training environment and the psychotherapist. *Psychotherapy, 50*(2), 139–149. doi:10.1037/a0028257

Gelso, C. J., Betz, N. E., Friedlander, M. L., Helms, J. E., Hill, C. E., Patton, M. J., Super, D. E., & Wampold, B. E. (1988). Research in counseling psychology: Prospects and recommendations. *The Counseling Psychologist, 16*, 385–406. Retrieved from http://dx.doi.org/10.1177/0011000088163006

Gelso, C. J., & Lent, R. W. (2000). Scientific training and scholarly productivity: The person, the training environment, and their interaction. In S. D. Brown & R. W. Lent (Eds.), *Handbook of counseling psychology* (3rd ed., pp. 109–139). Hoboken, NJ: Wiley.

Gelso, C. J., Mallinckrodt, B., & Judge, A. B. (1996). Research training environment, attitudes toward research, and research self-efficacy: The revised research training environment scale. *The Counseling Psychologist, 24*, 304–322. Retrieved from http://dx.doi.org/10.1177/0011000096242010

Gerstein, L. H., Heppner, P. P., Ægisdóttir, S., Leung, S. A., & Norsworthy, K. L. (2009). *International handbook of cross-cultural counseling: Cultural assumptions and practices worldwide*. Thousand Oaks, CA: Sage.

Gibbons, J. L., Hamby, B. A., & Dennis, W. D. (1997). Researching gender-role ideologies internationally and cross-culturally. *Psychology of Women Quarterly, 21*, 151–170. doi:10.1111/j.1471-6402.1997.tb00106.x

Giorgi, A. (1970). *Psychology as a human science: A phenomenological based approach*. New York: Harper & Row.

Giorgi, A. (1985). Sketch of a psychological phenomenological method. In A. Giorgi (Ed.), *Phenomenology and psychological research* (pp. 8–22). Pittsburgh, PA: Duquesne University Press.

Giorgi, A. (2009). *The descriptive phenomenological method in psychology*. Pittsburgh, PA: Duquesne University Press.

Glaser, B. G. (1978). *Theoretical sensitivity: Advances in the methodology of grounded theory* (Vol. 2). Mill Valley, CA: Sociology Press.

Glaser, B. G. (1992). *Basics of grounded theory: Emergence vs. forcing*. Mill Valley, CA: Sociology Press.

Glaser, B. G., & Strauss, A. L. (1967). *The discovery of grounded theory*. London: Weidenfield & Nicolson.

Glass, G. V., Willson, V. L., & Gottman, J. M. (1974). *Design and analysis of time-series experiments*. Boulder, CO: Colorado Associated University Press.

Glick, I., Weiss, R. S., & Parkes, C. M. (1974). The first year of bereavement. New York: Wiley Interscience.

Glock, C. Y. (Ed.). (1967). *Survey research in the social sciences*. New York: Russell Sage Foundation.

Gold, R. L. (1958). Roles in sociological field observations. *Social Forces, 36*, 217–223.

Goldapple, K., Segal, Z., & Garson, C. (2004). Modulation of cortical-limbic pathways in major depression. *Archives of General Psychiatry, 61*, 34–41. doi:10.1001/archpsyc.61.1.34

Goldman, L. (1976). A revolution in counseling research. *Journal of Counseling Psychology, 23*, 543–552. Retrieved from http://dx.doi.org/10.1037/0022-0167.23.6.543

Goldman, L. (1982). Defining non-traditional research. *The Counseling Psychologist, 10*(4), 87–89. doi:10.1177/0011000082104016

Goldman, L. (Ed.). (1978). *Research methods for counselors: Practical approaches in field settings*. New York: Wiley.

Goldstein, A. P., Heller, K., & Sechrest, L. B. (1966). *Psychotherapy and the psychology of behavior change*. New York: Wiley.

Good, G. E., Robertson, J. M., O'Neil, J. M., Fitzgerald, L. F., Stevens, M., DeBord, K. A., Bartels, K. M., & Braverman, D. G. (1995). Male gender role conflict: Psychometric issues and relations to psychological distress. *Journal of Counseling Psychology, 42*, 3–10. doi:10.1037/0022-0167.42.1.3

Goodman, J. K., Cryder, C. E., & Cheema, A. (2013). Data collection in a flat world: The strengths and weaknesses of mechanical Turk samples. *Journal of Behavioral Decision Making, 26*(3), 213–224. doi:10.1002/bdm.1753

Goodyear, R. K., & Benton, S. (1986). The roles of science and research in the counselor's work. In A. J. Palmo & W. J. Weikel (Eds.), *Foundations of mental health counseling* (pp. 287–308). Springfield, IL: Charles C Thomas.

Gottman, J. M. (1973). N-of-one and N-of-two research in psychotherapy. *Psychological Bulletin, 80*, 93–105. doi: 10.1037/h0034803

Gottman, J. M. (1979). Detecting cyclicity in social interaction. *Psychological Bulletin, 86*, 338–348. doi: 10.1037/0033-2909.86.2.338

Gottman, J. M., McFall, R. M., & Barnett, J. T. (1969). Marital interaction and parenting. *Psychological Bulletin, 72*, 299–306. doi: 10.1037/h0028021

Gould, S. J. (1994). The geometer of race. *Discover, 15*, 65–69.

Graham, J. R. (1990). *MMPI-2: Assessing personality and psychopathology.* New York: Oxford University Press.

Green, H., Barkham, M., Kellett, S., & Saxon, D. (2014). Therapist effects and IAPT Psychological Wellbeing Practitioners (PWPs): A multilevel modelling and mixed methods analysis. *Behaviour Research and Therapy, 63,* 43–54. doi:10.1016/j.brat.2014.08.009

Green, J. (2000). *Introduction to transgender issues.* Washington, DC: National Gay and Lesbian Task Force.

Greenberg, L. S. (1986). Research strategies. In L. S. Greenberg & W. M. Pinsof (Eds.), *The psychotherapeutic process: A research handbook* (pp. 707–734). New York: Guilford Press.

Greenberg, L. S. (1986). Change process research. *Journal of Consulting and Clinical Psychology, 54,* 4–9. doi:10.1037/0022-006X.54.1.4

Greene, J. C. (2007). *Mixed methods in social inquiry.* San Francisco: Jossey-Bass.

Greene, J. C., Caracelli, V. J., & Graham, W. F. (1989). Toward a conceptual framework for mixed method evaluation designs. *Educational Evaluation and Policy Analysis, 11,* 255–274. Retrieved from http://dx.doi.org/10.3102/01623737011003255

Greyser, N. (2014). Writing through writer's block. National Center for Faculty Development and Diversity. Retrieved from https://facultydiversity.site-ym.com/?writersblock

Grummon, D. L., & Butler, J. M. (1953). Another failure to replicate Keet's study, two verbal techniques in a miniature counseling situation. *Journal of Abnormal and Social Psychology, 48,* 597. doi: 10.1037/h0057442

Grundy, C. T., & Lambert, M. J. (1994b, June). *Assessing clinical significance: Application to the Hamilton Rating Scale for Depression.* Paper presented at the annual meeting of the Society for Psychotherapy Research, York, England.

Grzegorek, J. L., Slaney, R. B., Franze, S., & Rice, K. (2004). Self-criticism, dependency, self-esteem and grade point average satisfaction among clusters of perfectionists and nonperfectionists. *Journal of Counseling Psychology, 51,* 192–200. doi:10.1037/0022-0167.51.2.192

Guba, E. G. (1990). The alternative paradigm dialog. In E. G. Guba (Ed.), *The paradigm dialog* (pp. 17–30). Newbury Park, CA: Sage.

Guba, E. G., & Lincoln, Y. S. (1994). Competing paradigms in qualitative research. In N. K. Denzin & Y. S. Lincoln (Eds.), *Handbook of qualitative research* (pp. 105–117). Thousand Oaks, CA: Sage.

Guba, E. G., & Lincoln, Y. S. (1998). *Fourth generation evaluation.* Thousand Oaks, CA: Sage.

Gullestad, F. S., & Wilberg, T. (2011). Change in reflective functioning during psychotherapy—A single-case study. *Psychotherapy Research, 21*(1) 97–111. doi:10.1080/10503307.2010.525759

Gushue, G. V., & Carter, R. T. (2000). Remembering race: White racial identity attitudes and two aspects of social memory. *Journal of Counseling Psychology, 47,* 199–210. doi:10.1037/0022-0167.47.2.199

Guthrie, R. V. (1998). *Even the rat was white: A historical view of psychology.* Boston: Allyn & Bacon.

Hage, S. M., Romano, J. L., Conyne, R. K., Kenny, M., Matthews, C., Schwartz, J. P., & Waldo, M. (2007). Best practice guidelines on prevention practice, research, training, and social advocacy for psychologists. *The Counseling Psychologist, 35*(4), 493–566. doi:10.1177/0011000006291411

Hagenaars, J. A., & McCutcheon, A. L. (2002). *Applied latent class analysis.* New York: Cambridge University Press.

Hair, J. F., Jr., Anderson, R. E., & Tatham, R. L. (1987). *Multivariate data analysis: With readings* (2nd ed.). New York: Macmillan.

Hair, J. K., & Black, W. C. (2000). Cluster analysis. In L. G. Grimm & P. R. Yarnold (Eds.), *Reading and understanding more multivariate statistics* (pp. 147–205). Washington, DC: American Psychological Association.

Hall, C. C. I. (2014). The evolution of the revolution: The successful establishment of multicultural psychology. In F. T. L. Leong (Editor-in-Chief), *APA handbook of multicultural psychology, Vol. 1: Theory and research* (pp. 3–18). Washington, DC: American Psychological Association.

Hall, G. N. (2001). Psychotherapy research with ethnic minorities: Empirical, ethical, and conceptual issues. *Journal of Consulting and Clinical Psychology, 69,* 502–510. doi:10.1037/0022-006X.69.3.502

Hamachek, D. E. (1978). Psychodynamics of normal and neurotic perfectionism. *Psychology, 15,* 27–33.

Hammer, J., & Vogel, D. (2010). Men's help seeking for depression: The efficacy of a male-sensitive brochure about counseling. *The Counseling Psychologist, 38,* 296–313. doi: 10.1177/0011000009351937

Hammersley, M. (1996). The relationship between qualitative and quantitative research: Paradigm loyalty versus methodological eclecticism. In J. T. E. Richardson (Ed.), *Handbook of qualitative research methods for psychology and the social sciences* (pp. 159–174). Leicester, UK: BPS Books.

Hanson, W. E., Creswell, J. W., Clark, V. L., Petska, K. S., & Creswell, J. D. (2005). Mixed methods research designs in counseling psychology. *Journal of Counseling Psychology, 52,* 224–235. doi: 10.1037/0022-0167.52.2.224

Harding, S. (1991). *Whose science? Whose knowledge? Thinking from women's lives.* Ithaca, NY: Cornell University Press.

Harmon, L. (1977). Career counseling for women. In E. Rawlings & D. Carter (Eds.), *Psychotherapy for women* (pp. 197–206). Springfield, IL: Charles C Thomas.

Harmon, L. (1982). Scientific affairs: The next decade. *The Counseling Psychologist, 10*(2), 31–37. doi:10.1177/0011000082102006

Harvey, B., Pallant, J., & Harvey, D. (2004). An evaluation of the factor structure of the Frost Multi-dimensional Perfectionism Scale. *Educational and Psychological Measurement, 64,* 1007–1018. doi:10.1177/0013164404264842

Haverkamp, B. E., Morrow, S. L., & Ponterotto, J. G. (2005). A time and place for qualitative and

Safran, J. D., & Muran, J. C. (2000). *Negotiating the therapeutic alliance: A relational* Dipboye, W. J. (1954). Analysis of counselor style by discussion units. *Journal of Counseling Psychology, 1,* 21–26.

Salsman, N. L., & Linehan, M. M. (2006). Dialectic-behavioral therapy for borderline personality disorder. *Primary Psychiatry, 13,* 51–58.

Sanchez, L. M., & Turner, S. M. (2003). Practicing psychology in the era of managed care: Implications for practice and training. *American Psychologist, 58*(2), 116–129.

Sands, R. G., Bourjolly, J., & Roer-Strier, D. (2007). Crossing cultural barriers in research interviewing. *Qualitative Social Work: Research and Practice, 6*(3), 353–372. doi:10.1177/1473325007080406

Sapsford, R. J. (2006). *Survey research.* London: Sage.

Sax, G. (1989). *Principles of educational and psychological measurement and evaluation* (3rd ed.). Belmont, CA: Wadsworth.

Schlosser, L. Z., Knox, S., Moskovitz, A. R., & Hill, C. E. (2003). A qualitative examination of graduate advising relationships: The advisee perspective. *Journal of Counseling Psychology, 50*(2), 178. Retrieved from http://dx.doi.org/10.1037/0022-0167.50.2.178

Schmidt, F. L., & Hunter, J. E. (1996). Measurement error in psychological research: Lessons from 26 research scenarios. *Psychological Methods, 1,* 199–223. doi: 10.1037/1082-989X.1.2.199

Schmidt, L. D., & Meara, N. M. (1984). Ethical, professional, and legal issues in counseling psychology. In S. D. Brown & R. W. Lent (Eds.), *Handbook of counseling psychology* (pp. 56–96). New York: Wiley.

Schmidt, L. D., & Strong, S. R. (1971). Attractiveness and influence in counseling. *Journal of Counseling Psychology, 18,* 348–351. doi: 10.1037/h0031234

Schotte, D. E., & Clum, G. A. (1982). Suicide ideation in a college population: A test of a model. *Journal of Consulting and Clinical Psychology, 50*(5), 690–696. Retrieved from http://dx.doi.org/10.1037/0022-006X.50.5.690

Schwandt, T. A., & Arens, S. (2001). Making sense of the epistemological landscape. *PsycCritiques, 46*(3), 302–303. doi:10.1037/002504

Scriven, M. (1980). *The logic of evaluation.* Inverness, CA: Edgepress.

Seeman, J. (1969). Deception in psychological research. *American Psychologist, 24,* 1025–1028. doi: 10.1037/h0028839

Seggar, L., & Lambert, M. J. (1994, June). *Assessing clinical significance: Application to the Beck Depression Inventory.* Paper presented at the annual meeting of the Society for Psychotherapy Research, York, England.

Serlin, R. C. (1987). Hypothesis testing, theory building, and the philosophy of science. *Journal of Counseling Psychology, 34,* 365– 371. Retrieved from http://dx.doi.org/10.1037/0022-0167.34.4.365

Serlin, R. C., Wampold, B. E., & Levin, J. R. (2003). Should providers of treatment be regarded as a random factor? If it ain't broke, don't "fix" it: A comment on Siemer and Joorman (2003). *Psychological Methods, 8,* 524–534. doi: 10.1037/1082-989X.8.4.524

Shadish, W. R., Cook, T. D., & Campbell, D. T. (2002). *Experimental and quasi-experimental designs for generalized causal inference.* Boston: Houghton Mifflin.

Shadish, W. R., Kyse, E. N., & Rindskopf, D. M. (2013). Analyzing data from single-case designs using multilevel models: New applications and some agenda items for future research. *Psychological Methods, 18,* 385–405. doi: 10.1037/a0032964

Shadish, W. R., Matt, G. E., Navarro, A. M., & Phillips, G. (2000). The effects of psychological therapies under clinically representative conditions: A meta-analysis. *Psychological Bulletin, 126,* 512–529. doi: 10.1037/0033-2909.126.4.512

Shaffer, J. (1995). Multiple hypothesis testing. *Annual Review of Psychology, 46,* 561–584. doi:10.1146/annurev.ps.46.020195.003021

Shafran, R., & Mansell, W. (2001). Perfectionism and psychopathology: A review of research and treatment. *Clinical Psychology Review, 21*(6), 879–906. doi:10.1016/S0272-7358(00)00072-6

Shapiro, D. N., Chandler, J., & Mueller, P. A. (2013). Using Mechanical Turk to study clinical populations. *Clinical Psychological Science, 1*(2), 213–220. doi:10.1177/2167702612469015

Sharpless, B. A., & Barber, J.P. (2009). The examination for professional practice in psychology (EPPP) in the era of evidence-based practice. *Professional Psychology: Research and Practice, 40*(4), 333–340. doi: 10.1037/a0013983

Shechtman, Z., & Pastor, R. (2005). Cognitive-behavioral and humanistic group treatment for children with learning disabilities: A comparison of outcomes and process. *Journal of Counseling Psychology, 52*(3), 322–336. doi:10.1037/0022-0167.52.3.322

Shih, T., & Fan, X. (2008). Comparing response rates from Web and mail surveys: A meta-analysis. *Field Methods, 20*(3), 249–271. doi:10.1177/1525822X08317085

Shimokawa, K., Lambert, M. J., & Smart, D. W. (2010). Enhancing treatment outcome of patients at risk of treatment failure: Meta-analytic and mega-analytic review of a psychotherapy quality assurance system. *Journal of Consulting and Clinical Psychology, 78*(3), 298–311. doi:10.1037/a0019247

Shirk, S. R., Karver, M. S., & Brown, R. (2011). The alliance in child and adolescent psychotherapy. *Psychotherapy, 48*(1), 17–24. doi:10.1037/a0022181

Silverman, M. J. (2013). Effects of music therapy on self and experienced stigma in patients on an acute care psychiatric unit: A randomized three group effectiveness study. *Archives of Psychiatric Nursing, 27*(5), 223–230. doi:10.1016/j.apnu.2013.06.003

Singh, R., Fouad, N. A., Fitzpatrick, M. E., Liu, J. P., Cappaert, K. J., & Figuereido, C. (2013). Stemming the tide: Predicting women engineers' intentions to leave. *Journal of Vocational Behavior, 83*(3), 281–294. doi:10.1016/j.jvb.2013.05.007

Skovholt, T. M. (2012). *Becoming a therapist: On the path to mastery.* New York: Wiley.

Slate, J. R., & Jones, C. H. (1989). Can teaching of the WISC-R be improved? Quasi-experimental exploration.

Professional Psychology Research and Practice, 20, 408–410. doi: 10.1037/0735-7028.20.6.408

Smedley, A. (1999). Race in North America: Origin and evolution of a worldview (2nd ed.). Boulder, CO: Westview Press.

Smith, M. L., & Glass, G. V. (1977). Meta-analysis of psychotherapy outcome studies. *American Psychologist, 32,* 752–760. doi: 10.1037/0003-066X.32.9.752

Smith, M. L., Glass, G. V., & Miller, T. I. (1980). *The benefits of psychotherapy.* Baltimore: Johns Hopkins University Press.

Smith, N. G., & Ingram, K. M. (2004). Workplace heterosexism and adjustment among lesbian, gay, and bisexual individuals: The role of unsupportive social interaction. *Journal of Counseling Psychology, 51,* 57–67. doi:10.1037/0022-0167.51.1.57

Snijders, T. A. B., & Bosker, R. J. (2012). Multilevel analysis: An introduction to basic and advanced multilevel modeling (2nd ed.). London: Sage.

Spanierman, L. B., & Poteat, V. P. (2005). Moving beyond complacency to commitment: Multicultural research in counseling. *The Counseling Psychologist, 33,* 513–523. Retrieved from http://dx.doi .org/10.1177/0011000005276469

Speight, S. L., & Vera, E. M. (2003). Social justice agenda: Ready, or not? *The Counseling Psychologist, 32,* 109–118.

Spiegel, D., & Keith-Spiegel, P. (1970). Assignment of publication credits: Ethics and practices of psychologists. *American Psychologist, 25,* 738–747. doi: 10.1037/h0029769

Spielmans, G. I., Gatlin, E. T., & McFall, J. P. (2010). The efficacy of evidence-based psychotherapies versus usual care for youths: Controlling confounds in a meta-reanalysis. *Psychotherapy Research, 20,* 234–246. doi:10.1080/10503300903311293.

Sternberg, R. J. (Ed.). (1982). *Handbook of human intelligence.* New York: Cambridge University Press.

Stewart, R. E., & Chambless, D. L. (2007). Does psychotherapy research inform treatment decisions in private practice? *Journal of Clinical Psychology, 63*(3), 267–281.

Stice, E., Fisher, M., & Martinez, E. (2004). Eating disorder diagnostic scale: Additional evidence of reliability and validity. *Psychological Assessment, 16*(1), 60–71. doi: 10.1037/1040-3590.16.1.60

Stiles, W. B. (2009). Responsiveness as an obstacle for psychotherapy outcome research: It's worse than you think. *Clinical Psychology Science and Practice, 16,* 86–91. doi: 10.1111/j.1468-2850.2009.01148.x

Stiles, W. B., Barkham, M., Mellor-Clark, J., & Connell, J. (2007). Effectiveness of cognitive-behavioural, person-centered, and psychodynamic therapies in UK primary-care routine practice: Replication in a larger sample. *Psychological Medicine, 38,* 677–688. doi:10.1017/S0033291707001511.

Stiles, W. B., Glick, M. J., Osatuke, K., Hardy, G. E., Shapiro, D. A., Agnew-Davies, R., Rees, A., & Barkham, M. (2004). Patterns of alliance development and the rupture-repair hypothesis: Are productive relationships U-shaped or V-shaped? *Journal of Counseling Psychology, 51*(1), 81–92.

Stiles, W. B., Shapiro, D. A., & Firth-Cozens, J. A. (1988). Do sessions of different treatments have different impacts? *Journal of Counseling Psychology, 35,* 391–396. Retrieved from http://dx.doi .org/10.1037/0022-0167.35.4.391

Stoltenberg, C. (1981). Approaching supervision from a developmental perspective: The counselor complexity model. *Journal of Counseling Psychology, 28,* 59–65. doi:10.1037/0022-0167.28.1.59

Stoltenberg, C. D., Pace, T. M., Kashubeck-West, S., Biever, J. L., Patterson, T., & Welch, I. D. (2000). Training models in counseling psychology: Scientist-practitioner versus practitioner-scholar. *The Counseling Psychologist, 28*(5), 622–640. doi:10.1177/0011000000285002

Stone, G. L. (1984). Reaction: In defense of the "artificial." *Journal of Counseling Psychology, 31,* 108–110. doi:10.1037/0022-0167.31.1.108

Strauss, A. L. (1987). *Qualitative analysis for social scientists.* Cambridge, MA: Cambridge University Press.

Strauss, A. L., & Corbin, J. (1998). Basics of qualitative research: Techniques and procedures for developing grounded theory (2nd ed.). Thousand Oaks, CA: Sage.

Strauss, A., & Corbin, J. M. (1990). Basics of qualitative research: Grounded theory procedures and techniques. Thousand Oaks, CA: Sage.

Stricker, G. (1982). Ethical issues in psychotherapy research. In M. Rosenbaum (Ed.), *Ethics and values in psychotherapy: A guidebook* (pp. 403–424). New York: Free Press.

Stricker, G. (2007). The local clinical scientist. In S. G. Hofmann & J. Weinberger (Eds.), *The art and science of psychotherapy* (pp. 85–99). New York: Routledge/ Taylor & Francis Group.

Stricker, G., & Trierweiler, S. J. (1995). The local clinical scientist: A bridge between science and practice. *American Psychologist, 50*(12), 995–1002. doi:10.1037/0003-066X.50.12.995

Strickland, B., & Suben, A. (2012). Experimenter philosophy: The problem of experimenter bias in experimental philosophy. *Review of Philosophy and Psychology, 3*(3), 457–467. doi:10.1007/s13164-012-0100-9

Strickland, O. L., Maloney, M. F., Dietrich, A. S., Myerburg, S., Cotsonis, G. A., & Johnson, R. V. (2003). Measurement issues related to data collection on the World Wide Web. *Advances in Nursing Science, 26,* 246–256. doi: 10.1097/00012272-200310000-00003

Strohmer, D. C., & Newman, L. J. (1983). Counselor hypothesis-testing strategies. *Journal of Counseling Psychology, 30,* 557–565.

Strong, S. R. (1968). Counseling: An interpersonal influence process. *Journal of Counseling Psychology, 15,* 215–224. doi:10.1037/h0020229

Strong, S. R. (1991). Theory-driven science and naive empiricism in counseling psychology. *Journal of Counseling Psychology, 38,* 204–210.

Strong, S. R., & Matross, R. P. (1973). Change processes in counseling and psychotherapy. *Journal of Counseling Psychology, 20,* 25–37. doi: 10.1037/h0034055

Strong, S. R., & Schmidt, L. D. (1970). Expertness and influence in counseling. *Journal of Counseling Psychology, 17,* 81–87. doi: 10.1037/h0028642

Strong, S. R., Welsh, J. A., Corcoran, J. L., & Hoyt, W. T. (1992). Social psychology and counseling psychology: The history, products, and promise of an interface. *Journal of Counseling Psychology, 39,* 139–157. doi:10.1037/0022-0167.39.2.139

Strupp, H. H. (1980a). Success and failure in time-limited psychotherapy: A systematic comparison of two cases—Comparison 1. *Archives of General Psychiatry, 37,* 595–603. doi: 10.1001/archpsyc.1980.01780180109014

Strupp, H. H. (1980b). Success and failure in time-limited psychotherapy: A systematic comparison of two cases—Comparison 2. *Archives of General Psychiatry, 37,* 708–716. doi: 10.1001/archpsyc.1980.01780180109014

Strupp, H. H. (1980c). Success and failure in time-limited psychotherapy: Further evidence—Comparison 4. *Archives of General Psychiatry, 37,* 947–954. doi: 10.1001/archpsyc.1980.01780180109014

Strupp, H. H., & Binder, J. L. (1984). *Psychotherapy in a new key.* New York: Basic Books.

Strupp, H. H., & Howard, K. I. (1993). A brief history of psychotherapy research. In D. K. Freedheim (Ed.), *History of psychotherapy* (pp. 309–334). Washington, DC: American Psychological Association.

Stulz, N., Thase, M. E., Klein, D. N., Manber, R., & Crits-Christoph, P. (2010). Differential effects of treatments for chronic depression: A latent growth model reanalysis. *Journal of Consulting and Clinical Psychology, 78,* 409–419. doi: 10.1037/a0019267

Stumpf, H., & Parker, W. D. (2000). A hierarchical structural analysis of perfectionism and its relation to other personality characteristics. *Personality and Individual Differences, 28,* 837–852. doi:10.1016/S0191-8869(99)00141-5

Sue, D. W. (2003). *Overcoming our racism: The journey to liberation.* San Francisco: Wiley. doi:10.1002/9780787979690

Sue, D. W., & Sue, D. (2003). *Counseling the culturally diverse: Theory and practice* (4th ed.). New York: Wiley.

Sue, D. W., & Sue, D. (2013). *Counseling the culturally diverse: Theory and practice* (6th ed.). New York: Wiley.

Sue, D. W., Capodilupo, C. M., Torino, G. C., Bucceri, J. M., Holder, A. M. B., Nadal, K.L., & Esquilin, M. (2007). Racial microaggressions in everyday life: Implications for clinical practice. *American Psychologist, 62*(4), 271–286. doi: 0.1037/0003-066X.62.4.271

Sue, S. (1999). Science, ethnicity, and bias: Where have we gone wrong? *American Psychologist, 54,* 1070–1077. doi:10.1037/0003-066X.54.12.1070

Super, D. E. (1980). A life-span, life-space approach to career development. *Journal of Vocational Behavior, 16*(3), 282–298. Retrieved from http://dx.doi.org/10.1016/0001-8791(80)90056-1

Sussman, J., Beaujean, A. A., Worrell, F. C., & Watson, S. (2013). An analysis of Cross Racial Identity Scale scores using classical test theory and Rasch item response models. *Measurement and Evaluation in Counseling and Development, 46*(2), 136–153. doi:10.1177/0748175612468594

Swagler, M. A., & Ellis, M. V. (2003). Crossing the distance: Adjustment of Taiwanese graduate students in the United States. *Journal of Counseling Psychology, 50,* 420–437. doi:10.1037/0022-0167.50.4.420

Swanson, J. L., & Gore, P. A. (2000). Advances in vocational psychology theory and research. In S. D. Brown & R. W. Lent (Eds.), *Handbook of counseling psychology* (3rd ed., pp. 233–269). Hoboken, NJ: Wiley.

Tabachnick, B. G., & Fidell, L. S. (2001). *Using multivariate statistics* (4th ed.). Boston: Allyn & Bacon.

Tanaka-Matsumi, J., & Kameoka, V. A. (1986). Reliabilities and concurrent validities of popular self-report measures of depression, anxiety, and social desirability. *Journal of Consulting and Clinical Psychology, 54,* 328–333. doi: 10.1037/0022-006X.54.3.328

Tasca, G. A., Foot, M., Leite, C., Maxwell, H., Balfour, L., & Bissada, H. (2011). Interpersonal processes in psychodynamic-interpersonal and cognitive behavioral group therapy: A systematic case study of two groups. *Psychotherapy, 48*(3), 260–273. doi:10.1037/a0023928

Tashakkori, A., & Creswell, J. W. (2007). The new era of mixed methods [Editorial]. *Journal of Mixed Methods Research, 1*(3), 207–211. doi: 10.1177/1558689807302814

Tashakkori, A., & Teddlie, C. (Eds.). (2003). *Handbook on mixed methods in the behavioral and social sciences.* Thousand Oaks, CA: Sage.

Task Force for the Promotion and Dissemination of Psychological Procedures. (1995). Training in and dissemination of empirically-validated psychological treatment: Report and recommendations. *The Clinical Psychologist, 48,* 2–23.

Teddlie, C., & Tashakkori, A. (2011). Mixed methods research: Contemporary issues in an emerging field. In N. K. Denzin & Y. S. Lincoln (Eds.). *The Sage handbook of qualitative research* (pp. 285–299). Thousand Oaks, CA: Sage.

Thomas, M. L. (2011). The value of item response theory in clinical assessment: A review. *Assessment, 18*(3), 291–307. doi:10.1177/1073191110374797

Thombs, D. L. (2000). A retrospective study of DARE: Substantive effects not detected in undergraduates. *Journal of Alcohol and Drug Education, 46,* 27–40.

Thompson, A. S., & Super, D. E. (Eds.). (1964). *The professional preparation of counseling psychologists. Report of the 1964 Grey-stone Conference.* New York: Bureau of Publications, Teachers College, Columbia University.

Thompson, B. (2004). *Exploratory and confirmatory factor analysis: Understanding concepts and applications.* Washington, DC: American Psychological Association. doi:10.1037/10694-000

Thompson, C. E. (1994). Helms white racial identity development (WRID) theory: Another look. *The Counseling Psychologist, 22,* 645–649. doi:10.1177/0011000094224010

Thompson, M. N., Cole, O. D., & Nitzarim, R. S. (2012). Recognizing social class in the psychotherapy relationship: A grounded theory exploration of low-income clients. *Journal of Counseling Psychology, 59*(2), 208–221. doi:10.1037/a0027534

Thompson, M. N., Nitzarim, R. S., Cole, O. D., Frost, N. D., Ramirez Stege, A., & Vue, P. (2015). Clinical experiences with clients who are low-income: Mental health practitioners' perspectives. *Qualitative Health Research.* doi: 10.1177/1049732314566327

Thompson, M. N., Nitzarim, R. S., Her, P., & Dahling, J. J. (2013). A grounded theory exploration of undergraduate experiences of vicarious unemployment. *Journal of Counseling Psychology, 60*(3), 421–431. doi:10.1037/a0033075

Thompson, M. N., & Subich, L. M. (2007). Exploration and validation of the Differential Status Identity Scale. *Journal of Career Assessment, 15,* 227–239. doi:10.1177/1069072706298155

Thompson, M. N., & Subich, L. M. (2011). Social status identity: Antecedents and vocational outcomes. *The Counseling Psychologist, 39,* 735–763. doi:10.1177/0011000010389828

Tian, L., Heppner, P. P., & Hou, Z. (2014). Problem solving appraisal and its relationship to career decision-making difficulties and psychological adjustment in China. *International Perspectives in Psychology: Research, Practice, Consultation, 3*(1), 19–36. doi:10.1037/ipp0000011

Tichenor, V., & Hill, C. E. (1989). A comparison of six measures of working alliance. *Psychotherapy, 26,* 195–199.

Tingey, R. C., Lambert, M. J., Burlingame, G. M., & Hansen, N. B. (1996). Assessing clinical significance: Proposed extensions to method. *Psychotherapy Research, 6,* 109–123. doi: 10.1080/10503309612331331638

Tinsley, D. J., Tinsley, H. E. A., Boone, S., & Shim-Li, C. (1993). Prediction of scientist-practitioner behavior using personality scores obtained during graduate school. *Journal of Counseling Psychology, 40,* 511–517. Retrieved from http://dx.doi.org/10.1037/0022-0167.40.4.511

Tinsley, H. E. A., & Tinsley, D. J. (1987). Use of factor analysis in counseling psychology research. *Journal of Counseling Psychology, 34,* 414–424. doi:10.1037/0022-0167.34.4.414

Toporek, R. L., Gerstein, L. H., Fouad, N. A., Roysircar, G., & Israel, T. (Eds.). (2005). *Handbook for social justice in counseling psychology.* Thousand Oaks, CA: Sage.

Toporek, R. L., Kwan, K. K., & Williams, R. A. (2012). Ethics and social justice in counseling psychology. In N. A. Fouad, J. A. Carter, & L. M. Subich (Eds.), *APA handbook of counseling psychology, Vol. 2: Practice, interventions, and applications* (pp. 305–332). Washington, DC: American Psychological Association.

Tracey, T. G., & Glidden-Tracey, C. E. (1999). Integration of theory, research design, measurement, and analysis: Toward a reasoned argument. *The Counseling Psychologist, 27*(3), 299–324. doi:10.1177/0011000099273002

Tracey, T. J. (1985). The N of 1 Markov chain design as a means of studying the stages of psychotherapy. *Psychiatry, 48,* 196–204.

Tracey, T. J. G., Wampold, B. E., Lichtenberg, J. W., & Goodyear, R. K. (2014). Expertise in psychotherapy: An elusive goal? *American Psychologist, 69*(3), 218–229. doi: 10.1037/a0035099

Tracy, S. J. (2010). Qualitative quality: Eight "big-tent" criteria for excellent qualitative research. *Qualitative Inquiry, 16,* 837–851.

Trepka, C., Rees, A., Shapiro, D. A., Hardy, G. E., & Barkham, M. (2004). Therapist competence and outcome of cognitive therapy for depression. *Cognitive Therapy and Research, 28,* 143–157. doi: 10.1023/B:COTR.0000021536.39173.66

Triandis, H. C. (1972). *The analysis of subjective culture.* New York: Wiley.

Trimble, J. E., & Fisher, C. B. (2005). *The handbook of ethical research with ethnocultural populations and communities.* Thousand Oaks, CA: Sage.

Trimble, J. E., & Fisher, C. B. (2006). *The handbook of ethical research with ethnocultural populations and communities.* Thousand Oaks, CA: Sage.

Trimble, J. E., Scharrón-del-Río, M., & Casillas, D. M. (2014). Ethical matters and contentions in the principled conduct of research with ethnocultural communities. In F. T. L. Leong (Editor-in-Chief), *APA handbook of multicultural psychology, Vol. 1: Theory and research* (pp. 59–84). Washington, DC: American Psychological Association.

Trochim, W., & Donnelly, J. P. (2007). *The research methods knowledge base* (3rd ed.). Mason, OH: Atomic Dog.

Trochim, W., & Land, D. (1982). Designing designs for research. *The Researcher, 1,* 1–6.

Truax, C. B., & Carkhuff, R. R. (1967). *Toward effective counseling and psychotherapy: Training and practice.* Chicago: Aldine.

Truax, C. B., & Wargo, D. G. (1966). Psychotherapeutic encounters that change behavior: For better or for worse. *American Journal of Psychotherapy, 20,* 499–520.

Tsai, C., Chaichanasakul, A., Zhao, R., Flores, L. Y., & Lopez, S. J. (2014). Development and validation of the Strengths Self-Efficacy Scale (SSES). *Journal of Career Assessment, 22*(2), 221–232. doi:10.1177/1069072713493761

Turnbull, H. R., III (Ed.). (1977). *Consent handbook.* Washington, DC: American Association on Mental Deficiency.

Turner, P. R., Valtierra, M., Talken, T. R., Miller, V. I., & DeAnda J. R. (1996). Effect of treatment on treatment outcome for college students in brief therapy. *Journal of Counseling Psychology, 43,* 228–232. doi: 10.1037/0022-0167.43.2.228

Underwood, B. J. (1966). *Experimental psychology.* New York: Appleton-Century-Crofts.

Van de Vijver, F. J. R., & Leung, K. (1997). *Methods and data analysis for cross-cultural research.* Thousand Oaks, CA: Sage.

Vandenbos, G. R. (1996). Outcome assessment of psychotherapy. *American Psychologist, 51,* 1005–1006. doi: 10.1037/0003-066X.51.10.1005

Vásquez, V. B., Minkler, M., & Shepard, P. (2006). Promoting environmental health policy through community based participatory research: A case study from Harlem, New York. *Journal of Urban Health, 83*(1), 101–110. doi: 10.1007/s11524-005-9010-9

Veit, C. T., & Ware, J. E. (1983). The structure of psychological distress and well-being in general populations. *Journal*

of Consulting and Clinical Psychology, 51(5), 730–742. doi:10.1037/0022-006X.51.5.730

Vera, E. M., & Reese, L. E. (2000). Preventive interventions with school-age youth. In S. D. Brown, R. W. Lent, S. D. Brown, R. W. Lent (Eds.), Handbook of counseling psychology (3rd ed.) (pp. 411–434). Hoboken, NJ, US: John Wiley & Sons Inc.

Vera, E. M., Caldwell, J., Clarke, M., Gonzales, R., Morgan, M., & West, M. (2007). The Choices Program: Multisystemic interventions for enhancing the personal and academic effectiveness of urban adolescents of color. The Counseling Psychologist, 35(6), 779–796. doi:10.1177/0011000007304590

Villodas, M. T., Litrownik, A. J., & Roesch, S. C. (2012). Latent classes of externalizing behaviors in youth with early maltreatment histories. Measurement and Evaluation in Counseling and Development, 45(1), 49–63. doi:10.1177/0748175611423536

Waehler, C. A., Kalodner, C. R., Wampold, B. E., & Lichtenberg, J. W. (2000). Empirically supported treatments (ESTs) in perspective: Implications for counseling psychology training. The Counseling Psychologist, 28(5), 657–671. doi:10.1177/0011000000285004

Waldo, C. R. (1999). Working in the majority context: A structural model of heterosexism as minority stress in the workplace. Journal of Counseling Psychology, 46, 218–232. doi:10.1037/0022-0167.46.2.218

Wallenstein, R. S. (1989). The psychotherapy research project of the Menninger Foundation: An overview. Journal of Consulting and Clinical Psychology, 57, 195–205. Retrieved from http://dx.doi.org/10.1037/0022-006X.57.2.195

Walsh, W. B., & Heppner, M. J. (2006). Handbook of career counseling for women. Hillsdale, NJ: Lawrence Erlbaum.

Waltz, J., Addis, M. E., Koerner, K., & Jacobson, N. S. (1993). Testing the integrity of a psychotherapy protocol: Assessment of adherence and competence. Journal of Consulting and Clinical Psychology, 61, 620–630. doi: 10.1037/0022-006X.61.4.620

Wampold, B. E. (1986). Toward quality research in counseling psychology: Current recommendations for design and analysis. The Counseling Psychologist, 14, 37–48. Retrieved from http://dx.doi.org/10.1177/0011000086141004

Wampold, B. E. (2001). The great psychotherapy debate: Models, methods, and findings. Hillsdale, NJ: Lawrence Erlbaum.

Wampold, B. E. (2007). Psychotherapy: The humanistic (and effective) treatment. American Psychologist, 62, 857–873. doi: 10.1037/0003-066X.62.8.857

Wampold, B. E. (2013). The good, the bad, and the ugly: A 50-year perspective on the outcome problem. Psychotherapy, 50, 16–24. doi: 10.1037/a0030570

Wampold, B. E., & Bhati, K. S. (2004). Attending to the omissions: A historical examination of evidence-based practice movements. Professional Psychology: Research and Practice, 35, 563–570. doi: 10.1037/0735-7028.35.6.563

Wampold, B. E., & Bolt, D. (2006). Therapist effects: Clever ways to make them (and everything else) disappear. Psychotherapy Research, 16, 184–187. doi: 10.1080/10503300500265181

Wampold, B. E., & Brown, G. S. (2005). Estimating therapist variability: A naturalistic study of outcomes in managed care. Journal of Consulting and Clinical Psychology, 16, 184–197.

Wampold, B. E., & Drew, C. J. (1990). Theory and application of statistics. New York: McGraw-Hill.

Wampold, B. E., & Freund, R. D. (1987). Use of multiple regression in counseling psychology research: A flexible data-analytic strategy. Journal of Counseling Psychology, 34, 372–382. doi:10.1037/0022-0167.34.4.372

Wampold, B. E., & Freund, R. D. (1991). Statistical issues in clinical research. In M. Hersen, A. E. Kazdin, & A. S. Bellack (Eds.), The clinical psychology handbook (2nd ed., pp. 313–326). Elmsford, NY: Pergamon Press.

Wampold, B. E., & Imel, Z. E. (2015). The great psychotherapy debate: The evidence for what makes sychotherapy work (2nd ed.). New York: Routledge.

Wampold, B. E., & Kim, K. (1989). Sequential analysis applied to counseling process and outcome: A case study revisited. Journal of Counseling Psychology, 36, 357–364.

Wampold, B. E., & Serlin, R. C. (2000). The consequences of ignoring a nested factor on measures of effect size in analysis of variance. Psychological Methods, 5, 425–433. doi:10.1037/1082-989X.5.4.425

Wampold, B. E., & Worsham, N. L. (1986). Randomization tests for multiple-baseline designs. Behavioral Assessment, 8, 135–143.

Wampold, B. E., Davis, B., & Good, R. H., III. (1990). Hypothesis validity of clinical research. Journal of Consulting and Clinical Psychology, 58, 360–367. doi:10.1037/0022-006X.58.3.360

Wampold, B. E., Minami, T., Tierney, S. C., Baskin, T. W., & Bhati, K. S. (2005). The placebo is powerful: Estimating placebo effects in medicine and psychotherapy from clinical trials. Journal of Clinical Psychology, 61, 835–854. doi:10.1002/jclp.20129

Wang, K. T. (2010). The Family Almost Perfect Scale: Development, psychometric properties, and comparing Asian and European Americans. Asian American Journal of Psychology, 1, 186–199. doi:10.1037/a0020732

Wang, K. T., Heppner, P. P., Fu, C. C., Zhao, R., Li, F., & Chuang, C. C. (2012). Profiles of acculturative adjustment patterns among Chinese international students. Journal of Counseling Psychology, 59, 424–436. doi:10.1037/a0028532

Wang, K. T., Heppner, P. P., Wang, L., & Zhu, F. (2015). Cultural intelligence trajectories in new international students: Implications for the development of cross-cultural competence. International Perspectives in Psychology: Research, Practice, Consultation, 15, 51–65. doi:10.1037/ipp0000027

Wang, K. T., Wei, M., Zhao, R., Chuang, C., & Li, F. (2015). The Cross-Cultural Loss Scale: Development and psychometric evaluation. Psychological Assessment, 27, 42–53. doi:10.1037/pas0000027

Wang, S., & Kim, B. S. K. (2010). Therapist multicultural competence, Asian American participants' cultural values, and counseling process. *Journal of Counseling Psychology, 57*(4), 394–401. doi:10.1037/a0020359

Wang, Y.-W., & Heppner, P. P. (2011). A qualitative study of childhood sexual abuse survivors in Taiwan: Toward a transactional and ecological model of coping. *Journal of Counseling Psychology, 58*(3), 393–409. doi: l0.1037/a0023522

Wasserman, R. H., Levy, K., & Loken, E. (2009). Generalizability theory in psychotherapy research: The impact of multiple sources of variance on the dependability of psychotherapy process ratings. *Psychotherapy Research, 19*, 397–408. doi:10.1080/10503300802579156

Watkins, C. E., Jr. (1994). On hope, promise, and possibility in counseling psychology, or some simple, but meaningful observations about our specialty. *The Counseling Psychologist, 22*, 315–334.

Watkins, C. E., & Terrell, F. (1988). Mistrust level and its effects on counseling expectations in Black-White counselor relationships: An analogue study. *Journal of Counseling Psychology, 35*, 194–197. doi:10.1037/0022-0167.35.2.194

Watson, J. C., Gordon, L. B., & Stermac, L. (2003). Comparing the effectiveness of process-experiential with cognitive-behavioral psychotherapy in the treatment of depression. *Journal of Consulting and Clinical Psychology, 71*, 773–781. doi: 10.1037/0022-006X.71.4.773

Watson, J. C., Schein, J., & McMullen, E. (2010). An examination of clients' in-session changes and their relationship to the working alliance and outcome. *Psychotherapy Research, 20*, 224–233

Webb, C. A, DeRubeis, R. J., & Barber, J. P. (2010). Counselor adherence/competence and treatment outcome: A meta-analytic review. *Journal of Consulting and Clinical Psychology, 78*, 200–211. doi: 10.1037/a0018912

Webb, E. J., Campbell, D. T., Schwartz, R. C., & Sechrest, L. (1966). *Unobtrusive measures: Nonreactive research in the social sciences.* Chicago: Rand McNally.

Webb, E. J., Campbell, D. T., Schwartz, R. D., Sechrest, L., & Grove, J. B. (1981). *Nonreactive measures in the social sciences.* Boston: Houghton Mifflin.

Webster-Stratton, C. (1988). Mothers' and fathers' perceptions of child deviance: Roles of parent and child behaviors and parent adjustment. *Journal of Consulting and Clinical Psychology, 56*, 909–915. doi: 10.1037/0022-006X.56.6.909

Wei, M., Alvarez, A. N., Ku, T., Russell, D. W., & Bonett, D. G. (2010). Development and validation of a Coping with Discrimination Scale: Factor structure, reliability, and validity. *Journal of Counseling Psychology, 57*(3), 328–344. doi:10.1037/a0019969

Wei, M., Heppner, P. P., & Mallinckrodt, B. (2003). Perceived coping as a mediator between attachment and psychological distress: A structural equation modeling approach. *Journal of Counseling Psychology, 50*, 438–447.

Wei, M., Vogel, D. L., Ku, T-Y., & Zakalik, R. A. (2005). Adult attachment, affect regulation, negative mood, and interpersonal problems: The mediating roles of emotional reactivity and emotional cutoff. *Journal of Counseling Psychology, 52*, 14–24. doi:10.1037/0022-0167.52.1.14

Wei, M., Wang, K. T., Heppner, P. P., & Du, Y. (2012). Ethnic and mainstream social connectedness, perceived racial discrimination and posttraumatic stress symptoms. *Journal of Counseling Psychology, 59*, 486–493. doi:10.1037/a0028000

Weisz, J. R., Rothbaum, F. M., & Blackburn, T. C. (1984). Standing out and standing in: The psychology of control in America and Japan. *American Psychologist, 39*, 955–969. doi:10.1037/0003-066X.39.9.955

Wertz, F. J. (2005). Phenomenological research methods for counseling psychology. *Journal of Counseling Psychology, 52*(2), 167–177. doi: 10.1037/0022-0167.52.2.167

Westen, D., & Bradley, R. (2005). Empirically supported complexity: Rethinking evidence-based practice in psychotherapy. *Current Directions in Psychological Science, 14*(5), 266–271. doi:10.1111/j.0963-7214.2005.00378.x

Westen, D., Novotny, C. M., & Thompson-Brenner, H. (2004). The empirical status of empirically supported psychotherapies: Assumptions, findings, and reporting in controlled clinical trials. *Psychological Bulletin, 130*, 631–663. doi: 10.1037/0033-2909.130.4.631

White, O. R. (1974). *The "split middle": A "quickie" method for trend estimation.* Seattle: University of Washington, Experimental Education Unit, Child Development and Mental Retardation Center.

Whiteley, J. M. (1984). A historical perspective on the development of counseling psychology as a profession. In S. D. Brown & R. W. Lent (Eds.), *Handbook of counseling psychology* (pp. 3–55). New York: Wiley.

Whittaker, V. A., & Neville, H. A. (2010). Examining the relation between racial identity attitude clusters and psychological health outcomes in African American college students. *Journal of Black Psychology, 36*, 383–409. doi:10.1177/0095798409353757

Wiley, M. O., & Ray, P. B. (1986). Counseling supervision by developmental level. *Journal of Counseling Psychology, 33*, 439–445. doi:10.1037/0022-0167.33.4.439

Wilkins, K. G., Ramkissoon, M., & Tracey, T. G. (2013). Structure of interest in a Caribbean sample: Application of the Personal Globe Inventory. *Journal of Vocational Behavior, 83*(3), 367–372.

Wilkinson, L., & Task Force on Statistical Inference. (1999). Statistical methods in psychology journals. *American Psychologist, 54*, 594–604. doi: http://dx.doi.org/10.1037/0003-066X.54.8.594

Willett, J. B. (1997). Measuring change: What individual growth modeling buys you. In E. Amsel & K. A. Renninge (Eds.), *Change and development: Issues of theory, method, and application* (pp. 213–243). Mahwah, NJ: Lawrence Erlbaum.

Willett, J. B., & Sayer, A. G. (1994). Using covariance structure analysis to detect correlates and predictors of individual change over time. *Psychological Bulletin, 116*, 363–381. doi: 10.1037/0033-2909.116.2.363

Wilson, L. S., & Ranft, V. A. (1993). The state of ethical training for counseling psychology doctoral students. *The Counseling Psychologist, 21,* 445–456. doi: 10.1177/0011000093213009

Wöhrmann, A. M., Deller, J., & Wang, M. (2014). A mixed-method approach to post-retirement career planning. *Journal of Vocational Behavior, 84*(3), 307–317. doi: 10.1016/j.jvb.2014.02.003

Wolcott, H. F. (1992). Posturing in qualitative inquiry. In M. D. LeCompte, W. L. Millroy, & J. Preissle (Eds.), *The handbook of qualitative research in education* (pp. 3–52). San Diego: Academic Press.

Wolcott, H. F. (1994). Transforming qualitative data: Description, analysis, and interpretation. Thousand Oaks, CA: Sage.

Wolf, E. J., Harrington, K. M., Clark, S. L., & Miller, M. W. (2013). Sample size requirements for structural equation models: An evaluation of power, bias, and solution propriety. *Educational and Psychological Measurement, 73*(6), 913–934. doi:10.1177/0013164413495237

Wolpe, J. (1969). *The practice of behavior therapy.* New York: Pergamon Press. doi: 10.1016/0005-7967(69)90040-0

Woolf, S. H., & Atkins, D. (2001). The evolving role of prevention in health care: Contributions of the U.S. Preventive Services Task Force. *American Journal of Preventive Medicine, 20*(3), 13–20. Retrieved from http://dx.doi.org/10.1016/S0749-3797(01)00262-8

Worrell, F. C., Andretta, J. R., & Woodland, M. H. (2014). Cross Racial Identity Scale (CRIS) scores and profiles in African American adolescents involved with the juvenile justice system. *Journal of Counseling Psychology, 61*(4), 570–580. doi:10.1037/cou0000041

Worrell, F. C., Vandiver, B. J., Cross, W. J., & Fhagen-Smith, P. E. (2004). Reliability and structural validity of cross racial identity scale scores in a sample of African American adults. *Journal of Black Psychology, 30*(4), 489–505. doi:10.1177/0095798404268281

Worthington, E. L., Jr. (1984). Empirical investigation of supervision of counselors as they gain experience. *Journal of Counseling Psychology, 31,* 63–75. doi:10.1037/0022-0167.31.1.63

Worthington, R. L., & Mohr, J. J. (2002). Theorizing heterosexual identity development. *The Counseling Psychologist, 30,* 491–495. doi:10.1177/00100002030004001

Worthington, R. L., & Whittaker, T. A. (2006). Scale development research: A content analysis and recommendations for best practices. *The Counseling Psychologist, 34*(6), 806–838. doi:10.1177/0011000006288127

Worthington, R. L., Dillon, F. R., & Becker-Schutte, A. M. (2005). Development, reliability, and validity of the Lesbian, Gay, and Bisexual Knowledge and Attitudes Scale for Heterosexuals (LGB-KASH). *Journal of Counseling Psychology, 52,* 104–118. doi:10.1037/0022-0167.52.1.104

Worthington, R. L., Savoy, H. B., Dillon, F. R., & Vernaglia, E. R. (2002). Heterosexual identity development: A multidimensional model of individual and social identity. *The Counseling Psychologist, 30,* 496–531. doi:10.1177/00100002030004002

Worthington, R. L., Soth-McNett, A. M., & Moreno, M. V. (2007). Multicultural counseling competencies research: A 20-year content analysis. *Journal of Counseling Psychology, 54,* 351–361. doi: 10.1037/0022-0167.54.4.351

Wright, K. B. (2005). Researching Internet-based populations: Advantages and disadvantages of online survey research, online questionnaire authoring software packages, and web survey services. *Journal of Computer-Mediated Communication, 10*(3). Available at http://jcmc.indiana.edu/vol10/issue3/wright.html

Wundt, W. (1916). *Elements of folk psychology.* London: Allen & Unwin. (Original work published 1900.)

Wyatt, S. B., Diekelmann, N., Henderson, F., Andrew, M. E., Billingsley, G., Felder, S. H., Fuqua, S., & Jackson, P. B. (2003). A community-driven model of research participation: The Jackson Heart Study participant recruitment and retention study. *Ethnicity and Disease, 13,* 438–455.

Yakushko, O., & Morgan, M. L. (2012). Immigration. In N. A. Fouad, J. A. Carter, & L. M. Subich (Eds.), *APA handbook of counseling psychology, Vol. 2: Practice, interventions, and applications* (pp. 473–495). Washington, DC: American Psychological Association.

Yalom, I. D. (2005) *The theory and practice of group psychotherapy* (5th ed.). New York: Basic Books.

Yang, K. S. (2000). Monocultural and cross-cultural indigenous approaches: The royal road to the development of a balanced global psychology. *Asian Journal of Social Psychology, 3*(3), 241–263. Retrieved from http://dx.doi.org/10.1111/1467-839X.00067

Yates, J. (2014). Synchronous online CPD: Empirical support for the value of webinars in career settings. *British Journal of Guidance and Counselling, 42*(3), 245–260. doi:10.1080/03069885.2014.880829

Yeh, C. J., & Inman, A. G. (2007). Qualitative data analysis and interpretation in counseling psychology: Strategies for best practices. *Counseling Psychologist, 35*(3), 369–403. doi 10.1177/0011000006292596

Yeh, Y., & Hayes, J. A. (2011). How does disclosing countertransference affect perceptions of the therapist and the session? *Psychotherapy, 48*(4), 322–329. doi:10.1037/a0023134

Zeidner, M., & Saklofske, D. (1996). Adaptive and maladaptive coping. In M. Zeidner & N. S. Endler (Eds.), *Handbook of coping: Theory, research, and applications* (pp. 505–531). New York: Wiley.

Zhang, J., & Goodson, P. (2011). Predictors of international students' psychosocial adjustment to life in the United States: A systematic review. *International Journal of Intercultural Relations, 35,* 139–162. Retrieved from http://dx.doi.org/10.1016/j.ijintrel.2010.11.011

Zhang, Y., Kube, E., Wang, Y., & Tracey, T. G. (2013). Vocational interests in China: An evaluation of the Personal Globe Inventory-Short. *Journal of Vocational Behavior, 83*(1), 99–105. Retrieved from http://dx.doi.org/10.1016/j.jvb.2013.03.009

Zilcha-Mano, S., Dinger, U., McCarthy, K. S., & Barber, J. P. (2014). Does alliance predict symptoms throughout treatment, or is it the other way around? *Journal of*

Consulting and Clinical Psychology, 82(6), 931–935. doi: 10.1037/a0035141

Ziman, J. (1968). *Public knowledge: The social dimension of science*. New York: Cambridge University Press.

Zimbardo, P. G. (2004). Does psychology make a significant difference in our lives? *American Psychologist,* 59(5), 339–351. Retrieved from http://dx.doi .org/10.1037/0003-066X.59.5.339

Zuckerman, M. (1990). Some dubious premises in research and theory on racial differences: Scientific, social, and ethical issues. *American Psychologist, 45,* 1297–1303. doi:10.1037/0003-066X.45.12.1297

Author Index

Subject Index